THE UNKNOWN PRIME MINISTER

Andrew Bonar Law from a sketch for an oil painting by James Guthrie

THE UNKNOWN PRIME MINISTER

THE LIFE AND TIMES OF ANDREW BONAR LAW 1858 – 1923

BY

ROBERT BLAKE

LONDON 1955
EYRE & SPOTTISWOODE

To
MY WIFE

First impression October 1955
Second impression October 1955

*This book is made and printed in Great Britain
for Eyre & Spottiswoode (Publishers) Limited,
15 Bedford Street, London, W.C.2, by*
STAPLES PRINTERS LIMITED
at their Rochester, Kent, establishment

CONTENTS

ILLUSTRATIONS

PREFACE

IN his will Bonar Law expressed the wish that, if it were deemed desirable to write his life, his youngest son, Richard (now Lord Coleraine), should be given the first refusal. The pressure of politics and business upon his time has, however, made it impossible for Lord Coleraine to do this, and with his full agreement the task has been entrusted to me by Lord Beaverbrook, who was Bonar Law's closest friend and sole executor, and to whom he bequeathed all his papers. I should like to take this opportunity of thanking him for all his help, encouragement, and kindness. Without his generous aid this book could never have been written.

The title of this book is taken from a remark attributed to Asquith after he had attended Bonar Law's funeral in Westminster Abbey. "It is fitting," he is reputed to have said, "that we should have buried the Unknown Prime Minister by the side of the Unknown Soldier." I have used this phrase, not because I consider that Asquith's remark was either just or true, but because, however unfairly, it has come to be the verdict of most people to-day. Even in his own lifetime Bonar Law's origins, career, character, and the reasons for his success acquired something of an aura of mystery which the passage of time has done nothing to remove. It is my hope that this book may help to dispel that erroneous impression.

The biography of an important political personage, especially when it is the first to be based upon his private papers, requires no special justification. The biographer must bear in mind that he is not only producing the first reasonably authoritative account of his subject's personality and impact upon events, but also that he is making available in the form of letters, memoranda, speeches, etc., the raw material upon which future historians of the period will have to rely. For these reasons such a book, if it is to have any real value, cannot be short, and I therefore make no apology for the length of this biography.

If this book has a theme, other than one of pure narrative, it is to illustrate some of the problems and difficulties facing the leader of a great political party, who believed in preserving his party's unity and, for good or ill, succeeded in doing so through twelve dramatic years of convulsion, crisis, and revolutionary change. Those who regard party politics with contempt as a paltry or ignoble pursuit will think little of Bonar Law and still less of this book.

The principal source upon which I have relied has been Bonar Law's private papers in the possession of Lord Beaverbrook. These have been admirably catalogued and calendared by Mrs. Elton whose work has greatly reduced my labours. Lord Beaverbrook has also allowed me access to the Lloyd George papers and his own political papers for this period. I would like to express my gratitude to him for giving me such a free hand in using these papers and also for all the personal recollections and other information which he has contributed.

The other principal collections of unpublished documents which I have used are the Royal Archives at Windsor Castle, Mr. Balfour's papers in the British Museum, Mr. Asquith's papers in the Bodleian Library, the papers of Sir Austen Chamberlain in the possession of the Chamberlain Trustees and the diary of the 17th Earl of Derby. Acknowledgements are made below.

I have used two forms of note references. Those of substance are numbered and appear at the foot of the page. The lettered references ([a, b, c, d,] etc.) refer to sources, documentary and printed, a full list of which appears at the end of the book. These are intended for historians and scholars, and can be disregarded by the ordinary reader.

I have had much useful information of a non-documentary nature supplied to me by individuals from their personal recollections. It is impossible for me to list them all, but I hope it will not seem invidious if I mention Lady Sykes (Bonar Law's elder daughter) and Lord Coleraine, whose kindness and help have been invaluable. I should also like to thank Lord Davidson, Sir Patrick Gower, Sir Geoffrey Fry, Sir Horace Hamilton, Dr. Thomas Jones, Mr. L. S. Amery, Lord Swinton, Lord Inverforth and Mr. Kenneth Lyon. It must not, however, be assumed that all or any of them would approve of all or anything which I have said.

Since the publication of the First Impression of this book my attention has been drawn to some evidence which conflicts with a story about Mr. Asquith on page 289. The matter is discussed in a footnote on that page.

ROBERT BLAKE

CHRIST CHURCH, OXFORD

ACKNOWLEDGEMENTS

I WOULD like first to express my gratitude to Her Majesty the Queen for her gracious permission to make use of material from the Royal Archives at Windsor. I would at the same time like to thank Sir Owen Morshead, the Librarian at Windsor Castle, for the helpful advice that he gave me in connexion with these papers.

I would like to acknowledge with gratitude the permission given to me by the following to quote from papers in which they possess the copyright: The Rt. Hon. Sir Winston Churchill for permission to quote from certain letters of his own to Bonar Law; Lady Curzon for permission to quote from Lord Curzon's letters; the Trustees of the British Museum for permission to quote from Mr. Balfour's letters; the Chamberlain Trustees for permission to quote from Sir Austen Chamberlain's papers; Sir Maurice Bonham Carter and the Master of Balliol College for permission to quote from the papers of Mr. Asquith; Mr. L. S. Amery for permission to quote from his private letters and from his autobiography, *My Political Life*, Vols. I and II; Mr. Wickham Steed for permission to quote from his letters to Bonar Law; General Sir Hubert Gough for permission to quote from his memoirs, *Soldiering On*; Sir Harold Nicolson for permission to quote from his *King George V, His Life and Times*.

I would also like to thank the following for permission to quote from documents in which they possess the copyright: Lord Lansdowne; Lord Salisbury; Lord Derby; Lord Long of Wraxall; Lord Crawford and Balcarres; Lord Younger of Leckie; Lord Fitzalan; Lord Birkenhead; Lord Fisher of Kilverstone; Mr. Geoffrey Keynes; Mr. Raymond Savage (for permission to quote from the writings of Sir Archibald Salvidge); The Rt. Rev. Bishop Gwynne; General Sir Ivor Maxse; Sir Basil Goulding; Lord Quickswood; Lord Cecil of Chelwood; the Duke of Rutland; Sir Patrick Gower; Lord Davidson; Sir Leslie Wilson; Lady Carson; Lady Sykes; Lady Cunliffe; Mr. Anthony Asquith; Lord Remnant; Lady Crewe; Mr. J. A. Arnold-Forster; Lady Bingley.

I would like to acknowledge with thanks permission from Cassell and Co. Ltd. to quote from: *The Life and Letters of Sir Austen Chamberlain* by Sir Charles Petrie; *Down the Years* and *Politics from the Inside* by Sir Austen Chamberlain; *The Life and Diaries of Sir Henry Wilson* by General Sir Charles Calwell.

I would also like to thank Hutchinson & Co. Ltd. for permission to quote from *The Life of Lord Oxford and Asquith* by J. A. Spender and Cyril Asquith; Victor Gollancz Ltd. for permission to quote from *The Truth about the Peace Treaties* by David Lloyd George; The Clarendon Press for permission to quote from the *Dictionary of National Biography*.

I would like to acknowledge the help which I have obtained from the only previous biography of Bonar Law – *The Strange Case of Andrew Bonar Law* by Mr. H. A. Taylor, published in 1932. Mr. Taylor did not have access to Bonar Law's papers, but he obtained much useful information about Bonar Law's early life.

I have received much valuable help from Lord Coleraine, who allowed me to make full use of the draft of an early chapter which he wrote at a time when he hoped that he might be able to undertake his father's biography. He has, in addition, put at my disposal all the notes and material that he had collected for this purpose. They have been of great assistance to me.

Finally I would like to acknowledge with gratitude the help that I have had from two unpublished papers which their authors kindly lent me. One is by Mr. Maurice Ashley and is entitled, *Bonar Law and the Overthrow of the Coalition in 1922.* The other is a thesis submitted to the Department of History at Princeton University by Mr. David Colwell, who is a grandson of Bonar Law. It is entitled, *The Restive Years: Bonar Law, the Unionist Party, and Ireland, 1912–1914.*

CHAPTER I

YOUTH

1858–1891

*Andrew Bonar Law born September 16th, 1858 – Reasons for his name – Life in
New Brunswick – Character of James Law – Frugality of Bonar Law's early life –
He goes to Scotland – His education – The Kidstons and their wealth – Helensburgh
– Bonar Law's life as a young man – His voracious reading – His love of Carlyle
and Gibbon – His Conservatism – The Glasgow Parliament – Bonar Law's tastes –
His fondness for games – His dislike of scenery, the arts, and alcohol – He becomes
a partner in William Jacks & Co. – Nature of the business – Bonar Law's
marriage to Miss Robley*

ANDREW BONAR LAW was born on September 16th, 1858, in
New Brunswick.[1] The actual place of his birth was the old
manse of Kingston (since renamed Rexton), a small town on
the Richibucto River which flows out on the north shore of the
province. His father, the Reverend James Law, was Presbyterian
minister of the Free Church of Scotland in charge of the parishes of
Kingston and Richibucto. His mother was Elizabeth Annie Kidston,
formerly of Halifax, Nova Scotia. He was their fourth son and fourth
child.

The reason why he was thus named is of some interest, and the
usual explanations are incorrect. Neither his mother nor his father
had any connexion with the then celebrated Bonar family which
produced two brothers, Andrew and Horatius, who both became
Moderators of the General Assembly of the Free Church. Nor was
he so named because his parents had any special admiration for the
Reverend Andrew Bonar. The reason was that his mother had recently acquired a great respect for the life and works of the Reverend
Robert Murray McCheyne, known as the "Saintly McCheyne", a
preacher already famous when he died in 1843 at the early age of
thirty. She would have named her newly-born child after this eminent
divine, but she already had a son called Robert. Therefore she
decided to do the next best thing and name him after McCheyne's

---

[1] New Brunswick was not in those days a part of Canada, which indeed had not yet
come into existence in the modern sense. It was one of the Maritime Provinces which,
together with Upper and Lower Canada, formed the Federal Dominion of Canada in 1867.

B   17

biographer who happened to be the Reverend Andrew Bonar.[1] As Bonar Law himself observed, writing to an enquirer sixty-two years later, "This is a curious way of getting a name, but my father gave me that account of it."

Of his two names, Andrew was hardly ever used. He was known as Bonar by his family and friends from his earliest youth to the end of his life.

The old manse at Kingston still stands. With its white façade, low verandah and single upper window, it is a typical Canadian dwelling of that day. It was surrounded by farm buildings, for the minister had to supplement his meagre stipend by farming on a modest scale. No human habitation was visible from its window. Only the white spire of St. Andrew's Church could be seen above the trees. A narrow stretch of turf separated the manse from the river. In those hard days the Richibucto River dominated the settlers' lives. There were few roads and no railways. In the summer the river was a thoroughfare, and till recently people were still living, who could remember funeral processions floating down its waters, the coffin lashed to a canoe, the black-coated mourners following in their boats behind. In winter the river froze. One of Bonar Law's earliest recollections, which he would describe to his children, was of skating with his brothers to school over the black ice.

Of the majestic scenery which formed the background to Bonar Law's boyhood little need be said here. He left it for ever at the age of twelve and it appears to have made no great impression upon him. All his life he showed a singular indifference to his physical surroundings. Nature in the semi-frontier existence of the New Brunswick settlers was an enemy to be conquered, not as in England - or even Scotland – an agreeable object of contemplation. Whether for this or for some other cause, Bonar Law's attitude to the beauties of nature and scenery remained to the end of his life one of distaste, amounting at times to positive aversion.

Far more important in their influence upon him were the personalities of the home in which he was brought up. We know little of his mother. She was connected with the wealthy Kidstons of Glasgow and Helensburgh – which was to be a fact of great significance in Bonar Law's life – but her own branch of the family was not well off. She was delicate, and her upbringing cannot have been the ideal preparation for the arduous and austere existence of a minister's wife at Richibucto. Nevertheless she brought to it courage and steadfastness,

---

[1] *Memoir of R. M. McCheyne*, by Andrew A. Bonar, 1844; 2nd edition, 1892.

and a sweet kindliness of character which made her long remembered. Bonar Law may well have inherited some of her qualities, but
it is impossible that she could have had much personal influence
upon him. She died shortly after the birth of her daughter Mary,
when Bonar Law was only two years old. Her place in the family
was taken by her sister, Miss Janet Kidston, who came out from Glasgow in order to keep house for James Law and look after his family.

Inevitably it was his father who loomed largest in Bonar Law's
early life. James Law was, indeed, a man of formidable and dominating personality. His very appearance suggested his power – the
commanding presence, the broad frame, the black beard, the deep-
set and sombre eyes. He was born in 1822 at Coleraine in Northern
Ireland, the son of a prosperous farmer whose forebears had migrated
to Ulster from the lowlands of Scotland at the end of the seventeenth
century. He was educated at Glasgow University, was minister at
Coleraine for a short time, and in 1845 went out to New Brunswick
where he remained as minister in Kingston and Richibucto for
thirty-two years.

The population of New Brunswick was largely Scottish or of
Scottish descent. The minister therefore had all the prestige which
a Presbyterian minister possessed in contemporary Scotland – and
this was considerable. The place which the Sunday service occupied
in men's minds at that time is difficult to conceive today. It not only
satisfied the deeply-felt religious and devotional needs of that simple
Scottish community, it also supplied the elements of drama and
emotion which were lacking in the drab hardworking lives of the
great majority of the settlers. People came long distances to St.
Andrew's Church. The service lasted from eleven to three, and
between those hours every Sunday there would be some twenty or
thirty saddle horses tethered to the posts outside the porch, patiently
awaiting the end of their owners' lengthy devotions.

There is general testimony as to the remarkable eloquence and
power of James Law both in extempore prayer and in preaching.
His delivery was dramatic in the extreme. He was speaking once of
the revilement of Christ: "You see me here a minister of the Lord.
You see the cloth that I wear. You may think me a meek man. I try
to be so, but if anyone were to spit upon me I should strike him in
the face." And he shot out a powerful arm in a gesture of illustration.
Again, he was picturing the remorse of Judas Iscariot, and describing
the terror of a man who has contracted a debt so fearful that it can
never be repaid on earth. His sermon came to an end with the

minister falling upon his knees, his arms outstretched above his head, and crying aloud in an agony of supplication: "A rope, a rope! I'll pay, Lord, with a rope."

Many years later Bonar Law once said that he had never in his Parliamentary career heard a single speech of real eloquence. This seems a surprising statement from someone who had listened to nearly all the greatest political orators of the time. But it may be that he was comparing, consciously or unconsciously, the speeches of his contemporaries with the sermons of his father which he had heard long ago in the days of his youth.

It would be wrong to envisage James Law as entirely dominated by the rigorous Calvinist creed in which he had been brought up. On the contrary there was in him, as in many people, a certain dualism of mind. His intellect might oblige him to preach his some-what gloomy and fatalistic theology, but his emotions rebelled at insisting upon every outward observance which orthodoxy demanded. For example, he did not see why Sunday should be made a day of joyless boredom for little children. On Sundays he used to shut his children in a barn. To his devout neighbours, who regarded the young as "limbs of Satan" and as particularly susceptible to the whisperings of the Devil, this must have seemed an admirable prac-tice. But in fact the minister's motives were less orthodox. He shut his family in a barn not to punish them, but to give them a place where they could play together, safe from the censorious eyes of his parishioners.

James Law was never a happy man. At times a strange darkness would descend upon his spirit. The effort of preparing himself for Sunday became a terrible ordeal, a nightmare which obsessed his waking thoughts. He was always a lonely man and he grew, as time went on, more and more remote from the settlers amongst whom he dwelt. Intellectually he might as well have been living upon a desert island. He knew no one with whom he could even discuss on equal terms the new and perturbing theories of Darwin and Huxley – theories which, as he perhaps dimly saw, threatened to bring the old universe crashing down in ruins upon his head. Whatever the cause, there were periods of weeks on end when he seemed sunk in apathy unable to perform, even perfunctorily, the duties of his office. For the last ten years of his ministry he never recorded the names of those whom he baptized or married. For day after day he would sit in his dark study, gazing vacantly at the peaceful flow of the river and the still reflections of the forest trees.

Such was the sombre yet beloved figure who dominated Bonar Law's earliest days. It has been necessary to describe the father's character at length because he transmitted a part at least of that character to his son. This did not, indeed, become apparent in Bonar Law's boyhood, for he appears to have been carefree and cheerful then. But in later life a certain melancholy, not to be explained solely by his tragic bereavements, obsessed his spirits. Many have commented upon the indefinable sadness which seemed to linger around his presence. He never succumbed to the malady which paralysed his father's mind, but he knew well enough what his father had been, and he may easily have feared lest he himself might fall a victim to the same strange affliction. Something of this fear can be seen in his almost unnatural anxiety to fill every waking hour of his life with an occupation – no matter what it might be. To brood in solitude was not only wrong; it was, in his case, dangerous too.

However, there was no peril of this sort in Bonar Law's childhood. As a boy he was energetic, vigorous, and mischievous. He had excellent health and a sturdy body. He enjoyed the simple open-air life on the farm. He was in fact a normal high-spirited boy, not particularly studious or devoted to books, but quick at his lessons and able to learn more easily than most children of his age. There is a story of his reciting, at the age of twelve, a poem one hundred lines long at an entertainment in the Temperance Hall of Richibucto. Those who search for examples of later qualities in early life may choose to see here an early sign of the powers of memory for which Bonar Law was to be famous. But in general it is not easy to discern in the robust and uninhibited boy any of the characteristics which marked the business man and politician of later years.

A contemporary who knew him in his days at Kingston writes:

"My vivid recollection is of a stocky, eager boy, tirelessly active and apparently frivolous beyond cure. He was quick tempered but unresentful, and there was about him a kind of impudent frankness which was very engaging. He was noticeable for his courage. I remember how, when he was playing in the big barn into which he and his brothers and sister were turned on Sundays to amuse themselves out of sight and earshot of easily scandalized neighbours, he fell from a rafter fifteen or twenty feet from the ground. Dazed as he was, he immediately challenged his companions to leap as he had done from the roof.

"On another occasion we were getting in the hay from the field. Bonar was astride the horse between the shafts of the hay wain when, without warning, the animal threw up its head and knocked the boy to the ground. He fell with one arm doubled up beneath him so that it sustained a slight fracture. In silence he picked himself up and in silence was led to the doctor, holding with his free hand the useless limb. Such self-containment was impressive in a child of his years."

The life that he and his brothers led was anything but luxurious. Their father was a poor man. It is difficult to say exactly what his income was, nor would a mere statement of figures have very much meaning, but it is clear that his children were expected to work on the farm in their holidays and spare time, that domestic servants, and labour of all kinds were difficult to obtain, and that the household, though never impoverished, was run with the maximum of economy and frugality. Bonar Law learned that meals do not appear by magic at regular intervals, but that food must be cooked and plates washed up. He learned that if he was not to starve and freeze in winter, he must work at the harvest and saw logs in summer.

It is impossible to say how much effect this frugal upbringing had upon Bonar Law's character. Its significance can easily be exaggerated. For in 1870, when he was only twelve, an event of far-reaching importance in his life occurred. His father married again, his wife being Miss Sophia Wood, a New Brunswick schoolmistress. There was clearly no longer any place for Miss Janet Kidston in her brother-in-law's household. She decided to return to Scotland, but before doing so she made an offer to James Law which was to reshape the whole career of his youngest son. She suggested that she should take Bonar with her to Scotland and that she and her Kidston relations would be responsible for his education and for starting him off in a business career. James Law, however sorry he was to lose a son, must have seen the advantages which this offer would give to his boy, and he may have welcomed having one less child to support from his exiguous stipend. At all events, he agreed to let Bonar go. In 1870, accompanied by his aunt, Bonar Law sailed to Glasgow. He never returned to New Brunswick.

It is convenient at this point to say briefly what became of the rest of the family. Bonar Law's father was compelled by ill health to leave New Brunswick in 1877. He returned to his native Ulster where he died five years later. Bonar Law's distress at his father's death was intense, indeed almost excessive in its expression – at all events by modern standards of convention. During these five years Bonar Law visited his father nearly every weekend. He thus came both to know and love the land of his ancestors – a fact destined to be of much significance in the political campaign which he was to fight thirty years later.

Bonar Law's stepmother died in 1914. Her two daughters – Bonar Law's half-sisters – outlived him by many years. Of his full brothers the eldest, Robert, remained in Kingston and farmed. The second brother returned to Ireland and practised as a doctor at Coleraine. The third brother eventually went into business with Bonar Law and became a partner in the firm of William Jacks & Company. The closest to him of all his family was his sister Mary. She came over from New Brunswick with her father in 1877, and when he died she came to live with Bonar Law until the latter's marriage in 1891. She was deeply devoted to her brother, and she never married. She died in 1929.

The world into which Bonar Law was so abruptly transported at the age of twelve was as remote as can be imagined from anything that he had experienced before. After an almost primitive life upon the edge of civilization he had abruptly moved near to the heart of one of the richest civilizations that had ever existed. Yet it may be doubted whether this transition made much impression upon a boy of his age. He may have observed that Sunday at Helensburgh, where the Kidstons lived, was even more dismal than at Kingston. There was no barn to play in, and one of his early memories was of long Sunday afternoons at his cousins' house "Ferniegair", when he would lie under a bed with the blind just raised enough to cast a dim light on to the novel of Sir Walter Scott that he was illicitly reading. But in general, new interests, a new school, and new companions must have absorbed his time sufficiently for him to take little notice of the great change in the circumstances of his life.

His education was resumed as soon as possible after their arrival in Helensburgh. At first he was sent as a boarder to a small school called Gilbertfield in Hamilton, which is today a suburb of Glasgow but was in those days a country town some eight miles from the city. Little is known about his progress there, but it was evidently quite good, for in his last term in May 1873 he won a first prize for Greek in the Junior Class. He then left Gilbertfield and went to Glasgow High School which both had – and has – a very high academic reputation. Once again he was successful at his work, and in September 1874 was awarded the first prize for French in the Junior Class of the Senior Division. His school reports were good, except in one respect: his handwriting was condemned as atrocious. If it was the same then as it became in later life, his biographer can testify to the justice of this judgment. In 1875 his school career came to an end, and he left at the age of sixteen before he had even matriculated.

His cousins had offered him a post in their Glasgow office, and there
he was to remain for the next ten years.

The Kidstons were first cousins of Bonar Law's mother and they
played a most important part in his early life. There were three
brothers, Charles, Richard, and William, all partners in a very
successful firm of merchant bankers which became merged in the
Clydesdale Bank in the eighteen-eighties. Two of the brothers –
Richard and William – remained bachelors and lived with their only
sister, Catherine, who also never married. The third brother, Charles,
was married but had no children. All four took the greatest interest
in their young cousin from New Brunswick and treated him with
every kindness, both personally and financially. They regarded him
not as a poor relation but, rather, as an heir. They were very wealthy.
Some idea of their means may be gained from the fact that Mrs.
Charles Kidston, who outlived her husband and inherited most of
her money from him, left nearly £200,000 when she died in 1896,
and Miss Catherine Kidston who died ten years later left over
£150,000.

Helensburgh, which was to be Bonar Law's home for nearly forty
years, is situated about twenty miles north-west of Glasgow on the
northern shore of the Firth of Clyde. Despite all that has happened
in the past eighty years, the place cannot have altered very much
since the days of his youth. Its wide and spacious streets slope gently
upwards from the Clyde. The upper windows of the houses command
a splendid view across the water towards Greenock. The town is
neatly laid out in rectangles according to the plan imposed by its
landlords, the Colquhouns of Luss, at the end of the eighteenth century. The houses are mostly of a later date. Large and solid, built of
grey stone in the mid-Victorian Gothic style – and built to last – they
have a sober and substantial appearance not always found in English
architecture of the same period. They stand in ample grounds, and
those which still survive with their inevitable conservatories, walled
gardens, and the monkey puzzles beloved of the Victorians, remain
silent witnesses to the sedate, prosperous – and now long-vanished –
way of life led by the rich Glasgow business men who built them and
lived in them.

It was a way of life in many respects peculiar to the Scotland of
that time. The Scots of all classes are highly conscious of their family
connexions, often extending to very distant cousins. In those days
one's circle of acquaintance tended to be confined to what was
known as "the connexion", but since families were large and "the

connexion" was held to cover all sorts of remote relatives together
with the families into which they had married, this circle was often
a very wide one. The Kidston "connexion" dominated Helensburgh, and, in his boyhood, the invitations and hospitality which
Bonar Law received must have come very largely from relatives of
one kind or another.

Miss Janet Kidston, with whom Bonar Law actually lived, owned
a small house by the name of "Seabank". It was built about 1830
in classical Palladian style, and, as the name suggests, was situated
only a few yards from the water's edge. It has now been demolished.
About half a mile away stood – and still stands – "Ferniegair", the
home of the unmarried Kidston cousins. It is a large Victorian mansion in spacious grounds, on the outskirts of Helensburgh, about a
hundred yards from the sea. Bonar Law spent much of his early
youth in this house. Outside Helensburgh proper, about a mile from
"Ferniegair" and high up the hill, was "Glenoran", the home of
Mr. and Mrs. Charles Kidston. It had beautiful grounds and a
magnificent prospect across the Clyde. Bonar Law was a frequent
visitor there. Had he lived long enough he would have inherited the
house, for his cousin had tied it up in an entail of which he was the
ultimate beneficiary, but he died before this could happen and it
went to his children. The house still stands somewhat forlornly amidst
its overgrown gardens. It has long passed out of the family into other
hands.

The Kidstons' world was very self-contained. The wealthy Scottish
middle classes to which they belonged were divided by a clear line
not only from the class below but from the class above also. Their
attitude, their prejudices, their pleasures, their voices even, were
quite different from those of the Scottish nobleman or laird. An even
deeper gulf lay between them and the territorial aristocracy of
England. They had their own values, and they had no desire to move
up into a class of whose outlook upon many matters they strongly
disapproved. The Kidstons were generous and rich. Had they wished,
they could easily have sent Bonar Law to an expensive public school
followed by Oxford or Cambridge. But they would have regarded
such a choice as ridiculous. They considered it more sensible to send
a boy who was destined to earn his living in business to Glasgow
High School, and give him a clerkship in their office when he was
sixteen.

The years which Bonar Law spent in the Kidstons' office were the
formative years of his life. He was a boy when they began; he was a

mature young man of twenty-seven when they ended. It is safe to
say that few people change fundamentally in character after that
age. It is disappointing therefore to have to admit that on the whole
we know very little about the processes and influences at work in
Bonar Law's inner mind during this period – far less than we do
about the great majority of eminent men who have lived in recent
times.

There are various reasons for this gap. He kept no diary, he wrote
few letters – at any rate scarcely any that have survived from this
time. He was not given to confidences. He was very self-sufficient,
with the reserve which often marks a boy who has been brought up
away from his parents by relatives however kind. Nor did he in later
life indulge much in reminiscence. It was characteristic of him that
he seldom went back either in mind or body to the scenes of the past.
He never revisited New Brunswick. After he finally moved to London
in 1909 he scarcely ever returned to Helensburgh except for family
events which he had to attend. All his life he lived very much in the
present. He neither looked back to the past, nor attempted to stare
far into the future. It was perhaps a part of the strange anonymity
of his character that he never bothered to reflect upon the events
which had made him what he was. He took little interest in his own
early days and saw no reason why anyone else should do so.

His external mode of life can be reconstructed easily enough.
Every morning he would travel up from Helensburgh on the 7.10
train. In winter the oil lamps which lit the carriages were so dim
that in order to play chess – to which he was even then addicted –
he and his companion used to bring little candle lamps which they
fixed to the cushions, so that they could see the board. The train
wound its way for about fifty minutes through some of Glasgow's
more dismal suburbs and finally deposited its passengers in the acrid
and sulphurous gloom of the station known as Queen Street Lower
Level. It was a brief walk from the station to the Kidstons' Queen
Street office. Bonar Law worked there in the morning, snatched a
hasty luncheon at Lang's Coffee House nearby and sometimes had
time for a game of chess before returning to work in the afternoon.
He went back to Helensburgh in the evening. It was a humdrum
unexciting sort of life. Thousands of clerks and young business men
led just such an existence then, and thousands from the same class
lead one not very different today.

But Bonar Law's leisure time was spent, at least in part, in a
manner which is less familiar now. It was still the age of Samuel

Smiles, of earnest self-improvement – anyway in Scotland. Bonar
Law was very much a Victorian in this respect, if not in others. He
was conscious of the gaps in his education, and he sought to fill them
by voracious reading and by attending lectures, debates, and essay
societies. He went to classes given under the auspices of Glasgow
University, and used to recall that the most interesting and memorable were the philosophy lectures of Sir Edward Caird, who later
became Master of Balliol. In 1879 he was present at the installation
of Gladstone as Lord Rector of the University. The spectacle fired
his youthful ambition. "I left that great meeting", he said, many
years later, "with the hope and indeed the intention of one day
occupying the post that was then filled by Mr. Gladstone." When
he said these words his ambition had come true: they are to be found
in his own Rectorial address delivered to the students of Glasgow
University in 1921.

During these early years Bonar Law was an avid reader. The
author whom he most admired was Carlyle, and throughout his life
on the rare occasions that he used literary quotations in his speeches,
it was almost invariably Carlyle that he quoted. He had an encyclo-
paedic knowledge of the works of that prolific writer, and could
often name not only the page on which a particular passage could
be found in the edition that he used, but the exact place where it lay
on the page. His favourite book was *Sartor Resartus*. Carlyle is not a
fashionable author today, and few people read him, but in the
'seventies and 'eighties of the last century he was very much in vogue,
especially in his own native land. To some extent the influence of
Carlyle may have contributed to Bonar Law's Conservatism. It is
not easy to define the exact political doctrine that emerges from the
cryptic utterances of the Sage of Ecclefechan, but whatever else it
may be, it certainly cannot be described as Liberal.

The other authors whom he greatly admired were Walter Scott,
Dickens, and above all, Gibbon. Austen Chamberlain many years
later in conversation with Bonar Law confessed that he personally
had never been able to finish the *Decline and Fall*. Bonar Law was
astonished and declared that he had read it through three times
before he was twenty-one. On another occasion he told H. A. L.
Fisher that Gibbon's narration of the extraordinary vicissitudes of
the Roman Emperors, of common soldiers achieving the highest
position only to fall to yet another successful adventurer, was a
subject of perpetual fascination to him.

When did his ambitions first lean towards politics? It is impossible to say for certain, but all who knew him agree that from a very early age he hoped ultimately for a political career. That goal may at times have seemed remote. It was necessary to command both money and influence in order to enter Parliament, and in his younger days Bonar Law possessed neither. But it seems clear that he never regarded his business career as an end in itself, rather as a means for acquiring the independence without which politics is neither a safe nor an honourable profession. Money-making did not attract him for its own sake. As a young man he once delivered a paper entitled "Is Life Worth Living?" to the Helensburgh Eclectic Society. He came to the comforting conclusion that on the whole it is, but in the process of reaching that conclusion he commented severely and somewhat rhetorically on the man who devotes his entire life to accumulating a fortune:

"He heaps up riches, and knows not, and does not dare to ask, who shall gather them. He spends his days like a mole in grubbing with blinded eyes in the mouldy earth, but unlike the mole his grubbing is altogether aimless."

There was never any doubt about the party which Bonar Law would join if he entered politics. The Kidstons, unlike the great majority of the Scottish merchant class to which they belonged, were ardent Conservatives. Middle-class Scotland was in general at that time a stronghold of Liberalism. Why the Kidstons should have been an exception it is difficult to say, but the fact is beyond dispute. Conservative politicians who came to speak at Glasgow were naturally glad to accept hospitality from such distinguished members of a group which normally opposed them. Bonar Law was, therefore, brought up in an atmosphere of Tory politics. He must have met at his cousins' houses many of the most prominent Conservatives of the day. There is even a tradition that Disraeli once visited "Ferniegair", and an expression used by Bonar Law many years later suggests that he may have met – or at least seen – the great man in person. However that may be, Bonar Law had all his life a profound admiration for Disraeli. He studied his speeches, and could quote long extracts from them. He was an ardent reader of Disraeli's political novels. He had a corresponding aversion to the personality and works of Gladstone whom he persisted in regarding as a fraud and a humbug.

It would of course be wrong to suggest that Bonar Law was a Conservative solely because of environment and family tradition. He had too independent a mind for that. But the political atmosphere in which he was brought up was, as it happens, congenial to his whole temperament and outlook upon life. A person who is by nature cautious, who views Utopian plans with scepticism, who believes that the art of politics lies in choosing the least disastrous course rather than discovering the panacea of human ills, is more likely to be a Tory than a Radical – and Bonar Law had all these qualities and beliefs.

The first necessity for anyone with political ambitions is to learn the art of public speaking. Accordingly, at an early age Bonar Law became a member of the Glasgow Parliamentary Debating Association which held its meetings at the Assembly Rooms in Bath Street. It was a mock Parliament founded by some enthusiastic young men in 1876. It copied as closely as possible the rules of procedure in the House of Commons, and its "Speaker", James Turnbull, spent some weeks at Westminster studying the proper way to manage debates. Members had imaginary constituencies; there was a Prime Minister and a Cabinet; bills were introduced, and carried, rejected, or amended. There was even for a time a sort of Hansard – a weekly journal called *The Mace* which devoted much of its columns to reporting debates and had, surprisingly, quite a wide circulation in Glasgow. A mock Parliament of this sort might easily have degenerated into farce but for the strong personality of the Speaker. In fact, however, it was taken very seriously, met regularly every week, and was as invaluable a training ground in politics for the young business men of Glasgow, as the Oxford and Cambridge Unions were for the sons of the upper classes in contemporary England.

Bonar Law was the "member" for North Staffordshire. He is first recorded as taking part in debates early in 1879, and shortly afterwards as occupying the post of Home Secretary in a Conservative "Government", which unfortunately only lasted for one night. However he was frequently to hold that position again when a Conservative majority prevailed. *The Mace* did not believe in flattering the members of the Association, and on more than one occasion Bonar Law was singled out for criticism:

"The hon. gentleman's style of delivery", said the paper, "reminds one of the verses of the 'Sexton's Daughter' as read aloud by its author and described by Carlyle. 'A drea·y pulpit or even conventicle manner; that flattest moaning hoo hoo of predetermined pathos, with a kind of rocking canter introduced by way of intonation, each stanza the exact fellow of the other, and the dull swing of the rocking horse duly in each'. Why does not Staffordshire give up this style which mars but does not altogether spoil the fine matter of his speeches?"

On another occasion he was accused of insufficient seriousness –
always a grave charge in Scotland:

"It is a great mistake for members who possess ability, as North
Staffordshire undoubtedly does, to devote themselves to uttering common-
places or jocularities. Frivolities, even from an able speaker, are still
frivolities, and are of no assistance in furthering argument in debate."

However, the comments are not all adverse. In September 1881
we find Bonar Law being held up as a model to be imitated by
maiden speakers:

"It is at once evident that he understands his business – down even to
the by no means unimportant detail of where to take his position for
speaking. He makes just enough of reference to preceding speeches to give
a colour of spontaneity to the carefully prepared attack which he is going
to deliver."

Bonar Law himself was always grateful for what he had learned
in the Glasgow Parliament. It was a most valuable experience, and
it taught him much that he could hardly have acquired in any other
way. He remained an active member for ten years, until his increased
business commitments, and finally his marriage in 1891 made regular
attendance impossible, but the result of his experience was that when
he entered Parliament in 1900 he was far more familiar with its
traditions and procedure, and had to learn far less, than most new
Members. His early success in the House can be attributed very
largely to the technique that he had mastered in the Glasgow Parliament fifteen years earlier.

It is perhaps convenient to record briefly what was happening in
the politics of the real world while Bonar Law was thus being appren-
ticed in the mock politics of the Parliamentary Debating Association.
From 1874 to 1880 Disraeli was in power. In 1880 Gladstone's
Midlothian campaign resulted in a Liberal victory. He was Prime
Minister till May 1885 when he was replaced by a Tory minority
administration headed by Lord Salisbury. The General Election of
autumn, 1885, put Gladstone back in office, but his decision to introduce an Irish Home Rule Bill broke his party in half and resulted
in his own defeat, first in the House of Commons and then at the
polls. Supported by the dissident Liberal Unionists, Lord Salisbury
was Prime Minister from 1886 to 1892.

Keen though he was on self-improvement Bonar Law devoted some
of his leisure during his time at the Kidstons' office to recreation. In
his early youth he liked walking, and with a companion would tramp

the roads round Helensburgh. He did this not from any love of scenery – though in fact there is splendid scenery in that district - but for the sake of exercise. He was very fond of lawn tennis, played with much energy, and in a deceptive style that made him surprisingly difficult to beat. Together with some friends, he founded a tennis club at Helensburgh and secured the hard courts upon which the club still plays. He also became a keen though not very skilful golfer, and after his marriage spent nearly every holiday near a golf course. He played off a handicap of about sixteen. During these early years he must have spent some of his holidays in France and Germany, though it is not clear exactly where and when. He certainly acquired a competent working knowledge of both languages, but the soft Scottish Canadian accent which betrayed his origin when he spoke his own tongue was equally apparent when he talked French.

He was devoted to indoor games, in particular to chess, billiards, and whist, later of course to bridge. He was a good performer at all of them, especially chess, in which he excelled. It was a game which fascinated him, and going up and down in the train, he would amuse himself by solving chess problems if he could not get someone to play with him. For an amateur player he was exceptionally good although inclined by expert standards to be rather reckless. Jacques Mieses, an Austrian chess master who played with him a good deal in later life, declared that he was one of the best performers of the amateur class whom he had ever encountered.

To certain categories of pleasure he was from the first totally indifferent. At a very early age he became a teetotaller and he never touched alcohol except on doctors' orders for the rest of his life. It is not clear why he made this resolution. He did not preach it to others, and later when he had a house of his own he offered guests wine or spirits as a matter of course. This abstinence made him an unusual Conservative, for it was in the ranks of the Liberal Party that the vast majority of Temperance men were to be found. Ginger ale or lime juice seems to have been his favourite drink. As a nightcap, when orthodox persons consumed a whisky and soda, he would invariably take a glass of milk and some gingerbread. Moreover he cared nothing for the other pleasures of the table. A meal was something that was necessary for human sustenance but should be despatched as quickly as possible. He scarcely noticed what he ate, and, when he could, he left the table as soon as he had finished. He was, on the other hand, a devotee of tobacco and smoked cigars and pipes incessantly.

Although he was fond of reading history and literature, he cared nothing for art or music. Theatres and operas bored him to distraction. He never attended if he could possibly escape them, and the daughter of the then Master of Trinity College recalls how special arrangements were made for him to be spared the music in King's Chapel when he received an honorary degree at Cambridge in 1920. All these aversions, which became a matter of amused comment when he grew famous, appear to have existed from his very earliest days.

The Kidstons' office gave Bonar Law a valuable insight into the methods and technique of business, but it did not fully occupy his time. The truth was that his cousins, who were getting on in years, did not wish to continue the firm for much longer. By 1885 they had for some time been contemplating a merger with the Clydesdale Bank, and it was clear that there was no real future for Bonar Law in their office. William Kidston & Company was largely concerned with the financing of the iron and steel trade, and one of the principal firms with which they did business was that of William Jacks & Company. William Jacks had started up as an iron merchant on his own in 1880. He was an active Liberal politician and in the early 'eighties he successfully stood as Liberal candidate for Leith. He often travelled up to Glasgow in the same railway carriage as Bonar Law. Anxious to find a suitable person to whom he could delegate his work, now that he was in Parliament, he decided in 1885 to offer Bonar Law a partnership, reserving to himself a right of veto.

Bonar Law consulted his cousins. They saw that it was an opportunity not to be missed, and they agreed not only to release him from their office but to put up the money needed to buy him his partnership. At the age of twenty-seven, therefore, he was suddenly transferred from a relatively subordinate position to that of the effective partner in an important and prosperous concern. It was a big step upwards and a clear indication that he was regarded as an able business man. It must, moreover, have meant almost immediately a large increase in his income.

Although economic historians have subsequently traced the beginning of its slow decline to this period, the Glasgow iron market appeared in the middle 'eighties to be in a flourishing condition. Indeed, the five years that immediately followed Bonar Law's entry into William Jacks were years of boom and strenuous activity. The essence of the system was somewhat similar to that of the Liverpool Cotton Exchange. The ironmasters – the firms which actually made the pig iron – deposited their products at Connal's Stores on the

Above, left: Bonar Law and his aunt, Miss Janet Kidston, *c.* 1873
Above, right: Bonar Law and his brother, Jack, *c.* 1876
Below, left: Bonar Law at the age of 22
Below, right: Mrs. Bonar Law, an early portrait

south side of Glasgow. Connal's issued what were called warrants against any iron deposited there, i.e. documents which entitled their owners to a specified quantity, usually 500 tons, of pig iron. The iron merchants, acting as intermediaries between the ironmasters and the firms which ultimately purchased the pig iron, made their profit by dealing in Connal's warrants on the Glasgow iron market. This was conducted at the Royal Exchange. Every day from eleven to twelve o'clock and from two to three, the iron merchants would sit on their chairs in a circle, their clerks standing behind them, and carry on their business. At the close of the day's transactions settlement was made in the basement. Warrants changed hands and balances were settled in cash. It is said of Bonar Law that he never needed to take a note of his purchases and sales but could remember every detail in his head when the time came for settlement.

It was a highly speculative form of business. Prices were liable to violent fluctuation. Scares, rumours, changing trade conditions, the monetary policy of the Bank of England, all affected the price of pig iron. Evidently the basic prosperity of the Glasgow iron market depended upon the ability of Scottish manufacturers to supply large quantities of cheap pig iron. The larger the supply in Connal's stores, the greater the number of warrants, and the more business conducted on the Glasgow market. But at just this time the primacy of Scottish pig iron was beginning to decline. The Cleveland iron industry based on Middlesbrough was beginning to rival it. The growth of the Bessemer process was another blow, for it required haematite or non-phosphoric ore, which in Britain existed only in Cumberland. This spread in the geographical basis of the iron industry inevitably reduced the importance of Glasgow. Towards the end of the century the London metal market became increasingly predominant.

These changes did not cause any immediate difficulties to William Jacks. For one thing pig iron was not their only business. They dealt with iron ore on a large scale and were agents in Britain for the Nova Scotia Steel & Coal Company. Among their clients was the great German firm of Krupps, and, although this fact was destined in 1914 to have serious consequences which will be described in due course, it was a source of high profit during the earlier years. Moreover, the firm endeavoured to meet the new conditions in the pig iron business. In 1888 a branch was established in Middlesbrough under the management of Bonar Law's brother Jack who had returned from tea planting in Ceylon. In 1894 another branch was set up in

London under the control of Mr. Gray Buchanan who was, as it happened, a connexion of Mrs. Charles Kidston. This branch soon became a totally independent firm, and William Jacks of London is today a very large and prosperous concern. William Jacks of Glasgow, however, was destined to fall on bad times towards the end of Bonar Law's life, and his large holding in its preference shares was, at his death, almost worthless. But during the period that Bonar Law was a partner in the firm it was a lucrative business from which he made a very comfortable income.

William Jacks's Glasgow office was at 7 Royal Bank Place, a stone's throw from the Royal Exchange. Mr. Gray Buchanan has kindly supplied an account of Bonar Law's working day which throws an interesting light on his mode of life and his character.

"He would arrive in his office at 8.50 from the early Helensburgh train, open all the letters himself, and have round him the various heads of departments, Foreign, Pig Iron, and Warrant. Some quotations would have to be made at once which he would attend to, taking a view of what the markets would do that day. Then the time sheet would be brought in to him and those clerks who had arrived after nine with their entries in red ink would get a wigging.

"By 10.55 he would be on his way down to the Royal Exchange where business on the Iron Ring was announced by a bell being rung. A circle of chairs and 40 or 50 brokers sitting with their clerks behind them – Warrants each for 500 tons of Pig Iron were dealt in . . .

"Back to the offices, lunch, a quick lunch, as a game of chess followed. Back to the Iron Ring 2–3 p.m., and then making of quotations for the post for pig iron, steel plates, generally for Canada.

"About 3.30 he came out of his private room and sat at a desk in the general office signing all the letters and quotations and contracts until 4.10, when he left for the Helensburgh train – a short day, but it began early and the pace was hot while it lasted. Glasgow business men who lived at Troon or Helensburgh liked a game of golf at night and worked for it."

Mr. Buchanan goes on to say:

"In business he did not like lieutenants. He wanted to guide everything, and this was not easy working from 8.45 to 4.10, while we were in the offices to 10 p.m. or later . . .

"Our memories of him are of a shrewd business man carrying on business on the lines of his favourite game of chess, forming his own opinions, and pinning his faith to them, using his pawns as pawns, straight, firm and upright in his own actions and insisting upon the same with others. He asked for absolute obedience and preferred that his orders should be carried out literally.

"He never asked for favours and therefore never expected to be asked for them. Perhaps because of that he stood more alone than most men."

Such was the way in which Bonar Law spent his working days for the next fourteen years from 1886 to 1900. Quick, efficient, hardworking, straightforward, a trifle dictatorial, he was a successful business man. He soon acquired the general respect of the Glasgow business world, and towards the end of the time received numerous directorships. By the time he was forty he had become both financially and in repute a man of substance, whose judgment was sought after and highly valued.

Meanwhile an important event occurred in his life. In 1890 he met and fell in love with Miss Annie Pitcairn Robley, the daughter of a Glasgow shipbroker who lived in Helensburgh at a house called "Kintillo", which was later to be Bonar Law's own home. She was twenty-four, and eight years younger than Bonar Law. Although the Robleys were residents of Helensburgh, they did not belong to the Kidston "connexion", and appear to have moved in a somewhat less austere circle than the grave society which was frequented by Bonar Law and his relatives. Annie Robley was fond of dancing and of such entertainment as Helensburgh and its neighbourhood provided in those days. Bonar Law was induced for a short time to relax from his rather solemn mode of life, and even to go to dances. It is recorded that he actually went to a fancy dress ball on one occasion, dressed as a sailor, Miss Robley being disguised as a Swiss peasant. With his hatred for music he must have found all this a strain and his elder daughter can remember being reproved at a dancing class for biting her lip in just the same way as her father used to do when he attended balls at Helensburgh years before. He became engaged towards the end of the year, and on March 24th, 1891, their marriage took place at the West Free Church of Helensburgh. It was followed by a honeymoon in Paris. When they returned the couple settled down to live at "Seabank", which Bonar Law's aunt had handed over to him. There is little to record about the marriage. Mrs. Law was a person of spontaneity, sweetness, and charm. She was universally loved, and he was a most devoted husband. They had seven children, the eldest being stillborn. This large family soon necessitated a move, and on his father-in-law's death Bonar Law bought "Kintillo". It was a biggish Victorian house standing in an acre of garden, about half a mile from the sea. There he and his family remained until in 1909 his political duties obliged him to move finally to London.

CHAPTER II

FIRST STEPS IN POLITICS

1891 – 1909

Bonar Law's finances – He becomes a candidate – The Khaki Election of 1900 – He wins Blackfriars Division of Glasgow – Aristocratic nature of politics in 1900 – Characters of Salisbury and Balfour – Position of Joseph Chamberlain – Bonar Law's admiration for him – Chamberlain's imperial creed – Bonar Law's maiden speech – His despondency at political life – His first successes in the House – He becomes Parliamentary Secretary to the Board of Trade – Tariff Reform – Divisions in the Conservative Party – Bonar Law as a speaker – The Election of 1906 – Bonar Law defeated at Glasgow but returned for Dulwich – His friends in the House – Party discontent with Balfour – Joseph Chamberlain's illness – Bonar Law as one of his political heirs – Bonar Law's coolness towards Churchill – His rising prestige in the Party – He moves to London and buys Pembroke Lodge

THE years that followed Bonar Law's marriage saw a steady rise in his prosperity. William Jacks & Company was flourishing and he was earning a substantial income. The financial independence which he deemed necessary for a political career was suddenly brought much nearer in 1896 when Mrs. Charles Kidston died.[1] As we saw, she left nearly £200,000. Among her many bequests was a legacy of £30,000 for Bonar Law. This, together with his directorships and the investment income from the money he had made in business, was enough for him to consider the possibility of abandoning his partnership in William Jacks and entering into politics. Early in 1897 he began looking for a constituency.

A good many errors are current about Bonar Law's finances. Even at the risk of anticipating the main narrative, it is as well to make the situation quite clear. When he entered Parliament in 1900 he gave up active business, but retained his directorships. He did not relinquish them until his election to the leadership of the Party in the House of Commons in 1911. Perhaps the most important was that of the Clydesdale Bank, and for many years he used to travel from London to Glasgow even during Parliamentary sessions, at considerable inconvenience, in order to attend board meetings. It is

[1] Her husband died in 1894. Richard Kidston died earlier in the same year. William Kidston died in 1889.

36

interesting to notice that in those days a post in the Government did not necessitate the abandonment of directorships, as it would today. Bonar Law retained his directorships throughout his three years as Parliamentary Under-Secretary at the Board of Trade. His income during his first ten years in the House seems to have been about £6,000 per annum, of which some £4,500 came from investments, the rest from directorships. During this period he received another legacy from the Kidston family. Miss Catherine Kidston, the last survivor of the cousins, left him £30,000, thus bringing his total inheritance from that family to at least £60,000. The income from this legacy almost exactly balanced the loss of directors' fees from 1911 onwards, and his income continued to be just below £6,000 until the war broke out. When he entered the Cabinet in 1915 it rose to over £10,000, and remained about this figure for several years.

Bonar Law's will was proved at £71,324 (after deduction of estate duty, £61,213), but he had been, for nearly all his political life, substantially better off than this figure suggests. Its relative lowness can be explained by the heavy losses that he sustained at the very end of his life owing to the collapse of William Jacks of Glasgow, and to the fact that he had personally guaranteed the overdraft of one of the partners.

To sum up: Bonar Law was not, as some people supposed, a man of great wealth, but on the other hand he was very comfortably off, in those days of low income tax and a pound worth three times what it is now. Nor was he, as others supposed, a purely self-made man who had accumulated a fortune by his own unaided efforts. He certainly knew how to make money, and was successful in doing so, but he received very substantial legacies, and but for that good fortune he might not have entered politics when he did.

Although Bonar Law took a good deal of trouble to prepare himself for a political career, he did not follow the orthodox path to national politics. He was not conspicuous in local politics for example, and even in the Helensburgh Conservative Association he occupied no higher post than that of a temporary acting vice-president. He preferred to train himself as a speaker first by attending the Glasgow Parliament, and in later years by the somewhat curious method of going to bankruptcy meetings. Whenever there was a bankruptcy in which William Jacks were creditors he used to make a point of attending and speaking. It was, he maintained later, a very useful, if unorthodox, training for Parliamentary debates. From 1892 onwards he began speaking at political meetings in and near Glasgow.

In April 1897 we find for the first time a reference in his correspondence to the possibility of his becoming a Parliamentary
candidate. His name had been mentioned by one of his colleagues
in the Glasgow Parliament to Mr. Lewis Shedden who was secretary
of the Glasgow Unionist Association, and Shedden suggested it to
the Blackfriars Conservative Association, which was seeking a candidate at the time. Bonar Law was not willing to commit himself at
once, because he did not wish to have the trouble of nursing a constituency for some years before the election. Nevertheless he agreed
to speak to the Association. Shedden recalls in a letter to Lord
Coleraine[1]:

"I do not think it is true to say that your father displayed great nervous-
ness on his first appearance as a candidate. He spoke without notes and
rapidly – too rapidly in fact. He showed no hesitation in his delivery,
never had to fumble for the right word and rather conveyed the impression
that his speech had been carefully prepared beforehand and memorised
perfectly."

Bonar Law had no rival claimant, and the local Association gladly
accepted him. Early in 1898 he allowed his name to be officially
announced as prospective Conservative candidate for the Blackfriars
and Hutchesontown Division of Glasgow.

The constituency, one of seven into which Glasgow was divided,
had, ever since its creation by the Reform Bill of 1884, invariably
returned a Liberal Member to Parliament. The sitting Member, one
A. D. Provand, even survived the General Election of 1895, although
the Liberals had fared very badly in most other places. Bonar Law's
prospects of success, therefore, were remote. It was reasonable to
suppose that the next Election would show some swing of the pendulum against the Conservative Government, and that seats like
Blackfriars would remain safely occupied by Liberal Members. It is
unlikely that Bonar Law expected to win. He probably hoped to put
up a good fight and establish his claim to a less difficult constituency
next time.

But events turned out very differently from anything that could
have been predicted early in 1898. For within two years the country
was engaged in a war with the Boer Republics of the Transvaal and
the Orange Free State. It is unnecessary here to discuss the highly-
disputed rights and wrongs of the South African War. It is enough
to say that whereas the Conservatives were united in believing that it
was a righteous war, the Liberals were deeply divided, an important

[1] Richard Law, Bonar Law's youngest son.

section bitterly opposing it on the ground that the whole affair was engineered by the capitalists of the Rand, and the financiers of the City. The Conservatives could therefore declare with some plausibility that a vote for the Liberals was a vote for the Boers. This opportunity of enlisting patriotic sentiment was too good to miss. As soon as the war seemed safely won – and this appeared (though incorrectly) to be the case by summer 1900 – Lord Salisbury recommended a dissolution. In October began what the angry Liberals later called "the Khaki Election".

These unexpected events greatly favoured the fortunes of the Conservative Party. It was easy to tar even those Liberals who supported the war with the brush of "Little Englandism". The Government in general held its ground throughout the country, only losing about twenty seats, and in some places they actually captured traditionally Liberal strongholds. One of these places was the Blackfriars Division of Glasgow, and Bonar Law found himself head of the poll, having converted a Tory minority of some five hundred into a majority of exactly 1,000, which for those days was large. The figures were: A. Bonar Law, 4,140; A. D. Provand, 3,140. The Election was in many places fought with great bitterness. Lloyd George, for example, was nearly lynched in Birmingham and had to escape from the town hall disguised as a policeman. But Bonar Law's contest, though vigorous, appears to have been fought with good humour, and the Glasgow Press commented upon his "genial temper" and his "equable manner".

And so Bonar Law crossed the first fence in a career of politics both more easily and more quickly than he could have expected. When he became a candidate early in 1898 there was little reason to anticipate an Election before the beginning of 1902, and still less reason to anticipate a Conservative victory in that particular constituency. However, having once taken the plunge Bonar Law was not the man to do things by halves. He promptly arranged to relinquish his active partnership in William Jacks. Politics necessitated a new mode of life and, although he did not at first give up his house in Helensburgh, he spent only half the year there from then onwards. During the Parliamentary session which normally lasted from February to the end of July he moved with his whole family to a furnished house in London. The duty of finding each year a satisfactory house for the children, and of arranging the annual move from Scotland to London and back again fell upon Mrs. Law. Together with the task of bringing up a family of six, it must have made her life a busy one, but she carried out her duties with zest and enjoyment. She was intensely proud of her husband and of all his successes. If she did not fully understand the intricacies of politics, she certainly understood how to organize a home and provide a happy if unobtrusive background to the career that he led.

The political world into which Bonar Law now moved for the first time was essentially an aristocratic world. Despite all the changes of the nineteenth century, the Conservative Party remained the party of the traditional landed governing class which had ruled England for two hundred years. The composition of the Liberal Party was indeed somewhat different though it too contained great Whig magnates like Lord Rosebery, Lord Spencer, and Lord Crewe. But the Liberal Party had been convulsed, ever since the resignation of Mr. Gladstone in 1894, by a series of bitter internal feuds, and had temporarily ceased to be an effective political force. For eleven of the last fourteen years the Conservatives had been in office, and in 1900 they seemed well set for another six years of tranquil power.

At the head of the Party, survivor of the battles of a vanished political era, towered a solitary figure, Robert Cecil, the third Marquess of Salisbury. Although he was an intellectual who despised Society and Clubland, Lord Salisbury believed intensely in the preservation of an aristocratic hierarchy. The progress of democracy he regarded with profound apprehension and, throughout his long political career, he steadily opposed almost every move made in that direction. His chief interest was in foreign policy. Until 1900 he had combined the post of Foreign Secretary with that of Prime Minister – a conjunction, with one exception, unique in modern political history. No one could have been more remote than Lord Salisbury from the "common man". This remoteness was enhanced, almost symbolized, by the fact that he was a peer and a great landowner, and conducted foreign affairs by personal correspondence from his vast and venerable mansion at Hatfield almost as if they were the private business of his own estate. Yet he was by no means unpopular in the country, and he was regarded with great respect, if not affection, by the public. His position in the Party was unchallenged; no rival had dared to threaten him since the day some fourteen years earlier when Lord Randolph Churchill crashed to disaster in a rash bid for the party leadership.

The future, however, could not lie with Lord Salisbury. He was old and his health was beginning to fail. The future lay rather with his two principal lieutenants in the Lower House. The first of these was his own nephew Arthur James Balfour, who was leader of the House of Commons and was generally expected to be his uncle's successor. He too was an intellectual, an aristocrat and a large land-owner. He too believed in the preservation of an order of society which would continue to entrust the government of the country to the abler members of the great landed families. Eton, Trinity, Hat-field, "the Souls" – these were the influences that moulded him. He possessed great talents, he was a most formidable debater, he was an able minister, he was a brilliant talker. His charm, his affability and his wit gave him a wide and devoted circle of friends. Yet behind all this glitter there lay a hardness. "He always seemed to me", wrote Neville Chamberlain in his diary, "to have a heart like a stone." Sir Winston Churchill has commented upon the "cool ruthlessness" underneath Balfour's unfailing courtesy. His conduct was always one of scrupulous honour and rectitude, but he was not the man to be easily outmanoeuvred by persons less scrupulous than himself. "Had his life been cast amid the labyrinthine intrigues of Renaissance Italy", writes Churchill,[a] "he would not have required to study the works of Machiavelli".

The other leading figure in the Party was Joseph Chamberlain. His background was marked by none of the effortless ease which had characterized the career of Balfour. He had fought all his life, and fought hard. He did not belong to the ruling class. He was, like Bonar Law, a business man who had made enough money to retire and who entered Parliament when he was over forty. He began as the leader of the radical group in Gladstone's Cabinet of 1880–85. Then, just when it seemed as if he would inevitably inherit the leadership from the G.O.M., he resigned on the question of Irish Home Rule. For ten years he wandered in the political wilderness, detested by his old colleagues, yet reluctant to join the Conservative Party. But in 1895 Lord Salisbury offered him any position in the Cabinet that he wished. To the surprise of the political world he chose the Colonial Office – a department hitherto regarded as a backwater. It soon ceased to be so under Chamberlain's régime, for he now devoted the same restless energy, with which ten years earlier he had prosecuted the cause of Social Reform, to the movement for consolidating, unifying and developing the British Empire. He put himself at the head of the imperialist sentiment which swept the country during the 'nineties. He was a master at the art of popular leadership, and a great platform speaker. By 1900 he was probably far better known in the country than either Salisbury or Balfour. In the events leading up to the Jameson Raid and in the South African War he was the most prominent member of the Government. Regarded with implacable hatred by the Liberals, adored by the imperialists, Joseph Chamberlain stood forth as the most controversial, and the most famous statesman of his time.

There could be no question as to which of these two great political figures would inspire the emulation of Bonar Law. Joseph Chamberlain had a personal background similar to his own. Both of them were business men who understood economic and industrial problems, both of them came from outside the traditional governing class, neither of them belonged to the Church of England – an unusual characteristic among Conservatives of those days. It was almost inevitable that a man who had entered politics in the way that Bonar Law had done would seek to model himself upon Chamberlain. When the great imperialist died in 1914 it fell to Bonar Law as party leader to pronounce an encomium upon him in the House of Commons. He said: "At the time when I first entered this House I was young enough – and indeed I hope I still am – to be a hero-worshipper, and for me at that time the very essence of my political faith was belief in Mr. Chamberlain."

What exactly did this belief entail? It was not simply a matter of personal devotion. Joseph Chamberlain was not only a brilliant leader, he had a political creed which inspired the thoughts and actions of all the more "progressive" members of the Conservative Party. That creed was above all else a belief in the vital importance of converting the heterogeneous territories of the British Empire into a vast political unit which, if properly developed both economically and strategically, would be able to face with equanimity a challenge from any other great power. The imperialism of this period must be seen against its world background. Britain's hitherto unchallenged industrial supremacy, the long lead which we had gained over other nations thanks to our early exploitation of modern industrial methods and to our island position, were beginning to be threatened at the end of the nineteenth century. Both the U.S.A. and Germany were formidable trade rivals, and the latter, though late in the field, seemed a menace to our whole imperial position too. During the South African War Britain had been isolated, and found herself one of the most unpopular nations in the world. Only our naval supremacy and the feuds of our enemies saved us from a hostile intervention by the European Great Powers.

Yet at this very moment when our international position had

become less secure than at any time since 1815, we seemed to be threatened with the loss of our overseas dominions. South Africa had only been preserved by war. Canada seemed to be drifting into the orbit of the U.S.A. It was necessary therefore – or so it seemed to the imperialist party – to revitalize the whole concept of Empire. The policy of Tariff Reform had not yet been adumbrated, but there was a widespread feeling that, whether by political federation or by economic unification, some method must be found to arrest the centrifugal tendency of the dominions. A powerful and consolidated Empire could face the rivalry of Germany or America, but a Britain bereft of her overseas territories would in the long run succumb to the greater resources of these formidable powers. Moreover a policy of imperial development would have immense internal advantages too. It would lead to a rise in the prosperity of every class in the community. Not for nothing had Joseph Chamberlain begun his political career as the tribune of the people, the champion of the have-nots against the haves. On his side were all those who believed that the old-fashioned Toryism of the Cecils was now obsolete, and that only a positive policy would save the Party from defeat sooner or later at the hands of the Liberal Radicals who could offer so much more to the discontented masses.

In other words, the Conservatism that appealed to Bonar Law was the imperialist Conservatism of Rhodes and Chamberlain, the creed of the successful industrialists, of the engineers and technicians who were opening up a new world by their enterprise and their not always over-scrupulous vigour – the Conservatism of which Rudyard Kipling was both prophet and high priest.

The first entry of a new Member into Parliament is often a dis-illusioning experience. Enthusiastic and anxious to make a mark by loyally expounding the philosophy of his party, he is all too apt to find, after his maiden speech, that what the party wants is not his voice but his vote. Bonar Law's maiden speech was delivered during the debate on the Address in February 1901. It was a perfectly com-petent reply to a bitter attack by Lloyd George upon the punitive measures taken by the British Army against the Boer farmers, but it received no publicity. Bonar Law was perhaps unlucky, for on the very same day Winston Churchill made his first speech in the House of Commons, and inevitably the début of the son of Lord Randolph Churchill excited more notice than that of a middle-aged business man from Glasgow.

Soon after this Bonar Law appears to have been in a despondent mood. He had little to do. Despite his experiences in the Glasgow Parliament, much of the ritual and procedure of the House of Commons must have seemed at first maddeningly futile to someone accustomed to the brisk conduct of business on the Glasgow iron market. The life of London was unfamiliar to him. He was utterly indifferent to the glittering world of Edwardian Society into which an aspiring Tory politician could so easily enter. He hated social functions, and the prolonged dinner parties of those days with their many wines and their endless courses bored him beyond measure. There were times when he wondered why he had given up the familiar routine of Helensburgh and Glasgow. On such an occasion he once confided in Austen Chamberlain who was one of his earliest political acquaintances:

"He was sitting alone with me", writes Chamberlain,[b] "in the old smoking-room of the House of Commons, a prey to one of those moods of depression which beset him from time to time in his life. I tried to cheer him up. 'No, Austen,' he replied, 'this is no place for me. It's all very well for men like you who came into it young; but, if I had known then what I know now, I would never have stood for Parliament.' "

The Parliamentary session of 1901 was calm and tranquil. The Liberal Party was still rent by internal feuds. The Government engaged in some placid domestic legislation of an unimportant nature, but the chief interest in affairs was the South African War. For, contrary to the expectations so confidently entertained at the time of the Khaki Election, the Boers continued to resist with surprising obstinacy and success. There was indeed much to criticize in the conduct of the war, but the Liberals were in no position to do so at all effectively. The session of 1901 saw little discussion of the subjects which interested Bonar Law, foreign and imperial trade, the promotion of Empire unity.

But in the next session a much more promising field was opened up for him. Sir Michael Hicks Beach, the Chancellor of the Exchequer, decided that the cost of war could only be met by imposing a duty of one shilling per quarter upon imported wheat. This was not intended to be in any sense a concession to the doctrine of Tariff Reform, which indeed had not yet been officially propounded by Joseph Chamberlain. The essence of that doctrine was Imperial Preference, i.e. the imposition of a general duty on imports in order that it might be remitted in favour of imports from the Empire. Hicks Beach was, however, a Free Trader. His proposed duty was intended for revenue only and neither for Protection nor for Imperial Preference. Nevertheless, Liberal speakers, for lack of any other argument, claimed to see in this proposal the thin end of a Protectionist wedge capable, they said, of breaking the whole structure of the Free Trade economy, upon which British prosperity was alleged to depend.

It was in reply to these criticisms that on April 22nd, 1902, Bonar Law made the first speech which singled him out from the rank and file of the Party. It was delivered without notes, and perhaps somewhat too rapidly – a defect which he later outgrew – but with a remarkable command of figures and facts which at once impressed the House of Commons. Sir Arthur Boscawen who was present writes:

"He seemed to speak with the full practical knowledge of a man of business but with the detached and theoretical method of a Scottish metaphysician. . . . Members were amused but also greatly interested; and from that day Mr. Bonar Law had the ear of the House."

The details of Bonar Law's speech are of no interest today. It was not an exposition of Imperial Preference, but rather a good-humoured rebuttal of the theory that Free Trade must always and invariably remain sacrosanct, like the articles of some theological creed. The question of Free Trade and Protection, of the imposition or remission of duties, was one to be decided not on grounds of dogma but of common sense in the light of changing conditions. Bonar Law was inclined to think that for Britain at present Free Trade was the best policy, but it did not follow that Protection would never be necessary, and he pointed to the example of German industrial prosperity built up under a system of high protective tariffs.

The effect of this speech on his career was important. Today almost every Member of Parliament is able – or considers that he is able – to discourse with authority upon industrial and fiscal topics, but in those days far fewer could do so. Economics was still to most educated men "the dismal science". The average Conservative M.P. might have learnt a smattering of classics, law, and history, but he knew very little about trade, interest rates, and tariffs. A man of Bonar Law's evident capacity in this increasingly important field was marked for promotion. He did not have to wait for long. In July 1902 Lord Salisbury resigned, and was succeeded by Balfour. A number of older ministers took the opportunity of leaving the Government, and in the resulting reshuffle Bonar Law was appointed as Parliamentary Secretary to the Board of Trade. After only eighteen months apprenticeship in politics he had done well to receive such early promotion.

His duties at the Board of Trade were not unduly arduous. The President was the Prime Minister's brother, Gerald Balfour, who was also in the House of Commons. To Bonar Law fell only the duty of answering questions on relatively minor matters, and of occasionally speaking on the business of the department when the President was for any reason absent. In November he had occasion to make a speech on the subject of the Brussels Sugar Convention and its effect upon the West Indies. Once again the content is not of any historical interest, but it was evidently a very effective performance. Joseph Chamberlain, speaking afterwards in the same debate, described it as "one of the most admirable speeches, short though it was, to which I have ever listened in the House of Commons". This was praise indeed from such a quarter, and it must have been intensely gratifying to Bonar Law to receive such warm commendation from his political hero.

It was not long before the fiscal problem came even more to the forefront in politics. In the autumn of 1902 a Conference of Colonial Prime Ministers met under the presidency of the Colonial Secretary. A substantial measure of agreement was achieved, and a declaration made in favour of a measure of Imperial Preference. Joseph Chamberlain's mind had for some while been moving in this direction. The core of the argument was that political unity could only be achieved if economic unity came first. Just as a *zollverein*, or customs union, had preceded the political union of the numerous kingdoms into which Germany had been divided fifty years earlier, so a great tariff union embracing the whole of Britain's possessions overseas would be the surest way of preserving the political unity of the British Empire. Now that he had the Colonial Prime Ministers on his side, Chamberlain resolved to hesitate no longer. He was determined to take a first step in the direction of Imperial Preference, and for this purpose Hicks-Beach's revenue duty on imported wheat supplied a perfect opportunity. Why not retain the duty in the next Budget as far as foreign wheat was concerned, but remit it in the case of wheat imported from the colonies? The public had become accustomed to the principle of an import duty, but would have no objection to its relaxation in the case of the colonies. In this way the principle of Imperial Preference could be gradually and painlessly introduced into the fiscal system. Chamberlain persuaded the Cabinet to agree to this plan, and then in late autumn of 1902 departed to South Africa.

But the Free Trade party in the Cabinet were not to be so easily overcome. Hicks-Beach had indeed retired, but his successor C. T. Ritchie was an equally ardent Free Trader and was reinforced in his views by Sir Francis Mowatt, the permanent head of the Treasury. Lord George Hamilton and Lord Balfour of Burleigh strongly supported this attitude. Balfour was on the merits of the case totally impartial, but he was determined not to allow the unity of the Party to be broken. Since the revolt of the Free Traders threatened to do this, he decided to reverse the policy which Chamberlain had advocated. On his return from South Africa early in 1903 Chamberlain was dismayed to find that the duty on wheat was to be wholly abolished and the policy of Imperial Preference definitely abandoned in the coming budget.

There is no occasion here to detail the elaborate political manoeuvres that followed. Chamberlain at once created a tremendous sensation by publicly declaring in May his adherence to Imperial Preference. Three months later he resigned in order to have a free hand to prosecute a great national campaign for tariffs. A series of intrigues and misunderstandings resulted in the resignation of several leading Free Traders – which Balfour wanted – and, a fortnight later, in that of the Duke of Devonshire – which Balfour would gladly have averted. The Prime Minister tried to hold his Party together by an ingenious compromise formula which pleased no one. He reconstructed his Cabinet in autumn and kept links with both the dissident groups, installing Joseph Chamberlain's son Austen as Chancellor of the Exchequer, and Victor Cavendish, nephew and heir of the Duke of Devonshire, as Financial Secretary to the Treasury. It was understood that Joseph Chamberlain would have Balfour's blessing in an attempt to convert the country to his views, but that no action would be taken until enough time had elapsed to gauge the effect of his propaganda.

Bonar Law was of course a strong adherent of the Chamberlain school. His own position at the Board of Trade remained unchanged. The presence of Austen Chamberlain in the Government indicated that there was no obligation for a Tariff Reformer to resign, or to conceal his views. From now onwards the theme of Bonar Law's ever more numerous speeches up and down the country was Imperial Preference and the fallacies of Free Trade. It would be wearisome to recapitulate the arguments that he used. As was natural for a business man, he dwelt not only on the subject of imperial unity but also on the advantages of protective tariffs from a purely industrial point of view, and it may have been this emphasis which induced Joseph

Chamberlain to say of him once to Mr. Amery,[c] "He is no Tariff Reformer." By this, Mr. Amery says, Chamberlain meant that Bonar Law was interested in trade figures, rather than "a national and imperial policy of expansion and consolidation". Bonar Law's opinions on Tariff Reform will be dealt with in a later chapter. It is enough to notice that his recorded speeches do not bear out Chamberlain's contention. He used, as a good debater should, all the arguments which he thought would appeal to his audience, but he never neglected the imperial aspect of the question, and, indeed, devoted many of his speeches to it.

It was during his three years at the Board of Trade from 1902 to 1905 that Bonar Law first emerged as an important figure in his Party, and since he did so almost entirely through his effectiveness on the platform and in the House, some account of his method of speaking should be given. He was never either an original or an eloquent speaker. He did not possess the ability of a Lloyd George or a Churchill to illumine a whole vista of thought by a single phrase like a flash of lightning on a black night. On the contrary, he was a master of the commonplace. His audience left him with the feeling that he had put into words exactly what they themselves had been thinking all the while. He never spoke above their heads. On the other hand, he never talked down to them. He had a great clarity of mind and he was adept at punching home with a series of hammer blows the arguments which he wished to put across to his listeners. He had much of the vigour and trenchancy which marked his hero, Joseph Chamberlain, and after the latter was incapacitated, Bonar Law came nearer than anyone else in the Party to replacing him.

His technique was unusual. He never needed any notes. His phenomenal memory enabled him to learn by heart with comparative ease a long and complicated speech. His experience on the Glasgow Iron Ring gave him the same mastery of figures and of swift arithmetical calculation which sixty years earlier another unorthodox Tory, Lord George Bentinck, had acquired through his speculations on the Turf. If he was ever challenged for a fact or a figure he would produce a small notebook from his waistcoat pocket and immediately give chapter and verse for his statement with a reference to Hansard or a Blue Book. His adversaries soon learned to be chary of disputing any quotations or statistics which he mentioned in his speeches. He spoke with a soft Scottish Canadian accent which sounded unusual in the House of Commons of that day. At first he was inclined, as we saw earlier, to speak too quickly, but with practice he soon cured that defect. In the whole question of tariffs and trade he was a genuine expert. His views were listened to with respect and attention, and he rapidly became one of the leading spokesmen in his Party upon that contentious topic.

But this same subject which brought Bonar Law into the political limelight was bringing the Conservative Party to disaster. It is impossible nowadays to realize how passionate an article of faith Free Trade had become to the great majority of Englishmen. Like the Welfare State today, Free Trade was a sort of sacred cow. To question it was to brand oneself as a heretic of the most dangerous type. The Liberal Party at once closed its ranks. Liberal Imperialists and Little Englanders alike believed passionately in the iniquity of Tariff Reform. The feud between Asquith and Campbell-Bannerman was quickly forgotten, and the Party rallied to the support of the doctrines which for sixty years had been at the very centre of its creed.

Every weapon was used against the Tories. Asquith followed Joseph Chamberlain up and down the country answering point by point the case for Tariff Reform. In the summer of 1903 a lengthy letter to *The Times* was signed by fourteen professors of economics. Worded in the language of a Papal encyclical, it denounced in grave terms the perils and fallacies of protectionism. Everywhere the Liberals prophesied dire consequences. One formidable recruit was gained by the Liberal Party. The young Winston Churchill, abandoning the political tradition of his father and his family, crossed the floor of the House and became a Liberal.

If the Conservatives had been united on the desirability of change they might perhaps have fared better. But despite all Balfour's efforts to preserve a façade of unanimity, it soon became clear to everyone that the Party was hopelessly divided, and that its leader had no policy of his own. In these circumstances victory at the next election was most unlikely, and every month that went by made the prospect blacker. In 1905 a new issue arose – the question of Chinese Labour, or, as the Liberals alleged, Slavery, on the Rand. Milner had recommended – and Balfour had agreed to – a policy of importing indentured Chinese workers in order to put the gold mines of the Transvaal into operation after the end of the war. The conditions in which these labourers were employed were, by any European standards, atrocious, though apparently not so bad by the standards of the Chinese themselves, for they were anxious to come and unwilling to go. The Liberals were soon able to raise an outraged protest from humanitarian sentiment in England, and when the General Election

C

came the country was plastered with pictures of manacled Chinamen in an attitude of piteous supplication.

On December 4th, 1905, encouraged by a speech of Rosebery which suggested that the right wing of the Liberal Party might refuse to serve under Campbell-Bannerman, Balfour suddenly resigned. His calculation was incorrect. Rosebery spoke only for himself. Campbell-Bannerman did indeed at first have some difficulty in enlisting the support of Asquith, Grey and Haldane, but they soon came over, as politicians nearly always do when confronted with the reality of their leader installed as Prime Minister. Campbell-Bannerman dissolved as soon as he had formed his Cabinet and the country went to the polls early in January 1906.

Bonar Law was in Scotland when the dissolution was announced. He at once began his campaign for it was quite clear that he would not find it easy to hold his seat. The only encouraging feature was the presence of a third candidate G. N. Barnes, who represented Labour and might be expected to split the anti-Conservative vote. On the other hand Glasgow was traditionally Free Trade, and Bonar Law's prominence as a supporter of Chamberlain was likely to do him harm with the floating vote. His prospects were none too good, as he was doubtless himself well aware.

At that time an election was spread over several days, and it was possible from the early results to gain an idea of the general trend of voting in the country. One of the first cities to poll was Manchester, and when the news was announced that Balfour had lost East Manchester by 2,000 votes it became clear that something like a landslide was in process. Up and down the country the same tale was told. Posters of Chinese slaves, of the big and little loaf (the little one being what the public could expect if Free Trade was ended) effectively advertised the electoral programme of the Liberals. Venerable working men would stand on Liberal platforms and, with an improbable accuracy of detail, testify in quavering voices to the horrors of the hungry 'forties, when Protection still prevailed. These tactics together with the swing of the pendulum after ten years of Unionist rule made Liberal victory a certainty.

Glasgow was among the later cities to vote and Balfour, in no way discouraged at his own defeat, came and supported Bonar Law on the eve of the poll. But nothing availed. For a moment during the counting it was believed that he was in by 33 votes, and to quote a local paper, "for five minutes wild jubilation reigned" in his committee room, but at eleven o'clock the bad news was announced:

Bonar Law was out; Barnes had defeated him by 310 votes. The figures were: G. N. Barnes, 3,284; A. Bonar Law, 2,974; A. D. Provand, 2,058. Bonar Law accepted defeat philosophically enough. He made a brief speech to his supporters regretting that Socialist views had made such progress in the constituency, but congratulating his victor on the way he had conducted the fight. He then retired to console himself with his usual beverage, and it is on this occasion that another Scottish Unionist Candidate who had just been hearing the news of the Party's defeats is said to have come in and exclaimed: "Ma God! Milk!"

At his home in Helensburgh the news was received less philosophically. His elder daughter, a keen partisan at the age of ten, cried herself to sleep that night, and, the following day, wrapped herself in a sack, poured ashes on her head and sat at the entrance of the drive, to the amusement of the many callers who came to condole.

The Conservative defeat had indeed been overwhelming. From 334 in the previous House their numbers had fallen to 157, of which 109 were Chamberlainites, 32 were supporters of Balfour's compromise, and 11 were out-and-out Free Traders. There were 401 Liberals in the new House, 29 Labour, and 83 Irish Nationalists. The Liberals thus had a conclusive majority over any combination of parties, and fortified by such a popular mandate were in a position at once to begin on a large scale programme of reformist legislation. In view of this débâcle it was not immediately possible to find Bonar Law a seat, although his services were badly needed. It was not till March 12th that even Balfour himself could get back into Parliament. Eventually, however, in May a safe seat was found for Bonar Law in Dulwich, where a Conservative had been victorious in the late election by 357 votes. He had little difficulty here and on May 15th was returned by 1,279 against the opposition of the same Liberal candidate who had fought in the General Election.

In the interval between the two elections he went to Canada, on a business trip. He appears to have asked Mr. Churchill, who was now Parliamentary Secretary at the Colonial Office, for some sort of introduction. Churchill gave it, and added:[d]

"Yes the wheel has swung full circle in the country and we may be at work for sometime. I resist all temptation to say, 'I told you so'. Perhaps if you had had a clear run you might have got across your fence, but the double objective was fatal. It would be great fun to be a Tory now. I expect you will not be out of the House for long. The wheel may swing again as suddenly and completely as before."

The three years following his re-entry into the House were perhaps the happiest period in Bonar Law's life. The Conservative Party was, it is true, in a parlous state, but on the other hand his own reputation was steadily rising, and he soon established himself as an important figure in the Party. The emptiness and lack of employment which depressed him when he first entered the House had long disappeared. He was a much-sought-after speaker, upon public platforms, and during the session he assiduously attended Parliament. His time was almost as fully engaged as if he had been in office. Moreover he had a theme which he understood and could expound far better than most Conservatives. He was soon regarded as one of the Party's leading spokesmen upon Tariff Reform.

His domestic life was placid and agreeable. In 1905 the last of his children, his daughter Catherine, was born. He now had six, four sons and two daughters. He liked to have them all around him, and was quite content to spend at home the evenings that he did not devote to politics. He went out in society as little as possible. During these years he continued to move between Helensburgh and London, taking a furnished house for the session – usually somewhere in the South Kensington or Chelsea areas. From late summer to Christmas would be spent at Helensburgh, and it was the place which his family regarded as their real home. His holidays were invariably devoted to tennis and golf. He would sometimes go for a week on his own golfing with friends. His brother Jack and his brother-in-law, Douglas McIntyre, who was also a competent chess player, were favourite companions on those occasions. It was a contented domestic existence. Bonar Law had no money troubles, and no serious worries. He could safely devote himself to the great game of politics which as the years went by began to enthral him more and more.

His talents and the palpable straightforwardness of his character soon gained him friends in the House of Commons, although he never became the centre of a wide circle. One of his earliest friends was Edward Goulding, later Lord Wargrave, a genial and wealthy Irishman who owned Wargrave Manor, an attractive house on the Thames. Goulding was one of those back benchers who are never serious aspirants for office, but who, by their hospitality, their energy in party manoeuvres, their love of gossip, and of intrigue in the better sense of that word, exercise an influence upon party politics which is apt to be overlooked by the historian. He liked Bonar Law, recognized his ability, and often invited him to stay. Of the more prominent Conservatives Bonar Law's chief friend was Austen

Chamberlain. He was friendly too at an early stage with F. E. Smith
who had entered Parliament for the first time in 1906 and had at once
made his mark by one of the most brilliant maiden speeches that the
House had ever heard. Of Walter Long who was later to be a prominent candidate for the leadership he saw comparatively little. The
two men represented the extreme opposite poles of Tory politics, and,
apart from an acrimonious exchange of letters early in 1907 concerning a statement of Bonar Law to which Long took exception, they
had few dealings. Nor at this time does Bonar Law appear to have
been at all intimate with Carson who was subsequently one of his
closest allies.

The political scene to which Bonar Law returned at the end of
May 1906 was calculated to inspire despondency in the hearts of
most Conservatives. The triumphant Liberal majority would have
been in a position to carry all their most radical measures but for
one weapon which the Conservatives still controlled – the House of
Lords. Yet to make use of this archaic institution in order to frustrate
the will of the nation as expressed in the Lower House was a perilous
course. It might all too easily end by bringing the already discredited
Tory Party into still greater obloquy and finally in wrecking the
House of Lords itself. Nevertheless this was the policy upon which
the Party leaders embarked. It was, declared Balfour during the
election campaign, the duty of everyone to see that "the great
Unionist Party should still control, whether in power or whether in
Opposition, the destinies of this great Empire". Asquith claimed to
see in this imprudent statement a threat to use the powers of the
Lords to wreck the whole legislative programme of the Liberal Party.
His claim was justified. It was precisely this policy which the Tory
peers – with the full agreement, indeed encouragement, of the Party's
leaders in the Commons – now proposed to carry out.

Bonar Law was not yet a sufficiently important person to be consulted on these matters of high policy. In 1906 and 1907 the most
that he could reasonably expect would have been a good chance of
appointment as President of the Board of Trade in the next Unionist
administration. He was consulted on financial and economic matters,
and his opinion given its full weight, but he had not so far strayed
outside this field. There is, however, nothing to suggest that he
differed from his leaders, or saw the perils which were involved in
the unrestricted use of the powers of the House of Lords. It is a
remarkable feature of the political climate of the time, and a striking
example of the intense partisanship which prevailed, that even the

left wing of the Conservative Party regarded the wholesale exercise of the Lords' veto as a perfectly legitimate move in party tactics.

Balfour's leadership was, indeed, much criticized in the Party for other reasons. It was widely believed that his vacillation over tariffs was the cause of the 1906 débâcle. Leo Maxse, editor of the *National Review*, was a friend and admirer of Bonar Law. He wrote at the end of January 1906:[e]

". . . unless the Party is prepared to realise the impossibility of recovering the confidence of the country under the present régime we may remain in opposition for half a generation. Your absence from the new House is most serious, but I trust an opportunity may soon present itself of your getting back."

On April 24th H. O. Arnold-Foster, the former Unionist War Secretary, referring to Balfour in a letter to Bonar Law said:[f]

"Indeed his intelligent mind and his excellent dialectic are of immense value in the House. But somehow he does not inspire – not me at any rate – and his leadership is simply the public expression of his family affections and personal preferences."

This last comment was a hit at the remarkable number of Balfour's cousins and relatives in the late Cabinet which had at one time been described as the Hotel Cecil. Bonar Law's reply to these letters has not survived, but, from all that we know of his later conduct, and his opinion of Balfour, it is very unlikely that he endorsed these criticisms. He remained throughout a loyal supporter of Balfour, and although his real hero was Joseph Chamberlain, his allegiance to the Party's official leader never faltered. There was, indeed, no question of divided loyalties. Chamberlain did not intend to challenge Balfour's leadership. Whether in the long run events would have obliged him to do so, it is impossible to say. For the day after the celebration of his seventieth birthday on July 8th, 1906, Chamberlain was suddenly struck down by a paralytic stroke. His powers of speech and movement were permanently impaired, and, although at first it was hoped that he might recover, after a few months it became clear that he could never again return to public life. His mind was perfectly clear, and for eight years he lingered on, the pathetic ghost of his former self, an impotent spectator of the political stage which he had so often dominated in the past.

This unexpected calamity had two important consequences. First, there could now be no question of Balfour's replacement. An alternative leader did not exist, and, despite grumbles and complaints, it was certain that Balfour would remain at the head of the Party for the time being. Secondly, Bonar Law's own position was at once affected. The disappearance of Joseph Chamberlain threw the principal burden of advocating Tariff Reform upon his son Austen and upon Bonar Law. Moreover it soon became clear that in some respects Bonar Law was the abler advocate of the two. His vigour and punch as a platform orator was very reminiscent of his hero and, as time went one, he effectively established a claim to be, if not the heir, at least one of the most prominent coheirs, of the great "Joe". Throughout 1907 and 1908 he was tirelessly active in speaking on fiscal reform at political meetings all over the country. At the same time he strengthened and consolidated his already high reputation as a most formidable Parliamentary debater.

Bonar Law did not confine his utterances exclusively to Tariff Reform. The session of 1908 was largely taken up with a Liberal licensing Bill which aroused much party feeling. Bonar Law in a speech made an unflattering reference to the malevolence of the Liberals towards the Liquor Trade, and credited Mr. Churchill with some remarks which seemed to confirm that malevolence. Churchill protested. Bonar Law replied,[g]

"Dear Churchill,

"The report which you enclose is a condensed one. . . . So far as I can now remember what I said was, 'The true spirit in which this Bill is being pressed on by the Government was shown incidentally by Mr. Churchill the other day in Wales when he said the Tory party were dependent on the Trade while the Government was independent. The Government are independent and they can be trusted to give no mercy to the publicans who are their political enemies.'

"I may add that in my opinion the sentences you quoted in your letter are an admirable summary of the attitude of the Government towards one section of the Trade that supplies the public with alcohol. Since the debate in the H. of C., however, on the question of including off-licences in the Bill there is room for improvement in such a summary which should now read: 'Death to the publicans, they are all Tories; bless the licensed grocers, they are mostly Liberals.'

"Yours very truly,

A. Bonar Law."

Not unnaturally this reply dissatisfied Churchill. He wrote:[h]

". . . But the words which you now tell me you employed and which purport to be a paraphrase if not an actual quotation are only separated by a small degree of inaccuracy and misrepresentation from the inaccuracy and misrepresentation of the condensed report. . . . I presume you will have no objection to the publication of this correspondence."

Bonar Law replied that he had no objection, but unfortunately at this stage some of the early letters in Churchill's possession were accidentally burned, and so the matter had to lapse. There is a certain acerbity in these letters which suggests that the two men did not get on particularly well. As we shall see it was one of the first episodes in a series of clashes. There was something about Churchill's flamboyance and panache which aroused a profound mistrust in Bonar Law. It was not merely the fact that Churchill had gone over to the other side, nor was it in any way a matter of Tory feeling against Liberal. The two men were to be involved in many issues which cut clean across ordinary party lines. Yet in almost every one of those issues Bonar Law is to be found on the opposite side to Churchill. They had numerous friends in common; they frequently met socially; Churchill did all he could to bridge the gap. But Bonar Law remained obdurate. He admired Churchill's great talents but he did not trust him, and he did not like him.

By the end of 1908 Bonar Law had definitely established himself as one of the most effective members of the Conservative Opposition. A letter from Goulding dated January 9th, 1909, is of some interest in this respect:[i]

". . . Don't you think that you should take the chairmanship of the National Union (of Conservative and Constitutional Associations) this year. . . . I think that it would strengthen your rapidly growing power in the country as second man to A.J.B.

"Let me know what you decide and I'll talk to Ridley and put the matter in motion. . . ."

Allowance must of course be made for Goulding's personal friendship for Bonar Law. It was no doubt an exaggeration to suggest that Bonar Law was already second in the Party to Balfour. Even two and a half years later when Balfour retired, Bonar Law was not in that position. But it is significant that such a statement could be made at all at this time, and the fact is part refutation of those who have seen in his election to the Leadership, the appearance of a dark horse, and the victory of a complete outsider.

Early in 1909 Bonar Law decided that the time had come to take a permanent house in London. The fatigue of moving from Helensburgh every year and finding a furnished house for the session was beginning to be too much for Mrs. Law. Moreover he was now so fully occupied with politics, even in opposition, that a permanent residence in London had almost become a necessity. Accordingly he sold "Kintillo" and bought for £2,500 the lease of Pembroke Lodge, a biggish house just off Edwardes Square in South Kensington. By London standards the house had a large garden and so was suitable for the children. Mrs. Law was busily engaged on redecorating and furnishing the house during the summer so that it would be fully prepared for occupation by the time the children had gone back to school after the end of the summer holidays.

CHAPTER III

THE CONSTITUTIONAL CRISIS

1909 – 1911

*The Session of 1909 – The Lords reject the Budget – Illness and death of Mrs. Law
– Overwhelming blow to Bonar Law – His intense grief – Mary Law comes to live
with him – Her forceful character – General Election of January 1910 – The
Constitutional Conference – Max Aitken makes the acquaintance of Bonar Law –
Their close friendship – General Election of November 1910 – Bonar Law agrees
to stand for North-West Manchester – His defeat – Returned for Bootle – Made a
Privy Councillor – The Lords and the Parliament Act – Hedgers and Ditchers –
Bonar Law's letter to* The Times

THE session of 1909 was the prelude to one of the most bitter
political battles of the twentieth century. The Liberals after
three years of rule with an unprecedented majority behind
them had accomplished very little. Bill after Bill passed the House
of Commons only to be rejected or amended out of recognition in
the House of Lords. Moreover these tactics, however partisan, were
remarkably successful. Campbell-Bannerman might move resolutions
asserting the supremacy of the Lower House and carry them by an
immense majority, but the country remained placid and unmoved
by the alleged iniquities of the peers. By-elections throughout 1908
went adversely for the Government, culminating with the defeat at
North-West Manchester of Winston Churchill who was seeking re-
election on being appointed President of the Board of Trade.[1]

The Liberals were therefore confronted with something of an impasse. They were pledged to far-reaching measures of social reform
and their supporters were becoming more and more restive. Yet
every important Bill was blocked by the House of Lords. Unless this
situation could somehow be changed, the Liberal Party would lose
its appeal to radical sentiment, and Labour would gain much of the
support which the working classes had hitherto accorded to the
Liberals. In 1908 an important change had occurred in the Cabinet:
Campbell-Bannerman resigned, and died shortly afterwards; Asquith
replaced him as Prime Minister, and the leading member of the

[1] He found a safe seat at Dundee almost immediately.

Party's left wing, David Lloyd George, replaced Asquith in the key position of Chancellor of the Exchequer. It had become clear by now that the only method left open to the Government was to bring forward a really radical Budget. Drastic taxation was necessary, in any case, to meet the increased cost of old-age pensions and naval rearmament. If the necessary money to meet social services could be raised by such imposts as death duties, super tax, and a tax on the unearned increment on land, the Budget would accomplish two valuable services: first it would rally the radical sentiment of the nation to the Liberal banner; secondly it would cut the ground from under the feet of the Tariff Reformers who had long been declaring that the necessary money could only be raised by a revenue tariff.

There was a further important consideration: although the Lords had an undoubted right to amend or reject ordinary Bills their status with regard to a Money Bill was different; ever since the seventeenth century a binding convention of the constitution prohibited them from amending such Bills. They could, in theory, reject a Money Bill outright, but they could not modify it. Despite subsequent claims it is doubtful whether Lloyd George framed the "People's Budget" with the deliberate purpose of inducing the Lords to commit political suicide by rejecting it. There is certainly no evidence that he had this intention, and it seems unlikely that he or any other Liberal minister seriously expected that the Upper House would act so foolishly. It is more likely that Lloyd George regarded the Budget as a genuine method of by-passing the Lords' veto, and that, though he was delighted when the Unionist leaders finally took their fatal decision, he did not originally expect that outcome.

The session of 1909 was one of the longest and most exhausting that the House of Commons has ever known.[1] The Conservatives fought every clause of the Budget with implacable determination. There was no summer recess, and the battle continued long into the autumn. Bonar Law took the orthodox party line. He maintained that the Budget was a confiscatory measure actuated by class hatred and spite and that it was the thin end of the Socialist wedge. Like all keen Tariff Reformers he was particularly irritated because Lloyd George seemed to have discovered a means of raising money, that was compatible with the retention of Free Trade. He was one of the most active of the Budget's critics. At length, after no less than

---

[1] There were 895 divisions, of which 554 were on the Budget. In the session of 1946-7, reckoned to be a busy one, there were only 383 divisions altogether. Roy Jenkins, *Mr. Balfour's Poodle*, p. 53.

seventy Parliamentary days, the Finance Bill was carried in the House of Commons on November 4th, whence it went to have its final fate determined in the House of Lords. Before this day, however, private tragedy had temporarily removed Bonar Law from the political scene.

Mrs. Law had for sometime been feeling unwell. When the summer holidays came she took a house at Monckton, a small place on the Ayrshire coast. All the children were there and, whenever he could snatch some time off politics, Bonar Law came down and played golf with his usual energy – two rounds a day, followed by bridge or chess in the evening. Mrs. Law was not as high spirited as she normally was on these occasions, and – unusually for her – rested every afternoon. However she said little about her illness and made no complaint for she was anxious to get the children back to school before consulting a doctor.

As soon as the holidays were over she saw a specialist in Glasgow who sent her to Leeds to see the eminent surgeon Mr. (later Lord) Moynihan. He advised an operation on the gall bladder, and, accordingly, arrangements were made for her to enter a nursing home in Leeds at the end of October. While these consultations were in process Bonar Law and his wife stayed at Harrogate. One day when they were together Mrs. Law suddenly came across a photographer, and had herself taken, telling her husband that "some of the children" had asked her for a new photograph. Rightly or wrongly Bonar Law always looked back to that day as the moment when his wife realized that she might not survive the operation, but this may have been a mere fancy. The operation took place at the end of October and appeared successful, but three days later on Sunday, October 31st, Mrs. Law collapsed and died.

The funeral took place at Helensburgh; the service was at "Ferniegair", and the burial at the cemetery two miles away up the hill on the outskirts of the town. So great was the crowd of mourners that the last carriages were only leaving the house when the first arrived at the cemetery. According to the Scottish custom Bonar Law and his sons (except for his youngest who was only a child) each held a cord as the coffin was lowered into the grave. The scene with the black-coated mourners all around, and the bright autumn sunlight glinting on the distant waters of the Clyde, must have remained indelibly printed upon his memory as it is upon the memory of his children.

To Bonar Law the loss was a blow from which, in one sense, he never recovered. It was a terrible shock, all the more terrible for being so sudden. He depended very much upon the unobtrusive but cheerful and happy domestic background which his wife supplied. As is often the case with men engrossed in a career of business or politics he had perhaps come to take this background too much for granted, and now that it had vanished for ever he was morbidly stricken by grief, and by a certain remorse. Moreover Bonar Law could never bring himself to accept death. Most men, however great their sorrow, come in the course of time to recognize the fact of death as a part of the common lot of humanity – something which, however tragic, is inevitable and must be faced. Bonar Law was unable to do this, not through want of courage, for he was a brave man, but through some curious streak in his temperament which compelled him all his life to dwell with an almost pathological despondency upon the loss of those who were dear to him. Nor had he any consolation from religion. The sombre faith in which he had been brought up did, indeed, leave a lasting impression upon his behaviour and his way of thought, but its actual content meant nothing to him. He did not believe in a life after death, and could not bring himself to do so merely because he had suffered such a grievous loss. Lacking both the cheerfulness of the pagan and the consolations of the puritan, he was a prey to a gloomy despair which threatened for a time to paralyse his whole existence.

A flood of condolatory letters poured in from every quarter. Among the most notable was one from Austen Chamberlain.

"I keep on thinking and thinking of you and wishing that I could help you. If deepest heartfelt sympathy could lessen grief you are assured of ours . . . I hope you may find some little comfort in the sympathy of friends and in the knowledge and regard which your wife inspired even in those who knew her so slightly as we did. For we could see all that she was to you and you to her and how beautifully your lives were knit together. . . .

"Time does heal our wounds – even in spite of ourselves – time and work. And when you are able to think about these things again you will find that there is much and great work for you to do. Your friends have need of you. You can help our cause as none of us can. You bring peculiar qualities and a special knowledge to the work and we shall claim your help again when the time comes, knowing indeed how hard and irksome it will be to you to resume it without *her* help but knowing also that it is a duty from which you must not and will not shrink, and hoping that – hard as that duty is – it may yet help you to bear the heavier burden of your private grief by occupying a part of your thoughts with public cares."

Bonar Law followed this advice. To abandon politics, as he perhaps recognized himself, would have been folly at a time like this, for it was the only thing that could occupy his mind and prevent him from becoming obsessed with his private tragedy. Moreover any inclination that he felt to give up public life was counteracted by an even more potent force than Austen Chamberlain. At Bonar Law's urgent request his sister, Mary, came to live with him and join his household at Pembroke Lodge. She was a woman of strong character. Tall, with dark hair and flashing blue eyes, she stood forth at once as a person who could not be forgotten or ignored. She was only thirteen months younger than her brother, was deeply devoted to him, and had an unbounded faith in his talents. She was highly intelligent and had a clear, if somewhat cynical, understanding of the intricacies of politics and the motives of politicians. Bonar Law discussed with her nearly all his problems, and, by influence rather than direct advice, she was able to affect many of his most important decisions. During the twelve years of Bonar Law's supremacy in the Tory Party she was perhaps the person upon whom he depended most for counsel and encouragement. Her influence upon him was profound, and no account of his life would be complete without some reference to it, though by the nature of things no written evidence of it has survived.

Fond though she was of her brother it was something of a sacrifice to join him, for she was not and, never pretended to be, fond of children. At first her nephews and nieces were a little frightened of her, but they soon came to regard her with deep affection. On social matters she made strict terms with her brother. She would be at home when he brought back friends to luncheon or dinner, but she refused to go out with him to parties and social engagements, and allowed it to be known that she did not expect to be asked. This arrangement suited Bonar Law. After his wife's death he was even more reluctant than before to accept social engagements, and it was much easier to refuse if no lady was involved.

It was perhaps fortunate for Bonar Law that in the winter of 1909–10 the political world provided ample distraction for anyone who wished to forget private sorrow by plunging into public affairs. A political and constitutional crisis of the first magnitude impended. At the end of November the Lords rejected the Budget – an action without precedent in British history. This meant an immediate dissolution and a General Election fought on the question of "the Peers against the People". Writs were issued on January 10th, and polling, spread over a fortnight, began on January 15th, 1910. The result disappointed the hopes of the more optimistic Unionists. The action

of the House of Lords did not completely reverse, but it greatly modified, the anti-Government trend of the by-elections. The Unionists
recovered a good deal of ground, especially in the south of England,
and made a net gain of 116 seats, giving them a total of 273. The
Liberals declined from 401 to 275. But their effective majority was
much greater than this figure suggests, since there were 40 Labour
M.P.s who normally voted against the Unionists and 82 Irish
Nationalists who would support the Government on certain conditions. Asquith thus had a majority of 124 but he was in a far less
secure position that he had been before the Election. He had to
manage the Irish Nationalists, and his enemies were not slow to
point out that Redmond rather than Asquith held the real balance
of power in the country. From now onwards it was the normal Conservative Party line to declare that the Government's actions were
wholly dominated by an immoral bargain with Redmond, whereby
the latter contrary to his true convictions agreed to support the
Budget in return for a promise by Asquith to destroy the veto of the
House of Lords and to carry Home Rule. This belief was sincerely
held, and it goes far to explain the extraordinary bitterness which
soon began to mark party politics.

Bonar Law personally had no difficulty in his own constituency at
Dulwich. He concentrated as much as he could on Tariff Reform,
which was a more congenial and also a safer topic than the rights
of the House of Lords. He doubled his previous majority and defeated
his Liberal opponent by 2,418 votes.

From the first the new Parliament was dominated by the constitutional question. The Lords, after the verdict of the election, no longer
contested the Budget, and passed it without a division, but the
Liberals naturally had no intention of letting the matter rest at that.
Asquith promptly announced the Government's intention of modify-
ing the veto power of the House of Lords, and early made it clear
that he intended to deal with this question independently of any
question of reforming the composition of the Upper House. On
March 21st he put on the paper of the House of Commons a series of
resolutions, depriving the Lords of any veto over Money Bills, giving
them a suspensory veto of two years over other Bills, and reducing
the duration of Parliament from seven to five years.

It is not the task of the biographer of Bonar Law to describe in
any detail the complicated manoeuvres which finally resulted in the
passing of the Parliament Act some sixteen months later. Bonar
Law took a vigorous part in these debates but he was not one of the

principal actors, and a history of that turbulent Parliamentary battle would have no reason to single out his name from among many others.

The course of events must, however, be briefly outlined. By the middle of April a Bill based on Asquith's resolutions had been drafted and sent to the King. Then on May 6th an unexpected complication arose. King Edward VII died suddenly. His successor had little or no experience of public affairs, and it was natural that the leaders of both parties should try to spare him an immediate constitutional crisis, and seek an agreed compromise. Accordingly on June 17th a constitutional conference met, consisting of Asquith, Lloyd George, Birrell and Lord Crewe from the Liberals, and Balfour, Austen Chamberlain, Lord Lansdowne and Lord Cawdor from the Unionists. For the next six months the crisis was transferred from the limelight of Parliament to the secrecy of the conference room. Agreement seemed near at times, but it broke down on a crucial point. The Conservatives wished to put certain measures of an "organic" or constitutional nature into a different category from other Bills and make them the subject of a referendum, if they had been twice rejected by the House of Lords. What the Unionists had in mind was of course an Irish Home Rule Bill. But on this the Liberals, with their dependence on the Irish vote, could not compromise.

On November 10th the conference came to an end. The King had made it clear that, like his predecessor, he would insist on another General Election in order to determine finally the verdict of the nation upon the powers of the House of Lords. He agreed that in the event of the Government receiving a majority he would, if necessary, use his prerogative to create enough peers to carry the Parliament Bill. But no public announcement of this promise was to be made until the occasion for implementing it actually arose. The dissolution was fixed for November 28th.

Meanwhile an important event had occurred which was to affect profoundly both Bonar Law's private and public life. Two years earlier he had made the acquaintance of a young Canadian financier by the name of Max Aitken[1] who had, like himself, been born in a manse in New Brunswick. In 1908 Aitken was in London and, wishing to place some bonds, decided to try Bonar Law on the strength of the connexion between William Jacks and the Nova Scotia Coal & Steel Company. The meeting was not a success. Bonar Law was

---

[1] William Maxwell Aitken, 1878—, created Lord Beaverbrook, 1916.

bored by his visitor and bought some bonds only in order to get rid of him. Aitken, who at that time had a theory about the relationship of ability with the shape of a man's head, decided that Bonar Law's head was the wrong shape and that he would get nowhere.

In September 1910 Aitken returned to England with the intention of settling down there and entering politics as a protagonist of imperial unity and Tariff Reform. In the previous two years he had emerged the victor of a fierce financial struggle in Canada. He was now, at scarcely over thirty, a millionaire and, to quote his own words, "was determined never to put these grave matters to the test again". On the strength of his former acquaintance he called on Bonar Law. This time their meeting was much more successful. Aitken's colourful conversation amused Bonar Law. He invited him to stay to lunch.

"The food", writes Lord Beaverbrook,[a] "was not very good, and I noticed with a little annoyance that I was given one glass of whisky and water, whereas my host helped himself twice to what appeared to be a special whisky out of his own bottle. This keeping of a special tap in one's own house is a thing I have a prejudice against.

"It was a week after that when I found out that he was a teetotaller and his 'special whisky' was a bottle of lime juice. I had remorse for my lack of charity. Henceforward I saw more of him and it was plain that my conversation amused him.

"Next, to my surprise I found him dining with me. But perhaps his surprise was greater than mine for he never dined with anyone if he could help it."

To Bonar Law, lonely and prone to despondency, still broken by his tragic loss of barely a year before, Max Aitken came as a welcome breath of fresh air. Here was someone who had not been concerned in any way with his past life, someone young, amusing, witty, often outrageous, but above all full of vitality and energy. Moreover, no one can entirely resist flattery and even Bonar Law was not indifferent to what was palpably a genuine hero worship. He began to enjoy the visits of his new friend, and soon saw more of him than he did of anyone else. This development did not inspire unmixed approval from his own circle. Miss Mary Law observed suddenly one day with her usual directness:[b] "I don't care about the growing influence of Max Aitken here." Bonar Law, who was lying on a sofa reading a book, paused, slowly took off his glasses, and quietly said, "Do let me like him." Miss Law resolved that she would never again try to interfere with her brother's friendships, and from then onwards made a point of welcoming his new acquaintance whenever he came to the house. Perhaps she thought that it would be wiser to ally her-self than quarrel with him. As time went on she too became a close friend of Max Aitken. When she died in 1929 she bequeathed to him a legacy of £3,600 and her house in London.

The forthcoming General Election resulted in an important change for Bonar Law. Lord Derby and a number of others decided that it would be a good thing to put forward one of the principal Tariff Reformers as a candidate in the traditionally Free Trade area of Lancashire. Bonar Law was selected for this role and he readily agreed to take the risk of abandoning his own safe seat at Dulwich. He was at first offered Ashton-under-Lyne, but in the end the choice fell on North-West Manchester which was a truly marginal seat. In 1906 Winston Churchill won it for the Liberals. In 1908 he lost it to Joynson-Hicks at a by-election. In January 1910 Joynson-Hicks was beaten in his turn, and the sitting Member was now a Liberal again. A Unionist victory here would be a great triumph, and since Man-chester was one of the first cities to poll it might set the tone for the whole election.

Balfour was at first uneasy about the proposal. He wrote privately to Lord Derby who exercised the patronage of the Conservative Party in Lancashire in a manner reminiscent of a great territorial magnate of the eighteenth century, and whose approval was regarded as an essential preliminary to any Conservative manoeuvres in that county. He observed that Bonar Law might be a member of the next Conservative Cabinet, and that his loss would be a very serious matter if he (Balfour) had to form a Government. Derby assured Balfour that in the event of Bonar Law's defeat he would at once find him a safe seat in Lancashire. If necessary his own brother, Arthur Stanley, would vacate Ormskirk. Thus reassured Balfour wrote to Bonar Law on October 15th:[c]

"I have been requested by Derby and others to ask you whether you would consent to stand for N.W. Manchester. They are of opinion that unless a man of 'light and leading' like yourself fights our battle in Lan-cashire we shall not be able to make a sufficient impression upon the mass of seats which now return Radical members in a part of the country where Unionism was once so strong.

"I replied to these requests in the first instance by saying that I was very reluctant to see you leave a seat which had always shown such splendid loyalty to the Unionist Party. If by any chance you fail in Manchester our Front Bench would be most seriously weakened in the House of Commons and highly as I estimate the services you could render as a candidate they can hardly equal those which you render as a Parliamentary debater. The electioneering authorities have, however, now convinced me that there would be no difficulty in finding you a seat, should things go against you in your new constituency, and, this being so, I no longer hesitate to lay the matter before you. . . .

"Of this I am sure, that if you accept Derby's invitation you will both deserve and earn the gratitude of the whole Party."

Bonar Law resolved to go ahead and fight the Unionist battle at North-West Manchester. Meanwhile there was still the question of Ashton-under-Lyne, where the local Conservatives were anxious to persuade him to stand. He could not now do this, but before their deputation arrived to see him he thought of an answer to their problem. Accordingly he wrote on November 14th to the chairman of the local Conservative Association:[d]

". . . As regards your constituency, if you want an outside man, there is a young friend of mine who, I think, would make a very good candidate. He is a young Canadian, not much over 30, who without any outside help has made a large fortune; he is a keen imperialist and for that reason wants to stand for Parliament. He has not had any political experience, but he has a distinct personality and, I believe, would be attractive in any constituency.

"Of course I always think that a good local man is to be preferred but if you have to go outside, it might be worthwhile to think of my friend, and, if there is a chance of your Committee favourably considering him, you might communicate with me."

The members of the deputation were introduced by Bonar Law to Aitken who promptly invited them to lunch. It was an instant success, and by the time the meal was over he had been selected as Conservative candidate for Ashton-under-Lyne.

The election in Lancashire was fought with much vigour. At an early stage Bonar Law was engaged in a clash with Churchill who came down to speak for the Liberal candidate. Bonar Law challenged him to fight in person for his old constituency, with a gentleman's agreement that whichever one of them lost should remain out of the House for the whole of the next Parliament. Fortunately for Bonar Law this challenge was not accepted. On one occasion they met in the evening at one of Manchester's principal hotels. Churchill was about to address a Liberal meeting. "I suppose", said Bonar Law,[e] "I had better speak to you tonight, because I imagine after I've read your speech tomorrow we shan't be on speaking terms."

Eventually, despite a strenuous campaign, Bonar Law was defeated by 445 votes. The figures were: Sir George Kemp, 5,559; Bonar Law, 5,114. It was a great disappointment, and Bonar Law felt it keenly though he did not show it. To C. P. Scott, the editor of the Liberal

Manchester Guardian, who observed a trifle sententiously, "You may have lost our votes but you have won our respect", Bonar Law merely replied that he would have preferred the votes. In fact his struggle had been by no means without effect. The Unionists won nine seats from the Liberals in Lancashire as compared with the previous Election and only lost one. F. E. Smith, who was also a Lancashire Member, wrote:[f]

"I think your great fight considerably increased your already high prestige in the Party. You didn't win in your own constituency but you damned nearly won all Manchester, which would have been stupendous."

One of the Unionist victors in Lancashire was Max Aitken who conducted a highly unorthodox campaign in which he scarcely mentioned the stock Tory topics of Home Rule, the Welsh Church, and the House of Lords, but concentrated exclusively on Tariff Reform and Imperial Unity.

In the Election as a whole the situation of the parties was almost unchanged. The Unionists fell by one, the Liberals by three. These losses were counter-balanced by two gains to Labour and two to the Irish Nationalists. A surprisingly large number of seats actually changed hands – altogether fifty-six – but as far as the House of Commons was concerned the Election made practically no difference. It was clear now to all except fanatical partisans that the Liberals had won the game and that the powers of the House of Lords must inevitably be clipped by the next Parliament.

Bonar Law was not out of the House for long. Within six weeks of the new Parliament's assembling a vacancy was created at Bootle, the sitting Conservative Member, Colonel Sandys, retiring through ill health. Bonar Law received the Conservative nomination and defeated his Liberal opponent by over 2,000 votes, doubling his predecessor's majority.[1] During the interval before he returned he seems to have been curiously reluctant to go near the House of Commons. It was almost as if he were ashamed of his defeat. At all events he declined to go into the precincts of the House and preferred to stay at home and hear political news and gossip from his friends, until he could enter again as of right.

On June 22nd, 1911, the Coronation of George V took place and this led to a temporary lull in party feeling. It is a tradition for some all-party honours to be given on this occasion, and Bonar Law's high position in the political world was recognized by the award of a Privy

---

[1] The figures were: Bonar Law 9,976, Max Muspratt 7,782.

Councillorship. F. E. Smith was similarly honoured at the same time. Among other coronation honours was the award of Knighthood to Max Aitken. He wrote to Bonar Law:[g]

"Dear Bonar Law,
    "To congratulate you on the P.C. seems hardly necessary. You know how pleased I am.
    "But I do want you to realize that I am deeply grateful to you for my own affair. Hood did me the kindness but you made it possible and in my selfish way I want you to know that I am always ready to serve you not because of what you've done for me but because you are yourself.
                            "Yours faithfully,
                                    W. M. Aitken."

It was not until Asquith was forced by the continued obduracy of the House of Lords to reveal the King's promise to create peers that party feeling really became bitter. For a long while the Unionists had been declaring that talk of creating enough peers to carry the Parliament Act was simply bluff, and that the King would never do it. The revelation that it was not an idle threat but an imminent danger produced something not far short of hysteria in the Unionist ranks, and a deep division in the counsels of their leaders. Bonar Law had been since the beginning of the year a member of the Conservative Shadow Cabinet. On July 21st, 1911, a meeting of that body was held to determine whether or not to surrender or to fight to the end, and dare the Government to carry out its threat. Bonar Law voted along with Balfour, Lansdowne, Curzon and Walter Long in favour of surrender. On the other side were Austen Chamberlain, F. E. Smith, Carson, Selborne, Salisbury and the aged Lord Halsbury who had been chosen as the leader of the "Die-hards" or "Ditchers" (die in the last ditch) against the "Hedgers", as those who favoured surrender were called.

Although Balfour commanded a majority, it soon became clear that the Ditchers did not intend to accept his decision which was finally given on July 26th. On the contrary, led by Lord Hugh Cecil, they determined to shout down the Prime Minister in the House of Commons – an episode without parallel in Parliamentary history. For half an hour the Prime Minister tried to speak amidst cries of "Divide, divide", "American dollars", "Traitor", and "Who killed the King". Eventually he abandoned the attempt. The demonstration was aimed almost as much at Balfour and Lansdowne as at Asquith. A great banquet in honour of Lord Halsbury was held at the Hotel Cecil. Such enthusiasm was aroused that the banqueters were anxious to draw Lord Halsbury, who was eighty-eight, in triumph from the Strand to his home in Kensington and only desisted for fear of the effect upon his health. The feeling between the two factions of the Unionist Party was almost as intense as the feeling between Unionists and Liberals.

Bonar Law regarded the actions of the Die-hards as foolish and on July 26th wrote a letter to *The Times* in support of Balfour and Lansdowne. Among other observations he said:

"I am certain that six months hence if Lord Lansdowne had allowed the House of Lords to be swamped and the Government to be carrying in a single session Bills to establish Home Rule, to disestablish the Church in Wales, and to gerrymander the constituencies, then the Unionists in this country would not be praising the courage but would be cursing the folly of their leaders."

He then considered what powers a Tory dominated House of Lords would still have. There was the two years' delay which might have some value. "Time, therefore, though it may not be worth much is worth something." There was an even more important consideration. The House of Lords, despite the cutting down of its powers, might still be able to force a General Election, and Bonar Law ended:

"They can delay for instance the Expiring Laws Continuance Bill or the Army Annual Bill, and such action on their part would undoubtedly make the continuance of the Government impossible and compel an election. . . . It might or might not be wise to use this power, but if I am right in thinking that the House of Lords, would have the means of compelling an election before Home Rule became law that surely is not a power which ought to be lightly abandoned."

In view of the feuds which were now raging in the Tory Party this letter is a significant declaration. It put Bonar Law definitely on the side of the Hedgers and in support of the Party's official policy. He had shown his loyalty to Balfour and Lansdowne and had definitely declared himself against Chamberlain, Carson, F. E. Smith and the Cecils on this issue.

In the event the policy of the Hedgers prevailed. After scenes of intense bitterness, and after one of the most exciting debates ever held in the sedate precincts of the House of Lords the Parliament Act was carried on August 11th by 131 votes to 114. The constitutional crisis had ended but its repercussions were to echo long afterwards, not only in the affairs of the nation but in the counsels of the Tory Party, with important and unexpected consequences for Bonar Law's own career.

CHAPTER IV

THE LEADERSHIP

1911

Dissatisfaction in the Party – Problem of the succession – Characters of Walter Long and Austen Chamberlain – Bonar Law's prospects – Beaverbrook's Letter – Resignation of Balfour – Bonar Law's tribute to Balfour – Bonar Law decides to stand – Animosity between Long and Chamberlain – Views of Balcarres – Confused situation – Tactics of Beaverbrook – Attempts to persuade Bonar Law to withdraw – Their failure – Interview between Balcarres and Chamberlain – Chamberlain and Long withdraw – Bonar Law's hesitation – His discussion with Chamberlain – Chamberlain's Chagrin – Bonar Law's conduct defended – He becomes Leader of the Party

I

THE events described in the last chapter caused profound dissatisfaction in the Conservative ranks. The Party had lost two General Elections in quick succession, had been utterly defeated over the Parliament Act, and was now confronted with another long period of fruitless opposition. As is usual in such circumstances the malcontents directed their attacks first and foremost upon the party leadership. Ever since the death of Disraeli in 1881 the Conservative Party had been governed by the House of Cecil, first in the person of the great Lord Salisbury, then of his nephew Arthur Balfour, but by the summer of 1911 it became clear that what J. L. Garvin once called "the Byzantine theory of Unionist leadership – the theory of speechless loyalty to an hereditary succession" was about to be seriously challenged.

Balfour's handling of the Parliament Act crisis – although today it seems that he pursued the only sensible course – provoked furious dissension in the Party. The activities of the Die-hards headed by Lord Halsbury have already been described. Moreover, among the followers of that venerable but by no means decrepit peer were several members of Balfour's own family. The House of Cecil was divided against itself. Lord Robert and Lord Hugh Cecil, Balfour's own first cousins, were among his severest critics. There was a vigorous agitation in the Conservative press, headed by Leo Maxse of the *National Review* who devised the celebrated slogan B.M.G. –

"Balfour Must Go". It is not surprising that Balfour's thoughts turned towards resignation and in September and October rumours began circulating to that effect.

The problem of the succession at once became a subject for intense speculation and assiduous intrigue. The two obvious rivals for the post were Austen Chamberlain and Walter Long. Since these two men, in various ways, played so large a part in Bonar Law's political life, a few words about the politics and character of each may be appropriate here.

Austen Chamberlain represented the Liberal Unionist wing of the Conservative Party. In general he was believed to stand for the more progressive and enlightened elements upon the opposition side of the House. He was the heir to all his father's doctrines. He preached the pure gospel of Tariff Reform and Imperial Preference in its most uncompromising form. He was also – surprisingly enough – a keen Die-hard on the question of the House of Lords. Together with Carson, Wyndham and F. E. Smith he was one of the foremost supporters of Lord Halsbury. Here too, however, he was following his father's views. For by a strange irony of fate Joseph Chamberlain, who had once described the Peerage in bitter terms as "the class that toils not, neither does it spin", had become in his old age a violent opponent of the Parliament Act, and from his sick bed at Highbury fulminated against the very measures which, thirty years earlier, he would have ardently supported.

But, although Austen Chamberlain was heir to his father's beliefs, he inherited a very different character. Joseph Chamberlain, who at times almost resembled Achitophel in Dryden's satire – "resolved to ruin or to rule the State" – was a man of vast ambition, iron will, and ruthless energy. But Austen Chamberlain, for all his talents, was only a thin echo of his formidable father, a mere shadow of that extraordinary figure who, rising from obscurity, had become the most famous, the most hated, the most admired, personality in English politics, and who in the course of his stormy career had smashed in turn both the great political parties of the country. Austen Chamberlain was altogether kinder than his father, more likeable, more honourable, more high minded – and less effective. The truth was that, although an able speaker and a good Parliamentarian, he lacked that ultimate hardness without which men seldom reach supreme political power. It was singularly easy to deflect him from his chosen path by the merest hint that he might be thought to aim at personal advancement. As a result at many critical moments of his life he missed the supreme chance; and the words which are said to have been applied to him by Sir Winston Churchill might serve as his epitaph: "He always played the game and he always lost it".

The other claimant to the succession was Walter Long. He had been Chief Secretary for Ireland in Balfour's Cabinet, a position inferior to that of Austen Chamberlain who had been Chancellor of the Exchequer; but Long was ten years older than Chamberlain and in every other respect senior in the Party hierarchy. A country gentleman of an ancient lineage, upon which he was wont to dwell at some length if encouraged, Walter Long represented the best tradition of what Lord Salisbury once described as "pure Squire conservatism". He was a lukewarm supporter of Tariff Reform, regarding it as an affair of Birmingham business men, nor had he the sort of mind which readily understood economic and financial arguments. Moreover he differed from Austen Chamberlain on the course to be followed over the Parliament Act, and he had warmly repudiated some of the actions of the Die-hards. Indeed the political position of the two rivals was somewhat paradoxical. Long, the representative of the old rural England, was an opponent of the food taxes, which might have been supposed to protect agriculture, and was hostile to the Die-hards. Chamberlain, the representative of the traditionally Free Trade business interest, was an ardent Tariff Reformer and a passionate supporter of the privileges of the House of Lords.

Walter Long was neither an intelligent nor a quick-witted man. He was hot tempered and inclined to be impulsive. He was an indifferent and discursive debater. Balfour observed of him,[a] "The compliments which he pays to his opponents are the only features of his speeches I ever recall". But, despite these defects, he had a substantial bloc of supporters in the Party. He was universally respected for his character, if not for his intellect. The old county families, although their influence had declined with the long decline of agriculture since the 'seventies, were still powerful on the Conservative back benches, and Walter Long seemed the ideal representative of that class which had for so many years been the backbone of the Tory Party.

2

Such were the political opinions and the personal characters of the two principal rivals for the succession. What was the position of

Bonar Law? It must be admitted that his chances of becoming leader cannot have seemed good. He had been a Member of Parliament for only eleven years, and, although his abilities as a debater were generally respected and he had recently been made a Privy Councillor, he had never held Cabinet rank, or any position approaching it. Moreover, he altogether lacked the subtle social influences which, spreading from Hatfield, Chatsworth, Bowood, Londonderry House, could make or mar the fortunes of political aspirants in those days. Nor did he have behind him, like Austen Chamberlain, the prestige of a great name and the well-disciplined support of a powerful political machine.

Nevertheless in the early part of October his name was already beginning to be mentioned as a possible leader. The following letter from Aitken, undated but evidently written about the middle of October 1911, shows the position.[b]

On Board the
Cunard R.M.S. Lusitania.

"My dear Bonar,

"I hope you like your own name in my handwriting – if not I will call you A.B. . . . . Goulding and I have had a row, first night on board, and none since. He hasn't bored me a bit. I can't answer vice versa. Our quarrel was over politics. He is a canvassing agent for Austen – or was. I told him Smith[1] had no chance at all and he agreed. I then said you had some chance even if only an off chance. He agreed. Then I charged him with disloyalty and further urged that, if Garvin and Smith now came out or came out at the critical moment for you, that you would win. He straightway wrote to Garvin posted his letter at Queenstown and since has talked of no other thing.

"I have stated that you told me you would take the leadership if the chance offered. That your present line of conduct was your best plan for winning, etc. He urged you promised Austen you wouldn't contest first place with him. I ridiculed this statement, if made, having any effect on your friends, using the obvious arguments.

"I don't know what influence Paddy[2] had with Garvin and Smith. If he has enough influence and strength to persevere something may come of this. I build no hopes on him. Smith dominates him entirely and I would rather deal with Smith. . . .

"Yours faithfully,
W. M. Aitken."

It is clear from the tone of this letter that Bonar Law's candidature had already been for some time the subject of discussion, and that Bonar Law himself was not averse to the idea. However he seems to

---

[1] F. E. Smith.   [2] Goulding.

have made no immediate reply to these suggestions. He was doubtless ruminating carefully upon the problem, examining it from every aspect, as was his custom, before coming to a conclusion.

It was indeed a difficult problem. Evidently some sort of understanding existed between Chamberlain and Bonar Law to the effect that the latter would not contest with Chamberlain the leadership of the Party. Bonar Law did not intend to go back on his word in the somewhat cavalier manner recommended by Aitken. On the other hand the situation was not the same as it had been when this pledge had been given. Chamberlain was no longer the undisputed heir to Balfour. On the contrary there was now a powerful challenger in the field – a challenger, moreover, who represented an old-fashioned rural Toryism which was anathema to the section of the Party supported by Chamberlain and Bonar Law. The relations between Chamberlain and Long, and between their respective groups of partisans were at this time extremely hostile – a fact not always sufficiently emphasized by subsequent historians. Might not the Party's interests – and the interests of the wing to which Chamberlain and Bonar Law belonged – be better promoted by the candidature of a third person acceptable to the friends of both Long and Chamberlain, than by allowing a straight fight between the two senior rivals – a fight which would leave bitter feelings behind, whoever won?

However, there seemed to be no hurry for Bonar Law to make up his mind. Balfour had not shown the slightest sign in public that he was even aware of the agitation against his leadership, and his well-known boast that he never read the newspapers made it seem quite possible that he really was ignorant of the attacks which were daily being made upon him.

In fact, however, he was deeply offended at the agitation against him. At the end of September he invited Lord Balcarres, the Conservative Chief Whip, and Arthur Steel-Maitland, the Party Manager, to his country house in Scotland, and informed them that he contemplated resignation. On October 7th the Die-hards declared open war on the Tory leader by forming the Halsbury Club, an organization evidently designed – at least by some of its members – to oust Balfour. A complete split in the Party now seemed imminent, and Balfour's resolution hardened. At the end of October he told Lord Lansdowne, the leader in the House of Lords, that his decision was irrevocable. It only remained to inform the public. The date for this was fixed for Wednesday, November 8th, and Balfour announced his decision that afternoon in a speech to the Conservative Association of his constituency in the City of London.

The exact course to be followed after the leader's resignation was not entirely clear for no obvious precedents existed. Balfour, as the only Conservative ex-Prime Minister, was naturally leader of the whole Party as well as of the Party in the House of Commons, but his retirement did not mean that a new leader would be elected for the Party as a whole. In those days when a party was in opposition and when there was no former Prime Minister to take command, the leadership went, as it were, into abeyance between the leaders in the House of Lords and in the House of Commons. Balfour's resignation, therefore, merely vacated the leadership in the House of Commons and there was no guarantee that his successor would be the next Conservative Prime Minister. That post might equally well fall to Lord Lansdowne. It was generally agreed that the sovereign body for electing the leader of the Party in the House of Commons should be a meeting of all the Unionist M.P.s. This had to be held as soon as possible, since a conference of Constituency Representatives from all over the country was due to meet in the following week, and it was important to settle the matter before that event, in case the Constituency Representatives endeavoured to claim some share in the choice. Accordingly Balcarres summoned a meeting of all Conservative M.P.s to be held in the Carlton Club on the following Monday, November 13th.

To the general public and to the rank and file of the Party the news of Balfour's resignation came as a great shock, but the principal figures in the Party were informed of what impended some days before the official announcement, and on November 4th Balfour personally told Bonar Law of his decision. Bonar Law was much disturbed at the news. He had a profound respect for Balfour and expressed it in a speech at York on November 6th, two days before the public announcement of Balfour's retirement:

"I have never admired him so much as in the hour when his fortunes and those of his party were at their lowest ebb. You remember the Manchester election. Directly after that election he came to Glasgow and addressed a great audience without a note of despair, a speech full of confidence and courage. It was a speech which, as I listened to it, recalled to my mind the words applied to Cromwell in his darkest hour just before Dunbar: 'He was a strong man. Hope shone in him like a pillar of fire when it had gone out of all the others'."

Bonar Law concluded:

"And now there is no member of the House of Commons in whatever quarter he sits who does not look upon Mr. Balfour as the greatest parliamentary figure of our times."

As soon as Balfour's resignation had been publicly announced on Wednesday afternoon, November 8th, Bonar Law telephoned to Aitken who was at his country house, Cherkley, near Leatherhead, and asked him to come at once to London. Aitken was his most active supporter and, as we have seen, had already been busy canvassing on his behalf. He promptly came up to London, for there was no time to be lost. That very evening, as chance would have it, Chamberlain and Bonar Law were billed to speak at a great dinner for the Tariff Reform League. It was likely to be the occasion of a lively demonstration by the various groups of partisans on behalf of their candidates. The dinner duly took place, the speeches were made, and the supporters of each candidate endeavoured to raise the loudest possible cheer for their man. It was a disappointing moment for those who favoured Bonar Law. The cheer for him was noticeably weaker than the cheer which greeted Chamberlain.

This was not surprising. Out of some 280 M.P.s it is doubtful whether at this stage more than 40 were supporters of Bonar Law. Nevertheless, at a meeting of his friends held after the dinner, Bonar Law decided to allow his name to go forward as a candidate for the leadership. Even if he failed on this occasion, which seemed more than likely, he would at least have made his name known as that of a potential leader, and this might be very useful when the next vacancy occurred. Moreover there was always the chance that he might succeed, and, as we have already seen, he had good reason to believe that his success would be in the best interests of the Conservative Party.

3

It is now necessary to return to the two rivals. Walter Long and Austen Chamberlain were at this time on the very worst of terms with one another. This fact should be remembered, for otherwise the course of events may seem more puzzling than it really was. The kindness and generosity which the two rivals referred to each other in later years must not be allowed to conceal the very bitter animosity which prevailed between them and their partisans in the autumn of 1911. The sort of feeling that existed is well illustrated by Chamberlain's own account of meeting Long outside the House of Commons on the very afternoon of Balfour's resignation. Chamberlain had just arrived in a taxi and was accompanied by Henry Chaplin, the senior Conservative ex-minister:[c]

" 'Ah, here is Walter,' said Chaplin who had just got out.

" 'Chaplin picked me up at the Tariff Conference,' I began. 'He was just telling me——'

" 'Oh!' interrupted Long, 'you don't think it is necessary to explain why you are in a taxi with a man, do you? You haven't come to that have you?'

"You may imagine my feelings. I made one step towards him and had it on my lips to tell him he was a cad and slap him across the face, but I got a grip on myself, turned round and went in with Chaplin. At the top of the stair I turned to Long and said:

" 'You interrupted me in the middle of a sentence. I was going to tell you that Chaplin was telling me of his conversation with you. Will you join us? We had better go into Balfour's room'."

The ensuing discussion was anything but cordial and it was quite clear that neither of the two men had the slightest intention of withdrawing in favour of the other at this stage. Only if a trial ballot showed a conclusive majority for one of the rivals would the other concede a walkover. Both agreed, however, that they would withdraw if there seemed to be a third candidate who had any substantial backing and who was reasonably acceptable to their adherents.

The following day, Thursday, November 9th, was one of crucial importance. The battle was now fully joined. Chamberlain had the backing of nearly all the Tory ex-ministers and also of the Party managers. Carson, F. E. Smith, and the leading members of the Halsbury Club were on his side, and naturally the whole weight of the Tariff Reform Party was behind him too. Long was supported by a solid phalanx of back benchers and – for what it was worth – the influence of Londonderry House, as soon as it became clear to Lady Londonderry that there was no chance of Carson standing. Balfour's views – as far as the public was concerned – remained veiled in a discreet silence. Privately, however, he favoured Chamberlain and had told Balcarres so, over a month earlier.[d]

Balcarres, upon whom fell the responsibility of conducting the election, seems to have been actuated by three main motives. First he was anxious to avoid an open contest at the Carlton Club. Such was the prevailing bad temper that there seemed every probability of angry speeches, bitter disputes, and a general exhibition of dissension which could only discredit the Party and delight the Liberals. Secondly he wanted if possible to get Chamberlain in. Thirdly he

wanted to keep Long out. "Where should I be", he said to Chamberlain,[e] "with him (Long) changing his mind every hour." Balcarres
hoped that, if an informal poll was taken of the opinions of the Conservative M.P.s, it might be possible to discover that one or other of
the two rivals had a clear lead. In that case he intended to press the
loser to withdraw his candidature and allow a unanimous election
at the meeting on Monday.

In view of the general confusion, and the very short time (only
four days including a weekend) before the Carlton Club meeting,
Balcarres' plan was evidently likely to run into serious difficulties.
The problem, awkward enough in the case of two candidates, became
even more awkward when the news was announced on Thursday
that Bonar Law was a runner too. How was the final vote to be
taken? Would it be on the basis of a simple majority, i.e. victory to
whichever of the three got most votes on the first ballot? Or would
there be a second ballot in which all but the top two would have
been eliminated? In that case how were the votes for Bonar Law
most likely to be distributed? Moreover the matter was further confused because the leading members of the Long party declared that,
if Long seemed likely to lose, they would transfer their votes to Bonar
Law in order to keep Chamberlain out at all costs. The final touch
was added to this complicated picture by the tactics of Beaverbrook
who, seeing that Bonar Law's best chance lay in a total deadlock
between Long and Chamberlain, urged the Bonar Law party to vote,
during Balcarres' successive attempts at canvassing, not for Bonar
Law, but for whichever of his two senior rivals seemed at the time
to be losing.

Bonar Law's candidature at once alarmed the Chamberlain camp.
There was already disturbing evidence about the quantity, if not the
quality, of Long's support and it seemed probable that Bonar Law
would still further reduce the numbers of Chamberlain's side. A
letter from Goulding to Bonar Law dated Thursday, November 9th,
shows the position, as it appeared to one of his strongest supporters:[f]

"My dear Bonar,

"I have seen several since and I also told Bal that you had decided to
comply with the request of many friends and stand and serve if the Party
so desired next Monday.

"Lowther, Thynne, Goldman are among those who will support you.
Enclosed letter Hope[1] gave me with a wish that I should convey same to
you. Read and destroy.

---

[1] James Hope, M.P., later Lord Rankeillour.

"I hear that Helmsley and party are going strong for Long and from what I hear he must have a very large if not the largest poll – the Irish Unionists will be divided, most, however, going Long.[1]

"The latter's friends are working and I hear little or no mention of Austen's name.

"Yours ever,

Edward Goulding."

The enclosed letter from James Hope read as follows:

"Dear Goulding,

"I confess I hear with consternation the idea of Law standing for the leadership – and that largely for his own sake. I like and admire him immensely, but I do not think that he has a chance of election, and his standing may gravely prejudice Austen's chances and in any case cannot fail to leave a nasty taste. I am hardly intimate enough with him to beg him to desist, but I hope that you will use your influence in that direction.

"Ever yours,

J. A. Hope."

Nor was Hope the only one to advise Bonar Law to withdraw. J. L. Garvin, editor of the *Pall Mall Gazette* and a person of much influence in Unionist circles, saw Bonar Law on this same Thursday and tried hard to dissuade him from standing. Bonar Law at the time showed no signs of yielding: according to Austen Chamberlain, Garvin reported "that he had found Law inflexible, quite determined to get the position if he could and quite satisfied that he was fully qualified for it". In fact, however, these appeals had more effect on Bonar Law than Garvin realized. Bonar Law did not really expect to get the leadership unless the others withdrew, and since there was no sign of this he was reluctant to appear in the role of one who, by his personal ambition, was spoiling the chances of the section in the Party, to which he himself belonged. His principal purpose – that of making his name known as a possible leader at some future vacancy – had already been achieved. Therefore, after reflecting upon the matter overnight, Bonar Law prepared a letter to Hope on the following morning, Friday, November 10th. The draft of this letter is among Bonar Law's papers.

After some preliminary courtesies it continues:[g]

"I am not in the ordinary sense a 'candidate' for the vacant position. It never occurred to me that I had a chance of obtaining it; but after the Tariff meeting[2] the other night some of our friends who are members of

[1] The Irish Unionists' first choice was Carson but he declined to run. He had no real chance of securing general support in the Party.

[2] The dinner on Wednesday night (November 8th) referred to above, p. 77.

Bonar Law as seen by
Max Beerbohm (*left*)
and "Spy" (*right*)

the House saw me and asked me whether I would be a candidate. Goulding was one of them and I told them I was not a candidate, but when I was further asked, 'would you accept it if it were offered to you?' I said, of course I would. I cannot see what other attitude I could possibly take. But, if I thought that the fact that some of my friends think that I might fill the post as well as anyone else available would have the effect you fear, that is of preventing Austen Chamberlain from obtaining it, I should at once say that I would not under any circumstances take it. I cannot see however that it can have that effect. . . ."

Bonar Law then discussed at length the method of voting at the Carlton Club, which he presumed would be by two ballots, the first eliminating all but the top two candidates, the second deciding which of those two should be leader. In such circumstances Bonar Law failed to see how his candidature could damage Chamberlain. But he ends his letter thus:

"If I find at the meeting that the question is not to be settled in that way (provided it comes to a vote) but is to be settled in favour of the candidate who in the first vote obtains an actual majority, then, if in my opinion my nomination is likely to damage C. and help L., I should be quite ready to say that I would not allow myself to be nominated.

"I am yours very sincerely,
A. Bonar Law."

"I have marked this letter 'private' because I am very friendly with Long and do not think it right to take sides strongly against him, but I should say to A.C. exactly what I have said to you and I should not object to his seeing what I have written."

However, before sending this letter, Bonar Law decided to consult Aitken and on Friday morning (November 10th) he went round to call on the latter at his flat in Knightsbridge. Aitken, both in those days and ever since, has possessed to a singular degree the capacity, as one of his friends once put it, "of recognizing political dynamite when he sees it". As soon as he had read the letter, which Bonar Law handed to him, he saw the danger of sending it. However much quali- fied, it was a definite agreement to stand down for Chamberlain in certain circumstances. Moreover the letter was to be shown to Chamberlain himself and, if Chamberlain or his allies saw it, they were almost certain to take advantage of the offer and claim that the circumstances envisaged had occurred. Bonar Law's friends would then have ceased to press his candidature, which many of them, anyway, regarded as a forlorn hope. The mere knowledge that Bonar Law might withdraw at the Carlton Club meeting would have been most discouraging to his supporters. There was a further point: the Party managers were above all things anxious to avoid a split vote

D

at the meeting on Monday. The correct course for Bonar Law's friends was clearly to play upon this fear in the hope that the other candidates would withdraw. It was therefore vital to press his nomination until the last possible moment. If he seemed to be wavering, however slightly, his chances would be ruined.

Aitken therefore urged him in the strongest terms not to send the letter. Bonar Law was at first most unwilling to take this advice. A brisk and at times acrimonious discussion followed. Nevertheless in the end he decided not to send the original letter. Instead a letter, much shorter and couched in very different tones, was dispatched to Hope. It reads as follows:[h]

"I am glad Goulding has sent me your letter for we certainly know each other well enough to more than justify you in speaking to me at a time like this. My position is very simple. I have not sought and do not seek the leadership, but friends of mine have asked me whether I would accept the position, if it were offered to me, and I have said that I would.

"I do not see what else I could do.

"I may add that I am quite satisfied that the fact that my name is put forward will not affect Chamberlain any more than it will affect Long."

This gave nothing away, and clearly showed that Bonar Law meant to persist. From now onwards there was to be no question of withdrawal.

On Friday morning, then, the situation seemed as obscure as ever. Long and Chamberlain were still locked in an apparently inextricable struggle. It was far from certain who would command most votes, but there was at least some evidence to suggest that Long was gaining ground. As for Bonar Law he had no chance on a straight vote but he was determined now to press his candidature to the bitter end, and an attempt on the part of Balcarres to persuade him to withdraw met with no success. Balcarres came round that morning to see Chamberlain whose account must be quoted:[i]

"Bal. came again at 11 o'clock this morning (Friday, November 10th). He said that Carson would not allow his name to go forward. Bonar Law was determined that his should be submitted. 'I am furious with him,' Bal. said,[1] 'of course it injures your chance. Mind, I think that if the vote could be taken on Saturday you would win . . . But the lobbying is all on Long's side.'

"By Monday, therefore, he could not say what the position would be. We should each poll something over 100 votes and the votes cast for Law would have to be distributed between us. What the result would be he

---

[1] Balcarres was subsequently on the very best of terms with Bonar Law and served him most loyally. His anger at this time was the annoyance of a party manager who encounters an unexpected hitch in his carefully arranged plans.

could not say. Either of us might be chosen by a majority of between 10 and 20."

This information decided Chamberlain's course of action. It was now quite clear that Long would never withdraw. Indeed, why should he when he appeared to have a good chance of winning?

Moreover, even if Chamberlain did scrape through by a narrow margin, he was convinced – rightly or wrongly – that it would be a barren victory. He disclosed his mind at some length the following night to Balfour's private secretary and *eminence grise*, Jack Sandars, who wrote thus to his chief on November 12th:[j]

"Austen told me he was persuaded that Walter would never be loyal to him, that from the moment the leadership passed into his hands there would be no intrigue too petty but Walter would be in it. He knew (somehow or other) of Walter's ill managed Cabals against yourself. Warned by this knowledge he was very satisfied that as long as Walter had any substantial number of friends who had failed to carry him into the leadership there was but little prospect of loyalty and peace so far as he, Austen, was concerned."

Chamberlain informed Balcarres that he would withdraw in favour of Bonar Law provided that Walter Long would do the same. Balcarres demurred. Bonar Law, he maintained, was "lamentably weak". Why not allow Long to take the leadership? He would be so incompetent that it would be vacant again in a few months and Chamberlain could then succeed without dispute. Chamberlain refused this proposal on the understandable ground that the few months, however propitious to his personal fortunes, might be ruinous to those of the Party. Balcarres agreed and undertook to act as an emissary. He promptly called on Long who was quite content to withdraw his candidature. After his conversation with Chamberlain in Balfour's room he could hardly have done otherwise. Balcarres telephoned the news to Chamberlain, and then hastened to Pembroke Lodge to inform Bonar Law.

At this point, however, an unexpected hitch occurred. To the surprise of Balcarres, Bonar Law, on learning the news that Chamberlain and Long had withdrawn in his favour, did not at once accept the proferred leadership. In the morning after talking with Aitken it had seemed as if he had finally cast aside his doubts. Now with the object of his ambition already in his grasp he once again paused and hesitated. He told Balcarres that he must have time to consider the matter and that he must see Chamberlain. Early in the afternoon, therefore, he drove from the House of Commons to 9

Egerton Place where Chamberlain lived. For the story of their interview we must once more rely on Chamberlain's account written at
the time.[k]

Bonar Law, according to Chamberlain, said, "Well, Austen, this
is a very serious thing for me. I am not sure I can accept."

"My dear Law", replied Chamberlain, "you must. You have no
choice now. You allowed your name to go forward. Don't think that
I blame or criticize you for it – I long ago said that there should be
no personal rivalry between you and me about offices – but you
altered the situation by doing so; you cannot now shrink from the
consequences."

Bonar Law apparently demurred at this statement, declaring that
his only intention in allowing his name to go forward had been to
stake a future claim as a possible leader. According to Chamberlain,
Bonar Law then said, "Now look here, Austen! Can't you let Walter
Long have it? He couldn't keep it for six months. He'd be an obvious
failure and in six months or less the leadership would be vacant and
the whole question would be open." This was the second occasion
on which that proposal had been made to Chamberlain. It is difficult
to believe that Bonar Law meant this suggestion very seriously.
Perhaps he was merely "thinking aloud" as he sometimes did.

At all events Chamberlain declined even to consider it. After further discussion Bonar Law said, "Well, I suppose that I shall have
to accept, but it will make no difference to our personal friendship,
will it?" Chamberlain replied that it would not. He writes: "And
that promise I must keep. I confess I feel a little grieved. I don't think
that if our position had been reversed I could have acted as he did
but I must get that feeling out of my mind and keep it out."[1]

It is not easy to say exactly what Bonar Law had in mind during
this curious discussion. Perhaps he really had only intended to put
his name forward for the leadership in order to show that he was a
"possible", so to speak, and was genuinely perturbed to find that he
had won on the first attempt. Perhaps he was merely endeavouring
to make his relations with Chamberlain as smooth as possible. Perhaps – and this is more probable – he was not actuated by any logical
or clear-cut motive, but was overcome by that strange diffidence
which blended so oddly with his ambition and was still trying to
decide what he ought to do, still half in doubt whether he could
adequately fulfil the high office which had come to him in so unexpected a fashion. But, whatever was in his mind, he could not go

---

[1] No doubt he had in mind Bonar Law's promise not to contest the leadership.

back. On his return from his interview with Chamberlain he told
Balcarres that he would accept.

And so Bonar Law, who on the Wednesday evening when the
struggle for the succession began could only muster some 40 positive
votes out of 280, had become within forty-eight hours the agreed and
only candidate for the leadership of the Conservative Party in the
House of Commons. Few more remarkable events have occurred in
the history of parties and the elevation of Bonar Law will long remain
among the most extraordinary transactions in recent English politics.

Was Austen Chamberlain's grievance at Bonar Law's conduct
justified? It was certainly understandable. Chamberlain believed
that he could have got a majority on a straight vote and that Bonar
Law's intervention had weakened his chances. It is true that Chamberlain was probably wrong and that in fact Long would have won
had the matter come to a ballot, but this did not of course lessen
Chamberlain's grievance. It is what men believe to be true – not
what is actually true – which most often matters in politics. Nevertheless, even if we allow for Chamberlain's natural feelings, it is
difficult to see why Bonar Law should not have competed for the
leadership. It was a perfectly legitimate goal for a man of ambition.
Moreover the event fully justified his candidature. Neither Long nor
Chamberlain had any chance of commanding unanimous, or even
overwhelming, support in the Party. The election of either would
have caused very great bitterness, and, as will become evident later
in this narrative, Bonar Law was probably a much more effective
leader than either of his rivals would have been. Long lacked the
capacity to lead. Chamberlain would almost certainly have split the
Party in two on the food tax controversy – a crisis which Bonar
Law himself only surmounted with great difficulty. The decision to
make Bonar Law leader of the Unionist Party was reached in a
strange and tortuous manner, but it probably saved the unity of the
Party in a way in which no other choice could have done.

On the following Monday, November 13th, the meeting of the
Unionist M.P.s took place at noon in the Carlton Club. Aitken
accompanied Bonar Law to the meeting. He urged the new leader
not to be too modest, "You are a great man now," he said. "You
must talk like a great man, behave like a great man." Bonar Law's
answer was characteristic. "If I am a great man", he pensively
replied, "then a good many great men must have been frauds."

The details of the meeting need not detain us, for by this stage
everything had been carefully arranged in order to preserve a façade

of unanimity. The animosities of faction were to be discreetly veiled by polite formulae and smooth phrases. There were probably many M.P.s who disliked the way in which the whole matter had been taken out of their hands by the Party managers, but it was too late to do anything now, and an exhibition of dissent would merely have given pleasure to the Liberals. The meeting was presided over by Henry Chaplin, the senior Conservative ex-Minister. Long proposed and Chamberlain seconded Bonar Law's nomination, explaining in their speeches their reasons – or some of their reasons – for withdrawing. Then Carson, whose name had also been mentioned as a possible leader, was deputed to go and bring in Bonar Law who was waiting outside. The new leader entered amidst a tumult of applause and made a brief speech.

". . . For the last two days the feeling which has filled my mind has not been elation at a reward which anyone might look forward to. I have been filled with a sense of the terrible responsibilities which I am undertaking and I have looked around eagerly for some other solution which I should have welcomed then and which I should welcome now. All my intimate friends told me yesterday that at the meeting I was to avoid saying anything depreciating myself but I cannot pretend that I am not afraid of this task. I am afraid of it. If I were quite sure that I am incapable of filling it, no power on earth should make me touch it. I am not quite sure for no man can know accurately either his capacity or his limitations. But I am sure of this, that with the disadvantages under which I labour, which everyone of you will understand, the disadvantage of never having been in the Cabinet, the disadvantage too of having had comparatively small experience even of the rough and tumble of the House of Commons – that under those disadvantages I cannot possibly succeed unless I receive from you all a support as generous and perhaps more generous than has ever been given to any leader of your Party."

The meeting ended at five minutes to one. A Presbyterian of Canadian origin, who had spent most of his life in business in Glasgow, had become leader of the Party of Old England, the Party of the Anglican Church and the country squire, the Party of broad acres and hereditary titles. Not since the days of Disraeli had so strange a choice been made; and certainly no choice more strange has been made since.

CHAPTER V

THE PROBLEMS OF THE LEADER
1911 – 1912

Bonar Law's mode of life – His dislike of entertaining – The quality of his table – Lady Londonderry – Bonar Law's attitude to Society – His personal position – Erroneous rumours about Lord Beaverbrook's part in his election – Bonar Law's relations with Lansdowne and Curzon – Attitude of Long and Chamberlain – His relations with Balfour – Bonar Law as a fighter – Aggressive tone of his speeches – Asquith's low opinion of him – Bonar Law's attitude to Asquith – Problems of party organization – Conservative funds – Steel-Maitland's memorandum – Question of honours – The Shadow Cabinet

I

BONAR LAW was a man of ambition and his elevation to the leadership was a vast and unexpected stride towards the fulfilment of that ambition. Yet he showed no great elation at his victory. By now, indeed, he seldom displayed elation about anything. His air of weary indifference to the turns of fortune – perhaps originally a pose – had with the course of time become so habitual as to be a genuine part of his character. Expecting little of life, and ever prone to gaze at the darker side of events, he greeted with singularly little emotion either political adversity or political success. Adversity after all only confirmed his pessimism. As for success, a cautious scepticism was the safest attitude: only thus could the prudent man be sure of avoiding subsequent disappointment and chagrin.

Holding these views Bonar Law had no intention of allowing his whole existence to be turned upside down by the alteration in his political fortunes. He continued to live, as he had done, quietly at Pembroke Lodge. Certain minor changes did indeed become necessary in his mode of life. Aitken, in pursuance of his theory that Bonar Law must behave like a great man now, procured a butler for him in order to add tone to the establishment at Pembroke Lodge. Fortunately the choice was most successful, and Pitts, the butler recommended, remained with Bonar Law till the latter's death. Hitherto Bonar Law had done very little entertaining. This was not because he was mean or disliked spending money, but because formal

87

luncheons and dinners bored him profoundly. In those days a dinner party seldom had less than five or six courses with appropriate wines, followed by dessert and port. But what Bonar Law liked was a quick meal, preferably soup and chicken followed by milk pudding, washed down with ginger ale. Having consumed this barbarous repast he was impatient to leave the table and smoke a large cigar. To someone of these strange tastes the ordinary routine of hospitality was a painful and tedious infliction.

Now that he was leader he was obliged to dispense rather more hospitality than he had before. On the eve of every session it was a traditional duty of the leader in the House of Commons to give a grand dinner to the whips and those members of the Shadow Cabinet who were in the Lower House – Lansdowne entertained the peers – and this tradition was continued by Bonar Law at Pembroke Lodge. But in general he contrived to entertain as little as possible. Perhaps it was just as well. The guests at Bonar Law's rare parties received almost as little pleasure as their host. Food and drink are never likely to be good at a house whose owner takes no interest in either. Lord Beaverbrook is perhaps unduly severe when he says that "the food on Bonar Law's table was always quite execrable. Its sameness was a penance and its quality a horror to me." But there can be little doubt that Pembroke Lodge was not a place to which gourmets competed for invitations.

Bonar Law was quite happy to leave the social side of Conservative politics to Lady Londonderry. She was a great hostess and, so the malicious averred, an unfailing political barometer. Austen Chamberlain once said that he could always tell the state of his own political fortunes by the number of fingers, ranging from two to all ten, which she gave him when they met. Naturally she had never bothered to cultivate Bonar Law before, and indeed she scarcely knew him, but she was not the only fashionable hostess who found it necessary to make a quick readjustment of social values as a result of his unexpected elevation. From now onwards she bombarded him with invitations. Before every session it was her custom to give a splendid reception to which the whole world of Tory politics and Society was invited. Bonar Law would stand beside her on these occasions and shake hands with the seemingly endless stream of guests. He must have appeared a sombre and perhaps slightly incongruous figure amidst all the glitter of diamonds and decorations in Londonderry House. But although he disliked Society and seldom accepted invitations Bonar Law appreciated the help of Lady Londonderry. She was always ready to entertain on his behalf, and she was kind to his family too. It was under her auspices that his eldest daughter, Isobel, "came out" in the season of 1914.

If Bonar Law had wished, he could at once have moved into the highest circles of the social world. There was scarcely a stately home in England or Scotland to which he would not have been invited had he so desired. The English aristocracy – and it is one of the secrets of their survival – has never been slow to accept "new men" in their midst. Usually the "new men" are gratified and delighted at their reception, but Bonar Law was an exception. He seldom accepted the numerous invitations which were showered upon him, unless he knew his host extremely well, or unless it was convenient for some political purpose. It must be admitted that on the rare occasions when he did spend a few days at some great house he cannot have been one of the easier guests to entertain. There is an amusing account in Lord Sysonby's diary[a] of a visit to Windsor Castle when all propoₑsals for amusing him were turned down, until eventually the problₑm was solved by arranging a chess game between him and Sir Walt r Parratt, the venerable ex-organist of Windsor Chapel, who, surprisingly enough, won easily. "I hear old Parratt beat your head off," the King somewhat tactlessly observed at dinner.

Bonar Law's attitude to Society should not be misunderstood. He certainly did not despise it. He was well aware of class distinctions and the important part which social prestige played in Tory politics. Indeed one of his principal apprehensions on becoming leader was that he might fail because he did not belong to the traditional upper class from which Conservative leaders normally came. Bonar Law was in no sense dazzled by social glamour, but, on the other hand, he had none of the rather aggressive egalitarianism which sometimes characterizes self-made business men. It was simply that social life did not interest him. He was neither a wit nor a conversationalist. Personal gossip which has always constituted nine-tenths of the talk in the grand world was of no interest, and any way largely incomprehensible, to him, since he knew none of the people concerned. He was content to be guided through the social and genealogical intricacies of Tory politics by his two Parliamentary private secretaries, John Baird and George Stanley, a brother of Lord Derby, who had both been chosen partly for their expertise in a field likely to be unfamiliar to the product of Glasgow's High School and Iron Ring. But he had no intention of posing as the habitué of a world to which he had never belonged and in which he took no interest whatever.

2

The political problems confronting Bonar Law were exceedingly difficult. They were partly caused by the particular circumstances of his own election to the leadership. There were others which would have confronted any Conservative leader at this time, arising as they did from the general political conditions of the day.

Bonar Law's election inevitably left sore feelings among many members of the Party. He was, as he himself admitted, very inexperienced, nor had he the personal magnetism, the flair and self-confidence of a Lloyd George or a Churchill, which might have enabled him to blind his followers to these defects. On November 16th, 1911, Lord Derby wrote to the King, describing Bonar Law:[b]

"He is a curious mixture. Never very gay, he has become even less so since the death of his wife to whom he was devoted. But still he has a great sense of humour – a first class debater – and a good, though not a rousing, platform speaker – a great master of figures which he can use to great advantage. He has all the qualities of a great leader except one – and that is he has no personal magnetism and can inspire no man to real enthusiasm."

A back bencher is quoted as giving an even less flattering and more succinct verdict on his new leader:[c]

"How Bonar Law can help us without any knowledge of Foreign Affairs, Navy, Church questions, or Home Rule, the Lord alone knows."

Sentiments of this sort, although unjustified by later events, were probably widespread in the early days of Bonar Law's leadership.

Moreover there can be little doubt that the part played by Sir Max Aitken in the election was the subject of much criticism. Jack Sandars, writing to Balfour on November 10th, said:[d]

"I have just heard that it has been settled that Bonar Law will be elected leader of the Party in the House of Commons. Much intrigue has been at work. . . .

"Bonar Law's own methods are open to much criticism. In this struggle I am told that he has been run by Mr. Max Aitken, the little Canadian adventurer who sits for Ashton-under-Lyne, introduced into that seat by him. Aitken practically owns the *Daily Express* and the *Daily Express* has run Bonar Law for the last two days for all it is worth. Bonar Law was inflexible throughout in his intention to stand no matter what harm to the party or dissension there might be.

"The real Bonar Law appears to be a man of boundless ambition untempered by any particularly nice feelings. It is a revelation. He found Goulding had committed himself to a heavy support of Austen. He went to Goulding and reviving memories and rash promises, he practically ordered his support, and this support and influence was then transferred by Goulding from Austen to Bonar Law. . . ."

This version of events was, as the account in the last chapter shows, highly garbled, but it contained just enough truth to be plausible.

It was true that Bonar Law was very ambitious. It was true that Aitken was one of his most vociferous supporters. It was also true that some pressure had been put upon Goulding, though not by Bonar Law himself. But there is a limit to what intrigue can do. The real cause of Bonar Law's success was, as we saw, the very bitter animosity which prevailed between Walter Long and Austen Chamberlain. If this element in the situation is forgotten – and it often is – then the whole process of Bonar Law's election becomes far more mysterious than it need be. Contemporary observers and later historians have felt obliged to seek strange and tortuous explanations and have fastened upon the manoeuvres of Aitken as the only solution to the problem. To do this is to attribute to him a degree of influence in the Conservative Party, which it was quite impossible for a young man of his standing to have possessed and which he himself has never claimed.

He did play an important part, it is true. But his importance was not in the field of political wire-pulling or even in that of Press propaganda. It was rather his personal influence in persuading Bonar Law to press his candidature and in advising him on tactics. To this day there are those who believe that Bonar Law was a mere puppet or mouthpiece of a sinister intriguer operating from behind the scenes. Such a version of events should find no place in serious history, but the fact that stories of this sort were current may well have affected Bonar Law's own position and reputation in the early days of his leadership.

Bonar Law's personal position was complicated by other considerations. Although he was Balfour's successor, he did not succeed to Balfour's full inheritance. Balfour was the acknowledged leader of the Party as a whole, but Bonar Law was theoretically only the leader of the Party in the House of Commons. In the event of a Conservative Government being formed it was by no means certain that the King would send for Bonar Law. He might equally well send for Lansdowne. It is true that Bonar Law himself did not regard this as likely. According to Sandars:[e]

"Austen told Bonar Law at the same interview that the man who in the Commons led the Party to victory would be the next Prime Minister. Was Bonar Law ready to face that responsibility? Yes, said Bonar Law, he was.

"Parenthetically let me say that neither Austen nor Bonar Law appear to recognize George Curzon for a moment as their superior. No Peer, Austen believes, will be tolerated after the events of August last: least of all Lansdowne."

However, this was merely Bonar Law's and Chamberlain's opinion. It did not follow that the King would act upon that opinion. There was certainly no insuperable barrier in those days to a Prime Minister from the Upper House.

What was the attitude of Lansdowne and Curzon? Probably Lansdowne, who was getting on in years, would not have wished to be Prime Minister. His treatment of Bonar Law was always marked by unfailing courtesy. Now and then perhaps there is a hint of superiority, but it would be wrong to read more into this than the undoubted fact that Lansdowne was an older and senior person in the Tory hierarchy. Curzon's attitude was different. He was a man of immense ambition who never concealed either his desire to become Prime Minister or his conviction that he would succeed. The resignation of Balfour with whom he had a long-standing feud brought him appreciably nearer his goal. He was still of course junior to Lansdowne but the latter might at any moment retire. It was important for Curzon to stake a claim in the Party councils which would put him above Bonar Law's other colleagues. His letter congratulating the new leader upon his election suggests this purpose. After referring to "the great honour conferred on you today" he concludes:[f]

"If I have any opportunity of co-operating with you and facilitating your task, you may rely on me to take it. I hope Lansdowne, you and I may have a confidential talk before long on some aspects of the political situation which call for enquiry and action.

"Yours sincerely,

Curzon of Kedleston."

It was a hint – a quiet and discreet hint – that Curzon was not to be regarded in the same light as Bonar Law's other leading colleagues.

The two men who had most cause to resent Bonar Law's elevation at once pledged him unqualified support. Chamberlain did indeed tell Bonar Law at their interview on November 10th that he regarded the leadership question as open to revision. Sanders, writing to Balfour, said:[g]

"Austen has some anxiety about Bonar Law. I can see he does not regard the new arrangement as final. He has told Bonar Law that while he is quite ready to support him he (Bonar Law) must clearly understand that, should the occasion arise, he (Austen) will have no hesitation in standing again for the highest post in the party."

However, Austen Chamberlain did not in fact make any attempt to challenge Bonar Law's leadership. He disagreed with him on occasions – especially over the food tax question – but in general showed a loyalty which was, in the circumstances, very generous. The same was true of Long who indeed was rather more friendly than Chamberlain, if we can judge by the tone of their letters. It is much to their credit that neither of them ever descended – or even approached descending – to the intrigues with which in the somewhat analogous circumstances of the Liberal Party in 1894–95 Sir William Harcourt plagued his unfortunate leader, Lord Rosebery.

Balfour, like Long and Chamberlain, promised his support to the new leader. But, if Balfour did nothing to hinder Bonar Law, it is also true that he did little to help him. Their relations remained always civil, but always cool and distant. Balfour, for example, made no attempt to instruct Bonar Law in his new duties or to advise him on the difficult points of etiquette, policy, and procedure which at once arose. No doubt, this was partly the result of a praiseworthy disinclination to meddle with matters which were no longer his business. Possibly also Balfour's feelings, when he saw the occasional errors into which his successor fell, were not those of unmixed distress. He would scarcely have been human, had it been otherwise. Whatever the reason for his remoteness, there can be no doubt of the fact. It is interesting to notice that in their slender correspondence to the end, Balfour never gets beyond "My dear Bonar Law", and till as late as 1915, Bonar Law invariably begins "My dear Mr. Balfour".

3

In the face of all these personal difficulties Bonar Law possessed one important asset which soon became evident: he was above all else a fighter. The rank and file of the Conservative Party were weary of the ingenious formulae, the dialectical subtleties, the elaborately qualified arguments of their former leader. They wanted someone who would show no sign of compromise with the enemy, who would state in blunt, and preferably rude, terms what the average Conservative thought about the Liberal Government. They wanted someone who would hit often and hit hard – and this was undoubtedly what they got in Bonar Law.

For, despite a diffident manner in private life and a certain tendency to hesitate, Bonar Law was in politics essentially a fighting man. His hesitation was not due to cowardice or weakness; it was rather the product of his innate sense of caution, his desire to assure himself beyond all reasonable doubt that his course of action really was the right course. As soon as that mental process had come to an end – and it sometimes took a long while – then Bonar Law would march upon his chosen path without further scruples or doubts. This was so at many of the critical moments of his career: his decision to bid for the Leadership, his decision to overthrow Asquith in 1916, his decision to overthrow Lloyd George in 1922. All these actions were preceded by long deliberation and a careful estimation of the consequences, but no one could describe them as the actions of a man given to feebleness or vacillation. The truth was that Bonar Law possessed behind his unassuming, almost shy, demeanour a core of toughness which came as a surprise to many people. It was this hardness, this refusal to compromise, this determination to strike at the Liberals without overmuch nicety as to the weapons employed, which delighted the Tory Party and in a short while went far to consolidate Bonar Law's hold over his followers.

His fighting quality was speedily displayed in his speeches. Bonar Law's voice was naturally of a soft and gentle character, his normal method one of argument and reason. But he now adopted a new technique. A harsh, almost a rasping tone would come into his voice, and his oratory contained a note of invective which had never characterized Balfour's speeches. At an early stage, indeed in the debate on the Address in February 1912, Bonar Law indicated that the era of polite forms was at an end. After congratulating, as is customary, the mover and seconder of the Address, he observed, "Now, Mr. Speaker, I have done with compliments, and I am sorry to say that I do not think they will be very frequent during the Session upon which we have now entered."

The event bore out Bonar Law's prophecy and few men did more to ensure its accuracy than the prophet himself.

A good example of his technique is his speech at the Albert Hall on January 26th, 1912 – one of his first as leader of the Party. After referring to the record of Asquith's government as "an example of destructive violence to which there is no parallel since the Long Parliament", Bonar Law continued:

"Some people have the idea that the members of the present Government, apart from their policy are unusually competent. That is a delusion. It depends of course on the point of view. In one department of their activity – the only department that interests them – in electioneering, in the small trickery of politics, they are indeed competent. They have never had equals; but fortunately for this country in the past they have had no competition."

He then claimed as a hit at Lloyd George that jobbery had been peculiarly flagrant in Wales:

"Wales returns thirty members to the House of Commons – not all of them Radicals. And during the last six years the Government have bestowed marks of their esteem varying from a peerage to a job upon eighteen Welsh members. . . .

". . . They [the Government] have succeeded in six years in creating a political spoils system which already rivals that of the United States. But there is this difference: for years the United States have been striving earnestly to put an end to that system; the Government have striven with equal earnestness – and with more success – to create it. If we have a few more years of Georgian finance, the only attractive, the only lucrative profession left in this country will be that of a Radical Welsh politician."

Bonar Law later dealt with the Church of Wales:

"The next object of the Government's destructive violence is the Church of Wales. They propose to take away from that Church endowments which it has enjoyed for centuries and which are as much the property of the Church as the coat on his back," Bonar Law paused for a moment, "the coat which he has turned so often, is the property of Mr. Winston Churchill."

This last sally was particularly well received. During the course of the speech he described the Liberals as "Gadarene Swine", "A Revolutionary Committee", "Gamblers who are always ready to double the stakes. They are not only gamblers but gamblers who load the dice." He claimed that they were addicted to "Trickery and the methods of the Artful Dodger."

Another example of Bonar Law's method was a speech at Belfast on April 9th, 1912. It is worth quoting because it prompted Asquith's well-known description of Bonar Law's language as the "New Style" which Asquith contrasted unfavourably with the style of Balfour. Bonar Law had said at Belfast:

"For more than two years the Government have been in office but they have not been in power. They have turned the House of Commons into an exchange where everything is bought and sold. In order to retain for a little longer the ascendency of their Party, to remain a few months longer in office, they have sold the constitution, they have sold themselves. . . ."

It was this remark which apparently angered Asquith. He quoted it a few days later in the House of Commons.

"This Mr. Speaker is the new style. . . . Am I to understand that the right honourable gentleman repeats that here, or is prepared to repeat it on the floor of the House of Commons?

"Mr. Bonar Law: 'Yes.'

"The Prime Minister: 'Let us see exactly what it is. It is that I and my colleagues are selling our convictions.'

"Mr. Bonar Law: 'You have not got any.'

"The Prime Minister: 'We are getting on with the new style!' "

It must be admitted that this particular exchange of civilities suggests small boys at school rather than grave statesmen deliberating in the foremost legislative assembly of the world, but that has happened often enough in the House of Commons. Bonar Law's supporters were delighted by this kind of thing. The feeling that their leader would not spare his punches was very welcome to a party faced with an apparently hopeless period of unsuccessful opposition; and Asquith's attempt to play upon the feelings of those who hankered after the days of Balfour's leadership, by contrasting the style of the two leaders, had no success whatever. What the Conservatives wanted at this time was plenty of sport and a good run for their money. The new leader gave them both.

It has been questioned whether Bonar Law's "New Style" came naturally to him. How far he deliberately put it on for the sake of encouraging his own supporters is a moot point. According to Asquith in his *Memories and Reflections*,[h] as he and Bonar Law were walking side by side away from the House of Lords, after listening to the King's Speech at the opening of the 1912 session, Bonar Law said to him: "I am afraid I shall have to show myself very vicious, Mr. Asquith, this session. I hope you will understand." This certainly suggests that the harsh and often violent tone of Bonar Law's speeches was to some extent assumed; and it is no doubt true that, like those rulers who go to war in order to shelve the internal conflicts of their country, Bonar Law was in part cultivating a deliberate hostility to the Liberals so that his followers might forget their own feuds in their hatred of the common enemy.

But there is every reason to suppose that Bonar Law was speaking with genuine feeling when he delivered many of his most bitter attacks on the Government. This was a period when party politics were characterized by a degree of acrimony unparalleled since – except perhaps in the disputes over the Munich crisis of 1938. The reasons for such bitterness are complicated, and it would require a lengthy analysis of English history over the previous twenty-five years to explain them in full. But broadly speaking the immediate cause of this extraordinary animosity was the General Election of 1906, which thrust the hereditary ruling class of England out of power for the first time since the Glorious Revolution of 1688.

The mere decline of aristocratic power did not greatly move Bonar Law. He was not, and never pretended to be, himself of that class, and he had none of the romantic reverence for things past, for the glamour of the old England, for the pomp and pageantry of a vanished era – a reverence which so often goes with Tory beliefs. On the contrary his views on such matters were almost iconoclastic. He was the least sentimental, the most unromantic Conservative that ever lived. But there was a by-product of the aristocratic decline which touched Bonar Law far more nearly than that decline itself. And this was the imminent passage of an Irish Home Rule Bill which the Lords could no longer stop – a measure which would put Protestant Ulster, the home of his ancestors, under the rule of their hereditary enemies in the Roman Catholic South of Ireland. On this subject – and after all it dominated politics until August 1914 – Bonar Law felt with genuine passion. He once told Austen Chamberlain many years later that, before the war, he cared intensely about only two things: Tariff Reform and Ulster; all the rest was only part of the game.[i] We may then safely take with a grain of salt Bonar Law's strictures upon such topics as Welsh Disestablishment or the Franchise Bill, but upon Irish Home Rule there is no need to suppose that his violence was in any way artificial or affected. On that topic he meant every word he said.

4

It may be appropriate at this moment to consider Bonar Law's relations with the rival leader. Asquith was now at the height of his power and reputation. His career had been one of almost unbroken success from his schooldays onwards: a Balliol scholarship; a first in Greats; a large and lucrative practice at the Bar; politics, first as Home Secretary, then as Chancellor of the Exchequer, and now (at the beginning of 1912) for the past three and a half years Prime Minister of England in a period of immense difficulty, stress and strain which he had surmounted with extraordinary adroitness. Small wonder that Asquith, possessing this formidable record, should tend to look upon the new Conservative leader with a touch of condescension, a hint of patronage. Why should he, who had passed through the whole Cursus Honorum of English politics, pay over much regard to a mere tyro who had never held an office above a Parliamentary Secretaryship?

There were other reasons for Asquith's attitude to Bonar Law. Although both were men of middle-class origin who had made their

way in an aristocratic world to the summit of their respective parties,
they had no tastes or inclinations in common. For by 1912 Asquith
had long forgotten his humbler beginnings. He had been educated
among the aristocracy of England – Balliol in those days was an
aristocratic college – and by his second marriage in 1894 to Margot
Tennant, the daughter of a millionaire, he joined a fashionable circle
far removed from the world whence he had sprung, far removed too
from the world in which Bonar Law spent all his life.

Indeed Bonar Law and Asquith had nothing in common. Asquith
loved society, dined out incessantly, was delighted by the company
of pretty women. Bonar Law hated social engagements, never dined
out of his house unless he had to, and, after the death of his wife,
displayed total indifference to feminine society. Asquith enjoyed good
wine – enjoyed it too much, according to his enemies. Bonar Law
was a teetotaller. About the only taste which the two men shared
was a partiality for bridge, although in Asquith's case it was never
quite the passion that it became for Bonar Law – and incidentally
he was nothing like so good a player.

Perhaps inevitably, Asquith tended to underestimate Bonar Law.
He soon perceived, it is true, that the new leader was a much more
formidable debater than he had previously realized, but to the end
he never acquired for Bonar Law the respect that he felt for Balfour,
Curzon, or Austen Chamberlain. Perhaps he found it impossible to
believe that someone, lacking his own wide intellectual background
of Bar and University, and brought up in the narrower world of the
counting house and the iron market, could ever really be his equal
in politics. "The gilded tradesman," was one of his favourite phrases
about Bonar Law. On one occasion, when Lloyd George pressed for
Bonar Law's inclusion on a Cabinet Committee, Asquith curtly
replied: "He has the mind of a Glasgow Bailie."[j] It is doubtful
whether even to the end he ever altered that opinion.

Bonar Law, however, did not reciprocate those feelings. On the
contrary he had a very considerable respect, even an admiration,
for Asquith's talents. The different way in which each regarded the
other is well shown when they were in office together after 1915.
Asquith did everything possible to belittle Bonar Law, partly no
doubt from political motives, but partly from a real contempt of his
talents, whereas Bonar Law's respect for Asquith was so great that,
despite these slights, it was only after prolonged deliberation and
with great doubts that he took the vital step at the end of 1916 of
overthrowing the Asquith Coalition.

The relationship between Bonar Law and Asquith has been discussed at length, because it was to be most important in Bonar Law's career, and the history of events, particularly after 1915, is incomprehensible without some knowledge of it. For the time being the two were on opposite sides – Asquith gazing at Bonar Law with a good-humoured contempt changing to a certain reluctant admiration for Bonar Law's powers of argument, Bonar Law looking at Asquith with deep respect, mingled with indignation at the Liberal leader's ingenuity and craft.

5

In addition to the more obvious political questions that arise, a party leader has to face a whole number of problems connected with the backstairs of politics, which the average man does not see and which historians usually ignore. The Party moves forward, but what of the levers, the cog wheels and pinions, all the intricate mechanism which makes that movement possible; and what of the oil with which the complicated machinery must be greased? These are subjects too often veiled in a discreet obscurity. Yet they have their interest, and to describe the life of the leader of a great political party without mentioning this side of his work would be misleading and inaccurate.

When Bonar Law became leader, the organization of the Party was still in a state of confusion, although some start had been made to reform the worst abuses by Arthur Steel-Maitland, the new Party Manager who took over in July 1911. The main difficulty was the existence of two distinct but overlapping organizations, the Conservative Central Office which was supposed to deal with candidates, agents and finance, and the National Conservative Union which in return for a central office grant of £9,000 per annum was supposed to be responsible for literature, speakers and general propaganda. Steel-Maitland submitted a lengthy memorandum to Bonar Law on the disadvantages of this dual system.[k]

"(1) There is great waste of money . . .

"(2) There is absolutely no adaptation of means to ends – i.e. no consideration of whether money at our disposal would have the best effect if devoted to literature or spent on Press articles or other objects which I might mention.

"(3) There is no real selection of the best and most suitable men for the various committees. . . .

". . . It is absolutely clear that the whole organization must be under one head. . . ."

On the Central Office Steel-Maitland observes:

"I was prepared for a lack of system but not for what I found. No attempt was made at departmentalizing work. There was no control of ordinary office routine . . . no proper system of reports from district agents; no control of their expenditure. What is more there was no annual balance sheet. They could not tell you within £10,000 what the year's expenditure had been, probably not within £20,000. There was no proper classifica-tion of expenditure, no recovery of loans, no following up of lapsed subscriptions. No note was taken (except as regards General Election expenses) of interviews at which promises were made, pecuniary or other-wise. Vague verbal assurances were the rule, not satisfactory at the moment and productive of trouble later. Engagements were practically never kept. . . . This sounds extravagant. It is literally true. Proof can be given of each statement."

On the other hand the raising of funds, as opposed to their expendi-ture, was in a more satisfactory state.

"As regards the getting of money", [wrote Steel-Maitland] "Lord St. Audries[1] was very good. It is true that the expenses of organizing (as far as I can ascertain) were much less in former years. But still he started without any invested funds, and left a nest egg of over £300,000. A year's peerages are hypothecated, but still this is a very fine performance.

"We thus have about £13,000 a year from invested funds, and about £4,000 a year from the existing subscription list. We *ought* to have £100,000 a year at least. Towards this, Lord Farquhar[2] and I have at present got about £30,000 a year more, mostly in a few big subscriptions. I am at present organizing with him systematic collections from (1) Peers (2) the City. We ought to reach say £80,000 a year by July, as the autumn has been an unfavourable time. After that I hope to tackle provincial centres, and perhaps from local funds in Lancashire, Yorkshire and Scotland, thus relieving the centre. It is preposterous that these rich places should, as now, come yelping to London for help. I may be too sanguine, but I hope by the end, say of 1913, to have an income, irrespective of the Liberal Unionists, of £120,000 to £140,000 a year. This should be to a large extent, but not wholly, irrespective of future honours.

"Perhaps the caution should be borne in mind that the above notes refer to normal expenditure only. Expenditure on a General Election is a thing apart, though of course an Election influences the annual expendi-ture of the year in which it takes place. An Election costs from £80,000 to £120,000."

Steel-Maitland's solution to the problems he outlined was a much closer amalgamation between the Central Office and the National Union. In the end this was facilitated by another organizational change, namely a fusion – between the Conservative and the Liberal Unionist Party. There are lengthy memoranda in Bonar Law's files on this subject. Eventually a satisfactory arrangement was achieved,

[1] The previous Party Treasurer 1902–1911.
[2] The new Party Treasurer. Dismissed by Bonar Law in 1923.

and, after a meeting held at Bonar Law's house on February 12th, it was agreed to amalgamate all three bodies, the Conservative Central Office, the Conservative National Union and the Liberal Unionist Council into a single organization under central control.

Bonar Law's files contain a good many letters dealing with what may be called the managerial side of the Party. No doubt most of the work was done by Steel-Maitland or by the Chief Whip – a post held by Lord Balcarres, and later by Lord Edmund Talbot[1] – but the ultimate decision in controversial cases had to be made by Bonar Law. For example, should Sir Philip Sassoon be chosen as candidate for Hythe? The seat was "one of those demoralized seats", as Steel-Maitland put it.[1] It was recognized as a pocket borough of the Rothschilds, one of whose relations always sat for it; and the Rothschilds regularly subscribed £12,000 per annum to the Party funds in addition to large sums at Election time, without asking for anything in return. They would be most hurt if Sir Philip Sassoon were passed over. On the other hand there was Sir Arthur Colefax who had been unseated at the last Election and had certain claims which he never ceased to press. Bonar Law had to know all the facts and if necessary decide which to back. Another category of problems concerned the Press. There was, for example, the question of placating Mr. W. W. Astor, owner of the *Observer* and the *Pall Mall Gazette* and a heavy subscriber to Party funds. Early in June 1912 Bonar Law was to lunch with him at the Ritz, but was warned that Astor had been disappointed at not receiving a peerage from Balfour and therefore it would be unwise to hint at any expectation of future benefits for the Party.[m] In view of this and the fact that, as noted above in Steel-Maitland's memorandum, a year's peerages had been already promised in advance, the arrival at about this time of a long memorandum from Lord Selbourne, urging the Party to pledge itself never to give honours in return for financial benefits, must have seemed somewhat inopportune. It is not surprising that Bonar Law and Lansdowne gave it a cool reception and replied that consideration of such a matter should wait until the Party was in power again.[n]

It should not be thought from these remarks that Bonar Law himself was influenced by pressure from the Press in matters of policy. On the contrary he habitually disregarded such pressure and, by so doing, acquired the respect even of the formidable Lord Northcliffe,

---

[1] Later created Lord Fitzalan, when he became the last Viceroy of Ireland in December 1920. He was a most devoted friend and supporter of Bonar Law, and was a pall bearer at his funeral.

who treated him with a deference that he extended to few other political leaders. But Bonar Law was a man of common sense, and it was his duty to see that the Press was not antagonized unnecessarily, and that newspapers hitherto of Tory persuasion should not by sale or transfer go over to the other side. Although he never bowed to the power of the Press magnates, he saw that the Press was a powerful element in modern politics and that to ignore it was folly in the twentieth century – however different conditions might have been fifty years earlier.

In addition to all these cares of a leader there was the delicate question of the personal claims of various colleagues. This is well illustrated by Bonar Law's first Parliamentary dinner. A long letter of instruction from Lord Balcarres shows the problems of etiquette and precedency involved. After detailing who should be invited Balcarres goes on:°

"Your two private secretaries must come, must arrange menu, take all responsibility off your shoulders, guard the King's Speech and exclude inquisitive domestics.

"This document will reach you in the afternoon with a letter of portentous solemnity from Asquith.

"The Speech should be communicated to us in accents more colourless and impartial than I expect you to use for many weeks to come! You should attend the House of Lords next day to hear the King deliver the Speech in propia persona. . . .

"Now let me come to business

"The Leader generally sits at the side of the table and his *vis-à-vis* is technically his second in command, hitherto Akers-Douglas.

"These dispositions will be noticed by those concerned. It will be necessary to settle the point.

"Of course if you like, the problem can for the moment be evaded by putting me there, and one private secretary at each end of the table but even so somebody must sit at your Right Hand! . . .

"All this is a tiresome detail of dinner party precedence but it none the less connotes the future complexion of ministries. . . .

"I hope to see you on the 23rd but I should like a further conversation with you as to preliminary arrangements I wish to make. We can talk about amendments to the address later on.

"Yours ever,

Bal."

Then there was the problem of the Shadow Cabinet. It was strictly Lansdowne's function to summon that body, but he only chose the peers who were to compose it; the commoners were left to Bonar Law. The exact rules as to who should be summoned were anything but clear. A memorandum given to Bonar Law by Balcarres states somewhat unhelpfully:[p]

"CONSTITUTION. There is no particular qualification and no definite membership."

Balcarres then gives the following list of persons usually summoned:

"Lords Lansdowne, Halsbury, Ashbourne, Londonderry, Chilston, Selbourne, Derby, Middleton, Curzon, Salisbury, Mr. Balfour, Mr. A. Chamberlain, Mr. A. Lyttleton, Mr. W. Long, Mr. George Wyndham, Mr. F. E. Smith, Sir R. Finlay, Sir E. Carson, Mr. Chaplin."

In fact the Shadow Cabinet gave perpetual trouble. To omit persons gave offence, to invite them gave rise to intangible claims for office which might be difficult to evade when the Party came into power. The following letters from Lansdowne show the difficulties:[q]

February 23rd, 1912.

Lansdowne to Bonar Law
"I would propose to convene the following Peers, Curzon, Selborne, Middleton, and I am inclined to think in view of what was said in your room the other evening that Derby might be allowed to come also. If you bring Balcarres I think Devonshire ought to be summoned too. He is very sensible with regard to all these questions.

"Please tell me exactly what you think. If you concur I will summon the Peers and I presume you will summon the members of the House of Commons."

Bonar Law's reply can be deduced from Lansdowne's next letter:[r]

February 23rd, 1912.

Lansdowne to Bonar Law
"All right for Thursday at 11.30. But if the House of Commons 'shadows' are to number 11, I don't see how I can leave out Londonderry (who is very touchy and at this moment on the war path) – and I fear old Halsbury will be furious.

"Sorry to be tiresome but I have to be careful."

These difficulties frequently arose. As a result, Lansdowne and Bonar Law endeavoured to call the Shadow Cabinet as rarely as possible, and only when important controversial issues like the Food Tax were at stake, and some sort of authoritative party pronouncement had become imperative.

With this we have perhaps said enough of the managerial side of Bonar Law's leadership. It is well to remember, however, that during all the bitter political battles which lay ahead the matters discussed above formed, as it were, a continuous background, a sort of ground bass to the main theme. Bonar Law could delegate much to the

Whips and Party managers, but he alone was in the last resort responsible for the well-being of the Party in the House of Commons with all the complications that this involved. He could not – or at any rate did not – regard this side of politics with the lofty disdain shown by some of his predecessors; and there can be no doubt that a considerable part of his success came from the care and attention to detail which he devoted to the management of the Party.

CHAPTER VI

FOOD TAXES

1911 – 1913

Dissension in the Party over food taxes – The contending factions – Birmingham against Lancashire – The Referendum Pledge – Dispute as to its meaning – Views of Austen Chamberlain and Lord Derby – Shadow Cabinet decides against Referendum – Protest of Lord Salisbury – Bonar Law's reply – Visit of Sir Robert Borden – His attitude confirms Bonar Law's view – Lansdowne's announcement at the Albert Hall – Protest of Lord Hugh Cecil – Dissension in the North – Bonar Law's speech at Ashton-under-Lyne – Intrigues of Lord Derby – F. E. Smith's warning – Bonar Law and Lansdowne decide to resign – Memorial signed by Unionist members urging them to stay – Bonar Law's decision to accept the memorial – Explanation of his conduct – His letters to Chaplin and Chamberlain – The case for his decision

I

As soon as Bonar Law became leader he was faced with an important problem of Party policy. What was the most satisfactory line to take over the vexed question of Tariff Reform, and, in particular, the even more difficult question of food taxes? The Party was divided upon this issue, and had been divided ever since Joseph Chamberlain proclaimed the new gospel in 1903. Indeed Balfour's dialectical skill had seldom been more severely tested than in the verbal acrobatics with which he endeavoured to reconcile the divisions in the Party. His successor was now to be confronted with the same problem, and since the tariff dispute very nearly brought Bonar Law's career as leader to an end, scarcely more than a year after it had begun, it is necessary to give some explanation of its nature.

On the question of Tariff Reform there were in the Conservative Party two sharply contending factions. One, headed by the influential families of Cecil and Stanley, at heart regarded the whole of Joseph Chamberlain's crusade as a grave error and responsible in large measure for the successive electoral defeats of the Unionist Party. Especially disastrous, they claimed, was Chamberlain's proposal to impose taxes, however light, upon imported foodstuffs. The accusation that the Conservatives intended to tax the people's bread had been fatal in the past and would be fatal in the future. If the Tariff Reformers continued obstinately to keep food taxes on the party programme, the far more vital struggle over Home Rule might be lost for ever. The Unionist Free Fooders, as they were called derived their strength from Scotland and the north of England. They were especially strong in Lancashire, traditionally a Free Trade area. The spokesman of Lancashire was the Earl of Derby, who was regularly received there with much of the deference usually reserved for Royalty. His great influence in the Conservative counsels was thrown heavily against Tariff Reform, especially against food taxes.

The Tariff Reformers, on the other hand, maintained that the abandonment of food taxes would be a fatal repudiation of all past policy. Food taxes, they claimed, were essential because only thus could a preference be given in the British market to colonial products – in particular to Canadian wheat; and only a policy of Imperial Preference could preserve the Empire from disintegration. To prove that this latter danger was no mere chimera, the Tariff Reformers pointed to the Reciprocity Agreement between Canada and the U.S.A., concluded early in 1911 by Sir Wilfrid Laurier's Liberal Government. This was an arrangement which provided for mutual reduction of tariffs between the two countries and seemed a first step on the part of Canada away from the Empire and into the orbit of the U.S.A. It is true that this particular argument lost some of its force when in the same year the Canadian Election swept Laurier's Government out of office and replaced it by a Conservative Administration under Sir Robert Borden who promptly repudiated the Reciprocity Agreement: all this without the slightest move in England towards Imperial Preference. Nevertheless the Tariff Reformers could plausibly argue that Canadian patriotism deserved reward, that the Reciprocity Agreement, though now repudiated, was symptomatic of trouble to come unless Britain made a serious attempt to unite the Empire by the creation of an imperial *zollverein* or customs union. Moreover, the Tariff Reformers refused to believe that their policy had caused the recent Unionist defeats. On the contrary, they argued, the real trouble was that Tariff Reform had not been pressed ardently enough. If it had been, the Conservatives would by now have been in power. By the nature of things such arguments can be neither proved nor disproved, but that fact in no way diminished the fervour of the disputants; the debate rolled merrily on, and neither side showed any sign of yielding.

The home of Tariff Reform was Birmingham, and the struggle

between the Protectionist and Free Trade Conservatives was, to some extent, a struggle between the Birmingham and Manchester elements of the Party. Joseph Chamberlain, the high priest of the Tariff Movement could no longer speak in public, but he could still think and make his views known in writing; a series of encyclicals poured forth from his sick bed at Highbury, while his faithful son continued the work in public meetings up and down the country.

The whole problem was greatly complicated by the so called Referendum Pledge. This was a bomb-shell dropped by Balfour during the General Election of autumn 1910. Speaking at the Albert Hall on November 29th Balfour offered, if the Unionists came into power, to submit food taxes to a referendum. "I have not the least objection", he declared, "to submitting the principle of Tariff Reform to a Referendum." "If Tariff Reform is anything it is a great and Imperial policy. . . . I am perfectly ready to submit it to my countrymen." The pledge was a last minute manoeuvre to persuade the Free Trade element in the floating vote that it was safe to support the Conservatives, since no tariffs would be imposed until the nation had been consulted again specifically on that issue.

The exact meaning of Balfour's pledge was not quite clear. He made the offer in carefully guarded words as a *quid pro quo,* if the Liberals would promise a referendum on Home Rule. The Liberals naturally did not, and it could be argued that, accordingly, Balfour's pledge lapsed. A great deal of hair splitting disputation took place upon this point, and all through 1912 Bonar Law's mail is full of ingenious suggestions – worthy of medieval schoolmen interpreting a text – as to the various ways in which Balfour's pledge could be understood. It is difficult to see the need for such subtleties. After all the Unionists were perfectly free to repudiate the pledge if they wanted to do so – whatever its meaning. The argument was really one of expediency, and here the two sections in the party differed profoundly. The Tariff Reformers were naturally determined to repudiate the offer of a referendum, because they saw in it a serious obstacle to their plans. Austen Chamberlain had personally dissociated himself from it at the Tariff Reform Dinner of November 8th while the question of leadership was still in the balance. The Free Fooders were equally determined to retain the pledge, since, without it, they believed that there was no hope of winning an Election. The matter was still undecided when Balfour resigned.

The advocates of the two sides lost no time in putting their case before the new leader. Austen Chamberlain was first in the field on

November 11th,[a] followed two days later by Lord Derby, the spokesman of Free Trade Lancashire.[b]

Bonar Law's own sympathies naturally lay with Austen Chamberlain, and, although he had not at first been as hostile to the referendum pledge as Chamberlain had been, his views had become more definite since the 1910 Election. Nevertheless, as leader of the Party he had to do his best to avoid a split. After all there was no immediate reason to make any declaration on the matter, for the Unionists were not in office and the likelihood of a General Election was remote. Bonar Law therefore took no immediate step and avoided making any public utterances on the subject. No copy appears to exist of his reply to Chamberlain. To Derby he wrote on November 14th:[c]

"Many thanks for your letter and for the very kind way in which you welcome me to my new position.

"If you are in town do come and see me. I think there is nothing for us but to go straight forward with the programme as it is, but I should like to speak to you about it. Until we have met I am sure you will say nothing to commit you in any way. I have to speak in Bootle on the 7th December, and, if it is convenient to you, I shall be delighted to stay at Knowsley but I hope to see you before then. . . ."

2

At the risk of going somewhat ahead of the main story we must now trace the tale of Tariff Reform down to the crisis of January 1913. Bonar Law received numerous letters from the supporters and opponents of food taxes, but it was not until April 1912 that he took a definite decision. Then at a meeting of the Shadow Cabinet it was agreed that the food tax must remain a part of Tariff Reform and further that the Referendum Pledge must be dropped. This decision instantly evoked a protest from Lord Salisbury, to whom the news was imparted by his brother-in-law, Lord Selborne, and by Lord Curzon, both of whom strongly disapproved. Salisbury's letter is too long to quote in full but an extract shows the arguments used:[d]

20 Arlington Street,
May 1st, 1912.

". . . I am frankly somewhat of an opportunist in the matter. I incline indeed to think the food tax to be bad policy, but in a world of compromise I should be content if it were likely to be a successful policy. Hitherto it has been very unsuccessful. If it may be said to have finally made possible the destruction of the constitution, the prostitution of the Prerogative, the Repeal of the Union and the Disendowment of the Welsh Church, it will probably rank as the most costly policy in history. But there seems a chance that some of these disasters may be spared to us if public opinion were to pronounce an emphatic desire to change the Govt. Overwhelming loss of public favour might break up the Govt. or in the last resort strengthen the hand of the King. But it must be overwhelming. If we are to be saved it must be manifest that the country prefers the Unionists to the Radicals . . . and as long as the food tax is our programme any such manifest public opinion is in the highest degree unlikely. . . ."

To this letter Bonar Law replied on May 3rd at what was for him unusual length: parts of the letter are worth quoting:[e]

". . . I have had talks with your brothers about this – especially Lord Robert with whom on, I think, almost every other subject I have found myself in complete agreement, though our previous experience has been so different. On this subject, however, we never get any further forward because, I am afraid, the differences in view between us are fundamental.

"I quite realize that food taxes are a handicap; but on the other hand they are part of our policy and to change it now would in my opinion increase our difficulty of winning the election rather than diminish it."

". . . I really believe, and it is here I think that I differ so much from you that there is a great deal in Tariff Reform; and I believe also that there is a great deal even in the food part of it. I do not now allude to preference though of course that comes first. . . . I believe also that even a small duty on food stuffs would be a great advantage to small holders, and also to Ireland. In fact my real belief is that in the troubles ahead of us connected with labour we are moving very fast in the direction of revolution; and though I am sure you will consider my hope a baseless one I still entertain it – that it is by Tariff Reform that we might, so to speak, get the train for a time at least shifted on to other lines. . . .

"Apart altogether from merits I am as certain as I can be of anything that if a proposal were made to drop the food duties or to submit them to a referendum there would be a large split in the party which would I think be a greater handicap than anything else could be. So far also as I am personally concerned, the way in which I have been identified with Tariff Reform and also my sincere belief in the advantages of it would make it quite impossible for me not to be on the side of those who refuse to allow the programme to be altered . . . if I believed that the Party as a whole would be more successful by changing this policy I should be quite willing to stand aside, and even to help as much as I could, though I could not possibly, if such a split did take place, continue as leader and oppose those with whom I have all through been working. . . ."

This letter states as well as any of Bonar Law's private papers his attitude to Tariff Reform at this time. He believed in it, first because of Imperial Preference; secondly, because he thought it would benefit both the agricultural and industrial labourers and so help to modify the revolutionary tendencies of the day; thirdly, because its abandonment would – in his opinion – split the Conservative Party from top to bottom.

However, whether as a result of Salisbury's suggestion about the Canadian Government, or for other reasons Bonar Law decided to avoid a public declaration of the Shadow Cabinet's decision until he had ascertained the views of the Canadian Prime Minister. This was convenient because Borden and Hazon were coming on a visit to England in June. Bonar Law was most anxious to see that the Canadian Ministers were entertained by the Opposition as well as the Government, and despite his hatred of social engagements, he even asked Lady Londonderry to arrange a party for them and their wives. "I have sent a cable", he wrote,[f] "asking them to dine with me; but human nature is the same in Canada as it is in England and, especially if there are ladies, they will appreciate enormously an invitation to Londonderry House."

Bonar Law did not know Borden very well, but they had a close mutual ally in Sir Max Aitken. Indeed on Bonar Law's election Borden had suggested that Aitken should become Bonar Law's Parliamentary Secretary, adding that such an appointment would be well received in Canada. Bonar Law had replied, Dec. 9th, 1911:[g]

"As regards Sir Max Aitken he is the most intimate personal friend I have in the House of Commons (in spite of the comparatively short time I have known him) and not only for that reason but because of his remarkable force and ability I should have preferred him as my Secretary to anyone else. Since I got my appointment he has been assisting me in the most effective way, but he does not himself wish to be announced publicly as one of my secretaries. . . . Later on if he should desire to have his connexion with me made public I shall be delighted to announce it."

Borden was invited by Aitken to Cherkley, and Bonar Law was able to discuss matters with him there. The Canadian Prime Minister made it clear that food taxes were regarded in Canada as essential for a proper policy of Imperial Preference. He promised to take an early opportunity both of saying so publicly and indicating that, if Imperial Preference were abandoned, Canada might be obliged to make Preferential arrangements with other countries outside the Empire. He also agreed to try to increase Canadian Preference for English manufactured goods. His views were decisive for Bonar Law. He now resolved to go straight ahead and disregard the complaints of the Free Fooders.

Bonar Law had always regarded the imperial argument as the most important part of the case for Tariff Reform. Partly perhaps on account of his own Canadian origin, he believed strongly in the unity of the Empire, and the necessity of Preference as a means of preserving that unity. It has sometimes been suggested that Bonar Law's belief in Tariffs was primarily the business man's belief in protecting his manufactures against foreign competition. Naturally in debate Bonar Law used many different arguments when putting the case for Tariff Reform – and like any good debater, he chose his arguments to suit his audience; but his private correspondence at this time leaves no doubt of the paramount importance that he attached to the Empire, especially Canada. In a letter to Lord Graham, dated August 6th, he said that before committing himself on food taxes he had waited to find out whether the Canadian Ministers really attached value to them. His letter continues:[h]

". . . and they not only do attach value to them but say that if we went back on our policy now it would be regarded as a serious blow to the whole cause of imperial consolidation. Under these circumstances I hope you will agree with me in thinking that, whatever the handicap, we have no alternative but to go on and hope to win in spite of it."

Accordingly Lansdowne and Bonar Law decided to make public the repudiation of the referendum decided upon at the Shadow Cabinet in April. The occasion of this declaration was to be a meeting of the Conservative National Union held at the Albert Hall on November 14th, 1912. Meanwhile, the Tariff Reformers redoubled their efforts. Aitken departed to Canada in order to keep Borden up to the mark. At home the Tariff Reform League organized an immense banquet at which subscribers to the League's funds would meet Bonar Law. Until the last minute it seems to have been uncertain whether Lansdowne or Bonar Law should make the declaration at the Albert Hall, but in the end Lansdowne insisted upon doing so on the ground that he had been a party to the original pledge and could therefore speak with greater weight.

Lansdowne's speech at the Albert Hall immediately produced a furore among the Free Fooders. Already, on November 7th, Bonar Law had received six pages of "final protest" from Lord Hugh Cecil ending thus:[i]

"We are like the French legitimists who in 1873 sacrificed the throne of France rather than accept the tricolour in place of the Bourbon white flag. Taxes on food are exalted into a kind of religion – even to postpone them is apostasy. If there were no Union or Church or Ulster at stake this would deserve to be called insanity. But when the highest national interests are involved, when those whom we are bound to succour and save by every consideration of honour and chivalry may have to pay the price of our folly, what word fitly describes our action?"

It soon appeared that many other Unionists shared Lord Hugh

Cecil's sentiments – if not his eloquence. A stream of letters protesting at the abandonment of the referendum pledge poured in upon Bonar Law. They came chiefly, though not exclusively, from those who depended upon votes in the North. Bonar Law was told that there was no hope of progress in Yorkshire, that Scotland was furious and that at least six seats would be lost in Lancashire; an unfortunate Conservative defeat at this time in a by-election at Bolton gave plausibility to the last contention.

These strictures did not deflect Bonar Law from his chosen course, but he realized that the unrest in the party was considerable and decided to clarify the policy laid down by Lansdowne at the Albert Hall. For this purpose he resolved to carry the war into the enemy camp, and on December 16th he delivered an important speech on tariffs in Aitken's constituency, Ashton-under-Lyne. In this speech Bonar Law expounded and emphasized a part of Lansdowne's speech which had not received much prominence. Lansdowne had said that no food taxes would be imposed unless the Colonies wanted them. Bonar Law dwelt upon this point.

". . . first I want to tell you exactly what it is that we propose in regard to food duties. It was stated very briefly but clearly by Lord Lansdowne in the Albert Hall the other day. . . . If our countrymen entrust us with power we do not intend to impose food taxes. What we intend to do is to call a conference of the Colonies to consider the whole question of preferential trade and the question of whether or not food duties will be imposed will not arise till those negotiations are completed. We are told the Colonies have made no offer, that they do not wish such an arrangement. Well, if that is true, we should find out. If it is true, no food duties will be imposed under any circumstances [cheers]."

He then dealt with the Referendum Pledge and reaffirmed the Conservative resolve to abandon it – on the grounds that to negotiate food duties at a Colonial Conference and then submit them to a referendum would be unfair to the Colonies. "That is the reason and the sole reason why we object to submitting these proposals to a referendum."

The speech was interpreted by some as a step away from the full rigour of the Albert Hall programme. Austen Chamberlain, in particular, appears to have received it with uneasiness. But there seems no reason to suppose that Bonar Law had any such purpose. He knew that food taxes were unpopular. He therefore emphasized the possibility that they might not be needed, but he in no way receded from the view that if the Colonies wanted them, they should have them – and he reaffirmed that there would be no question of a referendum.

Aitken was anxious to ensure that the speech would be received with enthusiasm. In this way it might be possible to overawe the Free Food rebels and show that, even in Lancashire, Tariff Reform had strong support. He therefore took certain precautions in the way of organizing the meeting. His efforts were most successful. Bonar Law received a splendid welcome, his speech was greeted with tumultuous cheers, and, somewhat to his surprise, he found himself escorted to the station after the meeting by a phalanx of a hundred torch bearers.

But, despite this demonstration, all was not well. The speech, far from intimidating the Free Fooders, only aroused their indignation. The rebels now had the powerful influence of Lord Northcliffe on their side. He was conducting a vigorous campaign through his two newspapers, the *Daily Mail* and *The Times*, against what he called "stomach taxes". Bonar Law's Ashton speech had a chilling reception in *The Times*. Emboldened by this support, and encouraged – or at least not discouraged – by Lord Derby, the Lancashire Unionists broke into open revolt. A meeting of the Lancashire Conservative Association was due on Saturday, December 21st, five days after the Ashton speech. It soon became known that resolutions hostile to Bonar Law's policy were to be set down and would probably be carried. In the circumstances the Lancashire leaders resolved to try to secure an adjournment in order to give time for reflection and consideration. For if the motion against food taxes was carried, by such an important body as the Lancashire Association, there was every likelihood of a major cleavage throughout the whole Party.

Meanwhile, Bonar Law, ignorant of these ominous developments, had returned to the South and went to spend a few days at Cherkley. His repose was speedily broken by a startling telegram from F. E. Smith. It ran as follows:[j]

"Lancashire serious. Chamberlain, you, I, Carson and if possible Long should meet immediately. Salvidge[1] joining D."

This somewhat cryptic message was followed by a letter:[k]

Blenheim Palace,
December 18th.

"Dear Bonar,

"You must think of politics. Things in Lancashire are on the verge of a smash. I think Salvidge will support Derby. You, I, Austen, Carson and if he is well enough, Long ought *to meet at once*. Unless effective steps are taken a resolution will be passed at the Lancashire meeting that the food

---

[1] Mr. (later Sir) Archibald Salvidge, a person of great influence in Lancashire Unionist politics. D. is of course Derby.

E

taxes recommended (if such be the case) at the Conference[1] should not become law without an election. Such a resolution – though personally I have under existing circumstances much sympathy with it – is wholly inconsistent, it seems to me, with your position; it can be dealt with; possibly it can even be controlled but you must move. I am going to the adjourned meeting. Max Aitken should immediately intrigue with all the Lancashire members in favour of the only amendment which I think could be carried to the hostile resolution, viz. – that a deputation should wait upon you – I mean of course a private one. . . . You know I am not an alarmist and have good nerves but unless the position is promptly dealt with we are going straight on the rocks.

"Yours, F. E."

Matters now moved rapidly to a crisis. The Lancashire meeting was stormy, but Lord Derby succeeded in adjourning it for three weeks, and preventing any definite resolution from being passed. It did not suit the Lancashire leaders to provoke an open breach with Bonar Law, if they could secure their objective by less drastic methods. Derby meanwhile circulated a tendentious questionnaire to the Lancashire Unionists. The questions were so framed as to make it almost certain that an overwhelming vote would be forthcoming against food taxes and in favour of the referendum.

The news of all this soon reached Bonar Law. He had an interview with Lansdowne and the two men found themselves in complete agreement as to their course of action. They would resign rather than go back upon their declared policy. Bonar Law was understandably angry with Derby.

Writing to Lansdowne on Christmas Day, 1912, he said:[1]

"At first my speech at Ashton did some good but the effect of it had been destroyed by two things; first by Northcliffe with his Papers and second, I am sorry to say, by Derby through the position he holds in Lancashire and the use he is making of it. They had their meeting on Saturday and Derby has written to me implying that he was doing everything he could in the interest of unity but I receive other accounts which show that he himself . . . is, I believe, the chief cause of the discontent there."

But it became clear as time went on that feeling in the Party was against Bonar Law. On December 31st writing to Henry Chaplin Bonar Law himself admitted it.

"Politicians", he wrote,[m] "are not the most stable of people but the change which has taken place is remarkable even for politicians. The strongest Tariff Reformers are all coming to me saying it is impossible to fight with food taxes. The position therefore is a very difficult one, and I really have

---

[1] The Colonial Conference which Bonar Law promised he would summon before imposing any duties in foodstuffs.

no idea how it will end; but so far as the present is concerned I am not going to depart in the least from the policy we have laid down, though (between ourselves) I am convinced that it must in the end be modified. I doubt whether this modification will be possible under my leadership, but that is a bridge which I need not cross till we come to it."

Bonar Law was to reach that bridge sooner than he expected. Feeling now was so strong against food taxes and the prospect of an adverse resolution in Lancashire so certain that Bonar Law and Lansdowne decided at the beginning of January 1913 that they must call a party meeting, and, since they could not conscientiously repudiate their past speeches, resign. They were fortified in this resolution by the extreme Tariff Reformers.

"I do not understand", wrote Austen Chamberlain on December 24th,[n] "how after your recent speeches anyone can think it compatible with your honour to withdraw from the position you have taken up and I am certain it would be fatal to both yourself and to the Party if you were to do so." Similar advice to fight it out, and resign rather than give in came from Mr. L. S. Amery and Henry Chaplin, both enthusiastic Tariff Reformers.

But as soon as the decision of the two leaders became known consternation spread through the Party. The last thing that the opponents of food taxes wanted was the resignation of Lansdowne and Bonar Law. The former could no doubt be replaced without great difficulty – although his inevitable successor, Curzon, was in many quarters not viewed with enthusiasm – but the replacement of Bonar Law at the beginning of 1913 would have created insoluble problems. Austen Chamberlain would have been out of the question. Long had become no more fit to lead the Party than he had been a year before, and his health was not good. Carson and F. E. Smith did not command the necessary trust and respect. Bonar Law's resignation, especially upon such an issue, would have left the Party even more disastrously divided than it had been when Balfour retired.

Therefore, at the instance of Carson, on January 7th, 1913, a memorial was drawn up for the signature of Unionist Members (the front bench being excluded) requesting Bonar Law and Lansdowne to remain in office, and accept a modification of the Party's declared policy over tariffs. After a good deal of hesitation the two leaders decided that, rather than break up the Party, they would do so, although with very considerable reluctance. Bonar Law's own account is given in a letter to Henry Chaplin who protested vigorously at the decision.[o]

January 10th.

". . . I can understand exactly how you feel about this whole business but, from what I have already written to you, you know what my feeling was. Lansdowne had been away and when he came back on Monday I went to see him and told him that in my opinion he and I had only two courses open to us – one was to go straight on with our policy and the other to resign.

"We both felt that to go on with the policy was impossible and as the simplest way of showing you exactly what our view was I enclose copy of a Memorandum which I gave to Lansdowne. He came down to the House of Commons on Tuesday with the intention that we should at once tell Balcarres to call a Party meeting, when we would resign. Carson happened to be there, and I got him in to talk with us as well as Balcarres. He felt that it was very difficult for us to take any other course but he pointed out to me what the effect of it would be. I had of course fully considered the difficulty of getting a successor but I did not attach as much importance [to it] as he did. There was of course another consideration which did and does seem to me vital. If I had to resign on this cause, then the section of the Party which thought our policy right would certainly not have acquiesced in the change, and there would have been an absolute impossibility of having a united Party. I do think therefore (and there is no question of egotism in this) that the only chance of a united Party in the meantime was that I should continue. When Carson and Balcarres urged us therefore to delay we agreed to do so; and as a result they suggested a memorial to me. . . . The substance of the memorial is loyalty to the leaders; a determination to continue Imperial Preference on the understanding that any preference which is possible without food duties should be carried immediately we obtain power; that any further preference including food duties could be arranged by us but would be subject to approval at another election.

"Of course I do not like this any more than you do, but after all one has to take into account the feeling of the Party; and the alternative before us, I think, was to give up something which we greatly valued on the one hand, or cause such a complete split in the Party as would endanger everything we value – including Tariff Reform and preference. . . ."

3

Thus ended the first important crisis in Bonar Law's leadership. Lord Derby and the Cecils had won the day; the policy of Imperial Preference received a set back from which it took many years to recover – some would even say that it never did recover from this blow. The disappointment of the keen Tariff Reformers was very great, especially in the case of Chamberlain. Before Bonar Law made public his decision, he had written to Austen Chamberlain on January 8th explaining his reasons. He ended:[p]

". . . I am sure you believe me that if you or your father wished it, I would gladly resign my position, but I have not the courage to go or and be responsible for a policy which, with the feeling of the party such as it is, I am sure is bound to fail. If I had been your father I might have carried it through successfully, but *I* cannot.

"In this crisis, as in the earlier one, you have acted as what I know you are – a great gentleman."

Austen Chamberlain's reply was friendly but unyielding on the main issue:[q]

"As you know I wish that you could have felt differently, and I still believe that the advice which I tendered you was the best for your reputation and for the Party, and that, if it had commended itself to you and been acted on at once, the position of the Party would have been stronger in three months than it is now and your own reputation immeasurably enhanced. But I recognize that if you couldn't believe what I believed, you could not advocate it with success. . . ."

The letter ends:

"I am deeply sensible of the difficulties of your position; I will try not to make them greater and if you do not altogether like what I have to say when I come to speak you must make allowance for a man whose dearest political hopes and personal affections have received from fate a cruel blow."

Only six Unionist M.P.s refused to sign the memorial to the two leaders. One of them was Mr. Amery and another Sir Max Aitken.

Did Bonar Law act rightly in thus reversing his own declared policy for the sake of Party unity? To answer this is to answer a problem in political ethics which has never yet been satisfactorily solved. But in acting as he did there is no doubt that Bonar Law was following the established tradition of previous Conservative leaders. Ever since the day when Peel's decision to repeal the Corn Laws had broken the Party and driven it into the wilderness for twenty years, successive Conservative leaders had felt it their duty, at all costs and at almost any sacrifice, to avoid repeating Peel's action. Disraeli, Salisbury, Balfour, had all regarded party unity as of paramount importance – and Bonar Law both on this occasion and, at several other critical moments in his life, took the same view. It is of course easy to attack such conduct on high moral grounds, but those who declare that principles should always remain uncompromised and that no one should ever change his course on account of pressure from others are living in a cloud cuckoo land far from the realities of politics. Politics is the art of the possible, and the man who refuses ever to change his course will soon run on the rocks – and deserve to. Before we criticize Bonar Law for abandoning his cherished beliefs in order to

keep the Party united, it is worth remembering that his policy both
on this occasion and later was among the chief reasons why – for
good or evil – the Conservative Party survives today; and that the
very different fate of the Liberals can, at least in part, be explained
by the failure of their leaders to pay sufficient regard to the importance of Party unity.

Finally, it must be remembered that almost all Conservatives re-
garded the question of Irish Home Rule as the vital issue of the day
and were endeavouring to force a General Election on that issue.
Bonar Law shared this view. Writing on December 9th, 1912, to
St. Loe Strachey, the editor of the *Spectator* and a Unionist Free
Trader, Bonar Law said:[r]

> ". . . So far as I am concerned, I entirely agree with your main proposi-
> tion. I think the Union is more important than Tariff Reform but the
> Union can only be preserved by a united party and, now at least, there is
> no chance of a united party in any other way than by adherence to the
> policy laid down at the Albert Hall."

It was in a sense consistent on the part of Bonar Law – or at all
events not palpably inconsistent – to change his policy when, as
became evident by the end of December, the Albert Hall programme, far from uniting the Party, was certain to split it; and it was
clear that his own resignation would make the conflict even more
disastrous. The real battle over Home Rule was still to come, and,
given Bonar Law's strong feelings on Ireland and Ulster, any course
which weakened the Party for that struggle seemed to be a betrayal
of a far more vital cause than Tariff Reform.

CHAPTER VII

THE IRISH PROBLEM — THE FIRST
ROUND

1912 – 1913

Past history of the Irish question – Crises of 1886 and 1892 – Position of Irish Nationalists after 1910 – Their bargaining power – Violence and bitterness of Irish politics – Reasons for opposition to Home Rule – Problem of Ulster ignored by Liberals – Their reasons – Lloyd George and Churchill differ from their colleagues – Bonar Law's feelings over Ulster – His early pronouncements on Home Rule – His reply to Asquith – Liberal time table for Home Rule Bill – Activities in Ulster – Role of Carson – Bonar Law's speech at Belfast on April 9th, 1912 – His speech at Blenheim on July 29th – His extremism – Reasons for his attitude – Question of a General Election – Scene in the House of Commons in November 1912 – Bonar Law's interview with the King – Asquith's policy – Bonar Law's relations with Carson – Character of Carson

I

THE story of the food tax controversy has taken us ahead of our main narrative. It is necessary now to return to the beginning of 1912. The Parliamentary session opened on February 14th. It was Bonar Law's first full session as leader of the Conservative Party, and it was an arduous beginning for his leadership. Except for a summer recess of two months Parliament sat continuously until March 1913. Like all subsequent sessions till the outbreak of war, it was dominated by the Irish question. That problem was to be of the greatest importance in Bonar Law's life, and his career cannot be fully understood, indeed his place in history cannot be finally assessed, without some knowledge of this, the most complicated and baffling issue in British politics for the past hundred years.

The Irish problem had vexed English political life ever since the Act of Union in 1800, but it was not until the General Election of November 1885 that the Home Rule question became a major political issue at Westminster. As a result of the genius of Parnell and the extension of the franchise, the Parliament which met at the beginning of 1886 contained eighty-six Irish Nationalist members, who regarded the English parties with impartial distaste, and whose sole objective was to use the bargaining power of their votes in order to

119

secure self-government for Ireland. Gladstone, already convinced of the justice of their claim and aware of the harm that such a formidable block of voters might do to English Parliamentary life, decided to commit the Liberal Party to the Home Rule cause. In April 1886 he introduced the first Home Rule Bill. His decision broke the Liberal Party in two. A combination of the Conservatives and the Liberal Unionists, as the dissident Liberals were thenceforth called, was strong enough to defeat the second reading of the Home Rule Bill in the House of Commons. Gladstone promptly dissolved Parliament, but his appeal to the nation failed. The Home Rulers were defeated and there followed six years of Conservative rule.

At the Election of 1892 the Home Rule cause fared better. Once again the Irish Nationalists held the balance of power in the House of Commons. Once again Gladstone introduced a Home Rule Bill. This time, despite his great age – he was over eighty-two – and his physical infirmities, he piloted the measure through every stage in the House of Commons, only to see it go down to overwhelming defeat in the House of Lords. The General Election in 1895 vindicated the action of the Lords. The Liberals were for a second time heavily defeated on the Home Rule question, and ten years of Unionist rule ensued.

Then in 1906 came the celebrated landslide Election. The Liberals found themselves in power with an immense majority. But, to the chagrin of the Irish Nationalists, the new Government seemed in no hurry to attack the Irish question. This was not surprising: Gladstone, the great Liberal crusader for Home Rule, was dead; twice already Liberal Governments had been wrecked by their Irish policy; there was the formidable barrier of the House of Lords; and – most decisive consideration of all – the Liberal majority was so large that they could afford to disregard the Irish Nationalist vote. For four years the Irish question remained in cold storage. But as a result of the Elections of 1910 the Irish Nationalists once again controlled the Parliamentary balance. Their great chance had at last come. Redmond, their leader, was determined that it should not be missed. In 1911 the Parliament Act was carried depriving the Upper House of its veto, and the way was clear for yet another Home Rule Bill. During the autumn and winter of 1911 the Cabinet engaged in protracted discussions of the new measure. The King's Speech in February 1912 announced the Government's intentions, and in April 1912 Asquith introduced the third Home Rule Bill.

No one can begin to comprehend the political history of England in the years preceding the First World War, unless he realizes the dominating character of the Irish struggle for Home Rule. Today this is not easy, for, except within Ireland's own shores, the great struggle has vanished into the realm of "old unhappy far-off things and battles long ago". In England the quarrels of Home Rulers and Unionists, Nationalists and Orangemen, have become as remote as those curious disputes with which Gibbon so agreeably entertains us in his chapters on the early Christian Church. But until 1914 – indeed until 1922 – the Irish question obsessed English Parliamentary life to an extent seldom equalled – and never surpassed – by any political issue either before or since. At times it seemed as if all other problems had faded into the background, as if the Home Rule question had become the sole theme of English politics, overthrowing governments, destroying parties, and distorting the career of every political leader who attempted to touch it.

Irish politics imported a new element of passion, and hatred, indeed of melodrama, into English public life. By some singular fatality whenever the affairs of that unhappy country impinged upon those of England, their impact was invariably signalled by events of so fantastic a nature as to seem incredible, had they been found between the covers of a sensational novel, let alone when written upon the sedate pages of English political history. The Phoenix Park Murders; the Piggott Forgeries; the Parnell Divorce; the Easter Rebellion; the assassination of Sir Henry Wilson: the whole story of Ireland in those years is an extraordinary compound of crime, intrigue, romance and murder.

These furious passions disturbed even the stuffy and somnolent atmosphere of Westminster, and the violent colours of Irish politics were reflected, even if in somewhat less lurid shades, upon the English scene. We find Privy Councillors recommending rebellion, former Law Officers of the Crown urging armed resistance to an Act of Parliament, prominent soldiers disregarding their oaths of secrecy, and Bonar Law himself, leader of the Tory Party, seriously considering whether to encourage a mutiny in the Army. Between 1910 and 1914 the British Constitution and the conventions upon which it depends were strained to the uttermost limit; and, paradoxically, it was the outbreak of the First World War which, although it imperilled Britain's very existence, probably alone saved Britain's institutions from disaster.

At first sight it may seem difficult to understand why the Irish problem should have aroused such bitter emotions in England.

Viewed in the longer perspective of history the Irish desire for self-government was merely another example of those nationalist aspirations which, in one form or another, constituted the principal political force in Europe during the nineteenth and early twentieth centuries. To such movements abroad Englishmen were traditionally sympathetic. Even within the Empire claims for self-government were not regarded by the Mother Country as unreasonable; Canada, Australia, New Zealand, even South Africa, had all by 1912 secured a substantial degree of control over their own affairs, certainly far greater than the Irish Nationalist Party had dreamed of demanding for Ireland. Why then did the claims of the Irish for a measure of Home Rule convulse English political life for nearly forty years?

The answer is twofold. First there was the peculiar class structure of Ireland: an English "Ascendancy" class, numerically small, Protestant, and aristocratic, owning great estates; and a Catholic "native" peasantry, forming the bulk of the population, sunk in poverty, working tiny holdings under an iniquitous system of land tenure. Racial, religious, and economic motives all led to a class struggle of the most bitter nature.

This struggle, moreover, could not be treated with the air of Olympian detachment which English Governments were wont to adopt towards similar Colonial problems in Asia or Africa. The "Ascendancy" had the closest links with the landed aristocracy which governed England until the 1880s and which still possessed immense influence – at any rate in the Conservative Party – for another forty years. The Anglo-Irish landlords were convinced that Home Rule for Ireland would be followed sooner or later by their own expropriation, and had little confidence that they would receive adequate – or indeed any – compensation from a Dublin parliament.

The privileged position of the Irish landlords was not however the only reason for the bitterness caused by Ireland in English politics. The second – and for the purposes of this story – by far the most important reason was the peculiar position of Ulster. In the north-eastern corner of Ireland lay a region whose social and religious structure differed profoundly from that of the rest of Ireland. Ever since the early seventeenth century the population in four of the nine Ulster counties had been overwhelmingly Scottish and Protestant. It was not merely a question of a Protestant aristocracy; the peasantry and the artisan class were as strongly Protestant as the landlords, and regarded the Catholics of the South with feelings of fear, detestation, and contempt. In two more counties, Fermanagh and Tyrone, the

Catholics and Protestants were more or less equally divided. A slight majority was Catholic, but all the more prosperous and influential elements in the community were Protestant. In the remaining three counties of the historic province of Ulster the situation resembled that of Southern Ireland: the Catholics formed an overwhelming majority; the Protestants were a small but wealthy minority.

It would therefore seem at first sight obvious that the Protestants of Ulster could not be treated in the same way as the Catholics of the South. If the South had a legitimate claim for self-determination, could not a similar case be made for the Ulster Protestants? If the population of the South had a right to be regarded as a nation separate from the rest of Britain, the population of the so-called "plantation" counties could surely claim a right to be regarded as a nation separate from the rest of Ireland. Nevertheless neither of Gladstone's Home Rule Bills took any account of the special status of Ulster. Had either of these measures become law the whole of Ireland would – with certain safeguards – have been subjected to a Parliament at Dublin. And precisely the same was true of the Home Rule Bill introduced by Asquith in 1912.

Why did the Liberals apparently ignore the position of Ulster? Certainly their opponents gave them no cause for doing so. The Unionists at once perceived that the English electorate, although it might survey with indifference – perhaps with relish – the ruin of the Anglo-Irish aristocracy, would profoundly dislike any attempt to put a homogeneous Protestant population under Catholic rule. England was in those days a deeply Protestant country, and no slogan had been more damaging to the Home Rulers than the cry, "Home Rule is Rome Rule!" Even before Gladstone introduced his first Home Rule Bill in 1886, Lord Randolph Churchill, that most astute of Conservative electioneers, had perceived the electoral value of Ulster. "I decided some time ago", he wrote in February 1886,[a] "that if the G.O.M. went for Home Rule the Orange Card would be the one to play. Please God it may turn out the ace of trumps and not the two." At the same time he coined the famous phrase, "Ulster will fight, and Ulster will be right." From that day onwards the Unionists made the fullest possible use of the Ulster problem as a means of combating Home Rule.

Nevertheless the Liberals' refusal to recognize Ulster's claims, although it turned out to be a disastrous error, was not so irrational as might at first appear. The Irish Nationalists who were their allies naturally did all they could to minimize the importance of Ulster.

They were moved partly by a mystical belief in the sacred unity of Ireland, partly by the more material consideration that an Ireland lacking the wealth and industry of Belfast would be economically unworkable. This belief has not in fact proved to be justified, but it was widely held both by Home Rulers and by Unionists, and its existence goes far to explain the refusal of the Liberals and the Irish Nationalists to make any concessions to Ulster sentiment.

Moreover it is only fair to remember that, until a late stage in the controversy, the partisans of Ulster demanded separate treatment not only for the four counties or the six counties but for all nine counties of the historic province of Ulster. This claim, confusing as it did the shadowy frontiers of history and tradition with the genuine frontiers drawn by religion and race, was so exorbitant that the Liberals may be excused for declining to take it seriously.[1] It seemed – and no doubt was – principally a device for obstructing Home Rule of any sort, even for the South. For these reasons, then, the Home Rule issue from 1886 to 1912 was invariably discussed on the assumption that partition was impracticable and that, whatever solution was ultimately adopted, it must embrace the whole of the island.

Of the two great obstacles to a peaceful settlement of Ireland – the position of the "Ascendancy", and the claims of Ulster – the latter was far the more important when Bonar Law became leader of his Party. For by 1912 the land problem had in a large measure been solved as a result of the Land Purchase Acts introduced by successive Conservative Governments between 1886 and 1905. Their effect had been to buy out the "Ascendancy" – at a handsome price – and Ireland was well on the way to becoming a relatively prosperous nation of small peasant proprietors possessing their own land. The Irish scene in 1912 differed profoundly from the impoverished and blood-stained background against which Parnell had manoeuvred thirty years before.

But the abolition of the land problem did nothing to modify the problem of Home Rule. The Irish still demanded self-government. The Anglo-Irish aristocracy was still irreconcilably hostile. In any case the problem of Ulster remained as formidable as ever. Time had done nothing to soften the bitter hostility of the Ulster Protestants towards any measure which forced them to submit to a Dublin parliament.

[1] In historic Ulster as a whole the Unionists at Westminster had a majority of only one in the House of Commons – 17 to 16. At the beginning of 1913 a by-election in London-derry reversed the position, and the Unionists actually found themselves in a minority of one.

There were indeed some Liberal Ministers who saw the danger of ignoring Ulster. During Cabinet discussions which preceded the drafting of the third Home Rule Bill both Lloyd George and Churchill urged some measure of exclusion for the Protestant counties of Ulster. Lloyd George, who drew his support from the Nonconformist element in the Liberal Party, was well aware of the suspicion with which most Englishmen – and Welshmen – regarded Roman Catholics. Churchill perhaps remembered his father's campaign in Ulster. The two Ministers were, however, unable to persuade their colleagues. Asquith's Bill, like its two predecessors, made no provision for Ulster. The stage was set for a protracted struggle between the two parties, a struggle of the most bitter and uncompromising nature.

2

Bonar Law, as we have already seen, felt more strongly about the Ulster question than anything else in politics at this time. He was after all himself the son of a Presbyterian minister who had been born in Ulster and had died in Ulster. Although the last man to whom the word bigot could justly be applied, he deeply sympathized with his compatriots' aversion to being ruled by Roman Catholics. He recognized – even if he did not himself share – the profound mistrust which the average Englishman and Scotsman entertained for Roman Catholicism. Moreover it seemed to him morally outrageous that his fellow countrymen, who claimed merely to remain under their traditional allegiance to the crown, should be forced to submit to the rule of their hereditary enemies in the southern provinces of Ireland.

Bonar Law, like other Unionists, would have preferred if possible to stop Home Rule altogether, for he felt strongly not only for the Protestants of Ulster, but for the small Protestant minority scattered all over Ireland. Nevertheless he was ready to recognize that in the last resort it was impossible to use the position of Ulster as a means of checking Home Rule for the South. If an offer of exclusion were made by Asquith, an offer acceptable to Carson and the Ulster Unionists, he realized that the Conservatives could not and should not reject it. Here he differed from the more extreme supporters of the Unionist cause, who cared little for Ulster save as a means of stopping Home Rule entirely, and who regarded with dismay any proposal for a compromise which might make the Home Rule Bill appear more reasonable, and hence more acceptable to the British electorate. For the moment, however, such differences were not of practical importance. The Liberals showed no sign of suggesting any compromise with regard to Ulster.

Bonar Law's own views are well expressed in a letter dated October 7th, 1912, to Lady Ninian Crichton Stuart, a Roman Catholic, who had urged him to avoid attacks upon her faith:[b]

"I have read your letter with the greatest interest, and I think I can sincerely say that there is no one who less likes to arouse religious bigotry than I do, and I do not think I have said a word in any of my speeches which would be open to the charge that I attacked your religion. . . .

"The real reason why in my opinion the Ulster point of view must be kept to the front is that, whether the cause be religious or not (and I do not think it matters), the population there is homogeneous and determined to be treated in the same way as the citizens of the U.K. In my opinion from every point of view they have the right to take that attitude. . . . Perhaps the clearest way in which I can show you how I feel in regard to the matter would be by reversing the picture. Suppose three-quarters of Ireland were of the exact class of which the Ulster minority is composed and suppose that in the rest of Ireland there were one-quarter of the population who looked with horror upon the idea of being governed by Orangemen and claimed the right to continue under the control of the British Parliament. In that case, whatever the reasons, I should think their claim was just; and in the same way, whether the reasons which actuate the people of Ulster are sound or not, I think that their claim is one which this country cannot without dishonour disregard."

Bonar Law lost no time in making public his attitude upon the question of Home Rule. Surprisingly enough, before his elevation to the leadership, he was not generally known to hold strong views on the Irish question. Indeed a letter which he received from A. P. Nicholson of *The Times* shows that the Irish Unionists were anxious to be assured of their new leader's soundness on Home Rule.[c] They need not have feared. Early in the new year – on January 26th, 1912 – Bonar Law made his first important pronouncement on policy, in his new capacity as leader. This was on the occasion of a speech at the Albert Hall, portions of which have been quoted in an earlier chapter. Bonar Law devoted much of his most vigorous invective to an attack on the whole principle of Home Rule. He accused the Government of trickery, of deliberately deceiving the electorate, of entering into a corrupt bargain with Redmond. He taunted the Liberal leaders with their reluctance to mention the subject at their public meetings and suggested – he had perhaps heard rumours of the Cabinet dissensions over Ulster – that their silence proceeded from the difficulty of framing a plausible measure.

Asquith did not introduce the Home Rule Bill until April 11th, 1912.

To his eloquent opening speech Bonar Law replied five days later in tones of uncompromising hostility. Like Lord Randolph Churchill he played the Orange card.

"I said earlier it is impossible to grant Home Rule. That is my opinion. I think it is impossible. The opposition of Ulster, or if you do not like to hear it called Ulster, of the North-East Corner of Ireland, makes it impossible. . . . The Nationalists of Ireland as compared with the whole of the United Kingdom are about a fifteenth of the population. In Belfast and the surrounding counties – where the feeling is overwhelmingly Unionist – they are a million of people – something like a fourth of the whole population of Ireland. If, therefore, there is any ground upon which you can say that the Nationalists of Ireland are entitled to separate treatment as against us, the ground is far stronger for separate treatment of Ulster. . . .

"As the House knows, I was present last week at a gathering of these people [Ulster Unionists at Belfast][1]. . . . I have been present at many political demonstrations, perhaps as large as have been held in this country in recent years. This gathering was not like any of them. It really was not like a political demonstration. It was the expression of the soul of a people – as I believe a great people. They say they will not submit except by force to such a Government. . . . I do ask Hon. Members to believe this – I think I am saying nothing that is not literally true – that these men believe and are ready in what they believe to be the cause of justice and liberty to lay down their lives."

Bonar Law continued, and here was the crucial point of his speech:

"Do Hon. Members believe that any Prime Minister could give orders to shoot down men whose only crime is that they refuse to be driven out of our community and deprived of the privilege of British citizenship? The thing is impossible. All your talk about details, the union of hearts and the rest of it is a sham. This is a reality. It is a rock, and on that rock this Bill or any Bill like it will inevitably make shipwreck."

3

It would, however, be tedious to repeat at length the speeches made on the subject of the third Home Rule Bill. They were tedious enough even for contemporaries. The protracted and bitter debates on the earlier Bills had drawn forth almost every conceivable argument that could be used both for and against Home Rule, and from 1912 to 1914 the discussions were for the most part an endless repetition of the same well-worn themes. In general, therefore, the detailed Parliamentary history of Home Rule will be omitted here.

[1] See below p. 129.

But it is, as well for purposes of clarifying the narrative, to outline the Parliamentary time-table which the Liberals envisaged for the Home Rule Bill.

It will be recalled that under the provisions of the Parliament Act of 1911 the vote of the Lords had been restricted in the following manner: a Bill would become law, even if the Lords rejected it, provided it had been passed in the House of Commons in three successive sessions, and provided that not less than two years had elapsed between the second reading of the Bill in the first session and its third reading in the last session. It was rightly assumed by the Liberals that the Home Rule Bill and the Welsh Disestablishment Bill would be rejected by the Lords. It therefore followed that neither could become law until approximately the middle of 1914. The first of the three necessary sessions lasted from February 1912 to March 1913; during its course both measures were passed through all stages in the House of Commons, only to be immediately rejected by the Lords. The second session followed directly upon the first. It ended in August 1913, and once again the two Bills passed the Commons and were rejected by the Lords. There followed a recess for the remainder of 1913. In February 1914 began the third and final session, during the course of which, unless some special action was taken, both Home Rule and Welsh Disestablishment would become law.

It was not, however, in Parliament that the Unionists intended to fight their main battle. In the existing House of Commons there was no hope of averting defeat. The Liberals could command a majority sufficient to carry any Bill that they saw fit to pass. But the two years' delay which the House of Lords could enforce under the provisions of the Parliament Act opened up possibilities which the authors of that measure can scarcely have foreseen: the Unionists might be able somehow to force a dissolution before the Home Rule Bill became law; alternatively they might be able to convince the Government that, however unassailable was its legal position in passing Home Rule, to do so would in practice be an act of folly. To achieve either of these purposes the best tactics were clearly to concentrate upon the grievances of the Protestants in North Ireland.

The earlier history of the Ulster agitation belongs to the life of Sir Edward Carson, rather than to the life of Bonar Law. For the purpose of this narrative we need not go back beyond 1910. At the beginning of that year Carson became leader of the Irish Unionists in succession to Walter Long. In July 1910 he was accepted as leader also of the Ulster Unionist Council, although he was himself in no

Unionist demonstration at Blenheim, July 29th, 1912

Above: General view of the delegates listening to Bonar Law's speech

Below: A discussion outside the hall. Left to right, the Duke of Marlborough, Lord Londonderry, Mrs. F. E. Smith, Bonar Law and F. E. Smith

sense an Ulsterman – he came from Dublin and sat in Parliament as Member for Dublin University. Shortly after the passing of the Parliament Bill in the summer of 1911, Carson announced to a great meeting of Ulster Protestants at Craigavon on September 23rd that the Ulster Unionist Council intended to set up a Provisional Government to take charge of the Province the moment the Home Rule Bill was passed. Soon after this meeting members of the Orange Lodges and Unionist Clubs began to learn military drill with a view to armed resistance against a Dublin Parliament – a movement which culminated in the formation of the Ulster Volunteer Force early in 1913.

Bonar Law threw himself heart and soul into the support of the Ulster cause. As soon as he became leader, the Ulster Unionists invited him to address a huge demonstration to be held at Balmoral, a suburb of Belfast, on Easter Tuesday, April 9th, 1912. Bonar Law was more than ready to accept the offer. On the appointed day he stood side by side with Carson and some seventy Members of Parliament on the platform, from which flew what was alleged to be the largest Union Jack ever constructed. A hundred thousand Irish Unionists marched past in military formation. The power of religion was invoked to add solemnity to proceedings. The Primate of all Ireland and the Moderator of the Presbyterian Church opened the meeting with prayers, and the whole concourse then sang the 90th Psalm. Bonar Law spoke with unusual eloquence, and the oft-quoted words of his peroration are worth quoting once again.

"I say it to you with all solemnity; you must trust to yourselves. Once again you hold the pass for the Empire. You are a besieged city. Does not the picture of the past, the glorious past with which you are so familiar, rise again before your eyes? The timid have left you, your Lundys[1] have betrayed you, but you have closed your gates. The Government by their Parliament Act have erected a boom against you, a boom to cut you off from the help of the British people. You will burst that boom. The help will come and when the crisis is over men will say of you in words not unlike those once used by Pitt, 'You have saved yourselves by your exertions, and you will save the Empire by your example'."

Two days later Asquith introduced the Home Rule Bill, and it was this demonstration at Balmoral which Bonar Law described, in his reply to Asquith's speech, as "the expression of the soul of a people".

[1] Robert Lundy was the famous governor of Londonderry who tried to betray that city to James II during its siege in 1689. His name has been regarded ever since by Ulster Protestants as the very prototype of the traitor, and for many years after 1689 he was annually hanged and burned in effigy.

Bonar Law was by now publicly committed to the most extreme course. The culmination of his efforts was perhaps the celebrated rally held on July 29th, 1912, at Blenheim Palace, the seat of the Duke of Marlborough. This was another great Conservative demonstration attended by Bonar Law, Carson and F. E. Smith, together with a hundred and twenty Unionist M.P.s and some forty peers, including – to the fury of the Irish Nationalists – the Duke of Norfolk who was generally regarded as the leading Catholic layman of England. Some of Bonar Law's remarks upon this occasion achieved a notoriety which makes them worth repeating. After declaring that the Unionists regarded the Government "as a Revolutionary Committee which has seized upon despotic power by fraud" he said:

"In our opposition to them we shall not be guided by the considerations or bound by the restraints which would influence us in an ordinary Constitutional struggle. We shall take the means, whatever means seem to us most effective, to deprive them of the despotic power which they have usurped and compel them to appeal to the people whom they have deceived. They may, perhaps they will, carry their Home Rule Bill through the House of Commons but what then? I said the other day in the House of Commons and I repeat here that there are things stronger than Parliamentary majorities."

He went on to express his doubt whether any government would dare to force the Ulster Protestants to submit to the rule of a Dublin parliament.

Then came the words which caused a storm of criticism:

"Before I occupied the position which I now fill in the Party I said that, in my belief, if an attempt were made to deprive these men of their birthright – as part of a corrupt Parliamentary bargain – they would be justified in resisting such an attempt by all means in their power, including force. I said it then, and I repeat now with a full sense of the responsibility which attaches to my position, that, in my opinion, if such an attempt is made, I can imagine no length of resistance to which Ulster can go in which I should not be prepared to support them, and in which, in my belief, they would not be supported by the overwhelming majority of the British people."

Undoubtedly in making a declaration of this sort Bonar Law was going far to break the conventions upon which Parliamentary democracy is based. He was in effect saying that the passing of Home Rule into law by a Parliamentary majority was not decisive, that the men of Ulster had a right to resist by force, and that, if they did so, they would have the Unionist Party in England wholeheartedly behind them. Such a tone had not been heard in England since the debates of the Long Parliament, and it certainly sounded strangely from the lips of a leader of the Party which traditionally stood for law and order.

On the other hand Bonar Law could argue that he was justified in breaking the conventions of the constitution because the Liberals had done so first; that in the last resort Parliamentary democracy depends upon a tacit but none the less real recognition by the majority of minority rights; that the Liberals were ignoring this convention when they used their majority to impose upon the Protestants of Northern Ireland the rule of their hereditary enemies in the South. There was a further point: Bonar Law's appeal to force was made only on the assumption that the Liberals were going to impose Home Rule without holding another General Election. For Bonar Law, in common with the rest of his Party, maintained that Irish Home Rule had never been fairly submitted to the British people at the Election of Autumn 1910. Much of the violence with which the leading Unionists attacked the Home Rule Bill can be explained by their belief that if a General Election was held on that specific issue, the Government would be defeated. It was this consideration which enraged them when they reflected upon the Parliament Act. But for that measure, they could have forced a General Election by using the veto power of the House of Lords. In the Unionist view, the Liberals, by a corrupt bargain with the Irish Nationalists, had destroyed the power of the House of Lords, and now, having concealed from the electorate that the price to be paid for this would be the destruction of the Union as well, were in the course of carrying the Home Rule Bill against the will of the people.

How far was this accusation fair? There was certainly some truth in it. The Liberals did not make Home Rule at all a prominent feature in their election addresses during 1910, but concentrated understandably on the more popular question of the Parliament Bill. 'The sole issue of the moment", declared Asquith in an election speech at Bury St. Edmunds, "is the supremacy of the people", and he alleged that the Unionists were trying "to confuse this issue by catechizing Ministers on the details of the next Home Rule Bill". Nevertheless it can hardly be argued that Home Rule had been completely ignored. Indeed the Conservatives themselves saw to that. Perhaps their insistence upon a fresh General Election proceeded less from a feeling that they had been tricked at the last one than from a conviction that, whatever the mind of the electorate had been in 1910, an appeal to the people in 1912 would result in a Conservative victory.

4

All during the summer and autumn of 1912 and on into the next year the Unionists repeatedly announced their intention of backing Ulster to the furthest limits. In September the Ulster Unionists began signing "the Covenant", a portentous document asserting the Ulster right to resist. In November an extraordinary scene took place in the House of Commons. The committee stage of the Home Rule Bill had been reached. On Monday, November 11th, the Government was defeated as the result of a snap division on a financial amendment proposed by a Unionist M.P. Asquith announced his intention to introduce next day a resolution rescinding the amendment. The Opposition regarded such action as an outrage.

When the debate was resumed on November 13th several Unionist members favoured the drastic course of shouting down the Prime Minister, but this Bonar Law would not allow. Amidst increasing excitement Asquith made his statement. Bonar Law then moved the adjournment of the debate. He claimed that Asquith was displaying a contempt for the rights of Parliament unparalleled since the days of Cromwell. His motion was defeated. Then the Speaker put the first part of Asquith's resolution to the House. Pandemonium broke out. Sir William Bull called Asquith a traitor and was ordered by the Speaker to leave the House. The debate continued, but in great disorder. Sir Rufus Isaacs, the Attorney-General, was howled down with cries of "Civil War", "Adjourn, Adjourn". Finally, to quote the *Annual Register*, "in view of the terrific uproar, mingled, it was said, with cries of profanity, the Speaker adjourned the House for an hour". The debate was resumed at 8.30, but disorder had in no way diminished. After ten minutes of shouting the Speaker again adjourned the House till the following day and the Unionists cheered wildly. As Mr. Churchill and Colonel Seely, the War Minister, left their seats they were assailed with cries of "Rats", and Churchill turned round to wave his handkerchief in ironical acknowledgment of these remarks. Enraged by this gesture Ronald McNeil, an Ulster M.P., seized the Speaker's copy of the Standing Orders and hurled it with great accuracy at Churchill's head. Thus ended one of the worst scenes of Parliamentary disorder in modern times.

Apologies were made the following day, and calm more or less restored. Eventually a formula was discovered whereby the traditional procedure of the House was not violated. It was, however, significant of the passions raised that Bonar Law in no way repudiated or condemned the conduct of his followers. On November 14th at the Albert Hall he said: "I did not suggest a disturbance, but I have this responsibility; I did not attempt in any way to interfere with what my colleagues desired to do . . . I did not try it, and under similar circumstances I never shall try it."

Bonar Law's violent public declarations during these months were not belied by his private remarks. He took, indeed, an extremely pessimistic view of the situation. He saw little hope of averting civil war, or, failing that, a degree of dissension in the country which would strain the constitution to its uttermost limit. So strongly did Bonar Law fear the consequences of the Liberal policy over Home Rule that he did not mince his words even in the highest quarters. The role of the King will be discussed in a later chapter. Evidently it was of great importance, for one way of obtaining a dissolution of Parliament would have been to persuade the King that it was his duty to insist upon it. There was also the question of the Royal Veto. Bonar Law was no courtier and was ready to speak his mind with vigour as the following conversation shows. It took place after a dinner given by the King on May 4th, 1912. Our authority is Austen Chamberlain who jotted down Bonar Law's account of the conversation that same evening. The King observed, "I have just been saying to Sir Edward Carson that I hope there will be no violent scenes this session." Chamberlain's account goes on:[d]

" 'May I talk freely to Your Majesty?' asked Bonar Law.

" 'Please do. I wish you to,' replied the King.

" 'Then I think, Sir, that the situation is a grave one not only for the House but also for the throne. Our desire has been to keep the Crown out of our struggles, but the Government have brought it in. Your only chance is that they should resign within two years. If they don't you must either accept the Home Rule Bill or dismiss your Ministers and choose others who will support you in vetoing it – and in either case half your subjects will think you have acted against them.'

" 'The King turned red and Law asked, 'Have you never considered that, Sir?'

" 'No,' answered the King, 'it is the first time it has been suggested to me.'

"Law added: 'They may say that your assent is a purely formal act and the prerogative of veto is dead. That was true as long as there was a buffer between you and the House of Commons, but they have destroyed that buffer and it is true no longer.' "

Describing this conversation to Austen Chamberlain, Bonar Law said: "I think I have given the King the worst five minutes that he has had for a long time."

It was certainly strong language to use, and the King, who had not yet seen enough of Bonar Law to become accustomed to his bluntness of speech, may well have resented it. Sir Harold Nicolson tells us, speaking of the situation a year later: "Moreover he [the King] had no personal desire at all to see Mr. Bonar Law succeed Mr. Asquith, for whom he had acquired (and for ever retained) feelings of warm affection." It is reasonable to surmise that the King's very different feeling towards Bonar Law originated from the episode just described, and the frosty interview, which Bonar Law was to have with the King when the latter invited him to form a Government in December 1916,[1] suggests that even four years later this feeling had not wholly vanished. But it need scarcely be said that, whatever his personal sentiments, the King invariably treated Bonar Law with complete correctness and gave him all proper support when he finally became Prime Minister.

What was the attitude of Asquith during these months? Naturally he was not going to let the inflammatory discourses of the Unionists pass without comment. Bonar Law's Blenheim speech aroused his special wrath. "The reckless rodomantade at Blenheim in the early summer", he declared, ". . . furnishes for the future a complete grammar of anarchy."

Asquith's biographers have revealed[e] that he seriously contemplated legal action on grounds of sedition against the extremists of the Unionist Party, particularly against Carson and F. E. Smith, and Craig, the leaders of Ulster. There was no doubt that a strong case existed under the law. But there was no doubt also that, whatever the law might be, an Ulster jury would never convict. Moreover it would have been difficult to avoid similar action against Bonar Law whose language was at least as violent as that of Carson; and, for a government in the twentieth century to initiate a criminal prosecution against the Leader of the Opposition, was an action at which the boldest Prime Minister might pause.

There were two further reasons for Asquith's reluctance. The Irish Nationalists were strongly opposed to such action. They regarded the speeches of the Ulster leaders as mere vapour; they refused to believe that Carson would really act when the crisis came. Asquith depended for office upon Nationalist support and was not willing to act against Redmond's advice. Further, such advice accorded well with Asquith's own beliefs. He himself was temperamentally a constitutionalist. He was deeply imbued with the tradition of Gladstonian

[1] See Chapter XXI.

Liberalism, the belief that all things can be settled within the framework of the constitution, that in the last resort a minority will always accept the decisions of a majority. For many years these assumptions had – at least in English politics – been well founded. After all, even the Parliament Bill had been carried in the end without undue commotion. Asquith did not recognize that the Irish question raised problems different in kind from any that had come before. He would no doubt have been a greater man if he had done so. But who can entirely blame him for his failure? At all events it is clear from Asquith's actions – and they can be explained in no other way – that he regarded the Ulster movement as largely bluff; that he simply could not believe in the reality behind the threats of Carson and Bonar Law.

There is no need to pursue the public controversy any further through the years 1912–13. Up and down the country, and in the House of Commons, the Party leaders continued to reiterate with parrot-like monotony the same cries: Carson declared that Ulster would never submit to Dublin; Redmond declared that Ireland was an eternal and indivisible unity; Bonar Law promised that the Unionists would back Carson to the limit; Asquith insisted that the Unionists were bluffing. And so the debate continued, neither side making – apparently – the slightest impression upon the other.

Meanwhile, to the accompaniment of frequent "scenes", the Home Rule Bill proceeded slowly through its various stages in the House of Commons. On January 16th, 1913, the third reading was carried by 367 votes to 257. On January 30th it was rejected on the second reading in the House of Lords by 326 votes to 69. On March 7th Parliament was prorogued, and on March 10th a new session began. The Bill once more began its weary way through the House of Commons. On July 7th the third reading was again carried. On July 15th it was again rejected in the House of Lords. Parliament was prorogued on August 15th and remained in recess for the rest of 1913.

During all these months, and indeed later, Bonar Law acted in the closest co-operation with Carson. He regarded Carson with great respect. The letters they exchanged were invariably of a most cordial nature. Carson reciprocated Bonar Law's feelings. "It is a great thing", he wrote to Lady Londonderry,[f] "that he is animated only by his love of the country and is not 'on the make'." And again, "I see B.L. almost daily and of course have great confidence in his judgment."

Carson has often been misrepresented and misunderstood. The

general impression of him, both in those days and later, was of a stern, austere, monolithic character obsessed entirely by a narrow and fanatical devotion to the Protestant cause in Ulster. This air of granitic rigidity was enhanced by his physical appearance; the powerful frame; the deep-lined countenance; the dark sardonic expression upon his face.

Carson's personality was, however, of a more complicated nature than this impression might suggest. Far from being narrow-minded he surveyed the world and its affairs with a broad comprehension. It is true that he had decided to take up the cause of Ulster, and he believed that the only way to preserve Ulster was to threaten the Liberals with rebellion if the Home Rule Bill became law in its original form. It was vital for his purpose that these threats should not be regarded as bluff. Carson was a superb actor and both in public and in private he preserved a demeanour of the most uncompromising and resolute nature – so successfully that to this day no one knows for certain what would have happened if the crisis had occurred.

But this did not mean that he was in reality a fanatic, or that he was incapable of negotiation. On the contrary, as will appear later, Carson, like Bonar Law, was much more moderate over the Home Rule question than many of the right-wing Conservatives. The rights of the Protestants in Ulster he would never sacrifice, but he was not prepared, like the extremists in the Conservative Party, to use the Ulster issue in order to wreck Home Rule entirely. It is true that he took this line in the earlier stages of the controversy, but his motives were tactical, and he withdrew later.

There were strange contradictions in Carson which would not at first sight seem obvious. He preserved the façade of a man of iron, but behind it he had many qualities of the neurasthenic. He was, for example, a hypochondriac. His letters to Bonar Law seldom conclude without a gloomy reference to his own health which would appear, from his account, to have been precarious in the extreme. Yet it is difficult to believe that a man who earns a huge income at the bar, and leads a major political campaign in the country, can really be very ill. Carson lived to be over eighty.

There were other contradictions. In public Carson appeared like another Cromwell, ready to sweep aside the laws of the land in order to defend what he considered to be right and just. He announced on one occasion that he proposed when he went over to Ulster "to break every law that is possible". And this was his habitual tone. It might therefore be expected that he would use every weapon in his fight against the Liberal Government, and give no quarter to his enemies if they made any error. Yet, early in 1913, Carson, along with F. E. Smith, accepted a brief to defend Lloyd George and Sir Rufus Isaacs in a legal action arising out of the Marconi Scandal. This caused great indignation among Unionist back benchers. Certainly Carson's conduct was not easy to square with his normal attitude of relentless hostility to the Government and all its works.

Then again at the time of the Curragh incident he was curiously reluctant to proceed to extreme measures. A problem arose as to the action that should be taken over officers who resigned rather than participate in hostilities with Ulster. Many Unionists considered that the proper course was to promise reinstatement if ever the Unionists went back in office. Carson, however, disapproved. Writing on March 21st, 1914, to Bonar Law he said:[g] "I do not think that we can say that officers resigning will be reinstated if we get in, as that would be very destructive."

The sentiment is of course to his credit as a man of sense. To encourage, or seem to encourage, the wholesale resignation of Army officers was indeed a perilous course. Nevertheless his attitude once again does not quite accord with that of a man who is prepared to stop at nothing in his determination to resist the Government. Perhaps Carson, who was after all a lawyer and a Parliamentarian like Asquith, could not really envisage himself breaking the constitution. Perhaps this was why in the last resort Asquith could not bring himself to take seriously the threats of someone whom he knew so well and with whom he had so often crossed swords in the law courts and the House of Commons.

CHAPTER VIII

THE MARCONI SCANDAL

1912 – 1913

Question of the Welsh Church – Bonar Law's views – Property rather than theology – The National Insurance Bill – Votes for women – The Marconi Scandal – Isaacs and Lloyd George buy American Marconi shares – Scandalous rumours – Attitude of Asquith – Attempt to conceal facts from the House – The Marconi enquiry – Libel action against Le Matin *– Attitude of Carson and F. E. Smith – Bonar Law's annoyance – The Chesterton case – Elibank departs to Bogota – Tory mockery – Report of the Marconi Committee – Its partisan nature – Bonar Law's speech in the House – His condemnation of Lloyd George and Isaacs – His attack on Mr. Falconer – Conservative motion of censure defeated – Isaacs becomes Lord Chief Justice*

I

THE Irish question, although the most important, was by no means the only subject to engage Parliament's attention during the sessions of 1912 and 1913. There was, for example, the question of the Welsh Church. The Liberals had for a long while past maintained the desirability of severing the link between Church and State in a country where the vast majority of the population did not adhere to the Anglican Communion. Lloyd George felt very strongly on this. A similar step had been taken in Ireland as long ago as 1869, and it seemed only logical to follow that precedent in Wales. But the Welsh Disestablishment Bill provoked intense feeling among the Conservatives, and a hostility almost as determined as that with which they greeted Home Rule.

Bonar Law was not a member of the Church of England and did not personally feel very strongly on the principle of disestablishment, but he objected as strongly as any Conservative to another feature of the Liberal Bill, namely disendowment. This was an interference with the rights of property, which he regarded as wholly unwarranted, and in the debate on the third reading of the Bill on February 5th, 1913, he pointed out the perilous precedent set: if corporate property, hitherto protected by ancient prescriptive rights, could be thus confiscated, might not the same treatment be meted out to ordinary private property? To us in the 1950s this argument may seem to have an archaic ring. Private property has been attacked on a scale un-dreamed of by Bonar Law. But in 1913 such arguments had more weight and commanded greater attention. The Conservatives decided to use every power that remained to them in order to obstruct the Liberal measure, and the Welsh Church Bill was, apart from the Home Rule Bill, the only measure to which the House of Lords has ever applied the full rigour of the two years delay permitted under the Parliament Act of 1911.

Another problem was the National Insurance Bill. Bonar Law had to deal with this almost as soon as he became leader of the Party. In the light of later history this measure seems merely to have been a very mild first instalment of the Welfare State. At the time, however, it was most unpopular in certain quarters whence the Conservatives drew support. Doctors, usually a Conservative class, were extremely hostile; and duchesses – who also tend on the whole to be Conserva-tive – were busy urging their housemaids in the name of Liberty not to submit to the indignity of compulsory insurance. Nevertheless, the Conservatives' attitude to the Bill was somewhat ambiguous. For if they opposed it root and branch, they ran the risk of being branded as incorrigible reactionaries. Therefore the Party did not formally oppose the third reading of the Bill which occurred very soon after Bonar Law became leader. Instead they criticized its timing and details: indeed a section of the Party, headed by Sir Laming Worth-ington Evans and counting Stanley Baldwin among its members, took considerable trouble in preparing counter-suggestions for a Con-servative Insurance Bill which, they said, would be far more effective than the Liberal measure.

There was therefore some perturbation in the Party when the following exchange took place during the debate on the Address at the start of the Session in February 1912.[a]

"THE PRIME MINISTER: . . . 'The Insurance Act became the law of the land under the old Constitution. (An Hon. Member: "No".) Yes it did, and it is in regard to the measure so passed that the right hon. gentleman [Bonar Law] has tonight hazarded the prediction that it will never come into operation. Why not? Who is going to prevent it? Is the right hon. gentleman, if and when he comes into power, going to repeal it?'

"Mr. Bonar Law replied by giving a nod and saying 'Certainly'.

"THE PRIME MINISTER: 'He is. Now we know. The first plank in the new platform of the Tory Party as reorganized under the new Leader is the repeal of the Insurance Act. We are getting on. I am very glad to establish that.' "

But the Conservative "social reformers" were far from glad, and Bonar Law had in fact exceeded his mandate by making such a statement. He personally believed that, for the Conservatives, social reform was not on the whole a profitable line to pursue. If the country wanted more and better social reform it would not vote Conservative. But a public declaration to that effect was unwise, and Bonar Law's inexperience and bluntness had led him into a trap, which Balfour would probably have avoided. He had to climb down a day or so later with a skilfully worded letter to the Press.

Another question which commanded much public and Parliamentary attention was the vexed question of votes for women. During 1912 and 1913 the activities of the "suffragettes" became ever more violent and sensational. Despairing of obtaining the vote by constitutional means, women, otherwise high-minded and honourable, sought to impress the public with their case by a systematic campaign of crime. It may well be doubted whether this policy achieved anything but the consolidation of the opposition, and female suffrage might have been carried considerably earlier but for the activities of the suffragettes.

It was an issue which cut across party politics. On balance a majority of Liberals supported, and a majority of Conservatives opposed, the giving of votes to women. Asquith, however, was hostile to female suffrage, whereas Bonar Law, unlike most of his own supporters, favoured it. When the question came up in May 1913, Asquith left the Bill to a free vote of the House, but himself spoke and voted against it. He was seconded by Walter Long and F. E. Smith. The Bill's most eminent supporter was Sir Edward Grey. In the end it was rejected by 267 votes to 219. One hundred and forty-eight Unionists voted with the majority, and only 28 supported the Bill. Bonar Law and Balfour decided that they ought to abstain, in view of the sentiments of their supporters.

2

1913 was a stormy political year. Quite apart from Irish Home Rule and Women's Suffrage, there was the important question of the Marconi Enquiry. Since the issues involved have been too often misunderstood by later historians, and since Bonar Law's part was considerable, it is perhaps worth describing this episode in some detail.

On March 7th, 1912, the Postmaster-General, Sir Herbert (now Viscount) Samuel provisionally accepted a tender from the English

Marconi Company for the construction of a chain of wireless stations in the Empire. This acceptance was subject to the signature of a definite contract, and the contract in its turn would only become binding upon the Government after it had been ratified by Parliament. The news of the preliminary acceptance resulted at once in a sensational boom in Marconi shares. That boom was further aided by the publicity given to the sinking of the *Titanic* on April 10th, which illustrated in a striking fashion the need for wireless telegraphy on board ship.

The Managing Director of the English Marconi Company was Mr. Godfrey Isaacs, a brother of the Liberal Attorney-General, Sir Rufus Isaacs. In addition to the English Marconi Company there existed a legally quite independent Marconi Company in America. But the English Company held a majority of the American Company's shares, and Godfrey Isaacs, who was Managing Director of both companies, resolved to expand the whole scope of the American Company and to finance it by a large new issue of American Marconi shares in the English market. The new issue was due to be floated on April 18th, 1912.

On April 9th Godfrey Isaacs invited two of his brothers, Mr. Harry Isaacs, a fruitbroker, and the Attorney-General to luncheon, and offered them a large block of the new shares at one and one-quarter, a price far below the market price that was anticipated for April 18th. The Attorney-General would not at first agree, for he disliked the idea of accepting a favour from a person who was not only his own brother but a government contractor on a very large scale. Harry Isaacs, however, took up 56,000 of the new shares. A few days later Rufus Isaacs swallowed his doubts and bought at £2 each 10,000 shares from his brother Harry. He appears to have felt that a purchase at one remove was morally different from a direct purchase off a government contractor – although the distinction seems somewhat nice – and he had been convinced by both his brothers' arguments that the American Company had no connection with the English Marconi Company. Moreover he seems to have believed that he was buying the shares at a fair market price, although on the day he bought them, April 17th, they could not be obtained by any member of the ordinary public at less than £3. Rufus Isaacs then on the same day disposed of 1,000 shares to Lloyd George, and another 1,000 to the Master of Elibank who was the Government Chief Whip. He made no profit on this deal which took place at the same price of £2 per share. The imprudence of these transactions staggers belief, and it is extraordinary that Isaacs and Lloyd George should not have realized how very questionable they were bound to seem.

On April 18th the new issue was floated and the shares at once leapt to nearly £4. All three Ministers promptly disposed of a considerable portion of their holdings. Subsequently, however, they bought further shares. In particular the Master of Elibank purchased 2,500 for the Liberal Party Fund. A slump soon followed and eventually on the total of transactions in American Marconi each of the three Ministers made a loss.[b] But before long rumours of the most fantastic nature began to circulate in the City and the clubs. It was freely suggested that Lloyd George, Isaacs, Elibank, and Samuel had used knowledge gained in their official capacity to make enormous profits on the Stock Exchange. Naturally the rumours made no distinction between speculation in English or speculation in American Marconi shares. These suspicions were voiced in print for the first time by an anti-semitic paper called the *Eye Witness*, edited by Hilaire Belloc and Cecil Chesterton, brother of "G.K." Samuel, who alone of the accused was genuinely innocent of any dealings in any Marconi shares, contemplated bringing a libel action but was dissuaded by Asquith and Isaacs. At the same time Isaacs took the opportunity of informing Asquith about the transactions in which he, Lloyd George and Elibank had engaged over the American Marconi shares. Asquith's biographers are curiously evasive on the question of the Prime Minister's attitude, and, indeed, their account[c] does not reveal the fact that Asquith was ever informed about the dealings in American Marconi at this early stage. The evidence of Isaacs himself and many others, however, leaves no doubt that Asquith was told what had happened, and that he did not take the matter at all seriously. Obviously the only wise and honest course was to reveal at once that, although the Ministers on whom suspicion fell had committed no action that was at all corrupt or venal, they had, no doubt innocently, engaged in some highly imprudent speculations which were subject to misinterpretation. An explanation and apology to the House would have been accepted, and the matter would probably have blown over.

Instead the accused Ministers, with Asquith's connivance, decided to pretend that the rumours had no connection at all with their dealings in American Marconi shares. On October 11th, as a result of an earlier debate on the Marconi contract, the Postmaster-General moved the appointment of a Select Committee to investigate the

whole story of the contract which had been provisionally signed in
July. During the debate on this motion, Isaacs and Lloyd George
specifically and indignantly disclaimed any dealings in the shares of
"the Marconi Company". They were most careful to word their
denials so as to cover only the British Marconi Company. No reference at all was made to the American Company. Nevertheless anyone who heard the debate was bound to go away with the impression
that the Ministers in question had never bought or sold Marconi
shares of any sort at any time; and only persons of remarkable
credulity can suppose that this impression was created accidentally
or by error.

Bonar Law, in common with most of the more responsible members of his Party, did not believe the wild accusations which continued
to be levelled by Cecil Chesterton and others against the Chancellor
of the Exchequer and the Attorney-General. He assumed that their
denials meant what any common-sense interpretation would suggest
that they meant, and took it for granted that the whole affair was a
mare's nest. He was, therefore, astonished early in the New Year,
1913, to learn from his old friend James Campbell, K.C., that in the
course of a forthcoming libel action to be brought by Samuel and
Isaacs against the French newspaper *Le Matin* it would be stated
that Lloyd George and Isaacs had bought shares in the American
Marconi Company. Campbell wished to know from his leader
whether he ought to take the brief for *Le Matin*. Bonar Law told him
that he should. He was far from pleased to learn at the same time
that Carson and F. E. Smith, neither of whom had consulted him,
were going to appear for Samuel and Isaacs against *Le Matin*.

It might be true that on this particular issue *Le Matin*, having
accused the two ministers of flagrant corruption, was unquestionably
in the wrong, but this did not alter the fact that the case would
reveal conduct by Lloyd George and Isaacs of a nature which was
at least open to grave censure. No one could predict what would
happen, but was it not possible that a concerted Parliamentary
attack on this issue might bring about the fall of the Government?
And had not this been the object which the Ulster leaders for months
past had been declaring that they would stop at nothing to attain?
Yet here were the two most vociferous partisans of Ulster and the
two greatest lawyers on the Tory side defending the accused Ministers
and creating inevitably the impression that they did not think that
there was really anything in the Marconi Scandal after all. No doubt
it could be argued that professional etiquette made it difficult for

Carson and Smith to refuse the briefs, but it could also be argued –
and indeed was argued in forcible terms – that the two men had no
right to preclude themselves, as in effect they had, from taking part
in a Parliamentary debate upon grave issues concerning the propriety of ministerial conduct. Sir George Younger voiced the general
indignation of the Party in a letter to Bonar Law in which he strongly
protested at the action of Carson and Smith and declared that to
ordinary men it was incomprehensible.[d] Bonar Law did not wish to
make matters worse by a public breach with Carson, but privately
he shared Younger's opinion.

The evidence given in court produced an immense sensation.
Isaacs and Lloyd George were at once summoned before the Select
Committee where they amplified their previous statements but added
nothing new of importance. One disagreeable revelation took place
however. The Government had to announce that the Master of Elibank was away on business in Bogota and would only be back when
the Committee's proceedings had ended. This looked all the worse
since Elibank had left after the enquiry began, and had had ample
opportunity to give evidence if he wished. Naturally no Tory of spirit
was going to let this opportunity go by, and references to Bogota
were repeated by Tory speakers and hecklers on every possible
occasion. They were repeated with even more fervour when it was
revealed that Elibank had invested as much as £9,000 of the Liberal
Party Fund in American Marconi shares. This fact, only elicited after
much probing, had the worst possible effect on public opinion and
gave a general impression that the whole Liberal Party was implicated in the Marconi Scandal. Not unnaturally members of the
public began to suspect that all manner of dubious dealings were
still undisclosed. Nor was this impression removed by the conduct of
the two leading Liberal members of the Marconi Committee, Mr
Falconer and Mr. Handel Booth. They had been privately informed
by Rufus Isaacs as early as January about his and Lloyd George's
purchases of American Marconi, but they used this information not
in order to help but in order to hinder the Committee at every stage
of its investigations. Indeed their obstructionism became so scandalous that, in April, F. E. Smith's brother Harold actually resigned
from the Committee in protest at the way it was being conducted.

3

When the Committee finally reported it did so upon purely party
lines. The Liberal majority headed by Falconer acquitted the Minis-

ters of all blame, declared that the American Marconi Company and the English Company had no connexion whatever, and alleged that the rumours of corruption were started recklessly by persons who had no reason to believe in their truth. The Chairman's report, while exonerating the Ministers from blame, mildly observed that Sir Rufus Isaacs would have been "well advised" if he had not bought the shares and if, having done so, he had disclosed the fact a great deal earlier. The Conservative minority led by Lord Robert Cecil also acquitted Ministers of corruption, and condemned the recklessness of some of the charges in the Press, but declared at the same time that there was in fact a material connexion between the two companies, condemned the Ministers' action as a "grave impropriety", and censured their reticence in the debate of October 11th, 1912, as "a grave error of judgment, and as wanting in frankness and respect for the House of Commons".

The majority report appears to have been more than even a highly complaisant Cabinet was prepared to defend, and Asquith intimated to the two Ministers that they must make some expression of contrition when the debate took place on a Conservative motion regretting their share transactions and lack of candour to the House. On June 18th the Conservatives, hampered, much to their indignation, by the absence of Carson and F. E. Smith who had been advised by Lord Halsbury against attending, opened the attack upon the two Ministers. Lloyd George and Isaacs made statements whose apologetic nature was, to say the least, somewhat diluted, and then left the House. The debate proceeded largely on party lines. Attempts at finding an agreed formula failed. Sir Ryland Adkins suggested an amendment to the effect that the House accepted the statements of regret made by the Attorney-General and the Chancellor of the Exchequer and reprobated the false charges of corruption brought against them.

To this Bonar Law wound up for the Opposition in a speech which the Annual Register describes as "violent", and proposed instead the following amendment:

"That this House, having heard the statements of the Attorney-General and the Chancellor of the Exchequer, acquits them of acting otherwise than in good faith and reprobates the charges of corruption which have been proved to be wholly false, but regrets their transactions in shares of the Marconi Company of America and the want of frankness displayed by them in their communications with the House."

Bonar Law, like nearly every Conservative and a good many

F

Liberals too, had been incensed at the cavalier tone of the explanation given by the two Ministers, who appeared to be regretting not so much their own conduct as the fact that their conduct had given rise to unworthy suspicion. Bonar Law did not think that this was enough.

"Well, Sir, we cannot accept it as adequate. I know thoroughly the difficulty in which these Ministers were placed. They had maintained up to the last minute that they had done nothing which they would not be entitled to do again tomorrow. It was therefore very difficult for them to come down and say something exactly the reverse, but I listened to every word which they said with the intention, after consulting with my colleagues, of changing what we had intended to be the order of the debate and getting up and speaking then and giving our views, if these Ministers had said what we thought they ought to have said: that they had done things which they ought not to have done; that they were sorry, apart from what happened afterwards, apart from all controversy, that they had done it. That is our reason for not accepting the form of words which was submitted."

Bonar Law disclaimed any desire to be vindictive or to drive Lloyd George and Isaacs out of public life, but he strongly felt that the House should, if only for the sake of avoiding perilous precedents for future corruption, put on record its disapproval of what had happened, and he ridiculed the notion that there was no material connexion between the British and American Marconi Companies. He then attacked the Ministers for their lack of candour. Why had they not at once given evidence to the Committee?

"Is it unfair to say that their feeling was this: 'We do not think there is anything wrong in what we have done but the public will probably take a different view – "the acrimonious public".' Perhaps at the back of their minds was the feeling: 'We may never have to tell it at all.' Is it unfair to suggest that? At all events I think that is the probable explanation. If you say it is not, if you say that these Ministers meant at all costs – whatever happened in the Committee or in the inquiry – to go to the Committee and tell it, remember this: that that defence of these two right hon. Gentlemen is the condemnation of Lord Murray[1]. It puts him on the black list by himself. The Committee was sitting for a month or more before he went away. He went away in the belief that before he came back the Committee would have ceased to exist. He did not mean to tell them. He took care in regard to the party funds to do his best to prevent the matter coming to light."

Finally Bonar Law pronounced a most severe condemnation of the private communications made by Rufus Isaacs to the leading Liberal on the Committee, Mr. Falconer, who had endeavoured rather unconvincingly to explain away the matter earlier in the debate.

[1] Elibank who became Lord Murray of Elibank in 1912.

"The Hon. Member spoke this afternoon for I think nearly two hours and he did not give us the smallest explanation as to why that communication was made. But he did tell us that there was a kind of analogy with a Court of Law. I do not know as much about that as many of my friends, but I am under the impression that if there was an analogy to a Court of Law he was in the position of a juryman and I am under the impression that if anyone interested in a case were to have any communication of any kind with a member of the jury he would render himself liable to criminal prosecution."

Bonar Law concluded:

"All we ask is that the House of Commons should express in the mildest terms you like its disapproval of what has been done and in voting for the Motion which stands in the name of my hon Friend tonight we shall in my belief be only expressing what is the almost universal feeling in the United Kingdom."

Whether or not Bonar Law was right about the "universal feeling in the United Kingdom" can never be proved. Probably there was a fairly general disapproval of what had occurred. But Parliament in an era of well-drilled partisan battalions can be just as effectively insulated from public opinion by the party machine as it was in the early days of George III by jobbery and corruption. Voting was on rigid party lines, and only three Liberals voted against the Government. A number of Labour members abstained. Bonar Law's amendment was rejected by 346 to 268.

What ought to be our considered judgment on these events? It is certainly true that anti-semitism and violent partisanship resulted in the spreading of outrageous rumours which grossly traduced not only the two Ministers but many others like Samuel who were wholly innocent. But the fact that Isaacs and Lloyd George were not guilty of the sort of charges which were levelled against them by Cecil Chesterton has tended to obscure in the eyes of posterity what they were guilty of – namely a degree of indiscretion and a subsequent disingenuousness which seem in retrospect almost incomprehensible. It is quite certain now that no Minister who behaved as they did would survive for a day. The relatively harmless and trivial indiscretion for which Mr. Attlee so promptly dismissed Dr. Dalton from the Chancellorship of the Exchequer does not begin to compare with the conduct of Isaacs and Lloyd George.

The impropriety of which Lloyd George, Isaacs and Elibank were guilty was twofold. In the first place they had, however innocently, put themselves in a position in which their public duty might have clashed with an undisclosed private interest, and had moreover done so by accepting favours from a government contractor. Had they speculated in British Marconi shares, this fact would have been flagrant and obvious, but in reality speculation in American Marconi shares was scarcely less dubious, for any serious inquiry would at once have revealed the close connexion between the two companies.

Secondly the Ministers, having made their initial error, treated the House of Commons with a deliberate evasiveness which no subsequent excuses can condone. Only the most obstinate Liberal apologists can seriously maintain that Lloyd George and Isaacs intended all along to reveal the truth. They evidently hoped that they would not have to tell the full story of their transactions, and but for the libel actions it is quite possible that they might never have been obliged to declare the truth.

The postscript to this strange story is not the least extraordinary feature of the whole affair. In October 1913, only four months after a debate in which he had escaped a condemnation for grave impropriety by a purely party vote, Sir Rufus Isaacs was elevated to the second highest judicial position in the land, and was appointed Lord Chief Justice of England. It is difficult to decide which is the more astonishing – Asquith's arrogance in offering, or Isaacs' imperviousness in accepting, a post of this nature at that time. It is not surprising that Tory indignation knew no bounds and that Rudyard Kipling should have circulated what is perhaps one of the bitterest political satires of modern times, comparing Isaacs with Gehazi, the servant of the prophet Elisha.

CHAPTER IX

THE IRISH PROBLEM — ATTEMPTS AT COMPROMISE

SEPTEMBER 1913 – FEBRUARY 1914

Autumn 1913 – Danger of civil war – Difference between opinions of English and Ulster Unionists – Bonar Law's memorandum for the King – Its questionable validity – King favours compromise – Bonar Law visits Balmoral – His account of discussions with King and Churchill – Lansdowne's hostility to exclusion of Ulster – Indiscreet conduct of F. E. Smith – Bonar Law repudiates compromise – Bonar Law's discussions with Carson – He becomes convinced that exclusion is possible – Overtures from Asquith – Bonar Law's first secret meeting with Asquith at Cherkley – His second meeting – Asquith unable to carry out his promises – Letter from Curzon – Irritation of the King – End of negotiations for compromise – Frosty correspondence between Bonar Law and Stamfordham – Letter from Lord Derby – Bonar Law's attitude less extreme than usually supposed – The blame for the breakdown

I

No sooner had the echoes of the Marconi Scandal begun to die away than the Irish Problem entered upon its most acute phase. With the end of the session in August 1913 the Home Rule Bill had twice been passed in the House of Commons, twice rejected by the House of Lords. It needed to pass the Commons only once more in order to become law, and on the Government's existing time table this was due to occur about the middle of 1914. Meanwhile in Ulster preparations were far advanced for armed resistance: Sir Edward Carson's arrangements for setting up a provisional government as soon as the Bill became law had been worked out to the last detail; thousands of Ulstermen were drilling and learning the practice of arms. The danger of Civil War loomed ever larger, and it is not surprising that the leaders on both sides began to search for some means of avoiding that catastrophe.

At the risk of repetition it is worth emphasizing again at this point that the question of a separate treatment for Ulster had not yet been seriously suggested. The majority of English Unionists had concentrated on the grievance of Ulster, not because they really wanted separate treatment for Ulster, but because they wished to stop Home

Rule entirely.[1] It was, as we saw earlier, widely believed by both sides that an autonomous Ireland, without the wealth of Belfast, would be unworkable, and from this each side drew opposite conclusions, the Liberals that Ulster must at all costs be kept in, the Unionists that Ulster must at all costs be kept out. The attitude of the Ulster Unionists was naturally rather different. Carson and Craig were primarily leading a struggle for national survival. They recognized that, in the last resort, Ulster could not prevent Home Rule for the South and West, but they were determined that Home Rule should not include the North. The Ulster Unionists were thus fighting for a cause not quite the same as that for which the majority of English Unionists fought, and although they co-operated with the latter, they did so as allies and independent partners rather than as subordinates. Naturally both English and Ulster Unionists wished if possible to stop Home Rule entirely, but, whereas Lansdowne, Long, and the Cecils were hostile to any compromise which would enable Asquith to carry Home Rule even in a mutilated form, Carson was ready to accept the exclusion of Ulster rather than risk total defeat at the hands of the Liberals. These divergencies of interest became important in the course of the negotiations with Asquith during the autumn and winter of 1913.

For the time being, however, the exclusion of Ulster was proposed neither by the Unionists nor by the Liberals. The immediate problem upon which the Unionist leaders were concentrating was how to force a dissolution before the Home Rule Bill received its third reading in the House of Commons. Obviously the key figure here was the King. The only method by which the Unionists could obtain a dissolution, assuming that Asquith would not recommend one, was to persuade the King to insist upon it. The precise extent of the King's power in such a matter was of course doubtful, and even if he possessed such a power, the wisdom of exercising it was even more questionable. But Bonar Law was, from an early stage, convinced that the King must take action. His conversation with the King in May 1912 has already been described.[2] In September of the same year, he was invited for the first time as a guest at Balmoral and he submitted a memorandum to the King on the whole question. His own rough draft of this has survived and deserves to be quoted in full:[a]

---

[1] At the beginning of 1913 Carson proposed an amendment to the Home Rule Bill which would have excluded the whole province of Ulster, all nine counties, from its operations. But this was clearly intended to wreck the Bill completely, and cannot be regarded as a serious compromise proposal.

[2] See p. 133.

"If the Home Rule Bill passes through all its stages under the Parliament Act and requires only the Royal Assent the position will be a very serious and almost an impossible one for the Crown.

"The Unionist Party will hold that, as the Constitution is admittedly in suspense (for the duty of carrying out the Preamble of the Parliament Act is admitted by the Government) and as it is at least doubtful, and in view of the by-elections more than doubtful whether the Government have the approval of the country, the position is precisely similar to what it would be if the Government supported by the House of Commons asked the Sovereign to use the Royal Prerogative to overcome the opposition of the House of Lords.

"In such circumstances Unionists would certainly believe that the King not only had the Constitutional right but that it was his duty before acting on the advice of his Ministers to ascertain whether it would not be possible to appoint other Ministers who would advise him differently and allow the question to be decided by the country at a General Election.

"The last precedent prior to the Parliament Act which B.L. can recall was the Reform Bill of 1832. On that occasion B.L. believes, without having the opportunity of refreshing his memory, that though an election had been fought specially on the issue of the Reform Bill the King did not consent to the creation of the new Peers till he had sent for the Leader of the Conservative Party and ascertained from him that he was not prepared to take the responsibility of forming a Government. Such would be the view of the Unionist Party.

"The Radical Party, on the other hand, would almost certainly maintain that the veto of the Sovereign had fallen completely into desuetude, and that the duty of the King was to regard the passage of the Home Rule Bill under the Parliament Act as final and give his assent to it as a matter of course.

"In reality it does not matter much which of these views is constitutionally sound. In any case, whatever course was taken by H.M., half of his people would think that he had failed in his duty, and in view of the very bitter feelings which by that time would have been aroused, the Crown would, B.L. fears, be openly attacked by the people of Ulster and their sympathisers if he gave his assent to the Bill, and by a large section of the Radical Party if he took any other course.

"Such a position is one in which the King ought not to be placed, and B.L. is of the opinion that if his Majesty put the case strongly to the Prime Minister he would feel that it was his duty to extricate the King from so terrible a dilemma.

"B.L. also ventures to suggest to H.M. that when any crisis arises it might be well to consult informally Mr. Balfour or Lord Lansdowne or himself, and he assures H.M. that any advice given under such circumstances would not be influenced by Party considerations."

This view may well seem open to some doubt on constitutional grounds, but Bonar Law was backed by powerful authorities in his opinion of the Crown's powers. Writing to Professor Dicey, the celebrated author of *The Law and Custom of the Constitution*, on March 26th, 1913, he said:[b]

"I do not think that it is a question really of using the veto; but in my view the one constitutional right which the sovereign undoubtedly still possesses is that if Ministers give him advice of which he does not approve, he should then see whether he can get other Ministers who would give him different advice."

Dicey replied deprecating any revival of the Royal Veto, but adding:[c]

"I entirely agree with your view of the King's constitutional position."

Bonar Law does not appear to have had any further discussion upon this matter with the King until the summer of 1913. By then the King was beginning to be understandably anxious about the whole situation, for it seemed that he would once again, as over the Parliament Act Crisis, be the centre of a furious political and constitutional controversy from which he could not easily escape without incurring the bitter resentment of one or other of the two parties. He therefore decided through Lord Stamfordham, his Private Secretary, to find out the views of the Unionist leaders. As a result Lansdowne and Bonar Law drafted a lengthy memorandum which they sent to the King on July 31st.[d]

The gist of it was that the Constitution was in a state of suspense; that a dissolution was the only method of averting civil war; that, if Asquith declined to recommend a dissolution, the King had a right to dismiss him and send for someone who would do so; that the King should address a formal memorandum to Asquith urging a dissolution, and, the writers assumed, in such circumstances Asquith would be bound to dissolve.

It must be admitted that Bonar Law and Lansdowne, however well backed by constitutional experts, were asserting a doubtful constitutional doctrine in certain parts of their memorandum. It could perhaps be argued that there was nothing unconstitutional in the King endeavouring to *persuade* Asquith to recommend a dissolution, and even addressing a formal letter to Asquith on that theme. But when the Unionist leaders asserted that in 1913 the King still had the undoubted right to *dismiss* Asquith and replace him by someone who would recommend a dissolution they were venturing on very uncertain ground. The last occasion upon which a King had dismissed a Prime Minister who possessed a majority in the House of Commons had been nearly eighty years earlier – and it was not a happy precedent. When in 1834 William IV dismissed Lord Melbourne and replaced him by Sir Robert Peel, the ensuing General Election did not give Peel a majority. He was soon forced to resign. The King was obliged to send for Melbourne again, and the episode was generally regarded as a rebuff to the Crown and a humiliating personal blow to William IV. No doubt in theory the Monarch had in 1913 – and has today – the legal right to dismiss his Ministers, just as he possesses in theory the right to veto a Bill. But to exercise it in practice would have been to revive a power which had lain dormant since 1834, and which had only been exercised successfully in the days before the Reform Bill of 1832, when an entirely different set of constitutional conventions prevailed.

2

Nothing further happened as far as Bonar Law was concerned until September. Then began a series of complicated conversations and negotiations which are worth following in some detail, for the light they throw upon the inner processes of party politics, upon the position of the Crown, upon the relations between the principal political leaders of the day. The initiative came from the King who, on receiving from the Unionist leaders advice so completely opposed to that tendered by his own Ministers, decided that he must work for some settlement of the apparently irreconcilable Irish conflict. Otherwise, as Bonar Law had earlier pointed out, he would be forced into such a position that whatever action he took would render him the object of bitter criticism from one half of his subjects.

Early in September Lansdowne stayed at Balmoral and had a lengthy discussion with the King about the memorandum which he and Bonar Law had sent. He wrote an account of that discussion to Bonar Law.[e] The King told Lansdowne that, according to Asquith, it was impossible for a Constitutional Monarch to do anything but follow his Ministers' advice: the most he could do, if he disagreed, was to put his own views on record.[1] On any question of dissolution or a referendum Asquith was adamant. An Election would turn just as much on the Marconi Scandal or the Insurance Act as on Home Rule, and a referendum was impracticable. Asquith had, however, suggested that a possible compromise might be reached by giving separate treatment to Ulster, and the King passed on this hint to Lansdowne. Finally the King, according to Lansdowne,

---

[1] See Spender and Asquith, *Life of H. H. Asquith*, pp. 29–34, for Asquith's memoranda to the King, and Harold Nicolson, *King George V*, pp. 225–9, for the King's reply.

"recurred several times to the possibility of a settlement by consent. He preferred not to talk about 'conferences', but he thought that 'meetings' between the party leaders might be useful and in reply to a question by me said that he thought that the question of according special treatment to Ulster might be considered in this manner".

Lansdowne's reply to this indirect overture was chilly. He did not think settlement by consent at all hopeful and declared that he would deprecate a conference on the basis of exclusion of Ulster. Lansdowne still reiterated his point about dissolution and maintained that this was the only proper course:

"I said that I was quite unable to see what legitimate objection His Majesty's advisers could take to a general election except that it was likely to result in their defeat."

(Asquith might reasonably have replied that this was an objection quite legitimate enough for him). Lansdowne concluded by urging the King to lay a reasoned expression of his (the King's) own views before the Cabinet, and the King promised to do so before the next Cabinet meeting in the second week of October.

Bonar Law had also been summoned to Balmoral a few days after Lansdowne left. On the way he paid a short visit to the latter's country house, Meikleour, in Perthshire. He was thus fully briefed when he met the King. On September 18th Bonar Law wrote a full memorandum describing his conversation with the King. According to his own account he informed the King that there were two possible topics which an inter-party conference might discuss. The first was that of general devolution – sometimes known as "Home Rule All Round", i.e. the possibility of creating subordinate legislatures for Scotland and Wales as well as Ireland. A recent letter to *The Times* by Lord Loreburn, the late Liberal Lord Chancellor, had drawn attention to this possibility, and Bonar Law indicated to the King that the Unionists would not refuse to take part in a conference with these terms of reference. The second possibility was to hold a conference on the basis of excluding Ulster but agreeing to Home Rule for the rest of Ireland. Upon this Bonar Law was far more sceptical. It would be impossible, he declared,

"unless it secured a large measure of approval from the Unionists of South and West Ireland, for I was sure that the leaders of the Unionist Party would not give their consent to any scheme which would be regarded as a betrayal by the loyalists of Ireland. . . . H.M. informed me, as he had previously informed Lord Lansdowne, that he intended to write a personal letter to his Ministers which he would reserve the right to make public after the event. In this letter he would point out the difficulty of the position in which the Crown would be placed and that this difficulty would be largely avoided if there were an appeal to the people before the Home Rule Bill became law and that in his opinion it was the duty of his Ministers to submit the question to the country. . . . I pointed out what in my belief would be the effect on the Army if the Government attempted to use troops in Belfast before they had behind them the moral force which could only be secured by the support of the electors. I reminded him that the leaders of the Unionist Party had pledged themselves in that event to give every possible support to the people of Ulster, that I had no reason to think that in this respect the policy of the Party would be modified and in these circumstances I thought it very doubtful whether the Army would obey the orders of the Government".f

The King therefore received little encouragement from the Unionist leaders. Both were dubious about the possibility of compromise although not prepared to refuse a conference entirely; both insisted that dissolution was the only possible course; both were sceptical about partition; and Bonar Law gave a clear indication, that the Conservative Party would not discourage the Army in a refusal to obey orders, if the Home Rule Bill went through in its present form without an appeal to the nation. This was the first hint of the troubles which were to culminate in the so called "Mutiny" of the Curragh in the following March. In fact the Unionist leaders were in a mood of uncompromising resistance – even to the point of rebellion – and the possibility of settlement seemed remote.

But, in addition to his discussions with the King, Bonar Law had a conversation to which he attributed greater importance. This was with Churchill who, it will be remembered, was at this time First Lord of the Admiralty, and who was staying at Balmoral. Churchill had been authorized by Asquith to speak to Bonar Law, and the discussion as reported by Bonar Law is of considerable interest. Bonar Law reported it briefly to Lansdowne and at greater length to Carson on September 18th:g

"I think it is necessary that you should know all that I know about the position, and as arranged with you, I am sending this letter by messenger.

"I had a long talk with the King, and he asked me to put in writing a summary of the conversation. I did so and enclose a copy of it for you which gives all the information so far as my talk with the King himself is concerned.

"Churchill was there, and we had a talk about the whole situation in the course of which he told me that he had a letter from Asquith suggesting that he should speak to me.

"My talk to Churchill was practically confined to this: I told him that it seemed to me the position was a desperate one for both political parties.

I said it was bad for us; but it seemed to me much worse for them. I told him that if the thing was to go on on their lines they themselves had taught us that no half measures were any use, and it was certain that we would stick at nothing when it came to the point. I told him that it was idle to suppose that they could leave you alone and trust to your movement breaking down from its difficulties. I said to him that most certainly the moment the Home Rule Bill was passed you would not only set up your provisional Government, but that you would allow no force of any kind in your area except the force appointed by you; that you would appoint your own police, and allow no other body to interfere with your action. He then spoke in a half-hearted way as if it would be possible to allow even this to go on without interference by force. He spoke, for instance, of stopping railway communication and stopping sea communication; but I pointed out the absurdity of this, as it would interfere not only with Ulster but the whole of Ireland and the whole of England and Scotland which traded with Belfast, and I think he realized that that was impossible. I told him also that here in England there would be no half measures; and I said to him, 'Suppose it comes to this: the whole of the Unionist Party say that Ulster is right, that they are ready to support them, and that if necessary all the Unionist Members are turned out of the House of Commons – does he suppose that the Army would obey orders to exercise force in Ulster!' I said to him that in that case undoubtedly we should regard it as civil war, and should urge the Officers of the Army not to regard them as a real Government but to ignore their orders. I said to him also that of course we realized as clearly as he did not only the seriousness but the actual calamity of allowing things to come to such a point. I said also that I saw no way out of the difficulty. . . .

"Now that is the position, and I feel sure that Asquith will suggest a private meeting either with Lansdowne or with me. If it is with me I am most anxious that before it takes place I should have a talk with you. As you know I have long thought that it might be possible to leave Ulster as she is, and have some form of Home Rule for the rest of Ireland . . .

"When do you come back? For it is really not possible to have a proper understanding by letters; and you know that I have not only so strong a personal friendship for you but so much belief in your judgment that I do not think in any case I would go on with a proposal to which you were strongly opposed. I think I would rather give up the whole thing than do that. I do not think you should show this to any of your Irish colleagues, but of course you are free to show it to F.E. and perhaps you could arrange for him to see me as soon as he comes back to England. I do feel, however, that it is vital that before there is any meeting with the other side I should personally see you. The whole question as to the exclusion of Ulster really turns upon this – whether or not it would be regarded as a betrayal by the solid body of Unionists in the South and West."

The letter is of considerable historical interest. It shows in the first place the lengths of resistance contemplated by Bonar Law. Whereas to the King he had merely spoken of the probability of the Army refusing to obey orders, to Churchill he declared that in the last resort the Unionist Party would positively encourage and recommend such refusal. Secondly, it reveals Bonar Law's own belief, which he admits to Carson, that exclusion of Ulster was a possible solution. Carson of course agreed and his reply to Bonar Law contains a memorandum from F. E. Smith suggesting the possibility of a conference with the Liberals based on this assumption.[h]

Bonar Law sent copies of his correspondence with Carson to Lansdowne at Meikleour, but immediately a frosty wind begun to blow from the direction of Perthshire. For Lansdowne viewed the policy of excluding Ulster with the greatest misgiving. He felt strongly that to exclude Ulster and allow Home Rule for the South and West would be to betray the whole past tradition of the Unionist Party. Lansdowne was himself a great landowner in Southern Ireland. It was as natural that he should take this view, as that Bonar Law, with his Ulster descent, should see the problem primarily in terms of Ulster nationalism. But there is no need to suppose that Lansdowne was influenced only or even principally by his possession of great estates in the South. Many other Unionists took the same view although they possessed not one acre in Ireland. The right wing of the Party had always objected to Home Rule, not merely because it was unfair to Ulster, but because they denied the whole concept of a separate Irish nation. To them Britain was a unity and to break up that unity by creating a national state in Ireland seemed almost an act of sacrilege. It was true, as Lord Randolph Churchill had observed, that the Orange card was the best card to play against Home Rule, but this did not mean that the majority of Unionists were prepared to accept a settlement which gave a national parliament and executive to the rest of Ireland, even if Ulster still remained a part of the United Kingdom.

Lansdowne was quick to make this plain:[i]

"The language Winston used", he wrote on September 23rd, 1913, "leads me to anticipate that an overture of some kind will be made to us and that it will take the shape of a proposal that we should go into a conference upon the assumption that the Government Bill holds the field and the only matter open for discussion is the exclusion of Ulster. The idea of a conference on those lines fills me with alarm and I gladly call to mind that you made it clear that we could not entertain the project unless it were consented to by the loyalists of the south and west. . . .

". . . Are you not a little horrified at the manner in which F. E. Smith is pledging not only himself but the whole Unionist Party to violent action in Ulster? . . . I see, for example, 'A Message from England' conveyed by F.E. in the course of which he says 'on behalf of the Unionist Party in Great Britain' that 'from that moment we hold ourselves absolved from all allegiance to this government' and 'shall stand side by side with you refusing to recognize any law and prepared with you to risk the collapse of the whole body politic to prevent this monstrous crime' . . . it may indeed in certain events be necessary to take strong measures but shall we not be placed in rather an awkward position if we are asked whether it really is the case that F.E. has been authorized to use such language 'on behalf of the Unionist Party in Great Britain'?"

Bonar Law replied to this letter in mollifying tones, but Lansdowne's suspicions about Ulster and irritation with F. E. Smith were almost at once increased by a curious episode. The latter, while serving in the Territorial Army on manoeuvres, saw the King at about this time, and appears to have given him an altogether unduly optimistic estimate of the chances of a compromise: so much so that Lord Stamfordham wrote an enthusiastic letter to Bonar Law on September 26th:[j]

". . . F. E. Smith informed the King that Carson is all in favour of such an arrangement (leaving out Ulster) and thinks a solution on these lines could be arrived at which would be acceptable to his (C's) friends. F.E. returns to Ulster today and will tell Carson exactly what His Majesty said during these conversations. He was sanguine as to a satisfactory settlement and that by it all question of H.M.'s visiting either Dublin or Belfast in the future would be happily set at rest."

Bonar Law was alarmed at the possibilities of misunderstanding implied in this letter. However much he himself inclined to a solution along the lines of exclusion, he was well aware of the opposition within the Party from such powerful figures as Curzon and Long, not to mention the whole Cecil clan. He had indeed felt some misgivings about communicating with Carson at all. His doubts now seemed fully justified, and he at once wrote again to Lansdowne enclosing Lord Stamfordham's note. "Stamfordham's letter", he wrote on September 27th,[k] "makes me feel that I made a mistake in sending the copy of the talk at Balmoral to Carson." He also enclosed a draft reply to Stamfordham. Lansdowne wrote back on September 30th:[l]

"Stamfordham's letter to you of the 26th and the draft reply which you were good enough to send me are very important. I am afraid F. E. Smith has not been discreet and that your instinctive misgivings as to the results of direct communications between yourself and Carson were not without foundation . . . the King has been led to believe that a reasonable settlement is within reach and that Curzon and I are obstructing it. It is, as you say, absolutely necessary that he should understand that F.E. was much too sanguine. Apart, however, from F.E. I doubt whether the King himself or Bigge[1] really grasps the difference between what they call 'leaving

---

[1] Lord Stamfordham.

out Ulster' and the kind of settlement which Carson could afford to consider or we to discuss. . . ."

To Stamfordham's proposals for a conference on the basis of
excluding Ulster from the operation of the Home Rule Bill Bonar
Law now returned an uncompromising refusal.

"I am sorry to say," he wrote,[m] "that I see no prospect whatever of an
arrangement on the lines of your letter.

"The proposal, as I understand it, is that before entering into a conference we should agree to the present Home Rule Bill if North-East Ulster
were excluded from it. . . . I am certain that if it were known from the
outset that the Unionist leaders had entered into a conference pledged
beforehand to such a proposal there would be wild outburst of resentment
against us in the South of Ireland which would be reflected with almost
equal violence in England. . . . If there is to be a conference it must be
perfectly free as suggested by Lord Loreburn. I should not ask as a preliminary that the Government should drop their Bill; we should not be
expected to give in advance any conditional promise to support it. . . ."

Writing a day or so later to Lansdowne Bonar Law said:[n]

"F.E.'s talk with the King seemed to me just about as unwise as anything could be.

"Probably I have looked upon the solution of leaving Ulster out much
more favourably than you have, for I have had the idea for many years
that that might perhaps in the end be a right method of dealing with the
situation. But I quite agree with you that such a solution is only a last
resort and nothing would be more foolish than to give the enemy the idea
that we were not only ready but anxious for a settlement on these lines. . . ."

There for the moment the matter rested. The King's intervention
had apparently achieved nothing. The two Unionist leaders regarded
any proposal for separate treatment of Ulster with deep suspicion.
But there was this difference between them: Lansdowne not only
feared a Die-hard revolt if a compromise took place, but he also
sympathized with the sentiments which would have inspired such a
revolt; Bonar Law feared the revolt but did not feel so strongly on
the iniquity of the whole concept of Home Rule. His doubts about the
actual merit of a partition settlement, as opposed to its danger to
party unity, came more from his reluctance to "betray" the Southern
Unionists than from a belief that Home Rule for the South was
fundamentally wrong. If he could be convinced on that point he
would be more ready to consider the exclusion of Ulster.

3

At the beginning of October Bonar Law had a highly important
conversation with Carson who had returned from Ulster, and he

promptly reported it to Lansdowne. Carson said that he now believed that a settlement on the lines of excluding Ulster would not be seriously opposed by the Southern Unionists. He had recently met a deputation of Southern Unionists who had indicated that they were not prepared to agitate strongly against Home Rule; they were afraid of intimidation and damage to their financial and business interests. When Carson urged them to come out into open opposition they refused.

"If this really represents the position," Bonar Law wrote to Lansdowne on October 8th,° "it seems to me obvious that we are not justified in risking civil war for the sake of people who will take no risks even of a financial kind for themselves. . . . I must say, therefore, that I am more hopeful than I was of a settlement of that kind [exclusion of Ulster]."

It is clear that his conversation with Carson had a great effect on Bonar Law's attitude to Ulster. It largely removed his own doubts upon the admissibility of partition as a solution. Of course the danger of a Die-hard revolt remained, and Bonar Law, with his intense feeling for Party unity, was always strongly influenced by that fear to the very end. But, provided that a settlement of Ulster could be made in a way which genuinely satisfied Carson and his followers, and provided that the Unionist Party could be persuaded to acquiesce, then Bonar Law was prepared to consider such a solution as perhaps the only means of avoiding civil war in the North of Ireland.

Lansdowne was not convinced although he admitted the force of Bonar Law's contention. He replied:ᴾ

"I feel the force of the considerations which you have urged so clearly in your memorandum. We may be driven to the kind of settlement you have in view but I cordially dislike the idea and I feel sure that it would be a bad settlement and one that would be pregnant with trouble. . . . I find it difficult to believe that Redmond would accept it. . . . It would, however, no doubt be worth risking a good deal to obtain a settlement by consent and if Redmond shipwrecks such a settlement we shall find ourselves in a much better tactical position."

Meanwhile Asquith had paid his visit to Balmoral and heard from Lord Stamfordham and the King how the Unionist leaders had received his overtures. He had also received Mr. Churchill's account of his discussion with Bonar Law. Aware perhaps that Bonar Law was less hostile than Lansdowne to the notion of excluding Ulster, Asquith wrote to him and suggested a meeting. Bonar Law consulted Lansdowne who agreed that he must accept the invitation, and thought it best for Bonar Law to see Asquith alone. It was important to keep the meeting secret. Bonar Law therefore decided that the best rendezvous would be at Aitken's country house near Leatherhead which was in an isolated position where there would be little danger of their privacy being disturbed. Accordingly, after luncheon on October 14th Asquith drove down from London to Leatherhead. He arrived to find Bonar Law, characteristically, engaged in a game of double dummy with his host – the need for secrecy precluding a four.

It was the first time that Asquith and Bonar Law had met on other than formal occasions, but after a sticky beginning their conversation became more cordial, and it lasted about an hour. Bonar Law wrote an account of it immediately afterwards and sent a copy to Lansdowne, also to Balfour. "I am sending a copy to Mr. Balfour," he wrote to Lansdowne, "for of course neither you nor I would dream of having secrets from him." Bonar Law's account is so interesting if only for the candour with which he appears to have expressed himself to Asquith that substantial extracts are given below:[q]

15th October, 1913.
"Notes on Conversation with the P.M.

"I had a conversation with Mr. Asquith which lasted for about an hour, The conversation was very frank, but the larger part of it quite irrelevant, dealing, for instance, with personalities in the House of Commons and general subjects of that kind. . . .

"On my part the conversation then took the form of my pointing out how difficult such an arrangement [exclusion] would be for us, and I called his attention to these difficulties; the chief of them being:

"(1) danger of the Unionists in the South and West thinking that we had betrayed them, which would make any action on our part impossible if they were unanimous in that view;

"(2) that the probable result of an agreement would be that the Welsh Bill would go through under the Parliament Act, and that, whatever may be the feeling of the party, it is my belief that a very much larger number of our Members in the House of Commons would, if they had to choose, prefer Home Rule rather than the disestablishment of the Church;

"(3) that if the question of Ulster were removed one of the strongest points in our favour in an Election would be gone and our chance of winning it would, in my opinion, be diminished, and that also (and with this he entirely agreed) there was still in our party a strong survival of the differences connected with the 'Die-hard' movement, and that if there was any suggestion of what would be regarded as a second climb down there would be much more danger of a split in the party than would be the case in ordinary times.

"He then discussed his difficulties which were of course connected with the Nationalist Party. He said that we of course were in the habit of speaking of him as absolutely dependent on the Irish, but as a matter of fact, it was really the other way; that the Nationalists without the support of the Liberal Party were powerless, and that if he or the Government decided on any course which commanded the support of their own party the Nationalists would have no choice but to accept it. . . .

"I pointed out to him that in our opinion the real way out was in a General Election. He then said: 'What would be the use of that?' – as Carson had clearly stated that Ulster would resist whatever happened at an Election. I said to him, that might be true, and it was obvious that Carson, or any leader of the Ulster people, must take that line because the chance of winning an Election would be increased by the strength of the belief among the people of England and Scotland that Ulster was irreconcilable in the matter. I told him, however, that since Carson had come back I had myself said to him that while we pledged ourselves to support Ulster to the utmost if there were no Election, that pledge was contingent, and if an Election took place and the Government won, our support would be withdrawn; and I added that Mr. Asquith must understand as well as I did that this made all the difference, and that it was really the certainty of British support which made the strength of the Ulster resistance. . . .

"We then discussed what would happen if they went straight on with their present programme. He said that what would happen in that case was purely speculative, that no one could tell what the effect on public opinion would be if they resolutely carried out what they believed to be the law. I agreed that nobody could know in advance; but I told him that in my opinion, at bottom one of the strongest feelings in England and Scotland was Protestantism, or dislike of Roman Catholicism, and that if Protestants of Belfast were actually killed, then in my belief, the effect in Great Britain would be not only that the Government would be beaten but that they would be snowed under.

"I then said to him that of course the prospect before us was not attractive. We should have to try by all means to force an Election, and to be successful we should have to take means which would be distasteful to all of us, and in saying that, I hinted at the possibility of disorder in the House of Commons, of using the letter of the Parliament Act, and as a result of all this of his finding that the Army would not obey orders. He very mildly expressed surprise that we had pledged ourselves so definitely to support Ulster in resistance. In regard to that I pointed out to him that before I had made the speech at Blenheim, which he thought so outrageous, I had carefully read what had been said on the same subject in 1886 and 1893 not only by Randolph Churchill but by Lord Salisbury, Mr. Balfour, the Duke of Devonshire and the Duke of Argyle; that in substance what I had said was simply a repetition of what had been said by them . . .

". . . Then Mr. Asquith said: 'We have had a very interesting conversation, and I shall write you again later;' to which I replied, 'Yes, we have had a very interesting conversation, but I do not see that the result of it is any change in the position.' He said, 'Yes, there is, for I clearly understand what your position is;' to which I replied, 'Well, to avoid misunderstanding, I would like to know what your understanding is.' 'Your position,' he said, 'is this: that subject to no general outcry that they are

betrayed on the part of your supporters in the south and west, and assuming that what is meant by Ulster is satisfactorily arranged, if we left out
Ulster then you would not feel bound to prevent Home Rule being given
to the rest of Ireland.' I replied that that was not quite the position, as I
had made it clear that the first thing we should have to do would be to
make sure that we had the support of the colleagues whose adhesion to
any scheme would be essential, as in my opinion it would be quite impossible to go on with any proposal if we found that any of the prominent
leaders of our Party would be disposed to fight against it. He accepted
this, and then repeated his declaration of our position, as far as I can
remember, in these words: 'Subject to the agreement of your colleagues
whose concurrence is essential to you, if there were not a general outcry
against you in the south and west of Ireland, if Ulster (which we can at
present call X) were left out of the Bill, then you would not feel bound to
prevent the granting of Home Rule to the rest of Ireland.' I accepted that
statement as correct, and that is where the interview ended."

The Cherkley conversation caused some perturbation among the
Unionist leaders. Writing to Lansdowne Bonar Law was most pessimistic:[r]

"I do not like the position, and I am sure that the next move will be for
Asquith to sound the Nationalists. There is therefore a very great danger
that we shall be invited into a Conference in which they have made up
their minds to exclude Ulster. They would, I am sure, be reasonable in
their definition of Ulster, and would probably propose something like this:
that the four counties remain in the Union and as regards the two counties
a plebiscite should be taken and if they decide not to join in the Irish
Parliament they would be free to remain as they are. I don't believe
Carson could possibly accept this solution;[1] and yet it would be so reasonable that I think we should be in a hopeless position if we had to refuse it.
I hope, therefore, that there will be no conference and the best thing that
can happen for us is that he (Asquith) should find that the Nationalists are
irreconcilable."

Lansdowne of course shared these views to the full, and was far
from happy about the last part of Bonar Law's memorandum. He
was himself only prepared to agree to exclusion because "unless I am
mistaken the omission of so important an area would virtually knock
the bottom out of the Bill and necessitate its transformation into a
different measure".[s]

The conversation with Asquith was followed by a pause during
which both leaders made public speeches. Asquith began on October
25th with a speech at Ladybank of Delphic obscurity. Bonar Law
replied from Newcastle a few days later. In the interval the King

---

[1] It is difficult to see why not; but at this time Carson was still talking in terms of the
whole Province of Ulster, the "historic" Ulster of nine counties. Perhaps Bonar Law had
that in mind.

endeavoured to persuade Bonar Law to answer in conciliatory tones to Asquith's speech. Bonar Law replied:[t]

October 28th.

"My Dear Stamfordham,

"Many thanks for your letter. I quite realize all you say and in my speech tomorrow I shall certainly say nothing to close the door against some attempt at settlement by agreement; but Asquith's speech seemed to me very partisan, and mine will not be more polite than his.

"Yours very sincerely,

A. Bonar Law."

The two speeches did not advance matters. Asquith therefore suggested another meeting at Cherkley, and on November 6th the two leaders met with the same careful precautions for secrecy which had been taken on the first occasion. The meeting was again friendly and this time the problem was discussed in much more concrete terms. Obviously in any discussion of "exclusion of Ulster", everything depended first on what was meant by "exclusion" and secondly, what was meant by "Ulster". Bonar Law recorded the discussion thus in a memorandum of which he sent copies to Lansdowne and Balfour:[u]

"Mr. Asquith then said that there were one or two ways in which separate treatment could be given to Ulster; one was the suggestion of Sir Edward Grey, Home Rule within Home Rule; a second that Ulster might be excluded for a definite term of years, to come in automatically at the end of that time to the Irish Parliament; and the third, exclusion with the right of the people of Ulster, if they chose, to come in.

"To this I replied, if there was to be any suggestion of a settlement at all it was utterly useless unless it would remove the determination of the people of Ulster to resist . . . and therefore I was certain that no proposal would even be considered by them which did not leave them in precisely the same position as the people of England and Scotland. To this Mr. Asquith replied that I had given the answer which he expected, and further conversation was on the assumption that the exclusion is only to be terminable by a plebiscite by the people of Ulster in favour of joining the Irish Parliament."

The question of what was meant by exclusion was to be of great importance in subsequent discussions, and indeed was the rock upon which these negotiations ultimately foundered. However, the upshot of Bonar Law's second conversation with Asquith was that the latter agreed to propose exclusion of either the four or the six counties at the next Cabinet meeting, exclusion with an option to come under Dublin after a term of years.

According to Bonar Law's memorandum Asquith said:[v]

"I shall definitely make this proposal to my Cabinet on Tuesday and I think I can carry my Cabinet and my own Party with me. I have had no communication with the Nationalists and what they will do I do not know. As soon, however, as I have got the agreement of the Cabinet, Birrell will approach the Nationalists.

"I then said: 'I am not in the least afraid, Mr. Asquith, of your trying to jockey me, but I am afraid of your colleagues.' To this he replied: 'You need have no fear. I shall say nothing to them except that I put this proposal before you and you replied that you could of course say nothing about it until you had an opportunity of consulting your friends.' "

Bonar Law appears to have understood from this conversation that if Asquith could not persuade the Nationalists to agree to the exclusion of Ulster he would dissolve Parliament. The following day he wrote to Walter Long:[w]

"He [Asquith] told me definitely that he would propose to the Cabinet the exclusion of Ulster, either the four counties or the six – probably the six; that if they agreed he would then see the Nationalists; and my impression is that he had definitely made up his mind that an agreement on these lines is the only alternative to a General Election.

"From a party point of view I hope the Nationalists will not agree, for, if they do, I am afraid that our best card for the Election will have been lost. On the other hand if he makes us a definite proposal on these lines I don't see that we could possibly take the responsibility for refusing."

Bonar Law's account of this discussion does not tally with the account given by Asquith's biographers and based on Asquith's own notes.[x] These suggest that Asquith was far less forthcoming and far more non-committal than Bonar Law appears to have recognized. At this distance of time it is impossible to determine who was right. What is quite certain is that Asquith never seriously attempted to put before the Cabinet the only proposal which would have been acceptable to Bonar Law and Carson – viz. exclusion of Ulster with the option to come in later if an Ulster plebiscite pronounced in favour of joining. From then onwards Bonar Law was convinced that Asquith had broken his word to him.

The Cabinet did indeed discuss the possibility of excluding Ulster for a term of years to be followed by automatic inclusion, unless Parliament in the interval amended the Home Rule Act, but it was admitted by everyone, including Lloyd George who made the suggestion, that the Ulster Unionists would never agree to such a proposal since it involved abandoning the whole principle for which they were fighting. Even this modified proposal was rejected by

Redmond whom Asquith saw on November 17th. He firmly declared his determination to accept nothing less than "Home Rule within Home Rule", i.e. a large measure of autonomy for Ulster, but an autonomy subject always to the final supremacy of a Dublin Parliament.

While Asquith was consulting his friends Bonar Law was meeting equally serious difficulties from his supporters. Gloomy predictions emanated from Lansdowne. Walter Long bombarded him with memoranda denouncing all compromise. The Cecils proclaimed their hostility to Home Rule of any kind even if the whole Province of Ulster were excluded. It became clear that Bonar Law and Carson would not find it easy to carry their own party even as far as the very limited compromise which they had put forward. Meanwhile from the enemy camp no news came through. A black fog seemed to have settled upon the deliberations of the Liberal leaders and all through November little could be discovered except dubious gossip and distorted rumour. Then at last Asquith broke silence and suggested yet another meeting.

The two leaders met for the third time at Cherkley on December 9th. Since Asquith was prepared to go no further than Redmond would allow him to go, their conversation was inevitably abortive. Bonar Law refused to consider exclusion of Ulster on either of the bases put forward by Asquith, and reaffirmed the Unionist view that if exclusion were to be a solution at all, it could only be exclusion with an option to join in, after a term of years and then only if a plebiscite in Ulster so declared. In communicating his account to Lansdowne, he observed:[y]

"I really do not understand why he took the trouble of seeing me at all. The only explanation I can give is that I think he is in a funk about the whole position and thought that meeting me might keep the thing open at least."

There was an irritation in Bonar Law's tone that is unusual with him. By now indeed tempers were beginning to become frayed everywhere and the Irish Problem was becoming an obsession. The following letter from Curzon shows that even the highest circles were not immune.[z]

Chatsworth,
December 10th, 1913.
"My dear Bonar Law,

"I rather wish the papers had reported what I said about the various possible solutions[1] at my public dinner on Wednesday, for Edmund Talbot who was there could tell you that it was not unacceptable to the audience.

[1] For Ireland.

But even our own papers are very bad about reporting anyone but you, Lansdowne or Carson, and it hardly seems worth while making speeches which can have no influence on public opinion. . . .

"I had a long talk with the King last night. He is particularly incensed just now with Harcourt who has apparently been using some very in-discreet, or as the King says, 'damned impertinent' language about the Royal Prerogative.

"The King talks vaguely about using that instrument in some formidable manner not so far disclosed (and I daresay not even discovered).

"The King was less temperate in language and more excited in manner than at Balmoral. He is of course greatly keen on a settlement.

"Forgetting, I think, that Lady Crewe was the wife of an eminent Cabinet Minister he poured into her astonished ear terrific denunciations of Lloyd George on the subject of pheasants and mangold worsels.[1]

"Yours sincerely,

Curzon."

Bonar Law concluded from his final discussions at Cherkley that Asquith had decided to let matters drift and was hoping that if the Unionists refused an offer of Home Rule within Home Rule they would get little sympathy from the British electorate. His irritation at Asquith's apparent change of front was undoubtedly tempered by the reflection that it saved him from an awkward situation. There seemed no likelihood of Asquith proposing a compromise which would split the Unionist Party. All shades of party opinion would be against Home Rule within Home Rule, and Bonar Law's task of preserving the party's unity was made easier. As for the conversations at Cherkley, they had at least narrowed the issues which divided Conservatives and Liberals, and Bonar Law had learned a good deal about Asquith's attitude. Asquith himself found Bonar Law much less ferocious than his public utterances suggested and wrote of the conversations:[2a] "if we did not make much progress it was certainly from no lack on his part of courtesy or of honest endeavour to under-stand and appreciate an opponent's point of view." But the truth was that the differences, however much narrowed, still remained im-possible to reconcile, and, even if the two leaders could have reached agreement, they would have had immense difficulty in carrying their own perfervid supporters with them.

Negotiations were now almost finished, although Asquith did make a somewhat tentative last minute overture direct to Carson. There was, however, nothing new that he could offer and Carson who con-sulted Bonar Law at every step had no hesitation in rejecting the

[1] Lloyd George had recently justified his Game Bill by alleging that whole fields of mangold worsels were devoured by pheasants – a complaint which not even the most crotchety farmer has ever made.

proposals. Bonar Law was by now convinced that Asquith's motives were purely tactical and designed to put the Unionists in as bad a position as possible if a General Election took place. On January 15th, 1914, in a speech at Cardiff, he officially announced that negotiations for a compromise were at an end. A frosty exchange of letters followed between Bonar Law and Lord Stamfordham.[2b]

Lord Stamfordham to Bonar Law   Windsor Castle,
                                      January 20th.

"My dear Bonar Law,

"The so far barren results of the conversations between the Prime Minister, yourself and Sir E. Carson, together with the tone of your respective speeches at Cardiff and Belfast, lead the King to fear that the prospects of settlement by consent are much less bright than they appeared to be a few months ago.

"His Majesty was sorry to learn from the Prime Minister that Sir E. Carson felt unable to consider the last proposals which the former had elaborated with much thought and care entirely on his own responsibility and which he hoped might have proved a basis for discussion, and that the only alternative acceptable to Sir Edward would be the total exclusion of Ulster.

"Assuming that the Prime Minister has gone to the limit of his concessions the position seems to be:

Government Proposal	*Opposition Proposal*
Prime Minister's veiled exclusion of Ulster.	Total exclusion of Ulster for Unlimited period.
– Declined by Opposition.	– Declined by Government.

"But the King recognizes, and takes comfort in, the fact that though for the moment there may be a hitch in the conversations, still the two parties have come nearer than could have been expected judging by the somewhat inflexible attitude mutually assumed at the close of the last parliamentary session.

"The Prime Minister is ready to make important modifications of the Bill and to introduce further guarantees which would grant almost practical autonomy to Ulster – but she refuses to come under an Irish Parliament.

"You, on behalf of the Unionists, would withdraw your opposition to an Irish Parliament so long as Ulster is not represented in it and is allowed to remain as she is. It is a question of sentiment and, to some extent, *amour propre*.

"His Majesty still clings to the belief in British common sense and trusts that by 'give and take' by *all* parties concerned an amicable solution may yet be found. For this reason His Majesty strongly urges upon you the importance of not allowing the negotiations to come to an end.

             "Believe me,
                     Yours very truly,
                       Stamfordham."

Bonar Law's reply was unyielding, for he regarded Stamfordham's letter as substantially incorrect on the facts.[zc]

Bonar Law to Lord Stamfordham.   January 26th.

"My dear Stamfordham,

"I have been for a short time on the Continent, and on my return I read with the greatest interest your letter of the 20th inst.

"It is hardly necessary to discuss the account which you give of the conversations; but in order to prevent any misunderstanding, I think it right to say that your summary does not accurately represent what took place. No 'proposals' of any kind were made by the Government. The Prime Minister, indeed, in the earlier interviews expressed, as I understood him, his intention of proposing to his Cabinet that Ulster, or part of Ulster, should be excluded from the operation of the Bill. He withdrew later from that proposal, and made instead a suggestion which, if we had agreed to it, would have meant that we should accept, as the basis of discussion, that the Home Rule Bill should apply to the whole of Ireland, with modifications which would indeed have given a large measure of autonomy to Ulster but which would not have removed the ground which has already induced the people of Ulster to take up arms – their determination to be governed by the British and not by a Dublin Parliament.

"On our part, also, no proposals were made, but I did indicate that while our objections to Home Rule remain unaltered, we were ready in order to avoid civil war to take as the basis of discussion the exclusion of Ulster from the operations of the Home Rule Bill, accompanied by the modifications which would thus be rendered necessary, including the consideration of safeguards, for the minority in the rest of Ireland.

"I am sorry to say, therefore, that I do not share the hopeful view which your letter expresses. So far from thinking that the possibility of agreement is greater than when Parliament rose, I now despair of any agreement between the two Parties. When I first met the Prime Minister, as I have already indicated, I had the hope that a basis of negotiations might be found; but the later interviews with myself and the subsequent conversations with Sir Edward Carson have convinced us that the Prime Minister will take no step which does not secure the approval of his Nationalist allies; and on that basis, as has been made clear by the speeches of the Nationalist leaders, no settlement is possible. I am convinced, therefore, that unless definite proposals are made which would prevent the armed resistance of Ulster any further conversations would serve no other purpose than to continue the policy of drift, which can only have the most disastrous results.

"In our belief there are now only two courses open to the Government: They must either submit their Bill to the judgment of the people, or prepare to face the consequences of civil war.

"In these circumstances, it would be a great misfortune if His Majesty were led to believe that there was any hope of the dangers with which the country is threatened being removed by delay. I would therefore respectfully suggest that His Majesty might now usefully consider whether the time has not come when he should write to his Ministers the letter which in the autumn he indicated to me that it was his intention to address to them.

"I wish to add that I have shown your letter and my reply to Lord Lansdowne and some of our colleagues at a meeting today, and that the views which I have expressed to you are entertained by all of us.

"Yours very sincerely,
A. Bonar Law."

Lord Stamfordham replied a few days later:^{zd}

Lord Stamfordham to Bonar Law.   Windsor Castle,
                                                  February 2nd, 1914.

"My dear Bonar Law,

"Please forgive my delay in acknowledging your letter of January 26th.

"The King was very sorry to learn from it that you despair of any agreement between the two parties; and that in the opinion of you and your colleagues there is no alternative other than a General Election and civil war.

"The King is not prepared to take so pessimistic a view of the situation though, as he always has done, fully realizing the very serious attitude of Ulster.

"As to any special communication to his Ministers, His Majesty's action will be guided by time and circumstances.

"Believe me,
Yours very sincerely,
Stamfordham."

Evidently the King had changed his mind about the advisability of even trying to persuade Asquith to dissolve Parliament. When the suggestion of a special letter to his Ministers had been made in September the King favoured it and indeed actually promised Bonar Law, at Balmoral, that he would send it. Some light on his change of mind is thrown by a letter which Bonar Law received from Lord Derby.^{ze}

Lord Derby to Bonar Law.   Knowsley,
                                                    Lancashire.
                                                 January 26th, 1914.

"My dear Bonar Law,

". . . I have been at Windsor this week and had some conversation with the King about the political outlook. . . . The line he takes is that though from his point of view an Election would take the responsibility off his shoulders it would be no real solution of the Irish problem, that, if we won, it would only mean trouble in the three Nationalist provinces and that, if we lost, Carson and his Ulster people would still refuse to obey the law, still fight and, except that they would be unofficially supported by English Unionists, the position would not be materially improved.

"But what evidently weighs most with him on this question of forcing an Election is that Asquith has apparently in so many words told him that as the Election of 1910 was Lords against the People so this Election would be King against the People and that he [Asquith] would certainly take that line himself in his speeches. Can you imagine anything more iniquitous – they are evidently using their 1910 tactics and bludgeoning the poor man with every sort of threat of revolution – that the Conservatives will be known as the King's party – that even if they win this time they would be beaten the next time – and that the King would then be looked upon by his new government as being hostile to them, etc.

"I did all I could to counteract these threats, but it is difficult to do so.

"Yours sincerely,

Derby."

It was clear now that there was no longer any hope of the King insisting on a dissolution. There can be little doubt that the King was well advised to follow Asquith's counsel. Any other course was liable to land him in a political controversy of the greatest difficulty. Bonar Law, however, was most indignant at Asquith's alleged conduct. "If Asquith is really talking to the King in the way you suggest," he wrote back to Derby,[zf] "it is even more disgraceful than I believed." But he had to accept the facts. From now onwards he turned his attention to a different means of forcing a dissolution, the history of which will be dealt with in the next chapter.

4

These negotiations have been described in detail, partly because this is the first occasion upon which the inner counsels of the Unionist Party during this period have been revealed, partly because of the light thrown on Bonar Law. Certain conclusions seem to emerge from these transactions.

In the first place Bonar Law, who has been often painted as an extremist on the Home Rule issue, was in reality a good deal more moderate than many of his colleagues. He and Carson were both ready to consider a compromise settlement. Neither was prepared to use Ulster in order to sabotage Home Rule for the rest of Ireland. It is true that Bonar Law was faced by the most complicated cross currents as he endeavoured to steer his course, the well-meant intervention of the King, the fanaticism of his own supporters, the indiscretion of F. E. Smith, the dangers of a party split, but he steered it as best he could with a strong sense of responsibility, ever aware of the danger to the nation involved in letting matters drift into civil war.

Secondly, although it was Bonar Law who in the end broke off negotiations, the blame for their failure lies far less with him than with Asquith. Had Asquith been ready, as he had promised, to brave the wrath of the Irish Nationalists, he could have made an offer on the lines of the second Cherkley conversation, that is exclusion of the six counties with an option to come in if a plebiscite so declared at some later date. Asquith led Bonar Law to believe that he would carry this proposal in the Cabinet, and that he would be able to force it on Redmond. Such an offer Bonar Law would have accepted, and it would have been a real solution – in fact the solution which in a modified form, after years of storm and tribulation, ultimately prevailed. But instead Asquith receded from his earlier position and refused to go beyond "Home Rule within Home Rule" or alternatively exclusion for a term of years with automatic inclusion at the end. These were solutions which Bonar Law could never accept.

Asquith's biographers suggest[zg] that the difference between the various ways of meeting Ulster's aspirations was trivial, and imply that the Unionist leaders, by insisting upon their own preference, were displaying unreasonable obstinacy. But surely this view underestimates the very great gap between the only solution acceptable to Carson and Bonar Law, and the solutions proposed by Asquith. The essence of Ulster's claim was that Ulster was a part of the United Kingdom. Neither of Asquith's proposals recognized this claim. Home Rule within Home Rule was obviously inacceptable, while exclusion with automatic inclusion at the end of a period of years made the fate of Ulster depend upon some future General Election in which the questions at issue for the bulk of the electorate might, as in 1910, be entirely irrelevant to the question of Ulster.

It should be further remembered that Bonar Law was being assailed inside his own party for discussing any compromise at all and that he would have had great difficulty in carrying even a policy of total exclusion of the six counties, if the price were to be Home Rule for the rest of Ireland. In the circumstances it is not surprising that he applied the closure to negotiations in a summary fashion at the beginning of 1914.

This biography is not intended to justify all of Bonar Law's conduct over the Irish Crisis. His views on the constitutional role of the King have already been criticized, and his views on the use of the Army as a means of coercing the Liberals will be discussed and criticized later. But it does seem that, given the immense complications of the situation at the end of 1913, he could not easily have acted otherwise than he did over the negotiations with Asquith, and that he is not the man to blame for their failure.

CHAPTER X

THE ARMY ACT

JANUARY 26TH – MARCH 20TH, 1914

Importance of the Army – Its legal position – Bonar Law considers plan to amend the Army Act – He refers it to Shadow Cabinet – His letter to Lansdowne – Opinions of Lansdowne and Balfour – Attitude of the Army – Views of Lord Roberts – Plan for Roberts to write to the Press – Rôle of Sir Henry Wilson – His character and love of intrigue – His relations with Bonar Law – Proposal to amend Army Act abandoned – Bonar Law's motives

I

BY the beginning of 1914 all attempts at a compromise over the Irish question seemed to have failed. Bonar Law therefore began to reconsider the tactics of the Unionist Party. The official doctrine of the Party throughout all this endless wrangling had been that the real crime of the Government lay not so much in the iniquity of the Home Rule Bill as in the iniquity of carrying so drastic a measure without an appeal to the country. The Party's main effort had therefore been directed at forcing a dissolution of Parliament. In order to bring this about Bonar Law and Carson had tried two methods: first, intimidation – the public threat of a civil war in Ulster backed by the whole Unionist Party; secondly, private pressure upon the King to force a dissolution. The failure of both these methods had led to the abortive negotiations for excluding Ulster, described in the last chapter.

Now, however, a third method of forcing a dissolution presented itself to the Unionist leaders – a method more perilous than either of the others. It had long been evident that the key to the situation lay in the Army. If the Home Rule Bill was passed and if Carson really did set up a provisional Government, the Bill could only be enforced by a military occupation of Ulster. As we shall see shortly, there were good reasons to suppose that if the Government ordered troops to Ulster the loyalty of the Army might well be strained beyond endurance. But, apart from this consideration, the Unionist leaders perceived in the position of the Army a method of forcing the Government to dissolve. They proposed the extraordinary course of amending the Annual Army Act in the House of Lords in such a way as to exclude altogether the use of the Army in Ulster.

To explain what the Unionists had in mind it is necessary to explain the legal position of the Army. The existence of military discipline depends upon an Act, sometimes called the Mutiny Act, which is passed every year. If this Act were not passed, the position of a soldier would be precisely the same as that of a civilian. For example, a refusal to obey orders could only be dealt with as an ordinary breach of contract, a soldier who struck his superior officer could only be punished by an action for assault in the ordinary courts of the land. In other words the entire basis of military discipline would disappear if the Army Act was rejected. The reason why the Act is passed annually dates from the days of the Revolution Settlement in 1689. The purpose was to prevent an arbitrary executive – in those days the King – from using the Army to destroy the liberties of the nation. By refusing to pass the Act, Parliament could make the Army useless as an instrument of oppression.

What the Unionist leaders now proposed to do was to amend the Army Act in the House of Lords in such a way that the Government would be unable to use the Army in Ulster until after a General Election. This would put the Government into a position of the utmost difficulty. If they accepted the amendment the Opposition would evidently have won a great victory, but even if they rejected the amendment their position was no better. The House of Lords could refuse to pass the Army Act at all, thus putting all military discipline into suspense, and depriving the Government for two years of the use of the Army everywhere. Since no Government could afford to carry on in such circumstances a General Election would become inevitable before the Home Rule Bill became law.

The price of such tactics on the part of the Unionists was a high one. They would have been tampering with military discipline for political purposes at a time when the international situation had become dark and lowering, at a time when a well-disciplined Army might be the only bulwark of national safety. On any view such tactics were reckless in the extreme, and it is an astonishing revelation of the extent to which the Irish problem had dazzled, almost blinded, the leading politicians of the Conservative Party, that they should have even considered such a perilous course; although in the end, it is only just to add, they did not adopt it.

It has long been known that some Conservatives contemplated action of this sort. Indeed, Lord Willoughby de Broke announced publicly in the House of Lords on February 10th, 1914, his intention of moving such an amendment. But he was notoriously a fanatical Die-hard. What has not hitherto been revealed is the extent to which even responsible Unionist leaders were prepared to go – Bonar Law not least among them. Understandably the biographers of the leading Conservative politicians have displayed a certain reticence over the matter. For example, Mr. Ian Colvin in his biography of Carson scarcely mentions it. It is true that Sir Austen Chamberlain in his reminiscences, *Politics from Inside*, is slightly more informative, and Sir Henry Wilson's diary refers to the Unionist proposal. But in general the subject has remained shrouded in the mists of discretion.

The plan was suggested to Bonar Law by a correspondent as early as December 5th, 1913.[a] There is nothing to show his reaction to the proposal. At that time he still hoped for a compromise over Ulster, which would have made such a drastic step unnecessary. But, by the middle of January, negotiations for a compromise were brought to an abrupt end. He now appears to have begun a closer examination of the Army Act. On January 26th, 1914, he discussed the matter with Lansdowne. Lansdowne was doubtful about the wisdom of amending the Army Act. How could the Unionists justify so drastic a method of forcing an Election, unless there was some guarantee that the Ulster Party would accept the verdict of the electorate?

But Lansdowne agreed that further investigation should be made. Both he and Bonar Law were afraid that the Government might discover some legal flaw and use the Royal Prerogative to circumvent an Act of Parliament, somewhat as Gladstone had when he abolished the purchase of Army commissions by use of a royal warrant. They decided to consult Sir Robert Finlay, a leading Unionist lawyer and later destined to be Lord Chancellor, and to lay the matter before the Shadow Cabinet on February 4th. Finlay advised them that a suitably worded amendment could not be evaded, and he submitted a specimen draft for the Shadow Cabinet to discuss.[b]

Meanwhile, even before he heard from Finlay, Bonar Law had become convinced that an amendment to the Army Act was the only effective weapon left to the Unionists. On January 30th he expressed his views at length in a letter to Lansdowne, who had departed to Bowood, his country house in Wiltshire:[c]

"You were quite right", he wrote, "that logically our case is not complete so long as the Ulster leaders do not undertake to abide by the decision of the electors but there is no help for that, for certainly no such pledge could be given by them. . . .

"I am myself becoming more and more convinced that we must take this step (amend the Mutiny Act), and so far everyone to whom I have spoken is of the same opinion, including the three Cecils, Selborne, Austen Chamberlain and Carson. It is indeed a serious step but after all it is not so serious as allowing the Government to drift into a position where force is used in Ulster; and it is the only step I see which we can take within the letter of the constitution. I trust therefore that you will take the same view and I should very much like to see you a little while before the general meeting (of the Shadow Cabinet) takes place.

"So far as I can judge if we take that action we shall compel an Election. They will of course attempt to raise the cry against the House of Lords, but really the effectiveness of that cry has always depended upon the subject upon which the Lords were attacked, and that is a risk we must take. . . . If we miss this opportunity then really no other is left except to put pressure upon the King, and of the two I am sure you will agree that the latter would be the greater evil.

"If this course is not taken then so far as I can see one of two things must happen. Either the Government will have an Election selected at their own convenience after they have made in the most elaborate way the proposals for the protection of Ulster which were suggested to Carson. Such an Election would seem to me to be as bad for us as anything could be . . . for I am afraid that a great many people would think these proposals so reasonable that Ulster would not be justified in resisting, and that it would settle the Irish question. The other possibility is that they would go on with their Bill, and from a party point of view that would be advantageous to us, I think, for it would mean bloodshed in Ulster; but I am convinced Asquith will not take that course.

"It seems to me, therefore, that it is a question between an Election more or less forced by us on what we will try to represent as the plain issue: Shall the Army be used to coerce Ulster without the consent of the electors? Or on proposals for Home Rule which to moderate men will not appear unreasonable."

Lansdowne replied:[d]

"I quite realize that we may have to take action on the Army Bill, although as you know, I rather dread the step. As at present advised I do not see any other way out."

On February 2nd, Bonar Law consulted Curzon whose views were similar to those of Lansdowne.[e] He disliked the plan but had no alternative to suggest.

There was one other important person to consult. Bonar Law wrote to ask the views of Balfour who could not come to the Shadow Cabinet. The ex-Conservative leader was at this time delivering the Gifford lectures at Glasgow University upon the subject of "The Knowledge of God". But the preoccupations of the philosopher did not extrude the counsels of the politician. He wrote back at once:[f] "The proposal to modify the Army Annual Bill is one of extraordinary interest and importance, and I am not greatly moved by Lansdowne's objections." But he went on to raise a subtle objection of his own. The effect of the proposed amendment would not only be to prevent the use of the Army to impose Home Rule on Ulster. Might it not also preclude the Army from protecting the Roman Catholics of Belfast against Orange bigotry? Or at all events might not the Government say that this was so?

"It would", wrote Balfour, "of course be no reply to this to say that there was never a time when mob violence was less to be feared in Belfast than at the present time. This is true; but it is no effective debating point."

Balfour went on to point out the dangerous precedent that such action might give in the event of labour unrest. He ended:

"As is usually the case when I write to you, I feel that my letter may perhaps rather add to your troubles than diminish them. But I need hardly say that whatever course you adopt I shall do all I can to support it."

The Shadow Cabinet met on Thursday, February 4th, at Lansdowne House to discuss this and other problems. Parliament was to open in six days' time, but there was no urgent need to deal with the Army Act. That measure did not have to be renewed until April 30th and so there was plenty of time to discuss the problem. The meeting decided, as meetings usually do over awkward questions, to delegate the matter to a committee. This consisted of Finlay, Carson, Lord Robert Cecil, Cave, and the venerable Lord Halsbury, sprightly still despite his great age, and ever ready to advocate an extremist policy.[g]

2

What meanwhile was the attitude of the Army itself during these months? The Army was not a mere passive automaton. It consisted of officers and men whose feelings on religious and political subjects were just as strong as those of their fellow citizens; and on the issue of Home Rule perhaps even stronger. The increasing impoverishment of the Anglo-Irish gentry had resulted in a high proportion of that class, especially the younger sons, making the Army their career. Moreover, then as today, Ulstermen were particularly numerous among Army officers. To all these officers any proposal for the "coercion of Ulster", as it came to be called, was profoundly repugnant. Already Bonar Law had told the King that he doubted whether the Army would obey the Government if ordered to attack Ulster. At the same time, it will be remembered, he told Mr. Churchill that

G

the Unionist Party would in such circumstances actively encourage
Army officers to disobey orders.

The situation was in fact full of danger. The Ulster volunteers were
commanded by General Richardson, a retired regular soldier, and
contained a number of half-pay officers. Field Marshal Earl Roberts,
the most beloved and respected soldier of his day, victor of the South
African War, was a violent opponent of Home Rule. It seemed more
than probable that an armed conflict with Ulster would provoke a
major cleavage in the Army, and that this cleavage would not be
confined to the officer class. Some soldiers would undoubtedly feel
obliged to obey orders however repugnant. Others would feel that
this was civil war and that an issue had arisen upon which a man
could only be guided by his own conscience. In fact it was clear by
the end of 1913 that, quite apart from any move in the House of
Lords to amend the Mutiny Act, the Army might prove a broken
reed if the Government tried to coerce Ulster. Bonar Law kept in
close touch with the leading opponents of Home Rule in the Army.
He corresponded frequently with Lord Roberts and there exists
among his papers a draft, corrected in both Bonar Law's and
Carson's handwriting, of a letter which was to appear in the Press
under Lord Roberts's name. Among other expressions it contained
these words:[h]

"Every day I receive letters from soldiers asking my advice, and in my
heart and conscience I believe it to be my duty in the interests of the
country to utter this word of warning. It is a soldier's duty to obey but if
and when civil war breaks out no ordinary rules will apply. In that case a
soldier will reflect that by joining the Army he has not ceased to be a
citizen and, if he fights in such a quarrel, he will fight on the side which he
believes to be right. If the attempt be made to coerce Ulster, Civil War,
and nothing else will inevitably follow. Ulster will not be fighting against
the Crown or the Flag, and it will be idle to describe such men as 'the
King's enemies'."

The plan was that this letter, which Bonar Law forwarded to the
Field Marshal on January 27th, 1914, would be published in the
Press simultaneously with the moving of an amendment to the Army
Act. In this way the maximum effect would be obtained upon public
opinion. The letter was never published, nor was the amendment
ever moved, for in the end events made such a step unnecessary. But
the episode is vivid evidence of the lines upon which the leading
Unionists were thinking in the early months of 1914.

There was another important military figure with whom Bonar
Law kept in the closest touch. This was Major-General (later Field

Marshal) Sir Henry Wilson who was at this time Director of Military
Operations at the War Office. He too was an Anglo-Irishman like
Lord Roberts, but, whereas the latter's role was to give his great
name and prestige to a public demonstration, Wilson's activities were
of a more clandestine nature. His key position at the War Office gave
him an intimate knowledge of military secrets, and he seems to have
regarded it as quite compatible with his official duties to pass confidential information to the Leader of the Opposition, where such
information might be of value in the struggle against Home Rule.
Wilson's activities in the cause of Ulster were indeed almost ceaseless. They are described in great detail by himself in his diary, lengthy
extracts of which were published by his biographer, General E. C.
Callwell.[1] These revelations were deplored by many grave persons on
the ground that they damaged Wilson's posthumous fame. This may
be true, but biographers should not – and fortunately do not always –
publish only what flatters their subject and gratifies his friends.
Wilson's diary is a document of the greatest interest, and history
would be the poorer had it been bowdlerized or suppressed.

No one could less have resembled the conventional picture of the
military man than Sir Henry Wilson. His very appearance was unusual; the enormously tall and bony frame; the intelligent, ugly and
curiously enigmatic countenance. His conversation was equally unorthodox – an extraordinary compound of gravity and buffoonery;
for even when discussing issues of life and death he would frequently
introduce into his discourse the language and the antics of the clown.
These characteristics did not endear him to his Army colleagues, by
whom he was, indeed, profoundly mistrusted as a schemer. Had they
been familiar with the poets they might well have applied to him
Dryden's famous couplet.

> "For close designs and crooked counsels fit
> Sagacious, bold and turbulent of wit"

Nor would they have been far wrong. For Wilson all his life was
devoted to the art of secret intrigue. Intrigue was the very fibre of
his being. He was never more at home than in the atmosphere of plot
and counterplot and labyrinthine manoeuvre, which prevailed in
high Army circles at this time. His partiality for intrigue did not in
itself differentiate him so greatly from other soldiers for, contrary to
popular belief, it is by no means an uncommon feature of the military
profession. What marked Sir Henry Wilson was his success at it. He

[1] E. C. Callwell, *Field Marshal Sir Henry Wilson,* 2 vols.

was of course an able man, and he possessed the gift of clear and lucid exposition which is so often denied to soldiers, but it is nevertheless remarkable that a man, whose actual military accomplishments were singularly small, should ultimately have reached the post of Chief of the Imperial General Staff, the most coveted and influential position in the British Army.

It is true that Wilson got on much better with politicians than with soldiers, and to this he doubtless owed much of his success. But politicians are not fools, and there must have been some real qualities in a man who so greatly impressed such otherwise diverse characters as Lloyd George, Bonar Law, Balfour and Mr. Churchill. Whatever those qualities were, they must have depended largely upon charm and personality, for they have not survived in the cold written words which are the historian's evidence. They have vanished into oblivion, extinguished for ever by the bullets of the Irish murderers who shot down Sir Henry Wilson on the steps of his London home in 1922.

Bonar Law met Wilson for the first time in July 1912. He formed at once a favourable impression of Wilson's character and intelligence. Wilson was equally impressed by Bonar Law.

"I was very much pleased", Wilson wrote in his diary,[i] "by his quiet unostentatious manner and his exceedingly logical and practical mind. . . . He gives me the impression of being thoroughly honest and upright, anxious and determined to do all in his power to save the country."

From this time onwards he regularly kept Bonar Law primed with information which would help him to ginger up the Government over military matters. Wilson was also well acquainted with the military preparations in Ulster and gave advice to the Ulster volunteers, visiting Belfast for that purpose early in 1914. In the middle of March he had a long discussion with Bonar Law over the question of amending the Army Act. Even Wilson had some doubts about taking such a step. He was better aware of the dangerous international situation than the Conservative leaders. But Bonar Law's arguments convinced him.

"We had an hour's talk and he entirely persuaded me to his side. The proposal is for the Lords to bring in an amendment to the effect that the Army shall not be used against Ulster without the will of the people expressed at a General Election. This gets over my difficulty. . . . We discussed it all backwards and forwards, the handle it will give against the Lords, the possibility of no Army remaining after April 30th, the effect abroad; and I am convinced Bonar Law is right. Desperate measures are required to save a desperate situation."[j]

In the end, however, the Unionists dropped the proposal. Even before the Curragh Incident Bonar Law seems to have had some doubts about pursuing the question any further. As late as March 16th, while still favouring the amendment, he admitted that he had not finally made up his mind. He wrote thus to a correspondent who objected to the plan:[k]

"We have undertaken as a Party to assist Ulster. Here is a method which is strictly constitutional, for nothing is clearer than that the method by which the Army is maintained has been adhered to for the express purpose of putting a check on the Executive Government and preventing it from using the Army against the 'will of the people'."

He went on to claim that such a step, far from bringing the Army into politics, was the only way of keeping it out, for if the Army was ordered by the Government to attack Ulster a real disruption would occur. He added, however, that he would not recommend such action if it seemed likely to divide the Party. He ended:

"This is as so often happens a question in regard to which any decision is fraught with great risk, but a decision will have to be taken by Lansdowne and myself, and even now the difficulties are so great that neither of us has made up his mind what decision we shall take."

The Curragh Incident, which made the whole plan obsolete, occurred on the afternoon of March 20th, and the news did not reach London until the evening. Nevertheless on the 20th, even before he heard this news, Bonar Law had changed his mind about amending the Army Act. Writing to J. P. Croal, the editor of *The Scotsman*, he said:[l]

"It would be fatal to do it if there were any serious opposition to it in our ranks, and I think there is a sufficient amount of that feeling to make it impossible to do it."

Bonar Law's papers do not show why he had come to this conclusion. There was, as we saw earlier, opposition of a somewhat inconclusive nature from Curzon and Balfour, and Lansdowne too disliked the plan. It may be that their objections were in the end decisive. Asquith's biographers hint at another possibility. They claim that Asquith knew what the Unionists were proposing, "but was able to bring influences to bear which caused it to be still-born".[m] But they give no evidence for this suggestion, and there is nothing in Bonar Law's papers to show that any pressure direct or indirect came from Asquith, or from the King. As late as March 18th many prominent Unionists still favoured the extremist course. That night Wilson spoke to Mr. Amery who supported it, and later dined with Carson, Milner and Dr. Jameson (of the Jameson Raid). "They all

agree", he wrote,[n] "the Lords must amend the Army Annual Act."
It is not a matter of great importance to decide why Bonar Law
changed his mind. The most probable reason is opposition from the
rank and file of his own Party, many of whom were retired officers
from one of the Services and who may well have been alarmed at
the implications of their leader's policy. In any case it is quite
possible that Bonar Law would again have changed his mind before
April 30th, the latest date at which the manoeuvre could be accomplished.

However that might be, late on the very day when he wrote the
letter to Croal, quoted above, news came through of a series of sensational events in Dublin. The Curragh Incident transformed the
entire situation. It was now no longer necessary to amend the Army
Act. As a means of coercing Ulster the Army had become useless.

CHAPTER XI

THE CURRAGH INCIDENT

MARCH 1914

Liberal plans – Lloyd George's proposal – Churchill's menacing speech – General Paget summoned from Ireland – Troop movements ordered – Motives of the Government – Suspicion of Carson – Carson fears arrest and leaves for Ulster – Bonar Law warns against using Army in Ulster – New evidence on Government's motives – Churchill's orders to the Navy – His bellicose observations about Belfast – Paget addresses his brigadiers on March 20th – His confused remarks – Alternatives presented to his officers – Gough and 57 officers resign – Alleged "misunderstanding" – Bonar Law's scepticism – Gough and Paget summoned to London – Bonar Law's plans to exploit the situation – His dealings with Wilson – Asquith tries to pass the matter off – Bonar Law refuses to give him time – Gough at the War Office – Memorandum by Cabinet – Seely adds the "peccant paragraphs" – Triumph of Gough – Fury of the Liberals – Was Seely a scapegoat? – Resignation of Seely, French and Ewart – Asquith becomes War Minister

I

To explain what followed we must abandon Bonar Law for the moment and examine the secret councils of the Liberal Party during these weeks. Bonar Law and Carson had finally rejected Asquith's proposals at the end of January 1914. There then began a series of complicated discussions between the Government and the Irish Nationalists. Lloyd George and Birrell, the Irish Secretary, represented the Cabinet, and from the fertile brain of the former emanated the following plan. The Government should propose an amendment to the Home Rule Bill, which would give a separate option to each county in Ulster to remain outside Home Rule for six years. At the end of this period they would automatically be included, unless of course Parliament should have determined otherwise in the interval.

The motives behind this proposal were tactical, as Lloyd George in his memorandum to the Cabinet, virtually admitted.[1] Any proposal, he said, "must have two essential characteristics:

(1) It must be an offer the rejection of which would put the other side entirely in the wrong, as far as the British public is concerned; and

[1] Lloyd George's Memorandum is printed in full in Denis Gwyn, *Life of Redmond*, pp. 256–8.

(2) It must not involve any alteration in the scheme of the Bill; so that if it is rejected the Unionists cannot say, 'Why you yourselves admitted that your Bill needed amendment.' "

It was highly improbable that the Unionists would accept – and it is most unlikely that Asquith, or Lloyd George, or Redmond, expected them to accept – such a proposal. On the other hand their reasons for rejection might well seem unplausible to the public. There was a further point. As Lloyd George observed in the same memorandum

"It would be almost impossible for them to justify armed resistance in these counties at the present moment if such an option were given to them; and the same observation applies even if they rejected it."

Such action, Lloyd George continued, would be a rebellion in anticipation of a hypothetical act of oppression which could not occur for six years. In this way the whole sting would be drawn from the Ulster movement. The plan was certainly ingenious and, after much running to and fro, it was ratified by Redmond. He did not like it and consulted with the Catholic Hierarchy before giving his assent. Moreover, he insisted that it should be the last concession which the Government would make. If the Unionists rejected it then the Bill must go through – the whole Bill and nothing but the Bill.

On March 9th Asquith unfolded his proposals to the House of Commons on the occasion of the second reading of the Home Rule Bill. They fulfilled Bonar Law's worst expectations. He left the main speech of rejection to Carson who could alone, he said, speak for Ulster. Bonar Law, however, put the position clearly:

"The message that the right hon. Gentleman [Asquith] really sends to the people of Ulster is this: 'You have by your organization extending over two years placed yourselves in an impregnable fortress and therefore I do not ask you to submit now to a Nationalist Parliament. What I ask is that you should destroy your organization, and that you should leave your fortress, that you should come out into the open and then when you are weak you will be compelled to do what today when you are strong you will not do. . . .'
". . . If you think it is wrong to compel them [Ulstermen] to come in today, how can you think it right to compel them to come in tomorrow. . . ?"

On behalf of Ulster Carson totally rejected the proposal. The time limit came in for his bitterest attack. "Ulster", he declared, "wants this question settled now and for ever. We do not want sentence of death with a stay of execution for six years."

The Unionists' refusal even to consider this la test compromise proposal appears to have roused the indignation of the Government – or at all events to have made the Liberals confident that they had at last put the Opposition in a bad tactical position. Events now moved rapidly to one of the most dangerous political crises in recent British history.

On March 14th Churchill made a speech at Bradford, which was widely interpreted as a declaration of war upon Ulster. He condemned Bonar Law as "a public danger seeking to terrorize the Government and to force his way into the Councils of his Sovereign". He described Carson's convention at Belfast as "a self elected body composed of persons who, to put it plainly, are engaged in a treasonable conspiracy". There were, he said, "worse things than bloodshed even on an extended scale". He finished on an ominous note:

". . . If Ulster is to become a tool in party calculations; if the civil and Parliamentary systems under which we have dwelt so long, and our fathers before us, are to be brought to the rude challenge of force; if the Government and the Parliament of this great country and greater Empire are to be exposed to menace and brutality; if all the loose, wanton and reckless chatter we have been forced to listen to, these many months, is in the end to disclose a sinister and revolutionary purpose; then I can only say to you, 'Let us go forward together and put these grave matters to the proof'!"

On the same day that Churchill made this important declaration, Colonel Seely, the Secretary of State for War, sent a letter of instructions to General Sir Arthur Paget, the Commander-in-Chief in Ireland.[a] The gist of this letter was that "evil disposed persons" might attempt to seize government stores of arms and ammunition, that special precautions should be taken to safeguard depots, and that the stores at Armagh, Omagh, Carrickfergus and Enniskillen – all places in Ulster – were especially liable to attack. Paget replied that it would be better to withdraw the stores – at any rate from Omagh and Armagh rather than reinforce the garrisons, because troop movements of this sort might precipitate a crisis in Ulster. Paget's reply, however, crossed with another letter from Seely summoning him to London for instant consultation. Paget spent Wednesday and Thursday, March 18th and 19th, in prolonged discussions with Seely, Churchill and Sir John French, the Chief of the Imperial General Staff. Unfortunately no written record of these discussions was ever made, and it remains uncertain even to this day exactly what was said. All that can be stated definitely is that Paget's refusal to reinforce the Ulster garrisons was overruled and he was instructed to send 300 men to Enniskillen, 100 men in two cruisers to Carrickfergus which commands the arm of the sea leading to Belfast, 300 men to Omagh and 100 men to Armagh. Furthermore, a battalion of infantry was to go to Dundalk in order to protect a brigade of artillery stationed there, and the Dorset Regiment stationed in Belfast was to move at once four miles out of the city to the Holywood Barracks. This latter move was to be made so quickly that if necessary the men were to leave their rifles behind, having first rendered them useless by removing the bolts.

Moreover, it is admitted by all parties that the discussions at the War Office dealt also with the wider question of the troop movements which would be necessary in the event of an open rebellion in Ulster. Paget was told that he could expect very heavy reinforcements from England, and his plan of campaign in such an eventuality was discussed in some detail. Both Asquith and Churchill however denied subsequently that any actual orders for troop movements on this scale were given. The conversations were, they said, purely hypothetical and precautionary. There was no question of an unprovoked attack on Ulster.

Neither then, nor later, have any really convincing reasons been given for the Government's sudden alarm about Ulster. After the Curragh Incident it became part of the Unionist case against the Government to claim that certain Ministers were engaged in a deliberate "plot" to provoke a situation in Ulster which would compel a large scale intervention by the Army. Under the excuse of restoring law and order, so the Unionists were to argue, Seely, Churchill, and Lloyd George were determined to smash the Ulster Volunteers, occupy all the key points in Ulster, and enforce the Home Rule Bill. This explanation was of course hotly denied by the Liberals who maintained that nothing was intended beyond purely precautionary moves against a possible attack from hot heads among the Ulster Volunteers.

The more extreme statements of the Unionists can be dismissed as the heat engendered fantasies of party strife. Nevertheless, it does remain curious that the Government at no time published any evidence for its fear that "evil disposed persons" were contemplating a seizure of arms in Ulster. If police reports to that effect existed, as Asquith's biographers claim, then why not publish them, and so refute the Unionist charges?

The only fresh evidence on this in Bonar Law's papers is a letter written to him by H. A. Gwynne, editor of the *Morning Post*, a month after the Curragh Incident. Gwynne was reporting a long conversation with Sir John French, the C.I.G.S., who had by then resigned. According to French, Seely told him about March 6th that the Government possessed secret information that certain hot heads among the Ulster Volunteers – not Carson or Craig – proposed to take matters into their own hands and move southwards to attack Dublin. Gwynne writes:[b]

"Sir John French at first pooh-poohed this information but when it was reiterated with many assurances that the Government had every reason to believe that it was quite correct he advised that Sir A. Paget should be sent for. . . .

"On Thursday, March 19th, Sir A. Paget was at the War Office discussing the final details [of the precautionary moves]. He also talked of the bigger operations which might become necessary and said in a wild kind of way:

" 'I shall lead my army to the Boyne'.

"Whereupon Sir John told him not to be a 'bloody fool'."

Sir John French's soldierly admonition did not, however, have any success, and there can be little doubt that much of the trouble which followed was due to Paget's own excessive fears of trouble in Ulster together with a muddle headedness and stupidity remarkable in an officer of his rank and position. It remains extraordinary that in so delicate a matter Paget did not obtain clear written instructions from the Secretary of State for War or from the Army Council. The situation was not helped by the personal character of Seely who, though possessing the qualities of loyalty and courage in an eminent degree, united with them those of vanity, flamboyance, braggadocio and a certain obtuseness. But whatever the explanation of the Government's motives may be, it is quite clear that no danger of a move by the Ulster Volunteers in fact existed. Carson had them well under control and the last thing that he would have allowed was a *coup de main* against Dublin. From his point of view such an act would have been lunacy.

However, events conspired to produce the maximum possible confusion on both sides. Carson and Bonar Law were well aware of the fact though not the details of the discussions at the War Office and drew the conclusion that drastic action was imminent. If the Government feared some sort of *coup* on the part of the Ulster Volunteers, it is equally true that Carson anticipated a *coup* on the part of the Government. It was widely rumoured that Asquith had at last decided to strike and that warrants were out for the arrest of Carson, Craig, and some of the leading Ulster Unionists. Bonar Law had tabled a vote of censure on the Government which was due to be debated on March 19th and 20th. Carson had intended to go to Ulster on the 20th and the plan was for him to wind up for the Unionists. But in view of the highly circumstantial rumours of his forthcoming arrest he decided to leave a day earlier, thus missing the division, but rendering his arrest as difficult as possible.

On March 19th Bonar Law set the tone of the Opposition by issuing a grave warning against the use of the Army to coerce Ulster:

"If it is only a question of disorder, the Army, I am sure, will obey you and I am sure it ought to obey you; but if it really is a question of civil war, soldiers are citizens like the rest of us (Hon. Members, 'No!'). It never has been otherwise in any country at any time. If it is civil war whether it is right or wrong . . . the Army will be divided and you will have destroyed the force, such as it is, upon which we depend for the defence of this country."

Carson, though determined to go early, had no intention of departing in silence. He was even more defiant than Bonar Law, he indicated his knowledge of the discussion with Paget, and he openly accused the Government of deliberately planning to provoke a conflict in Ulster. He challenged the Government to use the Army if it dared:

"You will have become brave in entrenching yourselves behind the Army. But under your direction they will become assassins."

Soon afterwards Carson and eight other Ulster Unionists left the House of Commons. As usual with Carson the departure was superbly stage managed. There was a great demonstration, the entire Unionist Party rising to their feet and cheering wildly for several minutes.

Carson's departure added even more confusion to a highly confused situation. It is hardly surprising that in the heat of the moment members of the Government concluded from his language, actions and demeanour that he meant to take some decisive step in Ulster and perhaps even proclaim the Provisional Government. Actually a moment's thought would have shown that this was most unlikely, for it was impossible to see what Carson could have gained by precipitate action of this sort before the Home Rule Bill became law. However, none of the political leaders on either side was in the mood for cool reflection. What followed is best described by Gwynne in his letter to Bonar Law, from which quotation has already been made:[c]

"It will be remembered that on Thursday afternoon Sir E. Carson left the House of Commons for Ireland somewhat dramatically. Sir John French that same evening was dressing for dinner when he was telephoned to come at once to 10 Downing Street, and he was enjoined to come by the garden entrance and not the Downing Street door. He hastily dressed – drove down arriving at 7.30.

"At 10 Downing Street he found the Prime Minister, Mr. Birrell [the Secretary for Ireland], Colonel Seely, Winston Churchill, A. Paget.

"He was informed that the Government believed that Sir E. Carson had gone over to Ireland to proclaim the Provisional Government, that this might mean civil war, that it therefore behoved the Government to take every precaution. Again the subject of the artillery at Dundalk was discussed. Sir John French was still of opinion that it should be recalled to the Curragh, but the Prime Minister over-ruled him and ordered a battalion of infantry to be sent to defend the batteries. . . ."

This account bears the stamp of truth and would go far to explain the alarmism of Paget, and his curious conduct which led directly to the Curragh Incident and which will be described shortly. Meanwhile one further episode should be noted.

The Cabinet had decided a week earlier, though without fixing a definite date, that the 3rd Battle Squadron, which was in Spanish waters, should move to Lamlash on the Isle of Arran some sixty miles across the sea from Belfast. On the same Thursday evening that Paget, confused and perturbed by his complicated discussions at the War Office, returned to Dublin. Churchill gave orders that the 3rd Battle Fleet should steam immediately to Lamlash. He did not tell Asquith of this decision which, though technically within his own sphere of discretion, was a matter upon which the Prime Minister might legitimately have expected to be informed. In his *World Crisis 1911–14*, p. 154, Churchill says:

"It was thought that the popularity and influence of the Royal Navy might produce a peaceable solution even if the Army had failed."

If Sir John French is right Churchill's language at the time was rather different. Gwynne writes:[d]

"On Friday (March 20th), just before dinner, Sir J. French was told by Winston Churchill that if Belfast showed fight 'his fleet would have the town in ruins in twenty-four hours'."

Gwynne ends:

"In conclusion it is only just to say that Sir J. F. warmly denies that there was a plot but he always adds, 'unless it was devised behind my back'."

2

We must now return to Paget who arrived at Dublin early on day morning, March 20th. At 10 o'clock he summoned all his adiers and addressed them at some length. Once again there exists no undisputed record of what was said, but Bonar Law's papers contain a full account[e] written at the time by Brigadier General Hubert Gough who commanded the 3rd Cavalry Brigade, and this can be supplemented by Sir Hubert Gough's recently published memoirs[1]. Paget began by announcing that active operations were imminent against Ulster and that he expected "the country to be in a blaze by Saturday".[2] Paget then looked pointedly at Gough and said:

"You need expect no mercy from your old friend at the War Office" – meaning Sir John French.

"The only effect of this menace", writes Gough,[f] "was to put up all my heckles at once. Why should I be picked out to be threatened?"

Paget had however extracted certain concessions from the Army Council to officers who had scruples about engaging in operations against Ulster. For once he had obtained something in writing and, although we do not know for certain exactly what he said, we do know the instructions which he held in his hand. They read as follows:

"The War Office has authorized the following communications to officers:

1. Officers whose homes are actually in the Province of Ulster who wish to do so may apply for permission to be absent from duty during the period of operations and will be allowed to 'disappear' from Ireland. Such officers will be subsequently reinstated and will suffer no loss in their career.

2. Any other officer who from conscientious motives is not prepared to carry out his duty as ordered should say so at once. Such officers will at once be dismissed from the Service."

Whether or not Paget actually read out these instructions he certainly conveyed their gist. He concluded by ordering the brigadiers to put these alternatives to their officers and bring back the answers to him that evening.

In view of the controversy which ensued it is as well at this stage to make two points clear – first, that officers who elected to be dismissed under paragraph 2 were in no conceivable sense guilty of mutiny or insubordination. They were presented with certain alternatives and ordered to make a choice. The authorities who gave that order had no right to complain at the choice which was actually made. The

---

[1] *Soldiering On*, Chapter VI.
[2] This is what Gough writes in his original statement in the Bonar Law Papers. In *Soldiering On*, p. 101, he says that Paget declared that he did not expect any bloodshed. The point is not of great importance. What is important is the fact that Paget announced "active operations" against Ulster.

second point is that such a hypothetical question ought never to have been put to serving officers. Whoever was responsible – and it is by no means clear who was – had made a grave error. The right thing to do, if the Government really expected trouble in Ulster, was to order such troop movements as were deemed necessary, give no choice at all, and rely on loyalty and military discipline to produce obedience. It should never be forgotten that Gough himself, who came to be regarded as the personification of Army resistance to the coercion of Ulster, declared both at the time and subsequently, that if *ordered* to move north he would have done so.

He writes in his memoirs:[g]

"The truth was that we had obeyed orders. We had been ordered to make a choice between two alternatives that had been forced on us."

Gough had no doubt about his own choice. Despite the fact that he was one of the youngest brigadiers in the Army, and had a brilliant professional career in prospect, he elected at once for dismissal. But he made no attempt to influence his officers. He put the alternatives before them, and told them that in this, perhaps the gravest decision of their lives, they must be guided by their own consciences. Fifty-seven out of seventy officers in Gough's brigade decided to choose dismissal rather than be involved in active operations against Ulster. But they resolved to make their position clear and Gough wrote on their behalf to Paget that he and all his officers were quite prepared to carry out their duty if all that they were being asked to do was to preserve property and maintain order.[h]

"But if the duty involves the initiation of active operations against Ulster the following . . . would respectively and under protest prefer to be dismissed."

On receipt of this letter Paget at once telegraphed to the War Office:

"Regret to report Brigadier and 57 officers, 3rd Cavalry Brigade, prefer to accept dismissal if ordered north."

This sequence of events shows beyond dispute that Paget himself believed that the operations contemplated were something far more than the enforcement of law and order. The point is of importance since Churchill later tried to argue that Gough had in some way misunderstood Paget and had received a false impression that active operations were contemplated against Ulster, although in fact nothing of the sort was intended by Paget. But if this had been the case Paget would at once have realized that there was a misunderstanding as soon as he received Gough's letter, and would presumably have had further discussions with him before accepting the resignations. Instead his immediate reaction was to send the above telegram to the War Office. The only reasonable explanation is that Paget himself rightly or wrongly believed that his orders entailed active operations against Ulster.

The following brisk exchange which took place in the House of Commons on March 30th shows what Bonar Law thought of the theory that Gough had misunderstood Paget.

"MR. CHURCHILL: '. . . It is admitted that a misunderstanding on the point arose.'

"MR. BONAR LAW: 'Rubbish!'

"MR. CHURCHILL: 'Do I understand the Rt. Hon. Gentleman to say, "Rubbish"?'

"MR. BONAR LAW: 'Yes.' "

It remains possible that the "misunderstanding" occurred at an earlier stage and that Paget misunderstood the orders given to him by Seely and French. But since the Government in all the lengthy debates which followed never gave any coherent account of what those orders had been, it is not surprising that Bonar Law and his colleagues became more and more convinced that sinister and discreditable secrets were being suppressed.

The news of the resignations, received on Friday evening, produced consternation at the War Office. If any orders existed for an attack on Ulster they were at once countermanded: it was clear that the Army could not be relied upon for drastic measures against the Ulster Volunteers. Seely at once telegraphed Paget to refuse to accept the resignations, and Asquith learning for the first time on the following morning of Churchill's orders to the 3rd Battle Squadron immediately cancelled them.[i]

Meanwhile on Saturday morning Paget, alarmed at these events, harangued Gough and his officers at the Curragh. His address to them, if Gough's account is correct, was not calculated to clarify the situation. He now stated that his operations were going to be purely defensive, that "he had no intention of making war on Ulster . . . that if fighting took place against Ulster forces he would order all his men to lie down and not return the fire and then he and his generals would advance alone through the firing line and parley with the men of Ulster". But he then went on to say that it would be necessary "to hold the line of the Boyne" while 25,000 men were being brought over from England; which sounded a somewhat drastic measure of "defence". He continued thus, according to Gough:[j]

"He said that if officers liked to indulge in the luxury of sentiment they must pay for it . . . he had expected that only 'a few religious fanatics' would accept dismissal. . . . He said that no resignations would be accepted . . . that senior officers would be tried by Court Martial. He said we must clearly understand that this was the direct order of the Sovereign[1] and asked 'if we thought he would obey the orders of 'those swine of Politicians'."

Gough and his colleagues understandably declined to pay any attention to this extraordinary farago, and persisted in their resolution to resign. A heated scene followed in which Paget apparently again told Gough that he need expect "no mercy from Sir John French", and Gough replied that he did not ask for any mercy.

Scarcely had this discussion ended than instructions arrived summoning Gough and his three colonels to report immediately to the War Office in order to explain their conduct. Paget too was ordered at once to London. By Sunday morning, March 22nd, therefore, all the principal actors in this curious drama were at the War Office. There can be little doubt that the original intention was to make an example of Gough and any other officers who could be regarded as ring leaders, but it soon became clear to Asquith and his colleagues that such action might well provoke wholesale resignations throughout the entire Army. Asquith was, therefore, in a dilemma. If he took disciplinary action against Gough and the three colonels, the Army might crumble entirely. If on the other hand he tried to persuade them to withdraw their resignations, it was all too probable that they would only do so on the explicit condition that the Army would not be used to coerce Ulster. But a bargain of this sort would be indignantly repudiated not only by Redmond and the Irish Nationalists but by a very large section of the Radical and Labour members, upon whose support Asquith depended. It was a most difficult predicament, and no easy solution seemed in sight. He decided that the wisest course was to pass off the whole affair as a misunderstanding.

Bonar Law was, naturally, determined to exploit this situation to the uttermost limits. He first heard the bare news of the events at the Curragh in an anonymous telegram which arrived on Friday night.

---

[1] This was quite untrue. The King knew nothing of all this till he read the news in the papers that morning.

At 9.30 on Saturday morning, the busy and ubiquitous Sir Henry Wilson came round to Pembroke Lodge with further details which he had obtained from Gough's brother. Bonar Law, though still in the dark about much that had happened, at once telephoned Lord Stamfordham urging him to warn the King of the dangers ahead and pressing once again the case for either a referendum on Home Rule or the complete exclusion of Ulster.

Meanwhile Sir Henry Wilson had been spending the day consulting Unionist politicians and leading soldiers about the terms to which the Army would agree.

"I told Sir John [French]", wrote Wilson in his diary for that day,ᵏ "that there was still time to stop the breakaway of the officers if he made Asquith take instant action, but it must be done at once or the General Staff would break away next. Sir John was not yet seized with the gravity of the situation. After much coming and going of Sir John to Seely the latter asked what the army would agree to and I was asked to put it in writing."

Wilson's terms were a promise on the part of the Government not to use the Army against Ulster and the reinstatement of all officers who had resigned. But he adds, "Sir John took this paper to Seely and I gathered it was not agreeable to Asquith and his crowd". Asquith was anxious to avert a general defection in the Army and to persuade Gough to withdraw his resignation but he was not prepared to allow the Army to dictate terms to the Government.

The following day, Sunday, March 22nd, was a busy day for Bonar Law. First, he saw the Archbishop of Canterbury who was somewhat surprisingly acting as intermediary for Asquith. To him Bonar Law declared that, although it would give great dissatisfaction in the Unionist Party, he would agree to accept the Home Rule Bill if the six counties were totally excluded from its provisions. Any offer less than that was out of the question. The Archbishop replied that Asquith could never persuade the Irish Nationalists to agree to such terms. The deadlock therefore remained unbroken. Then Bonar Law saw Wilson who gave him the full story of what had happened at the Curragh as derived from Gough and his colleagues, and secondly, the terms which he, Wilson, was endeavouring to negotiate for the Army. Bonar Law backed Wilson strongly, and agreed that, in view of the Government's apparent anxiety to reinstate Gough and his brother-officers, it was vital for them to refuse to return except on a clear understanding in writing that the Army would not be used to coerce Ulster.[1]

That evening Bonar Law dined with his principal colleagues at Lansdowne House. Wilson was invited but thought it prudent to decline. The Unionist leaders were all agreed that the Government had intended to provoke a crisis in Ulster; that Paget's blunders had put the Government in a false position, from which they were anxious to withdraw; that Bonar Law had been entirely right in promising full Unionist support to the resigning officers. If Gough and Wilson played their hands correctly, it would now be impossible to coerce Ulster. There would be no need to worry about amending the Army Act. Ulster would be secure.

Bonar Law, with the full concurrence of his colleagues, wrote at length to Asquith that afternoon.[m] He declared that he intended to raise the whole question of the Army on the motion for the adjournment the following evening. He repeated his pleas for either a referendum on the Home Rule Bill or an amendment wholly excluding the six Ulster counties. He warned Asquith that if a Unionist Government came to power it would certainly reinstate any officers who were dismissed as a result of the Curragh Incident. He told Asquith that he was sending a copy of the letter to Lord Stamfordham so that the King would be informed of his proposals.

Later on the same day Bonar Law wrote to Carson forecasting with some accuracy the dilemma in which Asquith would be placed, if, as now seemed probable, he endeavoured to avoid trouble in the Army by reinstating Gough:[n]

". . . after what he has done I do not see how Gough could agree, if he were reinstated, to take his regiment to Ulster, except on the distinct assurance that he would not be asked to use his troops to coerce Ulster to accept a Home Rule Bill, and that pledge of course the Government could not give."

The Curragh Incident inevitably produced a crop of the most lurid rumours in London. All Saturday and Sunday stories were rife of large scale mutinies, of a head-on conflict between the Army and the Government. On Monday morning, however, there appeared in *The Times* an authorized communication from Asquith. Asquith stated that the troop movements were purely precautionary, that the Government did not intend – and never had intended – to arrest the Ulster leaders, that the Government did not mean to institute "a general inquisition into the intentions of officers in the event of their being asked to take up arms against Ulster", that the trouble over General Gough was due to an "honest misunderstanding". At the same time Asquith replied to the letter in which Bonar Law had warned him that the Opposition would demand an explanation in the House on Monday afternoon.

"There has been", wrote Asquith on Monday morning,[o] "much exaggeration in the statements that have been published and the incident at the Curragh (which was due to a misunderstanding) is at an end. . . . Would it not be more convenient to everyone that the discussion (if desired) should take place on the 2nd reading of the Consolidated Fund Bill on Wednesday rather than a motion for adjournment at 8.15 (on Monday)?

"Yours very truly,
H. H. Asquith."

Bonar Law had no intention of allowing Asquith another two days in which to wriggle out of his predicament. He replied immediately to Asquith's letter:[p]

"I am much obliged by your letter but I shall feel bound to press upon you the course I suggested yesterday. The feeling is so strong that I am confident that it will not be possible to go on with business in the ordinary way till the position of the Army has been discussed."

We must now return to Gough and his colonels. On Monday morning, March 23rd, Gough was summoned to the War Office. He firmly refused to withdraw his resignation without a written guarantee that his troops would not be used against Ulster.

French told Gough that if he would return to his brigade he (French) would give him the guarantee demanded.

"This put me into some difficulty," writes Gough, "because I had no faith in Sir John's promises but I did not at all want to say so. I explained rather lamely that a mere verbal report by me to my officers would not convince them."[q]

Deadlock having been thus reached, French took Gough to see Seely who delivered a long and pompous harangue on the principles of the Army Act. Gough still refused to move without the written guarantee. Seely declared that no Government would submit to such dictation from a servant of the Crown. Gough goes on:

"At this moment Sir John rescued everyone from a very difficult impasse by saying: 'Perhaps General Gough has not made it quite clear that he feels he would not be able to reassure his officers unless he shows them something *in writing*.'

"I knew this was nonsense but I felt it gave Seely the chance of extricating himself. . . .

"Seely then said, and his relief could not have been more obvious though his manner was still very condescending: 'This puts a new light on your request.'"

Seely then went across to a Cabinet meeting at 10 Downing Street, having first instructed the Adjutant General to draft and send across a memorandum in reply to Gough's request. Before the draft arrived Seely was summoned to Buckingham Palace in order to placate the King who was – understandably – in a fury because the War Office had neglected to inform him on the Curragh Incident and he had learned about it for the first time when he opened his morning newspaper. Seely therefore missed the Cabinet discussion of the Adjutant General's draft, for, when he returned, the meeting had broken up for lunch. Only Lord Morley remained behind. The first three paragraphs of the memorandum as revised by the Cabinet read as follows:[r]

"You are authorized by the Army Council to inform the Officers of the 3rd Cavalry Brigade that the Army Council are satisfied that the incident which has arisen in regard to their resignations has been due to a misunderstanding.

"It is the duty of all soldiers to obey lawful commands given to them through the proper channel by the Army Council either for the protection of public property and the support of the civil power in the event of disturbances, or for the protection of the lives and property of the inhabitants.

"This is the only point it was intended to put to the officers in the questions of the General Officer Commanding, and the Army Council have been glad to learn from you that there never has been and never will be any question of disobeying such lawful orders."

Seely was under the impression that he could, if he wished, add further words to explain the memorandum, and apparently Lord Morley, who had been present throughout the discussions, was also under that impression. Seely, accordingly, sent it over to Sir John French at the War Office, who showed it to Gough. Gough would not at once commit himself and asked time for reflection. He promptly consulted Sir Henry Wilson who perceived that the memorandum left a loophole for the Government, as was no doubt intended. For the Army might well be ordered to enforce the Home Rule Bill when it became law, under the plea of protecting public property in Ulster. He, therefore, urged Gough to have the matter clarified in writing. At the same time he sent a message to Bonar Law telling him what had happened.[s]

As a result of Gough's request and his insistence upon obtaining an answer in writing, Seely, French, and Ewart (the Adjutant General) added two further paragraphs to the Cabinet memorandum for Gough – the "peccant paragraphs" as they afterwards came to be known. They read thus:[t]

"His Majesty's Government must retain their right to use all the forces of the Crown in Ireland or elsewhere to maintain law and order and to support the civil power in the ordinary execution of its duty.

"But they have no intention whatever of taking advantage of this right to crush political opposition to the policy or principles of the Home Rule Bill."

Wilson was not quite satisfied even with this assurance. The word "political" was a qualification to "opposition", which might still leave a way round for the Home Rulers. It could be argued that the Ulster movement was seditious, or rebellious, and not political. He persuaded Gough to write a further note asking whether the amended document "relieved him from a liability to order his Brigade to assist in enforcing submission to a Home Rule Bill". Sir John French, without consulting Seely, wrote below Gough's note the words "I should so read it".[u]

This of course constituted a complete surrender to Gough and Wilson. Armed with this document Gough and his colonels returned in triumph to Dublin and Gough received an ovation from his officers at the Curragh. Suspecting that the Government might repudiate the guarantee, he at once had the papers made over to his eldest daughter under a trust drawn up by his solicitor in Dublin.[v] When he was asked later to hand the document back he politely replied that it was not in his power to do so but that the Government should apply to the trustee. No application was ever made.

Through Henry Wilson Bonar Law was aware of the principal facts about the Guarantee when he raised the question of the Army in the House of Commons on Monday evening. Asquith, however, neither knew the exact wording of the paragraphs added by Seely and French, nor of the assurance given by French personally, until after the debate. Bonar Law naturally did not dwell on this aspect of the matter. Instead he concentrated on the "plot", and accused members of the Government of having deliberately planned to provoke a revolt in Ulster, and then to use the pretext of that revolt in order to destroy the whole Ulster movement; and he read out extracts from Gough's account of Paget's statement. He acquitted Asquith personally, and his speech was evidently aimed at Seely and Mr. Churchill. The discussion which followed was stormy. Asquith denied all these allegations, and declared that the whole business had been a misunderstanding, that Gough and his colleagues had returned to Ireland fully satisfied. There was no question of rein- statement because they had not been dismissed. To Bonar Law's question whether any conditions had been made by the officers who returned to Dublin, Asquith gave an evasive answer.

On Tuesday the Unionist leaders endeavoured to elicit further explanations from the Government, but the most that they could obtain was a promise from Seely to produce a White Paper giving all the relevant documents in the Curragh Incident. Fuel was added to the Conservatives' wrath when they learned for the first time of the orders which Mr. Churchill had sent to the 3rd Battle Squadron.

On Wednesday the White Paper was published.[w] The information that it gave was meagre in the extreme, and its clarity was not enhanced by the fact that some vital letters were printed in the wrong order, but it did reveal for the first time the paragraphs added to the Cabinet memorandum by Seely. That afternoon the scene in Parliament was more violent than ever. Proceedings opened with a question from Lord Charles Beresford about the orders given to the 3rd Battle Squadron. Mr. Churchill gave the details and also the information, new to most members, that the orders had been countermanded on Saturday, March 21st, on the ground that the "precautionary" troop moves in Ireland had been successfully accomplished. Actually the Admiralty's orders, as we saw earlier, had been countermanded by Asquith who had not known of them until that day. But this fact was not revealed for another month. Mr. Amery asked whether the First Lord had hoped to provoke hostilities and bloodshed in Ulster. Mr. Churchill repudiated this insinuation as "hellish". An uproar followed in the House.

But if the Conservatives were indignant at the "plot" the Government's supporters were equally angry at what appeared to be a complete surrender on the part of the Cabinet to Gough and the three colonels. One of the most bitter of the many bitter speeches made on that Wednesday afternoon came from a Labour member, John Ward:

"This debate is the best illustration that we workmen have ever had in this House that all the talk about there being one and the same law for the rich and the poor is a miserable hypocrisy. Hon. Gentlemen belonging to the wealthy classes have no more intention of obeying the law that is against their interests than of flying to the moon."

In these circumstances it soon became clear to Asquith that the Government would never survive, unless the "peccant paragraphs" were repudiated. Accordingly it was arranged that Seely should hand in his resignation but that Asquith should refuse to accept it and at the same time define the attitude of the Government to the Army.

It is still a matter of dispute whether Seely's "peccant paragraphs" were the result of a Cabinet decision, which was now being reversed, or of a blunder for which Seely was personally responsible and which was now being repudiated.[1] The official Liberal version was that Seely had blundered, and this has since come to be the most generally accepted view. But there are considerable difficulties in following it. If the "peccant paragraphs" were a complete reversal of the Cabinet's intention, why did Lord Morley who was present throughout the Cabinet meeting on Monday agree to them? Unless we attribute a remarkable stupidity not only to Seely – which is perhaps plausible – but to Lord Morley too, the only rational explanation is that the Cabinet had agreed to the substance of the "peccant paragraphs", but left their detailed wording to the two ministers. Indeed, unless Seely had been under that impression, it is scarcely conceivable that he would have drafted the paragraphs without at least consulting Asquith who was after all lunching in the next room. The most likely explanation is that Asquith had come to realize by Wednesday how precarious his position would be unless he promptly abandoned all semblance of a bargain with the Army. The only way to do this was for Seely to accept responsibility and act as a scapegoat, originally hoping no doubt that he would not be forced into actual resignation.

At all events whether he was a scapegoat or a blunderer, Seely made a statement on Wednesday afternoon describing the genesis of the peccant paragraphs, and he informed the House that he had placed his resignation in Asquith's hands. It was not a particularly lucid speech, for Seely did not make it clear whether his resignation had been accepted. Nor did he reveal whether the difference over the "peccant paragraphs" was a difference of substance or one of mere form. In other words did Asquith and the rest of the Cabinet object because the new paragraphs gave the *impression* that the Government had bargained with Gough, or because the new paragraphs actually did involve a bargain with Gough, a bargain which Asquith now repudiated? Seely said that he himself stood by the paragraphs and did not recede from them one inch.

Balfour then spoke and elicited from Asquith that Seely's resignation had not been accepted, and that he was still War Minister.

Asquith's explanation, though clearer than Seely's, did not allay the rising passion in the House. Bonar Law replying was frankly

[1] See Asquith's own account in *Fifty Years of Parliament*, Chapter VII, and Mr. L. S. Amery's very different version in *My Political Life*, Vol. I, pp. 448–50.

contemptuous of the whole episode of Seely's proffered resignation.

"We have heard", he said, "of people being thrown to the wolves but never before have we heard of a man being thrown to the wolves with a bargain on the part of the wolves that they would not eat him."

But, five days later, Seely really did resign. His hand was forced by French and Ewart who resigned on the ground that they had signed the "peccant paragraphs" which were now apparently being repudiated by the Government. The Government's attitude was, however, still obscure since Asquith took good care not to send any official repudiation of the Guarantee to Gough. Had he done so, he would have raised the whole question of the coercion of Ulster and perhaps provoked widespread resignations in the Army, and this he meant to avoid at all costs. But in view of the resignations of French and Ewart, Seely felt obliged to resign too, and Asquith produced a great ovation from the Liberal benches by announcing that he himself would take the War Office and combine it with the Premiership. He also announced that he would have to seek re-election on the ground that he had accepted another office, and thus, to Bonar Law's indignation, was able to escape parliamentary inquisition for the time being.

CHAPTER XII

AFTERMATH OF THE CURRAGH INCIDENT

APRIL 1914

*The "plot" – Conservative allegations – Bonar Law demands a judicial enquiry –
The Larne gun running – Government's position – Asquith refuses to submit to
further questions – Unionist grounds for believing in plot – Circumstantial evidence
– Truth still uncertain – Bonar Law's genuine belief in the plot – Accusations
levelled at him – Subversion of the Army – His conduct admittedly unconstitutional –
Reasons for his attitude – Ulsterman's feeling towards the south – His determination
to stop Home Rule – Nature of nationalist problems – Their rarity in Britain –
Question of civil war*

I

For the next month the debates in Parliament were characterized
by a degree of bitterness which surpassed even what had gone
before. The Unionists were by now convinced that Churchill,
Seely, and one or two other Ministers had planned behind Asquith's
back to provoke a crisis in Ulster which would give them the excuse
to call Carson's bluff and to suppress the whole Ulster movement.
Day after day Mr. Churchill and Asquith in his new capacity as
War Minister were bombarded with questions designed to expose
this alleged "plot" to seize Ulster. The Liberal Ministers hotly denied
these accusations, but Asquith in the end promised to produce
another White Paper giving fuller details.

On April 17th the Ulster Unionist Council issued a statement purporting to give the actual facts of the "plot". The Liberals declared
that the whole statement was a pack of lies. But Bonar Law took the
excuse of those new allegations to demand a judicial enquiry on the
unflattering ground that Asquith and his colleagues had lied so
repeatedly that their statements could only be trusted if they were
put upon oath. This not unnaturally provoked yet another scene,
and Asquith refused to consider such procedure. He offered instead
a day for a vote of censure, but Bonar Law refused. On April 22nd,
however, the second White Paper appeared.[a] It was much fuller
than the first one and contained a number of details which had not

before been made public. Bonar Law now decided that he must move a vote of censure on the Government, and this was set down for April 28th.

But in the interval an event occurred which greatly changed the situation. On the night of April 24th a ship named the *Mountjoy* landed a cargo of 35,000 rifles and 3,000,000 cartridges at Larne for the Ulster volunteers. The arms had been bought at Hamburg. The whole affair was managed with great skill, the authorities were completely outwitted, and the weapons were quickly distributed throughout Ulster. Bonar Law was not informed of the Larne gun-running until after the event. Writing several years later to Ronald McNeil, he said that Carson had deliberately kept him in the dark on the ground that it might be awkward for the Leader of the Opposition to know beforehand that such a flagrant breach of the law was imminent.[b] But Bonar Law at once associated himself with Carson and took full responsibility for what had happened.

These events created an immense sensation in the country. Asquith denounced the conduct of the Ulstermen as a "grave and unprecedented outrage", but there was very little that he could do to implement his condemnation. The Curragh Incident had made it impossible to use the Army against Ulster, and there was no hope of securing a verdict of guilty from any jury in North Ireland in the event of criminal prosecution against the Ulster leaders. Meanwhile the Unionists were jubilant. Lord Roberts hastened to offer his congratulations to Carson. The Ulster Volunteers now constituted a force which no government could easily disregard. It is not surprising that the leading Liberals began to search for some compromise formula over Home Rule.

The episode did, however, strengthen the Government in one respect. For the past month they had been to a large extent on the defensive in the House of Commons, but now they could reasonably assume a more aggressive attitude. It was not easy for the Unionists to move a vote of censure in the new circumstances. They might claim that the Larne gun-running was justified as a precaution against further Liberal "plots", but the Government could reasonably argue that it gave an *ex post facto* justification to their precautionary moves in March. If this was the sort of thing the Ulstermen had in mind, then the naval and military moves of March 20th–21st could only be censured for their inadequacy. When the Unionists brought forward their motion on April 28th Mr. Churchill declared that it was like "a vote of censure by the criminal classes upon the police".

Balfour in reply observed, "There is one character disgusting to every policeman and which even the meanest criminal thinks inferior to himself in point of morals, and that character is the *agent provocateur*." Mr. Churchill declared that this was "a charge as shocking as it is possible to make". And in this now characteristic tone the debate went on to an inconclusive end.

Meanwhile in the same debate Asquith declared that he had no intention of answering any more questions about the Curragh Incident.

"The time honoured practice of the House", he said, ". . . has been perverted and degraded in a manner reminiscent of the worst traditions of the Old Bailey, and it reminded me more than once of the saying of an eminent Scottish judge when Counsel who appeared before him apologized for the length of the cross examination and said, 'I hope it was not too long'. The Judge replied, 'Sir, it exhausted time and it encroached upon eternity'."

As the Prime Minister had by now replied to some 500 questions on matters connected with the Incident of the Curragh his attitude was understandable. This debate more or less terminated the immediate repercussions of the Curragh Incident. The House now began to turn its attention once more, though in a greatly changed political climate, to the details of the Home Rule Bill.

Two questions arise from the tangled story of this strange episode: Was Bonar Law correct in suspecting the existence of a "plot" to coerce Ulster? Did he act rightly in exploiting so fully the conflict of loyalties which the Curragh Incident created in the Army?

On the first question no final answer can be given even today, after forty years of "revelations", memoirs and biographies. We have already seen how strong the circumstantial evidence was, which almost inevitably roused the deepest suspicions of the Unionists – Churchill's menacing speech at Bradford, the sudden summoning of Paget to London, his extraordinary language when he addressed his brigadiers in Dublin, the rumours of Carson's forthcoming arrest, the flamboyant orders given by Churchill to the 3rd Battle Fleet. The attempt by Churchill and Asquith to pretend that this latter move had nothing to do with their orders to Paget met with complete disbelief from every Unionist. As for the notion, also given currency by the Government, that the whole business was a result of a misunderstanding on Paget's part of the discussions which he had with Seely, Churchill and French, Bonar Law regarded it with contempt. He found it hard to believe that the Government would have retained

Paget, if the Curragh Incident had been due merely to his incompetence, and he made ironical play of the suggestion that they were
chivalrously protecting the general.

"Here we find twenty gentlemen all willing to sacrifice the Army, the
Commander-in-Chief of the Armed forces,[1] their colleagues, and themselves, for the sake of General Paget. Such self sacrifice was never known
in history before. We have here a score of St. Sebastians who are willing
to be the target of undeserved errors all for the sake of the career of
General Paget."

The prevarication and disingenuousness of some members of the
Government, and the militancy of others – especially Churchill who
was widely regarded as the villain of the piece – combined to convince every Unionist of the genuine existence of the "plot". Bonar
Law's private correspondence with his colleagues shows beyond
doubt that his convictions were sincerely held, and were not assumed
merely in order to discredit the Government. But convictions however sincerely held are not evidence, and the Unionist accusations
no more prove the Government's guilt than the Government's denials
prove its innocence. We can never know for certain exactly what was
said to General Paget on March 18th and 19th, and still less what
were the secret hopes of some of the Ministers concerned. No direct
evidence of a "plot" has ever emerged, but that is scarcely surprising.
If there had been any such orders drafted in the War Office or the
Admiralty, they could – and certainly would – have been suppressed.
The circumstantial evidence for the Unionists' suspicions was very
strong and it is hard to believe that the whole affair was merely a
misunderstanding.

At all events, to comprehend Bonar Law's policy it is necessary to
realize not only that he genuinely believed in the existence of the
plot but that he regarded it as an outrage too. He believed that a
monstrous plan had only been thwarted by Paget's mishandling and
by the resolute conduct of General Gough. Throughout proceedings
he acted in the closest collaboration with Sir Henry Wilson who
was himself convinced of the existence of the plot. This liaison with
Wilson enabled Bonar Law to obtain secret information by which he
was able again and again to expose Asquith's prevarications. Every
time Asquith misled the House of Commons, Bonar Law and his
colleagues felt a mounting suspicion that there was some dark secret
which the Government had been trying to conceal. As the facts were
elicited – and the process was as slow and painful as drawing teeth –

---

[1] Bonar Law must have meant the C.I.G.S. The post of Commander-in-Chief had been
abolished by this time.

the Unionists, who were by now in a state of feverish and frenzied rage with the Government, became more and more convinced that Gough's action alone had frustrated a sinister conspiracy on the part of Seely and Churchill.

The latter indeed was in a most belligerent frame of mind and his speeches seldom failed to provoke an uproar and a scene in the House of Commons. Much of the intense animosity with which the Unionists regarded Churchill for many years after these events can be explained by the part which they believed him to have played in the "plot".

2

It would be wrong to think that the Liberals were purely on the defensive during this month. On the contrary the more radical members – especially of the Irish Party – were quick to claim that there had been a Unionist "plot" to suborn the Army.

"The Ulster Orange plot", declared Redmond in a message to his Irish supporters in Australia, "is now fully revealed. . . . The plan was to put up the appearance of a fight and then by society influences to seduce the Army officers and thus defeat the will of the people. . . . The issue raised is wider than Home Rule. It is whether the Government are to be browbeaten and dictated to by the drawing rooms of London, seconded by officers who are aristocrats and violent Tory partisans."

Much was made of the fact that the officers who resigned came from fashionable cavalry regiments. A Labour Member asked whether Gough was now going to form a Government. The Curragh Incident was described as a mutiny so often that it will probably go down to history under that misleading name. Bonar Law aroused special wrath. His speeches were combed by indignant Radicals for passages which would suggest that he had urged the Army not to obey orders, and Churchill accused him of instigating "an organized campaign to seduce the Army".

How much truth was there in these allegations?

Any notion that Bonar Law and his colleagues directly instigated the resignations of Gough and his officers can be dismissed at once. Bonar Law knew nothing of the events at the Curragh until late on Friday evening. He could not possibly have had the opportunity to influence Gough and his brother officers.

Nevertheless on one count the Radicals could reasonably, from their own point of view, attack not only Bonar Law but most of the leading Unionists. There is no doubt that Bonar Law had frequently expressed in public his doubt whether the Army would agree to coerce Ulster. He had, for example, quoted the analogy of James II's failure to impose despotic rule, a failure due to his Army's refusal to support him. This was not quite the same thing as positively urging the Army to disobey the Government's orders, but it was, perhaps, not very different. Moreover, behind the scenes, as we have already related, Bonar Law, in close collaboration with Wilson and Lord Roberts, had been considering the amendment to the Army Act, which would have precluded the Government from ordering the Army to Ulster. Rumours of these proposals were widely circulated. They undoubtedly reached many officers in the Army, and it cannot be denied that in encouraging such ideas the Unionists were going far beyond the limits of constitutional opposition.

Further, when once the crisis had broken, Bonar Law had no hesitation in exploiting the situation in order to make the coercion of Ulster impossible. As we have seen, he kept in the closest touch with Wilson, and Wilson advised Gough at every step in the latter's negotiations with Seely. Undoubtedly Bonar Law strongly backed Gough's efforts to obtain a written pledge that he would never be ordered to coerce Ulster, and Gough must have known that he had the full support of the Opposition, as well as a powerful group in the Army, when he made terms with Seely which rendered the imposition of Home Rule on Ulster impossible. It is in these negotiations - and not over the events at Dublin – that the Unionists can fairly be accused of using the Army for political purposes. The *Morning Post* expressed nothing more than the truth when it declared: "The Army has killed the Home Rule Bill and the sooner the Government recognizes the fact the better for the country."

Bonar Law's conduct cannot be understood unless it is remembered that he was himself an Ulsterman, and deeply felt the character of a measure which would put his fellow countrymen under the rule of their hereditary enemies in Southern Ireland. He really believed that a Dublin parliament would ruin Belfast, that the liberties of the Ulsterman would vanish, that a prosperous enlightened community would be subjected to intolerable treatment at the hands of Southern bigots, that it was an outrage to drive out from their allegiance to the Crown a population which was so clearly determined to remain loyal. Thinking like this – whether rightly or wrongly does not matter – he was bound to regard as legitimate almost any means of wrecking the Home Rule Bill.

The truth is that Parliamentary democracy depends on certain conditions, which, because they have usually prevailed in England over the last two hundred and fifty years, tend to be taken by English-men for granted. In the last resort it depends upon a minority accepting majority decisions, and this acceptance in its turn depends upon the majority not taking decisions which the minority regards as genuinely intolerable. In England, the remarkable homogeneity of the population, the absence of violent disputes, the general agree-ment over the fundamentals of society, have made such conditions prevail. Minorities accept majority decisions, because they know that these decisions will not be insufferable and because they know that the majority of today will become the minority of tomorrow. As a result we have the swing of the electoral pendulum, the political neutrality of the Army and the Civil Service, the whole tradition of peaceful change which is England's greatest contribution to the science of government.

But in Ireland these conditions did not apply. Ireland was – and is – a land of bitter, irreconcilable, racial and religious conflicts. The Protestant minority could never hope by any swing of the pendulum to become the majority. The two nations in Ireland were separated by the whole of their past history. They were divided by rivers of blood and bitterness. It was absurd to expect that the conventions which prevailed in placid England would be accepted by the Ulster Protestants with all this fear, suspicion and hatred in their hearts. For of all political disputes, nationalist disputes are the most bitter and recalcitrant. They are very seldom settled by peaceful means within the framework of a liberal constitution. On the contrary, they are usually solved, as Bismarck observed, not by Parliamentary majorities but by blood and iron. The history of the struggles in South Africa, India, Palestine, to say nothing of the terrible conflicts upon the frontier lands of Europe, testifies to this unpleasant truth.

Bonar Law at an early stage saw that the problem of Ulster was a genuine problem of frontier nationalism. As he repeatedly declared, it was ultimately a question of civil war; and in civil war the con-stitutional conventions do not apply. In a civil war you cannot expect from the armed forces that unquestioned political neutrality which is found in normal conditions. If a government, however lawfully, endeavours to pass a measure which genuinely shocks the consciences of those who have to carry it out, there will be a conflict of loyalties which cannot be dismissed by platitudes about the constitution. Much can be said – and rightly said - in condemnation of the Unionist tactics during these stormy years. But it is only just to remember that Bonar Law and his supporters genuinely believed that, in imposing the rule of the Southern Irish upon the Protestant counties of Ulster, the Government was pursuing a course which was both morally outrageous and politically calamitous. Who can say that this belief was wholly wrong?

H

remember that Bonar Law and his supporters genuinely believed that in imposing the rule of the Southern Irish upon the Protestant counties of Ulster, the Government was pursuing a course which was both morally outrageous and constitutionally iniquitous. Who can say that this belief was wholly wrong?

CHAPTER XIII

THE BUCKINGHAM PALACE
CONFERENCE

APRIL – AUGUST 1914

Proposals for a compromise – Abortive discussion between Bonar Law and Asquith – Scene in the House of Commons – Bonar Law's sharp reply to the Speaker – Ingenious plans for Tory tactics – Death of Joseph Chamberlain – Murder at Sarajevo – The Buckingham Palace Conference – Its failure – Reasons for impasse – Shooting at Bachelor's Walk – Shadow of the Great War – Bonar Law persuades Asquith to postpone the Amending Bill – Was Ulster resistance bluff?

I

THE reader is probably by now thoroughly weary of the Emerald Isle. He must, however, bear a little longer with the Irish scene. For, until August 1914 when world wide cataclysm raised far graver issues, Bonar Law's political life continued to be dominated by the Home Rule struggle.

The effect of the Curragh Incident and the Larne gun-running had been to render the forcible coercion of Ulster virtually impossible. The Liberals realized this as clearly as the Conservatives; but for Redmond's pressure, they would willingly have come to a compromise. On April 28th Mr. Churchill at the end of an otherwise violent speech did indeed let drop a hint of such a possibility. He claims that his words "gave the debate an entirely new turn". Both Balfour and Carson expressed sympathy, and on May 5th Asquith invited Bonar Law and Carson to a private discussion of the problem.

Like all such conferences in the past it produced no result. Both Bonar Law and Carson expressed their doubts as to the possibility of any compromise acceptable to Redmond. They did agree however that, if such a compromise was to be attempted, the best procedure would be an amending Bill in the House of Lords to be placed on the statute book simultaneously with the Home Rule Bill, but naturally they strongly deprecated the Home Rule Bill being passed at all in any form. One comfort the Unionist leaders did gain. According to Bonar Law's account of the discussion, Asquith "stated more than once in a most emphatic way that he would be no party to the coercion of Ulster".[a]

On May 12th Asquith announced that he intended to take the third and final reading of the Bill in the House of Commons before the Whitsun recess. He promised at the same time to introduce an amending Bill in the hope that an agreed settlement could be achieved. Bonar Law fiercely attacked this proposal on the ground that it would mean the certain enactment of the original Home Rule Bill, with no guarantee except the word of the Government that the problem of Ulster would be adequately dealt with. Nevertheless Asquith's proposal was carried by the usual majority. On May 21st a notable scene occurred during the debate on the third reading of the Bill. The Unionists endeavoured vainly to elicit from Asquith some hint of the proposals which he intended to insert in the promised amending Bill, but Asquith declined to do so. Infuriated by his refusal they started an uproar of the sort all too familiar in the House during these stormy sessions. The Speaker, unable to quell it, took the unusual – and improper – course of asking Bonar Law whether the demonstration had his assent and approval. Surprised at such a question Bonar Law rose and answered: "I would not presume to criticize what you consider your duty, Sir, but I know mine, and that is not to answer any such question." He then sat down. After making a pained comment on this reply the Speaker adjourned the House amidst continued uproar.

Bonar Law's answer was vigorously applauded by his supporters. His papers contain many letters – the most important being from Walter Long and Lansdowne – congratulating him on his conduct.[b] Indeed if any episode can be said to mark the moment when Bonar Law emerged from the inexperience and hesitancy of his earlier days into a position of undoubted ascendancy as leader of the Party this was probably the occasion. A typical expression of Conservative feeling came from Mr. L. S. Amery. "You can have little idea", he wrote, "of the enthusiasm and warmth of affection which your action on Thursday has created right through the Party."[c] A few days later the Speaker made a handsome apology for what he fully admitted to have been an error of judgment on his part.

Bonar Law needed all the prestige that he could command, for the situation still remained one of extraordinary delicacy and difficulty. There was still a strong possibility of a Die-hard revolt if the Conservative leaders agreed to any compromise on the Ulster question, however generous it might be. Indeed a letter from Lord

Middleton to Lansdowne forwarded by the latter to Bonar Law shows that Lord Middleton was engaged in planning just such a revolt.[d] It is clear too that many extremists regarded both Carson and Bonar Law as less "sound" than Lansdowne on the Home Rule problem – a notion which Lansdowne himself was quick to repudiate.

Meanwhile Asquith had announced his intention of bringing in an amending Bill in the House of Lords. At the same time the Home Rule Bill having passed its final reading in the House of Commons went up to the Lords, and, whatever its fate there, was bound to become law within a short period. A most complicated tactical problem now arose for the Unionists. Bonar Law was bombarded with memoranda and counter memoranda full of ingenious suggestions. Ought the House of Lords to reject the Home Rule Bill on the second reading, or pass it with amendments? If the latter course were adopted what should these amendments be? Alternatively, should they concentrate on amending the Amending Bill? What sort of Amending Bill had Asquith in mind? Then there was a subtle plan to hold up the Amending Bill until the Home Rule Bill reached the stage when it had to receive royal assent or lapse under the Parliament Act. If this occurred could the King give assent to a measure which, even its own sponsors admitted, would provoke civil war unless substantially altered? Another alternative, emanating from the ingenious mind of Balfour, was to pass the Amending Bill with one amendment only – that it must be followed by an immediate General Election. Small wonder that in rejecting this latter plan Bonar Law gloomily commented: "Whatever course we take will be open to the gravest objections, and is almost certain to produce great differences of opinion among our own friends."[e] For the moment, however, he could relax. The Whitsun recess had arrived. Bonar Law devoted his time to the more congenial occupation of playing golf by day and bridge by night.

As soon as Parliament reassembled the battle began again. The Amending Bill was introduced by Lord Crewe on June 23rd. Its provisions were almost identical with those proposed by the Government in the House of Commons on March 8th that is a separate option for each county in Ulster to remain outside Home Rule for six years, with automatic inclusion at the end of the period, unless Parliament had decided otherwise in the interval. We have already seen the reasons which made this proposal totally unacceptable to the Unionist leaders. Lansdowne at once repudiated the Amending Bill, and in response to Lord Crewe's request to the Unionists for constructive suggestions proposed instead the complete exclusion of the whole province of Ulster, all nine counties, from the provisions of the Home Rule Bill. The Amending Bill thus entirely transformed was due to go down shortly to the House of Commons. There was of course no possibility of Asquith, let alone Redmond, agreeing to such a drastic change.

The fury of party strife was hushed for a moment by the death on July 2nd of Joseph Chamberlain. For the past eight years a paralytic stroke had tragically removed him from the political scene, but he remained clear in mind to the end. Opinions still conflict as to the merits and defects of his character, but of the impact which he made upon English history during his thirty years of political life there can be no question. Bonar Law felt for him a deep and sincere admiration. On July 6th Asquith, showing that courtesy which mitigates even the bitterest struggles of English politics, moved the adjournment of the House as a tribute to his dead opponent. Bonar Law spoke next.

"At the time when I first entered this House I was still young enough, and indeed I hope I still am, to be a hero worshipper, and for me at that time the essence of my political faith was belief in Mr. Chamberlain. . . . He almost alone has changed the whole spirit of the relationship of the different parts of the Empire towards each other and has thus laid strongly the foundation on which other men may build. I think there is no instance in our history of any statesman who has not filled the highest post, whose name has become, like his, a household word."

Another death of far greater significance had occurred a few days earlier. On June 28th the Archduke Franz Ferdinand was murdered at Sarajevo. Yet, such was the frenzy provoked by Home Rule politics, that this grave event seems to have been scarcely noticed in Unionist circles.

At the beginning of July Asquith began to make serious overtures for a compromise, for in many ways his position was even more difficult than that of Bonar Law. He was far more closely aware of the dangers in the international situation. He knew that he could not coerce Ulster, and he knew that the Liberal Party could not afford to provoke violent resistance from the Ulster Unionists. Yet at the same time he could not remain in office without Redmond's support. The only hope seemed a compromise to which both Carson and Redmond might agree.

The first negotiations appear to have been made through Lord Murray of Elibank, the former Liberal Chief Whip, and Lord Rothermere. Bonar Law's papers contain no account of these conversations and for Bonar Law's attitude we have to rely on Redmond's note of what Lord Murray said. It is printed in Denis Gwyn's *Life of Redmond*, pp. 327–30. According to this account, Bonar Law and Carson were most conciliatory in tone, but declined to make any proposal which Redmond could accept. Their minimum terms, according to Redmond's note on July 2nd, were (1) abolition of plebiscite by counties, and substitution of an artificial area carved out of Ulster, to include Antrim, Down, Derry, Tyrone, North and Mid-Armagh, North Fermanagh, and Derry City. (2) Abolition of the Government's time limit clause and substitution of an option to decide by plebiscite whether, and if so when, this area should come under Home Rule. (3) If these terms were agreed, Carson and Bonar Law guaranteed to support Home Rule for the South, and promised that they would not repeal it if the Conservatives came into power. Redmond declined even to consider such a proposal.

There matters remained for a fortnight. Then Asquith took up the question again, and again Lord Murray interviewed Bonar Law and Carson. Bonar Law made a detailed memorandum of this and subsequent conversations.[f] This time Murray conceded the point about plebiscite by counties, and proposed that an area in Ulster should be excluded en bloc from the Home Rule Bill. But the discussion broke down on the demarcation of the area, for Carson insisted upon all of Tyrone, while Murray insisted that the Nationalists could never agree to give up the whole county. Shortly after this, on July 17th, Asquith asked Bonar Law to see him in Sir Edward Grey's room in the House of Commons. The same arguments were discussed. Asquith maintained "That it would be a crime if civil war resulted from so small a difference". Bonar Law replied that although Asquith "might say it was our action which had created such a position, the people of Ulster know that they had a force which would enable them to hold the Province and, with opinion divided in this country, it was quite impossible that any force could be sent against them which could dislodge them, and therefore they knew that they could get their own terms, and it was certain they would rather fight than give way on such a point as this". Asquith then declared that he would give up the time limit clause altogether, but even this concession did not move Bonar Law and the meeting ended.

About two hours later, however, Murray got in touch with Sir Max Aitken and asked him to convey a message to Bonar Law. The gist of this was that the Prime Minister still thought there was a chance of a settlement and he proposed to ask the King to convene a conference. Bonar Law did not welcome this proposal. He writes:[g]

"I asked Sir Max Aitken to give this message: that we thought a conference was useless, but that if the Prime Minister on his own responsibility gave such an invitation in the name of the King we should be bound to accept it."

His reply to Lord Stamfordham's letter of invitation was equally pessimistic.[h]

Such was the origin of the well-known Buckingham Palace Conference which began on July 21st and lasted for three days. It is clear that from the start the Unionist leaders had no expectation that it would succeed, and that they only attended in deference to the King's wishes. The Liberals were represented by Asquith and Lloyd George, the Conservatives by Lansdowne and Bonar Law, the Nationalists by Redmond and Dillon, the Ulstermen by Carson and Sir James Craig. The King made an opening address and then departed leaving the Speaker to preside.

Bonar Law has left a detailed account of the discussion which followed.[i] On the whole it tallies fairly closely with the account given by Denis Gwyn in his *Life of Redmond* (pp. 336–42) and based on Redmond's papers. The Conference began with a lengthy discussion on the nature of the procedure to be adopted if it failed to produce any agreement – which was not a very encouraging start. Then followed a dispute as to what should be discussed first, area or time limit. The Unionists wanted to discuss time limit, while Redmond insisted that he could not discuss that, unless the area had been settled. Eventually Bonar Law and Carson gave way on this point. In the end the question of time limit was never discussed at all, since the problem of area proved insuperable. There is no need to go into the details of the discussions which followed. Redmond declared that county option was the only method. Carson declared that the whole province of Ulster should be excluded, adding, as a bait, that, the more Catholics there were in the excluded area, the more likely it was to opt ultimately for inclusion under a Dublin Parliament. Redmond with remarkable candour agreed that if he had been a free agent he would have accepted such a plan, but in fact to do so would lose him all support in Ireland. The conference then adjourned.

The following day, July 22nd, was devoted to an abortive discussion about Tyrone. When this was finished Bonar Law suggested the clear exclusion of the six counties. Redmond declared that it was useless even to discuss such a proposal. On the third day, July 23rd, Asquith came forward with a new proposal on his own initiative.

This was the exclusion of an area consisting of the six North-Eastern counties with the exception of South Armagh, South Fermanagh and North Tyrone.

"After this statement", records Bonar Law,[j] "we sat and looked at each other for some time without saying anything. I then said that I did not know whether the Prime Minister thought that this proposal was worth serious discussion, for it seemed to me that it amounted to little more than giving to the Ulster Unionists the four north-eastern counties. Both Asquith and Lloyd George shook their heads but did not say anything."

Then Redmond intervened to say that in any case he could not accept such a plan even if the Unionists did. After some further discussions about Tyrone it became clear, as Bonar Law had believed all along, that no agreement was possible. The conference then discussed for the second time how its failure should be announced and it was agreed that only a bare statement of the fact should be given to the public.

It has sometimes been said that the conference broke down solely upon the question of partitioning the county of Tyrone. But it should be clear from the foregoing account that this was by no means the only cause. The question of time limit, for example, had not even been discussed, and the gap between Carson and Redmond was far wider than the question of Tyrone. On the one side the Ulster Unionists were in a powerful bargaining position. Bonar Law and Carson were well aware of the dangers of a Die-hard movement, and they were most reluctant to abandon the Protestant minority in the three Catholic counties of the Province of Ulster. On the other side Redmond found it extremely difficult to give up the principle of county option, and would not even accept Asquith's last proposal which was about as favourable to the Nationalists as any policy involving the exclusion of Ulster could be. Those writers who endeavour to give the impression that the issues which divided the parties were foolish or trivial are unfair to the statesmen concerned.

No sooner had the Buckingham Palace Conference ended than a disastrous event occurred in Dublin. The Irish Volunteers, following the precedent of the Ulster Volunteers over the Larne gun-running, decided upon a similar exploit for themselves. On July 26th a cargo of rifles was landed at Howth on the north side of Dublin Bay. Unfortunately a fracas ensued in Dublin and resulted in a conflict between British troops and the Dublin crowd. Shooting began in Bachelor's Walk. Three people were killed and thirty-eight wounded. These events produced a violent reaction in Ireland, and

Redmond at once saw there would be no hope of persuading his followers to compromise. But the Amending Bill, sent down from the Lords in a form quite unacceptable to the Nationalists, was due to be debated almost at once in the House of Commons. This was the last chance of reaching some sort of agreement. Redmond, therefore, asked Asquith for delay in view of the passions raised by the shooting in Bachelor's Walk and the Prime Minister agreed to postpone the debate until Thursday, July 30th.

Meanwhile the shadow of the impending European War had grown so black and formidable that even the Unionists began to be alarmed. On July 23rd the Austro-Hungarian Government had presented its ultimatum to Serbia and by now the armies of Europe were everywhere mobilizing. The question of British intervention became a burning issue in the Cabinet. In the circumstances an exhibition of disunity and party strife was most undesirable. Yet a debate on the Amending Bill was as certain as anything could be to produce furious scenes in the House of Commons. Bonar Law and Carson therefore decided that it would be wiser to postpone the Bill for the time being even though such action might prejudice the cause of Ulster. On the morning of July 30th Asquith, while endeavouring to absorb religious statistics about Ulster in readiness for his speech that afternoon, received a telephone message from Bonar Law. The latter asked him to go round at once to Pembroke Lodge and sent his motor car to convey Asquith there. On arrival he found Carson present as well. Bonar Law declared that to advertise domestic strife would merely weaken the Government at a critical moment, and, with Carson's full agreement, he suggested that the Bill should be postponed.[k] To this proposal Asquith gratefully agreed, and announced the fact in the House of Commons in the afternoon.

In the event the Amending Bill never did come before the House. It is worth noting what Asquith would have done if the second reading had gone on in the ordinary way. He informed the King that he intended to restore county option, but without the proviso for automatic reinclusion at the end of a fixed period.[1] Instead he would have substituted a further option. Such a proposal was per-haps as reasonable as any that could have been devised, but it would undoubtedly have encountered violent opposition both from Red-mond, and from Bonar Law and Carson. We can only surmise what would have happened in Ulster, if the European War had been averted. The Liberals then, and their biographers since, have inclined to the view that Ulster's resistance was all a gigantic bluff.

Bonar Law's papers naturally are not conclusive on such a topic, but it can be safely asserted that Bonar Law himself did not believe that there was any bluffing in Carson's threats. He was all through this period in the closest touch with Carson and, although negative evidence is always dangerous, we would expect to find some sort of hint in Bonar Law's correspondence if in fact the Ulster Unionists were consciously engaged in a game of bluff. On the contrary it seems highly probable that Ulster would have resisted and at least possible that such resistance would have been successful. But it might well have been accompanied by riots and even civil war, while the passions raised in England would have been scarcely less violent. It is a small – though very small – consolation for the horrors of the First World War that England was at least spared a convulsion calculated to wreck the very foundations of her parliamentary system.

With this reflection we may leave for a while the tale of Bonar Law's dealings with Ireland and turn our attention to the mighty hurricane which had already begun to blow from the direction of Europe.

CHAPTER XIV

WAR

AUGUST AND SEPTEMBER 1914

Bonar Law's attitude to foreign affairs – He favours support of France irrespective of Belgian question – His weekend at Wargrave – He and Lansdowne support Asquith – Effect of their letter exaggerated – Asquith's opinions – Britain declares war – Importance of Bonar Law's part in war-time politics – Unionist attitude to Government – Appointment of Kitchener – Position of Balfour – Asquith puts the Home Rule Bill on the Statute Book – Anger of Bonar Law – His bitter speech in the House – Indignation of the Liberals

I

INEXHAUSTIBLE volumes have been written to describe the origins of the First World War. Fortunately there is no need for the biographer of Bonar Law to contribute any further pages toward the elucidation of that dark topic. As leader of the Opposition Bonar Law could have little say in the details of the diplomacy which preceded August 4th, 1914. Indeed he does not on the whole appear to have taken much interest in foreign policy before the war. No doubt he left such matters largely to Balfour, and to Lansdowne who, as a former Foreign Secretary, knew far more than Bonar Law could hope to know about European affairs. Certainly Bonar Law displayed no particular prescience with regard to the impending disaster. Until the last week in July, for him as for most Unionists, the Irish problem filled the horizon to the exclusion of almost everything else.

In general the Unionist attitude in foreign affairs was one of broad support for the policy of entente with France – a policy which after all owed its origin to Lansdowne and Balfour. One of the strongest traditions in English foreign policy is continuity from one government to another. Sir Edward Grey's policy was no exception to this rule. He represented the right wing of the Liberal Party, and the Unionists had no desire to see him displaced by a Radical. Therefore Bonar Law's rare utterances on foreign affairs were usually in support of Grey and Grey's policy.

When the Austrian ultimatum to Serbia, by setting in motion the

cumbrous levers and cogwheels of the European alliance system,
seemed certain to cause war between France and Germany, Bonar
Law's chief fear was that the British Government might fail to come
to the aid of France. For at first it was far from certain that the
Liberals would intervene. Whatever understanding might exist
between the naval and military authorities of the two countries, no
formal alliance bound Britain to act. Moreover, there was a strong
pacifist element in the Cabinet including at one time its most formidable member, Lloyd George. Indeed there can be little doubt that
but for the question of Belgian neutrality the Government would
not have intervened at all – or only have intervened when it was too
late. Even the Conservatives were by no means united on this question. Bonar Law told Grey, a few days before the war began,

"that it was not easy to be sure what the opinion of the whole of his party
was. He doubted whether it would be unanimous or overwhelmingly in
favour of war unless Belgian neutrality were invaded; in that event, he
said, it would be unanimous".[a]

Whatever might be the attitude of other members of his Party,
Bonar Law himself was quite clear that England ought to fight at
once on the side of France. Apart altogether from the Belgian
question, he considered that honour and interest alike demanded
that we should not permit the destruction of France as a great power.
There can be no doubt that this view, which was shared by all the
leading Unionists and by the whole of the right wing element in the
Liberal Government, was entirely correct. Failure to come to the aid
of France would have had incalculable consequences upon our position as a great nation. It would have been a disaster of the first order,
and we can be thankful in retrospect that the Germans did in the end
invade Belgium, thus converting even the pacifist wing of the Cabinet
to the need for prompt intervention by a united Great Britain.

All this was, however, still uncertain when on the evening of
Friday, July 31st, Bonar Law motored down to Wargrave Manor to
spend a long promised weekend with his old friend Edward Goulding.
Among others in the party were Carson, F. E. Smith, and Aitken.
Discussion soon turned to the international crisis and the correct
policy for the Opposition to follow. F. E. Smith, who had been in
touch with Churchill the evening before, informed the meeting that
the Cabinet was deeply divided, and that in the event of war numerous resignations could be expected. He therefore asked on Churchill's
behalf what the Unionist attitude was and whether they would be

prepared if necessary to fill the gaps thus caused and enter a coalition government. Churchill believed that he had the support of Grey and the unspoken agreement of the Prime Minister in making this offer.[b]

Bonar Law did not greet this overture with any cordiality. He disliked indirect communications of this nature, and, although he was a close friend of F. E. Smith, he regarded Churchill both then and later with profound mistrust. If there was to be any negotiation for a coalition he preferred to deal directly with Asquith. Moreover, he was by no means convinced that a coalition was necessary – yet. Here he differed from many of his supporters, notably F. E. Smith who was an ardent advocate of co-operation between the parties. As a result, then, of these discussions all that F. E. Smith could bring back to Churchill was a general assurance that the Unionist leaders would support the Government.

On Saturday afternoon (August 1st) the guests at Wargrave motored up to London. Bonar Law declined an invitation to dine that night with Grey and Churchill. He suspected that a further offer of coalition might be made, and he did not wish to discuss the matter again. Having arrived in London he proceeded to consult Lansdowne and Balfour at Lansdowne House. George Lloyd, M.P. (subsequently Lord Lloyd) and Sir Henry Wilson, were also present. The Unionist leaders decided to inform Asquith that they would be ready to see him whenever he wished in order to discuss the Unionist attitude towards the crisis. Meanwhile Austen Chamberlain had come up from Westgate where he had been staying. He arrived about 1 a.m. on Saturday night and was met on the platform by Lloyd who had come straight from Lansdowne House.[1]

Lloyd, according to Chamberlain, had gained the impression that, although Balfour understood the gravity of the situation, neither Lansdowne nor Bonar Law seemed to do so. Chamberlain writes: "I at once said that Lansdowne would obviously appreciate its full meaning – he must have misunderstood him." Chamberlain was evidently not so sure about Bonar Law, of whose opinion and ability he did not perhaps think very highly just then. As a matter of fact Bonar Law was well aware of the nature of the crisis. He had been seeing Grey almost every day during the past week to hear the latest news and his views were quite clear. Grey writes:

---

[1] The fullest account of what follows is in a memorandum written by Austen Chamberlain at the time and published in *Down the Years*, Chapter VI. The brief account given by Lord Newton in his life of Lansdowne contains serious errors and should be disregarded.

"As to Bonar Law's own opinion he never expressed it to me at this stage. Nor do I remember that I expressed mine to him. Each of us probably assumed the other to be convinced that we ought not to stand aside if France were attacked."[c]

Grey's assumption was correct. But Bonar Law was the last man to be excited or panicked by a crisis. He was inclined to seem lethargic and almost indifferent on such occasions and this may account for the impression received by Lloyd.

Lloyd's account seems to have worried Austen Chamberlain. Early next morning he went round to Lansdowne House, even before its owner had finished breakfast, and urged an immediate *démarche* to Asquith. Lansdowne replied that he and Bonar Law were waiting for a reply from Asquith to whom they had already sent a message. The two men then went to Pembroke Lodge to see Bonar Law. Bonar Law shared Lansdowne's view that it would be right to wait for a reply from Asquith. Chamberlain insisted that a statement of Unionist policy should be made at once. The conversation continued, and then "rather suddenly to my surprise," writes Chamberlain, "Law said 'I am not sure that after all Austen is not right. I think we ought to write to the Prime Minister'."

The Unionist Leaders then agreed upon the following letter to Asquith:[d]

2nd August 1914

"Dear Mr. Asquith,

"Lord Lansdowne and I feel it our duty to inform you that in our opinion, as well as in that of all the colleagues with whom we have been able to consult, it would be fatal to the honour and security of the United Kingdom to hesitate in supporting France and Russia at the present juncture; and we offer our unhesitating support to the Government in any measures they may consider necessary for that object.

"Yours very truly,

A. Bonar Law."

One point is worthy of note in this letter: there is no mention of Belgium. The letter clearly shows that the Belgian question was not the reason why the Unionists pressed for intervention. It was, rather, the whole question of our informal understanding with France, and the perilous isolation in which we would find ourselves if France and Russia were crushed.

The letter reached Asquith in time to be read out at the meeting of the Cabinet held at 11 o'clock that Sunday morning.

How much influence did it have on the course of events? Both

Bonar Law, and Austen Chamberlain who regarded himself with some reason as its true author, seems to have thought that it played an important part in Asquith's decision to stand by France. But the evidence suggests that it did not in fact make much difference. Both J. A. Spender in his *Life of Asquith* and Grey in *Twenty-Five Years* state that the letter had relatively little effect on the Cabinet's decision. Grey pays generous tribute to the Conservative leaders'

"resolution and courage in making this contribution to decision at a moment when they had not before them as we had before us the compulsion of the imminent menace to Belgium. But the message was first read and then laid aside; it could have no influence on our discussion."[e]

The truth would seem to be that although an Opposition can probably prevent the Government going to war, because in war a democracy must be united, it cannot force a Government into war. By Sunday, August 2nd, it is fairly clear that the Government did not intend to intervene unless Belgian neutrality was violated. But if Belgian neutrality was violated and the Belgians called for the implementation of the treaty of 1839, the Government was certain to intervene. That being the case, Bonar Law's declaration, although he was quite right to make it, did little beyond recording the Conservative attitude.

Asquith's reply, which is of some historical interest and has not been hitherto published, makes it clear that he was not greatly influenced by the Unionist communication. It confirms too that the Government had no intention of giving anything more than a very limited support to France, unless Belgium was invaded too. It took the form of a memorandum on Government policy, and reads as follows:[f]

"Secret.   10 Downing Street.

"We are under no obligation, express or implied, either to France or Russia to render them military or naval help.

"Our duties seem to be determined by reference to the following considerations:

(1) Our long standing and intimate friendship with France.

(2) It is a British interest that France should not be crushed as a great Power.

(3) Both the fact that France has concentrated practically their whole naval power in the Mediterranean, and our own interests, require that we should not allow Germany to use the North Sea or the Channel with her fleet for hostile operations against the Coast or shipping of France.

(4) Our treaty obligations (whatever their proper construction) in regard to the neutrality and the independence of Belgium.

"In regard to (1) and (2) we do not think that these duties impose upon us the obligation at this moment of active intervention either by sea or land. We do not contemplate, for instance, and are satisfied that no good object would be served by, the immediate despatch of an expeditionary force.

"In regard to (3) Sir E. Grey this (Sunday) afternoon sent the following communication to the French Ambassador."

Asquith goes on to say that the Cabinet guaranteed to protect the French coast against the German fleet. He continues:

"In regard to (4) we regard Mr. Gladstone's interpretation of the Treaty of 1839 in the House of Commons on 10 August 1870 (203 Hansard 1787) as correctly defining our obligations. It is right, therefore, before deciding whether any and what action on our part is necessary to know what are the circumstances and conditions of any German interference with Belgian territory.

2 August 1914."

Naturally the Unionists regarded this as most unsatisfactory. It even seemed to cast doubts on the question of intervening if Belgium were invaded. Lansdowne, together with Chamberlain and the Duke of Devonshire, was at Brook's Club that evening. Bonar Law came round from the Carlton with the letter and suggested that he and Lansdowne should see Asquith the following morning. They interviewed the Prime Minister at 10.30 the next day, Monday, August 3rd. They found him extremely tired and anxious not to prolong the discussion. He was however able to make it clear that the memorandum of the previous day did not fully represent his present views. In fact Asquith knew by now that a German invasion of Belgium was as certain as anything could be, and he was determined to play for time, confident that once the invasion had occurred, he would be able to carry nearly all the Cabinet with him. Unionist demands for an immediate declaration were therefore merely an embarrassment at this stage.

Indeed that very morning events moved rapidly. In the afternoon Grey spoke in the House of Commons and gave a clear warning that England would almost certainly be at war very soon. The following day, August 4th, the news came through that the Germans had definitely invaded Belgian soil. Already the Belgian Government had appealed to the Treaty of 1839. By midnight on August 4th Great Britain was at war with Germany. Only two members of the Cabinet, Morley and Burns, had resigned, and they were not among the men who counted most. Asquith's able management, aided by German

folly, had achieved the seemingly impossible – a united Liberal
Cabinet convinced that England must fight.

2

The war was destined to bring profound changes to Bonar Law's
life, as to the lives of so many million of his fellow men. It affected
him personally in his deepest feelings. No man was more devoted to
his family than Bonar Law, but he was destined to lose his two eldest
sons before the war had ended, and to lose them in peculiarly
harrowing circumstances. Like Asquith and Lansdowne, who both
suffered a similar tragedy, Bonar Law never wholly recovered from
this overwhelming blow. He had been a man of ambition. The war
brought him high office and great power, but these rewards were
no consolation. By the end he cared neither for office nor for politics.
Only a sense of duty and perhaps the anodyne which hard work gave
to his wounds kept him still in public life.

In the world of politics remarkable transformations were to take
place. Some men were to climb the glittering peaks of prosperity and
fame, others were to recede into the darkness of failure and obscurity.
The old party divisions were to blur and fade. New alignments were
to arise, new allegiances, new enmities. In this strange and unmapped
political territory every step was fraught with difficulty and peril.
The old landmarks had vanished, the familiar scene had disappeared.
In its place was a new and unknown landscape full of false tracks
for the imprudent and snares for the unwary.

During these extraordinary years Bonar Law had to take decisions
of the greatest importance both for his country and his party. It is no
part of his biographer's task to claim that those decisions were invariably correct. But it is a part of the thesis of this book that, correct
or not, Bonar Law's decisions were important. Their consequences
were of the first magnitude. Without them history would not have
been the same. The numerous accounts of the war – with a few
exceptions – have not done justice to Bonar Law's part. His own
self-effacement and modesty, his hatred of the limelight, his preference for the shadows, the grey and rather bleak aspect which he
presented to a world ever prone to love colour and romance, all have
combined to make him a forgotten figure in the great events through
which he lived. But it will be found on examination that his attitude
was of vital significance in nearly all the most important decisions
taken during the war, the formation of the First Coalition, the withdrawal from the Dardanelles, the appointment of Lloyd George to

the War Office, the fall of Asquith. On all these occasions a different decision by Bonar Law would, for good or ill, have altered the course of history.

His attitude to the problems of war will emerge as this narrative proceeds. One or two points should be remembered at the outset. Bonar Law was not and never claimed to be an expert on strategy. In the years before the war he left the problems of defence to others. Early in 1912 he did, it is true, briefed by Lord Roberts, make a strong public attack on Haldane's administration of the War Office. Later he used to receive information from Sir Henry Wilson which he sometimes used in order to ginger up the Government on Army matters. Moreover, he was well aware, from the numerous and violent memoranda sent to him by Lord Charles Beresford, of the criticisms levelled in some quarters at Mr. Churchill's régime in the Admiralty. In general, however, he does not seem to have concerned himself much over naval and military affairs. This did not mean that he was lukewarm or defeatist over the progress of the war. On the contrary, just as he was a fighter in politics, so he was a fighter against the German menace. He was totally unable to share or understand the views of those who believed in a negotiated peace. On this he found himself profoundly differing from Lansdowne who by the end of 1916 became convinced that the war could not be won decisively by either side. Bonar Law appreciated the sincerity of his old colleague's views, but from then onwards their paths led far apart. It is notable that, although Bonar Law expressed highly pessimistic views on almost every other subject, he never wavered in his belief not only that the war must be won but that, despite everything, it actually would be won in the end.

Finally, it should be emphasized that Bonar Law was singularly little influenced during these years by considerations either of party or personal advancement. Until 1914 he was an intense partisan. We shall shortly see that even after the war had begun it took him longer than some people to recover from the passions raised by party strife. But when once he had done so, his attitude was conditioned wholly by what he considered to be the national interest. We shall find him refusing to bargain with Asquith for the full quota of places to which the Unionists were entitled in the First Coalition; we shall find him declining to press his own claims to the Chancellorship of the Exchequer; finally we shall find him refusing the offer of the post which is the goal of every politician, refusing to become Prime Minister of England.

3

The outbreak of the war rallied all parties to the support of the Government. On the afternoon of August 3rd Redmond followed the speeches of Grey and Bonar Law by pledging the support of Nationalist Ireland against Germany. He urged the Government to remove all troops from Ireland declaring that the Nationalist Volunteers were ready to join with the Ulster Volunteers in defence of Ireland's shore against invasion. This bold and generous gesture, fraught with much risk to Redmond's own position as leader of his party, received general applause. For the moment the Irish problem seemed to have fallen into the background.

Meanwhile Bonar Law and his colleagues agreed that the normal functions of the Opposition should be suspended. The Government must be allowed a reasonably free hand in the running of the war. This would be impossible if every action were the subject of questions in Parliament or votes of censure. The machinery of opposition was dismantled. Party meetings up and down the country were cancelled. Instead the Unionists and Liberals stood together and made recruiting speeches from the same platform.

This self-imposed abstention from party polemics might have produced a greater strain upon Unionist forebearance but for two important appointments. Asquith could clearly no longer hold the War Office in conjunction with his other duties, as he had done ever since the Curragh Incident. He decided to give the post to the great Lord Kitchener. Kitchener had a prestige surpassing that of any soldier since the days of the Duke of Wellington. Moreover, although his appointment was non-political, it was widely believed that as a great imperialist, he sympathized more with the Conservative point of view than with that of the Liberals.

The other appointment – it was not new but now became important – was that of Balfour who had been ever since 1906 a member of the Committee of Imperial Defence. As such, Balfour was invited to meetings of the War Council and was in a position to press his views upon the Government.

Although Balfour's presence in the inner counsels of the Government had obvious advantages, Bonar Law expressed in private a certain anxiety.[g] An ex-Prime Minister and former Unionist leader closely co-operating with the Liberal Cabinet might in some circumstances have endangered Bonar Law's own position, might have produced, for example, a premature coalition, and so have split the

Unionist Party. In fact no such threat materialized. Balfour's relations with Bonar Law continued to be marked, as they always had
been, by an impersonal, but impeccable correctitude. On the whole
the two men moved along parallel lines, but, like parallel lines, they
would only have met at infinity.

The honeymoon period in Conservative-Liberal relations was
abruptly broken about a month after the outbreak of war. The
trouble as usual came from the Irish question. When the Unionists
postponed the Amending Bill, they had understood that Asquith
would in return postpone putting the unamended Home Rule Bill
upon the Statute Book. Bonar Law therefore was greatly perturbed
when he learned through Carson and Redmond that the Nationalists
meant to insist upon the Home Rule Bill being placed on the Statute
Book at once. He immediately protested personally to Asquith and
wrote to Grey on August 6th:[h]

> "I am sure you will agree that the Prime Minister could not now adopt
> the course desired by the Nationalists without a breach of honour which is,
> I am sure, impossible to him. . . . I wish you if possible clearly to under-
> stand what our attitude must be. If the Government should decide (which
> I do not think possible) to do what the Nationalists wish, they can do it;
> for under no circumstances would we take a factious part in hindering the
> Government in circumstances such as exist today; but if that course were
> taken we should have to say that in our opinion the Government have
> acted dishonourably, that we cannot trust them, and that though we will
> not hamper them it will be impossible for us to co-operate with them."

The Unionist leaders now proceeded to bombard Asquith with
letters and memoranda. Asquith was himself uncertain what to do
and decided to temporize, by making counter suggestions, one of
which was that the Home Rule Bill should be passed with an amendment excluding the six counties.[i] It was an unfortunate move, for
although Bonar Law agreed to it, Asquith soon discovered that he
had no chance of persuading Redmond to agree, and he was therefore obliged to withdraw the offer.[j] When Bonar Law charged him
with going back on his own proposal Asquith pointed out that it was
not actually a proposal or offer, but only a tentative suggestion.
This was strictly true for Asquith had drafted his original letter to
Bonar Law with lawyerly caution, but the withdrawal naturally
created the worst possible impression upon the Unionists.

But it would be tedious to go further into the details of the dispute.
It is enough to say that Asquith decided in the end to put both the
Irish Home Rule and the Welsh Church Bill on the Statute Book and

to pass at the same time a one-clause Act postponing their operation until the end of the war. It now seems a fair enough solution. After all it did not really matter whether the Bills were enacted or not. In the conditions which were likely to prevail after the war, it was almost certain that the Irish Bill at any rate would have to be greatly modified. It is difficult to avoid the conclusion that the Unionist leaders – Bonar Law not least among them – had lost all sense of proportion over this question.

As soon as Bonar Law heard Asquith's decision he wrote to him the following bleak letter.[k]

11 September 1914.

"Dear Mr. Asquith,

"I am in receipt of your letter of today and I learn with the deepest regret that you have determined at such a time as the present to revive party controversy.

"The decision which you announce is also, in the opinion of all the colleagues whom I have been able to consult, and of myself, a distinct breach of the definite pledge given by you in the House of Commons and repeated to me by yourself in conversation.

"Yours very truly,
A. Bonar Law."

Bonar Law decided that something must be done to mark the indignation of the Unionists when Asquith introduced the postponing Bill in the House of Commons on September 15th. On the other hand he wanted to avoid prolonged debate. He decided, therefore, that only one speech should be made and that he should make it. It was possibly the most bitter of all Bonar Law's speeches. Much to Asquith's annoyance he read out parts of the letter in which Asquith had made alternative suggestions for dealing with the Home Rule Bill, and he compared the Prime Minister's conduct to the bad faith shown by the Germans in invading Belgium. At the end of his speech he announced that the Unionists would walk out of the House and take no further part in the debate. Asquith wrote of the scene:[l]

"it was not really a very impressive spectacle, a lot of prosaic and for the most part middle-aged gentlemen, trying to look like early French revolutionists in the tennis court. Still it was unique in my or anybody else's experience".

Bonar Law's speech was greatly admired by his own party, and he was expressing, however violently, sentiments which were widespread.[1] The Liberals naturally took a different view. Asquith declared

---

[1] See, for example, the extremely acrimonious correspondence between Austen Chamberlain and Churchill – Petrie, *Austen Chamberlain*, II, pp. 6–13.

that he had never known Bonar Law "sink so low". McKenna
and Illingworth, the Liberal whip, had to leave the House for fear
that an uncontrollable gust of fury would oblige them to hurl
missiles at the Conservative leader's head.[m]

Thus ended for the time being the Irish controversy. That it
should have occupied so much time and raised so much dust and heat
at a moment when the whole issue of the European war was in doubt,
may well seem extraordinary today. But it is not easy for men who
have been engaged for three years in bitter strife on a question which
they regarded as vital for the existence of the nation to abandon it or
forget it even in the face of the gravest danger from outside. The
passions raised by Asquith's action took some time to cool. Writing a
month later to Lady Lugard, who had suggested that he should
appear on the same platform as Asquith, Bonar Law replied that he
would not refuse, but he added:[n]

"After what happened at the end of the session I should prefer not to
speak on the same platform with a member of the government and I have
no doubt that their feeling is the same as regards myself."

One thing was abundantly clear: the chances of a coalition, bad
already, became much worse now. It required a whole series of
drastic changes before Bonar Law and his colleagues were ready to
sit side by side with their political enemies in the same Cabinet.

CHAPTER XV

PATRIOTIC OPPOSITION
AUGUST 1914 – MAY 18TH, 1915

Embarrassing position of the Unionists – Their mistrust of the Government – Criticism of the Admiralty – Unionist hostility to Churchill – Bonar Law's personal dislike of Churchill – The Antwerp episode – Fisher becomes First Sea Lord – His extraordinary character – He confides in Bonar Law – Bonar Law's difficulties in restraining his colleagues – Curzon's letter of protest – Bonar Law's reply – Lloyd George's plan to nationalize liquor trade – Bonar Law agrees – The plan fizzles out – The King's pledge – Constantinople – The increasing discontent of Fisher – His disapproval of the Dardanelles Expedition shared by Bonar Law – Fisher resigns – Bonar Law sees Lloyd George and Asquith – Coalition agreed – A remarkable letter from Fisher – Churchill displaced – End of the Liberal rule

I

THE next eight months were to be a frustrating and vexatious period in Bonar Law's career. He had pledged himself and his Party to abstain from factious criticism, and to support the Government in order that a clear impression of national unity should be conveyed both to allies and enemies. He was loyally determined to fulfil this pledge. But at the same time he was determined not to enter into any form of coalition – at least for the time being. Even if he had favoured coalition he would not have received any welcome from the Liberals who – with the exception of Churchill – were determined to keep the Conservatives out for as long as possible.

The resulting situation soon proved embarrassing for Bonar Law. The military setbacks, inevitably suffered by a nation so ill-prepared for war as Britain in 1914, became at an early stage the subject of anxiety and criticism. The Unionists had no access to the confidential information which might have relieved their doubts or justified the apparent errors of the Government. They merely saw a series of reverses, for which there was no obvious explanation except the incompetence of an Administration which they had always mistrusted. Bonar Law and his colleagues were in the awkward position of being unable to remedy the shortcomings of the Government either by co-operation or by censure. Bonar Law himself sympathized with many of the criticisms levelled by his more vociferous supporters

against the Liberal Cabinet. As time went on, it became more and
more difficult for him to damp down the smouldering embers of a
revolt ever prone to flare into flame.

In theory, criticism should have been concentrated upon the
Cabinet as a whole. In practice it was concentrated upon the triumvirate which actually controlled war policy – Asquith, Kitchener
and Churchill; and of these three it was the last-named who
soon became the target for the sharpest arrows of the Opposition.
Kitchener escaped such attacks at first, largely because his was a
non-party appointment, and he was believed to be more sympathetic
to the Unionists than to the Liberals. Moreover the progress of the
war on land seemed reasonably satisfactory; at any rate the defeats
which did occur could not be attributed solely to British incompetence. The case of the Navy was very different. Since it was a crisis
in the Admiralty, which ultimately brought the Government down
and created the First Coalition, the reasons for the Opposition's
hostility to Churchill are worth discussing.

In the first place the Navy suffered a series of disasters which came
as an unpleasant shock to a nation accustomed to unchallenged
supremacy upon the seas: there was the loss of the cruisers *Hogue*,
Cressy and *Aboukir*; there had been the failure to prevent the German
cruiser *Goeben* from reaching Constantinople, a failure which cost us
Turkey's hostile entry into the war; then occurred the sinking of one
of our newest battleships, the *Audacious*; and finally, though soon
reversed, the disaster of Coronel. The public forgot the valuable
negative work of the Navy, the potential dangers which had been
averted, and saw only these sensational misfortunes. It is not surprising that the Prime Minister himself on one occasion told Lloyd
George at lunch that he thought one of the paradoxes of the war
was that the Germans "are so much better than we are on the
sea".[a]

These naval disasters might have been forgiven but for the personality of the man ultimately responsible for the Navy to Parliament.
It is not easy for those who have lived through the era of Churchill's
ascendancy, through a period when criticism of him seemed barely
short of treason, to comprehend the intense and bitter animosity
which he inspired forty years ago. Yet the merest glance at the private
papers or public utterances of that time shows that Churchill was an
object of deep distaste to almost every Unionist – except Balfour –
and, for different reasons, to very many Liberals too. What is the
explanation of this hostility?

It was not merely that he had crossed the floor of the House; not merely that he had become the most witty and merciless assailant of his old Party; not merely that he had played – or was believed to have played – so sinister a part in the Irish crisis. It was rather the feeling, however unjustified and unfair, that behind brilliant oratory, great talents, and prodigious energy, there lay a ruthless love of power, a passionate determination to reach the summit of English politics, no matter what changes in allegiance and loyalty this ambition might cost. No doubt such feelings were unwarrantable, but the history of the times cannot be understood unless their existence is recognized. Churchill, like Shelburne, like Disraeli, was at this period a person who inspired, for all his great virtues, a profound sense of *mistrust*; and there is perhaps no handicap more fatal to an English politician.

This mistrust was felt by no one more deeply than by Bonar Law. He recognized Churchill's great ability, but he regarded him at the same time with ineradicable doubt and suspicion. To Bonar Law Churchill seemed erratic, unbalanced, and overbearing. Nor were his doubts assuaged by any of that susceptibility to Churchill's personal magnetism, which influenced many of those who were otherwise hostile to his ideas and plans. On the contrary Bonar Law regarded him with a cool indifference amounting on occasions to a positive dislike. Moreover by a singular fatality the two men found themselves at variance on almost every great political issue which emerged both during and after the war. Again and again Bonar Law was destined to frustrate Churchill's dearest ambitions. His exclusion from the Admiralty in 1915, the abandonment of Gallipoli, his exclusion from Lloyd George's Government in 1916, the overthrow of the Coalition in 1922, were all due in no small degree to Bonar Law's attitude. Had Bonar Law lived it is unlikely that Churchill would either have wished, or been able, to return to the Conservative fold and carve out a new and brilliant career in the Party which he had left twenty years before.

There are many examples of the difference in outlook which existed between the two men on almost every subject. Their correspondence is cool, formal, and sometimes tinged with acerbity. Churchill writes on one occasion to Bonar Law:[b] "You dance like a will-o'-the-wisp so nimbly from one unstable foothold to another that my plodding paces can scarcely follow you." Nor did Bonar Law spare Churchill. For example, in the autumn of 1916, during a debate he said:

"Mr. Churchill has given the House two valuable lessons which came
with great effect from him. One is that we should all conduct ourselves
with becoming modesty." (Laughter) "That is good advice from whatever
quarter it comes. The other is that the Government are committing an
unpardonable offence in putting on Government Whips for a Government
Bill. That is from the same right hon. gentleman who told us yesterday
the Government should lead the House." (Laughter)

This sally annoyed Churchill who wrote to Lord Beaverbrook:[c]

"It is a pity Bonar should be *personal* in rejoinders to me. I do not make
personal attacks on him or try to decry his personal behaviour or qualities.
Surely the wide field of political argument should afford sufficient scope
at the present time when everything is so uncertain."

Why did Bonar Law hold so adverse an opinion of someone
destined to become perhaps the greatest war leader in all our long
history? There is no easy answer. Obviously Churchill, with his
colour, rhetoric, and flamboyance, would have had little in common
with Bonar Law. It might therefore be tempting to explain their
incompatibility as the incompatibility which one would expect between someone like Churchill and a sedate, prudent, and rather
unsociable teetotaller. But this clearly will not do. Bonar Law was
an intimate friend of F. E. Smith, and an even closer friend of Beaverbrook, and no one could ever have described them as either sedate,
unsociable or hostile to alcohol. Indeed Bonar Law appears to have
got on admirably with people of an entirely opposite temperament
to his own. His close and long alliance with Lloyd George is a good
example. Far from being repelled by persons of brilliance and wit
he seems to have been attracted by them.

Whatever the reason, the fact is undoubted. Bonar Law's opinion
of Churchill is tersely expressed in a letter to a correspondent who
criticized the conduct of the Admiralty:[d]

"I agree with the estimate you have formed of Churchill. I think he has
very unusual intellectual ability but at the same time he seems to have an
entirely unbalanced mind which is a real danger at a time like this."

Later events did not soften Bonar Law's judgment. In December
1916 Lloyd George, when forming his Government, endeavoured
vainly to persuade Bonar Law to consent to Churchill's inclusion.
Bonar Law refused. Lloyd George argued that although Churchill
might be troublesome in the Government he might be even more
troublesome outside. He compared the problem to that of briefing
a brilliant but unreliable barrister. The question to be decided was

this: "Is he more dangerous when he is *for* you than when he is against you?" Bonar Law replied:[e] "I would rather have him against us every time." And he never deviated from this opinion.

Early in October 1914 there occurred the celebrated Antwerp episode – an exploit which did nothing to improve Churchill's status in Unionist eyes. Churchill and Kitchener sent an expeditionary force to help the Belgians in their resistance at Antwerp, and Churchill went there himself in order to stiffen the failing morale of the Belgian High Command. Having arrived he telegraphed to Asquith offering to resign from the Admiralty and take personal command over the forces at Antwerp. Asquith promptly declined the offer. But he was obliged to read out Churchill's telegram in the Cabinet – suppressing incidentally the fact that Churchill had nominated Runciman to be his successor as First Lord.[f] The offer was received with roars of laughter. But laughter turned to something more serious when eventually the whole resistance at Antwerp collapsed with the total loss of one of the Naval Brigades which had formed part of the British force, and which was obliged to retire into internment across the Dutch frontier. This reverse was very unfairly attributed to Churchill; although in fact it was equally as much the responsibility of Asquith and Kitchener.

Bonar Law strongly disapproved.

"It seems to me", he wrote on October 14th,[g] "an utterly stupid business, and what makes it worse is that, I am told, the Belgians had decided not to defend Antwerp, and Churchill persuaded them to do so by the promise of sufficient assistance from this country."

Feeling perhaps that his position was somewhat shaken, Churchill now proceeded to make an appointment which, though designed to strengthen him, was destined ultimately to be fatal to himself and to the Liberal Cabinet. An ignorant wave of Germanophobia had enforced the resignation of the First Sea Lord, Prince Louis of Battenberg.[1] On October 30th Churchill appointed in his place the aged and formidable Lord Fisher.

Fisher was one of the most extraordinary and eccentric figures of modern times. A glance at his character should effectively dispose of the notion that Service Chiefs are necessarily conventional, hidebound, or slaves to rigid tradition. He had been First Sea Lord from 1904 to 1910. During that period he had carried through immense and long-needed reforms in the entire organization and equipment of the Navy, but, in doing so, he had provoked the most furious

[1] Father of Earl Mountbatten.

dissension and the most bitter animosity. Fisher's language and demeanour were indeed calculated to produce storms wherever he went. "Favouritism", he once wrote, "is the secret of efficiency." He openly declared his intention of ruining the professional careers of those who resisted him, whatever their rank. "Their wives should be widows, their children fatherless, their homes a dunghill," he would declare again and again.[h] The result of these methods had been a violent schism in the Navy. Fisher's chief enemy was Lord Charles Beresford, Commander-in-Chief of the Channel Fleet. Eventually Fisher went too far, and in 1910 he left the Admiralty, and retired with a peerage into private life. Not long after Beresford retired also. He at once entered the House of Commons where he conducted a ceaseless vendetta against Fisher's reforms and against Churchill, who, as First Lord of the Admiralty from 1911 onwards, continually consulted Fisher about Naval policy.

Churchill's decision to recall Fisher to the Admiralty at the age of seventy-four did not go unchallenged. Lord Stamfordham protested to Asquith on behalf of the King who had grave misgivings about Fisher. But Asquith was firm and, whatever his doubts about Antwerp, now proceeded to declare his complete confidence in the First Lord of the Admiralty, pointing out that the First Sea Lord must be someone who possessed Churchill's confidence. The King gave way, but put his views in writing in a formal letter of disapprobation.[i] Politically the appointment seemed a wise move. The majority of Unionists were in favour of Fisher, and regarded his presence at the Admiralty as a guarantee against the whims of the First Lord.

Bonar Law had been for some time on friendly terms with Fisher. He had a standing invitation to lunch at the Admiralty with the First Sea Lord. On one occasion there is a note from Fisher:[j] "*No one else coming.* So that I may be free to explain all things to you after lunch by ourselves." It is not clear from Bonar Law's papers quite how much Fisher was in the habit of disclosing, but, in view of the explosive nature of the First Sea Lord's character, it is unlikely that he erred on the side of undue discretion. On January 31st, 1915, he wrote:[k]

"Private and personal
"Dear Mr. Bonar Law,
    "I am making enquiries as to what has been told you but this being Winston Churchill's own special department I have so far kept entirely clear of it.[1]

---

[1] To judge from later correspondence between Churchill and Bonar Law, this probably refers to the allegations of Admiralty mismanagement of chartered shipping.

"I take this opportunity of enclosing for your private eye a paper I submitted to the Prime Minister but as he has decided not to circulate it to the War Council I must ask you not to quote it in any way. Why he has suppressed it is beyond my comprehension. Anyhow he is Prime Minister and there's the end of it. . . .

"Yours very truly,

F.

"*Secret*. I sent a paper last February to the Prime Minister warning him that German submarines would sink our merchant ships off Liverpool and I was flouted. That paper also suppressed. *This is very secret.*"

The paper which Fisher enclosed is too long to be quoted here in full,[1] but its purport is significant. It was a strong plea against naval bombardment of fortified coastal defences, an argument against two of Churchill's pet plans, the bombardment of Zeebrugge and the operation against the Dardanelles. Fisher was disclosing to Bonar Law the existence of an important divergence of opinion within the inner councils of the Government. The whole question of the Dardanelles expedition has been thrashed out at immense length elsewhere. We are only concerned here with the attitude of Bonar Law. His opinions on the Dardanelles expedition had not yet crystallized – they were later to be extremely hostile – but even from the beginning he viewed the plan with some misgiving. Fisher's letter naturally tended to confirm these doubts. Bonar Law now realized that, behind the apparent unanimity of the Admiralty, there lay a deep but hidden conflict. The Unionists were relying upon Fisher to keep the vagaries of the First Lord in check. It now became clear that Churchill and his principal adviser viewed matters with ever-increasing disharmony. When the final breach came, with Fisher's sensational resignation in May 1915 on this very issue, Bonar Law and his supporters were determined to see that Churchill did not prevail.

Almost at the same time as he received this disquieting information from the Admiralty, Bonar Law came under heavy pressure from his leading colleagues to make a drastic change in his relations with the Government. The Unionists had for some time regarded the party truce with dissatisfaction. It seemed to them that all the advantages lay with the Government. Already the Home Rule and Welsh Church Bills were on the statute book. The Liberals appeared to be still pursuing many of their most partisan measures under the cloak of national necessity. To understand the Unionist attitude we must

---

[1] It is published in full by Churchill together with his own counter memorandum in *The World Crisis, 1911–18*, p. 581 et seq. Churchill presumably did not know of Fisher's communication with Bonar Law.

imagine what would have happened during the recent war if a Labour Government had been in power and had introduced the numerous controls and the heavy taxation which even a Conservative administration soon felt obliged, however reluctantly, to enact. There would undoubtedly at first have been indignant protests from the Conservatives if they had been in opposition.

Early in January Unionist discontent came to a head. The immediate cause was a debate in the House of Lords in which some criticism was made of the Government by Curzon. Replying for the Liberals Lord Crewe declared that the Unionists had a joint responsibility with the Government for war policy. Bonar Law at once wrote to the papers on behalf of himself and Lansdowne disclaiming any such responsibility. But this declaration was not enough for some of his colleagues. Walter Long, who now led the Die-hard section of the Party, sent a seven-page memorandum urging a far more decisive repudiation of the Government.[1] Curzon also indited a characteristic letter in portentous tones:[m]

"If we ask perfectly legitimate questions in the House of Lords we are treated as though we were naughty children, to be snubbed even by Lord Lucas. The Secretary of State for War [Kitchener] reads us exiguous Memoranda of platitudes known to everybody, is acclaimed by the Liberal Press as having delivered an almost inspired oration and scored off his impertinent antagonists. He interpolates a curt affirmative or negative to the solitary speech to which he deigns to listen, and he then marches out and leaves the rest of the debate to colleagues who either affect to know nothing or screen their silence behind his authority."

Curzon continued in similar vein at great length and concluded by demanding either more vigorous debate and criticism, or alternatively a closer sharing of the Government's confidence. Both Curzon and Long, however, firmly repudiated any idea of coalition.

Bonar Law, replying to Curzon, made it clear that no middle course existed between their present conduct and a genuine coalition. He wrote on January 29th:[n]

"I know how unsatisfactory the present position is for it means that we are conducting the most difficult war in which we have been engaged, in regard to which the nation is united, but half the nation distrusts the men who are carrying it on. That is a very difficult position and may be found impossible but in my judgment, much as I dislike the present position, there are only two real alternatives open to us. One is to go on as we are doing without responsibility and with only a very limited amount of criticism, such as was made at the meeting of your House; or to face a coalition. The latter proposal I should certainly be against; and on the whole therefore I am reluctantly driven to the conclusion that the only proper course for us in the meantime is to continue on the lines on which we have acted since the war began."

But events were soon destined to force Bonar Law into a different attitude towards coalition. The first event which brought about a certain rapprochement between the Parties was a curious by-product of Lloyd George's effervescent mind. This was nothing less than a proposal that the State should buy up the entire liquor trade. Lloyd George had become convinced that the production of munitions was being slowed down because of the British working man's excessive addiction to alcohol, and he came to the conclusion that the only way to reduce this evil was to nationalize the brewing and distilling industries, so that the Government could impose whatever restrictions it saw fit. Such a drastic proposal could scarcely be contemplated unless the Opposition were prepared to give it their support. Lloyd George therefore opened up negotiations with the Unionists.

The Unionist leaders were not so hostile to the plan as might at first have been expected. They had grave doubts about its practicability but they did not reject it out of hand.

Writing on April 17th, 1915, to J. P. Croal, editor of the *Scotsman*, Bonar Law said:°

"If it were possible, but as a matter of fact I hardly think it is, that such a scheme should be carried out, it would ultimately have, I think, great advantages. It would free us as a party from the incubus of being tied to the Trade, which has done us far more harm than good, and the thing itself, I really believe, would be a great reform."

The sentiments are typical of Bonar Law's empirical and non-doctrinaire attitude to social problems. It might have been thought that the leader of the Party, behind which ever since 1874 the great brewing interests had been ranged, would have repudiated with horror a scheme which could scarcely fail to alienate this support, and which moreover embodied state socialism of the kind that would be anathema to believers in private enterprise. But Bonar Law was always willing to consider a new proposal upon its merits, and so far persuaded his colleagues that he was able to write to Lloyd George on April 7th, 1915:ᴾ

"Dear Mr. Lloyd George,

"If the information in possession of the Government causes them to decide that it is necessary for the successful prosecution of the war that the State should take over the production and distribution of alcohol with adequate compensation to the existing interests we shall not as a party oppose the proposal.   "Yours very truly,

                                            A. Bonar Law."

It is true that many of Bonar Law's colleagues were lukewarm upon the matter, Lansdowne, Chamberlain and Long all regarding it with considerable doubt. Moreover the Liberals themselves were divided: Asquith was sceptical; Edwin Montagu expressed strong opposition. The House of Commons resolutely refused to pass any self-denying ordinance about alcohol for M.P.s. From the opposite extreme there was violent hostility on the part of the fanatical teetotallers who objected to any compensation being paid to the liquor interest. The brewers and distillers naturally opposed the whole idea of nationalization. Finally, what was always a somewhat chimerical scheme came to disaster through the premature publicity that it received in the *Daily Express*, which asked in large headlines whether England was to be drowned in beer or methylated spirits. Lloyd George abandoned it almost as quickly as he had taken it up, and nothing further was done towards nationalizing the liquor interests.

In the end the only person to take abstinence seriously was the King. "The King's pledge", a resolution that no alcohol should be consumed at the Royal Table, persisted until the end of the war, to the discomfort of those who were either His Majesty's hosts or guests. But the example was not generally followed, least of all by the leading figures in the political and military world.

The only other attempt at bringing the Parties together during this period was in March 1915 over the question of Constantinople. The early stages of the Dardanelles expedition had been highly promising. Constantinople seemed to be within our grasp. What was its future to be? The Government, anxious to encourage the Russians, wished to announce publicly that in the event of a victorious peace Russia would be allowed to annex the city. So important a decision could not properly be made without consulting the Opposition. Accordingly Churchill, seeing in such consultation a chance of bringing about the coalition for which he had long hankered, urged Asquith to invite Lansdowne and Bonar Law to attend a War Council meeting upon this subject. The Conservative leaders accepted, but the meeting was not successful. Bonar Law behaved with extreme caution, for, although he was unaware of Churchill's plan, he suspected that there might be an ulterior motive behind the invitation and he was still extremely unwilling to join a coalition. Asquith was equally unforthcoming. He did not yet consider that he needed Conservative participation in the Government. The result was a frosty meeting and, although agreement was reached on the question of Constantinople, Churchill's hopes for anything in the nature of a coalition were frustrated.

2

Nevertheless two months after the events just described Bonar Law
was a member of a coalition government and, what is more, a coalition government formed largely at his own insistence. What produced
so remarkable a change in so short a time?

It has been usual to couple together two principal causes: (1) the
shell controversy, (2) the resignation of Admiral Fisher. But there
can be little doubt that the shell controversy was never comparable
in importance with the crisis in the Admiralty. No doubt it had some
effect in weakening the Government's prestige, and perhaps, if Fisher
had not resigned when he did, the trouble over munitions might
eventually have brought down the Government in any case. Such a
supposition must remain a matter of conjecture, for the resignation
of Fisher was undoubtedly the immediate reason for the reconstruction of the Government. By the time that the shell shortage first
became a matter of public outcry, the Liberal Cabinet was already
dead.

We have already seen how Bonar Law was aware of the widening
gulf between the First Sea Lord and the First Lord of the Admiralty;
and aware too that one of the principal bones of contention was the
Dardanelles expedition. Bonar Law's own doubts about its wisdom
had increased. Writing on April 9th, 1915, to Sir Henry Wilson, he
said:[q]

"As regards the Dardanelles I have not received any information beyond
reports which are more or less gossip; but as far as I can gather, your views
as to the seriousness of the operations are being amply justified. As I wrote
you before, I was satisfied that the Government had jumped into all this
without at all counting the cost."

But Bonar Law's doubts were as nothing compared with the increasingly bitter feelings of Fisher upon this subject. He favoured as
an alternative a plan of his own which involved the British Navy
breaking into the Baltic and landing troops somewhere on the German coast with the object of capturing Berlin. This plan naturally
competed with the Dardanelles expedition, and much of Fisher's
hostility can be explained by that fact rather than objections to the
Dardanelles expedition in itself. Fisher was not the man to keep all
those notions to himself. Before long it became widely known in
Opposition circles that he was at variance with his Chief. This knowledge merely confirmed the Conservative mistrust for Churchill. It
became more and more certain that, in the event of an open breach,

I

the Opposition would espouse the cause of the Admiral, and that it would be extremely difficult for Bonar Law, even if he so wished, to hold his followers in check.

In addition to his hostility to the Dardanelles expedition Fisher had another grievance. Kitchener, the leading soldier of the land, was a Minister with a seat in the Cabinet and a vote on the War Council, supreme in his own sphere and subject to no civilian except the Prime Minister himself. Why should he, Fisher, England's leading sailor, be confined to the rôle of a mere adviser to a civilian First Lord? Fisher failed to appreciate that Kitchener occupied a unique place in public esteem, a place far superior to his own – high though that might be; and his grievance continued, adding further fuel to an already combustible situation.

Churchill has given us in his Memoirs his own detailed account of his relations with the First Sea Lord. It is clear that he did not realize until too late how strongly Fisher felt, clear also that his failure to do so was at least in part Fisher's fault. The old Admiral was like some quiescent volcano. There would be occasional rumblings, and, every now and then, a sinister puff of sulphurous smoke, but the inhabitants dwelling upon its slopes have long been accustomed to these familiar phenomena, and little dream of the fearful eruption which is imminent.

By the beginning of May it had become clear that the landings at Gallipoli had failed in the sense that no quick military victory was likely. A struggle of attrition similar to the war in France seemed almost inevitable. All the opponents of the Dardanelles expedition found their worst misgivings confirmed. On Saturday, May 15th, the volcano erupted. Lord Fisher resigned.[1] In a curt note to Churchill he stated that he did not believe in explanations – "Jowett said – 'never explain' . . . I am off to Scotland at once to avoid all questionings."[2]

The First Sea Lord, eccentric though he could often be, had surpassed himself both in his method of resigning and in his method of communicating that fact to others. When Churchill informed Asquith of the letter he had received, the Prime Minister at once sent a peremptory note to Fisher commanding him in the King's name to

---

[1] The specific reasons need not detain us. They are given in Mr. Churchill's account, *World Crisis*, 1915, Ch. XVIII.

[2] It is frequently stated in accounts of this episode that Fisher forthwith left for Scotland. Whatever he may have threatened he did not in fact do so at once. There are several letters from him to Bonar Law in the next week with the Admiralty address. He was still in London on May 22nd when J. A. Spender interviewed him. See below, p. 255.

return. After some hours Fisher reappeared, but remained obdurate to all attempts to persuade him to withdraw his resignation. Lloyd George, Asquith, and finally McKenna tried their blandishments in vain. The First Sea Lord refused to come back to office, and remained locked in his room in the Admiralty with the blinds drawn.

Bonar Law first learned of Fisher's resignation from a curious communication. It was a letter addressed to him in Fisher's unmistakable handwriting, containing nothing except a brief cutting from the *Pall Mall Gazette*, which stated that Fisher had had an audience with the King lasting half an hour.[r] After puzzling over this cryptic missive Bonar Law decided that Fisher must be intending to convey the fact of his resignation, and early on Monday, May 17th, he called upon Lloyd George at the Treasury. He was on more friendly personal terms with Lloyd George than he ever was with Asquith, which may explain why he chose to interrogate the former rather than the latter. He asked Lloyd George point-blank whether Fisher had resigned. Lloyd George answered that he had. Bonar Law replied, "Then the situation is impossible." If Fisher resigned and Churchill remained, he, Bonar Law, could not, and indeed would not wish to, restrain the Conservatives from demanding a public debate upon the issues that had provoked the crisis. If Churchill remained as First Lord, the Opposition would deliver an attack upon the Government whatever the consequences might be.[s]

Lloyd George was never an enemy of coalition, and he was most unwilling to have an open rupture with the Opposition. "Of course we must have a coalition", he replied, "for the alternative is impossible." He promptly took Bonar Law across to number 10 Downing Street to see the Prime Minister. A very brief discussion convinced Asquith that a complete reconstruction of his Cabinet was now inevitable, and he promptly agreed to the proposal. Bonar Law had already consulted Lansdowne. He now asked for time to collect as many members of the Shadow Cabinet as were available in order to inform them of Fisher's resignation and the gist of his discussions with Asquith and Lloyd George.

Any doubts that Bonar Law may have felt about the fact of Fisher's resignation or its reasons were dispelled by a remarkable letter which he received on this same day.[t] A facsimile of the first page is given on p. 244 in order to show the extraordinary style in which Fisher was wont to write. The letter continues in similar vein for another four pages including such expressions as these:

"Don't be cajoled privately by the P.M. to keep silence. The danger is

This letter and its contents must not be divulged now or ever to any glass. Sent to your letter

My dear Michael - In reply to your letter to the P.M. this morning - After repeated refusals I have written giving to say that now my definite decision is I am absolutely unable to remain with W.C. (He's a real danger!) He is going to be kept - (& I do so at once today) only they are "forcing" me till Parliament rises for 3 weeks or more. I regret to say your A.J.B. has been breaking W.C. all through and I have refused to have anything to do with him (A.J.B.) any consequence! - Keep this private - I must not see you but Parliament should not rise till the fact of my going is extracted - Lots of people must know. for instance see enclosed from

244

imminent and vital. . . . Be careful of W.C. [Winston Churchill] with
F. E. Smith and others. Be prepared for the *suppressio veri* and *suggestio
falsi* . . . W.C. is leading them all straight to ruin. . . . *A very great national
disaster is very near us in the Dardenelles!* . . . W.C. is a bigger danger than the
Germans by a long way in what is just now imminent in the Dardenelles.
Concentrate on the Dardenelles!"

Finally there was a postscript headed "Please burn and don't mention."[1] It read as follows:

"Very *Secret* and Private

"This evening Winston sent Lambert the Civil Lord of the Admiralty to
offer me a seat in the Cabinet if I would return as his First Sea Lord with
him (Winston) as First Lord! I rejected the 30 pieces of silver to betray
my country."

This letter, for all its eccentricities, was bound to confirm Bonar
Law in the view that Churchill must leave the Admiralty. It was
clear that matters had reached a crisis which could not be resolved
by the resignation of Fisher and the substitution of a First Sea Lord
who would be a mere tool of Churchill. It must be remembered that
Bonar Law, however much he might deplore Fisher's extraordinary
mode of resignation, sympathized with him on the actual issue of the
Dardanelles, and his views would have been further reinforced had
he known of a resolution communicated to Asquith and Churchill
the previous day (Sunday, May 16th) by the other Sea Lords.[u] They
did not go so far as to resign, but they associated themselves both
with Fisher's objection to the Dardanelles expedition and with his
allegation that Mr. Churchill interfered too much in matters which
should have been the province of the First Sea Lord.

Churchill meanwhile had seen Asquith at the latter's country
house on Sunday, May 16th, and had proffered his resignation.[2]
Asquith refused to accept it, and, when Churchill stated that he was
able to reconstruct the Board of Admiralty and had persuaded Sir
Arthur Wilson to take the post of First Sea Lord, Asquith was content
to leave the situation as it was. But all this occurred before Bonar
Law's démarche on the Monday morning (May 17th).[3]

Asquith now saw that the situation had been transformed, and
that there was little chance of saving his First Lord of the Admiralty

---

[1] The frequency with which the recipients ignore such instructions is of great assistance
to historians.
[2] It is interesting to note, and typical of Asquith, that even in a crisis of this sort he had
not forgone his weekend at Sutton Courtenay, in Berkshire.
[3] Asquith maintained afterwards, *Memories and Reflections*, Vol. II, p. 97, that his
decision to form a coalition was arrived at entirely independently of Bonar Law's representations. In view of Asquith's discussion with Churchill on Sunday, it requires much
credulity to accept this statement.

from the wrath of the Unionists. Meanwhile the unfortunate Churchill, having, as he says,[v] "no knowledge whatever of the violent political convulsions which were proceeding around me and beneath me", went to the House of Commons on the Monday afternoon ready to vindicate his policy and his new Board in public debate. He received a disagreeable shock when he learned from Lloyd George and Asquith that a Coalition Government was to be formed, that he was to leave the Admiralty, that no debate would take place in Parliament.

Churchill has recorded his view that the Prime Minister should not have surrendered to the Opposition's demands, but should have laid the whole question of the Government's war policy on land and sea before a secret session of the House of Commons. He maintains that Asquith would have been supported by large majorities, and "could then with dignity and with real authority have invited the Opposition to come not to his rescue but his aid".[w]

Such a weighty opinion cannot be disregarded. It may well be conceded that Asquith would have done better to have allowed a debate in the House of Commons. But it is doubtful whether even this course would have saved Churchill personally. It is certain that Bonar Law and the Unionists would have made his exclusion a condition of their entry into the Government, and it is certain too that Asquith could not have kept them out much longer in any case. Moreover, Churchill never realized the extent to which his prestige had been diminishing over the past eight months in the eyes of the most important personage of all – Asquith himself.[1]

It is time to revert to Bonar Law. After his discussion with Lloyd George and Asquith on Monday morning he went to Lansdowne House to consult with Lansdowne and Chamberlain. They agreed not to make a formal offer of a coalition but to despatch the following letter to Asquith.[x]

Lansdowne House,
17th May 1915.

"Dear Mr. Asquith,

"Lord Lansdowne and I have learned with dismay that Lord Fisher has resigned and we have come to the conclusion that we cannot allow the House to adjourn until this fact has been made known and discussed.

"We think the time has come when we ought to have a clear statement from you as to the policy which the Government intends to pursue. In our opinion things cannot go on as they are, and some change in the con-

---

[1] A number of private letters written by Asquith at this time make it clear that he had come to regard Churchill as a liability. For reasons of copyright it has not been possible to quote from these verbatim.

stitution of the Government seems to us inevitable if it is to retain a sufficient measure of public confidence to conduct the war to a successful
conclusion.

"The situation in Italy makes it particularly undesirable to have anything in the nature of a controversial discussion in the House of Commons
at present, and if you are prepared to take the necessary steps to secure the
object which I have indicated, and, if Lord Fisher's resignation is in the
meantime postponed, we shall be ready to keep silence now. Otherwise I
must today ask you whether Lord Fisher has resigned and press for a day
to discuss the situation arising out of his resignation.

"Yours very truly,
A. Bonar Law."

Mr. J. A. Spender describes this letter as "a pistol at Asquith's
head".[y] This seems a somewhat highly coloured statement. In fact
Bonar Law had agreed with Asquith and Lloyd George to write such
a letter in order that Asquith could show it to his colleagues and
make the situation clear to them.[z] The letter certainly did not come
in any way as a surprise to the Prime Minister who had already in
conversation with Bonar Law agreed to reconstruct the Government. The following day Asquith replied informing Bonar Law that
he had received the resignation of the whole Cabinet and offering
to form a Coalition Administration in which the Unionists would be
fully represented. Bonar Law and Lansdowne promptly accepted the
offer.

Thus the long reign of the Liberal Party came to an end. The last
purely Liberal Cabinet to govern Britain had fallen. The first of the
war-time coalitions had begun.

CHAPTER XVI

THE FORMATION OF THE FIRST COALITION

MAY – JUNE 1915

The division of places – Asquith's reluctance in joining with Unionists – Bonar Law's claims to the Exchequer or Munitions – Austen Chamberlain's sound advice – Asquith resolves to make Bonar Law Colonial Secretary – His motives – Divide and Rule – His exaltation of Curzon – Unionist hostility to Haldane and Churchill – Latter appeals in vain to Bonar Law – Self-sacrifice of leading Conservatives – Thirst for places among minor office seekers – Complications over Irish Law Offices – Problem of Lord Fisher – Aitken refuses a baronetcy – The new Government – Bonar Law's part in negotiations discussed – The Jacks Case – Trading with the Enemy – Bonar Law's distress at the verdict – His own innocence

I

ON May 19th Bonar Law and Asquith announced in the House of Commons that a Coalition Government would be formed. The next week was occupied in the delicate, invidious, and sometimes unpleasant task of distributing offices. Bonar Law claimed on behalf of his Party an equal share in the important posts and in all government patronage. The claim was conceded in "principle" by Asquith, but it soon became clear that a wide gulf lay between principle and practice. In fact Asquith did not intend to yield an inch more than he had to. Such an attitude was natural, even if in the long run it was unwise. Asquith still found it most repugnant to join forces with those who had been belabouring him so vigorously over the past ten years; he still possessed a comfortable majority in the House of Commons; the new arrangement involving, as it did, the jettisoning of many old friends and supporters was bound to be disagreeable to him.

The first great problem concerned Bonar Law himself. As Leader of the Opposition he had eminent claims to one of the key positions in the Cabinet. These, apart from the Premiership, were the War Office, the Admiralty, the Foreign Office, the Exchequer, and the newly created Ministry of Munitions. According to his own account Asquith decided from the start that there should be no change in the

War Office or the Foreign Office.[a] But he seems to have forgotten
that at one time he seriously considered getting rid of Kitchener.
He told Churchill on Monday, May 17th, when breaking the news
of Churchill's own removal, that Kitchener would go too, and
apparently both he and Lloyd George said the same thing to Bonar
Law.[b] But in the end he seems to have decided that Kitchener's
prestige with the public, both at home and abroad, outweighed his
admitted defects as War Minister.

This decision meant that the only positions available for Bonar
Law, if he was to be given his proper status, were the Exchequer or
Munitions, for Asquith had already decided that the Admiralty
should go to Balfour who was Churchill's nominee for the succession,
and who, through his membership of the Committee of Imperial
Defence, seemed better qualified than anyone else to take over the
vacant post. At first Asquith appears to have favoured giving Bonar
Law the Exchequer, and indeed to have said so to Bonar Law himself. Austen Chamberlain strongly urged Bonar Law to take it, and
in a letter of May 17th waived any supposed claim that he himself
might have to the post:[c]

"... I presume that tomorrow you will give no hint at our shadow
cabinet as to who is to be in and who out beyond saying that Asquith has
offered you a fair share of places and has proposed that you should be
Chancellor of the Exchequer, Lansdowne President of the Council, and
A.J.B. 1st Lord.

"I attach great importance to your being Ch. of the Ex. That office
gives its holder great authority and power. There is none other except the
Prime Ministership which gives such influence, or such a starting point
for influence in the whole field of policy. It is second in the Govt. when in
the right hands. I beg you to take it. Don't for one moment think that it is,
as you said, 'hard on' me. I have no ambition for it, and I think that there
are special reasons why *in a Coalition Govt.* I should *not* take it. ...

"If I have had an ambition it has been (ever since I was Civil Lord in
'95–1900 except for a moment, I confess, when I thought the leadership
was falling to me) to be 1st Lord of the Admiralty. That is out of my reach,
and I only mention it to show you there is nothing 'hard on' me in being
sent elsewhere than the Treasury. If you take office I will go anywhere
where I can be useful."

But on reflection Asquith thought better of his original proposal.
What is more, he decided not only to keep Bonar Law out of the
Exchequer but to keep him out of Munitions too. The latter post
was to go to Lloyd George. For a moment Asquith contemplated
taking the Exchequer himself, but to hold it along with the Premiership – a task which even in peace-time had strained all Gladstone's

great abilities to the limit – was evidently impossible in war. The Unionists made it clear that they would never agree. The Liberal leader therefore resolved to give the post to McKenna, who was then Home Secretary, on the understanding that he would make way for Lloyd George when and if the latter wished to return. Accordingly the argument was spread abroad that it would be impossible to have a Tariff Reformer as Chancellor of the Exchequer in a House of Commons with a large Free Trade majority.

This argument had some faint plausibility as far as the Exchequer was concerned, but it could not conceivably apply to the Ministry of Munitions. There, indeed, Bonar Law's claims were overwhelming. The job of the new Minister would be largely one of negotiating with the world of business and securing the co-operation of the great industrialists. Bonar Law was among the very few prominent politicians, perhaps the only one at that time, to have had a business career before he entered politics. On grounds of personal suitability and Party claims he should have been given the post. Both Balfour and Kitchener wanted him to take it, and Austen Chamberlain, when he heard that the Exchequer was not available, held the same view. Writing on May 20th he urged him to insist upon it.[d]

"1. Because it is the biggest thing you can do in this country.
"2. Because it can *now* be made a success. . . .
"3. Because what Balfour said shows that Lloyd George is not equal to it and this is confirmed by what we know of him as an administrator.
"4. Because you are, as I said today at Lansdowne House, the only one of us who has been in business and had a business man's knowledge and training."

Bonar Law agreed with these arguments. He promised his colleagues that he would not give way. The question had already held up the announcement of the new Government, and now after nearly a week a decision had to be taken. Asquith was in an awkward position. Unless Bonar Law agreed, he could not form a Coalition Ministry at all, and the Prime Minister must have realized that, quite apart from the personal slight to Bonar Law, the Conservative Party might well feel indignant if out of the six most important Cabinet posts they only received one (the Admiralty for Balfour).

When Bonar Law came to see Asquith, the latter referred him to Lloyd George. Lloyd George made a vigorous appeal in the name of patriotism, unity, and other noble abstractions, to Bonar Law to withdraw his claim.[e] Always reluctant to push himself, Bonar Law gave way. He returned to his friends with the news that he had accepted the post of Colonial Secretary – a position which, whatever its peace-time status, was in time of war only in the second rank of importance. That the exclusion of Bonar Law was a deliberate and planned manoeuvre is shown by the following memorandum among Asquith's papers. It is published by Asquith's biographers but they have prudently omitted the words in italics.[f]

"On the morning of Tuesday, May 25th, I commissioned Ll. George to see B. Law and point out:

1. The resentment of our party at the exclusion of Haldane.
2. Their resentment at the inclusion of Carson.
3. The impossibility from a party point of view of both the Admiralty and the War Office[1] being in Tory hands.
4. The impossibility of having a Tariff Reformer at the Exchequer.

"*This was intended to prevent B. Law taking the office of either Munitions or the Exchequer.* [Author's italics.]

"Later in the day the Tory leader in substance accepted the position, Ll.G. going to Munitions, McKenna to Exchequer.

                                          H.H.A.   26th May."

What were Asquith's motives? He appears to have left no account of his reasons for acting as he did. Therefore any conclusion must be a matter of surmise. It is reasonable to suggest two principal causes. As we have seen, Asquith neither found Bonar Law a congenial character nor thought highly of his talents. He had far more respect for men like Balfour, Lansdowne or Curzon. He may, therefore, have genuinely considered that Bonar Law's abilities did not warrant anything more important than the Colonial Office.

Moreover it is easy to see that from a political point of view there was something to be said for giving the leader of the Opposition a depressed status. On the principle of "divide and rule", Asquith's own position in a Coalition Government might be strengthened if the principal Conservatives had no definite leader to represent them, if in fact the whole question of Tory leadership seemed to be thrown open. After all there was much sore feeling when Bonar Law became leader in 1911, and Asquith knew that those feelings had not been entirely forgotten. If this was Asquith's calculation, it was to some extent justified. Long and Chamberlain, it is true, remained entirely loyal to Bonar Law, but there can be no doubt that his position was weakened in some quarters. Curzon in particular was a prominent exponent of the view that the Coalition had put all the Conservative

---

[1] The War Office was actually in the hands of Kitchener who did not officially belong to any party, but Asquith was probably thinking of the Ministry of Munitions as a part of the War Office, and no doubt regarded Kitchener as a virtual Tory.

Ministers on the same level, owing allegiance to the Prime Minister but to no one else; that the position of Conservative leader had lapsed – at least for the duration of the war. Such a theory suited Curzon's own secret ambition. As time went on and as Lansdowne became less and less important in the world of politics, Curzon's stock began to rise. Asquith, whether or not his motives are correctly estimated here, undoubtedly tended to exalt Curzon at the expense of Bonar Law and Lansdowne, the official leaders of the Conservative Party.

Bonar Law's position was far from being the only matter of contention in the formation of the new Cabinet. The Unionists were particularly anxious to exclude Haldane, the Lord Chancellor, and McKenna, the Home Secretary, from the Government. In the case of the former they were successful. He had once observed that Germany was his spiritual home, referring in fact to the cloudy metaphysicians of that country, to whose works he was addicted; but this was a fatal admission to have made, now that public feeling condemned everyone who had ever, in any context, spoken well of Germany. Bonar Law made his exclusion an absolute condition. But McKenna, as we have seen, was able to survive, and indeed to rise to the even more elevated post of Chancellor of the Exchequer.

The other object of the Conservatives' wrath was, of course, Churchill. They were determined to keep him out of the Admiralty at all costs. But he was not the man to retire at all willingly. If he was to sink, it would be with guns blazing to the end. He felt – and with some reason – that he was being most unjustly treated. As a last expedient he even wrote a long letter to Bonar Law to justify his policy and demand an enquiry.[1]

This was a truly desperate measure, for he had already been told by Aitken, who acted as a link between the two men, that Bonar Law would never agree to his retention, and Bonar Law confirmed it personally soon after. Bonar Law replied to Churchill's letter on the same day (May 21st):[g]

"My dear Churchill,
"I thank you for your letter which I shall show to my friends beginning with Austen Chamberlain but, believe me, what I said to you last night is inevitable.
"Yours sincerely,
A. Bonar Law."

Austen Chamberlain agreed with Bonar Law.

[1] Published in full in *Politicians and the War*, Vol. I, pp. 126–9.

"I return Winston's letter," he wrote,[h] "I wish him nothing but good and can sympathize with his feelings; but, as you said, his proposal is impossible.

"1st because he has not the confidence of *either* the Navy or the country.

"2nd because it demands a full enquiry by a cabinet and there is no cabinet to enquire."

Accordingly Churchill yielded his place to Balfour and became Chancellor of the Duchy of Lancaster with the consolation of a seat on the War Council. It was indeed a melancholy decline. He, who had moved fleets from ocean to ocean, and surveyed with an all-embracing eye the entire strategy of the war, found himself in an office whose routine business consisted of such grave matters as the appointment of a new Commission of the Peace in Bootle.

The leading members of the Conservative Party, despite their long absence from office, showed a commendable spirit of self-sacrifice in pressing their claims. We have seen how Austen Chamberlain be-haved over the Exchequer. Indeed he went further, and, suggesting to Bonar Law that Lord Milner should be given office, he declared that he would himself accept a mere under-secretaryship if it made matters easier. Walter Long was equally co-operative, "I leave my-self in your and his [Lord Edmund Talbot's] hands", he wrote; although he added:[i]

"I cannot pretend that I shall not feel it acutely if I am obliged to take an office below the rank of a Secretary of State after all these years and all that has happened. Balfour offered me the Admiralty in 1905, and you know all about the leadership."

Unfortunately it was not possible to accommodate him with a Secretaryship of State, but having made his protest Long loyally accepted the post of President of the Local Government Board. Two other examples of self-sacrifice were Finlay, who readily abandoned a strong claim to the position of Lord Chancellor, and Lansdowne who offered to remain out of office altogether if his inclusion pre-judiced the appointment of Curzon or Selborne. In the end, however, he became a member of the Cabinet without portfolio.

But when we descend to the less important posts the position becomes somewhat different. Here the thirst for office resembled that of travellers who have for many days journeyed in a parching desert and see for the first time the thin trickle of water in an oasis. Bonar Law was bombarded with letters from his supporters pointing to their many years of service, to the debates in which they had taken part, the sacrifices that they had made for the Party, the Bills which they had supported or opposed. To the passion for office, inevitable in a Party that had been so long in opposition, was added a burning desire to serve their country in time of war. Further, when it is remembered that only half the places normally available to a Party entering into power were at the disposal of the Conservatives, there is no need for surprise at the intense competition that followed.

Nowhere was this more evident than in the case of the Law offices. It was generally agreed that Carson had overwhelming claims to become Attorney-General – despite the bitter opposition of Redmond and the Irish Members. Moreover, Bonar Law was determined to see that F. E. Smith received proper recognition of his great talents – a determination shared to the full by F. E. Smith himself. Bonar Law was successful and F. E. Smith became Solicitor-General. This meant that the Lord Chancellor had to be a Liberal. Since Sir John Simon had refused it, the only other candidate was Lord Buckmaster who thus found himself elevated, surprisingly young, to the highest judicial post in the land.

But it was the Irish Law offices which created the greatest difficulty. Asquith had agreed during certain preliminary discussions that James Campbell (later Lord Glenavy) should be made Lord Chancellor of Ireland, a position to which Campbell's standing at the Irish Bar undoubtedly entitled him. Bonar Law told Campbell, who was an old friend, of this offer. All seemed well, but in the meantime Asquith received angry protests from Redmond who objected on the grounds that Campbell had signed the Ulster Covenant. The Prime Minister had been compelled already once to disregard such protests – in the case of Carson. He did not feel that he could do so a second time. There followed a most protracted and embittered dispute. Asquith wrote to Bonar Law withdrawing the offer to Campbell.

"I have received your letter", replied Bonar Law,[j] "with the greatest regret and indeed dismay. It is not merely a question of disappointing Campbell, though that is serious to me after I told him that he would receive the appointment; but it means that we have no voice in the Irish Administration and therefore no knowledge of what is being done."

But Asquith remained firm in his refusal. At one time, indeed, it seemed as if the Cabinet might break up upon this apparently trivial incident. Bonar Law's own position was made no easier by the importunate attitude of Campbell himself, who pressed the claims of friendship to almost indecent lengths. He wrote to Bonar Law on an average every other day for three weeks. He even offered to accept a reduced salary, or none at all, for the duration of the war, provided he obtained the post – with its valuable right to a pension on retirement of £4,000 p.a. Bonar Law was pained, and indeed shocked, by this avidity on the part of his old friend, but he did his best for him and only accepted defeat when it was clear that Asquith would not yield, and that the only alternative was a break up of the Government, which would in such circumstances have been nothing short of scandalous.

Another problem was the position of the First Sea Lord. The Unionists had insisted that Fisher's resignation should be postponed, as a condition of entering into negotiations with Asquith. Bonar Law endeavoured to persuade the old Admiral to stay on, or at least to reconsider his resignation. But Fisher was determined to go. He considered that Balfour was scarcely better than Churchill as First Lord, and he was indignant that the latter remained a member of the Cabinet in any capacity at all. Also he was furious at the appointment of Sir Arthur Wilson as his successor. The end of his final letter to Bonar Law written on May 22nd is perhaps worth quoting:[k]

"I told him [J. A. Spender who was acting on behalf of Asquith] . . . that I would only serve under *you* or McKenna. *With either of you I want no guarantees.* Sir John Jellicoe has written the letter of his life against Sir A. K. Wilson being First Sea Lord and he says the whole fleet is unanimous and deeply stirred. I can only hope Jellicoe will not resign in consequence – that indeed would bring down the British Empire. *For the matter of that so will Sir A. Wilson if First Sea Lord!*[1]

"Yours truly,
Fisher."

In reality Fisher had already burned his boats when he sent an astonishing ultimatum to Asquith three days earlier. Fisher laid down six conditions which would guarantee victory. One of these was:[1]

"That I shall have complete professional charge of the War at sea, together with the absolute sole disposition of the Fleet and the appointments of all officers of all rank whatsoever, and absolutely untrammelled sole command of all sea forces whatsoever."

If Fisher was going to behave in so megalomaniac a fashion his retention was clearly impossible.

Next to the problem of appointments was the problem of honours. The Conservatives stipulated for their share of peerages, privy councillorships, baronetcies, and knighthoods. The question of these

---

[1] Wilson, in fact, though Fisher did not know it, had resigned refusing to serve with anyone but Churchill.

awards was the subject for much tiresome and not always very edify-
ing negotiation; and, as in the case of offices, the claimants far out-
numbered the vacancies. Most of the details are of no interest today,
but there was one letter which deserves to be recorded. Bonar Law
had obtained Asquith's consent to offer a baronetcy to Aitken, who
replied thus:[m]

Hyde Park Hotel,
June 2, 1915.

"My dear Bonar,

"I need not say how much obliged I am to you for the proposal made in
your letter today but, as I feel certain that the honour would be criticized
on the ground that it was given to me on account of personal friendship,
I must definitely decline it, because I think even a small thing like this
might weaken your position at the present time.

"Yours faithfully,

W. M. Aitken."

The Cabinet was announced on May 26th, just over a week after
the crisis had begun. The details are as follows:

*Prime Minister and First Lord of the Treasury	H. H. Asquith (L)
Lord Chancellor	Sir S. Buckmaster (L)
Lord President of the Council	Marquess of Crewe (L)
Lord Privy Seal	Earl Curzon of Kedleston (U)
*Chancellor of the Exchequer	R. McKenna (L)
Home Secretary	Sir John Simon (L)
*Foreign Secretary	Sir Edward Grey (L)
Colonial Secretary	A. Bonar Law (U)
*Secretary for War	Earl Kitchener
Secretary for India	Austen Chamberlain (U)
*First Lord of the Admiralty	A. J. Balfour (U)
*Minister of Munitions	D. Lloyd George (L)
Chancellor of the Duchy of Lancaster	W. S. Churchill (L)
President of the Board of Trade	W. Runciman (L)
President of the Local Government Board	W. H. Long (U)
First Commissioner of Works	L. Harcourt (L)
President of the Board of Agriculture	Earl of Selborne (U)
President of the Board of Education	A. Henderson (Lab)
Secretary for Scotland	T. Mackinnon Wood (L)
Chief Secretary for Ireland	A. Birrell (L)
Attorney-General	Sir Edward Carson (U)
Minister without Portfolio	Marquess of Lansdowne (U)

It can be seen that in a Cabinet of twenty-two there were twelve
Liberals, eight Unionists, one non-party (Kitchener) and one Labour.

This preponderance of the Liberals is even more obvious if we consider the six offices which really mattered. They have been marked with an asterisk. Four were held by Liberals, one was non-party and one by a Unionist. This inequality, together with the hard bargaining which had preceded the formation of the Government, did not promise well for harmony and good feeling in the next few months.

What of Bonar Law's part in these transactions? That he was right to press for a reconstruction of the Liberal Cabinet is beyond question. His attitude on the question of coalition had been consistent throughout. He opposed it as long as two conditions prevailed: (1) that he could keep his followers content with their rôle of "patriotic opposition", (2) that the Government conducted affairs sufficiently well to command the necessary prestige at home and abroad. The two previous attempts at coalition – at the outbreak of war, and over the question of Constantinople in March 1915 – had been rejected by Bonar Law because these conditions continued, in his opinion, to prevail. But with Fisher's resignation this was no longer the case. Bonar Law could not have restrained his followers, even if he had wished, from moving a vote of censure in the House of Commons. Moreover the open dispute between Churchill and Fisher was certain to shake an already tottering Government to its very foundations.

Ought Bonar Law to have bargained more keenly with Asquith for Unionist representation in the Cabinet? Some would say that he should have done so, and, above all, procured a better place for himself. But Bonar Law, though often accused of being a purely party man, was in fact singularly indifferent to these considerations during the war. He genuinely regarded the national interest as paramount, and he was not prepared to make Asquith's task more difficult by insisting too much upon party claims. Asquith himself had no such inhibitions. He undoubtedly resented the necessity of coalition and he was prepared to use the formidable powers of his office to the full in order to preserve as many Liberal places as he could. It is not surprising, therefore, that the Conservative Party seemed to come off badly in the delicate negotiations which preceded the formation of the First Coalition.

2

There was one personal matter, in no way connected with politics, which gave Bonar Law the greatest anxiety during this period. This was a criminal prosecution against the firm of William Jacks &

Company, in which Bonar Law had until the end of 1901 been an active partner. The prosecution was launched on the grounds that the firm had broken the laws which forbade trading with the enemy during time of war.

The facts were briefly as follows. William Jacks acted as selling agents for the Nova Scotia Steel & Coal Company. When war broke out on August 4th, 1914, a ship, the *Themis*, chartered by William Jacks, was *en route* from Nova Scotia to Rotterdam with a cargo of iron ore for certain German firms, among them Krupps, the great armament manufacturers. The defendants did indeed try to divert the *Themis* to an English port – not because they had in mind the danger of breaking the law about trading with the enemy, but because they saw very little chance of being paid by any German firm. Owing to a misunderstanding their efforts failed. The *Themis* docked at Rotterdam and began to discharge her cargo on August 11th. Six days earlier the Government had issued its first proclamation against trading with the enemy.

So far no offence had been committed, but there now followed an extremely complicated exchange of telegrams between the defendants and their Rotterdam agents [the latter pressing for delivery to the German firms, the former demurring on the ground that the German firms could not pay], the upshot of which was that William Jacks authorized, in return for the settlement of all outstanding debts, the delivery of about 7,500 tons of iron ore to Krupps and two other German firms. Some of the telegrams were intercepted by the Censorship, and the Lord Advocate's department proceeded to investigate the whole matter. By May 1915 it became clear not only that there would be a prosecution, but that Bonar Law's brother John Law, who was still a partner, might be among the accused.

Scurrilous rumours soon began to circulate about Bonar Law, though admittedly not in any quarters which commanded the slightest respect. On May 6th H. M. Hyndman, the elderly apostle of Marxism in England, wrote a letter to the paper, *Justice*, in which he implied that Bonar Law was implicated along with his brother. Bonar Law appears to have been greatly disturbed at this accusation. In fact he himself no longer had any executive connexion with the firm. He had ceased to be a partner and his only link with the firm was that he used them as bankers, leaving with them on deposit such surplus sums as he possessed, and drawing a fixed rate of interest.[1]

---

[1] He later acquired a block of preference shares in the firm but he does not appear to have had these at this time.

The sum to his credit with William Jacks fluctuated greatly from
year to year. In 1907 it was only £590. In 1915 it was £19,057. But
in reality the quantity was quite irrelevant. Bonar Law had no direct
interest in the profits or losses of the firm, except in the very general
sense that any depositor has an interest in the solvency of his bank
- if it goes bankrupt he loses his money. Nor of course had Bonar
Law any knowledge of, or control over, the firm's business transactions.

Stung by Hyndman's accusation Bonar Law prepared a statement
for the House of Commons. It was never actually delivered, but a
draft exists among his papers. After briefly reciting the facts about
his connexion with the firm Bonar Law concludes:[n]

"My relationship with my brother has always been so close and so
intimate that anything, which affected his honour, would not leave me
untouched. He has been accused of this great crime. To be accused does
not necessarily imply guilt. But if it should be proved that he has been
guilty I should not be willing to continue in public life, and I should at
once resign the position I now hold."

Bonar Law's brother was, however, taking the whole affair less
tragically. E. H. Robb, the firm's solicitor, wrote to Bonar Law.
After saying that there was no chance of the case being dropped, he
observed that the only bright feature was John Law's sense of
humour, the latter having told him that "if it were a matter of
imprisonment and there was any talk of leaving him out and taking
Wilson and Hetherington [two of the partners] he would much
prefer imprisonment to the worry of running William Jacks & Company in the absence of Wilson and Hetherington!"

In fact the prosecution did in the end decide to leave John Law
and the other partners out, and to proceed only against Wilson and
Hetherington, who had dealt with the question of the *Themis*. John
Law gave evidence in the trial and it was abundantly clear that he
was in no way responsible for what had happened. The trial began
on June 16th, 1915, at Edinburgh, before the Lord Justice General.
The leaders of the Scottish Bar were engaged for the defence but
their efforts were of no avail. Wilson and Hetherington had undoubtedly committed what was technically a crime, although it was
obvious that they did not intend to do so, that their minds were not
directed to the proclamation of August 5th, and that they were under
the impression that a transaction, begun before the war was even
contemplated, could be completed without criminal consequences.
Unfortunately some of the letters, which had been written a few days

after war began, and contained the ordinary expressions of courtesy to their German customers, made a bad impression, read out in court ten months later, when Germanophobia was at its height. The two defendants were found guilty and received brief terms of imprisonment.

Bonar Law was playing bridge, as he often did, at the Baldwin Club, on the day the verdict was announced. On learning the news Aitken went round at once to break it to him. He persuaded Bonar Law to leave the table – never an easy task – and told him what had happened. Bonar Law was deeply distressed. Indeed he was for a time in tears. The two partners were old friends of his and their plight greatly disturbed him. Moreover he felt that they had been hardly treated.

Four months later he wrote to Sir George Cave urging the War Trade Department not to persecute the firm. Referring to the two partners who had been sent to prison he said:°

". . . in spite of what has happened I think they are as honourable as other men . . . and though I think they were guilty technically I really believe that ninety-nine business men out of a hundred at the time would have done as they did."

On June 24th L. Ginnell, Irish Nationalist M.P. for North Westmeath, asked in the House of Commons whether any member of the Government had any financial interest in the firm of William Jacks & Company recently convicted for trading with the enemy. Bonar Law rose and replied, briefly stating the facts about his connexion. He was heartily cheered in the House. The *Morning Post* probably expressed the general opinion when it said in a leader the following day:

"No one but the parliamentary pariah who sits for North Westmeath would have dreamed of asking a question of the kind. Whatever may be thought of his political views or his political talents, there is no man in the House whose personal reputation is higher than that of Mr. Bonar Law."

With that we may end the story of an episode which, although it did no harm whatever to Bonar Law's repute, added very greatly to the worry and anxiety which he felt during this difficult period.

CHAPTER XVII

THE DARDANELLES

MAY – DECEMBER 1915

Bonar Law's duties as Colonial Secretary – The Dardanelles Committee – Bonar Law's brush with Asquith, and annoyance with Lloyd George – His doubts about the Dardanelles – Attitude of the French – Imminence of Bulgarian attack on Serbia – Courses open to Cabinet over Dardanelles – Recommendations of the General Staff criticized by Bonar Law – Carson resigns – Bonar Law objects to Asquith taking the War Office – He opposes sending Kitchener to the Dardanelles – He threatens resignation – Bonar Law gets his way – Churchill resigns – Efforts of Curzon to reverse decision to evacuate Dardanelles – Bonar Law's reply – Discussion of his actions – Reorganization of the War Office – Robertson becomes C.I.G.S. with special powers – Twilight of Kitchener

For the next year and a half Bonar Law occupied the position of Colonial Secretary. In those days no clear line was drawn between Dominions and Colonies. The Colonial Secretary dealt with the whole of the British Empire except India and Burma. Nevertheless, in time of war the post was not one of great importance despite the vast territories which came within its sphere. The biographer of Bonar Law need not devote much time to this side of his career. He performed his functions efficiently and quickly, winning at an early stage the approval of that most critical class, his permanent civil servants. In the House of Commons he gave a good account of himself, answered the various questions put to him with courtesy, clarity, and accuracy. It must be admitted that the subjects with which he dealt were not those upon which the fate of the nation depended. Such topics as the location of Archdeacon Birley in East Africa, the damage done by the grass louse in Jamaica, the remarks made upon the Nigerian Spirit trade by Mr. R. E. Dennett, were among the less pressing problems in a great war. Bonar Law's administration at the Colonial Office was quiet and competent. Beyond that there is little to be said.

Far more important during these months was Bonar Law's position as leader of the Unionist Party and a member of the War Council, or, as it was now termed, the Dardanelles Committee. This was an inner cabinet, concerned with war strategy, and so

named because the most important problems which it had to consider were those arising from the Dardanelles expedition. The
membership consisted of the following: Asquith, Kitchener, Balfour
Lloyd George, Bonar Law, Carson, Churchill, Crewe, Curzon, Sel
borne, and Lansdowne. As an instrument of policy it had from the
first grave defects. It had, for example, no power to take decision
binding upon the rest of the Cabinet. Yet there was little point in the
existence of the Committee, if all its decisions were liable to be
thrashed out again at length in full Cabinet. Moreover, it was too
clumsy a body and contained too many powerful personages for there
to be any chance of unanimity. An aggrieved minority could and did
appeal to the full Cabinet with the result that upon all controversia
issues there was a wasteful duplication of debate. Bonar Law was
soon aware of these defects, but he was in no position to remedy them

Quite apart from the question of governmental machinery there
was the question of politics and personalities. Indeed the cumbrou
mechanism was itself the product of a political situation which made
any speedy agreement upon policy extremely difficult. The Unionists
having, as it were, entered the Government by storm, viewed their
late antagonists in no friendly spirit. They deeply distrusted the
Prime Minister. In their early discussions there had been some debate
as to whether they could serve under him at all. A similar hostility
prevailed towards Lloyd George. Bonar Law himself was better
disposed than most Unionists towards the Minister of Munitions, bu
events were soon to make him share their sentiments. In general the
Conservative Ministers surveyed Asquith and the Liberals in the
spirit of a hostile court of enquiry rather than that of cordial col
leagues in the same Cabinet.

Two episodes occurred in the summer of 1915 ill-calculated to
improve Bonar Law's personal relations with the two principa
Liberal leaders. In August Asquith decided to appoint a Cabine
Committee to consider the advisability of introducing conscription
He omitted Bonar Law's name from the list. Bonar Law was under
standably annoyed at the fact that he was not even consulted, and
even more annoyed when he discovered that the Prime Ministe
had consulted Curzon and the latter had recommended his omission
The ensuing correspondence, which all took place on August 12th
speaks for itself:[a]

"Dear Mr. Asquith,
"I am greatly surprised to learn that you have not included my name in
the Committee which was decided upon in yesterday's cabinet. It is the

most important Committee which has been set up since the present
Government was formed and as the leader of our Party in the House of
Commons it is difficult for me to understand on what principle you left me
out of it without previously consulting me.

"Yours very truly,
A. Bonar Law."

Asquith replied at once:[b]

"My dear Bonar Law,

"I, of course, included your name in the first list of the Committee
which I showed to Curzon. We both thought it looked too long. So I left
out you and Simon as being both heavily occupied with departmental
work. But I need not say that I shall be very delighted if you will serve on
the Committee, and I have given instructions accordingly.

"Yours very truly,
H. H. Asquith."

Bonar Law was not mollified at learning that Curzon had been
thus consulted:[c]

"Dear Mr. Asquith,

"I have your note but my object in writing to you was not to ask that I
should be added to the Committee, and in the circumstances I prefer not
to serve on it.

"Yours very truly,
A. Bonar Law."

Asquith answered:[d]

"My dear Bonar Law,

"Just got your note – I very much regret that in the hurry I did not
consult you. You may be sure that it was not from any want of personal
consideration. I should be obliged if you would see your way to reconsider
your decision. I am sure that your co-operation would be a great gain to
the Committee.

"Yours sincerely,
H. H. Asquith."

Bonar Law maintained his refusal and declined to join the committee. The incident was trivial perhaps, but none the less symptomatic of Asquith's attitude to Bonar Law.

In September there occurred a second misunderstanding between
Bonar Law and one of his Liberal colleagues – this time Lloyd George.
Asquith had frequently to be away from London attending conferences in France and making visits to the front. In his absence who was
to act as Leader of the House of Commons? Clearly Bonar Law had
a strong claim to do so. He actually led the largest party in the House,

the Conservatives outnumbering the Liberals by one or two votes –
although the Labour and Irish parties normally gave Asquith a
comfortable majority. When Lloyd George became Prime Minister
at the end of 1916, Bonar Law became Leader of the House, an
arrangement which might well have been made long before. Now in
September 1915 Asquith appears to have agreed to make him deputy
leader, though it is not clear from whom the suggestion originated.
But Bonar Law had apparently omitted to consult Lloyd George,
who, ever since he became Chancellor of the Exchequer in 1908, had
held the position of Deputy Leader. On September 15th Bonar Law
received the following letter from Lloyd George:[e]

"My dear Bonar Law,

"Thank you for your note, but the P.M. whom I have just seen tells me
what you said to him yesterday on the subject of the Deputy Leadership
of the House, which you were anxious to secure.[1] As you are aware I have
held that position for 8 years. I have no objection to surrender it to you.
I wish, however, you had mentioned the matter to me. It would have been
more friendly and – having regard to our conversation yesterday – more
candid.

"There are grave issues to be settled involving the fate of the Empire,
and these personal arrangements, as I told the Prime Minister today, will
not weigh with me in the estimation of a hair. But I felt not a little hurt
that you had not thought to mention to me your desire for the position I
have so long occupied.

"Ever sincerely,

D. Lloyd George."

Bonar Law gave way as he had over the Ministry of Munitions.
A skilfully worded appeal of this kind was nearly always successful
with him. There was no further discussion of the position. Lloyd
George remained Deputy Leader. But Bonar Law's relations with
him became appreciably cooler – a fact destined to have important
consequences in the course of the next year.

Throughout the summer and autumn of 1915 the issue, which
dominated all discussions of strategy in the Cabinet, was the Dardanelles expedition. Since Bonar Law's attitude was of the greatest
importance in the decision ultimately taken it is necessary to summarize very briefly the course of events. The early stages lie outside
the scope of this narrative – the dramatic story of muddle and missed
opportunities, which is related with such eloquence by Churchill in
his *World Crisis*. By the time the Coalition had come into existence

---

[1] Apparently, however, Bonar Law disclaimed having made any such demand, for the
following day Lloyd George wrote to Asquith and said that Bonar Law had denied doing
so in conversation with him (Lloyd George).

hopes of an early victory had been frustrated. Sir Ian Hamilton's forces had, after desperate fighting, come to a halt on the Gallipoli peninsula. On the night of August 6th the attack was renewed, and a large force landed at Suvla Bay under the command of General Stopford. The Turks were taken by surprise, but a melancholy series of mishaps, combined with a display of incompetence on the part of the British Commander, seldom equalled in the annals of our military history, resulted in a miserable failure. Once again there was complete deadlock. Once again the Imperial forces were condemned to a dreary war of attrition upon the torrid and inhospitable shores of the Gallipoli peninsula.

Bonar Law found his worst apprehensions confirmed. He had not, at any time, been an enthusiastic supporter of the expedition. He was partly influenced by the letters he received from Sir Henry Wilson who was at this time liaison officer with the French and a strong advocate of concentration upon the Western Front. Replying to him on July 15th, 1915, Bonar Law wrote:[f]

"I have seen Amery and, like you, dread the whole Dardanelles business; but I am afraid we cannot abandon it. If Hamilton does not succeed with the troops he now has, I see nothing better in prospect than that he should hold his ground. I am a little more hopeful about it than when you were here, because we have very clear indications from our representative at Bucharest that the Turks are really short of ammunition."

Throughout the war Bonar Law was on good terms with the leading figures in the Army – far better terms than for example Lloyd George ever was. He listened to their opinions, and, rightly or wrongly, Army opinion was in general strongly hostile to diversions in the East. Bonar Law did not accept these judgments in any blind or uncritical spirit, but his natural instinct was to regard the generals as experts in their own profession, and to be most hesitant in supporting any policy which ran flatly against military opinion.

The failure at Suvla Bay had given a strong impetus to all the supporters of evacuation from Gallipoli, when suddenly a most unexpected event occurred. On September 1st, 1915, the French Government, hitherto uniformly hostile to the Dardanelles expedition, declared its willingness to despatch four divisions under General Sarrail to Gallipoli. The motive of the French in making so striking a *volte-face* was not obvious, and it only later dawned upon the British Cabinet that strategy was the least important of the considerations which prompted this startling decision. In fact it was based upon French internal politics, a desire to give an independent and important command to General Sarrail, the only sound anti-clerical Republican among the higher ranks of the French Army. The Cabinet was astonished at the news, especially when they remembered that Joffre had only recently brow-beaten the British into supporting his plan for a grandiose offensive on the Western Front. But whatever the French motive, their decision was welcomed. Even Bonar Law took a more favourable view of the Dardanelles. "Mr. Bonar Law", writes Churchill, "joined with me in pressing the despatch of still larger British forces to 'make a good job of it'."[g]

These optimistic sentiments were somewhat damped when it was learned that General Joffre had only agreed to the diversion of the four divisions on condition that he could retain them until the results of his forthcoming offensive in Champagne had become known. This was due to open on September 26th.

Meanwhile, yet a further complication appeared. The German victories in Russia, and the Allied failure at Suvla Bay convinced King Ferdinand of Bulgaria that the moment had come to throw in his lot with the Central Powers. Evidence accumulated to show beyond doubt that a combined Austro-German and Bulgarian offensive was imminent against Serbia early in October. The only power capable of aiding Serbia in time was Greece. It was argued accordingly that the Allies must at all costs procure the entry of Greece into the war, and that the only means of doing so was to send a substantial Allied force to Salonika. It would be a political rather than a military move, since there was no chance of an Allied army actually reaching Serbia in time to save the Serbs from being overrun. But it was hoped that such a move would stiffen the Greeks into fulfilling their obligations under their treaty with Serbia. So far so good, but where were the troops to come from? Not from France, where by the end of September the offensive was in full swing, and Joffre firmly refused to allow the departure of a single man. The only possible theatre which could be raided was Gallipoli.

Therefore the Cabinet was confronted at the end of September with three possible courses of action: (1) Complete withdrawal from the Near East and exclusive concentration upon the West. (2) The immediate transfer of some troops from Gallipoli to Salonika and, as a corollary, since there was no point in merely preserving a deadlock in Gallipoli, the ultimate withdrawal of all forces from that peninsula. (3) The reinforcement of Gallipoli in a last desperate effort to secure a decisive result. This of course meant disregarding the plea to send troops to Salonika.

Plan (1) was favoured by the weight of Army opinion and had some, although not much, support in the Cabinet.[1] Plan (2), or variants of it, was supported by Bonar Law, Carson, Lloyd George, Walter Long, and Austen Chamberlain. Plan (3) had the backing of Asquith, Balfour, Curzon and, above all, Churchill. With such redoubtable combatants there was certain to be a hard and fierce fought contest. Throughout October and November a ferocious paper warfare convulsed the Cabinet. Memoranda flew to and fro. Resignations were frequently threatened. It seemed that the Government could never survive.

The pro-Salonika party received valuable support when the French Government, reversing its original offer to send troops to Gallipoli, pressed instead, in the most urgent manner, for an expedition to Salonika. So far did they go that Joffre actually came to London and threatened to resign his command of the French armies if the British refused to support the Salonika plan. Joffre's attitude was the product of complicated political pressures, ill-comprehended by most Englishmen, but what Churchill calls "this outrageous threat" inevitably had the strongest influence upon the Cabinet. On October 6th the Cabinet was so deeply divided that it referred the whole question to the combined opinion of the War Office and Admiralty Staff. The Staffs produced a paper which began by strongly recommending plan (1), i.e. complete concentration of all resources on the Western Front. They then argued, consistently with this general doctrine, against any diversion to Salonika. But, they concluded, quite inconsistently with the rest of the paper, by recommending the continuance of the Gallipoli campaign. This recommendation when brought before the Dardanelles Committee resulted in such irreconcilable conflict that the Prime Minister decided to postpone the crisis by a characteristic and ingenious compromise; to send to Egypt as soon as possible 150,000 troops from France, and to decide later whether to employ them in Gallipoli or Salonika, the decision to be made after sending out some eminent soldier – Kitchener or Haig was suggested – to examine the situation in the Near East and report upon the best policy.

Neither Bonar Law nor Lloyd George was willing to accept this compromise. On October 12th each circulated a lengthy memorandum to the full Cabinet, and both seriously contemplated resigning. Bonar Law claimed that the so-called compromise was tantamount to complete abandonment of the Salonika plan, because the delay

[1] Lord Buckmaster was one of its advocates.

involved would mean the certain ruin of Serbia. He strongly urged that the troops should be sent to Salonika, not from France but from Gallipoli. He condemned the General Staff's proposal to reinforce Gallipoli as "quite indefensible". He pointed out,

"The whole tendency of the Staff paper is to recommend that all our efforts should be concentrated on France, and the suggested expedition to Gallipoli is against the whole spirit of the paper. I must also say that I am not in the least satisfied that this proposal represents the best military opinion."

He suggested that Sir William Robertson and Sir Douglas Haig should be so consulted. Bonar Law ended:[h]

"The decision of the Dardanelles Committee, if sanctioned by the Cabinet and adopted, would in my opinion be a fatal mistake."

Lloyd George wrote on similar lines but in more racy language. He described the idea of sending reinforcements to Gallipoli as "insane". "It is quite clear to anyone who reads the document prepared by the General Staff that this was no part of their original plan. It has simply been spatchcocked into their document by strong Dardanellian influences."[1] As a result of these representations General Munro was sent out to report on the advisability of withdrawing from the Dardanelles.

On the same day that Bonar Law and Lloyd George made their protests, Carson wrote a letter of resignation to the Prime Minister. His grounds were the failure to honour our pledge to Serbia and a general discontent with the whole way in which the war was being run. Bonar Law endeavoured to persuade him to withdraw, but Carson would not be shaken. His resignation was announced briefly on October 20th, although he postponed his full resignation speech until November 2nd. Here he put his resignation on the more general ground that the machinery of government was fundamentally defective, that it was no use having a War Council, even a small body of four or five, unless it had powers to bind the other Ministers, in other words unless it *was* the Cabinet. The Salonika episode, he claimed, was simply one example of the consequences of this defective machinery. Although Bonar Law sympathized with Carson's opinions on Salonika, he did not consider the resignation opportune or necessary at this particular moment, nor could he have looked with equanimity upon the presence of such a formidable member of his party standing outside the government, a focus for all the discontents inevitable in time of war.

[1] The whole Memorandum is printed in *War Memoirs*, pp. 298–304.

Meanwhile Bonar Law was assailed by more immediate worries. On November 1st Asquith broached privately to him a proposal that he (Asquith) should take over the War Office and combine it with the Premiership. Bonar Law at first agreed with this idea. Like most members of the Government he had become more and more disturbed at the way in which Kitchener was conducting affairs, and it was evident that a person of Asquith's calibre would at least bring some sort of order into what had become the most chaotic department in the Government. But having slept on the idea Bonar Law perceived its grave defects, and wrote to Asquith:[i]

Bonar Law to Asquith, November 2nd, 1915

"My dear Prime Minister,

"Your proposal to take the War Office yourself came to me so much as a surprise that the not unfavourable view which I expressed to you about it is entirely changed by further consideration. I quite recognize that so far as the work of the W.O. is concerned, nothing could be better than that you should be at the heart of it; but in my opinion it will be so badly received by the country that the whole benefit of the new departure will be lost.

"The criticism which is directed against the govt. and against yourself is chiefly based on this – that as Prime Minister you have not devoted yourself absolutely to co-ordinating all the moves of the war because so much of your time and energy has been directed to the control of the political machine. Now you are proposing to undertake duties which in the view of the country, as I believe, ought to be performed by a man who does nothing else, and thinks of nothing else, at the same time that you are continuing to do the work (and it is necessary work) which has already made you almost the busiest man in England. . . . I feel it would be impossible for anyone like myself to defend the arrangement.

"You will remember that at the time the coalition was formed all your Unionist colleagues refused to join the Govt. if you undertook the duties of Chancellor of the Exchequer as well as P.M. The objections to your present proposal are far stronger, and if anyone wished to find a reason for leaving the Govt. – and it is not impossible that some of your colleagues may be in that position – you are giving them an excuse which would have immense weight both with the House and the country. I am sorry that I did not express this view to you at once, but for the moment I thought only of the administrative work at the W.O. and overlooked other considerations.

"Now I feel in the strongest possible way that you could not make a greater mistake and I urge you to reconsider it.

"I should have preferred to discuss this matter with you, but I cannot ask you to spare the time to see me when you have today's speech in your mind.

"Yours sincerely,
A. Bonar Law."

On receiving this letter Asquith decided that he must abandon the idea of taking over the War Office as a permanency. He resolved however to send – or persuade the Cabinet to send – Kitchener to report on the Dardanelles, and during his absence, to act as temporary War Minister himself. His intention was not so much to get a second opinion on Gallipoli – General Monro had already by then pronounced decisively for evacuation[1] – as to get rid of Kitchener. Writing to Lloyd George on November 3rd, Asquith said that he was confident that he could put things on a better footing at the War Office. "We avoid by this method of procedure the supersession of K. as War Minister, while attaining the same result. And I suppose even B.L. would hardly object to such a plan."[j]

Bonar Law did not object to Asquith's temporary occupation of the War Office, and he approved of the changes which Asquith was able to make in its organization. Nor did he raise at first any objection to Kitchener's mission to the Near East, when the matter was discussed in Cabinet the following day, November 4th. But, as in the case of the Asquith's original proposal to become War Minister, a night's reflection made him change his mind. It was indeed a surprising proposal which Asquith had made. After all by now the Cabinet already had before it a clear military verdict from General Monro in favour of evacuation. The situation had been transformed since Bonar Law's protests of mid-October. Serbia had been utterly defeated and overrun. Direct communication through Bulgaria was now possible between the Central Powers and Turkey. Substantial Allied forces were being landed in Salonika; and, apart from the need to reinforce Salonika, there was reason to suppose that our positions in Gallipoli might become untenable, as soon as German supplies began to reach the Turks in large quantities. General Monro anticipated heavy casualties (30 or 40 per cent) in the event of a withdrawal but he thought that an even greater disaster would recur if the Army remained. In all these circumstances the sending of Kitchener seemed to Bonar Law merely a waste of time, a sop to the opponents of evacuation, a cause of dangerous delay in taking a vital decision.

Accordingly he wrote to Asquith the following day, November 5th, protesting at the decision of the Cabinet and demanding that the whole matter should be reopened.[k]

"You will perhaps remember", he wrote, "that when it was proposed that General Monro should be sent out I stated to the Cabinet that in my opinion we ought to evacuate the Peninsula . . . I consented to the delay

[1] "He came, he saw, he capitulated", writes Churchill with some acerbity, *World Crisis 1911–18*, p. 108.

necessitated by General Monro's visit and now it is proposed to have further delay, for which there is, I think, no justification, and which is only to be explained by the desire to postpone a disagreeable but inevitable decision. . . . If, as is at least possible, this delay may result in the destruction of our force, a weight of responsibility will rest upon the Cabinet, which I am reluctant to share. I therefore earnestly request you to call at once a meeting of the cabinet so that a definite decision may be taken on the subject."

Unfortunately Kitchener had already left, and even the supporters of evacuation were unwilling to cancel his entire mission, when they had, however reluctantly, agreed to it in Cabinet the day before. Bonar Law could not have put himself in a worse position. For whatever arguments he used, he could always be answered with the cry - "Why, if you believed all this, did you not say so on Thursday? It is too late now to reverse a unanimous decision. If we are to adopt such methods the conduct of business will become totally impossible?"

The Cabinet meeting held on November 6th resulted in complete deadlock. Bonar Law was in a minority of one but refused to be shaken. The following day was spent in prolonged discussions with Asquith, and vigorous appeals from his Unionist colleagues, in particular from Chamberlain and Long, against taking the irrevocable step of resignation. Bonar Law remained obstinate. On November 8th he actually sent his letter of resignation to Asquith,[1] who persuaded him to withdraw it and wait for Kitchener's report. But at the same time Asquith undertook to support Bonar Law over evacuation, and to join with him in pressing this policy upon the Cabinet.[m] On November 8th, Bonar Law wrote:[n]

"My Dear Prime Minister,

"In view of the discussion at the cabinet on Saturday (November 6th) and the appeal made to me by yourself and supported by our colleagues I have determined to postpone the consideration of my position in relation to the Gallipoli policy until Lord Kitchener's report has been received.

"Yours sincerely,
A. Bonar Law."

"I feel sure", wrote Asquith in reply, "you will not repent your wise and loyal decision."

But the struggle had resulted in a victory for Bonar Law on the real matter at issue. With Asquith on his side he was sure of defeating the Dardanelles Party, whatever the nature of Kitchener's report. A significant change in the composition of the War Committee showed the direction in which the wind now blew. On November 2nd the

Prime Minister had reconstituted the War Committee, reducing its members to five, Asquith, Balfour, Lloyd George, McKenna and Kitchener,[1] who departed on his mission two days later. But the names were not announced until November 11th. In the interval, presumably as a result of the events just described, Asquith thought it wise to add Bonar Law to the number. Scarcely less significant than the inclusion of Bonar Law was the exclusion of both Curzon and Churchill, the leading opponents of evacuation. The latter, indeed, was quick to see the implication of his own omission. On November 15th he resigned declaring his intention to go out on active service in France.

Bonar Law's observations on his resignation speech are of some interest.

"I entered the Cabinet, to put it mildly, with no prejudice in favour of the right hon. Gentleman. I have now been his colleague for five months. He has the defects of his quality and, as his qualities are large, the shadow which they throw is fairly large too, but I say deliberately, in my judgment, in mental power and vital force he is one of the foremost men in our country, and I am sure that every hon. Member of the House wishes him success, and every kind of success in the new sphere in which he is engaged."

The evacuationists were now victorious, and their position was greatly reinforced when Kitchener, who had gone out convinced that Gallipoli should be retained, cabled back on November 22nd advising withdrawal. The War Committee had no difficulty in coming to a unanimous decision on November 23rd in favour of carrying out this recommendation. Nevertheless, the Dardanelles Party was not ready to admit defeat. The decision still had to be ratified by the full Cabinet, and the opponents of evacuation fought a brisk rear-guard action with all the forces at their command. The ponderous artillery of Lord Curzon was brought into action and on November 25th he fired the first of two heavy salvoes in the form of lengthy memoranda for the Cabinet. In these the rotund eloquence, and rhetorical imagination of the Lord Privy Seal were given ample scope. A terrible picture was painted of the consequences of evacuation:[o]

"I ask my colleagues to picture the situation . . . a moment must come when a *sauve-qui-peut* takes place and when a disorganized crowd will press in despairing tumult on to the shore and into the boats. Shells will be falling and bullets ploughing their way into this mass of humanity. . . . Conceive the crowding into the boats of thousands of half crazy men, the

---

[1] Grey also attended when matters of Foreign Policy were discussed.

swamping of craft, the nocturnal panic, the agony of the wounded, the hecatombs of the slain. . . . It requires no imagination to create a scene that, when it is told, will be burned into the hearts and consciences of the British people for generations to come. What will they say of those who have brought about this supreme and hideous disaster?"

Five days later Curzon circulated a second memorandum with an equally fearful picture of the final scene on the beaches, which he described as "a welter of carnage and shame".[p]

By the time the reader had finished these effusions he might be pardoned for thinking that Curzon was describing something that had actually taken place before his own eyes rather than making an imaginative prediction which, incidentally, turned out to be wholly false.

Bonar Law was stimulated into replying to this second memorandum. He refers to Curzon's fearful picture of the evacuation and his description of that picture as a "welter of carnage and shame".[q]

". . . if this were an accurate picture, it would also be an accurate description. But I do not think it is an accurate picture. It implies an absence of discipline and a frenzied cowardice of which there are few examples in the British army and which is rarely found even in the crew of a merchant vessel when shipwreck overtakes her."

Bonar Law pointed out the dangers of remaining, and the evidence of German weapons arriving in increasing quantities.

"If the Central Powers attack us at Gallipoli with their own troops there is every reason to fear that our whole force will be destroyed: if not, then by remaining we shall not cause these powers to expend any energy whatever. It seems to be assumed, by a strange process of perverted reasoning, that by merely holding on at Gallipoli we should paralyse the whole offensive of the enemy in the East. . . ."

He concluded by asserting that every successive military authority consulted had advised in favour of evacuation, that the War Committee, although it included Asquith and Balfour, both strong opponents of evacuation, had now recommended unanimously in favour of abandoning Gallipoli, that the whole purpose of a small War Committee was to enable speedy decisions to be taken.

"Their recommendation was brought before the cabinet with the result that on a matter in regard to which delay must be dangerous and may be fatal no decision has been reached.

"I hope my colleagues will agree with me that the war cannot be carried to a successful issue by methods such as these."

The rearguard action of the Dardanelles Party had been the result of telegrams from Admiral Wemyss, the Naval C-in-C at Gallipoli, who made a last minute attempt to reverse the decision for evacuation, claiming that he could carry the Dardanelles by naval power alone. But Bonar Law's intervention was decisive. The British Government now at last ceased to vacillate. A final decision was taken to evacuate, and despite Curzon's melancholy predictions, the Army was withdrawn on the night of December 19th from Anzac and Suvla Bay, with scarcely a casualty.

These events have been discussed in some detail for two reasons. In the first place the importance of Bonar Law's influence in bringing about the evacuation of Gallipoli has rarely been given sufficient recognition.[1] Secondly, the whole story throws a curious sidelight upon Bonar Law's character. One of his weaknesses was a tendency to be out-manoeuvred in argument, especially when some unexpected proposition came up for the first time and caught him by surprise. On such occasions he was all too apt to agree with proposals to which on closer examination he would find himself deeply hostile. Both in the matter of Asquith taking the War Office as a permanency, and the question of sending Kitchener to report on the Near East, Bonar Law changed his mind abruptly, and protested with vigour against a policy to which he had consented only twenty-four hours earlier.

Naturally such a *volte-face* laid him open to the charges of inconsistency and vacillation. Anyone who wishes to resist a policy which the majority of his colleagues favour puts himself in a much weaker position if he fails to resist at once. To the general arguments against him there is then added the weighty consideration that almost anything is preferable to such violent fluctuations of opinion. Most men confronted with such a situation would swallow their doubts and, having once agreed, abide by their original compliance, hoping for the best. But Bonar Law was not the man to do this. His hesitation proceeded from a certain slowness in making up his mind. It did not stem from moral weakness or any inability to hold firm when once his mind was made up. It is a remarkable testimony to Bonar Law's tenacity, and the respect which his colleagues had for his tenacity, that he was able to win the day on the question of evacuation. A Liberal colleague gave away the secret of Bonar Law's success when he said, "Lloyd George is always threatening to resign, and we don't believe him. Bonar Law said he would resign and we knew he would."[1]

[1] Except by Lord Beaverbrook, *Politicians and the War*, Vol. I, pp. 157–74.

Although Bonar Law differed from Asquith on the issues of evacuation and the War Office, there was one matter upon which they, and most members of the Government, were agreed. This was a growing mistrust of the Secretary of State for War. The Unionists had entered the Cabinet as strong supporters of Kitchener, whose presence at the War Office they rightly regarded as the result of Unionist pressure. But the next six months had given them a less rosy picture of his abilities. The truth was that Kitchener endeavoured to do far too much himself. The War Office controlled until May 1915, war strategy, munitions and recruitment. Each was alone a whole-time occupation for an able man. Moreover, Kitchener totally lacked the inclination or the capacity to delegate work to others. The General Staff was reduced under his autocratic régime to a mere rubber stamp endorsing with obsequious regularity his own inscrutable, and increasingly capricious decisions.

To those defects may be added another. When war broke out Kitchener had not spent a winter in England for forty years. The great imperial proconsul was strangely ignorant of his own country. That same oriental remoteness which gave him his vast prestige with the British public – that awe and reverence which so often attaches to the unknown – was a grave disadvantage for a professional soldier, who, suddenly and without experience, found himself a member of the British Cabinet. Kitchener once said to Carson: "I don't know Europe, I don't know England, and I don't know the British Army." This ignorance, combined with a certain inability to express himself fluently, made Kitchener curiously reluctant to explain his policy to his colleagues. "It is repugnant to me", he once observed, "to reveal military secrets to twenty-three gentlemen with whom I am barely acquainted." But the Cabinet, obliged to take responsibility for the disasters which all too frequently followed upon Kitchener's decisions, was understandably incensed at this attitude.

By the end of October Bonar Law and Lloyd George were both convinced that Kitchener must go, and they made a strong protest to Asquith upon the subject. An undated note by Bonar Law to Lloyd George shows their views.[8]

"My dear Lloyd George,
"Have you any objection to my telling the P.M. that you had said to me that in your opinion as long as Lord K. was at the W.O. nothing but disaster was in front of us, that you had told me you had written to the P.M. that you could not continue to share responsibility if conditions at the W.O. were unchanged and that I had replied that if this question

were raised as a clear issue I should be compelled to take the same course."

Asquith agreed, and when he decided to send Kitchener to the Near East he undoubtedly hoped that it might be possible to supersede him, giving him instead some high position such as Commander-in-Chief of all Eastern forces. This plan was frustrated by the accident of a newspaper indiscretion. The *Globe* announced that Kitchener had resigned because of disagreements with his colleagues. The resulting uproar convinced Asquith that it would be politically dangerous to dismiss the War Minister. There was also the difficult problem of the succession. Therefore Asquith resolved to achieve his end by indirect methods. The Cabinet decided to elevate the Chief of the Imperial General Staff to the position of a second War Minister. The C.I.G.S. was to be responsible to the War Council for strategy, and from now onwards would have direct access to the Cabinet, where he could put his own views without having to submit them first to the Secretary of State. This really meant that the C.I.G.S. became the originator of strategy and the Secretary of State, though nominally his superior, declined into a mere administrator dealing with such problems as recruitment and man power.

In order to ensure that the change was really effective, Sir Archibald Murray, the existing C.I.G.S., was transferred to another post. Sir William Robertson, a far more formidable personality, replaced him. At his insistence the new arrangement was put in writing and, thus provided against all contingencies, Robertson entered upon his new domain with powers nominally inferior but in practice far superior to those of the War Minister himself. Kitchener offered to resign, but he was persuaded to remain. Only his strong sense of duty induced him to do so when his powers had been thus truncated. The new organization had little to recommend it in theory, but, as an *ad hominem* arrangement with the object of keeping Kitchener as a figurehead and transferring real power elsewhere, it had certain merits. Indeed, while Kitchener and Robertson were there it worked without any trouble, for the two men at once established the most friendly relations. It was only later that the real defects of the machinery became apparent.

The arrangements for the new organization were approved by Bonar Law. They became effective before the end of 1915. Another important change occurred at the same time, when Asquith replaced Sir John French by Sir Douglas Haig. The result of all these changes may be summarized thus. Until May 1915 war strategy had been run by Asquith, Kitchener, and Churchill. From May to December Churchill and Kitchener fought a losing battle against Bonar Law and Lloyd George, with Asquith as umpire. By the end of December they had been decisively beaten. But their defeat did not mean a victory for their opponents. Asquith saw to that. A third party had stepped on to the scene; the Army, in the persons of Robertson and Haig, was now in effective control and, backed by the Prime Minister, dictated the strategy for 1916.

As for Kitchener, his great career was moving into the twilight. In May he had lost his control over munitions to Lloyd George. In December he lost his control over strategy to Robertson. With his colleagues, as he well knew, his prestige had sadly fallen. Only with the public did his repute remain as high as ever. There he towered like some mountain peak above his fellows. Dusk approached, but, gazing at the summit bathed in sunlight, men were oblivious of the shadows creeping up from below.

CHAPTER XVIII

POLITICAL DIFFICULTIES

JANUARY – JUNE 1916

Bonar Law's private worries – Relations with his sons – Bonar Law's doubts about Asquith – His correspondence with Wilson – His reluctance to act against Asquith – Conscription – The Derby Scheme – Resignation of Sir J. Simon – Bonar Law insists on Conscription – Carried easily in Parliament – The Easter Rebellion – Chaos in Ireland – Proposals for Home Rule – Revolt of the Die-hards – Hostility of Lansdowne and Long – Bonar Law's speech at a Party meeting – His position as Leader imperilled – Death of Kitchener – Bonar Law and Lloyd George agree at Cherkley that Lloyd George should succeed – Bonar Law seeks Asquith at Sutton Courtenay – An interrupted bridge game – Bonar Law shocked at Asquith's levity

I

1916 was destined to be a gloomy and worrying year for Bonar Law. In his private life he experienced for the first time the anxiety of a father whose son is exposed to daily peril in the front line. Bonar Law was deeply devoted to his eldest son, Jim. At the outbreak of war he even tried to persuade his son not to join up at once, and displayed great distress when he discovered that Jim had done so without telling him. Afterwards Bonar Law was ashamed of this attitude. As if to make amends he resolved not to exert any influence towards procuring a staff appointment for his son. Nor did he raise any objection to his second son, Charlie, joining the K.O.S.B.s, although he was barely seventeen. Early in 1916 Jim, who had transferred from the Royal Fusiliers to the Flying Corps, completed his training and joined an Observation Squadron in France. From then onwards Bonar Law lived in constant fear of the dreaded War Office telegram announcing his son's death in action – a fear all too tragically justified eighteen months later.

Moreover, he had difficulty in reconciling himself to the changes which he found in his son's character. In July 1916 Jim had a serious crash, endeavouring to avoid a convoy of motor lorries which crossed the airfield as he was taking off. He had bad concussion and was given prolonged sick leave in England. Bonar Law saw much of him and discovered, as many fathers have done, that the experience of war matures the young out of all recognition. His son, writes Lord Beaverbrook,[a]

"had gone out a boy whom Bonar understood, he returned a man whom Bonar failed to understand. . . . There was no question of disagreement, but his father found a difficulty in adjusting himself to the new relationship".

To these private worries was added a heavy weight of public and political anxiety. The war showed no sign of ending. A long series of disasters attended Allied efforts in almost every field. At home the political situation grew darker and more perplexing, Bonar Law's own position increasingly precarious. Before the year had ended he was to be faced with one of the most complicated conflicts of personal and political loyalty which could confront any statesman. This will be described in its proper place, but it should be recorded from the outset that Bonar Law did not possess that happy gift of some politicians, the ability to take a hard and ruthless decision, and carry it through without further doubts or qualms of conscience. On the contrary with his natural melancholy, and his somewhat sombre view of life, he tended to brood about such problems in a manner incomprehensible to persons of sanguine temperament like Lloyd George, Asquith, or Churchill. Such a happy temperament is undoubtedly an advantage in politics. So also is a certain toughness of skin and an indifference to false or perverse criticism. Bonar Law lacked these qualities too. He was not indeed as hyper-sensitive to aspersions upon his honour as for example was Austen Chamberlain, but he hated to act in a way which could be represented even by the malicious as being dishonourable or discreditable. "That is the difference between Bonar Law and me," Lloyd George once said to Baldwin. "Poor Bonar can't bear being called a liar. Now I don't mind."[b]

Herein lies the clue to much of Bonar Law's dealings with Asquith. He viewed, indeed, with increasing alarm many features of the Prime Minister's administration. Some of their disagreements have already been recorded in the previous chapter. In addition to specific differences upon such matters as the Dardanelles and conscription, Bonar Law felt a more general mistrust of the whole way in which the war was being conducted, especially of the clumsy machinery of government, which Asquith refused to modify. But he was most unwilling to engage in anything which could be construed as an intrigue against the Prime Minister. To take any step against Asquith Bonar Law had to be convinced not only that Asquith's method of conducting the war was very bad, but also that some alternative could be found that was not even worse. Early in 1916 he was beginning reluctantly to be convinced upon the first point, but he remained wholly unconvinced on the second. In his opinion Asquith, despite grave defects, remained indispensable, the one man who could unite the nation in the great struggle against Germany.

Nevertheless, Bonar Law was well aware of the mounting hostility felt in many quarters for the Prime Minister. Early in March he observed to Lloyd George, "Asquith has no idea how unpopular his Government is".[c]

One of Asquith's bitterest enemies was Sir Henry Wilson. He wrote to Bonar Law at the end of March from France:[d]

"My dear Bonar Law,

"That old ramshackle of a coalition is, we all hope and trust, going to fall to pieces very soon. It has not been a success and the reason appears to me to be quite simple. We have at the head of it a man who has never gone to war, who has no intention, even now, of going to war, and who has no intention either of allowing anyone else to go to war.

"Now in spite of Squiff[1] we happen to be at war, and there is only one way of winning in war, and that is by going to war heart and soul. This, Squiff is both mentally and physically incapable of doing. Now I am fond of you – many of us are – and I don't want to see you go under when the crash comes. . . . You owe Squiff no loyalty, absolutely none. You saved him once when you joined him – and a bad day's work it was – whereas you owe the whole of your loyalty to our country, and you know as well as I do how shamefully, how disastrously, Squiff has tried to govern us. . . .

"Ever H.W."

But Bonar Law could not regard the situation in this light. He replied on March 31st:[e]

"My dear Wilson,

"I need not say that I am always glad to receive a letter from you; but I wonder if your own profession seems as plain to you as mine!

"What you say would do for an article in the *Daily Mail*, and I fancy expresses the view of the majority of our Party. The position, however, does not seem to me quite so simple. I wonder whether you have thought out the consequences of such a step as you propose? If we broke up the present Government, it is obvious that a new Government could not exist in the present House of Commons. There would therefore be the immediate necessity of a general election; it would be fought, in spite of the war, with almost the usual amount of party bitterness; and if our Party succeeded in getting a majority we would be faced with an opposition of precisely the

[1] A nickname for Asquith, widely used by those who disliked him. It had reference to the alleged conviviality of his habits.

same nature as that at the time of the Boer War. This would really mean in my opinion that in a very short time we would have martial law all over the country; for not only would there be strong Opposition in the House of Commons but that Opposition would encourage every form of opposition outside. . . . It may be that something of this kind may become necessary: it may be also that if we faced the danger and made up our minds that the best way of carrying on the war is by considering only the military position and ruthlessly dealing with all opposition, the best results would be obtained.

"In my belief however that is not what would happen, and we should find that the first effect of such a change, when it was obvious that instead of even the appearance of unity the nation was bitterly divided, would be to discourage our Allies and make our enemies feel certain that we could not stay the course. In other words my view is that with all its disadvantages the best chance of winning the war is by a Government such as the present, and of course as long as I hold that view I shall not do anything to change it. [The Government.]

"Do not suppose that I don't fully realize that the other – what I may call the ruthless – method may be best, but that must be a matter of opinion and my judgement is against it.

"Yours very sincerely,

A. Bonar Law."

Bonar Law had summed up his attitude rather more succinctly, a week earlier when writing to J. P. Croal.

"The whole political situation is as bad as it can be; so bad indeed that it seems to me very doubtful if the present condition of things can continue; but on the other hand I do not see the possibility of any change which would be an improvement."f

As long as Bonar Law envisaged the problem of change in terms of a break up of the Coalition, a General Election, and a return to party warfare, it was natural that he should take this view. There was, indeed, another solution: it might be possible to discover an alternative Prime Minister who would be able to unite the majority of both parties in support of a reconstructed coalition. In this way the whole machine of government might be overhauled without the need for a General Election and all the difficulties consequential thereon in time of war. But who would be the new Prime Minister? There were only two real possibilities – Lloyd George or Bonar Law himself. If those two could come together and agree upon (1) the need to overthrow Asquith and (2) which of themselves should replace him, then a change could take place without the dismal consequences contemplated by Bonar Law.

Yet, in early 1916, the chances of any such agreement seemed most remote. Bonar Law may have had his doubts about Asquith, but he certainly did not regard Lloyd George with any favour. On April 24th, Bonar Law had a long talk with Lord Riddell, and, if Lord Riddell's account is correct, spoke with considerable candour.[g]

They had both been guests at dinner with Sir Reginald Brade, the permanent Under Secretary for War, one of those civil servants whose influence upon events is all too likely to be forgotten by historians. "Bonar Law spoke much of L.G. He said that L.G. recently came to him and remarked that there was no real confidence between them, and that he would like a heart to heart talk. B.L. replied, 'I do not confide in you because I do not agree with you.' " These feelings were reciprocated by Lloyd George. A few days before, April 19th, Lord Riddell had dined with Lloyd George who said that he would not be prepared to replace Asquith by Bonar Law. "He thinks Asquith much superior to B.L. in every way – a much bigger man."[h]

As long as his two potential successors regarded each other in this light, Asquith was safe.

2

The two principal political problems in the first half of 1916 were conscription and Ireland. Fortunately the biographer of Bonar Law is not obliged to discuss either in very close detail. The question of conscription would indeed be a tedious topic to pursue through all its ramifications. The endless discussions, the attitudes taken by public men at various times, the compromises, the disputes, constitute a chapter in English history to which no doubt in years to come dull history professors will direct their duller research students. Here we need only notice a few salient points.

In general the Conservatives favoured and the Liberals opposed conscription. Lloyd George was an exception to this rule. He was a keen advocate of compulsion, and owed much of his unpopularity in Liberal circles to that fact. After the formation of the First Coalition it seemed highly probable that conscription would be enforced, and so it would have been but for the reluctance of the War Minister. Kitchener, for reasons not easy to understand, viewed conscription with a strange hostility. The Conservatives found it difficult to press for compulsion without a clear lead from the Minister most closely concerned, especially when they remembered that he was a great soldier and certainly could not be accused of Liberal sympathies.

In the autumn of 1915 the Government made a last effort to

exploit the voluntary system; this was the famous Derby scheme, so
called because its sponsor was Lord Derby who became Director-
General of Recruiting. By the end of the year the scheme had clearly
failed to produce the numbers required by the War Office, and
Kitchener at last began to press for some measure of compulsion.
Unfortunately one of the features of the Derby scheme had been a
virtual pledge by the Government that married men would not be
required for military service until the great majority of single men
had enlisted. This absurd differentiation, founded neither on justice
nor common sense, seriously hampered the first efforts of the Government to introduce compulsion. As regards voluntary recruiting it had
the effect which might be expected: large numbers of married men
attested their readiness to enlist, confident that they would not be
required for a long time, if at all, whereas on the best estimates over
a million single men remained outside the Derby scheme.

Early in 1916, after prolonged debates in Cabinet, Asquith brought
in a measure compelling the attestation of all unmarried men between
the ages of 18 and 41. He could not introduce general conscription
without seeming to betray the pledge given to the married men under
the Derby scheme. Even this modest measure of compulsion was
too much for some Liberals. Sir John Simon resigned from the
Cabinet, hoping perhaps to carry a substantial number into opposition.[1] If so he badly misjudged the war-time temper of the nation.
Not a dog barked, and the Bill was passed by overwhelming majorities in both Houses of Parliament.

The first Military Service Act was clearly only a temporary
measure. Bonar Law and his Conservative colleagues in the Cabinet
were anxious to bring in universal conscription at the earliest opportunity, for they were convinced that the Army's requirements could
be met in no other way. The Conservatives outside the Cabinet were
strong for the same course, especially the Unionist War Committee
whose chairman was Carson. But Bonar Law, aware of the political
difficulties involved, did not intend to be brow-beaten by any
external agitation into arriving at a premature decision on this
matter. Writing to Carson on April 4th, 1916, he said:[i]

"I am sure you will agree with me that I cannot allow myself to be
influenced either as to the decision which I shall think it my duty to take,
or as to the time which seems to me necessary before coming to that decision – even by my desire to meet your own views and those of the

---

[1] At one time it looked as if McKenna, Runciman, and Grey would all resign too, not
on the specific principle of compulsion, but on financial problems consequential upon its
introduction. They were, however, in the end induced by Asquith to remain.

committee which, as I know, is largely representative of the Party of which I have the honour to be the leader in the House of Commons."

There is a cool formality in Bonar Law's tone, which suggests that he was no longer on terms of cordial friendship with Carson. It was perhaps inevitable that Carson's position as the leading political figure outside the Government should bring him into collision with his leader. As we shall see, this divergence was soon to become even more significant.

Meanwhile, in the Cabinet the question of conscription was rapidly producing a crisis. The Liberals were still most unwilling to countenance universal conscription, and the Conservatives were divided on the matter, some favouring it whatever the political results, others reluctant to force it through at the cost of disrupting the Government. For a time Bonar Law belonged to the second category, but careful examination of a memorandum submitted by the Army Council convinced him that conscription was vital; further, that he would be placing an impossible strain on the loyalty of his own supporters, if he asked them to vote against a policy so strongly advocated by the military experts.

On April 17th Bonar Law addressed a long letter to Asquith. He argued that the only logical course now was to enforce universal conscription for all men of military age, married or single. He severely condemned the compromise proposals (the details do not matter) brought forward by a Cabinet committee over which Asquith had presided. He had been willing to oppose conscription, despite his own conviction of its necessity and his knowledge that nearly all his party favoured it, if such opposition was the only way to secure national unity. But the verdict of the Army Council seemed to him conclusive. He ended:[j]

"I think it is easier for you to carry your supporters in favour of compulsion than it is for us to obtain the support of our Party against it. . . . I think it right to send you this letter at once, before I have had the opportunity of consulting my Unionist colleagues, not as my final decision – for in that I shall be influenced by the views of my colleagues – but as an indication of what I think that decision must be."

Meanwhile, Lloyd George was bringing all his guns to bear upon the anti-conscriptionists. The Cabinet seemed again and again on the verge of dissolution. On April 25th, a Bill embodying a new series of compromises was introduced by Walter Long on behalf of the Government. It satisfied no one, and was withdrawn the next day. Finally on May 2nd Asquith, yielding to the pressure of Lloyd

George and Bonar Law, announced that he intended to bring forward a measure conscripting all able-bodied men between 18 and 41. Bonar Law's judgment turned out to be correct. There was no split in the Liberal Party. Sir John Simon's "cave" numbered a mere 27, to which could be added 10 followers of Ramsay MacDonald. No one resigned. The Bill received the Royal Assent on May 25th. For the moment the Government was safe.

3

The attitude of the Cabinet to conscription was considerably affected by the other great question agitating the political world at this time – the question of Ireland. Once again with that strange mixture of tragedy and farce, of folly and heroism, which so often colours their history, the Irish stepped into the limelight. On April 22nd, Sir Roger Casement, who had been landed in Kerry by a German submarine, was arrested. On the same day a German vessel laden with arms was seized off the Irish coast and scuttled by her crew while being conducted under naval escort to Queenstown harbour. Two days later, on Easter Monday, an armed insurrection broke out in Dublin; Sinn Fein forces seized the Post Office and other public buildings; P. H. Pearce proclaimed himself President of the "Irish Republic"; a number of British soldiers were murdered in the streets, and a large part of the centre of the city was consumed by flames. After a week of fighting the rebellion was suppressed with considerable bloodshed. Martial law was proclaimed in Ireland. Several of the leading rebels were summarily court-martialed and executed.

The Easter Rebellion was repudiated at first by the overwhelming majority of Irishmen. Many people have claimed that, if a greater degree of clemency had been displayed, then the extremist party in Ireland would have died a natural death, and the fearful bitterness of the years to come might have been avoided. It may be so. But it was difficult for any Government in the midst of war to display such magnanimity. In the next few weeks the Cabinet was assailed with equal fury by those who declared that it had been far too harsh and those who asserted that it had been far too weak. Believers in the doctrine of the Golden Mean will perhaps conclude that the Government had behaved with sense and moderation in circumstances of great difficulty.

Asquith visited Ireland in May and came to the conclusion that the existing system of government had broken down entirely, and that the only way to prevent the Sinn Fein extremists securing all the support previously accorded to Redmond and the moderate Nationalists would be to concede some measure of Home Rule. The Conservatives viewed such a step with much scepticism but Bonar Law agreed to Asquith's proposal that Lloyd George should endeavour to negotiate a settlement between Redmond and Carson. Lloyd George was successful as far as the Irish leaders were concerned. Redmond and Carson agreed to a settlement involving the immediate enforcement of the Home Rule Act, subject to an amending Bill excluding the six Ulster counties for the duration of the war. At the end of the war an Imperial Conference would be held in order to consider the whole government of the Empire including the government of Ireland. For the duration of the war the Irish Members would continue to sit in full numbers at Westminster.

Carson and Redmond hastened to Ireland in order to secure the support of their respective parties for the new proposals. But in the meantime a furious storm began to rise within the Coalition Cabinet. Lloyd George's plan encountered the fiercest opposition from the old guard of the Conservative Party. As we have already seen, Bonar Law was himself by no means a fanatic upon this subject – although he has frequently been regarded as such by subsequent historians. He disliked Home Rule, but he did not believe that it could be indefinitely postponed. What chiefly concerned him was the question of Ulster, and Lloyd George's plan seemed to him to give all that could reasonably be required for the duration of the war.

But Bonar Law could not go too far ahead of the sentiments of his Conservative colleagues. It soon became clear that a powerful group of Unionists would fight to the death rather than give way on the question of Home Rule. The leading figures of this group were Lansdowne, Walter Long and Selborne. The latter indeed resigned as soon as he learned of the proposals which Lloyd George, Carson and Redmond were making, and did not even wait for the Cabinet's verdict. The first two – more wisely perhaps – remained in the Cabinet and asserted their views there. Once again the Government seemed on the verge of collapse. Bonar Law returning from Paris toward the end of June found himself in the midst of a perilous crisis. Along with Carson and Balfour he fought as best he could for the Lloyd George plan, but the opposition was too strong. On July 7th Bonar Law summoned a Party meeting at the Carlton Club and tried to persuade the rank and file of his supporters. He concluded:

"I quite admit there is a danger in setting up this Government in Ireland, but there is a danger always with regard to Ireland: there is only a choice of evils. It may be that to do this is a gamble, but the alternative is not a gamble: there is not even a gambler's chance if we do not. . . .

"It is now nearly five years since in circumstances which you all remember you chose me to be your leader. Before the outbreak of war neither Lord Lansdowne nor I thought that our task was especially easy, but it was child's play in comparison with the difficulties we have had to face since. Until that time we had been going along the beaten track of ordinary party warfare: we were engaged in that party warfare but we had our Party behind us, and none of us cared what was said by our opponents – in fact perhaps we rather liked it. With the outbreak of war all that has changed: there is now no beaten track for us to walk on. Since then we have been sailing on an uncharted ocean with no compass to guide us except this, that we are bound to do what we think right in the national interest without regard even to the interests of our Party. (Hear, hear) Whether I am right or wrong that is what I am doing now. I am bound to do what I think right and as long as I am in the position in which you placed me I am bound to tell you what my conviction is, and it is this, that if we go back on these negotiations now as a Party we shall make a terrible mistake."

But, although Bonar Law was supported by Balfour and other important Unionists, it was far from certain that he carried a majority of his party with him. Lansdowne who also addressed the meeting made no secret of his hostility to Home Rule. There can be little doubt that he and Long represented the feelings of most Unionists: that to set up Home Rule, even with Ulster excluded, was a dangerous concession in time of war, a concession moreover which had all the appearance of being extorted by rebellion and revolution instead of being based upon a just assessment of the merits of the case. The meeting adjourned without coming to any conclusion, Bonar Law shrewdly perceiving that to take a division might be unwise and merely crystallize opposition.

In any case the scheme was destined very soon to founder. Lansdowne attacked the proposals openly in the House of Lords, and Bonar Law himself declared that he could not agree to the full number of Irish Members remaining at Westminster. All the Unionist Members of the Cabinet were firm on this point, for they feared that otherwise the 80 Irish Nationalists would continue to be able in certain circumstances to determine who should govern England – and this seemed an intolerable position *after* Home Rule had been granted. Redmond, however, regarded the maintenance of Irish representation as an indispensable guarantee that the settlement was temporary, and that the permanent exclusion of Ulster had not yet been conceded. Bonar Law declined to give way. The negotiations were brought to an end, and late in July the old system of government was restored, with a Unionist Chief Secretary, H. E. Duke (later Lord Merrivale), in place of the discredited Birrell.

The Irish negotiations had brought Bonar Law into closer touch with Carson and Lloyd George, but had alienated him from the bulk of the Unionist Party. We have already seen how Asquith, whether by chance or design, had weakened Bonar Law's position as leader. These latest events – though of course Asquith had no responsibility for them – had an even more unfavourable effect upon Bonar Law's prestige. He was bombarded with angry and abusive letters from Conservatives in every walk of life. It was perhaps fortunate for his personal fortunes that the negotiations broke down as they did. Otherwise he might have been the object of still greater wrath on the part of his colleagues and supporters. Even as it was, the summer of 1916 saw him acutely conscious of his dangerously isolated position. This refusal to swim with the main current of Conservative thought, or to bow to the antiquated idols which the Party had so long been worshipping was to his credit as a statesman, but to his peril as a politician and party leader.

4

Before these events came to their melancholy conclusion an important change had occurred in the Cabinet. On June 5th the *Hampshire* in which Kitchener had sailed for Russia struck a mine off the Orkneys. Kitchener and all his staff were drowned. The news spread a thrill of horror and dismay throughout the country. Even members of the Cabinet who had long surveyed with increasing doubts the conduct of the War Minister were stunned by the shock of this disaster. Kitchener's death left a most important vacancy. Who would succeed him at the War Office?

The two obvious claimants were Bonar Law and Lloyd George. There was indeed a third possibility. Many prominent soldiers fearing that Lloyd George might make difficulties with the Army Chiefs, favoured the appointment of Lord Derby, but the latter indicated at once that he did not aspire to such an elevated position. He would however be willing to serve as under-secretary to Bonar Law. Such an offer strengthened Bonar Law's claim to the post, for Derby possessed much prestige at this time. Bonar Law's own feelings were mixed. He did not particularly want to be War Minister. The Kitchener-Robertson agreement had deprived that office of much of its effectiveness. On the other hand he did not wish to be slighted again by Asquith and would have resented the offer being made to any Unionist other than himself.

On Sunday, June 11th, Aitken entertained Bonar Law and Lloyd George to luncheon at Cherkley. The avowed purpose was to achieve agreement on this important topic for, on the following day, Bonar Law had to leave for France, and it was necessary to settle the matter as soon as possible. The War Office was temporarily in the hands of Asquith who had so far come to no decision.

The two Ministers arrived quite early. "The conversation between them", writes Lord Beaverbrook,[k] "began extraordinarily badly as is often the case between two public men who are not on close terms of friendship with one another." Bonar Law apparently taxed Lloyd George with being too ambitious, too much on the make, and thus disturbing the harmony of the Cabinet. Lloyd George skilfully avoided these complaints. Declaring that the past was not worth discussing he diverted the conversation to the immediate problem – who was to be War Minister? He maintained that a weak man, a mere satellite of Asquith would be impossible, that the choice lay between himself and Bonar Law, and he offered to give full support to Bonar Law. "Yet even to this gesture", writes Lord Beaverbrook, "Bonar Law did not respond very readily." But the discussion was resumed after lunch, and eventually the two men agreed that Lloyd George should be War Minister, provided he could get some modification of the Kitchener-Robertson agreement, and that Bonar Law would see Asquith, and back his claim, if necessary with the threat of resignation.[1]

Bonar Law now endeavoured to get in touch with Asquith, only to be informed that if he wanted to see the Prime Minister he must go to the latter's house, The Wharf, at Sutton Courtenay in Berkshire. Bonar Law was naturally irritated at this news. It was too late to go that evening and the next morning he and Aitken were due to leave for Paris together. However, he could not risk Asquith making the appointment before he had time to put the case for Lloyd George. Accordingly on Monday morning he motored with Aitken from Leatherhead to Sutton Courtenay. Bonar Law went into the house leaving his companion in the car. He subsequently told Aitken that he found the Prime Minister engaged in a rubber of bridge with three ladies.[m] Asquith genially requested him to wait till the hand was finished.[1] Bonar Law, by now considerably annoyed, declined to

[1] Lady Violet Bonham Carter says that Mrs. Derenburg, a guest at The Wharf, states

wait and informed him of the discussion with Lloyd George. Asquith immediately offered the War Office to Bonar Law. Bonar Law replied that it was too late: he would have taken it had it been offered before his discussion with Lloyd George, but by now he was committed to the latter; and in any case he considered Lloyd George the best man for the job. Faced with this situation Asquith agreed to offer the post to Lloyd George.

The episode left a lasting impression upon Bonar Law's mind.[n] His doubts about Asquith were more than confirmed. It seemed to him that the Prime Minister displayed a levity which was inexcusable in so serious a matter. Moreover, he regarded it as wrong that the leader of a nation engaged in a struggle for its existence should oblige one of his principal colleagues to put off all arrangements in order to visit him at his country house fifty miles away from London, and then keep him waiting when he arrived. Earlier in the year Bonar Law had observed in a letter to Asquith:[o] "In war it is necessary not only to be active but to seem active." These were words that Asquith would have been prudent to heed. They might well be the epitaph upon his war administration. Bonar Law was austere and serious minded. Such an appearance of frivolity on the part of the Prime Minister surprised and shocked him. Moreover, it made him wonder whether appearance and reality were in fact so different as he had hitherto hoped and believed.

that Asquith was upstairs in his bedroom when Bonar Law arrived and sent down a message with his butler asking other guests to entertain him until he (Asquith) came down.

She also says that the Visitors' Book at The Wharf does not contain as many as three bridge-playing ladies among those staying in the house at the time in question. She further states her own belief that Asquith never played bridge before dinner.

In view of the lapse of time, it is difficult to regard any of these points as conclusive, but, nevertheless, I have thought it only fair to state them. Lady Violet Bonham Carter explains her father's presence at The Wharf on a Monday morning by the facts that it was the Whitsun weekend, and that he had an important speech to prepare.

CHAPTER XIX

THE TRIUMVIRATE

JULY – DECEMBER 1ST, 1916

Discontent at progress of the war – Defects of Governmental machinery – Bonar Law suggests a reform – Asquith's defects as a chairman – Asquith's enemies, Carson, Northcliffe, Lloyd George – Their differences – Churchill returns to England – Bonar Law's hostility to Asquith's opponents – His bad relations with Carson – Asquith's calm confidence – The debate on Nigerian palm kernels – Its intense bitterness and secret significance – Aitken advises Bonar Law to resign – He refuses – Misconceptions over rôle of Aitken – Its true nature – He sees the need to bring Carson, Lloyd George and Bonar Law together – Bonar Law threatens a General Election – Alarm of Churchill – Bonar Law changes his attitude towards Carson and Lloyd George – His reasons – The Triumvirate agrees on a policy – Asquith rejects it – Bonar Law's stormy meeting with Unionist Ministers – His isolation and doubts – Fresh proposal by Lloyd George – Bonar Law resolves to bring matters to a head with Asquith

I

As the autumn of 1916 darkened into winter, discontent at the progress of the war became ever more widespread. It had indeed been a dismal year for the fortunes of the Allies. Admittedly the French had been able to prevent the German armies breaking through the Western Front at Verdun, but only at heavy cost. Moreover, the great counter offensive launched by Haig on July 1st, the campaign of the Somme, seemed bitterly disappointing. Gains were few. Losses were immense. It is now known that the German suffered almost as badly as the Allies and that the balance was by no means as one-sided as it appeared at the time. But, during the autumn of 1916, there seemed little consolation for the lengthening casualty lists which brought home the fact of war in its most cruel and personal form to thousands of British homes.

In the east the picture was equally sombre. At the end of April, after a series of tactical and administrative errors seldom rivalled in our military history, the British force under General Townsend was obliged to surrender to the Turks at Kut. Of ten thousand prisoners less than one-third were destined to survive the fearful conditions of their captivity. On the plains of Galicia Brussilov's great offensive achieved early successes but died away without any lasting results. In August Rumania entered the war upon the Allied side, only to meet a swift and conclusive defeat. Before the end of the year Bucharest and three-quarters of the country were in German hands.

To all these calamities must be added the Easter Rebellion at Dublin described in the last chapter. We have seen how it weakened Bonar Law's personal position with his own supporters. Moreover, it seemed a clear proof of the bankruptcy of the Government's Irish policy. It further increased the hostility felt for Asquith by the right wing of the Unionist Party, a group which in any case regarded the Prime Minister with acute dislike and distrust.

Although many of these disasters were not the fault either of the Prime Minister or of the Cabinet, it was natural that criticism should focus upon the Government. A widening circle of politicians, soldiers, and journalists began to regard the Coalition Government with profound dissatisfaction. Again and again, so the hostile critics averred, events moved too fast for its slow deliberations, opportunities were missed, and instead of driving straight to its objective, the Government became lost in a morass of vacillation and indecision. How much truth was there in these accusations?

There can be no doubt that the Cabinet was an unsatisfactory instrument for achieving quick results. Bonar Law had perceived one of its weaknesses almost as soon as he entered it. He wrote to Asquith on June 22nd, 1915:[a]

"Might I suggest that you should have for every cabinet an agenda, and not permit any of our colleagues to raise any subjects, not previously submitted to you, until the agenda has been completed."

Asquith replied:[b]

"I am afraid this is a counsel of perfection in wartime. I try as far as possible to rule out secondary discussion but it is very difficult."

No doubt it was difficult, but Bonar Law had seized upon a defect which was ultimately to be in some degree responsible for Asquith's fall. Partly from a genuine reluctance to overrule the Unionists whom he felt he must treat with special courtesy, partly because he possessed what his biographers call "a certain arrogance"[c] which made him regard with contemptuous tolerance the ramblings of his colleagues, Asquith was curiously unwilling to closure debate in

Cabinet or to force a decision. This was particularly unfortunate in a Government which contained so many powerful and clashing personalities. Winston Churchill writes of the Coalition:[d]

"The progress of business therefore became cumbrous and laborious in the last degree and, though all these evils were corrected by earnest patriotism and loyalty, the general result was bound to be disappointing . . . every operative decision was obtained only by prolonged, discursive, and exhausting discussions. Far too often we laboured through long delays to unsatisfactory compromises."

This picture is confirmed from other sources. Austen Chamberlain noticed that Asquith was an indifferent chairman, and often could be observed writing letters while the discussion was in progress.[e]

". . . when he at last intervened with a statement 'Now that that is decided we had better pass on to . . .' there would be a general cry, 'But what has been decided?' and the discussion would begin all over again."

The truth was that Asquith had become a tired and weary man. He had been Prime Minister for nearly nine years – a longer continuous period in office than had been enjoyed by any of his predecessors since the days of Lord Liverpool. It had moreover been a period of intense stress and difficulty. Only a man with Asquith's iron constitution could have stood the strain so long. Then, in September 1916, came the death in action of his brilliant son, Raymond, to whom he was devoted. It was a terrible blow to Asquith upon whom, write his biographers, it left "an indelible scar". Such a tragic loss had inevitably a most unfavourable effect upon his capacity to carry on the Government, and it came moreover, at a moment when Asquith needed all his powers in order to surmount the difficulties which lay ahead. Lloyd George later wrote:[f]

"It was a misfortune for Britain that the great statesman who had the supreme responsibility was less equal to his task than he had ever been in the whole course of his distinguished career. Mr. Bonar Law, who was well disposed to him, was of that opinion, and expressed it repeatedly in the course of conversations I held with him."

But the various people who were hostile to Asquith's Administration were agreed neither upon how to bring it to an end, nor upon what should take its place. It is necessary here to give some account of these divergences, and then to consider the position of Bonar Law.

There existed a formidable group which frankly wanted Asquith's removal. Its two most important members were Carson and North-cliffe. Carson regarded the situation as hopeless while Asquith remained Prime Minister. It was not, Carson believed, merely a change in the machinery of government that was needed. The creation of a small War Council with real powers in the place of the cumbrous War Committee would be some help, and indeed it was partly on this issue that Carson had resigned in 1915. But this reform, though desirable in itself, would be ineffective, as long as Asquith was at the head of affairs. Carson was supported by Milner who had great influence with certain sections of Unionist opinion, and by Sir Henry Wilson who regarded Asquith with a personal hostility which was heartily reciprocated.

Northcliffe too favoured the removal of Asquith, and he was at this time a most formidable enemy. Indeed he possessed a power such as no newspaper proprietor has ever wielded before or since. Owning both *The Times* and the *Daily Mail* he could spread his opinions among the classes and the masses with equal effect. In his heyday he controlled half the circulation of the entire London Press. It must be remembered that the wireless, as a means of disseminating news, had not yet come into existence, and the Government had no alternative method of communicating with the public. The power of the Press was greater in those days than it ever has been since, and Northcliffe's share of that power was proportionately far larger than the share of any newspaper owner in more recent times. Asquith, however, regarded the sensationalism of the Northcliffe Press with a silent contempt. He declined to take the trouble of refuting the virulent charges which were constantly being brought against him, and made no attempt to present his own case to the newspapers. It was an attitude which reflected his personal integrity, but it was not wise.

Northcliffe's view of the situation was not quite the same as Carson's. He favoured the removal of Asquith because he considered that greater power should be given to Haig and Robertson in the direction of the war. At times he used language suggesting that he almost favoured a military dictatorship,[1] and the temporary suspension of Parliamentary Government. Carson would certainly not have supported any change as drastic as this. The link between North-cliffe and the Carson-Milner group was Geoffrey Dawson, editor of

---

[1] "To the right soldiers he would have given almost unlimited power." *History of the Times*, Vol. IV, Part 1, p. 274. See also *Politicians and War*, Vol. II, p. 122, for Northcliffe's remarks to Lord Beaverbrook.

The Times. He had a great dislike for Asquith, and a passionate admiration for Milner. He too consistently advocated the creation of a small War Council or War Cabinet.

If Asquith's opponents had come only from the right wing his position would have been much safer, for he still controlled a Parliamentary majority, even in the event of the Coalition breaking up. But his Achilles heel was in his own party. Lloyd George, the most powerful member of the Liberal Party next to Asquith, was deeply dissatisfied with the conduct of the war. His dissatisfaction was not, indeed based on the same grounds as that of Northcliffe. What Lloyd George wanted was to give the soldiers not *more* power but *less.* He believed that Haig and Robertson were entirely wrong in seeking a decision on the Western Front. A confirmed Easterner, he considered that the war could only be won by flank attacks through the Balkans or the Alps against Germany's weaker allies. In particular he chafed at his own position as War Secretary. Despite his original resolve, he had accepted that position without cancelling the Kitchener-Robertson agreement which, it will be recalled, gave to the Chief of the Imperial General Staff the substance of power over strategy and left the Minister controlling only man-power and administration.

Lloyd George differed from Northcliffe – and in this respect from Carson too – on another point. He did not want to see Asquith disappear from the scene. He hoped that Asquith would remain as Prime Minister while he (Lloyd George) acted as Chairman of a small War Council responsible for the strategy of the war. He did not at this time, autumn of 1916, wish to displace the Prime Minister, whereas Carson, Milner and Northcliffe from their differing standpoints believed that Asquith's removal was the essential preliminary to any further reforms.

Lloyd George was not the only prominent Liberal to view the Government with a jaundiced eye. There was also Churchill. As soon as he had resigned from office he had departed to France to command a battalion. It was scarcely a field worthy of his great talents. In the spring of 1916, at the instigation of Carson, and Aitken, who as Canadian Government Representative with the Canadian Forces made frequent visits to France, Churchill decided to return home and help to form a patriotic opposition with the object of "gingering up" the Government.

What was Bonar Law's attitude to, and relationship with, these various opponents of Asquith? At the beginning of November 1916, it is safe to say that he was on cordial terms with none of them. He viewed Lloyd George with much mistrust. Their co-operation over the War Office and over Irish Home Rule had not led to any close alliance. Indeed Bonar Law had regarded Lloyd George with more approval, when the Coalition had first been formed, than he now did after eighteen months of sitting with him in the same Cabinet. "When we joined the Cabinet", said Bonar Law at the end of 1915, referring to himself and his Conservative colleagues, "there was no man we disliked more than McKenna and no man we trusted more than Lloyd George. Now the case is precisely reversed."[g]

Bonar Law thought that Lloyd George was an ambitious, and none too scrupulous colleague. "The root cause of the trouble", writes Lord Beaverbrook,[h] "was that Bonar Law had formed the opinion that in matters of office and power Lloyd George was a self-seeker and a man who considered no interests except his own." It is unnecessary here to recapitulate Bonar Law's reasons for this belief: it was, after all, an impression widely shared by his colleagues in both parties. Moreover, Bonar Law had no sympathy with Lloyd George's complaints about strategy. He was on the contrary at this time a supporter of the Army chiefs. It was largely for this reason that he had pressed so strongly – and successfully – for the evacuation of Gallipoli.

As for the other opponents of the Government, Bonar Law's attitude can be quickly summarized. He had no use for, or dealings with, Northcliffe. More than a year before he had expressed himself thus when writing to Lord Maclay about a newspaper article:[i]

"For once I have no sympathy whatever with the Press as represented by the 'Mail'. It is all Northcliffe, who is one of the most jumpy of men and rushes at everything without any regard to anything except his own vanity."

And the succeeding fifteen months had given him no cause to modify this severe – though perhaps unfair – judgment. Northcliffe and Churchill were on the worst possible terms, but Bonar Law's disapproval of the former did not make him think any the more highly of the latter. He had social relations with Churchill through their mutual friends, F. E. Smith and Aitken, but any idea of political collaboration was out of the question.

Far more important to Bonar Law than either Northcliffe or Churchill were the intentions and attitude of Carson. The relations between the two men had been marked by increasing coldness ever since Carson's resignation. That episode in itself had lowered Carson in Bonar Law's estimation, for he regarded Carson's motives as insufficiently weighty in time of war. All through 1916 Carson had been emerging as the most dangerous enemy of the Government. In some ways he seemed to be acquiring a greater control over the Unionist Party than Bonar Law himself. His formidable oratory lashed the Cabinet again and again. Although he had never held any executive post to justify such a belief, the notion became current that he possessed a drive, a remorseless determination, and unrelenting hostility to the Germans, which contrasted strongly with the dismal procrastination attributed to Asquith and his colleagues. In fact there was no truth in this idea. Carson was not particularly effective when he became First Lord of the Admiralty in Lloyd George's Government, but he was undoubtedly one of the most formidable leaders of the Opposition that ever spoke in the House of Commons. More than any single person he was responsible for Asquith's fall.

Thus, then, the stage is set at the beginning of November. The various opponents of Asquith are divided among themselves as to strategy and tactics. Lloyd George advocates one policy, Carson another, Northcliffe a third. But they can do nothing, unless they gain the support of Bonar Law. As long as he remains allied to Asquith the Government is safe; and for the time being Bonar Law still believes that he must sustain that alliance. He regards Asquith, indeed, with a critical eye, but considers every alternative fraught with even greater danger.

And what are Asquith's feelings? He thinks, as so many others do, that he is indispensable, and that no one can overthrow him. He is sustained by consciousness of the powerful groups that support him: the Liberals, McKenna, Grey, Runciman, Crewe, Samuel, Montagu; the Conservatives, Curzon, Chamberlain, Cecil, Long, Lansdowne. He is perhaps a little weary. His son's death has dealt him a shattering blow, but he has no intention of abandoning the great post to which the nation has called him. Duty and inclination alike demand that he should remain. As for troubles and criticisms they are inevitable in war. An overwhelming majority supports him in Parliament. The ignoble machinations of the Press can be disregarded. The captiousness of Lloyd George can be ignored. The last of the Romans, as he was once described, sits presiding week after week in the Cabinet room, courteous, lucid, powerful and serene.

2

The curtain for the curious drama to be played during the next month[1] rises upon an apparently unimportant and irrelevant prologue. On November 8th, the House of Commons debated a topic as remote from war as can well be conceived. The question concerned the sale of enemy businesses confiscated in Nigeria, mainly firms which dealt with Nigerian palm kernels. Carson put down a resolution that "such properties and businesses should be sold only to natural born British subjects or companies wholly British".

This apparently innocent motion had been chosen with no small degree of craft. For it was certain to bring on to Carson's side and against the Government, which favoured a free auction to all bidders, the maximum number of Conservative Protectionists. It was also nicely calculated to aggravate those nationalist, anti-foreign, anti-neutral, sentiments which always predominate in time of war. It had, moreover, an inner significance which wholly escaped the general public. Bonar Law had declared at the time of the Coalition's formation that he would cease to be a member of the Government the moment that "the Party to which I belong has lost confidence in me" – in other words always a party man, he would not hold office by virtue of Liberal votes. This meant that the ostensible result of a division would be irrelevant. Supported by Liberal votes the Government was certain to win easily. What mattered was the way in which the Conservatives voted. If more voted for Carson than for the Government, then, whatever the technical result of the division, Bonar Law would resign – and his resignation would at once precipitate the fall of the Government.

The debate was marked by extraordinary bitterness. Bonar Law, as Colonial Secretary, had the task of winding up for the Government. Following immediately after a ferocious speech from Carson, Bonar Law began:

[1] The history of the crisis which resulted in Asquith's fall has been related in great detail by Lord Beaverbrook in *Politicians and the War*, Vol. II. Lord Beaverbrook played a most important personal part in the crisis. His narrative, based upon his own contemporary record and upon Bonar Law's papers, has in the main never been seriously challenged. The only important criticisms of it came from Austen Chamberlain, who has given his own account in *Down the Years*, pp. 107–31, and maintains that Lord Beaverbrook misunderstands the motives of the group of Unionist Ministers with whom Chamberlain acted, and from the biographers of Asquith who, while accepting in substance Lord Beaverbrook's story, consider that he attributes over subtle political intentions to the Prime Minister. These criticisms will be considered in their place. Carson and Lloyd George, the principal participants in these events still alive when Lord Beaverbrook's account was published, accepted it as accurate. In what follows I have based my account on Lord Beaverbrook's book, and, except where otherwise stated, it must be taken as my authority.

"This is a Motion of want of confidence in the Government, moved –
and this I must say I do regret – with a violence which to my mind is
hardly in keeping with the serious situation in which the country stands
. . I at least will never question the sincerity of the motives by which my
right hon. friend (Carson) is actuated and I hope and believe that our
personal friendship will stand the strain of political opposition and even
of speeches such as that to which we have just listened. . . ."

Nevertheless, it soon became clear that Bonar Law was opposed by
many members of his own party. He was repeatedly interrupted by
Carson with such observations as: "Nonsense". "I never made any
such statement." "Absolutely untrue." Bonar Law wound up with a
warning of the possible consequences of pressing a division. The
Carsonites ignored it. In the result the Government was supported
by 231 votes to 117. Churchill voted with the minority – a clear
indication that the real issue at stake was nothing to do with Free
Trade or Protection. But the true significance of the debate lay in the
way the Unionists voted: 65 supported Carson, 73 supported Bonar
Law, out of a total representation in the House of 286. Thus by a
narrow majority Bonar Law was upheld. The passions raised by the
debate were fierce. One of the Carsonite whips meeting Sir F. E.
Smith in the lobby told him that Bonar Law had been saved by the
votes of "the paid members". "We will cross off the votes of the
members who are paid," replied Smith, "if you cross off those who
want to be paid."[j]

Bonar Law was much disturbed at the result of the debate. Unlike
those who poured congratulations upon him after the division he
was well aware of its real significance. It was an alarming milestone
upon Carson's road to ascendancy in the Unionist Party. If such
attacks continued, Bonar Law would sooner or later be forced to
resign. Aitken, indeed, urged him to lose no time and resign at once.
But Bonar Law was unwilling to do so. Such action would be dis-
loyal to Asquith, however advantageous it might be for Bonar Law
to stand forth as an alternative Prime Minister and disentangle himself from a discredited Government. He refused to listen to Aitken's
advice.

An appropriate moment has arrived for the consideration of
Aitken's part in the events which followed. There have been many
who, both then and later, have maintained that he exerted a malign
and sinister influence upon the political scene at this time. It has
even been suggested that Bonar Law was a mere puppet in his hands
and that, but for Aitken's intrigues, Asquith would never have
fallen; his Government would have sailed on, buffeted and weather-

beaten perhaps, but victorious in the end. The Asquithian Liberal
were sedulous in spreading this view; but it was echoed in othe
quarters too. The *Morning Post* summed it up in a phrase adopte
from the title of a once well-known play, "Bunty pulls the Strings".

Yet a moment's thought is enough to convince anyone of th
essential unplausibility of such a theory. Opinions may conflict abou
the character, the attainments, and the influence of Lord Beaver
brook in the years between the wars, and during World War II, bu
it is an historical error to think of Sir Max Aitken in the same ligh
during 1916. At that time he was a Conservative back bencher
admittedly very wealthy, but this was not in itself of great signifi
cance. He had never held office. His influence upon the Press wa
relatively unimportant. For although the *Daily Express* was under hi
control it had but a tiny circulation compared with the paper
controlled by Northcliffe and Rothermere. Bonar Law was 58 year
of age and had been leader of the Conservative Party for five years
Aitken was 36 and had only been in Parliament for six years. He wa
in no position to use Bonar Law as a puppet, and the whole theory
has a high degree of inherent improbability. Bonar Law enjoyed
staying at Cherkley, liked talking about politics to his friend, an
was amused at his picturesque, entertaining, and, on occasions, out
rageous, conversation, but he was at no time a mere tool of Aitken

Nevertheless, it would be very wrong to go to the opposite extrem
and underestimate the part which Aitken played. Although Bona
Law's views on general political objectives were not much affected
by his friend's opinions, he was far more ready to take his advice or
tactics, on the means of securing those objectives. We have already
seen how shrewd that advice had been at a critical stage in the
negotiations which resulted in Bonar Law becoming leader of hi
Party. It was to be equally shrewd in the manoeuvres which led to
the displacement of Asquith. For Aitken had, and has, to an un
canny degree the art of perceiving and exploiting those weak – anc
strong – points in men's characters which can be played upon in
order to secure their friendship or support. Moreover, he possessed
immense energy and astonishing resourcefulness in the pursuit o
any project upon which he set his heart. No trouble was too great
no detail too small, when he devoted himself heart and soul to the
successful accomplishment of a political intrigue. He had a profound
intuitive understanding of the secret fears, vanities, aspirations, and
cupidities of those whom he knew well. His judgment on wide issues
of general policy was sometimes at fault, and, on occasions, wildly

:rratic, but it seldom erred in matters of individual personality. And
t was precisely a problem of individual personalities which had to
be solved if a change of Government was to be brought about. How
:ould the conflicting beliefs and prejudices of Carson, Lloyd George
and Bonar Law be brought into harmony? It must have seemed an
almost insuperable problem. There was, possibly, only one man who
:ould have solved it. In this sense, perhaps, the partisans of Asquith
were right, when they saw in Sir Max Aitken their hero's most
formidable foe, the true author of his downfall.

Aitken frankly believed that under Asquith's rule the country
would never win the war. That view may have been right or wrong,
but it was sincerely held, and it was shared by many others who
belonged to the inner circles of politics at that time. He saw, that, if
Lloyd George, Carson and Bonar Law could be brought together
and could agree upon a common programme of reform to present
to Asquith, some sort of crisis must ensue. The result might not
necessarily be the resignation of Asquith, but at the worst it would
mean a reconstructed Government which would run the war more
efficiently. At the best it would mean a new Government and a new
Prime Minister; and Aitken, with his intense devotion to his friend,
naturally hoped that the new Prime Minister would be Bonar Law.

But Bonar Law was still very far from joining in any opposition
movement against Asquith. His attitude was strikingly displayed a
few days later when on Sunday, November 12th, he drove down to
Cherkley to discuss the political situation with Aitken. Both F. E.
Smith and Churchill were there for the weekend and had already
been engaged the previous evening in a warm altercation on the
merits of the Government, Smith strongly supporting it, Churchill
expressing bitter hostility. At Bonar Law's arrival Churchill promptly
launched a great oratorical tirade against the Government. He spoke
as if he were addressing a mighty audience rather than a small
group of political friends and acquaintances. Bonar Law, like Queen
Victoria, did not enjoy being addressed as if he were a public meeting
and began to show signs of irritation. Finally, when Churchill came to
a pause in his allocution, he said, "Very well, if that's what the critics
of the Government think of it - we will have a General Election."

According to Beaverbrook, Churchill afterwards declared that
his suggestion to hold a General Election in the midst of war "was
the most terribly immoral thing he had ever heard of".[k]

Whether or not it was immoral it was undoubtedly a formidable
threat. For a General Election in which both Bonar Law and Asquith

appealed to the country against Carson and the Tory Die-hards could have had but one result – an overwhelming victory for the Coalition. In time of war the patriotic cry of rallying to a government supported by the leaders of both parties would have been irresistible. Moreover it would have had disastrous results for the Conservative Party. In effect it would have broken the Party in two, in something the same way that the Election of 1918 was destined to break the Liberal Party. Aitken reflecting after the departure of his guests came to the conclusion that it was vital to avoid this danger. An Election held at this time would confirm Asquith's power, destroy all chance of a successful reconstruction, and probably break up the Conservative Party. It became more than ever urgent to bring not only Lloyd George but Carson too into collaboration with Bonar Law.

Asquith's biographers deny that Asquith in fact seriously contemplated a General Election at any time during these events, though they admit that he might in conversation have used the expression "What if I were to dissolve?"[1] It may be, therefore, that Bonar Law was speaking without Asquith's authority when he made his threat. Nevertheless, whatever Asquith's real views, those who were contemplating his overthrow had to take into account the likelihood of such a counter-move on the part of the Prime Minister. And since they could not see into Asquith's mind they could scarcely be blamed for drawing conclusions from his casual observations. At all events the possibility of a General Election was a potent element in the calculations of the anti-Asquith group during the succeeding three weeks.

The next day, November 13th, Aitken saw Lloyd George at the War Office. Their interview is fully described in *Politicians and the War*. It now became clear for the first time to Aitken that Lloyd George and Carson were acting in close collaboration. They were agreed upon the reform that was needed: the control of war policy should be taken away from the Cabinet and the War Committee and given to a small War Council[1] of three or four members; this

---

[1] At this point a question of terminology should be made clear. In this narrative the word "committee" will be used to describe any body which is a mere committee of the Cabinet, to which the Cabinet may have delegated powers, but which is responsible to and can be overruled by, the Cabinet. All the successive war committees of the Asquithian régime had been of this character: their decisions could always be challenged in the full Cabinet. The word "council" on the other hand will be used to describe a body which has real executive powers and does not need to refer its decisions to the Cabinet, except perhaps on a few well defined specific subjects. This distinction between "committee" and "council" will be followed in this narrative, but the reader should be warned that in the contemporary letters and documents it is frequently disregarded. The words are often used indiscriminately and the context has to be examined before it is clear exactly what is meant.

council should sit from day to day with Lloyd George as its chairman, and Asquith would not be a member. Lloyd George hoped that Asquith would remain as Prime Minister and Leader of the House, Carson preferred that he should be superseded entirely. But both Carson and Lloyd George agreed that, whatever form the new arrangement took, its effect should be to take the day to day conduct of war out of Asquith's hands.

Having learned Lloyd George's intentions Aitken, on the following evening, Tuesday, November 14th, imparted them to Bonar Law. The latter's reception of these suggestions was frankly hostile. He regarded the whole plan as a device on the part of Lloyd George to get round the Kitchener-Robertson agreement about the War Minister's powers. Lloyd George's proposals seemed to him intended, as so often, only to exalt the position of Lloyd George. Bonar Law conceded that the Government was most unpopular and that the machinery of the Cabinet badly needed to be overhauled if there was to be any hope of obtaining quick decisions and a unified policy. But he was not prepared to agree to a plan which seemed likely to diminish the power of Robertson whom he favoured, and exalt the power of Lloyd George whom he distrusted. Nor was he prepared to take any part in an intrigue against Asquith.

Such was the situation on Tuesday, November 14th. Yet eleven days later Bonar Law is presenting to Asquith a memorandum drawn up by Aitken and agreed upon by Lloyd George and Carson, embodying almost precisely these suggestions. What had occurred to change his mind?

The biographers of Asquith give an unflattering explanation. According to them Bonar Law was influenced not so much by the bad progress of the war, or the merits of the proposals,

"but by a succession of personal appeals and inducements: appeals to his ambition, when it seemed to be flagging, reminders of the precariousness of his own position, and of the popular wrath supposed to be rising against the Government, and those whom the public might hold responsible for its failures."m

The writers do not claim any special insight into the working of Bonar Law's mind. They are purporting to summarize the account given by Lord Beaverbrook in *Politicians and the War*.

It should at once be stated that their version will barely be recognized by anyone who has read that book with care. Lord Beaverbrook traces in detail – far more detail than is possible here – the discussions which took place between himself, Bonar Law, Carson, and Lloyd George. He makes it quite clear, (1) that from the first Bonar Law favoured the general idea of putting the control of the war into the hands of a small body, (2) that Bonar Law was most dissatisfied with the existing method of deciding war policy, not because of his own personal position but because he really believed that disaster lay ahead. Bonar Law has himself left a somewhat bare memorandum of the events leading up to the fall of Asquith. It is dated December 30th, 1916, and so was written while the events were fresh in his memory. Bonar Law begins:[n]

"After the Nigerian debate I had very strongly the feeling that the Unionist Party in the House was not only hostile to the Government but was fast reaching a point where their hostility would make it impossible for me and probably for other Unionist Ministers to remain in the Cabinet. This view was strengthened by the number of political friends both in the House and out of it who came to me constantly with this complaint – that I alone was keeping up a Government which was not acting with sufficient energy and which in any case was so discredited that it had lost the power of effectively prosecuting the war. Among others Sir Starr Jamieson came to me urging strongly that I alone had the power to end the situation, which if it were not altered, would be disastrous for the country.

"In consequence of this feeling I came definitely to the conclusion that some radical change must be made, or that the Government would go straight on the rocks with consequences that no one could foresee.

"Early in November, therefore, I said to Mr. Asquith that in my judgment we could not go on as we were and that some radical change must be made in the Government and must be made at once. He did not accept this view, but thought, on the contrary, that I was simply exaggerating a passing discontent due to a want of military success in the war. I however adhered to my opinion but added that there was no object in talking about it until I had something definite to propose, and that, when I had, I would speak to him again.

"Afterwards I met Sir Edward Carson and asked him to come to my room . . . when I asked him in what respect a change was needed his reply was that the first essential was that the conduct of the war should be in the hands of a small body. I replied that I entirely agreed with this view but that there was one particular in which I thought we could not agree, and that was that, in my opinion, under such a Constitution as ours the control of the political machine, even from the point of view of the conduct of the war, was as essential as the preparation of big armies; and I added that in the present House of Commons no one, I thought, could control that machine so well as Mr. Asquith. Sir Edward Carson said that he did not altogether disagree with that view, and I then said to him that if we started on that basis – Mr. Asquith to continue as Prime Minister then I was prepared to take any measures and to exercise any pressure that it was in my power to exercise, in order to improve the existing state of things. . . ."

Bonar Law does not make it clear exactly when this discussion occurred - except that it was in early November, but it seems from Beaverbrook's narrative to have been shortly before November 14th, the date on which he, Beaverbrook, first put the case for Lloyd George to Bonar Law. It would appear then, that Bonar Law was from the first in sympathy with the idea of a small War Council. Beaverbrook's narrative makes it clear that the real obstacles in Bonar Law's mind were his personal suspicion of Lloyd George's ulterior motives[1] and his great anxiety to behave with loyalty to Asquith. His discussion with Carson and Lloyd George convinced him eventually that Lloyd George did not aim at displacing Asquith, and that a plan for a War Council could be drawn up, which would safeguard Asquith's position as Prime Minister, abolish the cumbrous deliberations of the existing War Committee, and give Lloyd George the chance of using his powers of drive and energy in the prosecution of the war.

Bonar Law's reluctance to do anything behind Asquith's back is shown by an incident which occurred during the course of these negotiations. He agreed to meet Lloyd George and Carson on November 20th and discuss their proposals for a War Council. These proposals had been communicated to him so far only through Aitken, and the latter had asked him to keep them confidential. Despite this injunction Bonar Law told Asquith what the proposals were and also that he intended to discuss them with Carson. Aitken was both surprised and annoyed when Bonar Law informed him of what he had done. Asquith's own reaction to the proposals was un-favourable but he raised no objection to the plan being discussed.

"The Triumvirate", as Lord Beaverbrook calls them (Bonar Law, Carson and Lloyd George), held several meetings. On November 25th they met at Pembroke Lodge and were at last able to agree upon a common formula. Aitken drafted, and Bonar Law amended, a document which took the form of a suggested announcement to be made by Asquith. It read as follows:°

"The War Council has in my [i.e. Asquith's] opinion, rendered devoted and invaluable service, but experience has convinced me that there are disadvantages in the present system which render a change necessary.

"Some Body doing the work of the War Council should meet every day. It is impossible that the War Council can do this while its members have at the same time to fulfil the exacting duties of their Departments. At the

---

[1] *Politicians and the War*, Vol. II, p. 142, "The trouble throughout was less a difference of principle than the view which the men took of each other's mentality", Bonar Law's memorandum surprisingly, makes no mention of his suspicion of Lloyd George.

L

War Council also we have felt it necessary to have the advantage regularly of the presence of the Chief of the Imperial General Staff and the First Sea Lord. Their time is in this way taken up sometimes unnecessarily when every moment is required for other work. I have decided therefore to create what I regard as a Civilian General Staff. This Staff will consist of myself as President and three other members of the Cabinet who have no portfolio and who will devote their whole time to the consideration day by day of the problems which arise in connection with the prosecution of the war.

"The three members who have undertaken these duties are:
[Here a blank is left for inserting the names]
and I have invited Mr. Lloyd George, and he has consented, to act as chairman and to preside at any meeting which, owing to the pressure of other duties, I find it impossible to attend.

"I propose that the body should have executive authority subject to this – that it shall rest with me to refer any questions to the decision of the Cabinet, which I think should be brought before them."

Although the names were left blank the Triumvirate in fact wanted the other members to be Bonar Law and Carson, unless the Prime Minister raised strong objections. Armed with this memorandum Bonar Law proceeded to No. 10 Downing Street to see Asquith. Bonar Law's own account of what followed must be quoted:[p]

"In giving it (the memorandum) to him I stated that, in my opinion, if this change were made by him entirely on his own initiative, and before there had been any pressure from outside, it could be made without the smallest loss of dignity; but if it came about as a result of pressure either in the Cabinet, or still worse, in the Press, it would be almost impossible to carry it out. I therefore urged upon him that if he saw his way to do it at all he ought to do it without a moment's delay. The Prime Minister did not seem to me altogether opposed to the idea but naturally did not give me any answer then."

According to Lord Beaverbrook, whose account is based on what Bonar Law told him that same evening, Asquith was rather more specific than this. He regarded the terms of the proposal as acceptable provided "they represented Lloyd George's final aims and were not merely an instalment of further demands for power. Personally he did not believe that this was a final demand. He went on to raise the former objections to Carson".[q]

Asquith repaired to his country house and spent Sunday in reflecting upon the problem. Then, as he had promised, he wrote a definite answer to Bonar Law's proposals. It took the form of a letter to Bonar Law which Asquith showed him in advance on Monday morning. What Asquith originally wrote is not known, since, at Bonar Law's request, he deleted some very adverse remarks about Carson, Bonar Law having pointed out that the letter would have to be shown to the other members of the Triumvirate. The references to Lloyd George, he considered, could be left in. The letter must be quoted in full:[r]

The Wharf, Sutton Courtney,
November 26, 1916.

"My dear Bonar Law,

"What follows is intended for your eyes alone.

"I fully realize the frankness and loyalty with which you have put forward the proposal embodied in your paper note. But under the present conditions, and in the form in which it is presented, I do not see my way to adopt it.

"I take a less disparaging view than you do of the War Committee. There is undoubtedly too much talk and consequent waste of time, but the Committee has done and is doing very valuable work; and is thrashing out difficult problems. I am quite open to suggestions for its improvement, whether in composition or in procedure. I may say, however, that I do not see how any body of the kind can be really workable unless the heads of the War Office and Admiralty are members of it. Our recent practice of sitting a good deal without the experts is a change for the better, and might perhaps be further developed.

"But the essence of your scheme is that the War Committee should disappear, and its place be taken by a body of four – myself, yourself, Carson, and Lloyd George.

"As regards Carson, for whom as you know, I have the greatest personal regard, I do not see how it would be possible, in order to secure his services, to pass over Balfour, or Curzon, or McKenna, all of whom have the advantage of knowledge of the secret history of the last twelve months. That he should be admitted over their heads at this stage to the inner circle of the Government is a step which, I believe, would be deeply resented, not only by them and by my political friends, but by almost all your Unionist colleagues. It would be universally believed to be the price paid for shutting the mouth of our most formidable parliamentary critic – a manifest sign of weakness and cowardice.

"As to Lloyd George, you know as well as I do both his qualities and his defects. He has many qualities that would fit him for the first place, but he lacks the one thing needful – he does not inspire trust. . . . Here, again, there is one construction, and one only, that could be put on the new arrangement that it has been engineered by him with the purpose, not perhaps at the moment, but as soon as a fitting pretext could be found, of his displacing me.

"In short, the plan could not, in my opinion, be carried out without fatally impairing the confidence of loyal and valued colleagues, and undermining my own authority.

"I have spoken to you with the same frankness that you use to me, and which I am glad to say has uniformly marked our relations ever since the Coalition was formed. Nor need I tell you that, if I thought it right, I have every temptation (especially now) to seek relief from the intolerable daily burden of labour and anxiety.   "Yours very sincerely,

H. H. Asquith."

This reply was of course a polite but absolute refusal to agree to Bonar Law's Proposals. The latter after some reflection saw Asquith again. To quote his own memorandum:[3]

"I told him that in my opinion the facts made it absolutely necessary to carry out such a change. I added that, as far as I could judge, he had no idea of the extent of the unpopularity of his government, and indeed, from the nature of the case, anyone in his position would find it difficult to realize the exact facts, for no one would be likely to tell him. I then put to him that, after all, the one thing, which seemed to me essential, was that he and Lloyd George should work together, with the close co-operation which existed at the time that the Coalition was formed, and I suggested that the best way would be for the two of them to have a frank talk and see to what extent they could come to an agreement. This was agreed to, and the meeting took place on Friday, December 1st."

The upshot of that meeting will be considered shortly. In the meantime Bonar Law was faced with another problem. Hitherto he had acted solely in concert with Carson, Lloyd George and Aitken. It was now time to consult his Conservative colleagues who, so far, knew nothing of what was in the air. The principal persons concerned were, Lansdowne, Balfour, Curzon, Austen Chamberlain, Walter Long, Lord Robert Cecil, and F. E. Smith. Balfour was ill, and so unable to come, but all the others attended a meeting summoned by Bonar Law in his room in the House of Commons on Thursday, November 30th.[1]

When Bonar Law put his proposals for a small War Council before his colleagues and told them that Lloyd George must be Chairman, and that he, Bonar Law, would back this plan with the threat of resignation if necessary, he met with very strong opposition. The Unionist Ministers disliked Lloyd George, and opposed the scheme not so much on its abstract merits as on those of the proposed chairman. So strong was this hostility that Bonar Law never even came to the point of mentioning Carson's name. If he had done so, the Conservative Ministers would have been even more hostile, for they regarded Carson by this time with almost as much mistrust as Lloyd George. However, the discussion broke up before this point had even been reached. Bonar Law's colleagues put forward, as an alternative, a scheme for two committees of the Cabinet – the existing War Committee and a Home Committee which would deal with domestic aspects of war policy. This scheme had already been discussed in Cabinet the day before, and it had very little to recommend it. Bonar Law pointed out forcibly the overlapping that would almost certainly

---

[1] Not November 27th, as stated in the *Life of Asquith*, Vol. II, p. 251, and repeated in *The History of the Times* Vol. IV, Part 1, p. 290.

occur if the plan was adopted. The meeting ended with no clear conclusion.

Feeling had however run high. F. E. Smith stigmatized the whole affair as "an intrigue". Lord Robert Cecil accused Bonar Law of dragging the Conservative Party at the coat tails of Lloyd George. Long and Lansdowne wrote afterwards to Bonar Law in protest. Lansdowne's tone was particularly sharp. "The meeting in your room", he declared, "left 'a nasty taste in my mouth'. " Bonar Law replied in mollifying tones.[1] He had not yet realized how deep a gulf was opening up between himself and his old colleague. First the Irish question and now Lansdowne's own sincere conviction that the war could not be won were driving the two men far apart. When the Second Coalition was formed Lansdowne alone of the Conservative Ministers declined to join it.

The result of his meeting with the Unionist Ministers was profoundly disturbing to Bonar Law. He felt obliged to reconsider the whole question of his attitude to Asquith, and he discussed the situation at some length that evening with Aitken. The forces arrayed against Lloyd George and Bonar Law seemed exceedingly formidable. Not only would Asquith be supported by nearly all his Liberal colleagues; it now looked as if he could rely upon all the Conservative Ministers too. It was true that many powerful forces supported Lloyd George and Bonar Law in their desire to bring about a change in the running of the war, but all these lay outside the Cabinet. The dissident Tory back-benchers, the discontented public, the anti-Asquith Press, even such important figures as Carson, Derby, and Milner could not intervene directly in the coming struggle. As far as their colleagues were concerned Bonar Law and Lloyd George had to fight on alone. "In these sombre and careful reflections", writes Beaverbrook, "Bonar Law passed the evening of Thursday."

We must now see what happened as a result of Bonar Law's suggestion that Asquith and Lloyd George should meet and discuss the position. The following day, Friday, December 1st, had been fixed for their interview. Lloyd George now drafted a new memorandum comprising what he considered to be the necessary reforms.[t] Having shown it to Aitken and to Lord Derby who had come out definitely upon the side of change, he proceeded to No. 10 Downing Street to see Asquith. The memorandum differed in one important respect from the memorandum which Bonar Law had presented to Asquith on November 25th. In Lloyd George's plan the Prime

---

[1] See *Politicians and the War*, Vol. II, pp. 169–70, for the full text of these letters.

Minister was not to be a member of the War Council, but could exercise from outside powers both of initiative and of veto, i.e. he could direct the Council to consider any topic, and if he disagreed with its conclusions he could refer the matter to the Cabinet which could override the Council's decisions.

Lloyd George handed this memorandum to Asquith. Apparently Asquith raised no immediate objection to the plan, or to the exclusion of the Prime Minister from the War Committee. He promised to let Lloyd George have his considered opinion in writing later. During their conversation which was entirely friendly Lloyd George told Asquith that he considered it was essential to remove Balfour from the Admiralty and that the Committee should consist of himself, Carson, and Bonar Law.

Lloyd George having finished his interview with Asquith promptly reported progress to Bonar Law. The latter seeing the memorandum for the first time at once pointed out that it gave the Prime Minister a less favourable status than in the original plan. His own account should be quoted:[u]

"Lloyd George's reply was that in his view the dignity of the Prime Minister was retained as much in the one case as in the other and that no exception had been taken to it by Mr. Asquith . . . he added that he had expressed the view to the Prime Minister that it was essential that Mr. Balfour should cease to be at the head of the Admiralty. I said at once that not only could I take no part in any attempt to get rid of Mr. Balfour from the Admiralty, but that in view of the relationship between us, if he were compelled to leave that position, I could not under any circumstances take his place, that, whoever else might be justified in doing so, nothing would justify me in treating him in such a way after the more than generous treatment I had received from him since the time he had ceased to be leader of our Party."

On this rather indecisive note the discussion ended.

Bonar Law spent the rest of the day, December 1st, brooding upon the problem. That night he dined alone with Aitken at the Hyde Park Hotel and went over the whole subject with him. Finally, he decided that he must see Lloyd George again, have out with him the question of Balfour, and finally decide what to do if Asquith procrastinated any further. Aitken happened to know that Lloyd George was dining out that night at the Berkeley Hotel with Lord Cunliffe, the Governor of the Bank of England, Lord Reading, and Mr. and Mrs. Edwin Montagu. Bonar Law insisted upon accompanying him to the Berkeley but agreed to wait outside in a taxi. Aitken went into the restaurant and beckoned from a distance to Lloyd

George who, to the surprise of the other guests, promptly got up and left. He knew that only a matter of the greatest urgency would have induced Aitken to act in this curious way. The three men returned in their taxi to the Hyde Park Hotel and they once again discussed the problem of what to do if Asquith refused to move. It must be remembered that Asquith's reply to Lloyd George's memorandum had not yet arrived.[1]

According to Beaverbrook Lloyd George behaved with great tact at the discussion and made no attempt to bully Bonar Law or to bring pressure upon him.

Bonar Law's own account is as follows:[v]

"I at once said to him [Lloyd George]: 'Now I want to know exactly to what extent you consider I am committed to you.' He replied that he did not consider me committed at all. I did not agree with that, but stated that I was committed to support him to the fullest extent in securing a small War Council of which he would be Chairman, but that I did not feel justified in dictating to the Prime Minister precisely the way in which that Committee should be constituted, and, therefore, I must be free to take whatever action I thought right, if the small Council were agreed to, and if the Prime Minister suggested other names to constitute it. Lloyd George agreed to this and, indeed, added that he himself had not made the names a condition in his conversation with the Prime Minister."

Lloyd George left late. He himself records the result of the meeting thus:[w] "it was decided that we should go forward with our plan of reorganization, whatever the consequences". Aitken accompanied Bonar Law to Pembroke Lodge. Late though the hour was, the two men continued the discussion even longer. "I can still hear him", wrote Beaverbrook, "speaking with that curious emphatic inflexion which always showed that he had come to the end of the period of interminable debate and made up his mind. So he had. He was going forward at any cost."[x]

---

[1] At least that must be presumed, although Lloyd George's own account, *War Memoirs*, pp. 587–89, seems to suggest that he had received Asquith's reply already. If so it is difficult to see why Lloyd George needed to write the following day to Bonar Law enclosing Asquith's reply; see below, p. 313. If it had already come, presumably it would have been discussed at the Hyde Park Hotel on Friday night.

CHAPTER XX

THE ATTACK ON ASQUITH

DECEMBER 1ST – 3RD, 1916

Asquith rejects Lloyd George's new proposal – Lloyd George's letter to Bonar Law – Rumours in the Press – Bonar Law calls a meeting of Conservative Ministers on Sunday, December 3rd – Sensational article in "Reynolds News" – Fury of the Conservative Ministers – Conflicting versions of their discussion with Bonar Law – Impossibility of reconciling Beaverbrook's and Curzon's stories – The Conservative Resolution – Bonar Law's own version – Bonar Law sees Asquith – Their apparent misunderstanding – Asquith agrees to come to terms – Conflict of evidence over the interview – Bonar Law's failure to show Asquith the Conservative Resolution – No ulterior motive – Significance of the omission much exaggerated by the Asquithians – Surmise as to what really happened

I

M EANWHILE what was Asquith's attitude to Lloyd George's proposal? Winston Churchill has subsequently observed that the Lloyd George plan was by no means as unfavourable to Asquith as it might at first sight appear. "Indeed if it is studied with attention it will appear to have contained many features of great advantage to him. Viewing the issue from a detached standpoint I reached the conclusion, as did Sir Edward Carson, that the position of the Secretary of State for War under it would become one both of difficulty and weakness."[a] Churchill points out that all the setbacks of the war would have been attributed to Lloyd George, that quarrels would certainly have arisen between him and the professional staff of both Army and Navy, and that in the case of appeals the Prime Minister would have had the final word, and thus been able to ensure that on all major and controversial topics his own view prevailed.

Asquith did not see the matter in this light. After reflecting upon his conversation with Lloyd George he wrote later on the same day, Friday, December 1st, a letter which was tantamount to a complete rejection of Lloyd George's plan. While agreeing that some sort of reorganization was necessary Asquith declared (1) that the Prime Minister must be Chairman of the War Committee, (2) that there must still be a right of appeal from its decisions to the Cabinet – a right which could be exercised, apparently by any aggrieved member of the committee, (3) that a second committee, called the Committee of National Organization, should be set up to deal with the domestic side of war problems.

"I purposely do not", Asquith added, "in this letter discuss the delicate and difficult question of personnel."[1]

It was clear to Lloyd George that an impasse had been reached. Asquith's counter-proposals were quite unacceptable. They destroyed the entire basis of Lloyd George's plan. But he could do nothing further until Bonar Law had first clarified the position with his Unionist colleagues and secondly presented his own final views to Asquith. Without Bonar Law, Lloyd George was powerless. Accordingly on Saturday morning he sent a copy of Asquith's letter to Bonar Law with this covering note:[b]

War Office,
Whitehall,
2nd December 1916.

"My dear Bonar,

"I enclose copy of P.M.'s letter. The life of the country depends on resolute action by you now.

"Yours ever,

D. Lloyd George."

On Saturday morning rumours of the impending trouble, and the probability of Lloyd George's resignation, began to appear in the Press for the first time. In the *Daily Express* and the *Daily Chronicle* these rumours were particularly detailed and accurate. This was not surprising: Aitken had informed their respective editors, R. D. Blumenfeld and Robert Donald, of the exact situation. Both papers not only announced the impending crisis but named Lloyd George, Carson, and Bonar Law as the essential members of a new War Council. Bonar Law now decided that he must summon a meeting of his Conservative colleagues to discuss their attitude to the rapidly approaching crisis. This meeting was fixed for Sunday morning at Pembroke Lodge.

The likelihood was that Bonar Law would find himself in a minority of one against all his colleagues, just as he had on the preceding Thursday. Admittedly no one knew what Balfour's attitude would be, but, as he remained ill in bed, his attitude for the moment did not matter. Lloyd George had indeed summoned Lord Derby from Lancashire, hoping thus to give Bonar Law at least one ally,

---

[1] For the full text see Lord Beaverbrook, *Politicians and the War*, II, pp. 186–7.

for Derby, who occupied the post of Under-Secretary for War, had
been won over to support the War Council Plan. Unfortunately
although Derby was a person of great weight in the Unionist Party,
he was not a member of the Cabinet. Bonar Law decided on balance
that he had better not risk the resentment which might be caused
if Derby were asked to attend.[c]

Before the critical meeting of Sunday, December 3rd, a discon-
certing and unexpected episode occurred. On Sunday morning there
appeared a leading article of a sensational character in *Reynolds News*,
a radical paper then owned by Sir Henry Dalziel. This article, which
looked "like an interview with Lloyd George written in the third
person",[d] stated plainly that Lloyd George would resign unless his
demands were accepted, that he was in close alliance with Carson,
that Bonar Law and Derby would back him up, and that, having
resigned, Lloyd George would appeal to public opinion against the
Government for its incompetence in managing the war.

The Unionist Ministers arrived at Bonar Law's house in a state of
fury. They were naturally very angry at what seemed a deliberate
attempt on Lloyd George's part to force their hands in the midst of
these delicate negotiations about the future of the Government.
Never friendly to Lloyd George they now became extremely hostile.
Bonar Law soon found that he had against him Curzon, Chamberlain, Cecil and Long. Lansdowne was in the country and unable to
attend but he would undoubtedly have agreed with the others.

What followed is far from clear. Indeed the accounts subsequently
written by some of the chief actors conflict in a manner impossible
to resolve. According to Beaverbrook, the Conservative Ministers,
with the exception of Bonar Law, were unanimous in their hostility
to Lloyd George, and any action which followed was, as far as they
were concerned, directed against Lloyd George in order to strengthen
Asquith, and not the other way round, as seemed afterwards to be
the case. Beaverbrook was not actually present in the room during
the discussion, but he was in another room at Pembroke Lodge and
Bonar Law at one stage came out and told him what was going on.
His account, therefore, must be regarded as an accurate reflection
of how Bonar Law viewed the situation at that particular moment.

Other accounts suggest that the difference between Bonar Law
and the rest of the Unionist Ministers was not quite so clear. There is,
indeed, a letter from Curzon to Lansdowne, published in the latter's
biography which gives a precisely opposite version, and suggests that
the Unionist Ministers were all determined on a course that would

result in Asquith's resignation and the substitution of Lloyd George as Prime Minister.

"We know", writes Curzon, "that with him (Asquith) as Chairman either of the Cabinet or War Committee, it is absolutely impossible to win the war."[1]

It is very difficult to accept Curzon's version, but, unless we suppose him to have been deliberately lying to Lansdowne – and it is hard to see what motive he could have had – we must assume that the discussion at Pembroke Lodge was of a more confused and ambiguous nature than has sometimes been claimed.

At all events, whatever the motives behind their action, the Unionist leaders, Bonar Law included, eventually passed the following resolution:[e]

"We share the view, expressed to the Prime Minister by Mr. Bonar Law sometime ago, that the Government cannot go on as it is.

"It is evident that a change must be made, and in our opinion the publicity given to the intentions of Mr. Lloyd George makes reconstruction from within no longer possible. We therefore urge the Prime Minister to tender the resignation of the Government.

"If he feels unable to take that step, we authorize Mr. Bonar Law to tender our resignation."

The resolution was evidently capable of being interpreted in more than one sense, and could have been legitimately supported by persons whose motives in so doing might well have been different. The important feature about the resolution was that it called upon Asquith to *resign*. As the biographers of Asquith point out, there is a great difference between "resignation" and "reconstruction". In 1915 Asquith had "reconstructed" the Government, that is to say, had himself remained in office while calling for the resignation of all his colleagues. But the resolution passed by the Unionist Ministers specifically declared that reconstruction was impossible, and demanded resignation.

This was a very different matter. When a Prime Minister tenders his own resignation along with that of his entire Cabinet, it is the King's duty to invite someone else – normally the leader of the next largest party in the House of Commons – to form a Government. The outgoing Prime Minister must stand aside while others are given a chance. Admittedly, if all other candidates fail to form a Government, he may return with greatly enhanced prestige and strength as the indispensable man. But it is a big risk. Men are very seldom

[1] The letter is published in full in Lord Newton's *Biography of Lord Lansdowne*, pp. 452–3.

indispensable in politics. Long and melancholy is the roll of those who "forgot Goschen".

If the Unionist Ministers, other than Bonar Law, really wished to strengthen Asquith's hand then they chose a curious way of setting about it. Surely they would have been better advised to have demanded that Asquith should reconstruct the Government as in 1915, rather than proffer his own resignation and so give someone else the chance of replacing him. Only a very firm conviction that Asquith was indispensable could have justified such a risk – always assuming that the Unionist Ministers genuinely wished to keep Asquith as Prime Minister, and not, as Curzon claimed, to get rid of him. However, a debate conducted in a crowded room by a number of angry and not always clear-headed men may easily produce illogical and incoherent results.

Bonar Law's own version of what happened must be quoted:[f]

"On the Sunday the newspapers were again full of Lloyd George's resignation, and when the Unionist members of the Cabinet met at my house I found to my surprise that they had all come to the conclusion that there was nothing for it but the immediate resignation of the whole Government, and it was proposed that I should communicate to the Prime Minister immediately a resolution to the effect that we unanimously urged him to resign on behalf of the Government, and if he could not see his way to do so the Unionist members would themselves resign in a body.

"This action (asking the P.M. to resign on behalf of the Government) was proposed mainly on the ground that the Unionist members of the cabinet did not wish to seem to have their position forced by the action of Lloyd George.

"The course proposed by them was not one which I desired to adopt. What I wished to say to the Prime Minister was that we considered it absolutely necessary that there should be a change in the conduct of the war, and that as Lloyd George was the only alternative the change should consist in practically putting the direction of the war in his hands, and that if the Prime Minister could not see his way to adopt this course then we should resign. I found my Unionist Colleagues were not willing to take this action and I therefore fell in with their view and agreed to communicate it to the Prime Minister.

*"I agreed to this because the action desired by them, though not in my opinion so good as the course I had suggested, would have the same effect of producing a crisis which would put an end to what seemed to me an impossible situation."

Up to a point this account bears out Beaverbrook's version of events – namely that the intentions of the Unionist Ministers and the intentions of Bonar Law were different. At all events it seems clear that Bonar Law himself believed that there was a difference. Whether the difference was in reality quite so definite as Lord Beaverbrook claims it to have been remains uncertain. If Curzon's attitude is correctly described in his letter to Lansdowne quoted earlier, then at least one other Unionist Minister besides Bonar Law seems to have wished to strengthen Lloyd George against Asquith. The account of these events given by Austen Chamberlain also suggests that the Unionist Ministers were influenced not so much by a desire to support Asquith against Lloyd George, as by a feeling that the present state of affairs was impossible and that Asquith and Lloyd George should fight it out between themselves.[g] It may be therefore that Lord Beaverbrook overstates the extent to which Bonar Law differed from his colleagues.

2

At 12 noon the meeting broke up, leaving Bonar Law to communicate its decision to Asquith in the afternoon. Despite the political crisis the Prime Minister had not intended to forgo his weekend in the country. It had been necessary to summon him that morning from Walmer Castle. Aitken remained at Pembroke Lodge for lunch, and then for the first time saw the actual text of the Unionist resolution. He was, he tells us, at once alarmed at the reference to Lloyd George's dealings with the Press. He feared that this paragraph would reveal the hostility felt by the Unionists for Lloyd George, and would suggest that Bonar Law shared this feeling. Asquith might in that case refuse to resign and simply reconstruct his Government by dismissing Lloyd George.

Feeling strongly on the matter he tried to persuade Bonar Law to repudiate this clause, or modify it, or if necessary to reconvene his colleagues in order to have it deleted. Bonar Law regarded the whole business as trivial, and became irritated at his friend's persistence. Eventually after lunch he agreed to summon F. E. Smith as a sort of umpire or arbiter. Smith, however, supported Bonar Law. He was adamant in the opinion that no change could be made. To do so would be to pervert the intention of the signatories and would be a breach of faith on the part of the Conservative Leader.

It was now about 3 o'clock, and time for Bonar Law to see Asquith. He was accompanied as far as the Colonial Office by Aitken. The afternoon was cold, dismal and foggy as only a December afternoon in London can be. Whitehall was bleak and deserted. "The attendant at the empty office", writes Beaverbrook,[h] "seemed uncertain whether Bonar Law really was Colonial Secretary or not." Eventually they

got in by a side door and Aitken lit the fire in Bonar Law's vast and
chilly room, while the Conservative leader walked across to No.
10 Downing Street for his momentous interview with the Prime
Minister.

The historian would give much to know exactly what was said at
the meeting which followed. For something of the fog and mist of
that gloomy afternoon seems to have drifted across the pages of its
history. There is a conflict of evidence which is by no means easy to
resolve, and we shall perhaps never know for certain precisely what
occurred.

According to Beaverbrook,[i] Bonar Law opened proceedings by
explaining carefully the difference which he believed to exist between
himself and his colleagues. *They* wanted Asquith to resign because
they believed that this action would result in a strengthening of his
position against Lloyd George. *He* wanted Asquith to resign in order
to produce a reconstruction of the Government, which would result,
not indeed in Asquith's deposition from the Premiership, but in the
transference of the direction of the war into the hands of Lloyd
George. But both sides, i.e. all the Unionist Ministers, were agreed
in demanding resignation as the only way out of what had by now
become an intolerable situation.

Beaverbrook does not directly discuss the question whether Bonar
Law actually showed the text of the Unionist resolution to Asquith.
But he vigorously repudiates any charge of bad faith against Bonar
Law. Bonar Law himself undoubtedly believed that he had made
the whole situation clear, and that he had told Asquith why the
Unionist Ministers demanded his resignation. On the other hand it
is fairly clear that, for whatever reason, Asquith did not fully grasp
the fact that some of the Unionist Ministers were pressing this course
of action in order to strengthen him against Lloyd George, and not
vice versa. Beaverbrook explains this failure on Asquith's part by his
alarm at the demand for resignation. "This single word RESIGNATION
frightened him. . . . The hostility of the Tories to Lloyd George and
the attack over trafficking with the Press seemed to be quite occluded
from his mind by the major issue of resignation."[j] The result of this
demand was to impel Asquith strongly in the direction of compromise
with Lloyd George. Asquith was far from sharing at this time the
view of his Unionist allies that he was indispensable. On the contrary, resignation by throwing the initiative into other hands might
well be a two-edged weapon. Suppose that, after all, Lloyd George,
or Bonar Law, or even Balfour found himself able to form an alterna-

tive Government. As we have seen there is a great difference between resignation and reconstruction, and it was the former which was being pressed upon Asquith. It is not surprising that he regarded the risk as too great.

The upshot then of Bonar Law's interview – and on this there is no dispute – was that Asquith decided to compromise with Lloyd George, and agree to the formation of a small War Council with Lloyd George as chairman. Assured that Asquith would send for Lloyd George that very afternoon, Bonar Law returned well satisfied to the Colonial Office. He had never wished to see Asquith ousted from the Premiership. The solution now envisaged seemed to him ideal.

The biographers of Asquith give a very different version of the critical interview at 10 Downing Street.[k] According to them Bonar Law wholly failed to explain the motives behind the Unionist resolution, and further he failed to show the text of the resolution to Asquith. They follow Asquith's own account – or rather, for Asquith never actually wrote an account of these events himself, that of Lord Crewe who was an intimate friend of Asquith. Lord Crewe's account was adopted and, as it were, officially authorized by Asquith. It must be taken as a correct representation of Asquith's views. According to Lord Crewe, "Bonar Law's message was curtly delivered but in further conversation it was implied that the demand for resignation was not made in Lloyd George's interest, but that the Government might be reconstructed".

Lord Crewe continues:[l]

"Assuming this to be the fact the action of the Unionist Ministers seemed disproportionate to the need, for reconstruction could quite well have proceeded as it did last year by the resignation of all the Prime Minister's colleagues, he himself retaining his place and commission to form a new Government. Still whatever the motive there the fact was, and it had been arranged that the Prime Minister would again see both Messrs. Lloyd George and Bonar Law later in the day."

Asquith's biographers do not openly impute any dishonesty to Bonar Law, but they plainly imply that he handled the matter badly and that, even if he did not intend to do so, he did in fact seriously mislead Asquith.[m] As a result Asquith believed that his Unionist colleagues were no longer prepared to support him against Lloyd George. This belief caused Asquith to compromise with Lloyd George, and, so his biographers argue, the attempt at compromise was in the end fatal to Asquith, since it alienated the very same

Unionist colleagues who might have supported him during the following two days when events forced him into an open struggle with Lloyd George. They dismiss Lord Beaverbrook's suggestion (which was of course based on what Bonar Law told him) that Asquith was so alarmed at the mention of the word resignation that he failed to appreciate Bonar Law's careful explanation of the intention behind the resolution.

"Such an explanation", writes Mr. J. A. Spender,[n] "can hardly be taken seriously by anyone who knew Asquith". If any man knew how to keep his head cool and his brain clear in an emergency it was he.

3

What justice is there in these criticisms?[1] It must be admitted at once that Bonar Law did not in fact show Asquith the Unionist resolution. On that point we have not only Asquith's testimony in *Memories and Reflections* but Bonar Law's own statement in the unpublished memorandum which he wrote on these events and which has been quoted on several occasions in this narrative.

Bonar Law writes:[o]

"I told him (Asquith) of the decision we had come to, but, though I had the resolution in my pocket, as I had not begun by handing it to him but had simply communicated its contents, I forgot to hand him the actual document. The Prime Minister was not only greatly shocked but greatly surprised by our communication, and asked me to treat it as if it had not been made, until he had an opportunity of discussing the matter with Lloyd George."

It may be conceded that Bonar Law would have done better to have handed the resolution to Asquith. The innuendo of dishonesty, which Asquith's friends did not hesitate to spread later, would then have been too absurd for belief. To that extent – but to that extent only – we must regret that Bonar Law kept the document in his pocket. But it is of course quite another matter to suggest that Bonar Law's action made any difference to the course of events or to imply that Bonar Law seriously misrepresented, by accident or design, the intentions of his Unionist colleagues. After all the very paper upon

[1] Mr. A. G. Gardiner reviewing J. A. Spender's and Cyril Asquith's Life of Asquith in the *Spectator* on October 22nd, 1932, described Bonar Law's failure to show Asquith the Unionist resolution as "one of the darkest blots on the page of history". This statement provoked a vigorous reply from Bonar Law's son Mr. Richard Law, M.P., who had himself reviewed the book in the *Evening Standard* on October 18th, and had described Mr. Spender as building up his charge "with a quite masterly combination of suppression and innuendo".

which Asquith's biographers rely – the Crewe memorandum quoted above – specifically states that Bonar Law made it clear that "the demand for resignation was not made in Lloyd George's interest, but that the Government might be reconstructed". Surely nothing can be more definite than this statement, which in itself disposes of any idea that Bonar Law gave Asquith the false impression that the Unionist Ministers had gone over to Lloyd George.

Nor do Asquith's biographers make any convincing case for the view that events would have gone differently if Asquith had seen the resolution. He would, it is true, have read the paragraph which implied a criticism of Lloyd George's relations with the Press. But, even if we assume that Bonar Law failed to communicate that point verbally, Asquith in any case knew that the demand for his resignation was not being made in Lloyd George's interest. It is not easy to see what else Asquith would have done even if he had read the text of the resolution. He might, perhaps, have resigned forthwith instead of waiting till Tuesday, thus compelling either Bonar Law or Lloyd George to attempt the formation of a Government immediately. But is there any reason to suppose that Lloyd George would have failed to do on Sunday what he achieved with ease three days later? The argument of the Asquithians appears to be that some of the Unionist Ministers – Curzon, Cecil, Chamberlain, Long are the names usually mentioned – might have declined to serve under Lloyd George on December 3rd, whereas on December 6th they were so irritated by Asquith's apparent attempt to compromise with Lloyd George that they were ready to serve under the very person with whom they had hitherto refused even to consider a compromise.

To this there are two answers. In the first place it is by no means certain that the Unionist Ministers concerned were in fact as hostile to Lloyd George and friendly to Asquith as has been represented. Curzon's letter to Lord Lansdowne, suggesting exactly the contrary, has already been quoted. Austen Chamberlain too makes it clear in his own account of these events that he was more or less neutral as between Asquith and Lloyd George. It is quite probable that patriotic desire to support a war-time Administration would, when it came to the point, have overcome the doubts of the Unionist Ministers, just as it did three days later. Secondly, even if the Unionist Ministers had declined to serve under Lloyd George and so had made it difficult or impossible for him to form a Government, it is inconceivable that they would have refused to serve under Bonar Law who was after all the leader of their own Party, and we know that Lloyd George would have been perfectly willing to have taken office under Bonar Law. Finally it is probably true to say that, even if the Unionist Ministers had taken the extreme step of refusing to serve under either Bonar Law or Lloyd George, it would still have been possible for one of them to have formed a Government. Powerful figures like Balfour, Milner, Carson, Derby and F. E. Smith would have rallied to the cause. The ship would have been launched, and once it was afloat there would have been plenty of persons willing to join the crew.

The only other action hypothetically open to Asquith on this critical Sunday was to remain in office and refuse to compromise with Lloyd George. But this would have been equally fatal, since Bonar Law would have joined Lloyd George, both would have resigned, and the Government could not have long survived the secession of two such important figures. There would have been a ferocious Press campaign, and the public withdrawal of the Conservative leader would have meant a return to party warfare which Asquith was now in no position to win. In this respect Bonar Law's attitude was evidently of critical importance, and by Sunday, December 3rd, it is quite clear that he had come to the view that Asquith must either agree to handing over the effective direction of the war to Lloyd George, or else resign the Premiership. Bonar Law preferred that Asquith should remain as Prime Minister, but only on condition that Lloyd George became the effective Chairman of the War Council.

Did Asquith himself feel a sense of grievance over the way in which Bonar Law had conducted the interview on Sunday afternoon? He certainly did not show any such feeling to Bonar Law. On the evening after Asquith's resignation Bonar Law went to see him. Beaverbrook noted down the exact words of their conversation as reported to him by Bonar Law immediately afterwards. Bonar Law bluntly began:[1]

"When a man has done another a serious injury no good can come from explanations."

Asquith replied:

"I have no feeling of hostility. You have treated me with complete straightforwardness all through."

Asquith's biographers, however, say – and presumably their state-

[1] *Politicians and the War*, II, p. 285. The same conversation in slightly different words is recorded by Bonar Law in his unpublished memorandum on the crisis.

ment is based on personal knowledge – that this was not his real opinion.

"It would be idle to pretend that this was Asquith's considered view of these transactions. He never concealed from his friends that he considered himself to have been seriously misled about material facts, or minced words in characterizing the parts played by some of the performers on this scene."ᴾ

Although Mr. J. A. Spender does not make the point quite clear it seems fairly certain that one of the "performers" in question was Bonar Law. If Asquith came to take this view it remains curious that he never committed it to writing. Certainly there is nothing in his published reminiscences or public speeches to suggest that he felt any such grievance, and there is no hint of it in the brief character sketch of Bonar Law which he wrote and published after the latter's death. However, it may well be true that Asquith came later to nourish a sense of grievance at having been, as it might seem, jockeyed out of office, and there were undoubtedly plenty of embittered Liberal Ministers who, joining their chief in reluctant political exile after 1916, were ready to fan any smouldering embers of indignation which Asquith may have felt. But this sense of grievance on Asquith's part, if it existed at all, was evidently not sufficiently specific for him to feel like issuing any charge of bad faith against Bonar Law. Possibly upon reflection Asquith came to realize that any misunderstanding which occurred was at least partly his own fault. Possibly, too, he may have come to the conclusion that the misunderstanding any way made little difference in the long run to the course of events.

Bonar Law's reputation for unflinching honesty and integrity is beyond challenge, even from those who belittle his political stature. It is inconceivable that anyone, except in the heat of the moment, could seriously maintain that he deliberately deceived Asquith, and sought to lure the Prime Minister to his doom by misrepresenting the true sense of the Unionist Ministers' discussion. It is equally improbable that Bonar Law, through accident, agitation, or incoherence, failed to make the situation clear. Lucid exposition was one of his strongest points.

What really happened in 10 Downing Street on that bleak December afternoon? The conflict of evidence makes certainty impossible, but some attempt can be made at a plausible reconstruction. It is clear that Bonar Law forgot to show Asquith the famous resolution. It is equally clear that he communicated the gist of it, and that he told Asquith – and Asquith understood – that the demand for his resignation was not being made in order to strengthen Lloyd George. Both sides appear to agree on this point. At this stage – and substantially Asquith's biographers do not disagree – Asquith appears to have seized upon the word "resignation", and to have seen in it implications of danger which the majority of the Unionist Ministers do not appear to have seen. He saw that, if he resigned and thus threw the initiative of forming a Government into other hands, he would really be putting the whole question of his indispensability as Prime Minister to the test. He was naturally not ready to do this, unless he had to. He therefore begged Bonar Law to treat the communication as not having been made, and terminated the discussion with a promise that he would see, and seek terms with, Lloyd George.

Both Lord Beaverbrook and Mr. Spender agree that Asquith did not fully realize how hostile the Unionist Ministers in fact were to Lloyd George. We have already seen that there is some reason to doubt the actual extent or universality of this hostility, but, if we assume that it did exist, the real dispute turns upon whether Asquith's failure to appreciate it was his own fault or that of Bonar Law. Clearly it will never be possible to settle this question authoritatively, but in balancing probabilities there is this point to consider. Both Bonar Law and Asquith were clear-headed men, and did not panic easily, but at this interview Bonar Law had all the advantage of coming ready briefed and knowing what he was going to say, whereas Asquith was in the unfavourable position of receiving a disagreeable and unexpected shock. After all, at its most favourable interpretation the demand for his resignation was a demand that he should do open battle with Lloyd George, and, even if he was sure of a majority of Unionist Ministers on his side, Asquith might well have been alarmed at such a demand. If anyone had an excuse for temporarily losing his head it was Asquith, and for this reason apart from any others, the balance of probability, granted, of course, complete honesty of purpose on both sides, is that Asquith failed to comprehend, rather than that Bonar Law failed to expound, the true sense of the message which he was delivering.

With these observations we may leave this much disputed topic. It has been necessary to discuss it at length because Bonar Law's reputation for competence, even for common honesty, has been seriously impugned, not – at least in public – by Asquith himself, but by his embittered partisans. Moreover a whole theory has been constructed of hypothetical means by which Asquith could have retained the Premiership if he had seen the Unionist resolution or had had it properly explained to him. We shall see that the episode has in retrospect been made far more significant than it really was. We shall see too that Asquith could easily have retained the Premiership, despite anything that happened at his famous interview with Bonar Law, if he had been prepared to play his cards differently. It was to his own friends – not his enemies – that he owed his downfall.

CHAPTER XXI

THE FALL OF ASQUITH

DECEMBER 3RD – 7TH, 1916

Asquith sees Lloyd George and Bonar Law – Their terms accepted – Relief of Bonar Law – Hostile leading article in The Times *on Monday annoys Asquith – Apparently inspired by Lloyd George – Asquith changes his mind over Lloyd George's terms – His motives – Bonar Law tries to dissuade him – Lloyd George resigns – The three "Cs" withdraw support from Asquith – Their stormy interview with Bonar Law – Reconciliation – The Unionist Ministers resign en bloc – Asquith resigns – Bonar Law sent for by the King – He declines the Premiership when Asquith refuses to serve – Conference at Buckingham Palace – Asquith unwilling to serve in any Government – Lloyd George becomes Prime Minister – Balfour joins – Great importance of his adherence – The three "Cs" and Long accept office - The Second Coalition is formed – Bonar Law becomes Chancellor of the Exchequer and Leader of the House of Commons*

I

O N his return to the Colonial Office Bonar Law at once summoned a meeting of Unionist Ministers to take place that evening at F. E. Smith's house. Bonar Law hoped to be able to convey to his colleagues the news that there had been a compromise. Meanwhile Lloyd George, who had come up from his house at Walton Heath, was waiting in the War Office for a summons from Asquith. Aitken took the opportunity to brief him in all the latest developments and Lloyd George fully realized the importance of the interview which lay ahead. When the message came he calmly waited till he had finished his cigar and then walked over to Number 10. The upshot of his discussion with Asquith was apparent agreement upon the status of the War Council. On this point Lloyd George had his way. The War Council was to have full powers over the direction of the war, subject to the Prime Minister's approval or veto. The Chairman would be someone other than the Prime Minister, but would report to the latter every day, and submit the agenda to him. The Prime Minister was entitled to attend meetings whenever he wished to do so. The only subject reserved for further discussion was that of personnel.

At 5 o'clock Asquith again requested Bonar Law to see him, and in Lloyd George's presence confirmed that complete agreement had been reached about the status and powers of the War Council, but that the question of membership remained open. It was, of course, understood that Lloyd George would be Chairman, but Asquith wished to exclude Carson and, though he did not say so, was by no means anxious to include Bonar Law, both of whom Lloyd George wished to see on the Council. However, there seemed no danger of a breakdown on this point.

Bonar Law writes:[a]

"This [the agreement] was a great relief to me as I had throughout worked with the one object of securing greater efficiency in the conduct of the war whilst retaining Mr. Asquith as Prime Minister."

It was agreed that the best way to create the new War Council would be for Asquith to request the resignation of all Ministers. He would in this way be able to reconstruct the Government as he had done in 1915. Bonar Law conveyed this decision to his Unionist colleagues who agreed to hold over their demand for Asquith's resignation. An announcement was released to the Press late that night informing the world that Asquith intended to reconstruct the Government.

The day which had begun so dramatically seemed to have closed in an atmosphere of peace and calm. Certainly Asquith appears to have been confident that the crisis had passed.

"I was forced back", he wrote that evening,[b] "by Bongie[1] and Montagu and Rufus[2] to grapple with a 'Crisis' – this time with a very big C. The result is that I have spent much of the afternoon colloguing with Messrs. Ll. George and Bonar Law and one or two minor worthies. The 'Crisis' shows every sign of following its many predecessors to an early and un-honoured grave. But there were many wigs very nearly on the green."

For Bonar Law, too, the day had been satisfactory. He had at no stage wished to oust Asquith from the Premiership. It would be idle to pretend that he had any great respect for Asquith's competence as a war leader, nor can he have been wholly insensible to the slighting manner in which Asquith at times treated him personally. But he still believed – wrongly as it turned out – that the country at large attached great importance to the presence of Asquith at the head of affairs. He was most anxious to avoid acting in a manner which would suggest disloyalty to the Prime Minister. A compromise solution of the nature arrived at on Sunday evening seemed to him admirable.

[1] Sir Maurice Bonham-Carter.
[2] Lord Reading.

Yet, only twenty-four hours later, the whole political situation was once again in a whirl. By Monday night Asquith had broken off all relations with Lloyd George, and was ready to do open battle with his formidable rival. The stage was set for a struggle which could only end in a complete defeat for one of the two men. Compromise was at an end.

What occurred on Monday, December 4th, to produce so extraordinary a *volte face* on the part of Asquith? To this question differing answers are given, but the problem belongs to the life of Asquith rather than that of Bonar Law, and will be only briefly discussed here. Asquith's biographers attach great importance to a leading article which appeared in *The Times* that morning and which seemed to be inspired by Lloyd George.[c] The article was in fact written by Geoffrey Dawson, the editor, and was in no way due to Lloyd George, nor did it contain anything which a well informed political journalist could not have known through his contacts. Nevertheless, the article described in some detail Lloyd George's proposals for reorganization, suggested that Asquith's power would be nominal only, and revealed the fact that Lloyd George, Bonar Law, and Carson were acting in concert. This information had been given to Dawson by Carson on Sunday afternoon, December 3rd.[d] The article ended on a note highly hostile to Asquith. "His closest supporters", wrote Dawson, "must have convinced the Prime Minister that his own qualities are fitted better, as they are so fond of saying, to 'preserve the unity of the nation' (though we have never doubted that unity) than to force the pace of a War Council."

It is not surprising that Asquith should have felt annoyance at these remarks. He was accustomed of course to hostile criticism from *The Times*, for Northcliffe was one of his bitterest enemies, but the details in this latest article might well have given the impression that they had been supplied by Lloyd George. In fact, as we have seen, this was not the case and Lloyd George had nothing to do with the article, but, if Asquith believed that *The Times* leader was an expression of Lloyd George's true intentions with regard to the rôle of the War Council, it is not surprising that he began to look upon the suggested compromise in a different light. This at any rate is the explanation given by Asquith's biographers for his change of front.

It may not, however, be the whole explanation. The announcement of the reconstruction, put out on Sunday night from 10 Downing Street, arrived as a complete shock to the political world at large,

and in particular to Asquith's Liberal colleagues who knew nothing
of the events which had occurred on Sunday. Only Crewe, Reading
and Montagu had been taken into Asquith's confidence. The rest,
McKenna, Grey, Runciman, Harcourt, Samuel, were disagreeably
surprised. They – or some of them – hastened to see Asquith early
on Monday morning, and pressed him strongly not to surrender thus
ignominiously to Lloyd George. McKenna, who hated Lloyd George,
was one of the most forcible advocates of this view. Moreover, at
some period on this same morning Asquith appears to have seen
certain Unionist Ministers – it is not clear exactly whom[1] – and to
have understood for the first time that the demand for his resignation
was not made in order to oust him but in order that he might return
all the stronger having proved himself the indispensable man.

It must have become clear to Asquith that he had a good deal more
support from Members of the Cabinet than he had realized on Sunday. Moreover, if, by compromising with Lloyd George, he had
hoped for peace and quiet, he was evidently in error. The anti-
Lloyd George wing of the Cabinet was going to agitate just as
vigorously as Lloyd George himself if their demands were not met.
Perhaps after all Asquith was indispensable. Certainly everyone said
so. But Asquith had already gone a very long way towards committing
himself to Lloyd George, and it was not easy to find a good excuse
to break off negotiations. Now it was precisely this excuse which *The
Times* article provided. The Unionists had condemned Lloyd George
for trafficking with the Press. It was too late to use the article in
Reynolds News, for Asquith had already, as it were, condoned that,
but *The Times* article seemed another striking example of Lloyd
George's alleged Press intrigues. Doubtless Asquith genuinely be-

---

[1] There is a conflict of evidence here. Lord Beaverbrook and Lord Crewe both state
that Curzon, Lord Robert Cecil, and Austen Chamberlain saw Asquith on Monday
morning. Austen Chamberlain, however, denies (*Down the Years*), p. 123) that he saw
Asquith before Tuesday. There is a letter from Curzon to Asquith written on the Monday
(published in the *Life of Asquith*, Vol. II, p. 260), which suggests that Lansdowne too had
seen Asquith that day. "Lansdowne has, I think, explained to you that my resignation
yesterday was far from having the sinister purpose which I believe you were inclined to
attribute to it." But, as Mr. J. A. Spender points out, the only "sinister purport" which
Asquith could have attributed to Curzon's resignation was precisely what Curzon had
himself attributed to it in his letter to Lansdowne the previous day. Lansdowne of course
may well have consulted others besides Curzon and so have been able to reassure Asquith.
But Curzon's two letters are impossible to reconcile unless he was behaving with quite
extraordinary duplicity. Finally, to add to the confusion of evidence, Lord Beaverbrook
tells us that Curzon gave Asquith an absolute pledge on Monday that "in no circumstances
whatever would he, Curzon, or those acting with him, take office under Lloyd George or
Bonar Law" (*Politicians and the War*, Vol. II, p. 256). Lord Beaverbrook's source appears
to be a member of the Government who attended a meeting of Liberal Ministers on Monday evening, at which Asquith made this claim. It is difficult to acquit Curzon of a considerable measure of sharp practice in all these transactions.

lieved that Lloyd George had inspired *The Times* leader.[1] "None the less," as Beaverbrook writes, "it wrongs Asquith to suppose him capable of changing his whole policy at the crucial moment of his life because of a leading article in a newspaper. Such a theory denies him the qualities of clarity of intellect, of a sense of relative proportion, even of personal dignity, which friend and foe alike have allowed him." In other words *The Times* article may well have been an excellent excuse for action which Asquith desired to take on other grounds.

Whatever his motives, Asquith now took prompt action. Despite repeated pleas and messages, he refused for the whole of Monday to find time for a personal interview with Lloyd George. All that he did was to write Lloyd George a sharp note[e] strongly hinting that the latter was responsible for – or at least able to prevent – attacks from *The Times*. Lloyd George replied in a conciliatory tone ending thus:[f]

"Northcliffe would like to make this and any other rearrangement under your premiership impossible. Derby and I attach great importance to your retaining the Premiership – effectively. I cannot restrain or, I fear, influence Northcliffe. I fully accept in letter and spirit your summary of the suggested arrangement – subject, of course, to personnel.

"Ever Sincerely,

D. Lloyd George."

Meanwhile Asquith had moved the adjournment of Parliament till December 7th in order that he might reconstruct the Government. Shortly before question time, Bonar Law, who was aware of the signs portending a change of front on the part of the Prime Minister, came to call on Asquith at his room in the House of Commons.

"I was disturbed", writes Bonar Law,[g] "to find that, as it seemed to me, he was not quite so decided as to the appointment of the small War Council as he had been the previous evening. We had not time to finish our conversation and immediately after questions I followed him to Downing Street in order to finish it."

Like Lloyd George, Bonar Law had some difficulty in getting an interview with the Prime Minister who, having now made up his mind was probably reluctant to discuss matters any further. But Bonar Law could be very persistent when he felt that the occasion called. He jumped the queue of waiting Liberal Ministers and found

[1] Asquith had been correctly told by Edwin Montagu that Northcliffe had visited the War Office on Sunday, December 3rd. It was not surprising that he drew an incorrect inference from this fact.

Asquith engaged in a private consultation with McKenna. The latter at once left. Bonar Law writes:[h]

"I only remained a few minutes and during that time urged the Prime Minister not, as I expressed it to him, to fall between two stools. I told him that in my opinion the only way to save the Government was to carry out the arrangement made the previous day. I added that the position had become extremely difficult partly through the action of the Press, and partly through his own delay which had made it difficult for the arrangement to be brought into effect without loss of dignity for him. I told him, indeed, that as the position was, there would be a certain amount of humiliation, but added that he had gone through this sort of thing before and in my opinion he was a big enough man to live it down."

This last characteristically blunt observation cannot have been much comfort to Asquith, and he relapsed into a gloomy silence. The interview, moreover, must have made it plain to him that he could not expect to separate Bonar Law from Lloyd George. If he ever hoped simply to reconstruct the Government without Lloyd George, that hope was shattered. He would have Bonar Law against him – and this in terms of power politics probably meant the whole Conservative Party machine which was after all under the control of Bonar Law – not that of Curzon, Lansdowne or Chamberlain. If Asquith really meant to fight Bonar Law and Lloyd George, his only weapon now would be either to accept their resignations and damn the consequences, or resign himself, force Lloyd George or Bonar Law to try to form a Government and, when they failed, demonstrate his own strength as the only possible Prime Minister.

By now, however, Asquith's mind was made up: he did not mean to compromise; perhaps in the last resort his own friends had made compromise impossible. Still resolutely declining even to see Lloyd George, Asquith that evening wrote him a letter completely repudiating the provisional arrangements for a War Council, and stating categorically that as Prime Minister he insisted on being its Chairman. This was open war at last. Lloyd George could only agree at the cost of total and humiliating surrender. He received Asquith's letter on Tuesday morning and at once informed Bonar Law. He then wrote to Asquith formally handing in his resignation, which Asquith promptly accepted.[1]

Bonar Law's doubts were now resolved. "Up to this point", he writes,[i] "I had been in a very difficult position – of being friends to

---

[1] The whole correspondence between Asquith and Lloyd George has been published in full by Lord Beaverbrook in *Politicians and the War*, Vol. II, and by Mr. J. A. Spender in the *Life of Asquith*.

both sides, and I was throughout greatly worried by the fear that each side might in the end think I had been false to it. After reading the Prime Minister's letter, however, I came definitely to the conclusion that I had no longer any choice, and that I must back Lloyd George in his further action."

2

On this same Tuesday morning, December 5th, a meeting took place in Austen Chamberlain's room at the India Office. There were present Lord Curzon, Lord Robert Cecil, Walter Long and, of course, Austen Chamberlain himself. These four apparently discussed events and came to two conclusions; first, that Bonar Law had mismanaged his interview with Asquith on the Sunday; secondly, that matters had now reached a point at which the present Government could continue no longer, and Asquith should be so informed. Moreover, they seem to have decided that any pledge which they had hitherto given to the Prime Minister was no longer valid in the new circumstances, since it was now plain that Asquith would have against him the combined weight of Lloyd George, Bonar Law, and Carson.[1]

Curzon, Cecil, and Chamberlain accordingly waited on Asquith early that afternoon.[2] Asquith had just held a meeting of Liberal Ministers and had been assured of their unanimous support against Lloyd George. He had, so his biographers inform us, expected similar support from the Unionists who now came to see him. But he received a disagreeable surprise. The three "Cs", as Lord Beaverbrook calls them, told Asquith that they would not be willing to remain in the Government if Bonar Law and Lloyd George both resigned. They saw no hope of the Government surviving if these two went into opposition backed, as they would be, by Carson, the whole of the Tory Press, and probably by the Party machine too. Lord Robert Cecil actually suggested to Asquith that "the finest and biggest thing that he could do would be to offer to serve under Lloyd George; but he (Asquith) would not allow Cecil to develop this idea which he rejected with scorn, even indignation".[j]

"It would be idle to pretend", writes Mr. Spender,[k] "that the decision which they announced at this final interview – coming as it

---

[1] It is only fair to say that Austen Chamberlain denies that any such pledge was given, *Down the Years*, p. 130.

[2] Austen Chamberlain is quite certain that this was the first and only time the "three Cs" saw Asquith during the crisis.

lid from men who had so recently expressed their distrust of Mr.
Lloyd George – was not a shock and surprise for Asquith." Nevertheless, it probably made no great difference to Asquith's ultimate
action. Long before this stage it was inevitable that he should resign,
and put the whole matter to the proof.

Meanwhile, the Tory Ministers had deputed Walter Long to
request Bonar Law to attend a meeting in Austen Chamberlain's
room in the India Office at 4 o'clock that afternoon. Long made
it clear that the object of this meeting was to extract from Bonar
Law an explanation of his conduct over the last two days. At this,
so Beaverbrook tells us, Bonar Law lost his temper. He gained
the impression that Long and the three "Cs" were endeavouring to
oust him from the leadership of the Party, and he informed Long
bluntly that, if this was so, he would appeal over their heads to the
Tory Party in the Commons and in the Country, and, what was
more, he would win. Finally, he refused to go to the India Office at
4 o'clock, but said that he would be ready to summon a meeting of
his own in the Colonial Office at 5 o'clock.

Austen Chamberlain has warmly denied in *Down the Years* that
he, or those acting with him, had any intention of trying to oust
Bonar Law. He declares that Lord Beaverbrook's chapter on these
events – entitled the "Court-Martial" – misinterprets the motives of
the Unionist quartet. Austen Chamberlain's denial must be accepted.
It is unlikely that the three "Cs" and Long had any serious intention
of removing Bonar Law, if only because of the extreme difficulty
which prevails under the English party system of ousting any leader
who refuses to resign; and Bonar Law clearly had no intention of
resigning. No doubt Chamberlain, Curzon and Long would all have
welcomed his voluntary retirement. Chamberlain in a letter to Lord
Chelmsford written shortly after these events says:[1] "We have little
confidence in Bonar Law's judgment and none in his strength of
character." But an open assault upon Bonar Law's leadership was
probably not considered a practical proposition.

It is, however, clear that Bonar Law thought that some such
intention existed. The earlier manoeuvres of Curzon, and the fact
that Long and Chamberlain had both had such strong claims to the
leadership in 1911 may have added colour to his belief. In any case
by now there was a general atmosphere of suspicion and hostility
in the whole political world, and it is not surprising that Bonar Law
should have mistrusted the "three Cs" just as much as they appear to
have mistrusted him.

The meeting at 5 o'clock cleared the air. Bonar Law was able to
convince the rebels that he had not misrepresented to Asquith the
true state of affairs. It was in the last resort a matter of his word
against Asquith's, and the Unionist Ministers had no hesitation –
such was Bonar Law's reputation for honesty – in accepting what he
said. The charge of misrepresentation was never raised again in
Conservative quarters – however assiduously it may have been
fostered among the infuriated Liberals.

The meeting now had no difficulty in agreeing on further action.
It was clear that the Government must resign. Accordingly with
the full agreement of his colleagues, Bonar Law wrote as follows to
Asquith:[m]

Dec. 5, 1916.

"My dear Prime Minister,

"Lord Curzon, Lord Robert Cecil, and Mr. Austen Chamberlain have
reported to a meeting of all the Unionist members of the Cabinet, except
Mr. Balfour who was unable to be present, the substance of their conversation with you. After full consideration we are of opinion that the course
which we urged on you on Sunday is a necessity, and that it is imperative
that this course should be taken today. We hope that you have arrived at
the same conclusion, but, if this is not so, we feel that we have no choice
but to ask you to act upon our resignations.

"Yours sincerely,

A. Bonar Law."

Asquith on receipt of this letter decided to resign forthwith. A last
attempt by Lord Derby to dissuade him was unsuccessful.[n] At
o'clock that evening Asquith went to Buckingham Palace and tendered the resignation of himself and the whole Cabinet to the King.
The Government at last was out. It remained to be seen whether an
alternative one could be formed.

3

As soon as Bonar Law received the news of Asquith's resignation
he hastened, together with Aitken, to the War Office to discuss
the problem with Lloyd George. It was clear that Asquith would
advise the King to send for either Bonar Law or Lloyd George
and all past constitutional usage suggested that the choice would first
fall on Bonar Law as leader of the largest party in the House of Commons. What was Bonar Law to do on receiving the Royal summons.

Bonar Law's own view was quite clear: the right man for the post,
the real protagonist in this struggle to reform the direction of the war
was Lloyd George, and, further, he was the person whom the country

wanted. Therefore the ideal solution was for Lloyd George to become Prime Minister. On the other hand there were certain grave difficulties in the way. To begin with, it was most unlikely that Asquith would serve under Lloyd George; and as we have seen, Bonar Law attached much importance to the prestige of Asquith's name. Might he not however be induced to serve under Bonar Law? Then there were the leading Unionist Ministers. They had regarded Lloyd George with profound mistrust at all events until very recently. Indeed the whole crisis had begun largely because of the indignation that some of them felt at Lloyd George's alleged trafficking with the Press. They might well refuse to serve under Lloyd George, but it was inconceivable that they would refuse office under their own leader. Nevertheless, despite these difficulties Bonar Law considered that it would be much better for Lloyd George to be Prime Minister if possible, and he told Lloyd George that, if summi ned to Buckingham Palace, he would put forward Lloyd George's name to the King.

Lloyd George was by no means enthusiastic at this prospect. H considered that there was much to be said for Bonar Law assuming the Premiership, while he, Lloyd George, became Chairman of the small War Council which would now be set up. He was sure of loyal support from Bonar Law, he felt that Bonar Law would in many ways find it easier to form a Government than he would himself, and all he aimed at was effective control over the war effort, not the honour and glory of being Prime Minister of England.

In the end the two men agreed that if Bonar Law's assumption of the Premiership would ensure that Asquith joined, and if, in other respects, it seemed the only practicable solution, then Bonar Law would accept the King's offer, but if, as seemed on the whole more likely, Asquith declined to serve under anyone, then Lloyd George should be the choice. Thus with very characteristic modesty and self abnegation Bonar Law threw away the certainty of becoming Prime Minister and the probability of going down to posterity as head of the Administration which brought Britain through to victory in one of the greatest wars in her long history.

At 9.30 Bonar Law was summoned to Buckingham Palace. The King had been much perturbed at Asquith's resignation. He wrote in his diary:°

"I fear it will cause a panic in the city and in America and do harm to the Allies. It is a great blow to me and will I fear buck up the Germans."

It may well be that the interview which followed was none too cordial. Fresh in the King's mind was Lloyd George's letter of resignation which had been shown to him by Asquith shortly before. In this Lloyd George had made it quite clear that he intended to appeal to the country in a fierce attack upon Asquith's Administration. The latter's resignation had, it is true, removed that immediate threat, but the King strongly deprecated electioneering of any sort during war-time, and he feared that Bonar Law might make his acceptance of office conditional upon the holding of an immediate General Election. Accordingly the King decided to consult Lord Haldane upon the constitutional issues involved. Haldane's opinion was "that the Sovereign cannot entertain any bargain for a Dissolution merely with a possible Prime Minister before the latter is fully installed".[p] His hand thus strengthened, the King proceeded to interview Bonar Law. Lord Stamfordham's account of what followed must be quoted in full:[q]

Buckingham Palace.

Tuesday, December 5th, 1916. 9.30 p.m.

"The King saw Mr. Bonar Law and asked him to form a Government. He did not hold out to His Majesty much hopes of his doing so, but would consult his friends, and give an early reply tomorrow. He told the King his own effort has been to keep Mr. Asquith and Mr. Lloyd George together as the combination for winning the War. But for long he has felt the Government was losing its position and reputation in the Country, while Mr. Lloyd George considers it going fast to perdition.

"The one essential thing is a reformed War Committee, which could meet daily, and if necessary twice a day; come to prompt decision upon which equally prompt action must be taken. The present War Committee has become almost impotent.

"Some weeks ago Mr. Bonar Law spoke to the Prime Minister pointing out the above state of things, and urging a reconstruction of the Committee, but the Prime Minister would not entertain the idea.

"Later on Mr. Bonar Law referred again to this serious state of things and pointed out that the matter could be satisfactorily settled on the initiation of the Prime Minister himself, without interference from the public or the Press. Mr. Asquith declined, and then followed the Press campaign of last week.

"Bonar Law told the King that he thought Mr. Lloyd George could orm a Government.

"The King mooted the question of dissolution, to which, however, he added he would not give his consent, if asked.

"Mr. Bonar Law questioned the advisability of His Majesty refusing, and hoped the King would consider before adopting that attitude. Indeed he, himself, might succeed in forming a Government if he appealed to the Country. He had come to the conclusion that he must decide between following Mr. Asquith or Mr. Lloyd George, and, as he believed the latter would win the War before the former could do so, he had decided to follow Mr. Lloyd George."

Sir Harold Nicolson, summarizing the gist of this memorandum, says that "the King informed Mr. Bonar Law that he would refuse, if asked, to accord him a Dissolution".[r] This statement, unless qualified, seems to go a little beyond what Lord Stamfordham actually says. Surely the King did not mean to declare in advance that he would refuse a dissolution to Bonar Law after the latter had become Prime Minister, but rather that he would not here and now guarantee a dissolution to someone who was still only a potential Prime Minister. He would be guided by circumstances and give no promise in advance to exercise his discretionary power until the new Prime Minister, whoever he might be, was properly installed in office and in a position to give formal, considered advice on the matter. In fact Bonar Law does not seem to have wished to make his acceptance of office depend upon any such bargain, nor to have attached any special significance to the King's refusal.

Bonar Law told the King that Lloyd George was the best choice but that he would not definitely decline the Premiership until he had seen Asquith who might possibly be induced to serve under him. Bonar Law writes:[s]

"I did not decline at once, explaining to His Majesty that my only reason for not doing so was that I thought it possible that Mr. Asquith and Mr. Lloyd George might both be willing to serve under a 'neutral' Prime Minister, although Mr. Asquith might decline to serve under Mr. Lloyd George.

"On leaving the Palace I at once went to see Mr. Lloyd George. He thought the best solution might be for me to be Prime Minister if Mr. Asquith would serve under me. I then went to Downing Street and saw Mr. Asquith."

Asquith was dining with Lord Crewe and others as his guests, and left the table to see Bonar Law. The latter asked him whether he would serve under a "neutral" Prime Minister. Asquith asked what was meant by "neutral".

"I said," writes Bonar Law, "that as His Majesty had sent for me I was the natural person, but that if he thought it would be easier ior him to serve under Mr. Balfour I would be delighted to fall in with such an arrangement. Mr. Asquith, after a moment's consideration, said that he could not agree to this."

Asquith was evidently determined to pursue his course of action to the bitter end. He was not going to help his rivals by offering to serve under them.

The following morning, Wednesday, December 6th, Bonar Law,

M

Lloyd George, Carson and Aitken met at Pembroke Lodge. They decided to consult Balfour. Balfour had been ill in bed throughout the last few days. But he had in fact been informed of developments, and, aware of Lloyd George's low opinion of his conduct at the Admiralty, had resigned on December 5th as soon as he heard that Lloyd George was likely to be Chairman of the War Council. Asquith's efforts to make him reconsider this decision had been unsuccessful. Balfour had been operating quite independently of any other cabals or groups. No one knew exactly how he viewed the changed situation. Yet as an ex-Prime Minister, and former leader of the Conservative Party, his position was of great importance. On being consulted Balfour advised that nothing should be done until the King had called a conference of political leaders in order to see whether a satisfactory National Government could be formed.

The conference took place at Buckingham Palace at 3 o'clock that afternoon. Those present were Balfour, Bonar Law, Lloyd George, Asquith, and Arthur Henderson, who represented Labour. Sir Harold Nicolson has published in full Lord Stamfordham's account of the meeting.[t]

The real object of the conference was to find out whether there was anyone under whom Asquith would serve. Lloyd George and Bonar Law with all forms of politeness had made it clear from the start that they would not serve under Asquith. Asquith replied by attacking the Press in vigorous terms and said that he would have to consult his friends before coming to a decision. Finally, on Balfour's proposal it was agreed that, if Asquith would serve under Bonar Law, then the latter would endeavour to form a Government. If not, Lloyd George would make the attempt. The conference broke up at 4.30.

There could be little doubt as to Asquith's answer. If he refused, the burden would fall on Lloyd George, and for a number of reasons it must have seemed highly questionable whether Lloyd George would succeed. Certainly his prospects seemed, on the face of them, less favourable than those of Bonar Law. After consulting the Liberal ex-Ministers Asquith wrote to Bonar Law:[u]

"They are unanimously of opinion – and I agree with them – that I, and probably they, can give more effective support from outside. They also think that we could not carry the support of the Liberal party for any such arrangement. I have no personal feeling of *amour propre* in the matter (as I believe you know) but I am more convinced, the more I think of it, that it would be an unworkable arrangement."

Bonar Law's reply was brief:[v]

"My dear Asquith,
    "I thank you for your letter and I greatly regret your decision.
                                    "Yours sincerely,
                                            A. Bonar Law."

Thus ended Bonar Law's prospect of becoming a war-time
Premier. At 7 o'clock together with Lloyd George he returned again
to Buckingham Palace. He informed the King that he must give up
the attempt to form a Government. The King accepted this decision
and at once sent for Lloyd George.

4

Lloyd George was by no means unprepared. He and Bonar Law
had been discussing all day the various offices and the best way to fill
them. It was clear that he could expect no more support from the
Liberal ex-Ministers than Bonar Law could. Whether or not, as has
been sometimes claimed, they had given an actual pledge to Asquith
against joining any other Administration, they were, with the exception of Edwin Montagu, extremely hostile to Lloyd George. Montagu
too felt that he could not serve, at least for the time being. The only
other prominent former Liberal Minister was Winston Churchill.
But his inclusion was vetoed absolutely by Bonar Law who was in
this matter backed by nearly every prominent Conservative. To his
great mortification Churchill was obliged to wait several months
before Lloyd George felt strong enough to bring him in.

The result of all this was that Lloyd George had to fill the principal
offices largely from the Unionist ranks, and here, of course, Bonar
Law's views and actions were of critical importance. The first person,
whose services the two were anxious to secure, was Balfour. His
adherence was of critical importance but the prospects were none too
good. Balfour knew that Lloyd George regarded his performance as
First Lord of the Admiralty in an unfavourable light. If he had resigned from Asquith's Government merely on hearing the report that
Lloyd George might be Chairman of the War Council, what would
his attitude be to an offer of a place when Lloyd George had actually
become Prime Minister? It did not seem likely to be favourable.

In discussion Lloyd George and Bonar Law had agreed that the
Foreign Office was the best position for Balfour. What followed must
be quoted from Bonar Law's own account.[w]

"... immediately on leaving the palace I suggested to Lloyd George
that I should go to Mr. Balfour and ask him to undertake that office. I

saw him and after a general conversation of about half an hour I said to
kim: 'Of course you understand that I have come from Lloyd George to
has you on his behalf to become Foreign Minister'. Mr. Balfour rose from
his seat and without a moment's hesitation said:

" 'That is indeed putting a pistol at my head,[1] but I at once say, yes.'

"Under all the circumstances I think that the part played by him was
the biggest part played by anyone in the whole crisis. It was quite plain to
me that he would have given anything, apart from his sense of duty, to be
free from the responsibility of being a member of the Government."

Balfour's decision was a notable triumph for the new Government.
His adherence lent an aura of respectability and authority to the
Administration, and it was bound to have a great effect both upon
the other Conservative Ministers and upon the rank and file of the
Party. It is perhaps too much to say that Balfour made the Second
Coalition possible, but it is certain that he made Lloyd George's
task very much easier. According to Lord Beaverbrook,[x] Asquith
"was completely thunderstruck" at the news. He must have seen its
significance at once, and realized the immense advantage given from
the very start to the new Government.

The following day, Thursday, December 7th, Lloyd George
opened negotiations with the other Unionist Ministers whose attitude was uncertain – the three "Cs" and Walter Long. At an earlier
stage Bonar Law had made some overtures to this important group,
but had met with no success. Lloyd George on the principle of
"divide and rule" tried them separately. He first approached Walter
Long, only to receive a rebuff. Long declared that he was not prepared to act apart from his group, and preferred to support the
Government from the back benches. Lloyd George then approached
Curzon with the offer of a seat on the War Council. Such a tempting
offer was too much for that great man. Unlike Long he promptly
accepted – without feeling it necessary to consult his colleagues.
Curzon's decision meant that the others were certain to come in too.
The whole of this group did, indeed, impose certain conditions before
they finally agreed to join. On no account was Churchill to be
included. Lloyd George could agree to this, since Bonar Law had
already vetoed his inclusion. Equally there must be no offer to
Northcliffe, and there must be no attempt to oust Sir Douglas Haig
from the Supreme Command in France. The interview between
Lloyd George and the Conservative Ministers was lengthy, but in the
end agreement was reached.[y]

[1] Asquith's biographers acidly observe that in the end there were not enough pistols to
go round.

Lloyd George was now in a position to announce his new Government. He decided to merge the Cabinet and the War Council into a single body called the War Cabinet of which he would himself be chairman. The other members were Bonar Law, who was also Chancellor of the Exchequer and Leader of the House of Commons, Curzon, Henderson representing Labour, and Lord Milner. The latter's appointment was a sensational promotion: it was a last minute switch from Carson, whom Lloyd George had originally designated. In addition Balfour, for the Foreign Office, Robertson for the War Office and Carson as First Lord of the Admiralty had a right to attend meetings of the War Cabinet when matters concerning their own departments were being discussed. But constitutional and ministerial responsibility for Cabinet decisions was vested in the small War Cabinet and in that body alone. Apart from those mentioned the other principal appointments were:

Lord Derby to be Secretary for War, but without a voice in the War Cabinet, Walter Long to be Colonial Secretary, Austen Chamberlain to retain the India Office, Sir F. E. Smith to remain Attorney-General, Sir George Cave to be Home Secretary, Lord Finlay to be Lord Chancellor, Sir A. Stanley at the Board of Trade, Dr. Addison to be Minister of Munitions, H. A. L. Fisher to be President of the Board of Education, Lord Robert Cecil to remain as Minister for Blockade.

Asquith's Coalition Government comprised 25 members, 14 Liberals, 10 Unionists, 1 Labour.

Lloyd George's Government, including under secretaries, consisted of 33 members, 15 Unionists, 12 Liberals, 3 Labour, and 3 who were not at the time of formation members of either House. But these figures do not give a real measure of the extent of the political change. The Liberals in Lloyd George's Government nearly all occupied posts of little importance, under-secretaryships and the like. All the key offices were held by Unionists. The change of Government was the death knell of the old Liberal Party.

CHAPTER XXII

CHANCELLOR OF THE EXCHEQUER
1916 – 1918

Bonar Law's position – His happy relations with Lloyd George – Lloyd George's respect for his judgment – Bonar Law's success as Leader of the House – His attitude to honours – The King's annoyance at his offer to Sir Samuel Hughes – Sir Max Aitken's peerage – Anger of the King – Erroneous rumours about Bonar Law's part – Bonar Law's disapproval of the Honours Scandal – His distaste for personal honours – Bonar Law as Chancellor of the Exchequer – The 1,000 million loan – He overrides his official advisers – His Budgets – His relations with J. C. Davidson – His support of Chalmers and Keynes arouses the hostility of Lord Cunliffe – Cunliffe's impudent demand – Bonar Law's reply –Bonar Law's ultimatum – Cunliffe's surrender – Bonar Law's sons – Death of Charlie Law – A pathetic postcard – Death of Jim Law – Bonar Law's prostration – He visits his son's squadron – His letter to Richard Law

I

FROM now onwards till his temporary retirement in 1921, Bonar Law stood at the very centre of events. He was, in effect, a second Prime Minister. As Leader of the House he had to deal with an immense variety of subjects, and to answer for the Government, when Lloyd George was absent, on all the major issues of war and peace. As Chancellor of the Exchequer and member of the War Cabinet, he occupied a position of power second only to that of Lloyd George himself. As leader of the Conservative Party, which constituted the great majority of the new Coalition's supporters, he was responsible for the political machine, whose smooth running was, as he had himself observed, essential even in time of war for the stability of the Government.

In his new rôle it was absolutely necessary that he should collaborate with Lloyd George on the closest and most intimate terms. The suspicion with which Bonar Law had undoubtedly in the past regarded the new Prime Minister might suggest that difficulties would soon have arisen. Yet, in fact, nothing of the sort occurred. Bonar Law and Lloyd George acted together with a harmony seldom found in high politics. Throughout their joint tenure of power their friendship was never marred by a single quarrel. It was justly described by Stanley Baldwin at Bonar Law's death as "the most perfect partnership in political history".

Bonar Law was clear from the first as to his own function in that partnership: the dynamic force in the new Administration, the man v hom the nation expected to infuse a fresh vigour into the battle was Lloyd George. Writing to Walter Long, who had observed that the new Government was really a dictatorship, Bonar Law said:[a]

"I agree with all you say about a Dictatorship. This is essentially George's Government and my own intention, like yours, is to back him to the fullest extent I can. There is, I think, no alternative."

Bonar Law had neither the desire nor the energy to emulate Lloyd George. He was content to be an auxiliary, an invaluable ally, but always a junior partner in the firm. He was convinced that Lloyd George's genius could, if suitably guided and restrained, bring the nation to victory. He was fully content to play the part of a cautious counsellor in the background, and, as always in his career, was utterly indifferent to public glory or prestige. Once, on a visit to G.H.Q., Bonar Law described his work in the war as "hanging on to the coat tails of the Little Man (Lloyd George) and holding him back". Lloyd George himself has described how he would invariably consult Bonar Law before putting forward a proposal to the Cabinet, since he could be sure that the latter would raise all possible criticisms and objections – not through defeatism, but through instinctive scepticism and caution. If a proposal could survive this searching test then it was worth pursuing. Lloyd George writes:[b]

"Sometimes I felt the force of his adverse criticisms was so great as to be insuperable and I abandoned the project altogether. . . . But if I came to the conclusion that his objections were not sufficient to deter the Government from initiating and carrying out the particular scheme I went away strengthened in my resolve as the result of our conversation. On these occasions I said to him:

" 'Well, Bonar, if there is nothing more to be said against this scheme, then I mean to put it before the War Cabinet today.'

"He usually acquiesced as he knew that I never failed to listen to his views and give full weight to them. Once I had secured his consent I had no more loyal supporter for my plans."

By the nature of things little or no documentary evidence of Bonar Law's influence upon Lloyd George has survived. As soon as he became Chancellor, Bonar Law gave up Pembroke Lodge[1] and moved to 11 Downing Street. Every morning, after breakfast, Lloyd George would walk along the corridor which connected No. 10 with the

---

[1] He offered it to Asquith but the latter had already made other arrangements.

Chancellor's residence and go into Bonar Law's room to discuss the business of the day. There amidst an opaque cloud of tobacco smoke, windows almost hermetically sealed, Bonar Law would be sitting in his favourite arm-chair sucking at his pipe and reading official documents. Files were scattered all over the floor. The atmosphere was often suffocating. For an hour or so the two men would discuss the war news, the business of the House of Commons and any proposals that had during the night leapt into the ebullient mind of the Prime Minister. Neither of them was in the habit of writing a word more than he had to. So inevitably no record of these discussions survives, but the testimony of those who knew the two men, and of Lloyd George himself, leaves no doubt as to their relationship. Dr. Thomas Jones, who was a member of the Cabinet Secretariat, writes in his admirable account of Bonar Law in the *Dictionary of National Biography*:

"For over four years the one never took an important step without conferring with the other, and to compute the contribution of Bonar Law to the partnership it would be necessary to know not only the policies and projects of his sanguine colleague which he approved, but also those which he resisted, modified, or defeated. That colleague has placed on record his sense of the value of Bonar Law's searching criticism and his real courage when together they were responsible for the momentous decisions of the European War."

It was in his capacity as Leader of the House of Commons that Bonar Law found his time most fully occupied. Lloyd George attended the House less and less as the war went on. He had to make frequent visits abroad, and at home an immense amount of work fell upon his shoulders both in the War Cabinet and elsewhere. He seldom came to the House of Commons except when really major issues arose, or when, as in the famous Maurice Debate of May 1918, the very existence of the Government was at stake. All the day-to-day business of the House was in the hands of Bonar Law, and his replies on behalf of the Government were recognized to be as authoritative and binding as if they had been made by the Prime Minister himself.

Bonar Law was undoubtedly a most successful Leader of the House. Before the war his style of debate had been anything but conciliatory, and his speeches were apt to produce an uproar rather than to calm down the furious passions which swayed the House at that time. But now he adopted quite a different approach. At a very early stage the combination of authority and courtesy with which he made statements and answered questions won him the ear of the House. The

sympathy felt for his tragic losses, his patent indifference to fame and
office, the restraint and modesty of his speeches, above all the transparent honesty of his character, gained for him a degree of affection
such as is rarely to be found in politics. From then till his death it is
safe to say that he was one of the most beloved figures in the House
of Commons.

His new duties meant long and late hours. Not the least important
function of a successful Leader is to keep his finger upon the pulse
of the House of Commons. It is all too easy for a politician who has
reached high office to forget this vital need, and to become insulated
by other seemingly more important cares from the sentiments and
prejudices of his own followers. One of the secrets of Stanley Baldwin's otherwise inexplicable hold over the House was that he never
fell into this error. Bonar Law bore little resemblance in other
respects to his successor, but he too had, to a singular degree, the
gift of knowing precisely what would or would not go down in the
House of Commons. Intensely conscientious he would sit hour after
hour in the stuffy atmosphere of late night sittings. Robert Monro,
then Secretary of State for Scotland, writes:[c]

"One remembers his war weary face in the course of a long night
sitting. Often the whips begged him to go home, on the assurance that his
presence was really not necessary, and that if the need arose he would be
sent for; but I cannot recollect that he ever acceded to the suggestion."

This deep knowledge of the susceptibilities of the House of Commons was to be a most valuable asset in the remaining years of the
war. There were many dark moments ahead when the fortunes of
war were adverse and the House became restive and querulous. On
these occasions Bonar Law's tact and management contributed at
least as much as Lloyd George's eloquence to the continued stability
of the Government.

2

Bonar Law's position as a sort of co-Prime Minister involved him
at a very early stage in a matter which he particularly disliked – the
question of political honours. He had, of course, already had some
dealings over honours during the First Coalition, but this is a convenient place to consider his attitude on the whole question, since
one of the most awkward of his problems arose almost as soon as the
new Government was formed. In general, Bonar Law, indifferent to
honours for himself, simply could not understand why other people
wanted knighthoods, baronetcies or peerages. He was most unwilling

therefore to put himself out in any way in order to procure honours for his friends. He regarded their aspirations not as being wrong or stupid but incomprehensible, and he hated the often shameless avidity for these marks of distinction which his political followers displayed. "Keep it till that wretched Honours List comes up again," he would instruct his secretaries when some particularly importunate aspirant wrote to him. On one occasion a certain individual was down for a knighthood on Bonar Law's list and Asquith asked whether it could be changed to a baronetcy. "Make him a duke if he wishes," replied Bonar Law.[d] He recognized that honours had to be distributed, and that they were a useful method of oiling the political machine, but he had no sympathy or feeling for those who sought them.

Holding this rather cavalier view of honours Bonar Law was not always as careful as perhaps he should have been to consult the King before offering them. Already while he was Colonial Secretary he had run into trouble by offering, at Aitken's suggestion in October 1916, an honorary lieutenant-generalship to Sir Samuel Hughes, who was Canadian Minister of Defence and a turbulent and somewhat controversial figure in Canadian politics. Lloyd George was associated with this offer too. Unfortunately they had not consulted the King who protested with vigour to Asquith. "I do feel it is rather a plant on the part of the two [Bonar Law and Lloyd George]," wrote Stamfordham to Sir Maurice Bonham Carter, Asquith's private secretary.[e] However the King had to give away.

Now in December there occurred an episode which enraged the King even more and which probably did Bonar Law a good deal of harm in some quarters. During the course of the tortuous intrigues which preceded the fall of Asquith, Lloyd George had promised to make Aitken President of the Board of Trade, if and when the new Government came into being. Relying on this promise Aitken informed the Chairman of the local Conservative Association in his constituency that a by-election would soon occur at Ashton-under-Lyne.[1] However Lloyd George decided that he could not, after all, give Aitken such a high office. Instead he appointed a great railway magnate, Sir Albert Stanley (later Lord Ashfield), and offered Aitken the post of Under-Secretary to the Ministry of Munitions. Aitken promptly declined. Then Lloyd George, partly because he wanted another Government spokesman in the House of Lords and partly

---

[1] In those days an M.P. who was given a ministerial post had to submit himself for re-election.

because he wanted Aitken's seat for Sir Albert Stanley who was not even an M.P. at the time, offered Aitken a peerage. The latter was not anxious to leave the House of Commons. On the other hand it was a very convenient way out of an embarrassing predicament over his constituency, and would save him the humiliation of explaining why there would not after all be any by-election. He decided that he would accept.

Seldom has the offer of a peerage caused more of a furore. Lord Derby was at once in arms and protested to Bonar Law that the award of a peerage to such a junior Lancashire M.P. would wreck all his careful arrangements for the "management" of the Unionist Party in that county. Bonar Law agreed, and hurried to Cherkley on December 10th to tell Aitken that he must on no account accept. "So on Sunday night", writes Beaverbrook, "I felt myself in a sense dis-Peered. The Peerage no doubt had been a phantom one but even the phantom had vanished."

The following day, however, saw yet another change in his variable fortunes. Lloyd George had seen Bonar Law and the two decided that Aitken should have his peerage—Derby or no Derby. They had, however, once again omitted to consult the King who was extremely angry that the offer should have been made without securing his prior consent. In fact, he declared, he would not have given his consent for he did not think that the "public services" of Sir Max Aitken "called for such special recognition". Lloyd George was disconcerted at this reply and requested Lord Stamfordham to discuss the matter with Bonar Law. When the latter informed Stamfordham that the offer had now been made and arrangements already started for a by-election at Ashton-under-Lyne, the King gave way with much reluctance.[1]

To most people in the political world the elevation of Sir Max Aitken to the peerage must have seemed either a flagrant piece of favouritism on Bonar Law's part, or else – if they were in the know – the price paid for his activities in bringing about Asquith's fall. As can be seen from the foregoing account neither explanation was true, but that did not prevent the currency of rumours which did Bonar Law's reputation no good at the time.

It should not be thought that Bonar Law ever shared the totally cynical attitude of Lloyd George towards the Honours List. He cer-

---

[1] See Harold Nicolson, *King George V*, pp. 511–12. Sir Harold Nicolson does not mention Lord Beaverbrook by name, but a comparison with the latter's own account in *Politicians and the War*, Vol. II, pp. 327–31, makes it clear who is meant.

tainly did not approve of the wholesale traffic in honours with which the latter celebrated the closing years of his Premiership. Bonar Law had by then ceased to be a member of the Government, and he undoubtedly disliked the whole business. During his own brief period as Prime Minister he did much to clean up the arrangements which had hitherto prevailed, and he was most careful in his choice of names to submit to the King. Nevertheless it remains true that he regarded peerages and lesser honours more in the light of a concession to human vanity than as a reward for meritorious public service. After all, what harm did it do to make someone (as long as he was respectable) a baronet or even a peer? Such elevation was, in his opinion, if anything a matter for condolence rather than felicitation. Writing to Lewis Harcourt, who was to be made a Viscount in the New Year's Honours for 1917, he said:[f]

"I hardly know whether the honour to be given to you is altogether a subject of congratulation, but at all events if I am ever to come into conflict with my old colleagues I shall have reason to congratulate myself on your removal from the House of Commons."

Holding this view of honours Bonar Law was naturally quite averse to receiving any for himself. He preferred to die as he had lived – plain Mr. Bonar Law with no letters after his name other than those which indicated his membership of the Privy Council and the House of Commons.

3

The post of Chancellor of the Exchequer was then, as now, one of great importance. Its importance, however, in time of war was of a somewhat different nature from its importance before 1914. In those days the Chancellor had been essentially the watch-dog on the nation's economy, surveying with a severe and sceptical eye his colleagues' proposals for fresh expenditure. But, in time of war, economy though never to be forgotten had not the first claim upon his attention. His first duty was to raise the money with which to finance the enormous national expenditure upon the armed forces and munitions of war. Cheese-paring was impossible in such circumstances and would have provoked righteous wrath. The pre-war rôles were reversed, and it was now the spending departments which called the tune. Within the limits of economic possibility the Treasury had to provide the money. To help him in his task the Chancellor had – as he has today – a formidable body of expert opinion. The Treasury constitutes a *corps d'élite* in the Civil Service and contains some of the ablest brains in the country, trained by a lifetime of experience in problems of finance. In addition the Chancellor can call upon the most authoritative opinions in the world of banking, commerce, and industry. The help of these counsellors is essential. To ignore or override their advice is perilous.

The first problem which confronted Bonar Law was the floating of a new War Loan. The prevailing policy, which had been based upon the best City and Treasury advice, was one of short-term loans at a rate of interest of about 6 per cent. Bonar Law was convinced that this rate was too high. His advisers, basing their opinion upon the state of the war and the existing market conditions, felt that there was no possibility of reduction and that it might be necessary to raise interest rates even further. Ordinary financial rules might warrant such a view, but Bonar Law believed that it underestimated the strength of war-time patriotism and he declined to accept this advice. On January 11th, 1917, he announced the terms of the new loan in a speech at the Guildhall. He reversed the previous policy and announced the floating of a long-term loan at 5 per cent, redeemable after twelve years, and repayable in 1947 at the latest. Although there had been a general expectation that the rate of interest would be substantially higher, the loan was an immense success. Over 1,000 million pounds were raised by the closing date on February 16th. Lord Cunliffe, the Governor of the Bank of England, was amazed at this result. It was a triumph on the part of the Chancellor of the Exchequer and a striking illustration both of his courage in relying on his own judgment, and of his financial acumen.

Bonar Law's next problem was the Budget. On May 2nd he announced in the House of Commons the arrangements to provide for raising the largest sum which had ever before been required by a British Government – almost £2,200 million. Bonar Law said in his Budget speech:

"These gigantic figures are not the subject for rejoicing though there is ground for thankfulness that we are able to bear the financial strain that is laid upon us. These figures represent a part only of the price, and not the biggest part, which we as a nation have to pay for the greatest act of madness – the greatest crime which has ever been committed in the history of the world."

The details of Bonar Law's two Budgets in 1917 and 1918 belong to the history of British finance rather than to the biography of Bonar Law. They were not in the main controversial and they passed with ease. It is perhaps of interest to note that in 1917 some 26 per cent of expenditure was provided out of revenue, which Bonar Law claimed to be a higher proportion than was to be found in any other belligerent country. The principal change that he proposed in that Budget was to raise Excess Profits Duty from 60 to 80 per cent, but owing to the lack of price control, even this heavy tax did not prevent immense fortunes being made during the war by those engaged in manufacturing munitions and other war necessities. In 1918, Bonar Law raised income tax from 5s. to 6s. in the pound and surtax to a maximum of 4s. 6d. in the pound on incomes over £10,000. He also lowered the exemption limit for surtax from £3,000 to £2,500. Even so it is interesting to note that the maximum effective rate upon the highest incomes was only 9s. 5d. in the pound. At the time this seemed an enormous burden, only to be tolerated in a period of desperate emergency when the nation was struggling for bare existence.

Bonar Law's gifts as a lucid expositor, and as a shrewd financier, were shown at their best in his Budget speeches. He had a remarkable, almost a freak memory for figures. Although it is not true, as sometimes averred, that he introduced his Budgets without any notes at all, it is true that such notes as he did have were extremely brief. It so happens that his notes on the Budget of 1918 survive – he gave them to his daughter Isabel[1] – and they must surely be one of barest *aide-memoires* ever to be used by a Chancellor of the Exchequer. They are all contained on two small double sheets of writing paper. Only someone with a quite abnormal memory could have delivered a Budget speech on the strength of such perfunctory jottings. There also survives from the same occasion a pencilled card in Lloyd George's characteristic sprawling hand, evidently tossed across to Bonar Law either at a Cabinet meeting or in the House of Commons: "Your speech last night was first rate. You had a great day, yesterday."

There can be no doubt that Bonar Law was a most successful Chancellor of the Exchequer.

When he moved to the Treasury, Bonar Law took with him the same private secretary who had served him at the Colonial Office, J. C. C. Davidson (now Lord Davidson). This action inspired protest from Walter Long, the new Colonial Secretary, but Bonar Law remained firm. He had, indeed, become deeply attached to Davidson, depended much upon his help, and treated him almost as another son. The Bonar Law papers supply ample evidence of the care with which Davidson looked after his chief's interests, and the tact with

[1] Lady Sykes.

which he kept importunate persons from bothering the Chancellor. In 1920 Davidson entered Parliament as M.P. for Hemel Hempstead. He then became Bonar Law's Parliamentary Private Secretary until his chief's temporary retirement from politics in 1921. He acted in the same capacity during Bonar Law's brief Premiership. He was a most valuable and helpful adjutant, and Bonar Law regarded him with much affection till the day of his death.

One of the joint secretaries to the Treasury at this time was Sir Robert (later Lord) Chalmers. He was a most able official, and Bonar Law who had a very high opinion of his talents induced him in August 1918 to stay on beyond the normal retiring age in order to see out the war. Behind a façade of cynical wit, which was apt to disconcert many people, Chalmers could be the kindest of men. His relations with his chief were, throughout, of the most harmonious character.

One other important member of the Treasury should be mentioned here. This was J. M. (later Lord) Keynes, the celebrated economist. Bonar Law soon acquired a good opinion of his abilities. Young though he was, Keynes had already become the leading authority upon external and inter-allied finance. In February 1917 he was made head of the new "A" Division of the Treasury which dealt with these problems, and in this capacity he had direct access to the Chancellor. Lloyd George on one occasion, when he was still Chancellor, asked Keynes what he thought of certain opinions which he (Lloyd George) had been expounding. Keynes replied that, with all due respect, he regarded them as "rubbish". It so happened that shortly after the change of Government Bonar Law used exactly the same words to characterize some propositions advanced by Lloyd George at a War Cabinet meeting. "Ah!" said Lloyd George, "I see you have learnt Treasury manners quickly."[g]

His strong support of Chalmers and Keynes involved Bonar Law in one of the very few serious disputes which occurred during his time as Chancellor. This arose from the conduct of the Governor of the Bank of England, Lord Cunliffe. Until the nationalization of the Bank in 1946, the relationship between the Governor and the Chancellor was not clearly defined. In practice harmony usually prevailed, and a close and friendly collaboration prevented difficulties arising. But Lord Cunliffe was of a choleric disposition. He came to the conclusion, after returning from a visit to America in the early summer of 1917, that the Exchange Committee, of which he was chairman and which had been set up by McKenna to deal with the difficult problems relating to foreign currency, was not being kept adequately informed by the Treasury. After protesting to Bonar Law he wrote to Lloyd George on July 3rd, 1917:[h]

"The late Chancellor . . . promised me verbally that Mr. Keynes should not meddle again in City matters, which promise was, as far as I am aware, kept until Mr. McKenna went out of office. . . . Yet the position today is that not only have all the means of controlling the Exchanges been taken out of our hands but all information is withheld from us even when we have the Chancellor's permission to obtain it, and requests for telegrams are not only refused but met with absolute incivility.

"The London Exchange Committee is therefore a mere cypher entirely superseded by Sir Robert Chalmers and Mr. Keynes who in commercial circles are not considered to have any knowledge or experience in practical exchange or business problems, and I am convinced that, short of a miracle, disaster must ensue . . . I cannot remain a mere figurehead acting under men in whom I have no faith, unless the Cabinet after this warning is prepared to accept the entire responsibility."

Lord Cunliffe concluded by referring to the kindness and help he had received from all other departments of the Treasury, "especially from the Chancellor of the Exchequer himself". In verbal discussion with Bonar Law, Lord Cunliffe demanded the dismissal of Chalmers and Keynes.

Bonar Law was, not unnaturally, enraged at such a demand. "Mr. Governor", he said,[i] "I hope you realize what you are doing. You are not asking for their dismissal but for mine. They are merely servants of the Chancellor and all they do is on my responsibility. Go to Number 10 and state your case to the Prime Minister." This was open war, and, quite apart from Cunliffe's unwarrantable interference, there were good reasons for Bonar Law's determination to force a crisis. Cunliffe was on very friendly terms with Lloyd George who had been much flattered by his declaration that Lloyd George's presence at the Treasury in 1914 had saved the financial situation. Cunliffe had found in Lloyd George a sympathetic listener to his bitter complaints during McKenna's tenure of the Treasury. Bonar Law was well aware that Cunliffe's presumptuous demeanour could be partly explained by his confidence in the backing of the Prime Minister, and he was determined to show Lloyd George that in all Treasury matters his word was absolute. He seriously contemplated for a time transferring the Government's account to one of the Joint Stock Banks.

At this juncture Cunliffe played into Bonar Law's hands. Without consulting the Chancellor he gave orders that the whole of the Bank

A leaf from Bonar Law's Budget notes, 1918, with an appreciative post card from Lloyd George

of England's gold in Canada should be at the disposal of Messrs. Morgan & Company from whom the Bank had a long-standing loan of 85 million dollars. At the same time, also without consulting Bonar Law he telegraphed to the Canadian Finance Minister that he was not to deliver any of the same gold at the request of the Treasury's representative in Ottawa, Sir Hardman Lever. When Bonar Law protested, Cunliffe made a reply which Bonar Law interpreted as meaning that this action was a "reprisal" for Cunliffe's alleged treatment by Keynes and Chalmers in the matter of the Exchange Committee.

Bonar Law's normal mildness vanished. He was now very angry indeed, and after a talk with Lloyd George on July 9th, put his views in writing in a letter to the Prime Minister couched in the strongest terms.[j] He described Cunliffe's action in sending the telegram to the Canadian Government as "an act of extraordinary disrespect towards the British Government and a direct insult to me who as Chancellor of the Exchequer had authorized Sir Hardman Lever to act for the Government". He said that Cunliffe "in suggesting that I should dismiss Sir Robert Chalmers . . . had taken an absolutely unwarrantable liberty", that Cunliffe's behaviour over the gold was "contrary to the whole principle upon which business has been carried on ever since I went to the Treasury", and was in any case quite unjustified since Morgan's were not in fact pressing for repayment in gold.

"For these reasons, I have, as already discussed with you in conversation, come to the conclusion that the present position cannot continue. There were three possible methods of dealing with it. One was that I should cease to be Chancellor of the Exchequer and leave the Government but this you have ruled out. The second is that Lord Cunliffe should cease to be Governor of the Bank of England. There is, however, a third possible alternative which is that Lord Cunliffe should agree to work with me in a reasonable spirit and with a full knowledge that the Chancellorship of the Exchequer is not in commission and that the views of the British Government as represented by me must be carried out. If you are willing to see him and find out whether or not he is ready to continue on these conditions I should be glad, but I cannot run the risk of a repetition of the friction of the last weeks. . . . I am therefore only willing to allow the present arrangement to continue on the condition that Lord Cunliffe sends to me in writing a declaration that he will at once resign the Governorship of the Bank if he receives a request from me to that effect.

"I hope you know me well enough to feel sure that I am not sensitive about my dignity, that I am not difficult to work with, and that therefore this impasse is not due to me. If Lord Cunliffe agrees to do as I suggest, I have not the smallest desire to humiliate him. No one would know of the arrangement except you, himself and me, and I should endeavour to work with him in harmony and with every consideration towards him. . . ."

To this devastating letter there could be only one reply, unless Cunliffe was prepared to resign at once. Presumably Lloyd George saw the Governor. At all events, on July 13th, the latter wrote in his own hand the required declaration. It was returned to him eventually but a copy was kept by Bonar Law, and the empty envelope addressed in Cunliffe's hand remains among Bonar Law's papers. After apologizing to the Chancellor, Cunliffe concluded:[k]

". . . if you felt there could not be complete and harmonious co-operation between yourself and me I should not think it compatible with the public interest that I should continue to occupy my position as Governor of the Bank of England."

In November 1917 the Directors of the Bank of England nominated Sir Brian Cockayne as Governor in place of Lord Cunliffe. There was no further trouble between the Bank and the Treasury while Bonar Law remained Chancellor of the Exchequer.

4

1917 was a tragic year for Bonar Law as far as his private and family life was concerned. He lost his two elder sons, both of whom were on active service. The first to be killed was his second son, Charlie. He was in Germany when war broke out but, since he was only seventeen, he was not interned and was allowed to return to England. He joined the 3rd King's Own Scottish Borderers and commissioned as a second-lieutenant was sent overseas to Egypt. His high spirits, zest for life, and unspoilt charm made him a favourite with all his family.

On April 16th he wrote:

"My dearest Father,

"We are just going into a large action and I hope it will be a success and that we shall scupper the whole lot of Turks. I shall write again as soon as possible, but it will last a good few days.

"Love to Auntie and all from your loving son,

Charles."

It was the last letter Bonar Law was to have from his son. On April 19th Lieut. Law was reported missing at the battle of Gaza. For many weeks it was thought on the strength of a German newspaper report that he might be a prisoner of war. About the middle of June, just when it seemed finally certain that he had been killed and hope had almost vanished, a message was received from the Vatican that his name was among those of prisoners in Turkish hands. Bonar Law had numerous letters of congratulations, but, alas, his hopes were yet again to be cruelly disappointed. There had been an unfortunate ciphering error and the word "not" had been omitted when the message was translated into clear.

A pathetic record survives of the period when Bonar Law still believed his son to be alive. It is a post card which was returned from the Ottoman Red Crescent many months later.

"My dearest Charlie,
"I am sending this on the chance of its reaching you. For three days until a German paper announced that you were a prisoner I was in utter despair, as we all were, and I knew then how dear you are to me."

Worse was to come. Like many fathers, Bonar Law regarded his eldest son with a very special affection. As we have seen, James Law was in the Royal Flying Corps. After his accident he had returned to France but had not so far been involved in combat. In July 1917 he was testing machines and wrote to his father complaining of boredom but adding: "It is a safe job any way which will commend itself to you." Then in September, at his own insistence, he was posted for the first time to a fighter squadron. At this period the casualty rate among fighter pilots was very high indeed. After a week of fighting he was shot down on September 21st. The body was never identified and his name is inscribed upon the memorial to Missing Airmen at Arras.

This second bereavement, following so soon upon the fluctuations of hope and despair over the first, came as a terrible, almost an overwhelming, blow to Bonar Law. Night seemed to have descended upon him. For the moment he was incapable of work, and could only sit despondently gazing into vacancy. All those dark clouds which were never far below the horizon of his thoughts came rolling up, obliterating light and happiness. Beaverbrook perceiving that something must be done persuaded him to go out to France in order to see his son's brother officers and find out what had happened. Bonar Law agreed to do so, and accompanied by Beaverbrook visited the headquarters of his son's squadron.

He saw the Squadron Commander, talked to some of those who had fought along with Jim, and then asked if he might see a plane which his son had flown. He was shown one riddled with bullets from a fight a few days earlier. Bonar Law climbed into the cockpit and then unexpectedly asked whether he could be flown in it. He was told that this was impossible. He continued to sit in the cockpit,

and, eventually, seeing that he wanted to be alone, Beaverbrook and
the Squadron Commander left him. For two or three hours Bonar
Law sat in the plane, apparently sunk in a sombre reverie.[1] Then he
climbed out, and, for some strange reason of temperament, he seemed
less melancholy than he had been. The clouds had not indeed rolled
away. They were destined perhaps to remain with him till his death.
But Bonar Law had recovered enough to carry on his heavy duties
and he seldom referred again to his loss.

From France he wrote to his son Richard Law, who was still a
schoolboy, describing his visit:[m]

"They all spoke of Jim as an exceptionally good pilot and the boy who
was with him the first day said to me, 'The Boches would not easily do
him in'.

"I was very proud to hear the way they talked of him and when the
time comes to harry me with the other politicians it ought not to be forgotten what my sons have done. . . . Keep this account of what they told
me about Jim for we have the right to be very proud of him."

CHAPTER XXIII

THE MISFORTUNES OF WAR

1916 – MAY 9TH, 1918

Bonar Law and the War Cabinet – His views on strategy – The Passchendaele Offensive – Bonar Law's scepticism – The Cabinet gives way to Haig – Lloyd George makes Churchill Minister of Munitions – Annoyance of Bonar Law – Renewed doubts about Passchendaele – The Lansdowne Letter – Bonar Law's attitude – The Supreme War Council – Extension of the British line to Barisis – The fall of Robertson – Vacillation of Lord Derby – The Germans break through in March 1918 – The rôle of the Opposition – General Maurice's letter – Asquith refuses to accept a Judicial Enquiry – Lloyd George and Bonar Law resolve to fight – The Maurice Debate – Vindication of Bonar Law – Lasting consequences of the dispute

I

BONAR LAW was not only Chancellor of the Exchequer, Leader of the House, and Leader of his Party. As if these duties were not onerous enough, he was in addition a member of the small War Cabinet which, under Lloyd George's reorganization, had sole responsibility for running the war. Indeed, strictly, this body was the Cabinet and bore the full constitutional responsibility normally carried by a Cabinet of fifteen or twenty members. It met nearly every day though rarely alone, for other Ministers and Service Chiefs attended when affairs concerning their departments came up for discussion. For the first time agenda of meetings were circulated beforehand, and regular minutes were kept of discussions and decisions. These were promptly sent to the departments concerned for information or action. There can be no doubt that these reforms enormously enhanced the efficiency of the Central Government.

The War Cabinet consisted at first of five members, the Prime Minister, Bonar Law, Curzon, Milner, and Henderson who represented Labour. In the middle of 1917 their number was increased by the addition of Carson and General Smuts. At about the same time Henderson was replaced by Barnes. In January 1918 Carson resigned. In April 1918 Chamberlain replaced Milner who had become Secretary for War and vacated his seat on the principle that departmental heads should not be members of the War Cabinet. The only exception to this rule was Bonar Law himself, and it was understood that he did not need to attend War Cabinet meetings if other duties clashed. In fact, however, he was nearly always present, and regularly presided over meetings when Lloyd George was away.

Nevertheless it was natural that Bonar Law did not figure among those who had most influence on war strategy. He was of course consulted by Lloyd George on every important topic, but he was chiefly preoccupied with his duties as Chancellor and Leader of the House. He had little time to consider the great strategical problems upon which the Prime Minister had to ponder. Moreover, unlike Lloyd George, Bonar Law did not hold any definite doctrine about the conduct of the war. He was more inclined than Lloyd George to leave the questions of strategy to the Generals and Admirals. As a result he was regarded by the Generals as being perhaps rather more friendly to their point of view than he actually was. It is, for example, worth noting that very soon after the formation of the new Government Robertson wrote to Bonar Law enlisting his support against further reinforcement of the Salonika expedition – a favourite project of the Prime Minister. Yet, in fact, Bonar Law was by no means an unqualified admirer of the professional soldier. Lord Stamfordham quotes Bonar Law as telling the King "that Robertson and the soldiers were all wrong, with the result that we have lost Serbia, Rumania and very likely Greece. The King expressed his entire disagreement with these views . . ."[1]

Bonar Law does not appear to have taken any prominent part in the War Cabinet discussions of early 1917 at which it was decided to endorse Nivelle's plans and place the British Army under the French Commander for the duration of the offensive. But with the failure of that offensive a new problem arose, and Bonar Law was now deeply concerned with its solution. Haig and Robertson laid before the Cabinet proposals for a large-scale offensive in Flanders to be undertaken by the British Army with the object of rolling back the right flank of the German Army, clearing the Belgian coast, and perhaps breaking right through the enemy front. At the beginning of June a War Cabinet Committee was set up to consider the whole question of allied strategy and in particular the Haig-Robertson proposals. Its members were Lloyd George, Curzon, Milner, and Smuts who was in England having attended the recent meetings of the Imperial War Cabinet. Bonar Law, though not strictly a member, frequently attended.

[1] Harold Nicolson, *George V*, p. 288 – The occasion was when the King sent for Bonar Law on Asquith's resignation.

The problem that confronted the Committee was perhaps the most difficult of the whole war. On the one hand Haig argued that there was a real chance of a success, that he could always halt the offensive if things went badly, that now was the time to act, before the Germans could reinforce with divisions drawn from the rapidly collapsing Eastern Front. He was backed by Admiral Jellicoe,[a] who appears at this time to have been plunged in gloom and who declared that, unless the British Army could deny the Belgian submarine bases to Germany, the war was lost. It is fair to add that this opinion was in fact unduly pessimistic, and that the submarine menace was already by June 1917 beginning to come under control. Nevertheless a judgment from such an authoritative source as the First Sea Lord could not be entirely disregarded.

On the other hand, as against Haig, Lloyd George maintained that it was better to wait until American aid arrived in 1918 before launching a major offensive in the West. The soldiers, he believed, had always been incurably optimistic about the prospects of success on this front, but so far their optimism had never been warranted. The only results of their strategy had been gigantic casualty lists and the capture of a few miles of devastated, desolate and useless terrain. If any offensive operations were to be conducted in 1917 why not try a new theatre of war, reinforce the Italian armies, and break through the Austrian defences? A great prize might be obtained. The Hapsburg Empire whose adhesion to Germany was known to be reluctant might well surrender and conclude a separate peace.

These issues were debated at great length and with most careful consideration. Bonar Law was sceptical about Haig's proposals.[b] He had no confidence that a sweeping victory was really possible on the Western Front during 1917. In the discussions he sided with Lloyd George and with Milner who was equally dubious about the prospects of success. On the other hand Smuts, who was the only member of the Cabinet Committee to have actually commanded in the field and who therefore had much prestige in military matters, favoured Haig's plan. He was supported, though somewhat less emphatically, by Curzon. The really critical discussion took place on the afternoon of June 20th. The Committee had listened during the morning to the views of Haig and Robertson and then discussed in private what attitude should be taken. Bonar Law, though sceptical, felt in the last resort that the Cabinet could not – or at all events should not – overrule the agreed and considered opinion of its principal military advisers. On balance Lloyd George and Milner were inclined to take the same view. Lloyd George had already discussed the matter with Balfour who, impressed by Smuts's views, also favoured giving way to Haig and Robertson.[c]

Thus, then, the ill-starred "Passchendaele" campaign had its genesis, and Bonar Law must take his share of responsibility for it along with the other members of the Cabinet. The offensive, as is well known, did not justify the more optimistic prophecies of its supporters. It lasted from July 31st to November 10th and at the end none of its territorial objectives had been gained, while casualties were immense. Lloyd George in his Memoirs states at length and in the vitriolic language of a prosecuting counsel the case against the campaign. This cannot be regarded as final. His casualty figures are far higher than those given by the Official History, and in general he spoils his case by gross overstatements. Although the Passchendaele campaign did not come near to fulfilling expectations, it may well have forestalled a German offensive against the demoralized French armies. Historians, moreover, will long argue as to whether Passchendaele on balance weakened most the British or the Germany Army. In other words, if there had been no Passchendaele, would the British have been better able to withstand the German offensive of spring, 1918, or would the Germans have been in a better position to exploit their early successes and perhaps roll the British Army into the sea? No clear answer has been – perhaps ever can be – given to this question.

In the middle of July an important change took place in the Government. Lloyd George had long been feeling his way toward the reinstatement of Churchill. Hitherto he had not dared to risk the Conservative resentment which would undoubtedly be caused. Now, however, he resolved to take the plunge and make Churchill Minister of Munitions. Rumours of his intention circulated at least a month before the final decision was announced. Tory indignation knew no bounds: Curzon, Walter Long and Derby protested bitterly; at the National Unionist Council a motion was carried amidst cheers that Churchill's appointment would be "an insult to the Navy and the Army". Bonar Law shared these feelings, and he was furious when he learned from Beaverbrook that Lloyd George had faced him with a *fait accompli* and without any consultation had announced the appointment to the Press. Lloyd George prudently avoided Bonar Law for the rest of that day. On reflection Bonar Law decided to make the best of a bad job and to back the Prime Minister in public.

He returned a stiff answer to a deputation of Conservative M.P.s who came to protest,[1] and eventually the storm subsided.

But Bonar Law did not mean to allow Churchill to become a member of the War Cabinet or interfere with general war strategy and matters which lay outside the sphere of munitions. He had evidently reassured Walter Long on this point, for on July 29th the latter wrote:[d]

"I am greatly relieved by your assurance: I think if W.C. were to join the Cabt. or if he tries to control policy and interfere in other Depts. there will be very serious trouble. Already there are uneasy rumours current among sensible men who do not listen to canards.

"The real effect has been to destroy all confidence in Ll.G. It is widely held that for purposes of his own quite apart from the war he has deceived and jockeyed us. The complaints come from our very best supporters, quiet, steady and staunch men and W.C. has made things worse by stating at Dundee that the opposition to him springs from his political opponents. This is a 'terminological inexactitude' and he knows it."

Soon after this there were complaints from the First Lord of the Admiralty, Sir Eric Geddes, who had recently succeeded Carson. Geddes evidently considered that Churchill was interfering with Naval matters. Bonar Law at once intervened. He wrote to Geddes:[e]

"I have spoken to the P.M. who assures me that he has already told Mr. Churchill that he must avoid anything in the nature of interference with the work of the Admiralty and that he (the P.M.) will make sure that there is no such interference.

"Yours sincerely,

A. Bonar Law."

"PS. I am sending a copy of this letter to the P.M."

Lloyd George was evidently taking no small risk in thus including Churchill in his administration. As he himself observes, "Tory antipathy was so great that for a short while the very existence of the Government was in jeopardy".

Nevertheless Bonar Law was clear in his mind that any alternative to the existing Government was impossible. On August 3rd he wrote to J. P. Croal, the editor of the *Scotsman*, who was one of the few people to whom he ever seems to have expressed himself at any length on paper.[f]

". . . There is no doubt that our Party is very seriously disaffected at the moment, mainly on account of Churchill, but as regards the Government

---

[1] For further details of the Churchill crisis, see the very full account in Frank Owen, *Tempestuous Journey*, pp. 410–16.

as a whole, and especially as regards the Prime Minister, I confess I am
surprised that after six months during which nothing has gone particularly
well in the war the unpopularity has not become greater than it is. I may
tell you also that personally Lloyd George has been a better Prime
Minister so far than I expected. He has devoted every moment of his time
and all his energy to the war and he has shown much greater patience than
I would have given him credit for."

The Passchendaele campaign was by now in full swing. It soon
became evident that the predictions of Haig and Robertson were not
being fulfilled. Whatever other justification the campaign had, no
prospect appeared of an immediate break through on the Western
Front. By early September Lloyd George was in a state of acute
depression, and retired to Criccieth to recover his health and spirits,
leaving Bonar Law to hold the fort. Bonar Law by now felt that his
and Lloyd George's initial scepticism had been fully justified. On
September 18th he wrote to Lloyd George:

". . . in speaking to Robertson yesterday, I said to him that I had lost
absolutely all hope of anything coming of Haig's offensive and, though he
did not say so in so many words, I understood that he took the same view.
I do not know when the next attack is supposed to take place but I
believe it may happen at any time. It is evident therefore that the time
must soon come when we will have to decide whether or not this offensive
is to be allowed to go on. . . .

"I have no doubt that you have been thinking of nothing except the
war during your absence and will come back full of ideas – and they will
all be needed. The Russian situation seems to get more confused every day,
but I am afraid that there is no hope of anything good emerging from there
within any reasonable time.

"*The Treasury:* I want to speak to you about this as soon as you come
back for I am really very doubtful whether it will be possible for me to go
on with the work here as well as the House of Commons. The financial
situation is getting increasingly difficult and the Bankers are not much
help."

This was not perhaps a very cheerful letter for the Prime Minister
to receive from his second-in-command, but undoubtedly Bonar Law
was right on the military situation. It remains surprising that Lloyd
George, who was at this very time seriously contemplating the
replacement of Haig, did not feel strong enough to insist upon the
Passchendaele offensive being halted. He expresses in his Memoirs
his own subsequent doubts as to whether he acted rightly, but excuses
himself on the ground that it would have involved the resignation
of Haig and Robertson and a political crisis in which he would have
had no support from the other members of the Cabinet, whom, he

says, he had sounded individually. Bonar Law presumably cannot
be included in this category. He would evidently have been on Lloyd
George's side. However, let no one underestimate the political risks
which would have been incurred by a peremptory order from Lloyd
George to Haig to discontinue the offensive. The fighting continued
until mid-November when the weather rendered all further progress
impossible.

2

The winter of 1917–18 was a profoundly depressing period for the
Allied cause. America had not yet intervened with any effect, total
defeat had been inflicted on Russia, the great Flanders offensive had
died away with little to show for the enormous losses involved. It was
not altogether surprising that the possibility of a negotiated peace
began to be considered in some quarters. Nevertheless a great sensation was produced when Lord Lansdowne, who had been in semi-
retirement from public life for the past year, wrote a letter published
in the *Daily Telegraph* on November 29th, suggesting that the time
had come to stop the interminable slaughter and consider whether
an honourable peace might be concluded with the Central Powers.
Lansdowne's letter expressed the same arguments that he had used
in a memorandum to the Asquith Cabinet a year earlier. His thesis
had much to commend it on general grounds and it may well be that
the world would in the end have been a happier place if his proposals
had been accepted. The trouble was that the late autumn of 1917
was a singularly bad moment to choose for making such proposals.
The German Government was not at that time likely to contemplate
peace on any terms remotely tolerable to the Allies, and we now
know that, even if the British Government had been prepared to
negotiate on the lines suggested by Lansdowne, there would have
been no response from the enemy.

In any case the British Government had no intention of negotiating
at this time, and Bonar Law felt obliged to take the first opportunity
of dissociating himself and his colleagues from Lansdowne's proposals. This he did in a speech addressed the following day to a
Conservative Party Conference. Bonar Law had much respect and
affection for Lansdowne. He did not like publicly repudiating his
former partner, but he felt that, unless Lansdowne's letter was
disavowed, the whole attitude of the Government might become
suspect both at home and abroad. He wrote the same day to
Lansdowne:[h]

"My dear Lansdowne,

"It is a strange thing and to me very distressing that you and I should differ in a matter so vital. There was a Party meeting today and I had to refer to the subject. I hope you will not think that anything I said was – I will not say offensive – but less friendly than it ought to have been, and I am sure that no difference of opinion on any subject will ever diminish the feeling of personal friendship and respect which we have always entertained for each other.

"Yours very sincerely,
A. Bonar Law."

Lansdowne replied two days later:[i]

"My dear Bonar,

"I was glad to receive your note of the 30th, for I should indeed have been distressed if my official excommunication at the party meeting had not been relieved by a word of personal goodwill from yourself.

"Please rest assured that so far as I am concerned, a difference of opinion such as that which has arisen between us cannot shake a friendship which I greatly value.

"Yours ever,
L."

Lansdowne and Bonar Law always remained on friendly terms, but their political paths now drew far apart. Lansdowne had written his letter with a full awareness of the consequences. He became one of the most reviled men in England. He intended, however, to continue his agitation for peace. He wrote further letters during the spring of 1918. A Lansdowne Committee was formed. Lansdowne himself made several speeches in the House of Lords and elsewhere on the subject of peace. His efforts, however, had little effect. He was pursuing a chimera.

Relations between the High Command and the Cabinet – or at all events Lloyd George – grew no better as the year came to an end. Each side viewed the other with profound distrust. Lloyd George was by now convinced that any reinforcements sent to Haig would merely be wasted in another Passchendaele. He therefore deliberately kept the Western Front short of troops during the early months of 1918 – a policy condemned even by Churchill, who was at least as sceptical as Lloyd George about the tactics of Haig. At the same time Lloyd George was determined to circumvent, even if he could not dismiss, Robertson. The first step was to furnish himself with an alternative set of military advisers. This he achieved by agreeing with Briand at the Conference of Rapallo in November 1917 to create a Supreme Interallied War Council. This body was to meet when occasion warranted, but – and here was Lloyd George's real objective – a permanent Committee of military advisers to the Council was to sit at Versailles. This Committee would provide a plausible alternative official channel for military advice to that provided by the Chief of the Imperial General Staff. In order to ensure that this new advice would be of a congenial nature Lloyd George appointed Sir Henry Wilson as British military representative on the permanent Committee. Wilson was a friend of Lloyd George and Bonar Law. He was greatly disliked by nearly all orthodox soldiers. His appointment was a definite blow to Haig and Robertson.

The creation of the Versailles Committee was regarded with no small distaste by the Army leaders and by their political and journalistic supporters. However, as long as its functions remained purely advisory, Haig and Robertson did not feel inclined to fight it, although they made no effort to conceal their contempt for its activities. But during the winter the Versailles Committee was concerned with an important military problem which, many months later, was to involve Bonar Law in a Parliamentary debate affecting the whole question of his own personal honour and integrity. The issues which led to the celebrated Maurice Debate in May 1918 have been the subject of much interested misrepresentation. It is therefore necessary to discuss them in some detail – at least in so far as they concerned Bonar Law.

At a meeting in September 1917 Lloyd George and Robertson had agreed in principle to a request from the French Government that the British Army should during the winter take over a section of the line occupied by the French. The details and timing were to be left to agreement between the British and French Commanders. Haig did not like this arrangement, but he met Pétain towards the end of October and the two Generals agreed in fixing the southern extension of the line at Barisis, a few miles south of the Oise. This meant an increase of the British line from about 100 to 128 miles, and a reduction of the French line from 350 to 322 miles. It was further agreed that the extension should take place early in November. It is important, in order to understand what followed and in particular the issues involved in the Maurice Debate, to remember that this extension to Barisis was the only extension of the British line which actually took place before the German offensive of March 21st, 1918, and that this extension was agreed between Haig and Pétain in October 1917 *before* the Supreme Allied Council had come into being.

For various reasons Haig was unwilling to fulfil his pledges at once. The French grew impatient and early in December Clemenceau and

Pétain strongly pressed, not merely that Haig should carry out his original promise to extend his line to Barisis, but that in addition he should extend it another 37 miles to his right as far as Berry-au-Bac. The War Cabinet, while agreeing that Haig must carry out the original promise to extend to Barisis, persuaded Clemenceau to refer the question of the proposed additional extension to the military advisers of Supreme War Council. On receipt of this news, Haig without waiting for the Council's decision – doubtless for the good reason that he might be pressed to acquiesce in the extra extension – promptly conferred with Pétain and agreed to fulfil his original pledge of October 1917 not later than the end of January 1918. This he duly carried out.

Meanwhile, the military representatives at the Supreme Council came to the conclusion that the proper place for the junction of the French and British lines was neither Barisis nor Berry-au-Bac, but the left bank of the River Ailette which lay about one-third of the way towards Berry-au-Bac, some 14 miles beyond Barisis. These recommendations were discussed at a meeting of the Supreme War Council on February 1st and 2nd, 1918, but were not accepted. The total result of all these deliberations was that Haig extended his line only as far as Barisis, in accordance with the original arrangement to which he and Pétain had agreed in October. No further change was made before March 21st, 1918.

The deliberations of the Supreme War Council were, however, not confined merely to the question of the line. Important decisions were taken on other matters. In particular it was resolved that a general reserve of thirty divisions should be created as soon as possible under the command of the military Committee at Versailles. This decision aroused the greatest hostility among all who supported the Haig-Robertson point of view. Robertson himself was deeply incensed at what appeared to him – quite correctly – to be a deliberate move to nullify his own position as the sole channel through which military advice was presented to the War Cabinet. The result was a major clash between Lloyd George and the C.I.G.S., the details of which do not concern the biography of Bonar Law. It is enough to say that early in February the Prime Minister at last decided to oust Robertson, and to alter the whole relationship between the military and civilian power. The position of C.I.G.S. was reduced to what it had been before Robertson's appointment, and Robertson himself was given the alternative of either becoming British representative at Versailles or retaining the post of C.I.G.S. with reduced powers. He refused both these alternatives, alleging that the position of military representative must be occupied either by the C.I.G.S. or by his deputy, and not by someone with independent powers and status. But on this point Lloyd George and the War Cabinet refused to give way. They appointed Sir Henry Wilson as C.I.G.S. in Robertson's place.

Great risks were involved in the War Cabinet's action. The enemies of the Government had the ear of Asquith who raised the whole question of the Versailles Committee in the House of Commons. On February 11th the egregious Colonel Repington published a most hostile article in the *Morning Post*. Evidently based on secret information it revealed details about the Versailles decisions which should never have been disclosed at this time. It was widely believed that Repington obtained his information from his close friend General Maurice of whom we will hear more later. Maurice was not only Director of Military Operations at the War Office but also a devoted admirer and confidant of Robertson. But the War Cabinet had no intention of giving way. Repington was promptly prosecuted under the Defence of the Realm Act and fined £100. Asquith's questions in the House were parried. The Cabinet was determined to fight the matter out.

Perhaps the biggest anxiety for the Government was the attitude of Haig. What would happen if he identified himself with Robertson and, as Robertson undoubtedly expected, insisted on resigning? No one could tell. The anti-Lloyd George forces would certainly have gained great impetus and the Administration would have faced a severe Parliamentary challenge. The Secretary for War, Lord Derby, had already sent in his resignation. The simultaneous departure of Robertson, Derby and Haig might well have shaken the Government to its foundations. However, as events turned out, the cloud that lowered so ominously was to pass by with scarcely a drop of rain. Haig had no intention of resigning, and, summoned from France, used all his influence to preserve the peace. He endeavoured to persuade both Robertson and Derby to withdraw their opposition. Robertson refused to budge, but Derby, who had already twice proferred and withdrawn his resignation, was persuaded to remain. In an acid moment Haig wrote that Derby "like the feather pillow bears the marks of the last person who has sat on him".[j] Poor Derby! So many people were sitting on him and in such rapid succession. Bonar Law, as his friend and Leader, was continually called upon for advice. In the end Derby offered to withdraw his latest and, allegedly final, resignation. When Bonar Law told Lloyd George, the Prime Minister agreed to accept the offer, but on one condition only – that Derby would promise never to resign again.[k] A few weeks later when the crisis was over Lloyd George quietly removed him to the embassy in Paris, and appointed Milner as War Secretary in his place.

Bonar Law was deeply involved in the whole of this crisis. He fully endorsed Lloyd George's actions. His past sympathy with Robertson did not affect his determination to put the whole system of military and political relations on to a different basis. Lloyd George was ill at this time and confined to his house at Walton Heath. It fell upon Bonar Law to deal with the vacillations of Derby and to arrange with Haig the announcement of the new system of co-ordination and command in France.

A month later the long-expected German offensive began. At first it met with striking success, and for many weeks the whole fate of the Allied Armies seemed in doubt. In these circumstances there can be little surprise that the same forces which had threatened the Government over the Robertson crisis once again made a concerted attack. It is important to remember that throughout these months there was a real opposition to the existing Administration. Lloyd George in his War Memoirs goes so far as to allege the existence of a "military junta" which aimed at nothing less than the creation of a military dictatorship with Robertson as its head.[1] This is an exaggeration, but there can be no question that, during the spring and early summer of 1918, powerful elements in Parliament and the Press, supported by much weighty military opinion, were on the look out for a chance to overthrow the existing Government. Moreover, despite the protest of his biographers, it is hard to believe that Asquith was averse to leading such an attack if the occasion arose. Certainly his supporters who had greatly resented his ejection from office, now regarded Lloyd George with bitter animosity. As for the military party, it was natural that they should look to Asquith. Had he not originally appointed both Haig and Robertson? Was he not the most vigorous Parliamentary opponent of the Versailles Committee and all its works? Asquith's own attitude remained – and remains to this day – enigmatic, but his very existence as an ex-Prime Minister, jockeyed out of office in circumstances which had caused great resentment, made him inevitably the focus of discontent against the Government.

This was the background against which on May 7th there was launched the last major effort to dislodge Lloyd George's war-time Administration. That morning there appeared a letter in the *Morning*

Post and *The Times*, written by General Sir Frederick Maurice who had recently been removed from his post as Director of Military Operations at the War Office by Sir Henry Wilson. He was, as we have seen already, an intimate friend of Repington, and an ardent supporter of Robertson. The letter was a most serious attack on the honour and veracity of Lloyd George and Bonar Law. It must be quoted in full:

"Sir,

"My attention has been called to answers given in the House of Commons on 23rd April by Mr. Bonar Law to questions put by Mr. G. Lambert and Mr. Pringle as to the extension of the British Front in France. These answers contain certain mis-statements which in sum give a totally misleading impression of what occurred. This is not the place to enter into a discussion as to all the facts, but Hansard's report concludes:

" 'Mr. Pringle: Was the matter[1] entered into at the Versailles War Council at any time?

" 'Mr. Bonar Law: This particular matter was not dealt with at all by the Versailles War Council.'

"I was at Versailles when the question was decided by the Supreme War Council to whom it had been referred.

"This is the latest of a series of mis-statements which have been made recently in the House of Commons by the present Government.

"On 9th April the Prime Minister said: 'What was the position at the beginning of the battle? Notwithstanding the heavy casualties in 1917 the Army in France was considerably stronger on 1st January 1918 than on the 1st January 1917.'

"That statement implies that Sir Douglas Haig's fighting strength on the eve of the great battle which began on 21st March had not been diminished.

"That is not correct.

"Again in the same speech the Prime Minister said: 'In Mesopotamia there is only one white division at all and in Egypt and Palestine there are only three white divisions; the rest are either Indian or mixed with a very small proportion of British troops in those divisions – I am referring to the infantry divisions.'

"That is not correct.

"Now, Sir, this letter is not the result of a military conspiracy. It has been seen by no soldier. I am by descent and conviction as sincere a democrat as the Prime Minister and the last thing I want is to see the Government of our country in the hands of soldiers.

"My reasons for taking the very grave step of writing this letter are that the statements quoted above are known to a large number of soldiers to be incorrect, and this knowledge is breeding such distrust of the Government as can only end in impairing the splendid morale of our troops at a time when everything possible should be done to raise it.

---

[1] The extension of the British line to Barisis referred to above.

N

"I have therefore decided, fully realizing the consequences to myself, that my duty as a citizen must override my duty as a soldier, and I ask you to publish this letter in the hope that Parliament may see fit to order an investigation into the statements I have made.

"I am,

Yours faithfully,

F. Maurice, Major-General."

This letter coming from the late Director of Military Operations naturally produced an immense sensation in the country. It does not appear that Maurice acted in concert with anyone else. He had thought of consulting Asquith, but in the end decided not to, and contented himself with informing Asquith the day before of what he proposed to do.[m] On the afternoon of May 7th, the day on which the letter appeared, Asquith asked Bonar Law in the House what action the Government intended to take over Maurice's allegations. Bonar Law replied that they proposed to invite two judges "to act as a court of honour to enquire into the charge of misstatements alleged to have been made by Ministers and to report as quickly as possible". This procedure was not liked by Lloyd George who, sensing the tone of the Opposition, saw that a real challenge to the Government impended and preferred to fight the matter out on the floor of the House at once. But Bonar Law had insisted in Cabinet that the matter affected the honour of Ministers, in particular his own personal honour, and that a judicial enquiry was essential.[n] However, as events turned out, Asquith played into Lloyd George's hands. He refused to accept a judicial enquiry and demanded, instead, a Select Committee of the House of Commons. It was agreed that Asquith's motion should be debated two days later.

Passions were by now thoroughly aroused. Maurice's letter raised issues far wider than the strict accuracy of ministerial statements. Behind that question lay the whole question of war strategy: the clash between Haig[1] and Lloyd George; the allegation that Lloyd George had overruled Haig and forced him, through the much criticized machinery of the Versailles Committee to extend his line, that he had kept the Army in France deliberately short of men – in short the whole question of responsibility for the Allied disasters since March 21st. It must be remembered that at the beginning of May the German offensive was still making formidable progress, and that, though it was soon to come grinding to a halt, no one could easily

---

[1] Haig was not personally involved, and indeed disapproved of Maurice' action. See Robert Blake, *Private Papers of Douglas Haig*, p. 308.

predict this at the time. There was a further point at issue. General Maurice believed that Lloyd George and Wilson contemplated dismissing Haig.[o] His letter was partly designed to forestall such a step.

The Liberal Press headed by the *Westminster Gazette* declared that the Government had lost the confidence of the country. "There must be a drastic change in all this and if it involves a change of Government that must come too." It was openly proclaimed in many quarters that the time had come for Asquith to take over the Government and reinstate Robertson as C.I.G.S. Nor was this hostility to Lloyd George confined to the Liberal ranks. At one time it looked as if there might be a Tory rebellion headed by Carson. Fortunately for the Government the average Conservative M.P., however much he might dislike Lloyd George, disliked Asquith a good deal more. In the end not a single Unionist supported Asquith's motion.

The problem of how to meet Asquith's refusal to accept a judicial enquiry was discussed at length in the War Cabinet on the morning of May 8th.[p] It was agreed by everyone present that a Select Committee of the House was a useless tribunal when political passion ran high. Lloyd George claimed that the general feeling of Government supporters favoured the earliest possible statement of the facts. Even a judicial enquiry could scarcely be concluded without some delay. As for a select committee its proceedings would be interminable.

Lloyd George's view prevailed. Bonar Law agreed to drop his demand for a judicial enquiry – in view of Asquith's attitude. The Cabinet was satisfied by Lloyd George that an answer existed to all Maurice's charges, even if it might be difficult to formulate for reasons of security. Ministers resolved to fight. If Asquith refused a judicial enquiry, very well – he would have no enquiry at all. The Prime Minister would state his case. The House could accept it or reject it, but rejection would mean a new Government. Lloyd George carefully prepared his speech and rehearsed it that afternoon to Milner and Austen Chamberlain.[q] He and Bonar Law allowed it to be known that the Government would regard Asquith's motion as a matter of confidence. Both sides sent out whips. The stage was set for a major battle the following day.

Asquith opened the debate in a speech which was moderate in tone. He disclaimed all intention of moving a vote of censure. He endeavoured to confine the issue to the respective merits of a judicial enquiry or a select committee. He begged members not to read into his proposal more than was intended. He dwelt on the fact that only two days earlier the Government, through Bonar Law, had admitted the desirability of an enquiry. His speech failed to gain the ear of the House. Mr. Amery described it in his diary as "the poorest speech that I have ever heard from him".[r]

Asquith's one opportunity came when Bonar Law made an interjection which suggested that he regarded a Select Committee of the House as incapable of impartiality.

"MR. ASQUITH: 'Well does the Chancellor of the Exchequer suggest that a Select Committee is not an unsuspect tribunal?'

"MR. BONAR LAW: 'I could not name a single Member of the House who is not either friendly or opposed to the Government, and who must therefore start with a certain measure of prejudice.'

"HON. MEMBERS: 'Oh! and Shame!' "

This was an interruption more candid than prudent. Asquith was able to express virtuous horror at such an allegedly cynical attitude on the part of the Leader of the House. But however tactless, what Bonar Law said was true. Quite apart from the real issues behind the Maurice Debate, Asquith's motion had serious disadvantages. The Marconi enquiry, where a select committee had divided on strict party lines when giving its verdict, showed the unsatisfactory nature of this procedure when political feelings are inflamed.

Lloyd George's reply to Asquith was devastating. It must rank among his most brilliant Parliamentary performances. Not only was Asquith demolished but the unfortunate Maurice was made to look ridiculous and, by the end of the debate, was wholly discredited. On Maurice's charge against Bonar Law Lloyd George's answer was conclusive. The extension of the line to which Bonar Law referred – the extension to Barisis – had been, as we saw earlier, agreed by Haig and Pétain before the Supreme War Council had even been created. Therefore it could not have been, as Maurice claimed, the result of a decision by that body. Maurice's letter seemed to imply that he had been actually present himself during discussions at Versailles about the extension of the line. Lloyd George was able to show from the Minutes of the Supreme War Council that, although Maurice was at Versailles, he was not actually in the Council Chamber when extension of the line was discussed, that the extension which had then been discussed was not the one to which Bonar Law had referred, and in any case had never been put into effect before March 21st. Lloyd George did not deny that Haig viewed any extension of his line with reluctance but pointed out that the pressure had come from the French Government and not from the War Cabinet, and that both Robertson and Haig had agreed in the end that this pressure could not be resisted. Bonar Law was thus effectively vindicated.

The other two charges which Maurice brought affected Lloyd George, and related to questions of manpower. As far as the House was concerned Lloyd George had a simple and conclusive answer: the figures upon which he had based his statements were supplied by General Maurice's own department, while General Maurice was still Director of Military Operations. Therefore if the public had been misled whose fault was it? In any case Lloyd George declared that the facts he stated were substantially true: the Army really was stronger on January 1st, 1918, than on January 1st, 1917; there really were only the four white divisions in Mesopotamia, Palestine and Egypt. The only difficulty was to argue away the awkward fact that the Government had already agreed to an independent enquiry only two days before. However, Lloyd George was able to sweep this aside:

"Since Tuesday it is perfectly clear from the action of the Press which is egging on my right hon. Friend, prodding him and suggesting that he ought to do this and the other to embarrass the Government, that no statement, no decision, of any secret tribunal would ever be accepted, but that this would go on exactly as before. We have therefore decided to give the facts in public and let the public judge."

Lloyd George concluded his speech by expressing surprise that Asquith had not seen fit to condemn the grave breach of military discipline of which Maurice had been guilty. He ended with an eloquent appeal for unity in the struggle against Germany.

"The national unity is threatened – the Army unity is threatened – by this controversy . . . I really beg and implore, for our common country, the fate of which is in the balance now and in the next few weeks, that there should be an end of this sniping."

Lloyd George's speech settled the issue. Carson, despite his previous doubts, rose to urge Asquith to withdraw his motion. There was, surprisingly, no speech from the Opposition Front Bench. Even McKenna whose name was associated with the motion remained silent. Yet Asquith made no attempt to withdraw. No doubt it would have been embarrassing and difficult to do so. Nevertheless he made a serious tactical error in pressing his motion to a division and it is far from clear what his motives were. He may genuinely have regarded the question at issue as being simply what he claimed it to have been in his speech. If so, one can but endorse the opinion of Dr. Thomas Jones.

". . . he must have been mesmerized by his own integrity if he imagined that the issue could possibly be limited as he wished."[8]

Possibly Asquith still hoped for Unionist support, and a real Parliamentary victory. If that was his intention it would have been better to have challenged Lloyd George openly and not in this somewhat indirect manner. Perhaps the whole affair was the result of muddle, drift, confusion, and vacillation – factors too often ignored by tidy-minded historians. Whatever his motives, Asquith had made a disastrous decision. He was indeed supported by nearly all the Liberal ex-Ministers who had resigned with him in December 1916, but only 98 Liberals voted for him in the division whereas as many as 71 voted with Lloyd George. A very large number must have abstained. The motion was lost by 293 votes to 106, and the general sentiment of the public and the Press was that Lloyd George had been triumphantly vindicated. For the Liberal Party this division was destined to have permanent consequences. Fierce feelings lay behind this ostensibly procedural debate. Asquith's supporters did not receive the "coupon" six months later, which meant – temporarily at least – political ruin. The cleavage in the Liberal Party never entirely disappeared. The echoes of the dispute have reverberated down the years even to the present day, and in the eloquent tones of those redoubtable daughters of the two combatants – Lady Violet Bonham-Carter and Lady Megan Lloyd George – can still be heard something of the authentic passion which animated the Maurice Debate.

On the manpower question Maurice had a far stronger case. It is not necessary to enter into the details here, since they concern the life of Lloyd George rather than that of Bonar Law, and are, moreover, extremely complicated. Briefly, Lloyd George based his refutation of Maurice and his case to the Cabinet upon War Office returns which were in fact incorrect and had been subsequently corrected. These corrections could have been known by Lloyd George. Whether they actually were known remains obscure, and Lloyd George's own memoirs throw no light on the matter.[1]

What is the final verdict upon Maurice's charges? As far as Bonar Law's statement was concerned Maurice was undoubtedly in the wrong. The questions which Bonar Law had answered in the House on April 23rd all referred to the extension of the line which had actually taken place before March 21st. They were designed to elicit whether or not this had been done because of intervention by the

---

[1] It is disappointing that Mr. Frank Owen, Lloyd George's most recent biographer, has not gone into this important problem in any detail.

War Cabinet and the Versailles Committee. Bonar Law was perfectly correct in saying that the Versailles Committee had not dealt
with "this particular matter". In fact the Committee had dealt with
other matters connected with the extension of the line, and doubtless
Bonar Law would have revealed this, had he been asked. But he was
not asked, and he was naturally not going to give away information
unnecessarily.

The real issue, however, was not the detailed figures – into which
Maurice was certainly very ill-advised to enter, given his own responsibility for them – but the wider question of whether the Government
could have reinforced Haig more effectively in the months immediately preceding the offensive of March 21st, 1918. The answer
undoubtedly must be that the War Cabinet could have done so, had
it willed. There were substantial numbers available in Britain, and
in various theatres of war overseas. Between March 21st and August
31st, 1918, about half a million men were sent to France from Britain
and the Dominions, and another 100,000 from other areas of battle.
Some of these, though by no means all, could have been sent out
before March 21st. Lloyd George – and Bonar Law must share the
responsibility too – can only be defended on the ground that he
feared another Passchendaele. Haig's diaries show that there was
some reason for this fear,[t] but it may well be questioned whether, for
all his mistrust of Haig, Lloyd George should ever have run so grave
a risk.

These facts do not excuse General Maurice. His action was one
of gross military insubordination for which he could certainly have
been tried by court-martial. It was a deliberate attempt by a soldier
recently serving in a most confidential capacity to make use of secret
information in order to discredit and bring down the Government.
No Government, worthy of the name, was going to tolerate such
conduct, and Maurice might well have regarded himself as lucky in
that he was merely placed by the Army Council on half pay and did
not receive a more serious punishment. It is significant that even
Haig himself disapproved of Maurice's action. It is not at all surprising that the apparent endorsement by Asquith and his followers
of so flagrant an attempt at military intervention in politics should
have aroused the deepest resentment in the House, and that this
episode still rankled six months later, when the General Election
took place on the morrow of the nation's victory.

CHAPTER XXIV

VICTORY AND THE COUPON ELECTION

MAY 9TH – DECEMBER 28TH, 1918

Victory in sight – Quiescence of the Opposition – Bonar Law's management of the House – The Pemberton Billing case – Bonar Law's brisk exchange with Lord Robert Cecil – Lord Beaverbrook's quarrel with the Foreign Office – Lloyd George dismisses Mr. Hayes Fisher – Bonar Law as a mediator – The need for a General Election – Bonar Law consults Balfour on tactics – He decides to continue the Coalition – A joint programme agreed – Asquith declines to join – Contrast between public opinion in 1918 and in 1945 – Arguments against the Coupon Election – The case for it – Attitude of Northcliffe – "Coupon" withheld from Asquith – Suggestion that Bonar Law drove a hard bargain with Lloyd George over allocation of "Coupons" – Its falsehood – Result of the General Election

I

THE fortunes of war which had for so long been moving against the Allies began at last to change. The German assault upon the British lines died away in the middle of May. True, it was followed by some alarming successes against the French, and the whole of Paris was thrown into dismay when the Germans came near enough to bombard the city with an enormous long range gun. But by early July it was clear that the principal German effort was at an end. Ludendorff's offensive at Rheims launched on July 15th, met with little success. Foch and Haig prepared their counter plans, and on August 8th, at Amiens, Haig dealt a blow from which the German Army never really recovered. For the remainder of the summer and autumn the Allied armies steadily advanced – the brunt of the struggle being borne by the British Army which remained the only really effective fighting force among the Allies.

The changed fortunes of the war were reflected in British politics. The Opposition was quiescent, content perhaps with the feeling that, even if they had not succeeded in ousting Lloyd George, at least they had probably prevented Lloyd George from ousting Haig. The long battle between Lloyd George and the soldiers had ended, neither in compromise, nor in a decisive victory for either side, but rather in a sort of frozen deadlock. Neither side ever forgave the other, but each was equally convinced that complete victory was impossible. And so they remained, glaring at one another with covert detestation, brooding upon their wrongs and sharpening their pens in readiness for the new battle that would begin as soon as the fight against the Germans had ended – the battle of the diaries and memoirs, which darkens even to this day the history of the First World War, and which is not over yet.

Bonar Law was not involved in any further major politico-military conflicts. He was busy as ever on the endless round of party management, House of Commons duties, Treasury business. His days and nights were filled. He had no time to reflect upon the cruel blows which the war had dealt him. There can be little doubt that during this period of his life he welcomed hard work, not only because it satisfied his sense of duty, but because it prevented him from brooding upon the past and because it kept away that deep melancholy which always threatened to obsess his thoughts. As he once told a friend, he was always content if he could at the beginning of each day see enough work and occupation to fill in every hour till it ended. He asked for no more than that.[a]

This was a period when tempers were easily frayed, when the weariness of four long years of war was beginning to oppress even the strongest spirits. Bonar Law, despite his bluntness, was a past-master at the art of giving the soft answer which turneth away wrath. He was always accessible, always ready to meet deputations on this or that subject, and to listen courteously to the recital of their grievances. He was nearly always able to placate the grumblers from the ranks of his own back benchers. This was partly because he had never allowed himself to acquire too much of that ministerial aloofness which is so often apt to encrust the minds of those who sit upon the Front Bench. Once when a particularly obstreperous delegation of right wing business men had been to see him, his private secretary, Sir Horace Hamilton, congratulated him on his skill in dealing with them. "You see," replied Bonar Law,[b] "I understand how those people think."

The Duke of Wellington, during his brief – and not very happy – tenure of office as Prime Minister, once complained that most of his time was spent in composing "what Gentlemen call, 'their feelings' ". Bonar Law certainly had his fill of this aspect of politics during the final year of war. It would, for example, be an amusing – though somewhat unprofitable – task to count the number of times that Lord Derby and Lord Robert Cecil insisted upon resignation, or the number of complaints which poured in from Walter Long at the Colonial

Office, or the number of letters that Sir James Campbell sent pressing his still unsatisfied claim to the Lord Chancellorship of Ireland.

That intransigent country was, as usual, producing endless trouble. The Government had decided early in the year to extend conscription to Ireland, and at the same time to couple it with a measure of Home Rule. No proposal could have been calculated to cause more difficulty. The Ulster Unionists were at once up in arms at the bare suggestion of Home Rule, while the Catholic Hierarchy gave its official blessing to resistance against conscription. Carson wrote a strong letter of protest to Bonar Law and threatened to publish it. Bonar Law replied stiffly:[c]

"My dear Carson,
"Your letter if it is to be published must be the beginning of conflict between us and my reply, if for publication, must be of the same kind.
"That may be inevitable but I should like to delay it as much as possible. . . ."

There was, however, no need for a breach between the two men. Affairs in Ireland took a turn which rendered the Government's proposals impossible. The discovery of treasonable connexions between the Sinn Fein leaders and Germany made Home Rule of any sort out of the question during the war, and the Government prudently decided to drop conscription at the same time.

Another matter which much disturbed the country in May and June of 1918 was the Pemberton Billing case. It was perhaps the most extreme and absurd expression of the Germanophobe witch hunting which had greatly discredited English political life throughout the war. Pemberton Billing, independent M.P. for East Hertfordshire, alleged in his paper, the *Vigilante*, that there was a simple explanation for German success in the war. They were winning by propagating among British public men and their wives, sons, and daughters "evils which all decent men thought had perished in Sodom and Lesbia". He went on to allege that there existed in Germany a Black Book with the names of 47,000 prominent people whom German agents had corrupted by means of homosexual vice. This rubbish might have gone unnoticed but for the fact that Pemberton Billing accused by name a certain Miss Maud Allan, a dancer who was appearing in a special private performance of Oscar Wilde's play, *Salome*. She prosecuted him for criminal libel.[1]

The ensuing trial must be among the most discreditable episodes

---

[1] For a most amusing account of this case see Joseph Dean, *Hatred Ridicule or Contempt*, Chapter I.

that have occurred in the English courts in modern times. It was grossly mishandled by Mr. Justice Darling who allowed Pemberton Billing to fling about fantastic accusations, to interrupt, and generally to behave in a manner which would have justified a severe sentence for contempt of court. A high point was reached when one of the witnesses for the defence, who claimed to have seen the Black Book, stated that it contained the name of Mr. Justice Darling himself, and added for good measure those of Haldane and Mr. and Mrs. Asquith. The judge's summing up was enlivened by Lord Alfred Douglas, who had already given evidence, and who shouted in the middle of the judge's speech, "damned liar". He was ejected, amidst applause, and was cheered by the crowd outside. The jury returned a verdict of not guilty.

Pemberton Billing, thus triumphantly vindicated, now proceeded to behave somewhat in the manner of Senator McCarthy, and made frequent and outrageous accusations of pro-Germanism in the House of Commons and elsewhere. Among others, F. Leverton Harris, the Parliamentary Secretary to the Ministry of Blockade, was accused of having given favourable treatment to a German firm. He resolved to hand in his resignation. His Chief, Lord Robert Cecil, wrote to Bonar Law:[d]

"My dear Bonar,

"I understand you have told Leverton Harris he ought to resign. If he does, I resign too. I had rather sweep a crossing than be a member of a Ministry at the mercy of Pemberton Billing and his crew.

"Yours ever,

Robert Cecil."

Bonar Law replied:[e]

"My dear Cecil,

"No – I did not advise him to resign. He told me he intended to do so and I did not dissuade him from doing so.

"His tendering his resignation is one thing, and from his point of view I think it is wise, but the accepting the resignation is another thing and I feel sure the P.M. will not accept it.   "Yours sincerely,

A. Bonar Law."

Lord Robert Cecil was mollified. He wrote back:[f]

June 25th.

"My dear Bonar,

"(I shall continue so to address you in spite of your 'Cecils'). I am quite sure that everything you did in the L.H. matter was kind and generous. If I said anything which could be differently construed, I am very sorry. . . .

"Yours ever,

Robert Cecil."

Leverton Harris remained in the Government and Bonar Law publicly declared that in his "deliberate opinion" Leverton Harris had done nothing that reflected on his honour. This provoked a virulent letter from Lord Cecil Manners who referred in abusive tones to the Jacks case and ended:[g]

"The deliberate opinion expressed by the Chancellor of the Exchequer and Leader of the House of Commons on the Leverton Harris 'indelicacies' probably came as a surprise to a good many men in the street. But when they remember, as I do that in this delicate matter we have probably had the advantage of the advice of Lord Beaverbrook – whose knowledge and experience of such cases is believed to be unrivalled – they will no doubt be satisfied that your attitude is sound and prudent – anyhow from the point of view of the comfort and security of your 'irreplaceable' Government."

Bonar Law was evidently amused at the letter or else he would not have bothered to keep it. Meanwhile, the Cabinet took the Attorney-General's advice as to legal action against Pemberton Billing. But F. E. Smith considered that nothing could be done. Bonar Law wrote to him:[h]

"I read your letter to the Cabinet this morning and they accept your view that it does not appear possible to take any action in the matter. The Cabinet wondered, however, whether it might not be possible to prosecute one or two witnesses for perjury with the certainty of success and I should be very glad to have your opinion on this point as soon as possible."

Evidently F. E. Smith advised against this too. At all events nothing was done, and the Cabinet took the wiser course of allowing the matter to fall into oblivion – a process made all the quicker by the resounding successes of Allied arms in France.

Another matter which exercised Bonar Law's talents for mediation concerned his friend, Beaverbrook. The latter had since February occupied the post of Minister in Charge of Propaganda, holding the office of Chancellor of the Duchy of Lancaster. At an early stage he ran into difficulties with the Foreign Office, the Admiralty and the War Office. The dispute with the Foreign Office was the most serious and concerned the exact boundary line between the functions of the two departments. The merits of the dispute cannot be discussed here, but Beaverbrook sincerely believed that all his efforts were being frustrated by the jealousy and obscurantism of the older Department. At the end of June he was so exasperated that he drafted a letter of resignation which he sent to Bonar Law for comment before it went to the Prime Minister. He wrote:[i]

". . . nothing could have been pleasanter than my relations with Mr. Balfour and Lord Robert Cecil to whom I am indebted for much kindness and wise advice. As to Lord Hardinge I met him twice at conferences. On each occasion he adopted an absolutely non-possumus attitude to every proposal. No matter what concessions I offered him he would never abate one iota of his demands, nor do I believe this matter will ever be settled so long as he remains Permanent Under-Secretary for Foreign Affairs."

It is interesting to note that Bonar Law advised the deletion of this last sentence. In the end Beaverbrook was persuaded to withdraw his resignation. But in August trouble flared up again and we find him writing to Bonar Law:[j]

"The resistance all round is so persistent that it is impossible for the Minister to carry out his duties effectively, and this unceasing opposition would be enough to break the spirit of a man of far greater moral courage than I claim to be."

Bonar Law did his best to help, and he succeeded in removing the causes of difference between Beaverbrook and the Admiralty by a personal intervention with Sir Eric Geddes. But the situation with the War Office and the Foreign Office remained as bad as ever. At this stage Churchill appears to have been worried about the dispute, and he wrote on September 8th to Bonar Law:[k]

"Look after Max or he will make a great mistake which all of us and he most of all will have cause to regret."

In October Beaverbrook became seriously ill and on the 21st he resigned from the Government. Twenty-two years were to pass before he was again in office, in another great war-time Administration, as Mr. Churchill's Minister of Aircraft Production.

At the end of October an even more delicate problem arose for Bonar Law. W. Hayes Fisher, who was a Conservative M.P., had occupied since June 1917 the post of President of the Local Government Board. Among his duties was the preparation of the new electoral register made necessary by the passing of the Reform Act of 1918, which was a measure agreed upon by all parties and which greatly extended the franchise. Lloyd George was disturbed to find that owing to defects in organization a considerable number of Service men would be disfranchised in the event of an early Election. He saw that nothing could be more damaging politically than this, and immediately drafted on October 28th one of the most devastating letters that a Prime Minister could pen to a subordinate minister. After a lengthy recital of Hayes Fisher's delinquencies the letter ended:[l]

"I regret that I have been forced to the conclusion that in the conduct of your office you have shown such lack of judgment and want of efficiency that I can no longer accept your services as a Member of the Government. I am advising the King to this effect and as to the appointment of a successor in your office. I should be greatly obliged, therefore, if you would place your resignation in my hands for submission to His Majesty as soon as possible, as I wish your successor to begin his work tomorrow at latest."

Fortunately for the future of the Coalition Lloyd George, who was in Paris at the time, had the prudence to submit his draft to Bonar Law before actually sending it to Hayes Fisher. Bonar Law was horrified at the peremptory tone of this dismissal. He at once telegraphed to Lloyd George:[m]

"Apart from the making of the change the method adopted of taking action without even seeing the individual will be, I believe, universally condemned. . . . If it is done I cannot accept any responsibility and must reserve complete liberty of action. . . ."

He refused to send on the letter until Lloyd George had reconsidered the matter, but he personally saw Hayes Fisher to warn him of what impended. He again telegraphed Lloyd George:[n]

"I have seen the individual. He has no money and this will mean ruin to him while the honour[1] is impossible. . . . I urge you to allow the matter to stand over till you return or at least till I see you tomorrow if I go to Paris. I believe that if the letter actually written were sent there is a likelihood of a resolution being moved about it and I do not think you could rely on the support of your own colleagues. . . ."

By now rumours of the forthcoming dismissal were widely spread, and a letter of protest reached Bonar Law from Curzon at what he considered to be the outrageous treatment of a Conservative by a Liberal Prime Minister.

Meanwhile, Bonar Law hastened to Paris to see Lloyd George. While he was there he received a vigorous telegram in defence of Hayes Fisher, signed by Curzon, Cecil, Chamberlain and Walter Long, but he decided that it would be unwise to show this to the Prime Minister. Even as it was their interview was none too friendly. Bonar Law wrote an account of it to Curzon. Lloyd George, he said, insisted that his position would be impossible if he were precluded on party grounds from dismissing a Minister whom he considered to be grossly incompetent. Bonar Law goes on:[o]

"I did not make that claim, which would be intolerable, but I insisted that, as the Unionists were asked to join the Government by me, I could not avoid responsibility for the way they were treated, and I had the right

[1] Presumably there was some question of consoling Hayes Fisher with a peerage.

to claim that they should be treated with every consideration not inconsistent with his right to make the changes he thought necessary. As soon
as I saw him we had a fairly heated conversation on the subject and it
ended on the basis that nothing further would be done until we – or at
least until I – returned. He will however certainly insist on his (Hayes
Fisher's) leaving the L.G.B. and I should not be prepared to contest his
right to do this."

This was indeed what happened. Lloyd George was content with
the substance of his demand, and asked for Hayes Fisher's resignation
in a much shorter and less wounding letter. His attitude is summed
up in his own words scrawled in red crayon and preserved among
Bonar Law's papers:[P]

"The P.M. doesn't mind if he (Hayes Fisher) is drowned in Malmsey
wine, but he must be a dead chicken by tonight."

On November 4th it was announced that Hayes Fisher had resigned and his place been taken by Sir Auckland Geddes. The
episode has been described at length since it is an excellent example
of the tact and skill with which Bonar Law mediated between his
impetuous Chief and the more rigid members of his own Party. There
can be little doubt that if Lloyd George had sent his original letter to
Hayes Fisher the Coalition would have been seriously endangered
at a particularly crucial moment. Bonar Law saw to it that Hayes
Fisher received some consolation. He was elevated to the peerage as
Lord Downham and given the valuable sinecure of a Suez Canal
Directorship.

The issue upon which Hayes Fisher fell was one of great importance. It had long been evident that a General Election would have
to take place soon, whether or not the war was over. The existing
Parliament had been elected in 1910 and had now outlasted by
three years the span alloted to it in the Parliament Act of 1911.
Moreover, the Reform Act of 1918, which more than doubled the
electorate, made the continuance of the existing House of Commons
highly anomalous. But if an Election were to be held, on what issues
would it be fought, and who would fight whom? Was there to be a
return to the old party warfare, or was the Coalition to continue in
being and appeal to the country for a general mandate not only to
win the war, but to solve the immediate problems of peace too? These
questions were agitating the minds of the principal political leaders
all through the summer and autumn of 1918. There was a further
complication. No one knew when the war would end. Until a late
stage the best military opinion was that it would continue into 1919.

This doubt added to the difficulties which stood in the way of any clear decision on the wisest course to pursue.

On October 5th Bonar Law wrote at length to Balfour asking his advice on the problem.[q] After stating his conviction that the Prime Minister would soon start manoeuvring for an Election, and that in any case it could not be delayed for long, he raised the awkward question of who, in the event of the Coalition appealing to the country, would be the Opposition.

"It would certainly seem extremely unfair that an election should be fought in the main on a Win-the-War policy, in which he (Asquith) – and the men who have acted like him – are to be opposed. On the other hand if we look at it from the point of view of the Prime Minister, it seems to me that he has a very strong case . . . he has reason to believe that the country supports his Government and . . . a right in that case to have a House of Commons which in this respect will represent the country and on whose support he can rely.

"While it is true also that Mr. Asquith and some of his friends have throughout been most patriotic in regard to the war, there really is no doubt that they are opposed to the Prime Minister, that they do not believe that he is the best man to conduct the Government, and that if the opportunity arose they would be hostile to him. This was shown not only for example in the Maurice Debate but on many other occasions in the House and it is shown still more clearly at this moment by the attitude of that part of the Liberal Press which is specially identified with Asquith. Every day now the *Daily News*, to a considerable extent, the *Westminster Gazette* and other papers are taking every opportunity of either openly or covertly attacking the Prime Minister."

But although Bonar Law recognized the strength of Lloyd George's case for an early Election he was not so clear about the wisdom of the Conservatives going along with him. The tariff question, the Welsh Church, Home Rule, were all issues that could be shelved temporarily, but what would happen after the war?

"Now on all these things L.G.'s view – quite naturally, and we can make no complaint about it – must be different from ours. It would obviously suit his views if the Party's solidarity all round were broken and I fancy that he would like personally nothing better than that there should be a split in our Party as a result of which a majority would support him. But that would be an impossible position for us."

On balance Bonar Law was inclined to the view that an early Election was desirable, that the responsibility should be left to Lloyd George, and that the Conservatives should support him for the duration of the war, but be free thereafter to act as they wished about the controversial questions which would have to be dealt with when the war ended. He went on:

"It would indeed be entirely against my own personal ambitions, if I were thinking of that, for obviously the probable result of it would be that, if an election were fought in this way, Lloyd George as the leader of the fight would secure a greater hold on the rank and file of our Party and he would also be so dependent on that Party after an election that he would permanently be driven into the same attitude towards our Party which (Joseph) Chamberlain was placed in before, with this difference – that he would be the leader of it. That would, however, I am inclined to think, be not a bad thing for our Party, and a good thing for the nation."

Bonar Law concluded by expressing the view that "our Party on the old lines will never have any future in this country". The circumstances had totally changed. After the war there would be many problems capable of arousing the greatest bitterness, unless they were solved by a combination of the two parties.

"The only chance of a rational solution of these questions is that they should be dealt with by a Government which is so secure of support not of one section but of both that there would at least be a chance that the reforms which undoubtedly will be necessary should be made in a way as little revolutionary as possible."

Balfour was in general agreement with these suggestions. "I think that whatever happens", he wrote, "the responsibility of a dissolution must rest with the Prime Minister. It always does so rest in fact; and on some previous occasions the Prime Minister of the day has not even gone through the form of consulting his colleagues."[r] But he agreed that this did not get Bonar Law out of the necessity for determining – and determining very soon – the programme and attitude of the Conservative Party. He agreed also that it would be most undesirable to resume party controversy at the same stage as it had reached when war broke out.

Bonar Law's papers throw no further light upon the exact date when he and Lloyd George finally decided to appeal to the country as a Coalition. It must have been sometime during October, for on November 2nd Lloyd George wrote a letter, the terms of which had been agreed in advance by Bonar Law, officially suggesting the continuance of the Coalition.

"If an election on these lines is to take place," wrote Lloyd George, "I recognize that there must be some statement of policy and a statement of such a nature as will retain to the greatest extent possible the support of your followers and of mine. My fundamental object will be to promote the unity and development of the British Empire and the nations of which it is composed, to preserve for them the position of influence and authority in the conduct of the world's affairs which they have gained by their sacrifices and efforts in the cause of human liberty and progress, and to bring into being such conditions of living for the inhabitants of the British Isles as will secure plenty and opportunity to all."

No one, whether Conservative or Liberal, could seriously cavil at such unexceptionable – if slightly platitudinous – aspirations. Everything, of course, depended on what was really meant, but here Lloyd George deemed it wise to be somewhat vague. "I do not think it necessary", he prudently observed, "to discuss in detail how this programme is to be carried out." Nevertheless, there were three subjects upon which he had to be rather more specific if he hoped to obtain any support at all from Bonar Law's adherents. These were Tariff Reform, Home Rule, and the Welsh Church. On the first named Lloyd George declared that he accepted "the policy of Imperial Preference as defined in the Resolutions of the Imperial Conference to the effect that a preference will be given on existing duties and on any duties which may be subsequently imposed". On the other hand he was not in favour of a tax on food. In general he hoped that the dispute between free trade and tariffs was dead – at least in the terms in which it had been fought before 1914.

"In order to secure better production and better distribution I shall look at every problem simply from the point of view of what is the best method of securing the objects at which we are aiming, without any regard to theoretical opinions about free trade or tariff reform."

As for Home Rule, Lloyd George declared that future policy was governed by two facts, first that Home Rule was already on the Statute Book, second that neither he nor anyone else would ever attempt to coerce an unwilling Ulster into accepting the rule of a Dublin Parliament. Finally, there was the vexed question of the Welsh Church. Lloyd George could not countenance any idea of the Welsh Church Act being repealed but he was prepared to reconsider some of the financial details of that Act.[1]

Bonar Law kept the letter secret for the time being, but consulted privately a number of his leading colleagues. He called a meeting of Conservative M.P.s for November 12th and resolved to announce his decision there. Meanwhile, rumours of what was impending had become widely current. Two important deputations from among the Liberals, understandably alarmed at the prospect of a permanent split in their Party, called on Lloyd George and begged him to come to an agreement with Asquith. According to his own account Lloyd George was more than willing to include Asquith in his new Govern-

[1] This statement satisfied the Conservatives with the exception of Lord Robert Cecil who felt it his duty to resign.

ment.⁸ He declined however to commit himself finally until he had
seen Bonar Law, but he was able to do this at once, and he returned
from 11 Downing Street with the news that Bonar Law was equally
glad to welcome Asquith and some of Asquith's immediate colleagues
in the Administration. It was suggested by one member of the deputation that Asquith should be Lord Chancellor – a proposal of which
both Lloyd George and Bonar Law entirely approved. But when this
offer was conveyed to Asquith he firmly declined. His biographers
do not say why, although they hint that one of his reasons was that he
refused to be a party to the sacrifice of his own friends, which, it is
alleged, would have been demanded by Lloyd George and Bonar
Law.ᵗ If Lloyd George's account is correct this can hardly have been
the real reason, for not only was no sacrifice involved but an offer
was made to include some of Asquith's colleagues in the Government. It is much more likely that Asquith was unwilling to take third
place in an Administration whose leaders he profoundly distrusted
and whose conduct in ousting him two years before he still deeply
resented.

Whatever Asquith's motives, his decision to fight the Election independently of the Coalition helped to clarify the situation. It was
already a foregone conclusion that the Labour Party would go into
opposition. Therefore, Lloyd George and Bonar Law could legitimately partition the Government nominations between their respective parties and treat both the Asquithian Liberals and the Labour
candidates as opponents. On November 12th – the day after the
Armistice – Bonar Law presided as arranged over a meeting of
Conservative M.P.s at the Connaught Rooms. He announced his decision, unanimously endorsed by the Conservative Ministers, that the
Party would go to the polls in support of the Coalition Government,
and he read out the letter of November 2nd in which Lloyd George
had outlined the Coalition programme. The arguments which Bonar
Law used need not be expounded here. They were in the main an
expansion of the theme of Lloyd George's letter – the importance of
unity in the post-war period, the desirability of solving bitterly controversial subjects in a non-revolutionary manner, the necessity for
the Government to receive a powerful mandate for its negotiations
over the peace treaties. In addition Bonar Law dwelt upon the
personal qualities of the Prime Minister:

"By our own action we have made Mr. Lloyd George the flag bearer
of the very principles upon which we should appeal to the country. It is
not his Liberal friends, it is the Unionist Party which has made him Prime

Minister, and made it possible for him to do the great work that has been
done by this Government. . . ."

Later he added:

"Remember this, that at this moment Mr. Lloyd George commands an
amount of influence in every constituency as great as has ever been
exercised by any Prime Minister in our political history."

Before he finished Bonar Law made one observation, which in view
of what occurred four years later, is worthy of note:

"What I propose does not mean that our Party is going to cease to exist.
We go into this election – at least if I have my way – as a Unionist Party
forming a portion of a coalition, I should be sorry if it were otherwise.
From the time that my colleagues in the House of Commons did me the
honour of electing me to be their leader I have felt that I was in the position of a trustee; and even throughout the war one thing that I have aimed
at constantly has been to preserve, if it could be done, the unity of our
Party. That does not mean of course that if at any time that interest had
conflicted with the national interest I should not have readily sacrificed
the Party interest. It does not mean that. . . ."

Bonar Law concluded by expressing the hope that eventually
Lloyd George and his friends would work with the Conservatives in
just the same way as the Liberal Unionists had come to do after their
split with Gladstone over Irish Home Rule. But it was quite clear
that he had no intention, then or at any time, of allowing the Conservative Party to be broken into pieces and to lose its identity as a
result of some new regrouping of the old political parties. It was
precisely because of this threat that, four years later, he felt obliged
to lead the revolt which resulted in the downfall of the Coalition and
the return to traditional party alignments.

2

The day before this important meeting took place had seen the
end of the war. The aftermath of victory in 1918 was in many important respects different from the years that followed Hitler's defeat
in the Second World War. Feelings were more bitter, the cry for
vengeance more strident, social stresses more violent. To those who
have seen the horrors of two world wars and who dwell from day to
day in the sombre shadow cast by the fear of a third more frightful
than any that have gone before, the passions which raged in Britain
during 1918 and 1919 may seem strangely artificial and unreal. After
all, it can be said, at worst the Germans in the 1914–18 war did not
adopt a policy of mass racial extermination, and surely on any view
the Kaiser was a cut above Hitler and the clique of criminals and

lunatics who controlled Germany from 1939 to 1945. This is undoubtedly true, but it must be remembered that the Kaiser's war
burst upon a far more secure and placid world than the uneasy hag
ridden Europe of 1939. For a hundred years before 1914 wars had
either been of short duration or fought by professional armies in
remote theatres.[1] The impact produced by the first "total war" of
modern times upon the peaceful and prosperous civilization of nine-
teenth-century Europe was bound to be devastating – and nowhere
so much as in Britain which had been both more peaceful and more
prosperous than any other country in the world. For all its horrors
Hitler's war burst upon a generation which already half expected
it and which had been hardened by bitter experience into a certain
insensibility.

There were other reasons for the difference between the impact of
the two wars upon Great Britain. The actual British casualties were
much higher in the First World War, and were concentrated in a
shorter period of time. Each year cost about twice as many dead
during the 1914–18 war as it cost in the war of 1939–45. Moreover,
the social stresses set up by the Kaiser's war were much more violent
than anything produced by Hitler's war. Heavy taxation had not
prevented the creation during 1914–18 of enormous fortunes out of
munitions and other war-time necessities. The high wages of the
average worker contrasted disagreeably with the low pay and the
wretched allowances of the soldier. To some extent the same pheno-
menon prevailed in England in 1945, and many a Service man smiled
cynically at the "sacrifices" which, his newspapers informed him,
were being made by miners and munition workers. But the contrast
was less blatant. Profiteering was less obvious.

Above all there was the feeling that during Hitler's war civilians
in many areas of Britain had endured in the form of aerial attack
perils far more acute and unpleasant than anything which befell that
numerous body of Service men whose duties never took them within
miles of the front line. But air raids were of negligible importance in
the 1914–18 war. On the whole, apart from food rationing, the civilian
population suffered little. A vast gulf yawned between their lives and
the nightmare of danger and squalor which brooded over the soldier
on the Western Front. It is not surprising that cynicism, disillusionment, and bitterness were ripe in the weeks that followed the Armistice. It is not surprising that the cry for implacable vengeance upon

[1] The one exception to this generalization is the American Civil War, and the aftermath
of that was just as bitter as the aftermath of the 1914–18 war.

Germany, for the ruthless expulsion of aliens from Britain, for enormous indemnities, for hanging the Kaiser, should have drowned the quiet voice of moderation and statesmanship.

It has been argued that, in view of all these circumstances, a General Election should never have been held in 1918, that an appeal to the nation should have been postponed till the following year when perhaps passion would have somewhat cooled, and the problems of peace might have appeared in a more rational perspective. The King, Sir Harold Nicolson tells us, strongly pressed the Prime Minister in this sense even at the time.[u] In retrospect many historians have severely criticized the Election and in some quarters it has been hinted, not obscurely, that Lloyd George and Bonar Law showed unscrupulous opportunism in seizing this moment to go to the polls. What truth is there in this charge?

We have already seen the powerful arguments in favour of an early Election. Indeed if the Coalition was to continue in being at all, any postponement of the date might well have been disastrous. Even as it was Bonar Law and Sir George Younger had the greatest difficulty in persuading local Conservative Associations to withdraw their candidates in favour of sitting Coalition Liberal M.P.s. In most cases they did eventually succeed, but only by an appeal to sentiments of wartime unity which would not long have survived the end of the war. In addition to this severely practical consideration Lloyd George and Bonar Law could fairly claim that they needed the nation's backing if they were to speak with real authority at the Peace Conference, and that, in any case, it was unconstitutional to go on governing when Parliament had already exceeded its proper span by three years, and when the entire electoral system had recently been changed. The case for an early Election was in fact very strong, and it is difficult to see how Lloyd George and Bonar Law could have defended a postponement, even if they had wished to do so.

More disputable is the way in which the Election was conducted and the nature of the political bargain struck between the two leaders. On the former point it may freely be conceded that the inflamed passions which swayed the voters received insufficient cold water from the Coalition leaders. Neither Lloyd George nor Bonar Law made the outrageous statements about Germany's capacity to pay, which have sometimes been attributed to them, but they could perhaps have done more than they did to discourage the vindictive sentiments of their audiences. Both were indeed personally sceptical about the astronomical sums which, certain experts declared, could be extorted from Germany. Since the expert whose estimate was most inflated happened to be Lord Cunliffe, it is safe to assume that Bonar Law was particularly sceptical in this matter. But neither he nor Lloyd George wished to incur public odium by too emphatic a denial of these absurd figures. It would no doubt have been better for their own reputations and for their later negotiations at Versailles if they had done so. It is only fair to add that Bonar Law and Lloyd George displayed far more moderation than the great majority of their colleagues and supporters.

There was a further difficulty. Lord Northcliffe had come out in bitter opposition to Lloyd George and the Coalition. It was largely a personal vendetta caused by Lloyd George's refusal either to give Northcliffe a seat on the Peace Delegation or to allow him to take charge of British propaganda during the Paris negotiations.[1] Their interview was stormy and ended in Lloyd George telling him "to go to Hades", whereat, as Bonar Law used drily to relate, "he promptly came to see me at the Treasury". He received an equally frosty welcome there, and from then onwards swore undying vengeance upon Lloyd George and Lloyd George's friends. His line of propaganda was straightforward: Lloyd George had become the prisoner of the Tory "nincompoops", and as a result of their weakness and secret pro-Germanism, the terms of peace would be far too lenient. These were the days before the myth of Press influence on politics had been punctured.[2] Politicians still tended to take the power of someone like Northcliffe at his own valuation of it – and this was not low. It was natural that Lloyd George and Bonar Law, though rightly refusing to tolerate Northcliffe's dictatorial claims, should be reluctant to say anything which might give colour to the propaganda of the *Daily Mail* and *The Times*.

Finally, there has been much criticism of the bargain between Lloyd George and Bonar Law. The gist of this agreement was that the Coalition should continue and that only those candidates to whom the two leaders sent a joint letter of support should be deemed to have the Government's approval. It was this letter which Asquith immortalized in the jargon of the then war-time rationing as "the

---

[1] See *History of the Times*, Vol. IV, p. 387, and D. Lloyd George, *Truth about the Peace Treaties*, Vol. I, pp. 268–70. It is possible that Lloyd George was wrong in believing that Northcliffe demanded a seat on the Peace Delegation, but Northcliffe did undoubtedly wish to control British propaganda. In any case he had already demanded, as a condition of his support, that Lloyd George should submit his proposed new Cabinet to him for approval, a claim which no Prime Minister could accept.

[2] The Election of 1918 went far to achieve this for Northcliffe's papers had no effect whatever on the result.

coupon". The coupon was to be withheld from all the Asquithian Liberals, and for the purpose of the Election the definition of an Asquithian Liberal was a Liberal who voted with Asquith in the division on the Maurice Debate. It is difficult to see why this decision should be condemned. Naturally, the Asquithian Liberals objected since, as they rightly foresaw, it meant their own political extinction, but after Asquith's refusal to join the Coalition he could hardly expect to be treated as a supporter. Moreover, it is not true, as sometimes alleged, that Lloyd George and Bonar Law manufactured, as it were, an opposition out of nothing, and hit on the division over the Maurice Debate as a plausible last minute excuse for dividing the sheep from the goats in the Liberal Party. Bonar Law's letter to Balfour quoted earlier – a private letter in which he had no reason to be other than politically realistic – shows that he regarded the Asquithian Liberals as genuine opponents. Nor, it may be added, did he consider this opposition as in any way reprehensible. An extract from his speech at the Central Hall, Westminster on November 16th is worth quoting:

"I say at once that the overwhelming majority of the House has been whole hearted in the prosecution of the war. But I do not forget – and there are many members of the House of Commons present who know it – that a large section of those who did take that patriotic view were not in favour of this Government . . . on many occasions, I do not say they were fractious – not at all – but by their speeches, and, on at least one occasion by their vote, they deliberately tried to get rid of this Government (Shame!). There is no shame. If they thought so they were entitled to do so. . . ."

In fact Bonar Law regarded the Asquithian Liberals as a perfectly legitimate opposition but an opposition none the less. It may be that in one or two cases the denial of the coupon worked unfairly, and that Liberals were excluded who in fact had been supporters of the Government. But Bonar Law could reasonably regard this as primarily a matter for Lloyd George rather than for himself, and it is safe to surmise that Lloyd George had a fairly accurate idea of who were his friends and who were his enemies.

Another criticism of the Election has been that Bonar Law drove an unduly hard bargain over the allocation of the "coupons" as between Conservatives and Coalition Liberals. It is quite true that the great majority went to Conservatives and also quite true that this division corresponded very closely to the arrangements proposed by Younger in a memorandum of September 27th. In this document he assumed that the Asquithian Liberals would be opposed, and suggested that whereas Conservative candidates should be induced to withdraw from contests with sitting Lloyd George Liberals, they should be allowed to fight Asquithian Liberals. In cases where there was no Conservative candidate already in the field then the Government candidates should be selected on a "give and take" basis agreed with Lloyd George. The operative factor here was the lack of Lloyd George candidates. Of the 600 Coalition candidates about 150 were Liberals and 450 were Conservatives. But this inequality did not occur because Lloyd George and his chief Whip, Captain Guest, were outwitted by Bonar Law and Younger. That indeed was most unlikely, given the character of the persons concerned. It occurred because Lloyd George could not find more than 150 candidates. A letter from Younger to Davidson, dated December 2nd, commenting on a Scottish newspaper's attack upon the Coalition shows how he regarded the situation:

"Heavens! What a demon I must be in the estimation of some of those scribes, when all I did was to agree to find for the L.G. lot the 150 seats they asked for.

"There was no haggling about it and no astuteness at all, still less the 'Scottish Grab' with which I am charged.

"My own idea is that the request for 150 seats made, be it remembered, not by Guest but by L.G. himself was governed by the number of candidates they had available.

"I've little doubt they would have asked for more if they could have put up the men, and as it is they have had the greatest difficulty in securing them. I have done my part quite fairly and I wish they had acted in the same spirit. . . . They have not played the game at all and in some cases have placed me in an impossible position and made a perfect fool of me. . . ."

No doubt these last sentences have their counterparts in the correspondence of Captain Guest, for the complicated arrangements must have provoked a certain amount of ill feeling on both sides. Nevertheless, Younger's estimate of Lloyd George's predicament was almost certainly correct. It was by no means easy for him to find new candidates – sitting members were in a different position – prepared to risk excommunication by Asquith who still controlled the official Liberal Party Organization. The truth was that the Unionists had good reasons to suppose that in a straight fight against a united Liberal Party they had an excellent chance of winning. The continuance of the Coalition meant that in many constituencies Conservative candidates had to withdraw, perhaps abandoning the harvest which they would have reaped after years of endeavour. Younger had to place as many of these candidates as he could. If Lloyd George was unable to furnish candidates from his Liberal supporters for more than 150 seats, it was certainly not Younger's job to help him out. He naturally took good care to fill the vacancies with Unionists. Certainly neither Younger nor his colleagues regarded themselves as having made a particularly successful bargain. At the end of some frantic correspondence in early December about the "coupons" for Scottish seats, in which it emerges that through an error the last six "coupons" had been given to Guest, Davidson gloomily writes:[w]

"It is clear from this that the pass has been sold and nothing can be done."

Younger was furious at this mistake which had occurred in his absence, but he agreed that no further action was possible.

The Election took place on December 14th. Votes were counted a fortnight later. Although it was universally expected that the Coalition would win, the extent of its victory came as a surprise to many people. The Coalition was supported by 474 members – 338 Unionists and 136 Liberals. In addition it had the independent support of 10 members of the so called National Democratic Party. The opposition parties totalled 222 members. But of these 73 were Sinn Feiners who repudiated the authority of Westminster and refused to take their seats. Labour with 59 members was the next largest party and became the official Opposition. As for the Asquithian Liberals they were utterly routed. Only 26 members were returned. All the leaders lost their seats including Asquith himself, although Lloyd George and Bonar Law had refused to give the coupon to his Tory opponent.

Bonar Law decided that the Election was an opportune occasion to return to the scene of his first entry into politics. Since 1910 he had been Member for Bootle. He now resolved to contest the constituency of Central Glasgow, his native city. During the latter stages of the campaign he contracted a bad chill and was unable to do much speaking. However, this made little difference. He defeated his Labour opponent by 17,653 votes to 4,736. He was delighted to be back once again in Glasgow and remained member for that important constituency during the rest of his political life.

Whatever the subsequent criticisms levelled at those responsible for the Election of 1918, Bonar Law himself felt no qualms of conscience. He considered that he had acted in the best interests both

of his country and of the party for which he regarded himself as
trustee. No doubt many things had been said in the Election, and
many arguments used, which might in the cold light of later reflection
seem intemperate and rash. But is not this true of every General
Election? And anyway Bonar Law had been among the most level
headed and moderate of those who took part. After all British General
Elections – even in the sedate 1950s – usually have something of a
touch of Eatanswill about them. A studious appeal to political reason,
a careful exposition of well ordered arguments have never, except in
the text books of political theorists, played the chief part in electoral
battles. The 1918 Election no doubt had many discreditable features,
but so has almost every Election in the twentieth century. It may
have been slightly worse, but it was certainly not very much worse
than a great many others.

CHAPTER XXV

PEACE AND REPARATIONS

DECEMBER 28TH, 1918 – AUGUST 5TH, 1919

Formation of the Government – Bonar Law becomes Lord Privy Seal – His influence on appointments – A brush with Austen Chamberlain – The new Ministers – Lack of public enthusiasm – Bonar Law's first ride on a motor bicycle – His relations with Beaverbrook – His private secretaries – Reparations – Recommendations of the Treasury – Inflated estimate of the Sumner Committee – Scepticism of Lloyd George and Bonar Law – Difficulties of the Reparations problem – French attitude – Political atmosphere in England – Bonar Law's efforts to pour cold water on public demands – Kennedy Jones's telegram – Lloyd George's riposte to Northcliffe – Keynes's criticism of the politicians – The final settlement – Unfortunate results of America's withdrawal – Bonar Law's part in procuring the O.M. for Lloyd George

I

O N December 28th the results of the Election were out. There was no time to waste in forming the new Government. The first full meeting of the Paris Peace Conference had already been fixed for January 18th and it was deemed prudent that the British delegation, of which both Lloyd George and Bonar Law were members, should attend at least a week earlier for preliminary negotiation and intrigue. January 10th was, therefore, the latest date when the Prime Minister could conveniently announce the composition of his Administration. Bonar Law had already settled his own position with Lloyd George. He was to relinquish the Treasury, to act simply as Leader of the House and in effect – though the title was then unknown – as deputy Prime Minister, with the sinecure office of Lord Privy Seal.

No Prime Minister, however carefully he weighs the competing claims of party loyalty and the public service, can avoid disappointing some legitimate expectations and incurring some righteous wrath. His task is even more difficult when he has not merely to consider his own party, but to placate the aspirations of another party too – especially where, as in 1919, that other party constitutes three-fourths of his supporters and is inclined to view him with mistrustful eyes. It is safe to assume that Bonar Law was consulted on all appoint-

nents and that none was made without his assent, but it is only here
and there that actual evidence survives of the part he played. We
find him for example pressing the claims of F. E. Smith to the Lord
Chancellorship despite the opposition of the King.[1] We find him
oning down the letter which Lloyd George intended to send in reply
o a rather peremptory demand from Winston Churchill, and so
perhaps preventing a serious breach between the two men.[a] We find
him involved in a delicate controversy with Austen Chamberlain
over the occupation of 11 Downing Street and the status of the
Chancellor of the Exchequer. Lloyd George had offered that post to
Chamberlain in a somewhat brusque fashion, and on condition that
he did not occupy the traditional residence, which Bonar Law was
o keep on the ground that it was essential for him as Leader of the
House to have easy access to the Prime Minister.

Chamberlain did not like this arrangement and went to call on
Bonar Law who replied "very stiffly that his occupation of that house
was a *sine qua non*". Chamberlain's account goes on:[b]

"We had a rather stormy conversation. In fact we both lost our tempers
for the first and last time in our long friendship, but the breach was healed
by some kindly words from Bonar Law the same afternoon and left no
scar on our relations."

Chamberlain gave way over the house, but he was most indignant
when he learned from Bonar Law that the Prime Minister did not
intend to make him a member of the Cabinet. What followed is of
some interest in English constitutional history, for, when Chamberlain
protested to Lloyd George, the latter replied that it was impossible
to have a proper Cabinet as long as he and Bonar Law and Balfour
were away in Paris, that they could not continually refer matters
back to the Cabinet in London, and therefore that they proposed
not to appoint any Cabinet at all.[c] This was certainly a surprising
plan, and it is difficult to know quite how seriously it was intended.
However, Chamberlain was adamant that he would never be Chancellor without a seat in the Cabinet, while Lloyd George was
equally adamant against having the full Cabinet which, he averred,
would be forced on him if the Chancellor was included – because of
the claims that would then be made by other Ministers. At this stage
Bonar Law who agreed with Chamberlain made a compromise

---

[1] Lord Stamfordham wrote to Lloyd George: "His Majesty does not feel sure that Sir
Frederick has established such a reputation in men's minds as to ensure that the country
will welcome him to the second highest position which can be occupied by a subject of
the Crown. His Majesty, however, only hopes he may be wrong in this forecast."

proposal. Why not simply preserve the old War Cabinet? Chamberlain was already a member and could continue, although no appointed specifically as Chancellor of the Exchequer. In this way the claims of other Ministers to membership could be postponed, and Chamberlain would be satisfied. The arrangement could prevail until the Paris negotiations had come to an end.[d]

Chamberlain acquiesced, and thus it came about that the small Cabinet continued in being for another ten months. It was not till late autumn that Lloyd George formed an orthodox representative Cabinet on the old lines. The whole episode is a good example of how what might seem to be an experiment in the machinery of government – the continuation of a small inner Cabinet in time of peace – was in fact the casual outcome of a compromise adopted largely on personal grounds to meet a particular political situation.

On January 10th the names of the new Ministers were announced to the public. They had nearly all been in the old Government although there was a substantial reshuffle in offices. F. E. Smith became Lord Chancellor with the title of Lord Birkenhead. Winston Churchill became Secretary for War and had the Air Ministry under his control as well. Walter Long went to the Admiralty. Balfour remained Foreign Secretary. Curzon continued as Lord President of the Council with a special responsibility for that section of the Foreign Office which did not deal with the Paris peace negotiations. He succeeded Balfour as Foreign Secretary in October. Milner became Colonial Secretary. E. S. Montagu retained the post of Secretary for India. Both the Geddes brothers held office, Sir Eric as Minister of Transport, Sir Auckland as Minister of Reconstruction. In May the latter succeeded Sir Albert Stanley at the Board of Trade. H. A. L. Fisher remained as President of the Board of Education. As in the case of the previous Government most of the really important places were occupied by Conservatives. This distribution merely reflected the balance of power in the Coalition. Lloyd George was for the moment in a position of great popularity but if for any reason his personal prestige waned, he would find himself and his own supporters perilously dependent on Conservative good will.

The new Ministry received but a lukewarm welcome in the country. Naturally it incurred malignant hostility from the Northcliffe Press but even when allowance is made for this factor, there can be no doubt that many who expected sweeping changes were bitterly disappointed. Of the 77 members of the Government, all but ten

had been members of the previous Administration. Criticism fastened
particularly on the appointment of F. E. Smith who was considered
by many to possess neither the experience nor the character to act as
'keeper of the King's conscience". Churchill's appointment was also
criticized – partly on personal grounds and partly because of the
inking of the War Office and the Air Ministry. Bonar Law's own
position did not, however, cause any adverse comment. There had
already been some suggestion that it was too much for one man to be
Chancellor of the Exchequer, Leader of the House, and a member of
the War Cabinet. His decision to relinquish the first of these posts
was welcomed. It was clear that he must do so if he was to act as
virtual Prime Minister during the lengthy periods of Lloyd George's
absence.

2

Grave though the problems were which lay ahead, Bonar Law,
like everyone else, felt that some relaxation was permissible from the
austere life of wartime. For the last few years work had confined him
almost entirely to London. He now decided for part of 1919 to take a
house on Kingston Hill where the air was supposed to be more
salubrious than in the heart of London. While he was there an episode occurred which might easily have brought his career to an
abrupt end. His younger son, Dick, had reached the age when the
possession of a motor bicycle becomes the dearest ambition of every
youth. Bonar Law duly presented him with one, and took a keen
personal interest in it, for he could never resist new mechanical
gadgets. On one occasion when Sir Auckland Geddes was visiting
him he decided to see if he could ride it himself. He persuaded Geddes
to sit on the pillion and, with his son in the sidecar to give instructions,
he set off down the steep drive which led from his house to the busy
main road. The machine, thus carrying the Lord Privy Seal and the
President of the Board of Trade, was approaching the gate with
gathering momentum when its passengers saw that a steam roller
was proceeding ponderously along the street at precisely the speed
which would ensure a collision, unless drastic action was taken. Unfortunately, although Bonar Law had learned how to start the motor
bicycle, he had not yet mastered the equally important knack of how
to stop it. An accident seemed inevitable, but he averted the worst
by swerving into the gate. Luckily he was still moving fairly slowly
and no damage was done – except to the machine. It was his first
and last venture in the art of riding a motor cycle.

With the advent of peace Bonar Law was able to enjoy his usual forms of relaxation. Early in 1919 we find him once again playing golf and tennis. He resumed his custom of visiting Lord Beaverbrook at Cherkley on most Sundays. In the summer he would come down in his car invariably dressed in white flannels for tennis, often accompanied by his daughter Isabel. He would stay to dinner, play bridge afterwards, often to a late hour and then return to London. He seldom spent the night there unless he had some special reason to do so. Beaverbrook was now devoting himself entirely to the building up of his newspapers. He had acquired a controlling interest in the *Daily Express* early in 1917 but had no time, while the war continued, to supervise its activities at all closely. Now his own resignation from the Ministry of Propaganda, and the end of the war, gave him the necessary leisure. Early in 1919 he launched the *Sunday Express*. Both newspapers achieved striking success in the years that followed although their circulation figures would seem trivial compared with the immense readership which they acquired later.

From this side of Beaverbrook's activities Bonar Law kept firmly aloof. The *Daily Express* vigorously supported the Coalition in the Coupon Election, but the negotiations for its support were conducted by Lloyd George and Churchill. Bonar Law was not even present at their meetings and took no part in their proceedings. Indeed as Beaverbrook himself reveals Bonar Law had little sympathy with his entry into Fleet Street. " 'Go back to politics', was his constant advice," Beaverbrook recalls in his entertaining book, *Politicians and the Press*. Bonar Law always maintained that the ideal of Imperial unity which Beaverbrook sought to promote would be better served if he worked through the orthodox Conservative channels. If he pursued an independent line he would "simply become an imitation Northcliffe".[e]

Holding these views Bonar Law at an early stage declined to exert any influence on the policy of the *Daily Express*. If Beaverbrook positively asked for his guidance he would be ready to help, but he was not prepared to press his own views or to take any initiative in the matter. His position is well summarized in a letter to Austen Chamberlain on June 28th, 1920:[f]

"Beaverbrook, whom I saw yesterday, said to me that he was willing to start a campaign in your support in answer to the malignant attacks of other papers.
"To do this he would require to be coached by you or your department and I said I would gladly see you about it.

"This is not my doing as I have ceased to try to influence him on political subjects, but I think it would be of great importance to help before and at the time the Budget is going through. His line would be that the attacks are all organized by those who object to pay what they ought. . . ."

But, however little pressure Bonar Law might in reality exert on the Beaverbrook Press, most people outside believed that the two men worked hand in glove, and, whenever the *Daily Express* indulged in attacks on Bonar Law's colleagues, he was invariably bombarded with protests. To these he always replied that it was not his business and that he had no power to influence his friend's newspaper policy. No doubt the policy of the *Daily Express* and that of Bonar Law did frequently coincide, but this merely reflected the respect which Beaverbrook undoubtedly had for the sagacity and judgment of Bonar Law.

There are, moreover, many examples of divergence. To take one: Beaverbrook campaigned vigorously during 1919 and 1920 for the imposition of a levy on capital, which would catch some of the immense profits made by armament manufacturers and others during the war. There was much to be said for such a measure, provided that it was a once-and-for-all levy and was imposed immediately. Bonar Law acknowledged the case in its favour, and he was not so fettered by Conservative orthodoxy as to maintain that it was impossible or ruinous for trade, but he came down decisively against it nonetheless. His reason was the perilous precedent that it might set for a confiscatory capital levy as a permanent feature of finance if ever a radical Government was in power. His opposition effectively killed the plan. Again in 1921 the *Daily Express* fought hard in favour of the Irish Treaty, and some people assumed that Bonar Law must have become converted to a far less stubborn attitude on the subject of Ulster. As we shall see, this was not the case, and, although he did not oppose the Treaty in its final form, his views on Ireland were very different from those of Lord Beaverbrook. These occasional divergences, however, in no way spoiled the relations between the two men, and their personal friendship remained as close as it always had been.

Bonar Law continued to reside at Number 11 Downing Street. No great changes occurred in his routine of life while the Parliamentary session was in progress. He saw perhaps rather less of Lloyd George than during the war, not because of any cooling off on the part of the latter, but because foreign affairs kept him away from England for

o

so long. Early in 1919 J. C. Davidson, who had served Bonar Law so well as private secretary, was obliged to go for three months to the Argentine where he had substantial property to look after. He procured as a substitute Colonel Ronald Waterhouse, a regular soldier who had been serving as private secretary to the Chief of the Air Staff, Major-General Sykes. Waterhouse continued to act as an additional secretary after Davidson's return. In November 1920 Davidson entered the House of Commons, winning a by-election at Hemel Hempstead, and Waterhouse became Bonar Law's principal private secretary. He was not a very happy choice. He possessed, no doubt, the virtues of assiduity and persistence, but he was indifferent at paper work, and wrote in a convoluted style which on occasions is so stilted as to be scarcely comprehensible. Moreover, he seems to have been intensely ambitious – not perhaps the most desirable qualification for a private secretary. He inspired little trust in the members of Bonar Law's family or his immediate entourage. The surprising fact about Waterhouse's appointment is that Bonar Law personally rather disliked him, and indeed said on one occasion that he did not care to have him in the same room. It is perhaps comprehensible that he tolerated the new secretary till March 1921 for the brief remainder of his time in office as Lord Privy Seal, but it is certainly strange that he should have asked for his services again on becoming Prime Minister eighteen months later.

Another – and much more satisfactory – addition to Bonar Law's secretariat was Mr. (now Sir Geoffrey) Fry. He had served under Bonar Law in the Treasury as a member of its celebrated "A" Division headed by Keynes. He now became an unpaid private secretary to Bonar Law for the remainder of the latter's political career. During Bonar Law's brief Premiership he dealt with the problems of patronage, civil and ecclesiastical, though his activities were by no means confined to this sphere. He performed similar functions for Stanley Baldwin after Bonar Law resigned the Premiership.

3

Three major problems faced the Government at the beginning of 1919, the peace treaties, industrial unrest, and Ireland. Of these three the first was the most urgent and the most difficult. Bonar Law's part in it was essentially a minor one. He was, it is true, one of the British delegates at the Peace Conference, the others being Lloyd George, Balfour, and Barnes, but in practice negotiation was left almost exclusively in the hands of Lloyd George and Balfour. Bonar Law was of course kept informed of their progress and from time to time flew to Paris when his presence was needed for deciding certain major issues. He was one of those who signed on Britain's behalf at the imposing ceremony in the Galerie des Glaces at Versailles on June 28th. It was characteristic of him that, to the subsequent indignation of his family, he gave the pen with which he signed to the pilot of his plane as a souvenir. But the credit or otherwise of the British achievement in Paris belongs above all to Lloyd George. Bonar Law's principal task was to deal with the House of Commons which, as the peace negotiations dragged on, became ever more impatient for results and ever more suspicious lest undue leniency on the part of the Prime Minister might mitigate the severity of the punishment which Germany was held to deserve.

The most intractable of all the questions which vexed the peace delegation was undoubtedly that of reparations. On no subject, except hanging the Kaiser – and the sturdy legalism of the Dutch soon rendered this merely academic – were passions more furious. On no subject could the Press provoke greater mass indignation. On no subject did even experts talk more unmitigated nonsense. Bonar Law played a rather more important part in this side of the peace negotiations than he did in the purely political discussions. It is as well to state what his views were.

Like Lloyd George he was entirely sceptical about the more extravagant figures which were being freely mooted at the end of the war. He had in the autumn of 1918 set up a Treasury committee under the auspices of Keynes to investigate Germany's capacity to pay. The committee thought that this might reach as much as £3,000 million, but that the Allies would be more prudent to reckon on £2,000 million. As to methods of payment the committee discussed two alternatives: (i) a ruthless levying of the maximum obtainable over the next three years to be followed by a relatively small tribute in the future; or (ii) a less ruthless immediate levy, and, instead, a substantial tribute over a long term of years. They reckoned under (i) that something over £1,000 million might be obtained in the course of three years, and, according to Lloyd George, this was the course recommended by Keynes's committee.[1]

Meanwhile, Lloyd George decided to appoint a really authoritative committee containing distinguished names in order to report to

---

[1] See *Truth about the Peace Treaties*, Vol. I, p. 455, where extracts from the Treasury memorandum are quoted.

the Government on the whole reparations question. He says in his memoirs (*Truth about the Peace Treaties*, Vol. I, p. 458) that he hoped thus to obtain "an authoritative report that would damp down the too fierce anticipations of an expectant public". Unfortunately he got nothing of the sort. The committee presided over by "Billy" Hughes, the Prime Minister of Australia, and containing among others Walter Long, Lord Cunliffe, Herbert Gibbs, who was a leading banker, and the economist W. A. S. Hewins, produced a report which was calculated to inflame the hopes of the ignorant public to an absurd degree. The report assessed the bill for damages at £24,000 million and considered that there would be no real difficulty in extracting this enormous sum.

"Mr. Bonar Law and I", writes Lloyd George, "regarded the conclusions of this Report as a wild and fantastic chimera . . . I was repelled and shocked by the extreme absurdity of this document. In view of the election then proceeding I decided not to publish it. It would be foolish to excite insane hopes that the enemy would shoulder the whole or even a substantial proportion of our heavy War burdens. Mr. Bonar Law was emphatically of the same opinion. As Chancellor of the Exchequer he did not want to be confronted with the statement that he had, like the French Finance Minister, misled the tax payer into the comfortable belief that Germany would pay."

In fact Bonar Law was most careful during the Election to discourage the idea that Germany could pay for the whole cost of the war. Like all political leaders of the day, including Asquith and Henderson, Bonar Law thought and said that, morally, the Allies had a right to claim every penny, but he never for a moment either believed or declared that such a right could in practice be enforced. In a speech at Mile End he stated that the task of the Allied experts would be

"to examine this question with precisely the same amount of scientific skill and energy, as an accountant examining the books of a bankrupt to find out how much he could pay his creditors. . . ."

"Whatever amount we get, it would be holding out a hope, the fulfilment of which I cannot conceive, to suggest that Germany could pay our whole war debt. Whatever amount we get, the burden upon this country will only be met, in my opinion, by something in the nature of a different way of living and reduced expenditure."

But the truth was that the political pressures under which the Allied statesmen had to work were such that a really sensible solution to the reparations problem was almost unobtainable. Keynes, who resigned his post in disgust, published at the end of 1919 *The Economic*

Consequences of the Peace – a masterpiece which will long live in the annals of literature and polemic. His case against the economic clauses of the Treaty is devastating and unanswerable. But he is far less convincing on the political aspects of the Treaty. He is, moreover, less than just in his treatment of the characters and motives of those who made the Treaty. Never a politician himself, indeed highly contemptuous of the whole breed, he does not allow sufficiently for the formidable difficulties that lay in the way of Lloyd George and his colleagues. Carried away by his own brilliant argument, he seems at times to forget that politics is in the last resort the art of the possible. His description of the Treaty and its makers cannot be regarded as a final verdict – nor, it is fair to add, was this Keynes's intention.

As far as the British were concerned the political difficulties can be divided into two categories – foreign and domestic. In the former came the problem of agreement with France. It must never be forgotten that the whole of France was obsessed by a passionate desire to exact the uttermost farthing from Germany, and a deep conviction that only the ruthless imposition of crippling peace-terms would prevent the revival of their enemy. Clemenceau, whom Keynes depicts as the embodiment of this avid spirit of implacable hate, was in reality widely suspected in France of being far too lenient. His position was the object of constant innuendo and intrigue on the part of Poincaré, the President, and of open hostility from Marshal Foch. At the end of the year he was to be rejected for the Presidency because he had not been sufficiently rigorous towards Germany. Lloyd George had to reckon on the high probability that, if he forced Clemenceau into resignation, any alternative French Government would be – not more liberal – rather, more narrowly rigorous, more determined than ever to insist on reparation clauses wholly impossible of fulfilment.

Then there was the home front to consider. It is not true, as we have already seen, that Lloyd George or Bonar Law were bound by election pledges to insist upon impossible terms. But it is true that many – perhaps a majority – of their supporters in the House of Commons had made wildly imprudent promises. It is true that the British public was in general wholly ignorant of those economic facts of life which render impracticable the payment of gigantic indemnities by one country to another. It is also true that no Prime Minister could have survived a day if he had submitted to the House of Commons as a final figure for reparations even the highest sum that was

actually within Germany's power to pay. These errors and delusions
under which the public laboured were carefully fostered by Northcliffe's papers as part of his vendetta against Lloyd George and Bonar
Law, and were presented daily with all the persuasiveness of skilled
journalism. In the House of Commons, Northcliffe's satellite, Kennedy Jones, assiduously repeated the same absurdities and soon
started a highly successful whispering campaign to the effect that
Lloyd George, through weakness and subserviency to President Wilson,
intended to betray the just demands of the British and French nations
for a severe and rigorous peace treaty.

Towards the end of March trouble flared into the open. Colonel
Claude Lowther, M.P., circulated a memorandum to all Members of
Parliament in which he claimed that Germany could easily pay the
£25,000 million which he reckoned as the cost of the war. Bonar
Law asked Keynes to produce a "light and airy" criticism of
Lowther's arguments, which were exceptionally ludicrous even by
the standards of the school of thought to which he belonged. Keynes
did so, demonstrating by exactly parallel arguments how if Colonel
Lowther had £5,000 p.a. it would be possible for the Chancellor of
the Exchequer to obtain a million pounds from him. He added this
cautionary note:[g]

"The only flaw I can see is that he *may* for all I know be easily able to
pay a million. If so, please cook up the figures to taste."

In his reply to a debate initiated by Lowther on April 2nd, Bonar
Law observed that Colonel Lowther had quoted from an election
speech of Lloyd George:

"The one part he did not mention was the part which was the basis, I
believe, of all the Prime Minister's speeches, and that was not that he
would make Germany pay the whole cost of the War but that we would
exact from Germany whatever Germany was able to pay. Every time this
subject has been raised I have had the feeling that I am more out of
sympathy with Members, who support the Government, on this subject
than on any other that has been raised. If that is due to any real difference
of opinion it cannot be helped because everything I have said in this
House is precisely what I have said during the Election. I have not
changed my view."

And Bonar Law went on to quote from his own speech at Mile
End, to which reference has been made above. He begged members
not to adhere to the "curious idea that if you have doubt about
arithmetical figures you are friendly to the Boche". He urged them
to believe that the Government had precisely the same ends in mind
as their supporters in the House. He ended:

"If we cannot come to the same conclusions it is simply because our minds will not allow us. . . . I remember reading in one of Carlyle's works, I forget which, he was describing a very bitter controversy about something – I think it was probably religion – and he said the protagonists were shouting at each other, 'God confound you for your theory of irregular verbs'. In this matter there is no difference of principle and I hope my Friends neither outwardly nor in their hearts will be inclined to say, 'God confound you and your rotten arithmetic'."

But Bonar Law was under no delusion that he had quelled the storm. As he wrote a day later to the Prime Minister:[h]

"I had a bad time about indemnities last night. I do not think I convinced anyone and probably nine out of ten, of the Unionist Members at least, were very disgusted."

He was right. A few days later Kennedy Jones forwarded in a telegram to Lloyd George in Paris a round robin from 370 M.P.s urging him to stand firm on the question of making Germany pay for the war. Even before this telegram arrived Lloyd George had been veering round to the view that the only solution, which was politically feasible and which offered any hope of common sense ultimately prevailing, would be to name no definite total figure in the reparations clause. The peace treaty would simply contain a general statement of Germany's liability to pay for the war, but the actual figure would be left for subsequent assessment by a Permanent Reparations Commission. The Kennedy Jones telegram convinced him that this was the best solution. It also convinced him that serious trouble impended at home. He returned to England and vigorously defended his conduct of negotiations before the House on April 16th. Lloyd George always believed that attack was the best form of defence, and his speech was memorable for his invective against Northcliffe. He did not refer to that great newspaper owner by name but everyone knew whom he meant when he castigated Kennedy Jones for using information from "a reliable source".

"Reliable! That is the last adjective I would use. It is here today, jumping there tomorrow, and there the next day. I would as soon rely on a grasshopper."

He then referred to Northcliffe's "ridiculous expectations", "diseased vanity", "black crime against humanity". He regretted that *The Times* was still believed in France to be a serious organ. "They do not know that it is merely a threepenny edition of the *Daily Mail*."

It was one of Lloyd George's most brilliant performances and for the time being disarmed criticism. But it was clear from the tone of the House of Commons that the Government could not afford to appear to err towards leniency in the peace negotiations. Keynes many years later referred with asperity in a review of Winston Churchill's *Aftermath* to the alleged way in which political leaders shrugged their shoulders at the Peace Treaty and consoled themselves with the reflection that nothing could be done about it anyway.

". . . the doctrine that statesmen must always act contrary to their convictions, when to do otherwise would lose them office, implies that they are less easily replaceable than is really the case. I believed then, and believe now, that it was a situation where an investment in political courage would have been marvellously repaid in the end."i

This is to ignore the political realities of the time. Neither Lloyd George nor Bonar Law had delusions about being irreplaceable, but they also had no delusions as to the sort of influences that would replace them. Suppose Clemenceau and Lloyd George had vanished from the political scene, who would have ruled in their place? In France a Government dominated by Poincaré and the extreme Right. In England one that was obedient to the whims of Northcliffe and Kennedy Jones. And would a peace concluded under such auspices have been more just than the Versailles settlement? It is a delusion to suppose that an effective alternative administration composed of high-minded Liberals existed even in England. It certainly did not in France.

4

And, after all, was the final settlement really so iniquitous? In the end no figure for reparations was inserted. Germany was declared responsible for all the loss and damage in the war, but it was recognized that she could not pay this in full. She was, however, obliged to promise "to make compensation for all damage done to the civilian population of the Allied powers and to their property". This was to be assessed in two years time by a Reparations Commission upon which Britain, France, America, Italy and Belgium would be represented. Lloyd George hoped that the delay would give time for passions to cool and for the inflated post-war prices to come down. He also expected that the chairmanship of the Commission would go to America, and that Britain, Italy and America holding a majority would prevent the French from pushing their claims too far. The Commission had wide powers to vary the method of payment and postpone dates. It could not however let Germany off any part of her obligations, as finally assessed, except with the permission of the several Governments represented. Meanwhile, Germany was to pay, on account as it were, £1,000 million over the next two years.

The indefiniteness of Germany's obligation was undoubtedly a grave defect rightly condemned by Keynes, but it was perhaps preferable to a definite sum of enormous magnitude which was the only practical alternative. The obligation to pay £1,000 million in two years has also been very severely criticized, especially by Keynes, but it is not, in fact, so very different from the calculation of the Treasury committee which he himself headed in autumn 1918. That committee considered that over the course of three years a sum of more than £1,000 million but less than £2,000 million could by drastic methods be extracted. Perhaps Keynes had changed his mind on reflection, but the figure which he now attacked so vigorously does not seem outrageous, assuming that the original Treasury estimate was reasonable.

It is no part of this book to deal with the general criticisms of the Peace Treaties – only to consider them so far as they concerned Bonar Law. There are other and graver charges against the final settlement, especially against the claim put forward successfully by General Smuts to include in civilian damage the cost of war pensions and separation allowances – a claim which trebled the total bill ultimately presented to Germany. Bonar Law did not worry about this, because, like Lloyd George, he hoped that the Reparations Commission would interpret its functions in a liberal fashion despite the clauses of the Treaty. Unfortunately – and this, rather than the economic clauses, was the real disaster – the Americans withdrew completely as a corollary of their refusal to ratify the Treaty. Accordingly the French claimed the chairmanship and hence a casting vote which, since Belgium was for these purposes a French pocket borough, ensured them a perpetual majority. As the first chairman was Poincaré it was inevitable that the Commission should interpret every dubious clause or discretionary power in the most harsh and exacting spirit. Lloyd George and Bonar Law can scarcely be blamed for failing to foresee the future in this respect.

The Treaty, which was finally signed on June 28th, had a good reception in England and the Prime Minister reached a high point in popularity and prestige. Bonar Law regarded his colleague's achievement with deep admiration. It was therefore with alacrity that he agreed to a suggestion from the King that Lloyd George should receive some signal honour or reward. The difficulty was to decide what this should be. Lord Stamfordham suggested the Garter or a Pension.[j] Bonar Law consulted Balfour, who pointed out that Lloyd George was entitled under the existing law to draw a pension of £2,000 but that this would involve no special distinction. A higher pension would need legislation and this might be embarrassing since the Liberal Party had set their faces against such pensions and "have played up to one of the small prejudices of democracy, which is in favour of the underpayment of their public men. In my opinion this is greatly to be regretted, but it is the fact".[k]

As for the Garter, Balfour saw no objection except that it was technically given on the advice of the Prime Minister,[1] and this might be rather awkward in the circumstances. He added a further difficulty – "That if we once begin giving the Garter for merit, irrespective of rank, the troubles of future Prime Ministers in recommending for that honour will be greatly increased!" Bonar Law decided against either of these courses and suggested to Lord Stamfordham that the Order of Merit might be the most appropriate honour since it was given entirely on the King's own initiative and not on ministerial advice.[l] There was a minor difficulty because the rules governing this particular honour seemed to preclude its award for political service, but in the end this was disregarded, and, on August 5th, Lloyd George received the Order of Merit.

---

[1] This is no longer true. Since 1946 the Orders of the Garter and Thistle have been the Sovereign's personal gift.

CHAPTER XXVI

AFTERMATH OF WAR

1919–MARCH 1921

Labour unrest – Bonar Law's detached and impartial attitude – Character of the new Parliament – Bonar Law and the Triple Alliance – His determination and courage – His support of Lloyd George – The Coalition in the doldrums – Suggestions for "fusion" – Balfour's draft letter – Unexpected snags – Opposition of Coalition Liberals – Bonar Law's relief – Sagacious observations by Lord Derby – Ireland and the Election – Sinn Fein in control – Irish Home Rule Bill of 1920 – Asquith's attack – Notable speech in defence by Bonar Law – The "Black and Tans" – Bonar Law's elder daughter marries – Bonar Law and the problem of unemployment – His busy life – He defends the Government for dismissing General Dyer – His low opinion of Edwin Montagu – He defeats Professor Gilbert Murray for the Lord Rectorship of Glasgow University – His Rectorial Address

I

DURING all these months and indeed for much of the remainder of the year Lloyd George's absence abroad left Bonar Law in virtual charge of domestic affairs. It was a period marked by much labour unrest and by frequent strikes. Looking back on it from the vantage point of thirty-five years we can see that the trouble was largely caused by post-war readjustment, and by the adverse effect of the war upon the purchasing power of money. At the time, however, it seemed due to more sinister influences, and there were many who saw in this unrest the prelude to far reaching, perhaps revolutionary, upheavals in society. The Bolshevik revolution in Russia with its aggressive ideology and its appeal to the working classes of the world appeared to be the hidden cause behind these alarming manifestations.

Bonar Law regarded much of this apprehension as mere alarmism. He was well aware of the grave threat which protracted strikes offered to the national economy, but he was well aware too of the grievances which lay behind the strikers' demands. He saw that it was not enough to attribute every working class demand to the subversive influence of Bolshevism. A story, perhaps apocryphal, but certainly characteristic, is told of Bonar Law at about this time. He was dining after addressing a political meeting in the country. His hostess referring to the strikers said, "Now do tell me, Mr. Bonar Law, what do these people really want?" Bonar Law looked at the table with its glittering load of glass and silver, at the portraits on the walls, at the silently efficient servants. "Perhaps", he said in his soft voice, "they want just a little of all this."[a]

It was fortunate that Bonar Law, a business man himself and leader of the party which its enemies accused of being the party of big business, should have held reasonably liberal views on the question of labour. Many of his supporters were of a very different persuasion. Everyone has heard of the famous description of the 1919 Parliament as "hard faced men who look as if they have done well out of the war" – a phrase sometimes attributed to Keynes and sometimes to Baldwin. J. C. Davidson on entering Parliament in November 1920 referred in a letter to Lord Stamfordham to "the high percentage of hard headed men, mostly on the make, who fill up the ranks of the Unionist Party. The old-fashioned country gentlemen, and even the higher ranks of the learned professions, are scarcely represented at all".[b] Asquith who returned to Parliament at a by-election early in 1920 always maintained that it was the worst Parliament he ever knew. These opinions are not of course final or conclusive, but there is plenty of contemporary evidence that the Coupon Election had produced a very different – and in some ways less satisfactory – House than anything in recent times. The change even struck Lloyd George himself who observed on one occasion that it was no longer the House of Commons that he was addressing, but the Associated Chambers of Commerce on one side and the T.U.C. on the other.

It certainly seems clear that a large number of M.P.s owed their prosperity to the war-time profits of business. They had not of course done anything illegal or corrupt, but their presence as supporters of the Government, at a time when profiteering was generally stigmatized as morally reprehensible, tended both to lower public esteem for the Government and to exacerbate class bitterness. Had they been led by anyone of the same rather narrow employers' outlook as themselves, the situation in 1919 and 1920 might well have been far more unpleasant than it actually was.

The first big crisis in industrial relations arose early in 1919. The railwaymen, miners and transport workers – the Triple Alliance as they came to be known – all put forward demands for higher wages and shorter working hours. The Government, having taken over responsibility for the railways and mines, was at once involved in the dispute with the first two of these groups. It was also involved in the other dispute, since the fulfilment of the trade unionists' demands involved legislation. There was, indeed, already in existence a Royal Commission presided over by Lord Justice Sankey, investigating the whole position of coal mines in Britain. Towards the middle of March a crisis seemed imminent, and, in Lloyd George's absence Bonar Law had to deal with it. The details of the negotiations have little interest today, but the memorandum which Bonar Law sent to Lloyd George deserves a few extracts:[c]

"We are having a Cabinet at 6 p.m. and what I propose if the Cabinet approve is to make a statement to the House as soon as possible on the general situation.

"As regards transport workers negotiations under the direction of the Minister of Labour have been going on, and the employers have made offers which seem to me reasonable and will I hope be accepted.

"As regards railways I hope to have a statement which will enable me to say, in effect, what the demands of the men are: give some idea of what the cost would be, and state what we have offered, which means an addition which cannot be estimated but may be as much as £15,000,000. . . .

"As regards the miners I shall give the substance of the three reports (coal owners', miners' and the Chairman's) and shall say that the Government intend to adopt Sankey's Report and to take all the necessary steps to carry it out without delay.

"As regards nationalization I shall give extracts showing that no one expected it to be decided now. . . . I am to see Sankey at 4 o'clock today and I propose to say to the House that I have his authority for stating that he would be prepared to give a report on nationalization within a given time, say 2 months.

"I shall then add that both miners and railwaymen are servants not of employers but of the State: that a strike would be against the State and that the State must win and must use all its power for that purpose, otherwise it would be the end of Government in this country. . . ."

Bonar Law then declared that he was prepared if a strike broke out to pass legislation empowering the Government to seize strike funds and arrest the leaders.

He ended:

"It is quite possible that your absence may be criticized and we may be asked whether there is anyone who is empowered to act with the authority of the Prime Minister in an emergency. I propose to say that I have full authority from you to act in that way and shall so act."

Bonar Law's tendency to efface himself and seek the shadows rather than the spotlights of political life has sometimes given him the reputation of indecisiveness and procrastination. The words of this document show that such a notion is far from correct. It is not the language of a man who feared responsibility or was reluctant to act. In the event no strike took place. Bonar Law's offers were accepted for the time being. The labour crisis temporarily disappeared and a serious threat to the national economy at a particularly bad time was averted. Bonar Law received many congratulatory letters after his speech in the House of March 20th. The King sent a particularly cordial message, and Lloyd George wrote from Paris:[d]

"I must once more congratulate on the extreme skill and success with which you handled the industrial situation. As you say I have no doubt there are plenty of troubles ahead of us [this was one of Bonar Law's favourite expressions] but it is very satisfactory to know that you have overcome the worst of them in England and I shall be very happy were I able to do so well with my troubles here."

This was by no means the end of industrial disputes during the Coalition Government, but it was perhaps the most serious crisis which Bonar Law had to deal with personally. The general prosperity of the country remained at a high level till the end of 1920. In December of that year unemployment figures suddenly climbed from the figure of about 300,000 to 700,000. By March 1921 they reached 1,300,000. In June they were over two million. The slump that thus convulsed English industrial life did not seriously affect Bonar Law's political career. He had resigned from the Government through ill health, within three months of the breaking of the post-war boom.

It might be reasonable to suppose that Bonar Law's role on the home front would have become less important with the conclusion of the Paris negotiations. In fact, however, Lloyd George continued to leave much to his colleague. It was not until November 13th that he appeared at question time in the House of Commons for the first time since the formation of the Government. He did indeed revert formally to a more orthodox machinery of government, and in October 1919 set up a fully representative Cabinet on peace time lines, but foreign affairs continued to absorb his attention. By the beginning of 1920 he was the sole survivor in politics of the Big Four who had made the Peace Treaty. This gave him a prestige which he did not fail to exploit. The affairs of Europe were still in chaos. In those optimistic days it was still believed that meetings of Prime Ministers or Heads of State were the panacea for all political ills. Now after thirty-five years of disillusionment we realize that this remedy may be more perilous than the disease, but no such gloomy forebodings bothered Lloyd George. Travelling in his special train from conference to conference, attended by an imposing retinue of friends, secretaries, and satellites, the Prime Minister seemed the very incarnation of the new diplomacy. Those who applauded his glittering progresses through the capitals of Europe gave little thought to the grey and colourless figure who hovered in the background. But Lloyd George did not forget – at least in his more reflective moments – how much he depended upon this faithful lieutenant for the political support at home, without which all this splendour would soon have been seen as the insubstantial pageant that perhaps it really was.

2

At the beginning of 1920 the Coalition Government was becoming less popular. By-elections had, indeed, gone adversely all through 1919, and early in the New Year two redoubtable opponents made their way back into Parliament. At Spen Valley Sir John Simon was victorious. At Paisley Asquith defeated the Labour candidate by 3,000 votes while the Conservative Coalitionist who had received a letter of support from Bonar Law – though not from Lloyd George – actually lost his deposit. Nor was the House of Commons always easy to manage. A huge majority is never very ready to accept party discipline. On one occasion in October 1919 the Government actually sustained a defeat – on a relatively unimportant amendment to the Aliens' Bill. It required all Bonar Law's tact as leader to induce the House to reverse this decision a few days later.

The adverse trend of by-elections, the general lack of co-operation between Conservatives and Coalition Liberals in the constituencies, suggested to both Bonar Law and Lloyd George the possibility of formally uniting the two parties. Early in 1920 there were widespread rumours that "fusion", as it was called, would soon be announced. Had anything come of these proposals the course of English political history might have been very different. There were many powerful figures who supported the plan. Churchill on the Liberal side, Birkenhead, Austen Chamberlain and Balfour on the Conservative side, all in varying degrees favoured some such union. It had obvious advantages for Lloyd George since it would open the way for him to secure what at the moment was the weapon that his armoury most lacked – control over a properly organized party machine and adequate party funds.

The whole question was brought to a head early in March 1920. A by-election impended at Stockport, and Lord Salisbury wrote a letter advising the local Conservative association not to support the

Coalition Liberal candidate. This episode seemed a striking example of the difficulties which would constantly arise until co-operation between the parties in Parliament was reinforced by a corresponding co-operation in the constituencies. Bonar Law and Lloyd George agreed that a real amalgamation between their respective parties was desirable, if it could be attained. Bonar Law was not, indeed, as enthusiastic as Lloyd George and accepted the idea as a disagreeable necessity rather than as a boon in itself. Meanwhile, on March 2nd, further pressure was brought on the two leaders in the form of a round robin from ninety-five M.P.s, forwarded by Captain Colin Coote, stating:

"that this group believing in the National necessity for the Coalition expresses the hope that it may develop into a Single United Party."

On March 10th Balfour submitted to Bonar Law the draft of a letter which he proposed to write to Lord Aldenham, the chairman of the Conservative Committee in the City of London, Balfour's constituency. The letter was intended for publication and was a vigorous exposition of the case for amalgamating the Coalition Liberal and the Conservative organizations.[e]

Bonar Law showed it to the Prime Minister, and they agreed that Lloyd George should sound out opinion among the Coalition Liberal Ministers. If it was favourable he would take the opportunity of hinting at the need for some degree of amalgamation when he addressed the Coalition Liberal M.P.s the following week. Bonar Law would throw out a similar hint at a meeting at which he was billed to speak a day later. But this plan ran into a wholly unexpected snag. Lloyd George found that the Coalition Liberal Ministers were far from favourable to the proposed fusion and on the contrary attached great importance to retaining the name of "Liberal". This attitude was surprising since they were, on the face of things, the very people who would gain most by the proposed change, but, however surprising, it was a fact to be reckoned with.

On March 24th Bonar Law wrote to Balfour an account of what had happened:[f]

"L.G. first of all met his Liberal Ministers and he found that they were much more frightened at the idea of losing their identity as Liberals than he had expected. In consequence when he met the Coalition Liberals as a whole he spoke only of the need for closer co-operation. . . . The result of this will probably be not to attempt any real fusion of the Parties but to get co-operation, something on the lines of the Liberal Unionists and Conservatives in the early days. This will be very difficult to arrange and will certainly not be efficient but personally I am not sorry at the turn events have taken.

"I do not like the idea of complete fusion if it can be avoided, but I had come to think, as you had also, that it was really inevitable if the Coalition were to continue. But it always seemed to me more important from L.G.'s point of view than from ours. As a Party we were losing nothing and, since the necessity of going slowly in the matter has come from L.G.'s own friends, I do not regret it. . . ."

Balfour's letter was, accordingly, never published. Bonar Law wrote on similar lines to Derby who, though Ambassador in Paris, took a keen interest then as always in the machinery of politics. Derby favoured "fusion", but he had shrewdly warned Bonar Law earlier that, unless it came at once, it would never come at all. He replied to Bonar Law's letter:g

"I quite understand now what the position is. This fuss in the Press undoubtedly will give you more trouble in bringing about a fusion than would otherwise have occurred, and holiday time is always a bad time as it is then when intrigues are got up. . . ."

In the end fusion was dropped. The reluctance of the Liberal Ministers postponed a decision, and postponement was in this case tantamount to rejection. As time went by, amalgamation became more and more difficult. The chance that the Liberals threw away in 1920 never recurred. Though they little realized it at the time, their political doom had been sealed – and, with theirs, that of the greatest of them all, Lloyd George himself.

3

No account of Bonar Law's career during these years would be complete without some reference, however brief, to events in Ireland. For the war had brought no solution to the problems of that unhappy land. Indeed it had only served to exacerbate the furious hatreds which had for so long poisoned the politics of the Emerald Isle. In a famous passage during one of his speeches on the Irish Free State Bill, early in 1922, Winston Churchill described the extraordinary persistency of the Irish feud.

"The mode and thought of men, the whole outlook on affairs, the grouping of parties, all have encountered violent and tremendous changes in the deluge of the world, but as the deluge subsides and the waters fall we see the dreary steeples of Fermanagh and Tyrone emerging once again."

An attempt had been made during 1917 to secure some basis of agreement between North and South, but the Convention appointed for that purpose achieved nothing. At the General Election of 1918 a new and disagreeable change in the character of Irish nationalism became manifest. The old Irish Nationalist Party, which, whatever its faults, at least stood for Home Rule within the Empire, was obliterated for ever. Instead there were returned 73 Sinn Feiners who repudiated the British allegiance and aimed at establishing an independent republic. They refused to take their seats at Westminster – thus missing another splendid opportunity of convulsing British Parliamentary life – and declared themselves the legitimate government of Ireland. Early in 1919 the extremists of the Party, a group of desperadoes and fanatics, began a campaign of arson and murder which grew steadily worse as the year went on, culminating with an attempt – nearly successful – at assassinating Lord French, the Viceroy. The Government of Ireland endeavoured to meet these tactics by the ordinary legal methods but had little or no success.

Bonar Law's attitude to these events was by no means one of blind resistance to nationalist aspirations. He had agreed with Lloyd George that the presence of the Home Rule Bill on the statute book made the preservation of the Union morally impossible. As long as Ulster was safeguarded from coercion he was prepared to agree to a substantial measure of Home Rule for the rest of Ireland. Meanwhile, he was determined to uphold law and order in Ireland. "For the present", he wrote on September 14th, 1919, in reply to a letter from Lord Stamfordham, "the policy of His Majesty's Government must be what it has been throughout – of supporting the Irish Government in taking whatever measures they think necessary to secure orderly government in Ireland."[h]

Throughout 1919 a Cabinet committee headed by Walter Long was busy preparing a new Irish Home Rule Bill. On March 30th, 1920, it received its Second Reading in the House of Commons. It fell to Bonar Law to reply to Asquith's attack upon the new measure. By common consent this was one of Bonar Law's finest Parliamentary performances. He sat listening to Asquith, his head thrown back, eyes riveted on the ceiling. Then he rose immediately afterwards and speaking for forty-five minutes without a single note dealt point by point with Asquith's speech. He received a great ovation at the end.

The new Bill created separate Home Rule Parliaments for Ulster and the South. It provided for the creation of an all-Ireland Council to which, if the two Parliaments could ever agree, almost complete Dominion powers might be assigned. It remains to this day the legal basis of the Government in Northern Ireland. But in the South the measure, which might well have been accepted ten years earlier, was blown aside with contempt – such was the changed temper of Irish nationalism. Although the Bill became law in December 1920 it was never put into operation in Southern Ireland.

Meanwhile, the British Government at last decided in favour of drastic measures against the Sinn Feiners. In April 1920 Sir Hamar Greenwood was appointed Irish Secretary. A man of great courage, clear-headedness, and determination, he saw at once that the existing methods of enforcing order were inadequate. He proceeded to recruit during the summer additional armed constabulary to reinforce the numbers in Ireland. They soon began to turn the tables on Sinn Fein. In the course of doing so they were driven to take reprisals and adopt many of the same methods as their enemies. This policy provoked much grave moral censure from high-minded persons in England. But it was effective. By the end of 1920, thanks to the "Black and Tans", the tide had begun to turn against the terrorist campaign.

In the spring of 1920 an important domestic event occurred in Bonar Law's life. For some time past on his visits to Cherkley he had been accompanied by his eldest daughter. Recently General Sir Frederick Sykes, formerly Chief of Air Staff and now the Controller of Civil Aviation, who was a friend of Beaverbrook, had been in the habit of going there too whenever Isabel Law was present. To everyone except Bonar Law it was quite clear what impended. At last Beaverbrook decided that it was time to enlighten Bonar Law. When he did so it was with that vigorous directness for which he is so well known. "Bonar," he said one day, "Sykes is after Isabel." Bonar Law – and this is a not uncommon failing among fathers – remained incredulous. Nevertheless, he thought that he ought to find out. His enquiry was anticipated by his daughter who, the same evening, told him that it was indeed true that she had become engaged to General Sykes. "Oh, Isabel", was the reply, "how could you, when you knew I was so worried about Ireland!" That evening he telephoned Beaverbrook who recalls his opening words:[i]

"Max, a dreadful thing has happened . . ."

However, this perturbation did not last for long and was in no way due to any disapproval of his future son-in-law. On the contrary Bonar Law had long been friendly with Sir Frederick Sykes, and treated him from then onwards as if he had been his own son. His alarm was caused by the prospect of losing a daughter to whom he was deeply devoted, and on whom he had come to rely for much of his domestic happiness. The wedding took place at St. Columba's, Pont Street, on June 3rd. The day before, a presentation of plate was made by the Speaker to Miss Law on behalf of 600 M.P.s. It was not only a tribute to her own popularity, it was also a sign of the respect and affection with which her father was regarded by members of all political parties.

The remainder of 1920 was dominated by the Irish question, which we have already discussed, and by continued labour troubles. In the latter Bonar Law played an active part as mediator. As has been seen, his views on labour were by no means those traditionally associated with the business man. Indeed one of Bonar Law's greatest assets was his ability to get on well with Trade Union leaders. This was largely because of his candid acknowledgement of the force of some of their arguments. Bonar Law never gave the impression of being impervious to their case even when it appeared to undermine the whole basis of the capitalist system. True, he did not agree with them, and never left any doubt about his own views, but the very fact that he would discuss the most revolutionary suggestion and appear to consider it purely on its merits without reference to traditional prejudice or political doctrine made him personally more liked and trusted than many Ministers who were in fact prepared to concede far more.

Bonar Law's days, like those of all political leaders in modern times, were filled with a constant round of pressing problems which required instant answers. As Leader of the House he had to deal with almost every variety of Government business – appointments, answers to questions, replies to debates, Cabinet meetings. Profound thought about long-term issues of policy was almost impossible. He was perhaps the busiest minister in the Cabinet. He seldom took a holiday. Even the newspapers began during the summer of 1920 to comment on the tiredness of his appearance, and it was perhaps a symptom of the same trouble that there were repeated complaints in the Press gallery of his inaudibility in the House of Commons. Fatigue did not however lead to irritability or testiness. Bonar Law continued to excite admiration by his smooth and masterly handling of the House.

In July 1920 there occurred an episode which tried his powers to the full. General Dyer, who commanded a brigade near Amritsar in the Punjab, had in April 1919 suppressed riots there with a degree of ruthlessness which was regarded as quite incompatible with the proper attitude of a British soldier towards the Indian population.

Dyer openly declared that his purpose in ordering his men to fire long after the danger of riot was over had been to strike terror by this example all over India. He was censured by Sir Charles Monro, the Commander-in-Chief, and removed from his command. Monro's action was upheld by E. S. Montagu, the Secretary for India. Montagu had long been suspected by many Conservatives as dangerously pro-Indian in his political views, and there were some who openly declared that this could be explained by Montagu's own racial antecedents. The debate on the case of General Dyer was characterized by great acrimony. Carson led the opposition and hinted that Dyer was being sacrificed as a scapegoat. A speech from Churchill in defence of Montagu did nothing to allay the fury of the High Tories. Even Bonar Law had some difficulty in carrying opinion with him but eventually he succeeded in doing so. He expressed every sympathy with General Dyer but said: "I hold that General Dyer's action was wrong and the Government is bound to declare that it was wrong." Although Bonar Law had thus as in duty bound rallied to the defence of Edwin Montagu, his private opinion of the Secretary for India was not high. Three months earlier he had written to Lloyd George a letter, whose precise context is not quite clear, but which evidently refers to the Dyer case:[j]

"I saw Max yesterday. E.M. is going to do nothing. With all his cleverness he has evidently some of the poorest qualities of his race."

Montagu had by now inspired the implacable animosity of the greater part of the Conservative Party. It was with something like a howl of delight that they were able to wreak their vengeance upon him two years later.

Public men sooner or later cannot escape – if they are sufficiently eminent – the ordeal of academic honours being thrust upon them. Bonar Law was the least academically minded of men. Keynes describes how at Cambridge he once made "a charming little speech given to undergraduates after dinner in which he dismissed with sweet-tempered cynicism everything a university stands for".[k] But this did not prevent him receiving in 1920 an honorary degree from that University. He was doubtless pleased with the compliment especially as the degree was conferred upon him by Balfour who had recently become Chancellor.

An honour which gave him even greater pleasure was his election at the end of 1919 to the Lord Rectorship of Glasgow University. It was particularly gratifying to be victorious in that Liberal centre especially as his rival was Professor Gilbert Murray who was not only a most eminent scholar, but a strong exponent of the purest Asquithian Liberalism. One of the tasks of the Lord Rector is to deliver an address on the occasion of his installation. Bonar Law had to postpone this until March 1921, owing to the pressure of political duties. He chose as his theme the subject of "Ambition". It seemed a surprising choice for someone who was widely but erroneously believed to be wholly without that quality. His address delivered as usual without notes contained no startling new thoughts, and does not lend itself to quotation.

It was, however, received with tumultuous applause. There were festivities and jollifications of every kind, at which he had to assist. There were torchlight processions in the cold and dank weather. There were luncheon parties, and even dances that he had to attend. It was noticed by some that Bonar Law looked on occasion very weary during these days. It was also noticed that during his address he did something most unusual for him: he hesitated more than once for words, as if he had for the moment forgotten what to say, and he seemed somewhat disconcerted by the boisterous efforts of his student audience to fill in the gaps.

CHAPTER XXVII

RETIREMENT

MARCH–DECEMBER 1921

Bonar Law's illness – Letter to Balfour – He resigns his offices – Goes to Cannes – A conversation with Balfour – His health improves – Austen Chamberlain's conduct as Bonar Law's successor – Letters from Beaverbrook, Birkenhead and Lloyd George – Bonar Law rejects an offer to attend the Washington Disarmament Conference – He goes to Paris – His time spent in bridge and chess – His style as a chess player – He takes up residence at Onslow Gardens – Keen interest in politics – Ireland again – Changed policy of the Cabinet – Peace negotiations with Sinn Fein – Bonar Law determined to protect Ulster – His fears on that score fully justified – He states his attitude – Pressure on Lloyd George – Lloyd George changes his mind – Ulster allowed to contract out – Bonar Law's speech on the Treaty – His apprehensions about its consequences

I

WITHIN a week of his resounding success at Glasgow Bonar Law astonished the political world by resigning from all his offices. He had not, in fact, been feeling well for some time past. On one occasion after a Cabinet meeting he had a brief black-out, and his health was at last beginning to show the strain of six years of exhausting official duties. During his visit to Glasgow he contracted a chill, and on returning to London he resolved to have a thorough medical overhaul. The result of this was decisive. On Tuesday, March 15th, 1921, Bonar Law wrote to Balfour warning him of what would happen.[a]

"I have talked to you about it, but I do not think you could possibly quite realize how irksome I have found my work for more than three years. While the war lasted I did not think of giving up but ever since I have longed for release. What, however, brought it to a point is that I got a slight chill the other day and I have been examined by my Doctor. I have felt that as long as it was only a question of my feelings it would be unfair to L.G. and perhaps cowardly to run away while the difficulties are so great, but Dr. May after examining me for blood pressure told me definitely that unless I could take immediately at least a three-months holiday a breakdown is quite inevitable.

"I saw L.G. and though at first he said that if I went he would certainly go also, he was afterwards very kind and considerate. He asked to be allowed to see my Doctor himself and the latter wishes to have some one else in consultation. If the expert confirms the opinion of my own Doctor I must go, and, to show you how I myself feel I may add that already the prospect of relief is making me feel much better.

"You have been so considerate ever since your own resignation that I not only wish to let you know, before I have spoken to any of my other colleagues, what is in my mind, but I am very anxious that you should not have the feeling that I am shirking my duty."

The specialist confirmed Dr. May's verdict: Bonar Law was suffering from dangerously high blood pressure; only a complete rest for several months would restore him to health. On Thursday, March 17th, Lloyd George announced the news in the House of Commons. He was overcome with emotion; his eyes were filled with tears; his voice was so inaudible that for some time Members believed him to be referring to the Speaker, James Lowther, whose resignation was well known to be imminent. When at last it dawned upon the House that Bonar Law was retiring from political life, amazement and sorrow were universal. There was no small degree of consternation, too. It was widely realized that the Coalition largely depended upon the personal relations between Lloyd George and Bonar Law. Both in the Press, and still more in the lobbies and the clubs, doubts were soon expressed as to whether it could long survive the loss of the junior partner whose role was not the less indispensable for its un-obtrusiveness. The *Financial News* probably echoed the sentiments of many when it wrote: "Mr. Bonar Law's resignation is more than a nine-days' wonder. It is probably the beginning of the end of Coalition Government."

A host of private messages from the King downwards, and in-numerable public tributes testify to the deep affection which people of every political party had by now come to feel for the Leader of the House. Bonar Law had acquired through his transparent honesty, his dry irony and humour, above all his essential kindliness, a reputa-tion in the House of Commons, which could never be shaken. His resignation was universally deplored.

He decided to make a clean cut with political life at once and on Saturday, March 19th, only two days after his resignation had been announced, he left for Cannes. Sir Frederick and Lady Sykes and Richard Law went with him. It was convenient to take a long holiday abroad, for, quite apart from considerations of health, he had for the moment no home of his own in England. His resignation meant giving up 11 Downing Street. He took a house at No. 24 Onslow Gardens, but there was much to be done before he could live in it.

At Cannes he stayed at his usual haunt, the Hotel Bellevue. It was quiet, unfashionable, very comfortable and by no means inexpensive. There he could relax, play golf and tennis by day and bridge and chess in the evening. It was not long before he began to feel very much better in health, and he soon resumed his interest in politics.

Balfour was also staying at Cannes. As is evident from the letter quoted at the beginning of this chapter, Bonar Law's relations with his predecessor had become very much closer than in the years immediately following his election to the leadership. Probably Balfour's adherence to the Coalition in 1916 – a decision as unexpected as it was welcome – had contributed to this change, and perhaps too Bonar Law had learned to penetrate behind the front of impartial, aloof, courtesy which Balfour presented to friends, acquaintances, and enemies alike. Moreover, it is likely that Balfour had come in the course of time to regard Bonar Law with more respect and esteem than in the years before the war.

A letter of April 2nd from Lady Sykes to her husband who had returned to London gives a vivid picture of the two men, and throws an interesting light on Balfour's attitude.[b]

"Father, Dick and I had tea upstairs with Mr. Balfour. He and Father discussed German indemnities and problems of exchange. There was an episode which you would have enjoyed very much, I think. Mr. Balfour was standing before the fireplace gently scratching his arm and talking to Father when a servant came in and gave him a letter. A.J.B. fumbled with the envelope and looked helplessly at the man who thereupon opened the letter for him. . . . Then he looked at the letter and said: 'Oh dear, this is from that man again. His name is So-and-So. Do you know anyone of that name? He seems to live in this hotel. I had a letter from him a few days ago asking if he might see me, because he knows George Younger's aunt, but I did not think that a sufficient reason and did not answer his letter.'

"Then he read out a part of the letter which gave as an additional reason that he had helped Gwynne. So A.J.B. asks Father if he knows who Gwynne is. Father says, 'It must be the Editor of the *Morning Post*, one of the greatest enemies of the Government.'

"Then A.J.B., still gently scratching, consults his servant as to whether he need see him and agrees to do so later in the day on his man's recommendation; but he still feels the reasons are insufficient . . .!

"Oh! I must tell you that Mr. Balfour was talking to me alone for a few minutes after Father went to bridge and says that he thinks it's an awful mistake his (Father's) giving up everything. I said I wished he had been in London to advise Father, whereupon he said he wished to goodness he had been, as he was quite sure he could have suggested arrangements which would have met the case (I suppose he meant that he would have led the House temporarily). He then said, or perhaps insinuated, that Father was not in a fit state to judge for himself and that in a few months he will be fit and well – and bored to death. He was very nice and I'm afraid I agree, don't you?"

The day after this discussion Bonar Law himself wrote to Miss Watson who was one of his devoted private secretaries at 11 Downing Street. "I am having a splendid time doing nothing and feel better than I have done for several years." Nearly two months later, on May 27th, he wrote again to Miss Watson:

"The French Doctor turned out to be Clemenceau's Doctor. He seemed to me to be very able and gave me the same account of my condition as the other Doctors. He said that it was quite evident that it was necessary for me to give up my political life, and, when my sister who was with me interposed, 'for the present', he said that from what he knew of politics he would not recommend me to return to it. At the same time he said that all I needed was rest and freedom from worry; and as a matter of fact I feel better in every way than I have for more than four years. Lord Beaverbrook and Goulding are coming over here tonight and perhaps I may return to London soon before deciding what to do during the summer. I have no doubt I shall get from them all there is in the way of gossip."[c]

2

Meanwhile, what of the political scene from which Bonar Law had made so sudden an exit? Inevitably his successor was Austen Chamberlain whose claims were overwhelming. He was unanimously elected leader of the Conservative Party at a meeting in the Carlton Club two days after Bonar Law had left for France. When taking leave of him Bonar Law warned him that he would inherit no easy position, and that the task of keeping the Party loyal to the Coalition would be even more difficult than it had been over the last four years.

The new leader was not so well qualified as Bonar Law to cope with this difficult situation. Upright, honourable, loyal, incapable of intrigue, an able parliamentarian, he had all the virtues of a leader. Yet there was something lacking. He was far less approachable than Bonar Law. He did not mingle to the same extent with back bench members. For all his ability there was in him a certain rigidity and aloofness, emphasized perhaps by his stiff appearance, impeccable dress and perpetual monocle – a parody almost, it seemed, of his famous father. Austen Chamberlain, warm-hearted though he was behind this rather bleak façade, never wholly succeeded in gaining the affections of his followers.

When he became leader he was generally regarded as a stricter party man than his predecessor, and more likely, therefore, to break up the Coalition through insistence on Tory orthodoxy. This was a delusion. It was not through excessive devotion to Conservatism that Austen Chamberlain damaged the Coalition. On the contrary he was to succumb more completely than ever Bonar Law did to the enchanter's spell. It was, rather, excessive loyalty to Lloyd George which blinded Austen Chamberlain to the signs of discontent in his own Party and caused him to steer far away from the opinions of his own supporters till he brought the Coalition crashing on to the rocks eighteen months later.

It would be idle to pretend that Bonar Law did not feel conscious of a certain neglect on the part of his friends during these first weeks of his retirement. It is true that he received plenty of letters from Beaverbrook with a characteristic and vigorous running commentary on politics. For example:[d]

"The P.M. is active and his interest in his own situation never falters. Evidently he never gets bored with power. Winston is very – very – very – very angry[1]. . . . L.G. continues to lead Govt. and Opposition. Asquith is his Deputy Leader – of the Govt. The old boy gets weaker and worse. He cannot fight but his speeches about Courteney Ilbert, and Lowther are unrivalled. . . ."

And again:[e]

"About politics, George has decided to do away with an intermediary in the leadership of the Tories. He gets on well with Austen who continues to make much of the need for loyalty. But George fears for the permanency of Austen's leadership. The latter gets tired at 10 p.m. and cannot lead with efficiency. He is like Asquith after dinner – but for another reason. In Cabinet he gives unswerving support but George is not content."

Others, however, were less mindful of their old friend. Bonar Law was hurt that he had received no letter of condolence from Birkenhead. The latter, apprised of this fact, hastened to write on May 5th. After explaining, somewhat unconvincingly, that he had written at the time but that the letter must have been mislaid on the Woolsack, Birkenhead continues:

"I cannot, my dear Bonar, recapture the moment of emotion in which I wrote and to attempt it would now sound extravagant.

"But I said – and it is permanently true – that neither politics generally nor the Unionist party in particular would ever be the same to me again. I have now lost a sure and faithful sheet anchor with whom I could discuss everything (the metaphor is mixed) in the most complete candour and friendship. There is none who can take your place and as our friendship is nearly fifteen years old it seems very unlikely to me that one will arise.

[1] On Bonar Law's resignation Austen Chamberlain became Lord Privy Seal, and Sir Robert Horne Chancellor of the Exchequer. Apparently Churchill expected that appointment for himself.

"I respect Austen very much but he is aloof and reserved. I seldom se
him and never seem to get to know him any better. . . .

"I shall be interested to hear when you return whether you miss th
great game or whether you get the repose and pleasure which you contem
plated when you used to talk to me about giving up. . . . The P.M. keep
at it in the most wonderful way: keeps his eye on the Press vigilantly an
is not, I think, quite disinterested in the leadership of the Unionist Party
Winston, I think, is very disappointed at not getting the Exchequer. H
and I are dining with Max tonight. Will you be able to play tennis whe
you come back? Or golf which I have taken up again? Anyhow we sha
at least have bridge. You will be amused (and not displeased) to hear tha
since January I have made £550 net at bridge. What cards, you will say
But in fact I am less venturesome.

"Goodbye, Bonar: Give my love to Isabel and buy her a new dres
(from you, not from me).

"I *do* hope you are really stronger.

"Yours affectionately,
F."

A few weeks later a *cri du coeur* came from Bonar Law's old frienc
and supporter, Sir James Remnant, M.P.

"I was glad to hear . . . that you are enjoying your freedom! Whether
or not you are, all I can say is that your friends are not enjoying you
absence! Come back again and lead us. Your successor won't do, and won't
lead many. We want *you* back badly."[g]

Soon after this Bonar Law heard from Lloyd George. Despite the
distress which he had shown when announcing his partner's resignation the Prime Minister was apparently too deeply immersed in
business to write to Bonar Law for over two months. This time the
verdict on Austen Chamberlain was more favourable.[h]

Chequers,
June 7, 1921.

"My dear Bonar,

"As you will have perceived from the papers – if you have time or
inclination to glance at them – whilst you are engaged in steadily bringing
your blood pressure down, events are conspiring to work mine up. One
perplexity after another.

"Crises chasing each other like the shadows of clouds across the landscape.
Miners, unemployment, Reparations, Silesia, and always Ireland. . . .

"It is a whirling world and you are well out of it. I often envy you. But I
am sincerely glad to hear accounts of the improvement in your health. I
miss your counsel more than I can tell you, although nothing could be
finer than the way Chamberlain is bearing his share in the partnership.
He is loyal, straight, and sensible.

"When are you returning? Let me know. I want to see you.

"Ever sincerely yours,
D. Lloyd George."

At the end of June Bonar Law, who was by now far fitter, paid a brief visit to England and spent a Sunday with Lloyd George at Chequers. But this was not a prelude to resuming "the great game". He was soon back in France, and during July and early August enjoyed the pleasures of the season at Le Touquet. He had by now completely recovered.

Towards the end of August he came over to England and stayed for two days at Lympne with Sir Philip Sassoon. Lloyd George was in the same party and suggested that Bonar Law might go to America to represent Britain at the forthcoming Washington Conference on Naval disarmament. Bonar Law replied that he would only consider it if, for any reason, Balfour, who had first claim, refused. In the event Balfour accepted.

In September Bonar Law was in Paris with his son Richard. He stayed at a quiet inconspicuous hotel. His son recalls how he signed the visitors' book "A. B. Law" to avoid recognition. His days in Paris were conducted according to a fixed routine. The mornings were spent on the golf course at St. Cloud. After lunch he played bridge at the Travellers' Club.

"Isabel", he wrote to Miss Watson, "says that the Travellers' Club has a bad name – like the Pope at Portadown; but it is like other places – exactly what you make of it, and bridge is played there for reasonable stakes as well as very high."

In the evenings he used to visit one of the cafés where he could rely on getting a game of chess. His favourite was the Café de la Régence in the Avenue de l'Opéra. Richard Law once asked one of the players how good his father really was at chess. To his surprise the answer was not – as one would expect – that he played a prudent and cautious game, but on the contrary that he played with great recklessness, flashes of brilliance, but in a manner dangerously unsound by ordinary standards. His technique was the exact opposite to his style of bridge or golf, or, indeed, to his normal attitude towards most things in life.

3

At the end of September Bonar Law returned to England, and took up his residence at 24 Onslow Gardens – in "these benighted suburbs", as Curzon described them. His health was now fully restored. For the first time since March he began to take a serious interest in politics. He had good reason to do so. The Irish problem like some vast thunder cloud had brooded over the English scene

ever since Bonar Law could remember. Sometimes, indeed, it would
drift toward the horizon, and only a distant rumble, an occasional
lightning flash, would remind the onlooker of its presence. But now
in the autumn of 1921, the cloud had come once again towering up
into the political sky. It is necessary to summarize briefly what had
happened since Bonar Law resigned.

When he had last sat in the Cabinet the Government's policy had
been one of utter refusal to negotiate with Sinn Fein, unless (1) it
leaders recognized the Crown and the Imperial connexion and (2
the murder campaign had been completely crushed. The method
employed by Sir Hamar Greenwood's Black and Tans had by then
gone a very long way towards achieving the second of these two
conditions. Lloyd George may have been premature in saying on
November 9th, 1920, "We have murder by the throat", but un
doubtedly the Sinn Feiners were, by the early summer of 1921
rapidly losing the battle.

The extraordinary process, whereby a Government still pledged a
the end of May 1921 to a policy of rigid refusal to negotiate with the
rebels had become at the end of June converted to one of appease
ment, or, as its enemies declared, surrender, forms no part of Bona
Law's biography. He was out of the country at the time and was no
consulted. It is impossible to say what his attitude would have been
but it is at least possible that the reticence, which Lloyd George and
Birkenhead displayed towards their old colleague during these weeks
was partly caused by a fear of what his reaction might be. In fac
there is no evidence that Bonar Law disapproved of what had been
done. On the contrary he seems to have welcomed the prospect
which now appeared on the horizon, of peace in Ireland.

But peace with Ireland did not mean to Bonar Law peace at an
price. He had no intention whatever of allowing the independence
Ulster guaranteed under the Act of 1920, to be compromised in the
slightest degree. Yet, as the negotiations between the Governmen
and the Sinn Fein leaders dragged on, the possibility that Ulster'
independence might be endangered began to appear more and mor
threatening. As early as October 31st, 1921, a group of Conservativ
M.P.s headed by Colonel Gretton moved what was virtually a vot
of censure on the Government for even negotiating with the rebels
Some forty-three members voted against the Government, an
Austen Chamberlain was received with particular hostility by thi
group of his own party when he defended the Cabinet's policy.

Hitherto, the details of these negotiations had remained unknow

o the public, but early in November rumours that Ulster would be
obliged to enter an All Ireland Parliament as one of the preconditions
of a settlement with the South became widespread. At the same time
here was a buzz of speculation in the Press as to the probable action
of Bonar Law. His recovery of health, his presence in London, his
known opinions on Ulster made it seem highly probable that he
would intervene against the Government. If he did so, the chances
were that he would carry a large part, perhaps a majority, of the
Conservative Party with him.

The rumours and gossip of the Press were by no means without
substance. In fact, at this time, the Cabinet does appear to have
seriously contemplated something little short of the "coercion of
Ulster" – that very measure against which the Unionist Party had
fought so bitterly for the past ten years. On November 10th Lloyd
George communicated to Sir James Craig, the Prime Minister of
Northern Ireland the terms of the settlement, "towards which His
Majesty's Ministers have been working". Among these terms, which,
it is fair to add, included numerous "safeguards" for Ulster, was one
which inevitably inspired the greatest alarm among the friends of
Ulster:

"The unity of Ireland would be recognized by the establishment of an
all-Ireland Parliament upon which would be devolved the further powers
necessary to form the self-governing Irish State."

Bonar Law was in close touch with all these developments and was
greatly perturbed by them. He wrote on November 11th to Miss
Watson:

"I am really very anxious for peace, but I am quite certain that Ulster
will not agree to go into an all-Ireland Parliament and, if the attempt is
made to force her to do so it will mean immediate civil war.

"I will certainly oppose such a proposal but whether I will undertake
the leadership of opposition to it I really do not know ... if the Prime
Minister tried for a settlement on the present lines he would make the
mistake of his life. . . . I am as certain as I can be that the overwhelming
mass of the Conservative Party will be against the P.M.

"I had a long talk with the P.M. last night. I am sure on personal
grounds he would dislike almost as much as I should that we should be in
opposite camps in what would be a horribly bitter fight.

"I am still in hopes that this will not happen and that he will find some
other way out of the difficulty."

On November 12th, in response to a request from J. P. Croal, the
Editor of the *Scotsman*, Bonar Law dictated to one of Croal's journal-

ists a very full account of his views on the situation. It is so important
that it deserves lengthy quotation.[i]

"I did not intend to have anything to do with politics till the beginning
of next session. But it now looks as if I might. . . . As regards my own
position in this business I have been a good deal worried, but it is not so
any longer for I have made up my mind, and as you know one is most
worried when one is not quite sure what is the right thing to do. If L.G.
goes on with his present proposals I will oppose them. I shall try to get the
Conservative Party to follow me. If I succeed we will simply be back on
the old lines. If I fail to get the majority, which means of course the control
of the Organization, I will simply drop out. . . . I am certainly not going
to do what Disraeli did after the passing of the Corn Law – attempt to
build up a new Conservative Party. . . .

"As regards the Conservative Party, to take the line that the Government are now proposing will be the greatest and most obvious breach not
only of particular pledges but of the whole political life of every Unionist
that has ever taken place in this country. . . .

"I am glad to say that as far as personal friendship goes there is no
breach between L.G. and myself. I saw him two nights ago and I am going
to dine with him again tomorrow."

Bonar Law then described the conversation which he had held
with the Prime Minister. He had pointed out that, whether Lloyd
George or he carried the day with the Conservative Party, the
difficulties would be enormous.

"I then said to L.G.: 'I want to suggest another alternative. Don't
confine your bullying to Ulster. Try it on the Sinn Feiners too. Say to them
"Ulster in spite of all the pressure I have put on is immovable, and not
only so but the party on which I rely will be hopelessly broken up.
However much I wish it, it can't be done. . . . I therefore make this
proposal to you – For your own part of Ireland frame your own constitution, and if it is within the Empire we will accept almost anything you
propose. Not only so, but if it is possible we will carry an act of Parliament
so that the moment Ulster is willing to join with you she can do so automatically". . . .' "

Bonar Law continues:

"I said to him [Lloyd George], 'if you take that line and they refuse
you will have the country behind you just as solidly as if the question of
allegiance were at stake'."

Finally Bonar Law stated to Croal his general opinion of the Ulster
situation.

"People say that Ulster has made no concession, won't move an inch.
As a matter of fact what is asked of them is not concession but the surrender
of everything for which they have been fighting for 35 years. That fight
has been on one simple issue – that they will not be put under a Dublin

Bonar Law playing chess at the Café de la Régence in Paris,
from a drawing by L. Berings, summer 1921

Parliament without their consent. In my opinion the fact that they do not consent is enough. It is not for us to judge whether they are wise or foolish in refusing. They are part of the United Kingdom. Under this proposal they would become a province of a Dominion with no more political connection with Westminster than has the Province of Natal."

Bonar Law concluded:

". . . after my experience as leader of the Conservative Party and second man in the Government, though I would never have competed against Austen Chamberlain in any sense, and would have supported him always, I would not have served under him. Now if these proposals go on and Chamberlain and the others say, 'we are prepared to go with the Prime Minister as long as there is a chance of convincing Ulster but, when it comes to a question of coercing Ulster, we go no further' – then I would serve under Chamberlain.

"Forgive this long screed. You who knew me so well at one time know that before the war there were only two things which I really cared for as matters of conviction – the rest was mainly a game. One of these was tariff reform; the other was fair play for Ulster, and I feel as strongly about it as I did then. So you will not be surprised, I am sure, that, if this issue is raised, nothing will move me from my present position."

It is impossible to say exactly what effect Bonar Law's arguments had upon Lloyd George and the other members of the Cabinet, but it must have been considerable. At all events the final agreement with the Sinn Feiners – the celebrated Treaty signed, in such dramatic circumstances, in the early hours of December 6th, corresponded remarkably closely to the suggestions which Bonar Law had made to Lloyd George at dinner. The Treaty, although it still aroused bitter hostility in Ulster, contained very different terms from those which Lloyd George had officially put forward to Craig on November 10th. The new proposals no longer involved the inclusion of Ulster without option in an all-Ireland Parliament. Instead Ulster was given the right to withdraw within one month of the Act coming into force, provided that an Address to that effect was presented to the Crown by the Ulster Parliament. It need scarcely be added that the Address was immediately presented.

Bonar Law did not have to make any public intervention in order to achieve this change. He took no part in the deliberations of the annual meeting of the National Union of Conservative and Unionist Associations which was held in Liverpool on November 17th. There a motion hostile to the Government was heavily defeated. Austen Chamberlain made it clear in his speech that there would be no question of including Ulster against her will under a Dublin Parliament. It seems clear that there had been much discussion behind the

P

scenes since Lloyd George's proposals to Craig only a week earlier. Bonar Law was in a position, if not to overthrow, at least to damage very seriously the Coalition Government. According to Lord Riddell who talked to the Prime Minister on November 5th Lloyd George said:[j]

"Things look very awkward. Bonar Law has come out as the advocate of Ulster. Whether he thinks he sees his opportunity to become Prime Minister or whether he is solely actuated by a conscientious desire to champion the cause of Ulster, I don't know, but I can hardly believe that he would desire to supplant me."

Austen Chamberlain was equally suspicious about Bonar Law's motives. He wrote just before the meeting at Liverpool:[k]

"And I might add to my catalogue of troubles Bonar Law, an Ulsterman by descent and in spirit, a very ambitious man, now astonished at what he thinks his own complete recovery and itching to be back in politics where he is disposed to think the first place might and ought to be his.
"I am fighting for my political life. . . ."

These suspicions were not warranted. Bonar Law had no desire to stand forth as an alternative Prime Minister. But he was well aware of the political threat which he constituted towards the Coalition and his purpose was to use that threat as a means of protecting what he considered the vital interests of Ulster. He did not break silence till the debate in the House of Commons on the Irish Treaty. This occurred on December 14th and 15th, and the attitude of Bonar Law was a matter of intense interest to the House. He spoke on the second day. He was received with great applause. Almost at once he allayed any doubts which members of the Government may have felt, and crushed any hopes which may have been entertained by the Diehards.

"Let me say at the outset that I am in favour of this agreement. . . . For a time it looked to me as though there might be an attempt to compel Ulster to go into an all-Ireland Parliament against her will. That would have seemed to me an impossible thing, and I am glad to see that the fear has turned out to be quite unjustified. For a time, however, it seemed to me a possibility – I will not go beyond that – that I might be one of those who would ask the country to condemn that policy."

Bonar Law's support of the Government was of decisive importance. Had he come down on the other side the Tory revolt, which brought the Coalition to an end in October 1922, might well have occurred ten months earlier. Yet his support was by no means uncritical. He condemned the Prime Minister and Cabinet for endeavouring to bring moral pressure on Ulster, and he condemned the pro-Government Press for encouraging the notion that an intransigent Ulster was the only obstacle to negotiations with Sinn Fein. He expressed sympathy with Ulster indignation that the Government had without consultation resolved on a boundary commission to revise the frontier.

"When I say that I am in favour of this Agreement I do not pretend to like it. I am sure the Government do not like it in many particulars. I do not pretend to like it but I ask myself this. What is the alternative? Are we to go back to the condition of things which prevailed over the last two years?"

Bonar Law voted with the Government, and the Treaty was carried by 401 to 58. Nevertheless, there can be little doubt that he, like many others who voted on the same side, viewed the Treaty with much scepticism. It might work. Ulster was safeguarded to all appearances. Perhaps the Sinn Fein leaders meant what they said, and could accomplish what they promised. Anyway things had gone too far for repudiation. At all events there was some chance that the long and fearful history of murder and reprisal would come to an end. Bonar Law felt that the experiment must be given a chance.

CHAPTER XXVIII

RETURN TO POLITICS

JANUARY 1ST–OCTOBER 19TH, 1922

Effects of the Irish Treaty on the Conservative Party – Lloyd George's offer to make Bonar Law Foreign Secretary refused – Younger opposes an election early in 1922 – Bonar Law's perturbation at the conduct of the Coalition – He urges Lloyd George to retire – Murder of Sir Henry Wilson – Bonar Law's menacing speech in the House – The "Honours Scandal" – Revolt of the junior ministers temporarily quelled by Birkenhead – Events leading to the Chanak incident – The Government's two ultimatums – Bonar Law's letter to The Times *– Its political implications – He again warns Lloyd George – Conservative discontent with Austen Chamberlain – Chamberlain's letter to Birkenhead – He resolves to test opinion at a meeting of Tory M.P.s – Bonar Law's hesitation – Resignation of Curzon – The forces against the Coalition – The attitude of Mr. Wickham Steed – Bonar Law decides to intervene – His speech at the Carlton Club meeting – Some erroneous myths about the meeting – The end of the Coalition*

THE Irish Treaty was in the end fatal to the Coalition. If it had been an immediate success, if the Sinn Fein leaders who signed it had been able at once to establish order in the South, perhaps the Conservative Party would have acquiesced. But it was not an immediate success. No sooner had it been signed than De Valera, heading a considerable though unrepresentative section of the Dail, at once repudiated it. Michael Collins and Arthur Griffith were unable – their critics said unwilling – to prevent a bloodthirsty terrorist campaign against Ulster conducted by gunmen from the South. One of the conditions of the Treaty had been the holding of free elections in South Ireland in order to ratify the Treaty. Instead an electoral pact was made between Griffith and De Valera whereby each section of Sinn Fein maintained its existing numbers in the Dail. This seemed to most Englishmen both incomprehensible and indefensible, especially since it gave the opponents of the Treaty a far larger representation than they would have obtained on a free vote. All through the spring and summer of 1922 resentment against the Cabinet, in particular against its leading Conservative members, Chamberlain and Birkenhead, grew ever more bitter in the ranks of the Tory Party.

Lloyd George had been anxious to hold an immediate General Election after the debate in the House in December 1921. A group of Coalition Ministers discussed the plan at a dinner party on December 20th. Beaverbrook was present, and also Sir Archibald Salvidge, the principal organizer of the Conservative Party in Liverpool. Salvidge advised the Cabinet to include Bonar Law before going to the country. He notes in his diary that Churchill and Birkenhead seemed not to relish this proposal.[a] Eventually it was decided to postpone a decision in view of the forthcoming meeting of the Supreme Council at Cannes, which the Prime Minister was due to attend in January. Early in that month the Prime Minister tentatively suggested to Bonar Law that he might care to rejoin the Cabinet as Foreign Secretary.[b] Bonar Law, while agreeing that an early Election was desirable, declined the offer to return, assuring Lloyd George at the same time that he had no intention of opposing the Government.

During the early months of the New Year there was general restiveness in the Conservative ranks at the leadership of Lloyd George. Something of this was conveyed to Bonar Law, who was staying at Cannes, in a letter from J. C. Davidson written on January 13th, 1922:

"There is no doubt that throughout the South and West the end of the Coalition and the revival of the in and out system is strongly desired. My constituency is quite definite in its views.

"I was talking to S.B.[1] the other day (he is against an election) and he is inclined to share the opinion that our own people fervently desire to know where they stand and what they stand for.

"The re-establishment of a great Conservative Party with
    Honest Government
    Drastic Economy
    National Security
    and
    No Adventures abroad or at home
would carry great weight in the country. . . .

"Derby in the Lords and you as leader and P.M. in the House of Commons has been mooted pretty widely. Naturally it is what I should like though I don't know whether D. is to be trusted. Birkenhead doesn't cut any ice with the public in the same way as D.

"I hope the election will be postponed but if it comes the Tories must go separately to the Country. . . ."

Bonar Law does not appear to have been wholly convinced by these arguments. He had been seeing Lloyd George frequently. He wrote on January 21st to Miss Watson:

[1] Stanley Baldwin.

"I don't think I shall stay here much longer as I am getting too many invitations. . . . I had a long letter from Davidson giving all his news. He is evidently becoming more and more of a Die-Hard.

"I see a lot of the P.M. here and I really think that even he is beginning to feel that he has had enough of it."[c]

Meanwhile the chances of an early Election suddenly receded. Austen Chamberlain early in January had asked the Principal Agent of the Conservative Party, Sir Malcolm Fraser, to report on the probable results of an immediate Election. The answer was very discouraging: the Coalition would certainly lose at least 100 seats, and the Conservative Party would be split from top to bottom. On hearing this Sir George Younger, the Chairman of the Party, publicly proclaimed his hostility to an early Election. Lloyd George was furious and Bonar Law too doubted whether this was a proper course on the part of Younger. Writing to Miss Watson from Paris he said:

"Isabel says that you think Younger was quite right. Between ourselves I do not. If anything had to be said about the Unionist attitude, it should, I think, have been said by Mr. C., but perhaps when I know the whole story I may take a different view."[d]

Chamberlain, however, defended Younger's action to Lloyd George and gave his own reasons for opposing an early Election. Nevertheless the decision was regarded as a victory for the Die-hards and a blow against the Coalition. At the end of February Lloyd George actually offered to resign in favour of Austen Chamberlain.[1] Chamberlain, however, still believed that Lloyd George's presence at the head of the Government was essential. He was by now an out-and-out Coalitionist. Only a fortnight earlier he had told a Die-hard deputation that his ultimate objective was to fuse the National Liberals and Conservatives into a single party. He, therefore, declined Lloyd George's offer.

For the malcontents Bonar Law's attitude to these problems was of critical importance. He was the only person outside the Government – and, therefore, uncommitted to its plans – who was capable of standing forth as an alternative Prime Minister. The dissident Tories could do nothing without a leader. But Bonar Law evinced no desire to play this part. On returning to England early in February he continued to give the Government a judicious, independent support on most major topics. He preserved enigmatic silence as to his views on the continuation of the Coalition and the future rôle of the Conservative Party.

[1] See Petrie, *Chamberlain* II pp. 174-8 for full text of Lloyd George's letter.

Yet behind his public reticence he was in fact much perturbed. He was well aware of the murmurings of the rank and file against Lloyd George's rule. He realized that the Cabinet was not as united as it seemed. With that deep instinctive knowledge of the sentiments of his Party – the knowledge which gave him so high a place in its esteem – he could see that the future was full of danger for the Government. Yet he could not intervene without appearing to show disloyalty to Austen Chamberlain and, in view of what happened over the leadership in 1911, he was particularly anxious not to incur this reproach. Nevertheless he felt bound to give some warning. Balfour made a note of a conversation which he had with Bonar Law at the end of December 1922 when the two men surveyed the history of the past year:[e]

"He informed me that when he returned to London in February he found a complete change of opinion in the Party with regard to Coalition; that he had seen Austen once but only once upon the subject; but Lloyd George frequently (I think he said ten times at least); that he had persistently told him that, in the present mood of the Party it was impossible that things should go on as they were; that he reiterated this opinion with great insistence; and that he had understood it was not dissented from."

It is difficult to say how far Lloyd George heeded these warnings. Probably he wrote them off as typical examples of Bonar Law's pessimism. After all, everyone else said that Lloyd George was indispensable. He still commanded the applause of the nation and the support of a great part of the Press. When he did offer to resign the only result had been a more fervent assurance than ever of loyalty from the leader of the Conservative Party. Why should he, Lloyd George, a statesman of world renown, the architect of Allied victory, give up the great game because a few Die-hard back benchers murmured at his rule?

Afterwards, when it was all over and Lloyd George had fallen from power – as it turned out, for ever – Bonar Law uttered some reflections upon these events to C. P. Scott, the editor of the *Manchester Guardian*. He said:[f]

"My experience is that all Prime Ministers suffer by suppression. Their friends do not tell them the truth; they tell them what they want to hear. It was so with Asquith. I remember, just before the change of Government, he would not believe that there was any general movement on the Conservative side against him. He thought I was the only Conservative Minister who would support Lloyd George. He asked me if I stood alone – I said: 'No; *all*, because the Party means it.'

"That is how George also was misled. People are always apt to think that what has been will be. I am less inclined perhaps than most men to that error because of my early training. I was in the iron trade, a highly speculative business with frequent violent fluctuations in prices. . . ."

Whether or not Bonar Law's explanation is correct, it is clear that Lloyd George was unwilling to act on the warnings which he received. He continued at the head of affairs, whirling from conference to conference, Cannes, Genoa, London. His appearances in the House of Commons were reserved for great occasions. On every important issue he was sustained by immense majorities. Meanwhile even as a forest fire can long smoulder unobserved until at length some change of wind or weather turns it into a fearful blaze, so the discontent of the Tory Party remained quiescent, unnoticed, yet ever present.

During the spring and early summer of 1922 the situation in Ireland steadily deteriorated. The Provisional Government of Southern Ireland, headed by the Sinn Fein leaders who had signed the Treaty, proved wholly incapable of preserving order. On April 13th a group of extremists headed by a certain Rory O'Connor took possession of the Law Courts in the centre of Dublin and proclaimed themselves the Republican Government of all Ireland. From this stronghold they organized a campaign of murder and terrorism throughout Ireland and Ulster. The Provisional Government was unable or unwilling to eject them. These developments seemed to justify the worst apprehensions of those who opposed the Treaty.

Then came an episode which caused a thrill of horror throughout the world, and shook the Government to its foundations. On June 22nd Sir Henry Wilson was shot dead by two Irish fanatics[1] on the steps of his own house in Eaton Place. Every detail conspired to make the crime appear one of peculiar atrocity. Wilson had just returned from unveiling a War Memorial at Liverpool Street Station. He was dressed in the uniform of a British Field-Marshal. The murder occurred in broad daylight and in full view of a number of people.

The shock caused by this monstrous crime at once produced a wave of indignation against the Government. Was this the result of pandering to the Irish Nationalists, of "shaking hands with murder"? It was widely felt that the Provisional Government of South Ireland through its failure to suppress the Republican terrorists of Dublin was morally responsible for Wilson's murder; and it was felt that the British Cabinet by condoning such a state of affairs bore some responsibility too. When Austen Chamberlain visited at Eaton Place

[1] The murderers were condemned to death in July and hanged in Wandsworth Prison on August 10th.

in order to condole, Lady Wilson greeted him with the word, "Murderer!"[g] She expressed a desire that no members of the Government should attend the funeral, and only gave way when it was pointed out that her refusal might look like a slight upon the Crown.

Sir Henry Wilson's aged mother wrote to Bonar Law requesting him publicly to deny that her son had ever been a friend of Lloyd George, as Lloyd George himself – quite correctly – had claimed in the House of Commons.[h]

Horrified at what had happened Bonar Law was determined to force the Cabinet into a firmer attitude towards the Irish Government. It was widely rumoured that he brought personal pressure on Lloyd George that weekend, by threatening to lead a Die-hard revolt, unless the Government insisted upon immediate restoration of law and order in Dublin. However that may be, the policy of the Government did in fact sharply change. A dramatic debate took place in the House of Commons on Monday, June 26th, only a few hours after many of those present had attended Sir Henry Wilson's funeral in St. Paul's Cathedral.

Winston Churchill, who as Colonial Secretary was the Government spokesman, delivered a public and categorical warning to the Irish Government:

"If either from weakness or want of courage, or for some other even less creditable reasons, it [the terrorist campaign] is not brought to an end, and a very speedy end, then it is my duty to say on behalf of His Majesty's Government that we shall regard the Treaty as having been formally violated . . . and that we shall resume full liberty of action in any direction that may seem proper and to any extent that may be necessary to safeguard the interests and rights that are entrusted to our care."

When Bonar Law rose to speak from what had now become his regular place, the corner seat of the third bench below the ministerial gangway, the House was tensely expectant. But those who hoped that he would come out as leader of the dissident Tories were once more to be disappointed. Bonar Law disclaimed any desire to overthrow the Government, but some of his remarks cannot have been pleasing to the Ministers.

"I am not prepared to say that we ought to scrap the Treaty. But I confess that for many months I have been very anxious about the position in Ireland – very uncertain whether the Government were dealing with it in the right way.

". . . I agreed with the Treaty, but I confess had I foreseen exactly what the position would have been today, I doubt whether I would have voted for it. That is not at all because of the anarchy in Ireland. It is not because of the murder of Sir Henry Wilson . . . I – certainly not by any intention on the part of the Government – was entirely deceived, or I misunderstood two vital things in connection with the Treaty. They were both vital. I thought that those who signed the Treaty . . . accepted the position that Ulster could never be brought in until they were willing to be brought in. Everything that has happened since has shown that I was wrong.

"The next point equally vital in which I was mistaken was that I assumed that the men who had signed the Treaty not only meant to keep it in good faith but meant to run risks, and all risks, in order to carry it out. I understood they meant to govern. We all know that they have not even tried. . . ."

Bonar Law expressed his approval of the firm line which Churchill had taken, but he ended on a menacing note.

"Just think of this. . . . There is in Dublin a body which has seized the Four Courts – to make the irony complete it is the centre of justice in Ireland – and from these Four Courts, undoubtedly emissaries are going out, trying to carry out in Ulster precisely the same methods which they think succeeded in the South, and are instigating murder in every direction. Is that tolerable for a moment? Suppose we found that there was a body in Paris . . . openly subsidizing murderers to come to this country and upset our Government. What would happen? We should not make representations to the Government in Paris, and say, 'We must make sure you do not approve of it.' We should say, 'You must stop this, or there is war'."

At these words Bonar Law had to pause as a burst of cheering shook the House. He ended:

"Now the position is clear. Much time cannot elapse before these grave matters – to quote a saying of the Colonial Secretary – are brought to the test. I for one say that I believe the Government means to see this through, but if they do not, I will be against them, and I hope the House of Commons will be against them too."

Bonar Law met Lloyd George and Churchill later that evening in the lobby. The latter's description of the meeting deserves quotation.

"Although always holding himself in strict restraint he [Bonar Law] manifested an intense passion. As far as I can remember, he said, 'You have disarmed us today. If you act up to your words, well and good, but if not . . .!' Here by an obvious effort he pulled himself up and walked away from us abruptly."[i]

The Cabinet was at last genuinely determined to act, and to eject O'Connor from the Four Courts, but their action was anticipated by Michael Collins. On June 30th after a three days bombardment he compelled O'Connor to surrender. Thus began an open civil war between the pro-Treaty and anti-Treaty sections of Sinn Fein, which lasted for several months.

By the middle of the summer of 1922 the Government was running into very heavy weather, and Ireland was not the only quarter whence it came. The Genoa Conference, upon which Lloyd George had pinned much hope, proved a failure, and its only upshot – a pact between Russia and Germany – seemed to most Englishmen fraught with sinister implications in the field of foreign affairs. Then there was the "Honours Scandal". Precise details are not easy to come by, but it is enough to say that for a long while past Conservative opinion had been disturbed at the quantity – and quality – of those upon whom the Prime Minister bestowed peerages and lesser honours. Sometimes honours had been given to Conservatives whom the Conservative Party Whips had already passed over as unsuitable. It was widely believed that the Whips of the National Liberal Party (Lloyd George's section of the Liberal Party) sold titles on a definite tariff system of contribution to Party funds, without any regard to the personal merits of the recipients.[1]

In June Tory discontent exploded into the open when the Birthday Honours list was announced. It included the award of peerages to Sir Archibald Williamson, Sir Samuel Waring, and a South African financier, Sir Joseph Robinson. All three were very rich, and all three had in some quarters a dubious reputation. The South African Prime Minister was quick to announce that his Government had not been consulted on Sir Joseph Robinson's peerage.[2] A debate followed in both Houses of Parliament. Eventually Lloyd George, while defending his past practice, agreed to appoint a Royal Commission to examine the procedure for bestowing honours. There the matter rested for the time being, but the facts revealed aroused much indignation in the Conservative Party. The whole affair marked yet another milestone on the Coalition's road to disaster.

Bonar Law took no part in the debate on the Honours Scandal. Clearly he had no ambition to stand forward as an alternative leader at the head of the dissident Conservatives. Privately he expressed his intention of returning actively to politics in the autumn session, but in the rôle of an independent supporter of the Government. He did not desire to challenge Chamberlain or Lloyd George.

By the end of July discontent with the Government had reached

---

[1] See Gerald Macmillan, *Honours for Sale*, a biography of that curious figure, Maundy Gregory.

[2] In the end Sir Joseph Robinson was persuaded – with some difficulty – to decline the peerage. See Frank Owen, *Tempestuous Journey*, p. 623, n. 1. The other two took their seats and were bitterly attacked by Ronald McNeil in the House of Commons. See Harold Nicolson's *Life of George V*, pp. 512–3, for the King's comments on these peerages.

such a pitch that a group of Conservative junior ministers formally confronted the Conservative members of the Cabinet and stated the case for ending the Coalition. Austen Chamberlain made the error of putting up Birkenhead to reply on behalf of his colleagues. He proceeded to lecture the junior ministers in his most hectoring and arrogant style. Mr. Amery noted in his diary:[j]

"Whatever chances F.E. may have had of the Unionist leadership of the future, they are not likely to have survived this unfortunate perform-ance. We dispersed – most of the juniors spluttering with indignation."

On August 4th Parliament adjourned for the summer recess. Few Members can have guessed that the old House would never meet again, and that when Parliament reassembled in the autumn the Coalition would have fallen for ever, and a General Election would have confirmed Bonar Law as Prime Minister of England.

The immediate cause of the Coalition's downfall lay in the Near East – in a train of events which culminated with what has come down to history as "the Chanak Incident". The full story is far too complicated for detailed description here. Briefly the root of the trouble was the inability of the victorious Allies to impose their peace terms upon Turkey. The Government at Constantinople did, it is true, sign the drastic and humiliating Treaty of Sèvres in August 1920, but this was a fact of little significance since by then real power resided not in the puppet administration of the Sultan but in Mustafa Kemal, who had raised the standard of nationalist revolt in Anatolia, and was determined to repudiate the Treaty.

The Allies possessed no army of their own on the spot to enforce the Treaty of Sèvres. They therefore accepted with alacrity an offer by the Greek Prime Minister, Venizelos, to employ the Greek Army in the task of crushing the Kemalist rebellion. No one was more enthusiastic in this matter than Lloyd George who had become a passionate philhellene, and possessed a boundless admiration for Venizelos. It was a fatal decision. Within a few months the young King Alexander of Greece was dead and the ensuing political revolu-tion resulted in the exile of Venizelos and the restoration of King Alexander's pro-German father, the ex-King Constantine. These events, which occurred in the autumn and winter of 1920–21, totally extinguished all pro-Greek sentiment among the Allies – apart from Lloyd George himself – and gave the French, who for various reasons were anxious to come to an agreement with Kemal, precisely the excuse that they needed for withdrawing support from Greece.

In these circumstances common prudence should have dictated a reversal of the Venizelist policy of expansion in Asia Minor. Instead, King Constantine determined to carry through the plans of the previous Government and to engage the Kemalist forces. He did not sufficiently reckon with the war weariness of armies that had been engaged in constant fighting for nearly ten years. In August 1922 the Greek forces on the Anatolian plateau were utterly defeated. Kemal pursued them to the coast, burned Smyrna to ashes, and massacred its Christian population. He then proceeded to turn his victorious armies in the direction of Constantinople and the Straits.

A desperate crisis now loomed ahead. The zone round the Straits had been declared neutral under the Treaty of Sèvres. It was guarded by scattered detachments of British, French and Italian troops. The destruction of the Greek armies meant that this thin line, supported, it is true, by the British Fleet in the Sea of Marmora, remained as the sole barrier against the capture of Constantinople and the invasion of Europe.

By mid-September the Turkish Nationalist Army was encamped close to the barbed wire protecting the neutral zone in the area of Chanak on the Asiatic shore of the Dardanelles. The Cabinet now decided to take firm action. Kemal had already (September 11th) been informed by the Allied High Commissioners that he must not invade the neutral zone. On September 15th – a Friday – the Cabinet held prolonged meetings which culminated in a number of decisions. A message, drafted by Churchill, was sent to the Dominions requesting their aid in the event of hostilities. All the great powers were informed of British determination to maintain the position at Chanak.

The weekend was still sacred at this time to the convenience of those who dwelt in country houses, and the Foreign Secretary accordingly departed on Saturday to Hackwood. In his absence Churchill and Birkenhead, at the Prime Minister's request, drafted that morning a communiqué for publication in the Press. This statement, the first serious intimation to the public of what was likely to happen, seemed to many people highly alarmist in tone. It referred *en passant* to the appeals already made to the Dominion Governments. Unfortunately the telegrams conveying these appeals, although transmitted late on Friday, were not received and deciphered in the Dominion capitals until after the publication of the communiqué, and the Dominion Prime Ministers were naturally furious.

Meanwhile yet another revolution took place in Greece. King Constantine fled the country. Venizelos returned to power. This belated change of heart on the part of the Greeks promptly aroused

warm sympathy in Lloyd George who had never abandoned his philhellene affections. It also inspired the alarm of Mustafa Kemal.
He feared that Lloyd George would endeavour to use Greek troops
against the Turkish Nationalists and so deprive them at the last
moment of the rewards of victory. The Kemalist troops proceeded
to violate the neutral zone. On September 29th the Cabinet, whose
policy was by this time entirely controlled by Lloyd George,
Churchill and Birkenhead, ordered General Harrington, the British
Commander at Chanak, to send another ultimatum to Kemal. Curzon protested but was overruled – his only supporters in the Cabinet
being Baldwin and Griffith-Boscawen. But Curzon was right. To
quote Sir Harold Nicolson:[k]

"The communiqué of September 16th had been a stroke of reckless
genius justified by the result: the ultimatum of September 29th, although
equally reckless, was not, at that moment, essential."

Had it been delivered, war might perhaps have followed. Luckily it
never was delivered. General Harrington, supported by Sir Horace
Rumbold, the British High Commissioner in Turkey, turned a Nel-
sonian blind eye to the Cabinet's orders. As Sir Harold Nicolson
writes:

"They saved us from a war which, as events proved, would have been
wholly unnecessary."

The situation remained precarious for several days, but eventually
on October 10th the Kemalists agreed to an armistice pending the
negotiating of a new peace treaty to replace the now long-dead
Treaty signed at Sèvres.

It has been necessary to describe this episode because, without a
knowledge of the antecedents and consequences of the "Chanak
Incident", the fall of the Coalition and the attitude of Bonar Law
cannot be comprehended. The Conservative Party, it must be
remembered, was, by a long tradition dating from the days of
Disraeli, pro-Turk. Lloyd George's attitude to the Greeks seemed to
most Conservatives a curious survival of Gladstonian Liberalism, a
piece of antiquated sentimentality which had no connection with real
politics of the modern world. That he should orientate British foreign
policy in this direction was a tiresome aberration; that he should
bring us to the verge of war for so irrelevant a cause was utterly
intolerable. Of course we can now see that issues far wider than
Lloyd George's philhellenism were involved, and it would have been
scandalous if Kemal had been allowed to invade Europe. Never-

theless, although a firm line at Chanak was fully warranted, such a perilous situation need never have arisen if Lloyd George had been less pro-Greek, and the second ultimatum – that of September 29th, which was never delivered – showed a reckless indifference to the danger of war, quite unjustifiable in the circumstances that prevailed.

Bonar Law followed all these developments with profound anxiety. It seemed to him, as to many Conservatives, that the Government was pursuing a highly perilous foreign policy. Whatever the reason, it was lamentable that we should be faced with the possibility of fighting alone an unpopular war in support of a cause which had no interest to most Englishmen. Bonar Law was, however, far too conscious of his responsibilities as a statesman to wish to weaken the Cabinet in its stand against Kemal. Wherever the blame might lie for the events which had led to the crisis, now that the crisis had arrived it was essential to support the Government.

On October 6th Bonar Law wrote a letter which was published in *The Times* and the *Daily Express* the following day. He began by supporting the stand taken at Chanak:

"It would serve no useful purpose to criticize or even to consider the circumstances which have led to the present situation. . . . When the Greek forces were annihilated in Asia Minor and driven into the sea at Smyrna, it seems to me certain that, unless a decisive warning had been issued, the Turkish forces flushed with victory would have attempted to enter Constantinople and cross into Thrace. . . .

"It would certainly have involved Thrace in horrors similar to those that have occurred in Anatolia, and the probability – indeed I think it is a certainty – of the renewal of war throughout the Balkans.

"It was therefore undoubtedly right that the British Government should endeavour to prevent these misfortunes. It is not, however, right that the burden of taking action should fall on the British Empire alone. The prevention of war and massacre in Constantinople and the Balkans is not specially a British interest. It is the interest of humanity. The retention also of the freedom of the Straits is not specially a British interest; it is the interest of the world. We are at the Straits and in Constantinople not by our own action alone, but by the will of the Allied Powers which won the war, and America is one of those Powers.

"What, then, in such circumstances ought we to do? Clearly the British Empire, which includes the largest body of Mohammedans in any State, ought not to show any hostility or unfairness to the Turks. In the Agreement arranged with the Allies in Paris by Lord Curzon, proposals were made to the Turks which are certainly fair to them, and beyond these terms, in my opinion, the Allies ought not to go.

"I see rumours in different newspapers, which I do not credit, that the French representatives with the Kemalist forces has encouraged them to make impossible demands. The course of action for our Government seems to me clear. We cannot alone act as the policemen of the world. The financial and social condition of this country makes that impossible. It seems to me, therefore, that our duty is to say plainly to our French Allies that the position in Constantinople and the Straits is as essential a part of the Peace settlement as the arrangement with Germany, and that if they are not prepared to support us there, we shall not be able to bear the burden alone, but shall have no alternative except to imitate the Government of the United States and to restrict our attention to the safeguarding of the more immediate interests of the Empire.

"Yours truly,

24 Onslow-Gardens, S.W.7.   A. Bonar Law."

This important letter could be interpreted in more than one sense. The beginning part appeared to be an endorsement of the stand taken at Chanak. To that extent it might seem as if Bonar Law was coming to the aid of the Government, and Austen Chamberlain, to judge from his congratulatory note to Bonar Law, thought that was the principal purpose of the letter.

But the letter had a wider significance which the opponents of the Coalition were quick to see. It was by implication a warning that Bonar Law was not prepared to support a policy of intervention abroad on issues which had no direct connexion with British interests. In other words, although he was ready to support the Government for defying the Turks single-handed at Chanak, he viewed with grave doubt the wisdom of the policy which had made such action necessary.

"We cannot alone act as policemen of the world. The financial and social condition of this country makes that impossible."

Here was a statement which appealed to the isolationist sentiment of a large section both of the Conservative and Liberal Parties. There was a general feeling that at Chanak the Government had been on the verge of dragging Britain and the Dominions into a war which had no direct relevance to the security of the British Empire. The country as a whole was in a thoroughly war-weary mood, and now at last a political leader of the first rank – indeed the only person who could stand forward as an alternative Prime Minister – had declared his belief that henceforth, unless the French Government took its share of the burden, Britain would "have no alternative except to imitate the Government of the United States and to restrict our attention to the safeguarding of the more immediate interests of the Empire".

It is not too much to say that Bonar Law's letter was the death-knell of the Coalition. From that moment onwards, although he had

Bonar Law and Lloyd George, summer 1922

Bonar Law with his son Dick, the present
Lord Coleraine, c. 1922

not yet decided personally to challenge the Government, events
moved in such a way that he could scarcely have avoided the challenge, unless he had been ready to retire completely from public life.
He was at once bombarded with letters urging him to return actively
into politics. One supporter writes:

"Do come forward and lead us. Nothing will induce me to vote again
for a coalition under Lloyd George."

Another, George Lane Fox, M.P., wrote:

"The one thing that would rejoice the hearts of all of us would be your
return to the leadership. If your health and your inclination permit this,
the whole party will, I know, do their utmost to spare you undue fatigue
and anxiety."

These appeals caused Bonar Law much perturbation. He was, as
we have already seen, most reluctant to resume the leadership, but
he was profoundly alarmed at the course of events. The Chanak
Incident had a double significance for him. He not only disapproved
of what he considered to be the reckless foreign policy of the Coalition, but he saw that a continuation of this policy was certain to split
the Conservative Party even more sharply than the Irish problem or
the Honours Scandal. He was very unwilling to interfere with Austen
Chamberlain, but, as an old and disinterested friend, he felt fully
justified in warning Lloyd George, and he did so on several occasions.
His admonitions had no effect. Perhaps Lloyd George had by now
come to regard Bonar Law as a Jeremiah who was always prophesy-
ing disaster. Perhaps he overestimated the control which Austen
Chamberlain had over the Conservative Party. At all events he seems
to have been quite confident that he could carry on.

Meanwhile what was happening in the inner circle of the Cabinet?
Austen Chamberlain had had ample warning of the storm that was
brewing in his Party. As early as September 1st, before the Chanak
Incident, he received a letter from that unfailing weathercock of the
political climate, Lord Derby. Derby had refused an offer from Lloyd
George to join the Government in March. He now wrote to Chamberlain declaring that he could no longer support the Coalition and
intended to join "Salisbury and his new party".

"For my own part the Foreign Policy of the Government will prevent
me from further supporting them. . . . That policy has always seemed to
me fraught with disaster.

" 'Your letter', replied Chamberlain on September 7, 'is a great shock
to me . . . it still seems to me that Salisbury has manufactured differences
where none ought to exist. The electoral results of the split must be bad
and may easily be disastrous.' "[1]

On September 16th the Cabinet resolved to spike the guns of the malcontents by holding an immediate General Election. The reason for this decision was that the annual conference of the Conservative Party was due to take place on November 15th, and it seemed highly probable that a vote would be recorded there against the continuance of the Coalition. But this decision in favour of an Election, taken the very same weekend as the Chanak Incident, had to be postponed on account of the Turkish crisis and the imminence of war. Nevertheless Austen Chamberlain informed the principal Party managers that the Election would take place as soon as possible. He received immediate protests. Sir George Younger wrote on September 22nd:[m]

"I have received from (Sir Malcolm) Fraser an account of your decision at Chequers last Sunday and I am frankly appalled at the results it must entail. . . ."

On the same day Sir Leslie Wilson, the Chief Whip, wrote:[n]

"I must ask you to consider the advisability of not making public your decision without consulting the Party first, and without informing all your colleagues in the Government (Junior Ministers, etc.) of your decision. . . . I know the feeling in the Party well and you will have very little support in the proposed continuation of the Coalition as it is with L.G. as its head. . . ."

A few days later he informed Chamberlain that so far 184 constituencies had declared their intention of running independent Conservative candidates, adding:

"this list is open to criticism as some of the members and candidates are certainly sitting on the fence."

Chamberlain was still convinced of the importance of continuing the Coalition and hoped that he could carry the day with his Party, although he was not quite as confident on this point as some of his colleagues. On October 10th a further meeting of the Cabinet took place, at which Sir Leslie Wilson was present. It was again decided to go to the country as early as possible on a Coalition basis. Baldwin was the only member of the Cabinet who dissented. Wilson strongly objected but was overruled. Matters were now at breaking-point. The following day both Younger and Wilson declared to Chamberlain that they would publicly repudiate his leadership if the Cabinet persisted in its decision and gave the Party no chance of expressing its views.

These protests did not deflect Austen Chamberlain from his path, but he now began to favour an early meeting of Conservative M.P.s, where he could put the whole issue to the vote and where he believed that his chances of victory would be more favourable than at a full Party conference. On October 12th he wrote a significant letter to Birkenhead:°

"The enclosed [Wilson's letter of protest] has just reached me.
"I think it would be unwise for the P.M. to commit himself on Saturday for under this growing pressure we may find some of our colleagues back-sliding. . . .
"I am not sure that it may not now be necessary to call a Party meeting and to tell them bluntly that they must either follow our advice or do with-out us, in which case they must find their own Chief and form a Govern-ment *at once*. They would be in a d-d fix! . . .
"I am not willing to step into L.G.'s shoes and to take any part in a Government formed in personal opposition to him. The malcontents assume that they can reject our advice and use us for their own purposes. They make a mistake and it may be well to prove it to them."

The letter shows clearly that the famous meeting of Tory M.P.s at the Carlton Club was not called under duress from the malcontents, rather that it was a counter-attack on the part of the Coalitionists who were far more confident of winning the day there than at the annual Party conference. The letter also shows that Chamberlain must have been unaware of Bonar Law's misgivings, or he could never have been so sure that his opponents would fail to find a leader. Like many before him and many after him, Chamberlain was suffering from the occupational malady which so often besets politicians – the hallucination of indispensability.

In fact Bonar Law was now beginning to move in the direction of intervention, although he had not yet finally made up his mind. He was convinced that the Conservative Party was on the edge of a disaster which would split it wide open. On the other hand he did not really wish to take office himself. His health seemed to be fully recovered, but who could predict what the consequences would be if he had to endure the strain of the Premiership? And it was becom-ing more and more clear that he could only rescue the Party from disaster if he was prepared to take on the onerous burden of leading it himself. There was no lack of counsellors to urge this course upon him. Beaverbrook was foremost in the field. Ever since the publica-tion of the letter in *The Times* his newspapers had been proclaiming that Bonar Law alone could save the situation. To this public pressure he added much private pleading and argument. The Party managers were equally anxious for Bonar Law to intervene. Bonar Law had dis-cussions with Younger and together they made careful calculations about the prospects of a General Election in which the Conservatives led by Bonar Law would fight as an independent party. They reckoned that the best that could be expected was a majority of 25 over all other parties.

Meanwhile events were moving rapidly. Curzon after promising to go along with the other Coalitionists had suddenly changed his mind, incensed by a speech of Lloyd George on Saturday, October 14th, in which the latter fiercely denounced the Turks and the French at the very moment when the Foreign Secretary was endeavouring to persuade the French to help him in obtaining peace with the Turks. A meeting of the leading Coalitionists took place at a dinner in Churchill's house on October 15th. Curzon refused to attend but Leslie Wilson was present, and pressed strongly for the view that the Coalition should wait until the Party conference before going to the country. Austen Chamberlain refused to agree and offered instead to summon a meeting of all Conservative M.P.s and Ministers to the Carlton Club on Thursday morning, October 19th. He would abide by the decision reached there. Wilson acquiesced in this compromise, although many Conservatives subsequently protested on the ground that such a body was not the true sovereign body of the Party and that the National Union, or at the very least its executive should be consulted first.

Now at last Bonar Law had to make up his mind. Only four days remained. It was clear at this stage that everything depended upon his attitude. The only members of the Cabinet who could be relied on to oppose Lloyd George were Baldwin, Griffith-Boscawen and probably – though in view of his frequent changes of heart not certainly – Curzon. None of these were national figures. Derby and the Duke of Devonshire were likely to come out on the same side, and there was the Die-hard group led by Salisbury. There was also the Party machine controlled by Younger and Wilson. In addition he could rely on a large number of Junior Ministers and Under-Secretaries who were anything but Die-hards and yet were deeply resentful of the Coalition. Their leading figure was Mr. Amery. Finally there existed a powerful group of back benchers headed by Sir Samuel Hoare (now Lord Templewood) and Mr. Ernest Pretyman. Against these dissidents – numerous, admittedly, but essentially light artillery – were all the heavy guns of the Coalition Cabinet. Its members included some of the most formidable and respected figures in the Party – Chamberlain, Balfour, Birkenhead, Worthington-Evans, Horne. It would not be easy in a Party, which by tradition was deeply respectful of authority, to overthrow nearly all the principal leaders.

Nevertheless Bonar Law had one important asset on his side – the Press. The newspapers owned by Lord Beaverbrook were naturally vociferous in his favour. Lord Rothermere, who controlled the *Daily Mail*, and believed himself with some reason to be on the verge of acquiring *The Times* as well, wrote an encouraging letter to Bonar Law on the eve of the Carlton Club meeting. Finally – and in the circumstances it was a more important support than any other – he had the backing of *The Times*. During the interregnum caused by the insanity and death of Lord Northcliffe, the editor, Mr. Wickham Steed, had sole control – for a brief period – of the paper's policy. He was a strong opponent of the Coalition. He believed that a restoration of the two-party system was essential. He saw Bonar Law for three successive nights culminating with the eve of the Carlton Club meeting. He was convinced that Younger and Bonar Law were pessimistic in believing that they had no chance of winning a majority of more than 25 at a General Election, and might even be defeated. He predicted – very accurately as it turned out – that an independent Conservative Party would win by 75 seats.[p]

Wickham Steed wrote to Bonar Law at 1 o'clock on the morning of the 17th:

"Since our brief conversation tonight, information has reached me which strongly confirms my conviction that unless you decide to lead the opposition at Thursday's meeting of the Unionist Members of the House of Commons, there will be no hope of maintaining the cohesion of the Party. You best know the course you ought to pursue; but looking at the situation as an outsider with some knowledge of national and foreign affairs, it seems to me that the maintenance of a strong Unionist Party is a pre-eminent national and Imperial interest. You have it, I believe, in your power to defend this interest and also to set such an example to the Liberal Party that it too would feel compelled by instinct of self preservation to close its ranks and thus to restore something like stability to the political life of the country. I need hardly say that whatever influence *The Times* possesses will be used in this sense. . . ."[q]

Despite everything Bonar Law's attitude remained uncertain up to the very night before the critical meeting. He felt profound reluctance at the prospect of breaking with Lloyd George with whom he had served in such a loyal partnership for so many years. To a late hour he hoped that perhaps Lloyd George might voluntarily retire in favour of Chamberlain. In that case the chief difficulty would have vanished. The Party would follow Chamberlain – its only objection to him was his excessive devotion to Lloyd George – and Bonar Law could remain in peace, confident that the Party's unity would be preserved. According to Balfour, Bonar Law said afterwards that he had seen Lloyd George as late as the "days which intervened between the summoning of the Carlton Club and the meeting itself", and urged on him the impossibility of continuing on the existing basis. But Lloyd George was unwilling to move.[r]

On Wednesday, October 18th, Bonar Law received numerous callers at Onslow Gardens. One of the first was Curzon, who stated that he had definitely decided to break with the Coalition and his resignation was now in Lloyd George's hands. He found Bonar Law in a despondent mood, doubtful whether he could face the burden of office, uncertain whether he would attend the Carlton Club meeting.[s] Indeed, at some period during the day, Bonar Law actually drafted a letter of resignation to the chairman of his constituency party.[t] He felt by now that, if he remained in politics at all, he must come out against the Coalition. Rather than do this and face the inevitable consequence – the Premiership – he seriously contemplated complete retirement from public life. Later that day – in the afternoon – Chamberlain called on him. Bonar Law spoke with sympathy of Chamberlain's position. As to his own he was still uncertain.

"It was a hateful position, he said. He thought he would plead the state of his health and keep away from the meeting altogether, but in that case he must leave Parliament and give up public life. If he came to the meeting he must speak against me. I told him that his speech would be decisive; the vote would go in his favour; the Government would have to resign and he would have to form a new one. 'Well,' he said again, 'it's a hateful position; I expect if I had remained in your place I should have acted like you.' "[u]

It is not clear precisely when Bonar Law made up his mind. He saw Wickham Steed sometime that evening and, although nothing definite was said, the editor of *The Times* was certain in his own mind that Bonar Law would attend the Carlton Club meeting. Later still Sir Archibald Salvidge, who supported the Coalition, came round to Onslow Gardens. He was astonished to discover that Bonar Law had now definitely decided that he would speak against the Coalition next day, and would indicate his readiness to resume the lead. Salvidge writes in his diary that Bonar Law thought that there was "a tidal wave of feeling in favour of a united Conservative Party". Salvidge continues:

"He concluded by asking whether I had not been surprised by the growth of this feeling within the last few weeks. I replied that whichever way he gave the lead – either for or against the coalition – would be equally effective. During the day I had discussed the matter with any number of people. A firm pronouncement from him could turn most of them in one direction or the other. . . . A man servant entered and whispered something to Bonar Law. When the servant had gone I made my final appeal. I reminded Bonar of the day in Downing Street just after the war when he told me of the tremendous gratitude the nation owed Lloyd George. . . . 'We must never let the little man go' . . . Bonar flushed deeply and made no attempt to hide how much the reminder had gone home. 'But I must surely realize the extent to which the whole position had changed. . . . The issues now at stake went far beyond the claims of personal loyalty. Lloyd George had failed to secure the adherence of the Conservative wing of the Coalition and our party must be kept together.' I retorted that Lloyd George retained the unswerving support of everyone of his Conservative colleagues in the Cabinet. Bonar puffed at his pipe for a few minutes. At last he said, almost regretfully without the slightest note of triumph in his voice, 'I may as well tell you that Curzon is here. He is waiting in another room.' It was an absolute bombshell. . . . There was no more to be said, and I rose to go. As I reached the door Bonar called me back. 'Tell Austen and F.E. to be moderate,' he said. 'Do you think I or Curzon imagine we can rule the country with the sort of people that will be left to make up a cabinet after the break tomorrow? I must have Austen and F.E. back at the first possible opportunity.'

"As Bonar stood there he looked a lonely perhaps even a forlorn figure. There was nothing about him suggestive of a man who tomorrow would have reached the pinnacle of ambition. He held out his hand, and I grasped it not without emotion, and wished him Godspeed in the great task to which, I felt certain, nothing but his sense of public duty had impelled him. Then I went out and he went in to meet Lord Curzon."[1]

Curzon's own account of the interview which followed confirms Salvidge's story that Bonar Law had by this time definitely decided upon his course of action. "He even gave me", writes Curzon,[v] "the substance of the speech he proposed to make on the morrow." This evidence together with that of Salvidge's diary should be enough to refute the myth, sedulously propagated by Bonar Law's enemies, that he only made up his mind at the last moment when he saw which way the wind was blowing at the Carlton Club meeting on the following day.

Who or what finally tipped the balance in Bonar Law's mind in favour of intervening? The argument that weighed with him most strongly was undoubtedly the fear that the Party would be irrevocably and decisively split if Chamberlain persisted in supporting

[1] Stanley Salvidge, *Salvidge of Liverpool*, pp. 237-8. This is a book of the greatest interest for all students of Conservative politics in this period.

the Coalition. Indeed it was not so much the reason for the revolt of
the rank and file as the mere fact of its existence which convinced
him that the Coalition must be ended. There is no reason to suppose
that any one individual swayed his judgment. Bonar Law was quite
capable of taking this critical decision independently of friends or
counsellors. Of course many people were urging him to intervene,
Beaverbrook, Younger, Wickham Steed, Baldwin, Hoare; but it does
not follow that any of them had the decisive say. Bonar Law himself,
writing after the event to Sir Robert Borden, said:[w]

"Up to the last moment I was very undecided and if my own family –
my sister and children – had not been so strong against my giving up, I
believe that is the course I should have adopted."

So perhaps Mary Law, whose influence had often before been
decisive with her brother, once again had the last word, not in convincing him that the Coalition ought to be ended but in persuading
him that it was *his* duty to end it. Certainly there were very few
people for whose advice he had greater respect.

As soon as he left Bonar Law, Salvidge hastened to 10 Downing
Street where an informal session of the leading Cabinet ministers was
in progress. The news of Bonar Law's decision was not unexpected.
That of Curzon, however, says Salvidge, produced consternation.
"So our punctilious Pro-Consul has ratted," someone observed.
Curzon had threatened resignation so frequently that no one could
really believe that he would do it. It is certain that from then onwards
he was regarded by his erstwhile colleagues with all the implacable
hatred which is reserved for the traitor in the camp. Balfour's attitude
to the news of Bonar Law's and Curzon's decision amazed Salvidge.

"He banged the table with his fist and shouted, 'I say, fight them, fight
them, fight them. This thing is wrong. Is the lead of Law and Curzon to
count as everything and the advice of the rest of us as nothing? This is a
revolt and it should be crushed.' "[x]

But to crush the revolt was easier said than done. If Bonar Law
spoke, the result of the Carlton Club meeting was virtually certain.
A last blow to the Coalition was delivered by the news on Thursday
morning of a by-election at Newport. An independent Conservative
was running against a Coalition Liberal and a Labour candidate.
Austen Chamberlain had confidently expected that the Labour man
would get in on a split vote, thus illustrating the danger of an independent Conservative candidature. But in the event, the independent
Conservative won by over 2,000, Labour was next, Coalition Liberal

a bad third. This news, carried in the later editions of *The Times*, arrived in time for most of the members who attended at the Carlton Club. It seemed to confirm the views of all those who wanted to end the Coalition.

The story of the Carlton Club meeting has been too often told to bear any lengthy repetition here. It began at 11 o'clock. Some 275 members attended. When Bonar Law entered he received a tumultuous welcome – far more vociferous than that extended to Chamberlain. The latter's opening speech was unconciliatory and was received without enthusiasm. Then Baldwin spoke strongly and very effectively against the Coalition. He was at once followed by Ernest Pretyman and Lane Fox, who proposed and seconded respectively a motion in favour of fighting the next election as an independent Party. After some desultory discussion there was a general cry for Bonar Law. He rose somewhat reluctantly and seemed at first to speak with hesitation, but he soon made it clear that he supported Pretyman's motion.

"I confess frankly," he said, "that in the immediate crisis in front of us I do personally attach more importance to keeping our Party a united body than to winning the next election

"The feeling against the continuation of the Coalition is so strong that if we follow Austen Chamberlain's advice our Party will be broken and a new party will be formed; and not the worst of the evils of that is this, that on account of those who have gone, who are supposed to be the more moderate men, what is left of the Conservative Party will become more reactionary, and I, for one, say that though what you call the reactionary element in our party has always been there and must always be there, if it is the sole element, our party is absolutely lost.

"Therefore if you agree with Mr. Chamberlain in this crisis I will tell you what I think will be the result. It will be a repetition of what happened after Peel passed the Corn Bill. The body that is cast off will slowly become the Conservative Party, but it will take a generation before it gets back to the influence which the Party ought to have."[y]

Bonar Law then declared that he would, though very reluctantly, vote for ending the Coalition. His speech was greeted with great enthusiasm and it carried the day. Pretyman's motion against the Coalition was supported by 187 votes to 87.

Both at the time and subsequently the decision of the Carlton Club meeting was stigmatized as the result of an intrigue carried through by a reactionary minority clique. The fact that the Tory M.P.s met at a West End club helped to give currency to this version of events, and naturally it was exploited to the full by Lloyd George and his friends in the ensuing General Election. It should be clear from the

foregoing narrative that this notion is a complete myth. Lord Salisbury and his diehards may have been "reactionary", and they
certainly supported Bonar Law, but they constituted only a minority
of his total support. They never numbered more than about 50, but
no fewer than 187 M.P.s voted in favour of the termination of the
Coalition. A large number of these could by no stretch of imagination
be fairly described as reactionaries. Indeed people like Baldwin,
Hoare (Lord Templewood), Wood (Lord Halifax) were destined
later to incur if anything the reproach of being too pink in politics
rather than too blue. The truth was that Austen Chamberlain had
lost the confidence of very widely divergent elements in the Party,
and no talk about "reactionary intrigues" can alter that fact.

As for the process of his overthrow it was certainly not an intrigue.
He would undoubtedly have been far more severely defeated at the
Party conference in November, and it was he, not his enemies, who
insisted upon securing an earlier verdict from the Conservative M.P.s.
He did this because he thought that there was a better chance of that
verdict being favourable, in which case he and Lloyd George would
certainly have forestalled the conference by an immediate dissolution. The decision of the Carlton Club meeting was taken after a free
debate, in which both sides could and did express their views. Far
from being the result of backstairs plotting it represented, to quote
one of the ablest of modern writers upon the British party system, "a
thoroughly healthy manifestation of internal party democracy".[1]

As soon as the result was declared Chamberlain announced that
he would have to consult with his friends. Their decision was to force
upon Bonar Law as soon as possible the task of forming a Government. That afternoon Lloyd George went to Buckingham Palace and
tendered his resignation to the King. The Coalition had fallen. A
new era in British politics had begun.

[1] R. T. McKenzie, *British Political Parties*, p. 109.

CHAPTER XXIX

PRIME MINISTER OF ENGLAND

OCTOBER 19TH–DECEMBER 1922

Bonar Law's belated reluctance to become Prime Minister – He declines to take office until elected Leader of the Party – Cabinet making – He offers Exchequer to McKenna who refuses – Baldwin appointed instead – The new Government – Its aristocratic composition – Wise advice of Mr. Wickham Steed – Attacks of Lloyd George – Attitude of the Asquithian Liberals – Bonar Law's cautious Election Manifesto – His unwillingness to hit back at Lloyd George – Vigorous support from Beaverbrook – He puts up candidates against the Liberal ex-ministers – Defeat of Guest and Churchill – Attitude of the Press – Unexpected friendliness of Lord Riddell – Lord Rothermere demands an earldom – Bonar Law's refusal – Beaverbrook and Mesopotamia – Bonar Law's pessimism about the Election results – His triumph – The Parliamentary session – The Irish Free State Bill – Trouble with the Daily Herald *– Birkenhead's attack on Curzon – Its total collapse – Indignation of Curzon – End of the session – Bonar Law's success*

I

"I HAVE climbed to the top of the greasy pole at last." In these words Disraeli, after a lifetime of political endeavour, greeted his appointment to the highest position of all. Few Prime Ministers have spoken with such candour, but many must have felt the same emotion. Ten years earlier Bonar Law too might have welcomed the glittering prize that now lay within his reach. He had been ambitious then, far more ambitious than anyone realized. But since those days his outlook had greatly changed. The death of his two elder sons had destroyed much of his zest for living. He remained in public life from a sense of duty – and perhaps a fear of the emptiness of any other existence – until at length his health broke down. Only a compelling sense of party loyalty and national necessity would have induced him to resume "the great game" once more.

Even at this late stage, on the afternoon of the momentous Carlton Club meeting, he seems to have been strangely reluctant to take the final plunge into the whirlpool of politics. At about 5 o'clock he was called to the telephone to speak to Lord Stamfordham who asked him to come at once to Buckingham Palace. Bonar Law demurred,

and requested Stamfordham to see him first at 24 Onslow Gardens.
At their interview, Lord Stamfordham writes:[a]

"He explained that he was not the leader of the Conservative Party,
that the party was for the moment broken up and, until he knew that he
could count on its undivided support he would not accept office. Therefore
it was indispensable that he should be present at a meeting of the representatives of the whole Conservative Party, where he would make the
above condition and others including one limiting his holding office to one
year.
"I ventured to suggest to him that the King sent for him independently
of these party considerations into which His Majesty did not enter; that,
having accepted Mr. Lloyd George's resignation, it was the King's duty
to form a new Government as soon as possible and to send for whoever he
considered was the proper person to carry out this great responsibility. . . ."

But Bonar Law remained firm. He refused to take office until the
Party had elected him as leader. Much telephoning followed between
Onslow Gardens and Buckingham Palace. Eventually the King
accepted the position, but requested that Bonar Law should at least
come and talk to him. Bonar Law promptly drove to Buckingham
Palace. He promised to call a Party meeting as soon as possible, and
meanwhile to consult with those who might help him to form a
Government. It was agreed that the Court Circular should state the
bare facts that Lloyd George had resigned and that the King had
granted an audience to Bonar Law.[b]

Was Bonar Law solely actuated by constitutional niceties during
these discussions? The situation was indeed highly abnormal, but it
is worth noticing that, neither before nor since, have potential Prime
Ministers deemed it necessary to await their Party's decision before
accepting the King's offer to form a Government – and this has been
the case, even when they have not already been leaders of their party.
Perhaps Bonar Law was hesitating, even as he had hesitated over the
leadership crisis in 1911, rather like a swimmer who dips his toes in
the water and finds it disagreeably cold. Perhaps he was hoping that
even now something might occur, some twist of fortune, that would
save him from the supreme responsibility which was being thrust
upon him.

If he had such thoughts they cannot have lasted for long. The
flood of events soon swept him on. All next day a steady stream of
taxis and motor cars brought callers to his door. The telephone –
there was only one, situated in a particularly awkward place – rang
incessantly. The house was besieged by photographers. Eventually
they were allowed in, and Bonar Law agreed to pose for them in his

dining room. "You want me to look cheerful?" he said, and did his best to oblige. Lord Salisbury, the Leader of the Die-hard group, stayed to lunch and discussed the claims of his supporters for office. All the busy hum of rumour and intrigue which normally centres upon Downing Street had shifted suddenly to Onslow Gardens. By the end of the day Bonar Law had gone a long way towards forming the Cabinet. On Monday, October 23rd, a meeting of Conservative Peers, M.P.s and Parliamentary candidates, was held at the Hotel Cecil. Proposed by Curzon, seconded by Baldwin, Bonar Law was unanimously elected leader of the Party. He immediately went to Buckingham Palace where he was formally appointed as Prime Minister and First Lord of the Treasury. The following day he announced the names of his Cabinet. On October 26th Parliament was dissolved, and a General Election was fixed for November 15th.

The five days that elapsed between the Carlton Club meeting and the announcement of the new Government were some of the busiest that Bonar Law ever spent. The formation of the Cabinet offered peculiar difficulties. Nearly all the most weighty and experienced figures in the Conservative Party, spell-bound under the enchanter's wand, had remained loyal to Lloyd George. They were filled with rage and chagrin at the Carlton Club revolt, and formed a compact under which they undertook to give no help to the new Government. Immediately after the meeting a manifesto was issued over the signatures of thirteen Conservative Coalitionist Ministers headed by Austen Chamberlain, Birkenhead, Balfour, and Horne.[1] The signatories declared:

". . . we advised the Unionist Party not to take a course which must repel powerful allies in the anxious campaigns which lie in front of it. The meeting today rejected that advice. Other men who have given other counsels must inherit our burden and discharge its consequent responsibility."

As a result of this boycott, Bonar Law was faced with an alarming lack of experienced politicians from whom to choose. Not since the secession of the Peelites had a Conservative leader been confronted by such a dearth of talent in his ranks. Even the Law Officers of the late Government declined to co-operate and an attempt to persuade them merely brought a chilling rebuff from Sir Ernest Pollock, the Attorney-General.

The two key positions on which any Government depends for

---

[1] Only four Conservatives from the late Cabinet were ready to join Bonar Law. These were Curzon, Baldwin, Peel, and Griffith-Boscawen.

success are the Foreign Secretaryship and the Chancellorship of the Exchequer. The former was no problem. Curzon's last minute resignation from Lloyd George's Cabinet – however treacherous it may have seemed to his late colleagues – ensured continuity in that most important post. Bonar Law at once confirmed Curzon in office. But who was to be Chancellor of the Exchequer? So difficult was this problem that Bonar Law decided to look outside his own party and offered the post to McKenna who had been the Chancellor in Asquith's last Government.[c] McKenna hated Lloyd George and it seemed possible that he would welcome a chance of lending his support to Bonar Law and so helping to consolidate the ruin of the Coalition. But he was now Chairman of the Midland Bank and was not ready to give up that lucrative post in order to join a Government whose political prospects seemed so uncertain. The most he could promise was to make a speech conferring the official blessing of "the City" upon the new Administration. So Bonar Law had to fall back on Baldwin. The latter had at one time been his Parliamentary Private Secretary. Bonar Law knew him well and liked him. Moreover, Baldwin had played a bigger part than any of its members in bringing about the downfall of the late Cabinet. He deserved a reward. Bonar Law appointed him, though not without misgivings about his lack of experience.[d] These misgivings were to be justified.

For the remainder of his Cabinet Bonar Law's choice was largely dictated by the circumstances of the Coalition's downfall. Two quite distinct elements in the Conservative Party had brought about the revolution at the Carlton Club – the aristocratic right wing which included Salisbury's Die-hard group, and those Ministers and Junior Ministers in the late Government who, more in touch with Party sentiment than their Chiefs, were determined to bring the Coalition to an end. These facts were reflected in the composition of the new Government. Including Curzon and Baldwin, four members of Bonar Law's new Cabinet had been members of the previous one and no fewer than five had been under secretaries or the like. The only Die-hard proper whom Bonar Law invited to join his Cabinet was Lord Salisbury, but the right wing of the Party was represented by as many as seven peers – among them such weighty representatives of the old territorial interest as Lord Derby and the Duke of Devonshire.

The final list announced on October 24th was as follows. Junior Ministers in the late Government are marked with an asterisk:

Prime Minister and First Lord of the Treasury	Mr. A. Bonar Law
Lord President of the Council	The Marquess of Salisbury
Lord Chancellor	Viscount Cave
Chancellor of the Exchequer	Mr. Stanley Baldwin
Secretaries of State:	
Home	Mr. W. C. Bridgeman
Foreign	Marquess Curzon
Colonies	The Duke of Devonshire
War	The Earl of Derby
India	Viscount Peel
Scotland	Viscount Novar
President of the Board of Trade	Sir Philip Lloyd-Greame*[1]
President of the Board of Education	The Hon. E. F. L. Wood*[2]
First Lord of the Admiralty	Mr. L. S. Amery*
Minister of Health	Sir Arthur Griffith-Boscawen
Minister of Agriculture	Sir Robert Sanders*
Minister of Labour	Sir Montagu Barlow*

A week later the names of the Ministers outside the Cabinet were published. The most notable were the Attorney-General, Sir Douglas Hogg who soon proved himself one of the ablest parliamentarians on the Government side, Sir Samuel Hoare who became Secretary for Air and who had been a leading figure among the anti-Coalition back benchers, and Neville Chamberlain who accepted the position of Postmaster General. Bonar Law was particularly gratified at this last appointment. Neville Chamberlain had been in Canada throughout the crisis and, although his detestation for Lloyd George was well known, it seemed probable that loyalty to his brother Austen would prevent him from joining the new Administration.[e]

"It is a real pleasure," wrote Bonar Law, "to have you in the Government and in saying this I am not thinking of the political advantage of your having joined us. My earnest hope is that, in spite of the soreness which must inevitably exist at present, it will not be long before we are all in the same boat again."

Although Bonar Law's Administration contained both in and out of the Cabinet many Ministers who were destined to make their mark in later years, it cannot have seemed a very impressive team at the time it was announced. Sir Winston Churchill has called it a "Government of the second eleven", and the description has some substance. There was a good deal of criticism at the number of peers in the Cabinet. It is certainly somewhat ironical that Bonar Law whose own elevation to the Party leadership had been the symbol

[1] More familiar as Lord Swinton.
[2] Lord Halifax.

of a revolt against the aristocratic and landed interest should have
found himself at the head of a Cabinet composed so largely of members of the House of Lords. But the truth was that circumstances left
him no choice. He frankly regarded the Administration as a care-
taker Government and looked forward to the day when the dissident
Conservatives would reunite under his leadership. Then he could
quietly fade away from the political stage to which he had so un-
willingly returned.

On one point, however, Bonar Law had been persuaded to give
way. His original intention, as he told Stamfordham and many
others, had been to announce publicly that he would only hold
office for one year. This seemed to some of his friends most unwise.
It was one thing to be resolved in his own mind to resign after a year,
but quite another thing to inform the world of this intention. On
October 19th Wickham Steed wrote to him:[f]

"On thinking over our conversation this evening, the objections to an
avowed and concerted time limit to your leadership of the Unionist
Party and to your tenure of the Premiership seem to me very serious indeed. Were it announced that you agreed to act only for a year there
would inevitably be some decrease of enthusiasm in the immediate future
and a considerable increase of uncertainty as to the position a year hence.
There would also inevitably be movements within the Party in favour of
this or that candidate for the succession – and of Elishas there would be
no lack. . . ."

This was undoubtedly very sound advice and Bonar Law gave
way. He decided to make no categorical statement as to the length
of time he would hold office.

But would the Government survive the coming Election? The very
suddenness of the crisis made prophecy extremely difficult. The
Conservatives had not won a victory on their own since 1900. And
now they were fighting without allies and contrary to the advice of
nearly all their principal leaders. The omens cannot have seemed
good, and many of Bonar Law's supporters, though putting on a bold
face to the world, must have wondered what would happen. It was
at least possible that the ship so hastily constructed would founder
as soon as it was launched – amidst the triumphant jeers of the
spectators.

One thing soon became clear. The fallen Ministers did not mean
to take their defeat lying down. Lloyd George led off in typical style
in a speech delivered at Leeds only two days after his resignation. He
referred to "the reactionary meeting" at the Carlton Club, which had
been engineered from "Mayfair and Belgravia". He regretted that

Bonar Law had allowed his judgment to be rushed by a clique of Die-hards, and stigmatized the whole affair as "a crime against the nation". Birkenhead and Churchill, who saw their dream of a great centre party shattered for ever, were equally vigorous. Birkenhead, alleging that the Conservative revolt had been caused by the Party machine, compared Sir George Younger to the cabin boy who had taken charge of the ship. He commented on the "second class intellects" of the new Ministers, and declared that their mediocrity frightened him. But Birkenhead cut little ice now in the Conservative Party. His jibes had alienated too many people. He was actually booed at the Carlton Club meeting, and Lord Robert Cecil won much applause when he pointedly observed in an election speech that England preferred to be governed by second-class intellects rather than by second-class characters.

Then there were the Asquithian Liberals or "Wee Frees", as they had come to be called. Their feelings towards Bonar Law were divided. They were of course overjoyed at the fall of Lloyd George. Civil war always stirs up the greatest hatred, and by now the official Liberals had come to regard the Coalitionist Liberals with implacable resentment. Mrs. Asquith wrote enthusiastically to Bonar Law:[g]

"You and Sir George Younger deserve every word of praise and thanks from *every* one of us from the lowest to the highest. It was a deplorable and cruel blunder the Coupon Election, and the Ll. Georgites had a good run, long and dangerous. You will find no lack of generosity in my husband if and when he has to criticize, and *all* of us wish you God Speed."

And again in a later letter:[h]

"Don't believe a word about Reunion.[1] Never was a greater lie. We would rather be out for *ever*. Smashing the sham of the Coalition was the right thing to do. Be firm and poke fun at these warriors."

Bonar Law thanked her for the first letter. "What the result of all this commotion will be", he wrote, "I cannot pretend to foresee, but in any case I am confident that the country will survive!"

On the other hand the Asquithian Liberals, however pleased they might be at Lloyd George's discomfiture, were in no sense allies of Conservatism. They were an independent party and put 348 candidates into the field. Though they could not hope for a clear majority they might well be in a position to control the Parliamentary balance and make their own terms for entering some sort of coalition. It was important therefore to stand apart from any other group. Lady Violet Bonham Carter gave the keynote to their programme in a

[1] Between Asquith and Lloyd George.

Q

speech at Paisley, her father's constituency. She declared that whereas Lloyd George's Government had suffered from St. Vitus Dance, Bonar Law's appeared to be suffering from Sleeping Sickness.

It must be admitted that the Conservative election manifesto, which was issued by Bonar Law on November 4th, gave some slight colour to this last accusation. Certainly it represented a reaction against the constant flow of legislative activity which had characterized the late Government. "The crying need of the nation at this moment", wrote Bonar Law, " – a need which in my judgment far exceeds any other – is that we should have tranquillity and stability both at home and abroad so that free scope should be given to the initiative and enterprise of our citizens, for it is in that way far more than by any action of the Government that we can hope to recover from the economic and social results of the war."

Tranquillity may not seem a very inspiring programme upon which to fight an Election, but there can be little doubt that it appealed to the unexpressed but no less deeply felt emotions of millions of voters. It was not so much any specific measure passed by the late Government as the general impression of "meddle and muddle", of uncertainty, of recklessness – especially in foreign policy – which had inspired such profound dissatisfaction with Lloyd George. There are occasions in the history of Britain when the public becomes, quite suddenly, tired of continual excitement, constant legislation, and perpetual crises. This was one of those occasions, and the final paragraph of Bonar Law's appeal shows how he gauged the sentiments of his supporters.

"There are many measures of legislative and administrative importance which in themselves would be desirable and which in other circumstances I should have recommended to the immediate attention of the electorate. But I do not feel that they can, at this moment, claim precedence over the nation's first need, which is, in every walk of life, to get on with its own work, with the minimum of interference at home and of disturbance abroad."

For the rest Bonar Law's programme contained no startling items. He undertook to reorganize the Cabinet Secretariat and return the conduct of Foreign Affairs to the undisputed control of the Foreign Office. This was a hit at Lloyd George's swollen personal staff – the celebrated Garden Suburb – whose intervention in the field of foreign policy had aroused such furious – if ineffective – passions in the breast of Curzon. He promised to impose drastic economies in Government expenditure in order to reduce taxation – in those

PARTY DISTINCTIONS.

Tax-Payer. "SPLENDID! PITY I CAN'T VOTE FOR ALL THREE OF 'EM."

days the orthodox panacea for bringing about a revival in trade
and the reduction of unemployment. He promised to implement
the late Government's policy with regard to Ireland, and to carry
into law the Irish Free State Bill, before the time limit had expired.
On the fiscal question he made no specific promises, but stated that
he would call a conference of Empire Prime Ministers to consider
the best way of promoting trade and economic development in the
Empire. During the election campaign, however, he went rather
further, and in the course of a speech made the same promise that
Balfour had made in 1910, namely that he would make no change
in the fiscal system until he had made a second appeal to the nation.
It was perhaps an unwise pledge and it has been much criticized,
although it may well have helped from an electoral point of view.
Baldwin claimed that he was fulfilling this promise when he recommended the premature – and, from the Conservative point of view,
disastrous – dissolution of 1923.

Few Elections in modern times have been fought in an atmosphere
of greater confusion and obscurity than the General Election of 1922.
Bonar Law was opposed by no less than four parties or groups all of
which had what purported to be divergent policies – though in fact
some of their programmes were virtually indistinguishable from one
another. First there were the Lloyd George Liberals with 138 candidates. It is difficult to discern any clear policy here apart from
personal support for the late Premier. Then came the Asquithian
Liberals whose position has already been described. More formidable than either of these was the Labour Party which regarded all
the older parties with equal aversion and did at least produce a
definite programme. But its principal item, the capital levy, proved
such a liability that the Labour leaders decided half way through
the campaign to drop it. This vacillation did them no good. In any
case the Labour Party at this time gave an impression of doctrinaire
rigidity which, together with the taint of Bolshevist influence, seriously
damaged its electoral chances. Finally, there were the dissident
Unionists, few in number, but possessing much prestige. Their
attitude was one of lofty contempt for the new Government. They
awaited the result of the Election confident that Bonar Law would
be defeated. They would then have the gloomy satisfaction which
always comes to those who can say, "I told you so".

Bonar Law was anxious not to alienate permanently either the
dissident Tories or the Lloyd George Liberals. His opening speech at
Glasgow on October 26th was studiously moderate in tone and con-

tained only the mildest references to the conduct of the Coalition
Government. At the same time the Conservative Central Office was
using its influence to prevent Conservatives standing against the
Liberals who had served in the late Administration. But it early
became clear that these kid glove methods would not pay. The
supporters of Lloyd George had no intention of responding in kind.
Bonar Law soon saw this himself. On October 30th Salisbury wrote
to him:[i]

"I have been thinking over what you said to me this morning that in
your next speech you will have to be more severe with L.G. I am sure that
is absolutely right. I find that it is expected and will be all the more effective in that your gentleness hitherto has not been responded to."

Sir Robert Donald, the former editor of the *Daily Chronicle* wrote
on similar lines the same day:[j]

"You must attack at once and dispel the illusion which Lloyd George
has created that he was kicked out of office by a trick and that there is
practically no change of policy, except in minor things. . . . Tell him he is
a liar and that he knows it. The harder you fight him the easier it will be
to deal with him when the fight is over. You offer him an olive branch and
he smites you with nettles."

Bonar Law replied to this advice:[k]

"I had hoped that Ll.G. would have used his sword openly and not
attacked by innuendo. Still, he was the first to begin and on Thursday I
intend to start fighting – which once begun will not stop."

To some extent Bonar Law's tactics did become rather more
aggressive. He made an occasional sally at Lloyd George's expense.
But in general he was reluctant to hit his old friend too hard. Writing
on November 6th to Sir Robert Borden he said:[l]

"As regards L.G. I feel as strongly as you do how great his service was –
greater than that of any other man anywhere – but the situation had become such that his Government could not continue with credit, and I met
him several times during the last six months and always urged him to resign.
If he had done so, he could have come back in six months or a year a bigger man than ever. We must of course say strong things of each other in
the Election but I earnestly hope that our friendship will not be broken or
even permanently impaired."

But if Bonar Law had scruples about attacking the members of the
late Government there was at least one ally who had no such
hesitancy. Beaverbrook plunged into the fray with all his accustomed
energy. It so happened that, on the evening of October 19th – the
day of the Carlton Club meeting -- he had a dinner engagement with

Birkenhead and Captain Guest. The conversation soon turned to politics and in particular to the Newport by-election where Beaverbrook had played a vigorous part in defeating the Coalition candidate. Before long "the discussion became extremely acrimonious".[m] It ended in an open breach between Beaverbrook and Guest, but not before Birkenhead had retailed a piece of gossip which he had learned the night before from Sir Archibald Salvidge. This was to the effect that some people attributed Beaverbrook's hostility to the Coalition to his alleged possession of oil interests in the Middle East which were being endangered by the Coalition Government's foreign policy.[n] Neither Salvidge nor Birkenhead believed the story themselves, but in the course of a heated conversation Birkenhead may not have made this point clear. At all events Beaverbrook was greatly annoyed. The allegation was, in fact, quite untrue, and Beaverbrook possessed no oil interests anywhere. But such an innuendo might well have had serious consequences, especially in view of the influence over Bonar Law, with which he was credited by many people.

A few days later he retaliated on Salvidge with a slashing leader in the *Daily Express* in which he dwelt upon Salvidge's past support of the Coalition. Salvidge wrote a protest to Bonar Law, who replied:[o]

"Lord Beaverbrook is personally one of my most intimate friends but he himself suggested to me at the very beginning, probably on account of the jealousy of other newspapers, that it would be better for him to leave me alone altogether during this crisis. I have not therefore attempted to influence him in anything, but if, as is possible, I should happen to see him on Sunday I will mention to him how strongly you feel the article in the *Express*."

He sent a copy of this reply to Beaverbrook first, who approved, observing:[p]

"Salvidge made some remarks to F. E. Smith. He should keep a civil tongue in his head. I am sorry you are troubled by these things."

At the same time Beaverbrook resolved to ginger up the whole election campaign. He saw no reason why the National Liberal ex-Ministers should be immune from Conservative opposition. They were hostile to Bonar Law. If enough of Lloyd George's supporters got back into Parliament they would join with the dissident Tories and either overthrow or at least seriously hamper the new Government. He resolved to disregard the arrangements made by the Central Office, and used his influence in support of independent Tory candidates against the Liberal ex-Ministers. The indignation of the latter knew no bounds, especially as Beaverbrook's tactics met with notable success. A striking case was that of Captain Guest himself. He lost his traditionally Liberal seat in East Dorset by over 5,000 votes to Hall Caine, the Beaverbrook candidate, who was a son of the famous novelist. Guest attributed this intervention to malice and spite; it was a long while before friendly relations were restored between him and Beaverbrook. Another case was that of Winston Churchill who was defeated at Dundee in similar circumstances.

Bonar Law had, throughout his campaign, strong support from the Press. The attitude of *The Times* under Wickham Steed was described in an earlier chapter. H. A. Gwynne, editor of the *Morning Post* which was the organ of Die-hard Toryism, pledged his help, incidentally restoring friendly relations with Bonar Law which had lapsed through a quarrel in the past. Sir Edward Hulton, the proprietor of the *Evening Standard* and many provincial newspapers, after an interview with Derby promised to come out on the side of the new Government. The *Daily Express* was of course a vociferous ally, and conducted an energetic campaign against the Coalition.

From one wholly unexpected quarter support came for Bonar Law. He was astonished, shortly after his assumption of the Premiership to receive warm congratulations from Lord Riddell, the Nonconformist, teetotal, proprietor of the *News of the World*. Riddell was a close friend of Lloyd George, and, although he had in general preserved political neutrality – possibly because the aspect of life, upon which the *News of the World* dwells, knows no political barriers – there certainly seemed no reason why he should support Bonar Law. However, the *News of the World* defended the new Government throughout the Election. Lord Riddell was, indeed, temporarily on bad terms with his old friend. He had recently visited Churt, and, Lloyd George being out, he was shown into an empty room to wait. No sooner had he sat down than a large black chow which Lloyd George kept came across to his chair growling in a menacing fashion. Whenever Lord Riddell moved the chow growled even more ferociously, and the unfortunate peer remained thus "pinned" for nearly an hour, until Lloyd George and his family returned from their walk and released him. Lloyd George was much amused at this episode, laughed heartily, and was wont to tell it as an excellent story to his friends.[q] Riddell was, however, most annoyed. Whether this or some grave issue of policy caused him to abandon the traditional neutrality of his paper must remain a matter of surmise, but, whatever the reason, it was Bonar Law and not Lloyd George who received the blessing of the *News of the World* in the Election of 1922.

A more doubtful question was the attitude of Lord Rothermere. Ever since the insanity and death of his brother, Northcliffe, in July 1922 he had been revolving in his mind a number of intricate schemes in connexion with *The Times* which he expected shortly to acquire. His political views were uncertain. At one time he appears to have contemplated installing Lloyd George as editor, but he was also at the same time, summer 1922, discussing the future of the paper with Bonar Law. In the end nothing came of these schemes, for on the very day of the Carlton Club meeting Rothermere's bid for *The Times* was beaten by that of John Jacob Astor, but Rothermere still controlled the *Daily Mail* which then possessed the greatest mass circulation in the country, and he also owned the *Daily Mirror*. On the morning of the Carlton Club meeting he wrote to Bonar Law:[r]

"Stick your toes in today. George and Chamberlain haven't one chance in a thousand of winning the election whilst the Conservative Party might and I think would."

This was encouraging but did not mean that Rothermere had pledged support. In any case Bonar Law had suffered in the past from Rothermere's attacks. He replied after the meeting was over:[s]

"You are a queer creature. You abuse me like a pickpocket, forget all about it and then write a most friendly letter for which, notwithstanding, I am obliged. Well – for good or ill this fence has been taken."

Rothermere's son, Esmond, was an M.P. and Bonar Law intended to offer him a minor post in the Government. But Rothermere had higher ideas than this. He called on Bonar Law, shortly after the latter's accession, and demanded as the price of his newspapers' support an earldom for himself and Cabinet office for his son. Bonar Law was far too hardened a politician to be greatly surprised at such a demand, but he was determined not to inaugurate his Premiership with an action which would rival Lloyd George's worst performances in the Honours Scandal. He pretended not to have heard what Rothermere said and rang for his visitor's car. As soon as Rothermere was out of the room he sent for his son, Dick, and dictated an account of the interview.[1] He also informed his Parliamentary private secretary, J. C. Davidson. If necessary he was prepared to reveal the episode to the public, and when Rothermere started to evince hostility in his papers he seriously considered doing so. In the end,

---

[1] The memorandum was kept by Bonar Law but has not survived. The facts given above are based on the personal recollections of Lord Coleraine (Richard Law) and Lord Davidson. The account given in the *History of the Times*, Vol. IV, Pt. II, p. 757 is not correct.

however, Rothermere deemed it prudent to come down on Bonar Law's side and support him during the Election.

Rumours of this episode soon began circulating in the clubs, often in a garbled form, and on one occasion Bonar Law was told that stories of his having given way to Rothermere's demand were current but generally disbelieved. In March 1923 the Duke of Somerset and Lord Willoughby de Broke seem to have contemplated raising the matter in the House of Lords, but they were dissuaded by Lord Salisbury, although it is not clear what arguments were used.[t]

Both Beaverbrook and Rothermere conducted an embarrassing campaign in favour of an instant declaration by the new Government that Britain should clear out of Mesopotamia. Beaverbrook wrote:[u]

"I think I ought to write and tell you that I really cannot follow you on Mesopotamia and Palestine. I am for the clean cut, as I have always been and I don't read your remarks to me in that sense.

"You must not imagine for a moment that this means that I, as a rare newspaper proprietor who does not want and won't take anything from you in the way of honours or office, mean to declare hostility to your administration. On the contrary I am going to help you all I can in the circumstances. But I feel so strongly on the Middle East question that I am going to try to bring public pressure to bear on the Conservative candidates in the constituencies to pledge themselves to the bag and baggage policy of evacuation in Mesopotamia and Palestine. I did not want you to read and perhaps misinterpret the question to candidates I am putting in tomorrow's *Daily Express* – so I send you this note in advance."

Bonar Law was sympathetic towards this demand, but he had no intention of making a declaration which would bind his Government in advance. He did not consider it possible to make any statement until he had had time to investigate the issues involved. Nor did he wish to trespass upon Curzon's province. He firmly refused despite much pressure to give the guarantee for which Beaverbrook and Rothermere asked.

As the election campaign proceeded, the volume of support for Bonar Law, and the degree of division among his opponents became more and more evident. Bonar Law was at first optimistic. In his letter of November 6th to Borden he said:[v]

"Though it is rash to prophesy I am inclined to think that we shall have a majority," characteristically adding, "but even so I know well that our troubles are only beginning."

But with the approach of polling day he became increasingly gloomy and depressed. His health had been giving him trouble and – ominous portent – his voice failed him on one or two occasions. His own seat in Central Glasgow seemed by no means safe. It would be little short of a disaster if his Party won but had no Prime Minister to lead them when Parliament opened. The dearth of experience on the Front Bench would then be shown in a particularly glaring light. And anyway would his Party win? Perhaps "Tranquillity" was not after all a very inspiring slogan for an election campaign in a modern democracy. Perhaps Lloyd George was right, and the nation dazzled by his firework display would vote in such a way that the House of Commons would contain no party with a clear majority, and everything would be in confusion again.

Bonar Law spoke at Glasgow on the eve of the poll, and then returned to London. Polling day was November 15th. The weather was abominable and much of the country was shrouded in fog. Despite a bad cold Bonar Law set out for the polling station at South Kensington and, heavily muffled in scarves, duly recorded his own vote. As the first news of the Election appeared it seemed as if his gloomier predictions were to be justified. There was much delay in announcing the result of his own contest and he thought that this must mean a recount. Moreover, the results of the boroughs – which always come in first – were inconclusive. It was not until the news from the county seats became known that Bonar Law realized the full extent of his triumph for the countryside had rallied to the Tory Party, and the good news arrived that he had held Central Glasgow by 3,000 votes. When the final result was declared Bonar Law found that he had a majority of 77 over all other parties combined. The Conservatives had 344 seats. Labour came next with 138 – almost twice its previous strength. The Asquithian Liberals had 60 seats, and the Lloyd George Liberals 57. But – such are the vagaries of the British electoral system – this sweeping victory was gained on a minority of the total votes cast. Bonar Law had been saved by the divisions among his opponents.

As the congratulations poured in Bonar Law could reflect with much satisfaction upon his victory. It was very largely a personal triumph for him. It was a gratifying vindication of his decision at the Carlton Club meeting. No longer could his enemies proclaim that the Coalition only fell because of an intrigue between the Die-hards and the disgruntled Under-Secretaries. Whatever the motives of the malcontents, there seemed little doubt that their action was endorsed by the country at large. Not merely had Bonar Law won but he had won by a sufficient margin to dispense with the need for any outside allies. For the first time in over twenty years a Conservative Administration was supported by a homogeneous Party with an overall majority in the House of Commons.

Several of Bonar Law's principal opponents lost their seats at the Election. Of the leading National Liberals, Churchill, Guest, Kellaway and Hamar Greenwood all succumbed. Of the Asquithian Liberals, Walter Runciman and Sir Donald Maclean were beaten. Maclean had been their leader during Asquith's temporary exile from the House after the Coupon Election.

"My dear Maclean," wrote Bonar Law,[w] "I am really very sorry the fortune of war has gone against you at Peebles, and I earnestly hope that it may not be long before you are back in the House.

"I always thought and I fancy I said it to you more than once that your time of leading your party very much resembled my own experience and in each case the success came because the House of Commons rather liked us."

Most of Bonar Law's leading supporters were victorious at the polls, but one Cabinet Minister, Sir Arthur Griffith-Boscawen, and two Junior Ministers, failed to get in. The problem of finding them seats was destined to cause a good deal of trouble early in the following year. Another casualty was the Chief Whip, Colonel Leslie Wilson, despite the part he played in overthrowing the Coalition.

2

The most immediate and urgent matter confronting the new Government was the Irish Free State Bill which set up the new Constitution for Southern Ireland. Under the terms of the Irish Treaty this had to be ratified by both sides within a year of the signing of the Treaty. It had already been ratified in Ireland. Parliament therefore had to pass the Bill before December 6th; otherwise the Constitution lapsed completely. Bonar Law had never regarded the Treaty with enthusiasm, and the ranks of his supporters contained some of its bitterest enemies. Nevertheless, even the Die-hards admitted that matters had now gone beyond recall, and that there was really no option except to pass the Bill as soon as possible and hope for the best. Accordingly Bonar Law decided to have a short Parliamentary session before Christmas, beginning on November 20th. This would be devoted almost exclusively to Ireland. All other measures could wait until the next session which was fixed to open in the middle of February.

On November 27th Bonar Law moved the second reading of the Irish Bill. His speech was one of masterly neutrality for he was anxious to avoid giving offence to the Die-hards. With that ability to limit the issues of debate, which had always been one of his strongest assets in argument, he carefully avoided any general discussion of the Treaty. The Treaty had already been approved by the late Parliament. No political party or individual Member at the recent Election, he said, "took any other view than that this Treaty must be given a chance, and everyone desires that this should be done". Having thus skated over the thin ice, Bonar Law proceeded to deal with the legal question as to whether the wording of the new Irish Constitution, set up in the Bill, accorded with the wording of the Irish Treaty. In this way he carefully lowered the whole temperature of the discussion before it had time to arouse those heated passions which normally swayed the House whenever the question of Ireland was debated. The Bill was eventually passed without a division – though not without many mournful groans and gloomy jeremiads from the Ulster and Die-hard members.

Since the Irish Bill aroused so little controversy it might have been expected that the session would pass by uneventfully, but, as Bonar Law himself observed in his first speech to the House, "I have never seen a session however short in which something does not turn up, which was not expected to happen." The session was in fact marked by two episodes which deserve to be recorded. The first arose indirectly out of Bonar Law's decision, taken as soon as he became Prime Minister, to restore the departmental Ministers to their proper constitutional rôle. Of late Lloyd George had conducted business almost as if he had been a popular dictator relying on the advice of a small clique of intimate friends. The Cabinet was habitually by-passed. Every delegation or deputation found its way sooner or later to 10 Downing Street. Bonar Law promptly signalized the reversal of this policy by refusing to receive a deputation of the unemployed who insisted upon laying the grievances before the Prime Minister. This decision was not prompted by callousness or indifference. Bonar Law viewed the conditions of the unemployed with every sympathy, but he considered that the Minister of Labour was the proper person to deal with them, and he wanted to make it clear to the world that the new Government was not to be a one man show. Moreover, he did not believe, or wish the public to think that he believed, in the existence of any simple panacea for unemployment. The problem could only be solved by an improvement in the national prosperity – an improvement which might be achieved gradually by reduction of taxes but which certainly could not come overnight.

The Labour Party, however, naturally resented this attitude. They considered that the Prime Minister should have shown more sympathy, but, since they could hardly deny that he was within his rights in refusing, they chose another matter upon which to attack him. Bonar Law had not only refused to see the leaders of the Deputation, he had also examined their police records. He came to the conclusion that, in view of their violent and subversive language, there was some danger of a riot in London. He therefore caused two of his secretaries to summon representatives of the London Press and convey a warning about the danger. Unfortunately, his secretaries omitted to include the *Daily Herald* among the papers thus informed – no doubt on account of its political hostility. The Labour Party was quick to move the adjournment of the House on the ground that this was a case of "tampering with the Press" – a practice of which the late Government was alleged to have been often guilty, and which, Bonar Law had in an election speech declared, would cease under his régime. In fact Bonar Law had not given orders to exclude the *Daily Herald*, and would have countermanded that exclusion, had he known in time. He explained this to the House with his usual candour, but firmly defended his right to communicate matters of this sort to the Press. His defence was convincing and the attack fizzled out.

Towards the end of the session a much more serious attack was made upon the Government, and from a very different quarter. This was the curious episode of the Gounaris letters. Gounaris had been the Prime Minister of Greece while King Constantine was King. He was held responsible by the new Greek Government for the débâcle in Asia Minor, and on November 28th to the horror of the civilized world, together with five colleagues he was shot at dawn. Gounaris had conducted a lengthy correspondence with Curzon from February 1922 onwards. This correspondence had – by means that have never been disclosed – fallen into the hands of Beaverbrook. On December 3rd he published in the *Sunday Express* extracts from a letter of February 15th, 1922, addressed by Gounaris to Curzon. The gist of it was a grave warning that, unless Britain could give support in arms and money to the Greek Government, the Greek Army would have to withdraw from Asia Minor before it was too late. The political significance of such a publication was of course to pin the blame for the Greek disaster and the judicial murder of Gounaris on to the Coalition Government.

But on reading this letter in the *Sunday Express* the leading ex-

Coalitionists thought that they had a golden opportunity of damaging Curzon. Birkenhead was confident that he had never seen the Gounaris letter. He consulted Lloyd George, Chamberlain, and Worthington Evans, who all disclaimed any knowledge of it. If this were really the case Curzon deserved severe censure for not having circulated to the Cabinet a communication of such importance. The Cabinet could not be held responsible for the Greek débâcle when the Foreign Secretary conducted policy on his own without giving them the vital information that they needed in order to form an opinion. On December 7th Birkenhead read the letter out in the House of Lords. He declared in the most emphatic terms that it had never been seen by him or by his ex-colleagues, and therefore that if any member of the late Government was responsible for the Greek tragedy it was Curzon who was one of the very few who retained his post in the new Cabinet.

Birkenhead, however, in making this attack had displayed a reck-lessness, remarkable in an ex-Lord Chancellor. His rashness was, indeed, shared by his former colleagues, for none of them appears to have taken the precaution of consulting the official records in order to see what had really happened. In fact the document had been printed and circulated to the Cabinet, and Birkenhead himself had actually returned it initialled as having been read. Bonar Law's own account written to Curzon in Lausanne, the day after the attack shows what had happened:[x]

"Our friends, your late colleagues, have made almost as big a mess of it as I have seen in the whole of my political experience. A paper published extracts from a letter to you from Gounaris of 15th February last. L.G., F.E., Austen and Worthington Evans – I do not know whether there were any others – came to the conclusion that here was a weapon to be used against you to prove that it was you and not L.G. who had led the Greeks on and caused the disaster. They had risked this by trusting to their memory. A question was put to me in the House whether this correspon-dence had been circulated to the Cabinet. I was able to reply, 'Yes'. They questioned it by supplementaries but without any result. F.E. had arranged to make an attack in force in the House of Lords, and apparently they had forgotten to tell him of the answer given.[1] He therefore made a violent attack which was quite successfully answered by Salisbury, and now a question is going to be put in the House of Lords and probably in our House too asking for confirmation of the statement made by me.

"We have the most absolute proof not only in the Foreign Office list, but Horne and Austen have left their papers with their successors and in

---

[1] Bonar Law's answer was given about three quarters of an hour before the House of Lords met.

both cases the document, which F.E. said none of them had ever seen, is found among their papers. Probably you have been informed of a lot of this, but, if you have had any idea that trouble might be caused to you, you may put that out of your head.".

In the face of this evidence Birkenhead and Lloyd George felt obliged to withdraw their charges, and Birkenhead made a full and handsome apology in the House of Lords. The ex-Ministers of the Coalition now appeared in a most foolish light. For they had not been content with merely denying all knowledge of the Gounaris letter. They had also dwelt, at length and with eloquence, upon the complete change in policy which they would have demanded had they seen so vital a document. But it seemed clear that they had all in fact seen it and yet had done nothing whatever. It is not surprising that the rest of the session passed without further attacks upon the Government from that particular quarter. It is difficult to explain what Lord Ronaldshay in his life of Curzon had justly described as "a truly remarkable case of collective amnesia". Evidently the ex Ministers genuinely believed that they had not seen the document. Any suggestion to the contrary would argue not merely dishonesty but a high degree of folly. It can only be supposed that the prospect of damaging Curzon, for whom they all felt a deep animosity at this time, was so exhilarating that they forgot to verify their references.

Curzon was understandably furious. Neither mild nor brief were the denunciations of his former colleagues, with which he regaled Bonar Law in letter after letter from Lausanne. On December 9th he wrote:[y]

". . . I am concerned at the malevolence exhibited by my late colleagues. Birkenhead daily fires off a number of poisoned shafts *in my absence* in the Lords. I will deal with him faithfully if he repeats it next session. But I am surprised at Chamberlain and W. Evans – tho' not at L.G. – joining in the manhunt.

"Of course the real paradox lies in the fact that I am represented as the author of Greece's remaining in Asia Minor whereas I had been struggling for a year to get her out (in the face of the machinations of L.G. and only wanted her to hold on until I could get to Paris and arrange an honourable evacuation)."

Bonar Law replied:[z]

"The Gounaris business is over for the present but in case it comes up again when you return there is a more deadly weapon left for you than has yet been used and that is a letter from Gounaris – dated February 27 I think – to the late Prime Minister calling attention to the letter to you and recapitulating all the facts contained in his letter to you. This is in the

Foreign Office because he sent a copy of it. I had arranged with Salisbury to read it yesterday but after L.G.'s withdrawal I thought it better not to use it and Salisbury agreed."

Curzon did not dissent from this. He merely observed in menacing tones:[za]

"If I am ever called upon to tell in Parliament the whole tale of the 10 Downing Street cum-Greek intrigue it will be a bad day for L.G. That was why he cooed like a dove in the H. of C. when the question last came up."

The need for these lurid revelations was, however, suddenly removed by the action of Beaverbrook. On December 16th, the day after the session ended, he published in the *Daily Express* some of the facts about Lloyd George's personal part in encouraging the Greeks to hold on in Asia Minor as late as ten days before the fall of Smyrna. Curzon was delighted. He had been priming Bonar Law with information to use against Lloyd George and now added: "But my information has been rendered unnecessary by the revelations in yesterday's *Daily Express*". Bonar Law, however, was displeased at Beaverbrook's action. He rang up his friend at 8 o'clock that morning and said: "This is a bombshell you have thrown. If you had published it yesterday the House would not have risen." Beaverbrook replied that he had postponed publication for that very reason. "Well whether the House is up or not," replied Bonar Law gloomily, "you can depend upon it you will hear more of this."[zb] In fact, however, Bonar Law was wrong. Lloyd George deemed it prudent to ignore the allegations in the *Daily Express*. For the time being the whole matter was dropped, and the ex-Coalition Ministers bided their time for further attacks on other issues.

Thus ended the first session of Parliament in Bonar Law's Premiership. It had been largely a personal triumph for him. He had carried nearly all the burden of the work. Indeed it was somewhat ironical that he who had from the first proclaimed the importance of Cabinet responsibility and the abolition of one man rule should have been forced to take so much upon himself. It was certainly not his wish, but the lack of experienced colleagues made it almost inevitable at first.

"I have been following your Parliamentary proceedings as closely as I could," wrote Curzon, "but I am afraid the strain upon you must be considerable as your Front Bench seems to shine more in silence than in speech."

"Thank you very much for your personal letters which were extremely interesting," replied Bonar Law, "but they were not exactly the kind which

I could read to the Cabinet in view of your compliment to the Front Bench. . . ."

It was still the duty at that time of the Prime Minister to send every day a letter in his own hand to the King describing what had happened in Parliament. On the last day of the session Sir Patrick Gower, one of Bonar Law's private secretaries, took the liberty of writing a personal letter to Lord Stamfordham, in order to supplement Bonar Law's account. He ended:[zc]

"The Prime Minister's success in the present House has been remarkable, and the most striking feature of this Session has been the extraordinary influence that he has exercised over the Labour Party. They are obviously very impressed with his sincerity and his powers of logical argument, and even the extremists would seem to be hushed into comparative silence when he is speaking. There may be exceptional occasions which I suppose are inevitable with such explosive material, but the Prime Minister undoubtedly exercises a growing sway over them."

CHAPTER XXX

FRANCE AND AMERICA

DECEMBER 1922 – APRIL 1923

Problem of reparations – Attitude of the French – Poincaré's severity – Bonar Law's attempts at compromise, first in London, then in Paris – Their total failure – The Rupture Cordiale begins – Bonar Law's relations with Curzon – He insists upon Curzon avoiding war with Turkey – Prickly attitude of Curzon – The American Debt – Folly of Baldwin – Bonar Law refuses to accept Baldwin's settlement – He contemplates resignation – He decides to remain – The Conservative Party funds – Lord Farquhar refuses to pay over the money – Lord Astor's £200,000 – Bonar Law dismisses Farquhar – Reopening of Parliament – Bonar Law's ascendancy – His firm conduct of Cabinet meetings – His empirical approach to politics – Abolition of the "Garden Suburb" – Unemployment and Housing – Unsatisfactory By-elections – Continued hostility of the Coalition Conservatives – Birkenhead's dinner in honour of Balfour – Bonar Law's throat gives trouble

I

THE calm which had attended Bonar Law in his early weeks as Prime Minister was of brief duration. Long before Parliament next met – mid-February – the storm clouds began to gather. It was in the field of foreign affairs – in particular relations with France and America – that the greatest difficulties were to arise. Bonar Law had never taken any very close interest in foreign policy. In the Coalition Cabinet Lloyd George had monopolized that side of the Government's activity. Indeed his propensity to disregard his Foreign Secretary had been a contributory cause of the Coalition's fall. Therefore, quite apart from personal inclination, Bonar Law was almost bound to leave foreign policy to Curzon. But no Prime Minister can wholly dissociate himself from such an important matter, and Curzon's absence from the country at Lausanne made it necessary for Bonar Law to deal with at least one major issue of foreign policy – that of German reparations.

Accordingly, while his Foreign Secretary endeavoured to restore British prestige and conclude a satisfactory peace treaty with the Turks, Bonar Law essayed the almost hopeless task of achieving an agreement with Poincaré over the treatment of Germany. This was an appropriate division of labour. Bonar Law had taken an interest in reparations ever since his days as Chancellor of the Exchequer. He understood economic and financial problems, whereas, to quote Sir Harold Nicolson, Curzon's "interest in finance was confined to his own income", and he had never played an important rôle in the interminable conferences on that contentious subject, which occupied so much of the European statesmen's time since the end of the war.

The situation when Bonar Law returned to office can be briefly summarized. In April 1921 the Reparations Commission – which was dominated by France – fixed Germany's total liability at £6,600 million, and at the same time gave official notification that Germany was in default on the interim payments which had been imposed in the Versailles Treaty. The Germans accepted this liability but protested that their economic condition made it impossible for them to pay for the time being. The British Government sympathized with the Germans, and informed British opinion, influenced partly by Keynes's famous book, inclined to the view that such sums were wholly out of the realm of practical politics. The French Government took a much more severe view. It was still believed in France that huge sums could be obtained from Germany, if only the Germans were bullied enough.

There was another consideration which influenced French policy. The French had in 1919 given up their insistence upon the frontier of the Rhine, in return for a joint Anglo-American guarantee against German attack. Unfortunately the British guarantee only came into effect if the American Senate ratified the Versailles Treaty. The Senate, however, to the dismay of the Allies, refused to do so. The British guarantee therefore automatically lapsed, and Lloyd George was not prepared to risk the unpopularity which would have followed any attempt to negotiate a military treaty with France, independently of America. The French therefore felt, with good reason, that they had been cheated out of their minimum requirements for security against future German aggression, and, from an early stage, a powerful section of French opinion favoured using the cat and mouse powers conferred by the reparations clauses of the Versailles Treaty as an excuse for seizing the Ruhr, establishing a puppet Rhineland State, and securing the Rhine frontier which the extremists had always demanded. Those who took this view did not really care about reparations at all, and regarded German default as a welcome excuse for their own ulterior purposes. In January 1922, the fall of Briand and the accession of Poincaré who represented this element of French

THE GOOSE THAT COULDN'T—OR WOULDN'T.

Mr. Bonar Law. "THE WRETCHED BIRD CAN'T LAY GOLDEN EGGS WITHOUT A NICE LONG MORATORIUM."

M. Poincaré. "AND I SAY SHE CAN. AND A GOOSE THAT CAN LAY AND WON'T LAY MUST BE MADE TO LAY—EVEN IF I HAVE TO WRING HER NECK!"

opinion made any hope of agreement between Britain and France extremely remote. During 1922 the Reparations Commission, the British member dissenting, had formally declared Germany to be in default over deliveries of timber. Poincaré therefore had the law on his side, and he announced that France would if necessary act alone, invade the Ruhr, and apply sanctions in order to extract reparations.

Various efforts were made during the remainder of the year to prevent Poincaré from fulfilling this threat, but by the beginning of December his patience – not a quality conspicuous in his character – had evidently become exhausted. It was finally agreed to hold a Conference of Allied Prime Ministers in London on December 9th in order to consider what should be done. Three days earlier Bonar Law gave an interview to C. P. Scott, the editor of the *Manchester Guardian* who kept a note of what was said:[a]

". . . He spoke of the extreme difficulty facing him at the Conference of Prime Ministers on Saturday – a far more difficult business than the Conference at Lausanne (at which I had said I wished he could have taken Curzon's place). . . . 'For the first time I am going into a conference without any policy in my own mind – I know I am suspected of being pro French and it is quite possible you may quarrel with me on that score (I admitted that I had my fears) – It is true that I attach the utmost importance to maintaining a good understanding with France. I may have to choose between two evils – between a breach with France which would mean chaos in Europe or concessions to France which would also involve great misfortunes'. . . .

"He mentioned that he had gone into the whole subject of Germany's capacity to pay with Keynes and I gathered that he intended to continue to consult him. . . ."

The Conference was wholly abortive. Indeed all Bonar Law could do was to postpone a final settlement until a further meeting of the Prime Ministers in Paris at the beginning of January.

The Italian Prime Minister at the London Conference was Benito Mussolini who had just brought off the successful *coup d'état* which was to put him in control of his country for over twenty years. Curzon, who had met him already, formed a most adverse opinion of him, and hastened to pen a letter in his best style to Bonar Law:[b]

"I must utter the most solemn warning about treating with such a man . . . I beg you, if the man attempts to discuss these Eastern questions or to extract any assurances about them, to decline to say a word on the subject. He is a thoroughly unscrupulous and dangerous demagogue – plausible in manner but without scruple or truth in conduct."

In fact, however, Mussolini appears to have behaved well in

London, and he made no attempt to extract assurances from Bonar Law. The Prime Minister found him, as many others have, a striking personality. "Look at that man's eyes," he said to one of his secretaries. "You will hear more of him later."[c]

At the end of December Bonar Law, armed with a compromise plan, crossed to Paris. He was accompanied by Davidson, Eyre Crowe, the Permanent Under-Secretary of the Foreign Office, and Lloyd-Greame, President of the Board of Trade. He stayed at the Crillon Hotel where he had discussions with Curzon summoned from Lausanne. Curzon agreed with Bonar Law's proposals for a compromise. The gist of this plan was that Germany's total liability should be fixed at £2,500 million – a not unreasonable sum – and that she should be dispensed from any payment for the next four years so that she might have a chance to restore her economic condition and her credit. The plan was put forward more as a means of convincing British and world opinion that the Government had made a real effort at producing a fair solution rather than in expectation that the French would agree. "I have no hope of the Conference of January 2nd," Bonar Law wrote to Curzon, "unless something unexpected happens."

Unfortunately nothing unexpected did happen. Indeed the Conference went precisely as might have been predicted. At the first meeting Poincaré made it clear that he was determined to occupy the Ruhr, and he refused to regard Bonar Law's plan even as a basis for discussion. Indifferent to diplomatic finesse, Bonar Law was strongly in favour of breaking off negotiations at once and returning to London. He was dissuaded from taking such a drastic step, and consented to attend two more meetings. These were characterized by complete courtesy and equally complete disagreement. In the circumstances further negotiation was useless, and the discussions ended on January 4th, 1923.

The French now fulfilled their long delayed threat. On January 11th their troops occupied Essen. What came to be known as the "Rupture Cordiale" had begun. It did not end in Bonar Law's lifetime.

2

Bonar Law was profoundly disturbed at the outcome of the Paris Conference, but he seems to have given Curzon an even greater impression of gloom than he in fact felt. "The feet of the Prime Minister were glacial, positively glacial," Curzon observed to Harold

Nicolson on returning from Paris to Lausanne.[d] Bonar Law's tendency to dwell on the darker aspect of affairs often made him seem
defeatist, and, in view of the breach with France, he was certainly
most anxious that Curzon should not commit the Government to an
armed conflict with Turkey, in which Britain might be completely
isolated.

Sir Harold Nicolson in his masterly account of Curzon's foreign
policy is perhaps unduly severe on Bonar Law and the rest of the
Cabinet. He refers to the Prime Minister's "pessimism", his "defeatist
opinions", his "faint but frequent bleatings".[e] No doubt these
reminders of public opinion in Britain were unwelcome and irritating
to the Foreign Secretary in Lausanne. Nevertheless, Bonar Law had
some reasons for his attitude. He was after all leader of the Conservative Party which had a tradition of being both pro-French and pro-
Turk. Already events had forced a rupture – however cordial – with
France. The last thing he wanted was a war with Turkey. It was
precisely the danger of such a war – at the time of the Chanak
Incident – which had been the immediate cause of Lloyd George's
downfall and the replacement of the Coalition by the present
Government. A war with Turkey would be a bad start for a policy of
"tranquillity".

There was a further point. Early in January it seemed – wrongly
as events turned out – that the only issue which prevented the signing
of a treaty was the question of Mosul. Was Mosul to belong to Turkey
or to the infant Kingdom of Iraq, which was under British protection?
Now the question of Mosul was one on which the Cabinet was highly
sensitive. For Mosul not only contained a hideously complicated
tangle of obscure and hostile races, it also contained a great deal of
oil, and in the company which owned the oil British interests had a
three-quarter share. If we took a firm line in favour of Iraq would
not the Liberals and the Left at once protest that this was an outrageous example of the financial imperialism which was popularly,
though incorrectly, believed to exercise a sinister influence over
British foreign policy? And was it not equally certain that the *Daily
Mail* and the *Daily Express* – or, more accurately, Lords Rothermere
and Beaverbrook – already engaged in a campaign to liquidate all
our Near Eastern commitments on grounds of economy, would attack
the Government with greater persistence than ever?

Bonar Law was not unduly sensitive to newspaper attacks, but in
this particular case he had strong sympathy with the critics. He was
anxious to get out of Iraq and very anxious to avoid even the mere

appearance of risking a war because of British oil interests. He therefore issued a categorical warning to Curzon on January 8th:[f]

"I am still as satisfied as we both were before you went to Lausanne that we cannot go to war for Mosul. Indeed, although, I think, from conversations you know exactly what my views are, it is perhaps as well to prevent the possibility of misunderstanding that I should again repeat that there are two things which seem to me vital. The first is that we should not go to war for Mosul, and second that, if the French – as we know to be the case – will not join us, we shall not by ourselves fight to enforce what remains of the Treaty of Sèvres. I feel so strongly on both these points that, unless something quite unforeseen should change my view, I would not take responsibility for any other policy."

This letter can hardly be described as a "faint bleat", and it made the position quite clear. Curzon did not disagree. In the end, with a skill and persistence which must excite the utmost admiration, he demolished the entire Turkish case for occupying Mosul, and contrived to take this problem out of the Lausanne discussions altogether. The Turks were obliged to agree to arbitration by the League of Nations, and Curzon was rightly confident that an impartial verdict would favour Iraq. Thus the question of Mosul did not finally prove an obstacle at Lausanne.

It should not be imagined from the foregoing account that Curzon was in any sense a passive recipient of admonitions from Bonar Law. On the contrary, elated at the eclipse of his enemy, Lloyd George, he had seldom been in better form. The effort of coping with French and Italian intrigues, and negotiating with Ismet Pasha in no way exhausted his activities, and, till a late hour, night after night, he would write from Lausanne in his own hand long letters to Bonar Law, complaining, exhorting, instructing, above all asserting the rights of the Foreign Secretary against every encroachment.

For example, Bonar Law had had a courtesy visit from the French Ambassador and Curzon detailed a long list of complications which, he alleged, ensued:[g]

"All this has arisen out of the 'courtesy visit', and when the F.O. ask me what has happened all I can reply is that I am entirely in the dark. Had this happened under the old régime there would have been nothing surprising, but you yourself put reparations back under the F.O. and I know you have not the slightest intention of doing or saying anything except with our full knowledge.

"But it makes me very suspicious of 'courtesy visits'. Can you tell me exactly what happened, and if you see an Ambassador again will you dictate, afterwards – as I always do – a brief account of the interview."

Bonar Law replied mildly:[h] "As regards the courtesy visit nothing could have been more formal or more indefinite." He assured Curzon that he had made none of the statements alleged by Curzon's informants. But when Curzon began to criticize his conduct of affairs at the Paris Conference, a certain note of acerbity is discernible in the Prime Minister's reply. Curzon wrote on January 6th:[i]

"I was surprised and sorry at the early breakdown in Paris, and I wonder whether it was altogether wise to publish our scheme in advance and expose it to the ruthless fangs of the Paris Press."

Two days later Bonar Law replied:[j]

"I note what you say about our Paris Conference, but you have evidently not had time to understand the situation, as you speak of our having published our scheme in advance when as a matter of fact it was only handed to the Conference simultaneously with the French scheme, and both were published together."

Curzon's complaints were not directed only at Bonar Law. He found Derby's activities very trying. The two men had never been on cordial terms. "He is the meanest man I know," Derby once said of Curzon in a letter to Bonar Law. On December 6th Curzon wrote to Bonar Law:[k]

"The quasi political activities of the W.O. are a perfect curse. You will remember that before I went to Paris Derby, without ever telling the F.O., had sent over Burnett-Stuart to Paris, and he had shown a W.O. memo on the whole question of peace with Turkey to Foch – many of the proposals being in violent disagreement with my policy. . . .

"Derby is particularly bad in this respect for he fancies that he is the only man who has influence with the French and that his mission in life is to vary attendance at Parisian race meetings with attempts to correct the blunders of the British Ambassador and Foreign Secretary."

It was not only on Foreign Affairs that Curzon meant to assert his rights.

"Before you fill the Regius Professorship of Divinity at Oxford," he wrote, "I hope you will consult me as Chancellor of the University. Ll.G. usually did so with these appointments."[l]

Bonar Law had no objection on this score. He replied:

"I shall certainly not appoint a Regius Professor without your advice. Indeed I would not myself have any idea as to the suitable person to choose."[m]

Towards the end of the Lausanne negotiations Curzon seems to have become somewhat overwrought. Bonar Law had warned him of the views of the Cabinet on certain matters.

"Have I not", protested Curzon,[n] "kept carefully in mind the views of the Cabinet throughout and have I ever misled or landed you?"

"I have been fighting here a battle the magnitude and difficulty of which you hardly realize at home.

"I am more than grateful for the free hand that you have given me. But I have sometimes felt a little hurt that from start to finish I cannot recall a word of encouragement of my labours, while I am continually being told to beware of situations of which I am just as conscious as any-one at home and perhaps am able to apprise more accurately."

Bonar Law's reaction to these letters is not known. But it is perhaps reasonable to surmize that their general tone may have implanted in his mind certain doubts – not about Curzon's ability as Foreign Secretary, for which he had great respect – but about Curzon's character. This doubt may at first have been a mere whis-per, a faint feeling that, for all his great talents, there was something not quite right about Curzon. The evidence is lacking to give a definite answer, but these letters should not be forgotten when we came to consider the circumstances of Bonar Law's retirement a few months later, and his attitude to the problem of who should succeed him.

On February 4th the Lausanne Conference came to an end. The Turks refused to sign the Treaty, and Curzon returned to England. But what seemed apparent failure was in reality success. Although the Treaty had not been signed British prestige in the East had been in a large measure re-established, war had been avoided, and in fact the Treaty with a few unimportant modifications was to be signed by the Turks five months later.

3

At the end of January 1923 a sudden wholly unexpected squall blew up and very nearly overturned the Government completely. This was the question of the settlement of the American debt, and, since it brought Bonar Law to the verge of resigning, the matter must be described in some detail. The British Government owed the Government of the United States a sum which amounted to nearly £900 million. This debt had been almost exclusively contracted in respect of munitions supplied during the war, and a very large part of these munitions had been used by France, Italy and other Euro-pean Allies. Indeed the total indebtedness of the other Allies to Britain was nearly four times as great as that of Britain to the United States. It was clear therefore that, although we had an indisputable legal obligation to repay our debt to America irrespective of any sums that we could recover from our debtors, common sense and justice demanded an all round settlement. This had, indeed, been the theme of the celebrated "Balfour Note" in August 1922. Balfour, temporarily in charge of the Foreign Office, informed our European debtors that we would only expect them to pay enough to cover our own debt to the United States. All the rest would be wiped out.

This declaration was ill received in America, and was followed by a demand that the British debt should be funded as soon as possible. Sir Robert Horne was on the point of leaving for America to discuss the matter with the authorities at Washington, when the Coalition fell. The problem was therefore temporarily postponed but it was clear that Bonar Law's Government would have to take some sort of action at an early stage.

Bonar Law's own attitude was the same as that of Balfour and Lloyd George. He considered that the only fair settlement was one which involved either cancellation all round or payment all round. He regarded it as most unfair that Britain should be faced with a huge one-sided burden. Yet this seemed all too likely, if the Americans insisted on the letter of the law, and if the French insisted that they could only pay Britain to the extent that they could successfully extract reparations from Germany – a prospect which was becoming ever blacker. Bonar Law made his own view clear in the House of Commons on December 14th, 1922. Referring to our need for American credit during the war he said:

"It is an undoubted fact that we were in that position because we had used all our securities and pledged them already to secure munitions for carrying on the War; and we had pledged them without any regard whatever to whether it was for the British Armies or the Armies of our Allies. I am sure there is no one in the world who will doubt that, from the point of view of justice, it cannot be right that we alone should make payment as the result of this. . . . I am convinced that to make that payment without receiving anything from outside sources would reduce the standard of living in this country for a generation, and would be a burden upon us, which no one who talks of it now has any conception of."

This categorical statement leaves no doubt as to Bonar Law's attitude, and it makes what subsequently happened all the more surprising. At the beginning of January Baldwin, the new Chancellor of the Exchequer, sailed to America with Montagu Norman, the Governor of the Bank of England. It does not appear that they had any written instructions, but it is quite certain that, whatever else they were empowered to do, they had no right to conclude an independent Anglo-American settlement without reference to the Cabinet. Yet this was in the end exactly what they did.

The situation when they opened discussions at Washington was that Britain had currently to pay about £46,000,000 annually as interest – quite apart from sinking fund, since the original debt had been contracted at 5 per cent. This was generally agreed to be absurdly high. The best of the various offers which Baldwin could obtain from the American Commissioners was 3 per cent for ten years and 3½ per cent thereafter. This with a sinking fund of 1 per cent meant annual payments of about £34,000,000 for ten years and, after that, £40,000,000. According to Dr. Thomas Jones, who wrote the notice of Bonar Law in the *Dictionary of National Biography*, and who was at this time a member of the Cabinet Secretariat, the maximum that Bonar Law was prepared to concede was 2½ per cent – giving an annual payment of about £25,000,000. Presumably – though Dr. Jones does not say so – even this payment was conditional as far as Bonar Law was concerned, upon the recovery of a comparable sum from our European debtors. Alarmed at the way negotiations seemed to be proceeding, Bonar Law telegraphed his views to Baldwin at some length. The Chancellor was under strong pressure from the British Embassy and the United States Government to conclude an agreement as soon as possible, for Congress rose on March 4th, and it was considered important to ratify any settlement of the debt before that date. Nevertheless, when all allowances are made, his final decision remains astonishing. He decided that the American offer was the best he could hope for, and he closed with it on his own authority without reference to the Cabinet. Then, as if determined to block all possibility of retreat, he informed the newspaper reporters, when he landed in England at the end of January, both of the nature of the terms, and of his own conviction that they were the best obtainable.

Bonar Law could scarcely have been placed in a more embarrassing position. He was convinced that the settlement was disastrous, that the burden of taxation thus imposed would make British economic recovery impossible, that, even if the terms were acceptable to public opinion now, they would be greatly resented in a few years' time. He considered that it was wholly wrong to conclude any arrangement about the American debt independently of the whole question of inter-Allied indebtedness. There was, he believed, no hope of recovering from our European debtors anything like the sum that Baldwin had contracted to pay to America. He frankly preferred to make no settlement at all. This might legally amount to default, but it could not be so described in equity. In the long run the Baldwin settlement would greatly damage Anglo-American relations. It was better to have a temporary difference now. The delay might mean that the American people would come to take a more generous view.[1]

Bonar Law was fortified in his opinions by expert advice from two sources. During the negotiations he had consulted both Keynes and McKenna who advised him against accepting the American terms. Keynes is quoted by Mr. G. M. Young in his life of Baldwin as writing:[o]

"I hope on the whole we refuse the American offer, in order to give them time to discover that they are at our mercy as we are at France's, France at Germany's. It is the debtor who has the last word in these cases. We could reply quite politely that we have made the best offer we can in the present circumstances of uncertainty and, if they want more, they must wait till the general situation clears up and we know what we are going to get from France and Germany. . . ."

But it was one thing to object to the American proposals while they were still a matter for negotiation, quite another to reject the *fait accompli* with which Baldwin's blunder had presented the Cabinet. Bonar Law was supported in his view by only two members of the Cabinet, Lord Novar and Sir Philip Lloyd-Greame. The rest either considered that the settlement was reasonable on its merits or else thought that it was now too late to reject it. Outside the Cabinet Bonar Law was supported by Beaverbrook who was very hostile to the proposed settlement, but by no one else – apart from McKenna and Keynes. Nevertheless, he declared at a Cabinet meeting held on January 30th that he would rather resign than be a party to such disastrous terms. This announcement made in gentle but firm tones came as a bombshell to his colleagues.[p] His resignation would infallibly break up the Government. There would be great difficulties over a successor. At this time and in these circumstances Baldwin would have been out of the question and Curzon, the only possible alternative, was disliked in many quarters. If the Government fell on an issue like this, barely three months after taking office, the Conservative Party would have sustained a disaster of the first magnitude. The Cabinet promptly adjourned in a state of no small consternation.

The following morning the principal members of the Cabinet held an informal meeting in the Lord Chancellor's room, without Bonar Law being present. They were all agreed, including Lloyd-Greame,

[1] For Bonar Law's views see *Sunday Times*, December 18th, 1932, for an article by Wickham Steed who saw Bonar Law on the evening of January 29th and made a summary of his opinions.

that however bad the terms of the settlement might be, to repudiate
it now would be even worse. Bonar Law's only firm supporter was
Novar. Accordingly the Duke of Devonshire, Baldwin and Cave were
deputed to wait upon the Prime Minister and implore him on behalf
of all his colleagues to withdraw his resignation.[q]

Bonar Law has left no account of this crisis, but it is reasonable to
surmise that he must have felt himself to be a very lonely man. He
was convinced that the proposed terms were disastrous. "I would
be", he is said to have declared, "the most cursed Prime Minister
that ever held office in England if I accepted those terms." Therefore, if all his colleagues were in favour of accepting, what could he
do but resign. He was tired. His health was not robust. He had never
meant to stay in office for long. Why not go now? Yet here were these
same colleagues who had forced him into this odious position implor-
ing him to stay. And not only his colleagues: McKenna, whose
judgment he respected and who personally disapproved of the terms,
urged the same course, asserting that the City favoured acceptance,
and his oldest and closest friend, Beaverbrook, who regarded the
settlement just as gloomily as he did, was using all his powers of
persuasion – and they were considerable – to induce him to remain
in office. Moreover, Bonar Law, modest though he was, could not
have failed to realize that his departure at this stage, from a Cabinet
containing so many untried and inexperienced ministers, and only a
fortnight before Parliament opened, was bound to cause a political
crisis which might well be ruinous to the Conservative Party. Perhaps his friends were right. Perhaps after all it was his duty to swallow
his scruples and remain. That afternoon Bonar Law informed the
Cabinet at a meeting which only lasted five minutes that he would
not resign, but would bow to his colleagues' opinion and accept the
American terms.[r]

Two questions arise from the foregoing account. Was Bonar Law
justified in his hostility to Baldwin's settlement? If so had he any
right to withdraw his resignation? It is certain beyond all dispute that
Baldwin ought never to have concluded an agreement without
reference to the Cabinet, and that he should never have made such
candid remarks to the journalists who interviewed him. His action
placed the whole Cabinet in an intolerable position. It is fair to add
that he recognized that fact himself, and is reputed to have said that
he would rather have bitten his tongue off than have made such a
statement.

But were the actual terms of the agreement as bad as Bonar Law thought? Opinions will continue to conflict on this point. It is no answer to say that in fact the standard of living in Britain was not lowered for a generation, for within ten years the settlement was repudiated by the British Government in circumstances which caused the maximum of damage to Anglo-American relations. Nor will anyone today seriously dispute Bonar Law's contention that an Anglo-American settlement should only have been concluded as part of a general settlement of inter-Allied debts. On the question of the actual figures it can be conceded that Baldwin was probably correct in believing that he had got the best terms obtainable *at that time*. Bonar Law had been led by the American Ambassador, Mr. Harvey, into the belief that Congress would agree to a rate of interest of 2½ per cent or even lower. This was a delusion. On the other hand, if no settlement at all had been made in 1923, it may well be that in a year or two's time American opinion would have come round to the necessity of conceding more generous terms.

The actual difference in figures between Bonar Law's maximum and the American Commission's minimum may not seem so very great – a difference of about £15,000,000. But it is necessary to remember that Bonar Law was against any settlement unless it included a settlement with our own debtors. What Baldwin had done was to commit us to paying annually about £40,000,000 with no certain prospect of recovering anything from France, Italy, or Germany. This was a time when the cry was for economy everywhere and Bonar Law's attitude must be judged in that context. Orthodox opinion held that a reduction of taxation was absolutely essential if trade was to recover and unemployment diminish. Hence the demand for liquidating any foreign commitments that were not immediately essential for British interests, for example, in Palestine and Iraq. In these circumstances a settlement, which added about 4 per cent on to the budget for the next 60 years, at a moment when reduction seemed essential, was naturally most unwelcome.

Ought Bonar Law to have persisted in his original resolution to resign? No one can finally answer so difficult and rare a problem in political ethics. A Prime Minister seldom differs so completely from his colleagues that he is in a minority of one. Resignation would probably have involved the break-up of the Conservative Party, and a major political crisis. To preserve the unity of the Party had been one of Bonar Law's principal reasons for returning to politics. The pressure brought upon him to remain in office must have been overwhelming. On the other hand – whatever the consequences of resignation – had he any right to stay, if it meant giving his approval to a settlement which he regarded as calamitous? It was a question, as so often in politics, of a choice between evils, and, in view of all the arguments on each side, can we blame him for the choice he made?

4

January was, indeed, a trying month for Bonar Law. In addition to his other troubles an awkward and embarrassing problem arose over the Conservative Party funds. The Treasurer of the Party was Lord Farquhar. He was well known as an intimate friend of the Royal Family, in particular of King Edward VII who had on accession made him Master of the Household. From 1915 to 1922 he was Lord Steward of the Household. Farquhar had been originally a Unionist M.P., and had been promoted first to a baronetcy, then through successive stages in the peerage, until in autumn 1922 he received an earldom from Lloyd George in the Resignation Honours list. He was generally reputed to be a man of considerable wealth and much financial acumen.

But early in January 1923, to the dismay of Younger and the managers of the Conservative Party, he suddenly refused to sign a cheque for £20,000, drawn on the Central Office account, for the payment of salaries and bonuses connected with the recent Election. Apparently he argued that the money in question had been collected for the Coalition and did not belong to the Party as such. On January 15th Younger wrote to Bonar Law:[8]

"I am not in a position to state definitely that he did collect money for the Election expenses and handed that money to the Lloyd George Executive, but I have every reason to believe that he did so, and hope to be able to prove this one of these days.

"The salient points of the position are:

(1) That he was Treasurer of our Party and had no right to collect funds for any other than our own Central Fund so long as he retained that position.

(2) That there has never been any fusion of funds during the existence of the Coalition, and that collections made by Farquhar either for elections or ordinary expenditure were paid into our own Central Fund, just as Lloyd George's Fund was used by his Treasurer and Executive.

(3) When any joint financial responsibilities were undertaken the costs were halved and each Party paid by cheque on its own Fund.

(4) In any case the Coalition had come to an end before the General Election and Farquhar's reported statement that he had collected money for the Coalition does not hold water."

A garbled version of Farquhar's behaviour had already appeared in the Press. In the circumstances it was necessary for Bonar Law to summon him and find out what had really happened. Apparently Farquhar was somewhat incoherent. On January 24th Bonar Law wrote to Lord Edmund Talbot, his former Chief Whip:[t]

"You have noticed the trouble there was with poor old Farquhar. I have seen him twice and there is now no question of his hesitating to sign cheques for the actual Party funds, but I have still a strong suspicion that he has handed sums – perhaps large sums – to L.G. for his party, while acting as our Treasurer. He is so 'gaga' that one does not know what to make of him, but among the many statements he made to me was one which he repeated several times – that he had given no money to L.G.'s funds that was not earmarked for that purpose. Hicks, the accountant, has been seeing him and he has now become sane enough to realize that this was not a wise thing to say; so that he has now said to Hicks that he has given no money to L.G. except £80,000 from Astor. He spoke to me also about this and said that at the same time he handed over £80,000 to you. This he did, so he tells me, on the ground that Astor had left him a perfectly free hand to deal with it as he liked. I said that in that case, provided you as representing our Party knew what had been done, I had not a word to say against it, but the poor old boy is so helpless that I would like to know whether even this story is literally accurate."

Talbot replied that Farquhar had indeed told him, about a year before Lord Astor's[1] death, that Astor had given him £200,000 to do exactly what he liked with, that he (Farquhar) had given £40,000 to a charity in which the King was interested and had divided the rest between the Conservative Party funds and Lloyd George. Talbot ended:[u]

"But no money was 'handed' to me as stated in your letter. I was not consulted as to what should be done with the money. The thing was a *fait accompli* when I heard of it. He simply happened to tell me what had been given and what had been done with it. . . .

"At the time of the election I heard Horace [Farquhar] talking in the wild way he was doing. I tried to speak to him seriously, but he would not listen and was quite hopeless and I don't think he is responsible. He certainly cannot be relied on."

Bonar Law was of the same opinion, and a further complication about Sir John Ellerman's contribution to the Party confirmed his view.[2] On March 15th he dismissed Farquhar from the Treasurership, and replaced him by Younger. Bonar Law's papers do not

---

[1] William Waldorf Astor, created a Baron in 1916, and a Viscount in 1917, died October 1919.

[2] It was £5,000 p.a. – not an excessive sum for a man who left over twenty million pounds.

R

reveal what had really happened to Lord Astor's £80,000, nor do they tell us how the problems arising from Farquhar's strange attitude were finally settled.

There is one curious footnote to this incident. On August 30th Farquhar died. His will was found to contain a number of lavish bequests to various members of the Royal Family, worded in suitably courtier like language. But admiration for this manifestation of loyalty waned somewhat when his executors came to distribute the estate. There was, alas, no money left to fulfil these generous provisions. Farquhar's great wealth, if it ever existed, had entirely vanished.

5

On February 14th Parliament reopened. Bonar Law had now been Prime Minister for four months. Despite repeated rumours to the contrary in the Press, his health, though not very good, was certainly not bad. His efforts in the forthcoming session were to be evidence of this. It would be absurd to claim that he enjoyed being Prime Minister, but it would be equally absurd to suggest that he found the task in any respect beyond his powers. He had always been a first-class Parliamentarian and an admirable Leader of the House. That side of his work came easily to him. A Churchill or a Lloyd George might be more eloquent and more impressive, but perhaps the very extraordinariness of their minds made them less able to gauge the prejudices and sentiments of the ordinary Member of Parliament. At all events despite the poverty of his Front Bench support Bonar Law conducted business in the House with an ease and smoothness which gained him universal praise. He remained till his final illness master of the House of Commons to an extent seldom rivalled in modern times.

In the Cabinet room too Bonar Law, despite his seeming mildness, dominated proceedings. He was a cool and efficient chairman.

"Bonar Law under his diffident manner", writes Mr. Amery,[v] "was much more of an autocrat than Lloyd George and much more set in his ways. He was a business man for whom an agenda was something on which decisions were to be got as soon as possible, not a series of starting points for a general discussion. Sooner than let discussion roam afield or controversy be raised, he would cut things short by suggesting a committee."

If it is a weakness to take little interest in the broad universal themes which underlie all political activity then Bonar Law must plead guilty. He had long ago arrived at certain conclusions about the scope and limitations of what a Government can do to ameliorate human woes and miseries. These conclusions coincided roughly with the doctrine held by the Conservative Party, but they had been reached by a very different route from that followed by most Conservatives. The process of thought which had made Bonar Law an adherent of the Conservative Party resembled in no way the corresponding processes in the mind of, say, Curzon on the one hand, or Neville Chamberlain on the other. But since they were all agreed on the final conclusion, why delve into the underlying reasons? It was a waste of time and might create difficulties. Much better concentrate on solving the practical problems as they appeared. The art of politics lay, not in applying some body of philosophical doctrine, but in dealing with the actual issues that came up. It lay above all in deciding which of those were capable of being dealt with at all by Governmental action. Bonar Law held the belief, unfashionable today, that there exists a wide field of human activity in which Government intervention does no good and may only make matters worse.

This view, and the candour with which he was wont to express it, sometimes made his policy seem negative and his attitude unsympathetic. This latter adjective is certainly unjustified. Bonar Law never lacked sympathy for social evils, and, for example, in the case of unemployment he was well aware of the suffering involved. To the T.U.C. deputation which saw him on January 16th, 1923, he said of these evils:[w]

"We all feel it. I said once before that obviously people who do not themselves feel hungry cannot feel it as acutely as those who have suffered that calamity. But it does not need much imagination to realize the seriousness of the present situation . . . and the evil is added to, I think, by the long continuance of the unemployment, to an extent which people hardly realize."

On the other hand Bonar Law considered that there were very serious limitations upon what any government could do to help, and that there might be even greater evils than unemployment.

"The difference which arises always . . . is as to the method by which the Government can effectually help the situation. I am convinced as of course you know, that the scheme which is recommended by so many members of the House of Commons, involving a complete upsetting of our present social conditions would not make things better but worse."

He then discussed the various remedies possible within the existing social and economic system.

"I do not hesitate to say that our situation as regards unemployment

has been made a great deal worse because, rightly or wrongly, not this
Government only but all Governments since the war came to the conclusion that in the long run the first essential to real prosperity was to pay
our way and balance the budget. We did that, and if we had not done it,
but had continued to borrow large sums in order to balance the Budget,
there would have been much less unemployment. But the view of the
Government was that such a course would have had to be paid for by
greater suffering afterwards. Other countries have adopted a different
system. You know what happened in Germany . . . I am certain that if,
in order to meet your views, we were now to borrow money, and employ it
in any way you like so as to set the stream of wages going, we should be
permanently destroying the chance of getting back to normal conditions.''

In other words it was, as so often, a choice of ills. Unemploymen
might be a grave evil, but a policy of reckless borrowing which
produced inflation and a total breakdown of ordinary economic life
would be even more disastrous.

The interview with the T.U.C. delegation illustrates another important aspect of Bonar Law's policy. As we have seen, he was
determined to return to normality, and to remove the impression
created by Lloyd George that the cure to all the nation's ills lay in
Westminster or Downing Street. The actual purpose of the T.U.C
delegation was to ask for an early reassembly of Parliament in order
to deal with the unemployment problem – a request already made
by Ramsay MacDonald, the leader of the Labour Party. Bonar Law
regarded this as a wholly useless proposal. It was the kind of thing
which might make a fine impression on the public but it did no good.
In fact Ministers were more likely to be able to get on with their job
while Parliament was in recess than when it was sitting. He therefore
refused to make a pointless gesture of this sort.

He was equally determined to reject another request of the T.U.C.
– namely that he should reconsider his earlier refusal to see a deputation of the unemployed hunger marchers. Demonstrations of this
sort, were, in his opinion ridiculous. "I can", he said, "imagine
nothing more foolish than that they should waste whatever money
they had, and their shoe leather, in coming to London to make a
demonstration." He had been frankly told that the purpose was
propaganda against the Conservative Government. "Well, in that
case you cannot expect me to assist it," he remarked. The demon-
strators could see the heads of the Departments concerned – the
Minister of Labour, etc., but they could not see the Prime Minister.

It was all part of a return to the ordinary machinery of Government. The period of the Coalition had been extraordinary and while

it lasted there had been neither Cabinet government, nor party politics in the normal sense. Bonar Law did not criticize what had happened in the past, but he considered that the time had come for a reversion to the traditional mode of British Government, with Cabinet responsibility, and each Minister dealing with the affairs of his own department. Another corollary of this was the dismantling of Lloyd George's immense secretariat. Bonar Law had no intention of abolishing this entirely. The great services of Sir Maurice Hankey and his subordinates he fully recognized, and he strongly favoured the innovations which Lloyd George had made on first becoming Prime Minister, but he saw no reason for perpetuating the "garden suburb", or for retaining the somewhat dubious and swollen train of personal secretaries, satellites, and hangers-on, whom the late Prime Minister encouraged or at least tolerated.

There is no reason, at this distance of time, to gloss over the un-doubted fact that, although Lloyd George enlisted many men of integrity and ability, some members of his entourage had a very doubtful reputation. A great deal of the resentment against his régime was caused by a feeling among people "in the know" that, even if no actual corruption had occurred, there had been a careless-ness and want of discretion which were incompatible with the high traditions of Number 10 Downing Street. How far these suspicions were justified is a matter for the biographers of Lloyd George, but their existence is beyond dispute, and they certainly contributed to the fall of the Coalition Government. In no field was this suspicion more strongly felt – and with greater foundation – than in that of honours. Bonar Law was determined to break with the practices of the immediate past. He therefore issued no New Year's Honours List until the Royal Commission, forced on Lloyd George in July 1922, had issued its report, at the beginning of February. His list when it did appear was much shorter than those of his predecessor and contained only names of unimpeachable respectability. The most notable was that of Sir George Younger whose elevation to a Viscountcy cannot have pleased the dissident Conservatives.

In the field of appointments and patronage Bonar Law was equally determined to break with the practices of the immediate past. He considered that the time had come to revert to the more cautious traditions of earlier times and to rely upon orthodox advice through the correct official channels, rather than upon intuition. This did not mean that he made dull or unimaginative appointments. For exam-ple, when it fell to him to recommend to the King the name of the first Governor-General of the Irish Free State he selected, instead of the usual elder statesman or retired Field-Marshal, T. M. Healy who had been for many years a fervent though somewhat unorthodox Irish Nationalist M.P. The other important non-political appointment made by Bonar Law was that of Lord Crewe, the former Liberal leader in the House of Lords, to be Ambassador in Paris. Both these appointments were highly successful.

It is unnecessary to discuss in any great detail the Parliamentary session which opened on February 14th and ended on March 28th. It was dominated by three principal questions, foreign policy, unemployment, and housing. The numerous debates on foreign policy resulted from the perturbation felt by M.P.s on two issues. First and foremost was the question of our attitude to the French occupation of the Ruhr. Secondly, there was the problem of the Near East. Since the Foreign Secretary was in the Upper House, Bonar Law had to deal with foreign affairs in the House of Commons. Some people thought that they detected a certain difference of emphasis in the attitude of the two ministers, Bonar Law dwelling rather more fully than Curzon upon the desirability of British withdrawal from Iraq and Palestine. These differences can easily be exaggerated. Bonar Law had no intention of being stampeded into a premature liquidation of British commitments in the Near East, but it is probably true that, in his concern for economy, he was more worried at our heavy expenditure in that area than Curzon who cared little about finance and whose Indian experience made him take a special interest in the affairs of the Muslim world. But, whatever the difference of emphasis, there was no real difference of principle involved, nor was any final decision taken while Bonar Law was Prime Minister.

Bonar Law's attitude to the question of unemployment has already been discussed. He was ready to encourage the heads of great employing corporations to undertake works which might set the wheels of industry turning, and did indeed interview the chairmen of the big Railway Companies for that purpose early in December 1922. But he would not press them to undertake projects unless those projects were in themselves sound business propositions. In general he continued to regard an improvement in world trade as the only real remedy, and he was encouraged in this belief, because during the winter of 1922–3 trade did in fact improve and unemployment fell by nearly half a million.

On housing, the third of the questions mentioned above, the Government ran into serious trouble. One of the ways in which the new Administration hoped to return to normality was by gradually repealing the Rent Restriction Acts. As we know today such a proposal is liable to be exceedingly unpopular, and this proved to be the case in 1923. The matter was further complicated by the absence from the House of Commons of the Minister of Health, Sir Arthur Boscawen, under whose department housing came. He had been defeated at the General Election, and had had the greatest difficulty in finding a seat. Even Lord Derby's normal skill at wire pulling seemed to have vanished, and he was unable to provide the displaced Minister with a Lancashire constituency. In despair Boscawen suggested that he might go to the Upper House, but Bonar Law was already under fire for the excessive number of peers in his Cabinet and refused.

Eventually what seemed to be a safe seat – Mitcham in Surrey – adopted Boscawen. At the same time two other by-elections pended, in both of which Junior Ministers, beaten at the General Election, were endeavouring to return to Parliament. Thus at the beginning of March the Government faced a trial of its popularity in three consti-tuencies. The result was disastrous. All three Ministers were beaten – and in two of the seats beaten because independent Conservative candidates, put up by the ex-Coalition Ministers, had contrived to split the Conservative vote. Boscawen was himself a victim of this manoeuvre. The affair was temporarily a blow to the Government's prestige, but in the long run strengthened Bonar Law in a way which could hardly have been predicted. For the defeated Ministers all resigned, and in place of Boscawen Bonar Law promoted Neville Chamberlain whose administrative and debating powers valuably reinforced the Cabinet and the Front Bench. He was a far abler man, and tackled the housing problem with much greater efficiency than his predecessor.

The attitude of the dissident Conservatives clearly showed that they had no intention of joining Bonar Law. Austen Chamberlain was opposed to his brother entering the Cabinet, for he regarded it as on the verge of collapse. Nor would he have regretted such an event, for his feelings towards Bonar Law were most unfriendly, as was perhaps inevitable in the circumstances. He wrote in his diary at the beginning of March:[x]

"Nor can I conceive that anything will make me join this Govt. under Bonar's leadership or take over his Govt. if he breaks down. I cannot join him for I think him unfitted to be Prime Minister, and I feel too deeply his conduct towards me to make it possible for me again to act under him."

On March 23rd the dissident Conservatives demonstrated their solidarity by that characteristic British method – a dinner. It was given by Birkenhead ostensibly in honour of Balfour, and included seven peers and twenty-four M.P.s.[1] Bonar Law received a report of the proceedings.[y] The general sentiment appears to have favoured continuing on a more or less independent line, although Sir Leslie Scott[2] made a strong speech against forming a "cave", and Bonar Law's anonymous informant considered that this view would have most effect in the long run. But Birkenhead summed up the discussion by saying that he proposed to remain a free agent and say what he liked. Undoubtedly the dissidents were intellectually a formidable body, and even in numbers not to be despised. The historical parallel which they and everyone else had in mind was that of the Peelites in the 1850's who, though only thirty or so strong, were able to form a Coalition Government in which they had the Premiership and half the places. As long as Birkenhead and his friends entertained hopes of this sort the prospect of unity under Bonar Law's leadership was remote.

However, this did not greatly matter for the time being. Even if one group of his opponents remained solid, there was another group which continued in the greatest confusion. The Liberal Party was still deeply divided. Lloyd George and Asquith seemed further apart than ever, and a tentative overture from the former was at once met with a freezing rebuff. Asquith had neither forgotten nor forgiven the past. These dissensions strengthened the Government, and on many occasions the National Liberals voted with the Administration while the Asquithian Liberals abstained or opposed.

And so the session, though turbulent and at times stormy, drew to an end without any serious danger to the Government. Bonar Law had carried a heavy burden, but there were now signs that some of his colleagues were beginning to find their feet. Baldwin, despite his lamentable conduct of the American Debt negotiations, details of

---

[1] Those present at the dinner were: The Duke of Marlborough, Lords Balfour, Farquhar, Crawford, Lee, Astor and Wargrave. M.P.s: Austen Chamberlain, Sir L. Worthington-Evans, Sir Ernest Pollock, Sir Leslie Scott, Sir Philip Sassoon, Sir William Bull, Sir Francis Lowe, General Hunter Weston, Sir Robert Chadwick, Sir Joseph Hood, G. W. H. Jones, Sir Walter Preston, Sir Howard Kingsley Wood, Sir Harold Smith, Sir Robert Newman, Sir Walter de Frece, Sir James Agg-Gardner, Sir Warden Chilcott, Colonel Grant Morden, Colonel Moore Brabazon, T. R. Remer, Patrick Ford, Commander O. Locker Lampson and Sir Robert Horne. The Press was represented by J. L. Garvin, editor of the *Observer*. Lord Farquhar's presence was not without significance. An attempt was being made at this time to induce him to hand over part of the Conservative funds to the Coalitionist Conservatives. It had no success.

[2] The Solicitor-General in the late Government.

which were of course unknown to the general public, began to show something of the Parliamentary ability in which he was later to excel. Neville Chamberlain's success has already been mentioned. Another most able Minister was the Attorney-General, Sir Douglas Hogg (later Lord Hailsham).

"Hogg, as you know," Bonar Law wrote to Curzon, on January 24th,[z] "is turning out to be a real discovery. He has an exceptionally good brain and I hope to be able to use him a great deal."

Altogether there were signs of improvement in the calibre of the principal Ministers. The Prime Minister could look forward to rather less exacting duties as time went on.

And meanwhile what of Bonar Law himself? His mode of life continued very much as it had been before his eighteen months of absence from politics – except that he was now in Number 10 instead of Number 11 Downing Street. He worked hard, his hours were long, his meals brief and hasty as if he resented the time snatched from the working day. Though he lived at his official residence he still kept on 24 Onslow Gardens, perhaps as a mental pledge to himself that his period in office was not to be of long duration. As might be expected – given his detestation of the country – he never resided at Chequers, the beautiful country house presented by Lord Lee of Fareham for the use of the Prime Minister of the day. He gladly relinquished it to Baldwin who as Chancellor of the Exchequer had the next refusal. Bonar Law remains the only Prime Minister so far to have declined this offer.

There was only one cloud on the horizon. He continued to have trouble with his throat. Off and on, this complaint had bothered him ever since the Election. It grew no better, and on the last day of the session his voice was temporarily so weak that he had to delegate Baldwin to answer for the Government on foreign policy. However the Easter recess was now at hand. It was hoped that Bonar Law would be fit again when Parliament met in the middle of April.

CHAPTER XXXI

THE SUCCESSION

APRIL 10TH – MAY 18TH, 1923

Prospects in April 1923 – Bonar Law's declining health – His decision to take a month's rest – The succession – Overture to Austen Chamberlain repulsed – Bonar Law's opinion of Curzon – His correspondence with Curzon determines him not to recommend Curzon as his successor – Bonar Law leaves for Mediterranean – His health grows worse – he goes to Paris – Cancer of the throat diagnosed by Lord Horder – Advice of Beaverbrook – Lord Crewe advises Bonar Law to make no recommendation as to the succession

I

At the beginning of April 1923 the prospect for Bonar Law's Government appeared considerably brighter than at any time before. The clouds that had lowered over his early weeks as Prime Minister were beginning to disperse. It was as if the warmer air of spring brought with it a similar change in the climate of politics. At home the formidable Tory Coalitionists were reduced to silence, apart from an occasional newspaper squib by Birkenhead. The Liberals remained hopelessly disunited. The Labour Party as yet showed few signs of becoming an effective opposition. Assured of a safe majority in the House of Commons, guided by the sagacity and experience of Bonar Law, this "Government of the second eleven", might well have enjoyed several years of tranquil power.

The immediate future was encouraging. In August Bonar Law was due to preside over an Empire Economic Conference. It would have been a symbolic occasion. The first Prime Minister in English history to be born in the overseas Empire would have directed the deliberations of the Dominion Prime Ministers. The statesman who had always put the greatness of the British Empire foremost among his aims might have had a chance of realizing some of the ideals for which he had entered political life twenty years before. The strange vicissitudes of Bonar Law's career might have been crowned by some decisive step in the direction of that imperial unity which had ever been his goal.

But it is, perhaps, idle to speculate upon what might have been.

No such golden future lay ahead for Bonar Law. Even at this moment he was under sentence of death. Not for him the knowledge of tasks accomplished, ambition achieved. Not for him an old age calm and bright. Fate which had already dealt him cruel blows, was to deal him a blow more cruel than all – an abrupt and hurried departure from the political scene, lingering months of torment, and a painful death.

The first symptoms of Bonar Law's fatal malady had appeared, as we now realize, immediately after the General Election when owing to a pain in his throat he was temporarily unable to speak in public. But during the next three months he seemed to get better. Now, however, his throat was giving him trouble once more, and he also began to suffer from severe, sometimes agonizing, pain in the side of his face. The true nature of his illness had not yet been diagnosed. It was believed that he merely suffered from the sort of sore throat which is common enough in elderly men after a London winter. He went to Torquay for the Easter holiday, accompanied by his sons, Richard and Tony, and by Lady Sykes and her husband. There he relaxed as usual, playing golf and tennis with his accustomed energy, and his family hoped that the mild air and rest from work would improve his health. Meanwhile rumours began to spread in the political clubs and in the Press that the Prime Minister would soon be obliged to retire. There was general perturbation at the prospect. It was widely felt that Bonar Law, through his popularity in the House and his experience of office, was the lynch pin of the Government. What would happen if he were to resign?

Public uneasiness was not diminished when Parliament re-assembled on April 10th. Although Bonar Law looked considerably better, his voice was still extremely weak. He was almost inaudible when he attempted to answer questions in the House and after a few attempts he handed over the task to Stanley Baldwin. Rumours of resignation now became stronger than ever, but on April 16th Bonar Law allowed an official denial to be issued. At the same time it was announced that the Prime Minister would not take part in debate for at least a fortnight. He did not, however, absent himself from the House of Commons. He would sit on the front bench during debates and sometimes whisper a reply to Baldwin or whoever was acting as his mouthpiece. He did not seem especially ill – apart from the trouble with his voice. On April 26th, wearing the gold lace and feather hat of a Privy Councillor, he attended the wedding of the Duke of York to Lady Elizabeth Bowes-Lyon in Westminster Abbey.

The *Daily Express* commenting on his entry observed "He walked like an athlete".

Meanwhile, there had been a further consultation with Sir Thomas Horder, his physician. He advised Bonar Law to try the benefits of a sea voyage; the warmer climate, the sea air, and a month's rest from duties might bring about a cure. On April 27th Bonar Law had an audience with the King and told him of his plan.[a] In his absence Curzon would preside over Cabinet meetings, Baldwin would lead the House of Commons. The King agreed to this arrangement which was announced officially the following day. It was announced at the same time that the Prime Minister intended to be back before the meeting of Parliament following the Whitsun recess. It was further stated that Bonar Law's medical advisers "assure him that there is every reason to suppose that his voice will be completely restored".

Although neither he nor anyone else realized the gravity of his illness Bonar Law was very far from sharing the optimism expressed in this bulletin. He was feeling extremely unwell, and suffering much pain. He was, as he well knew, in no real condition to carry the heavy responsibilities of his great office. Moreover, he clearly could not remain Prime Minister unless he recovered his voice in the near future. Only the urgent entreaties of his colleagues and friends prevented him from resigning at once, and it was with reluctance that he agreed to postpone his retirement until he had tried the effects of his cruise. But on one point he was quite clear: he was more determined than ever to keep to his original resolution of not remaining in office for more than a year, and of retiring at the latest by the following October. This decision meant that Bonar Law had for the first time to give serious thought to a most delicate and awkward problem. Who was to be his successor as Prime Minister and leader of the Conservative Party? During the last fortnight of April there occurred two episodes, unknown to the general public but fraught with highly important consequences for the succession. These must be recorded.

Bonar Law had always hoped that he might eventually be able to reunite the dissident Conservatives under his leadership. If he could do this the choice of a successor presented no difficulty: Austen Chamberlain had every claim on grounds of prestige, experience, and seniority to succeed Bonar Law in command of a reunited Conservative Party. But the difficulty was that Austen Chamberlain along with Birkenhead and the other ex-Coalitionists showed no signs of wishing to return to the Party fold. Nevertheless, about the middle of April, Bonar Law resolved to make an overture to Chamberlain. He authorized Beaverbrook to offer on his behalf the post of Lord Privy Seal to Chamberlain on the definite understanding that Bonar Law would resign in the autumn, and recommend Chamberlain as his successor with a free hand to reconstruct the Government.[b]

Perhaps in all the circumstances Beaverbrook was not the ideal intermediary to choose. He was regarded with much hostility at this time by Austen Chamberlain and all the ex-Coalitionists, who believed that his public propaganda and private intrigues had been in no small measure responsible for their downfall. Doubtless aware of this hostility, Beaverbrook decided to approach Chamberlain through Rothermere. He too, however, was scarcely more likely to gain Chamberlain's confidence, for the latter regarded all Press magnates with considerable distaste and had indeed led a much applauded attack upon their activities during the war. Whether for this reason, or because he still felt acute resentment at Bonar Law's part in the Carlton Club meeting, Chamberlain firmly declined the offer.

Chamberlain's uncompromising attitude at once raised a question which must have been at the back of Bonar Law's mind for some time – at least since the Cabinet crisis over the American loan three months earlier. What would happen if he had to resign before he could bridge the gulf between himself and the dissident Conservatives? Who among the members of the existing Cabinet could succeed him as Prime Minister? At first sight the answer seemed obvious. In terms of long service, vast experience, distinguished record, intellectual calibre, Curzon stood far above all his colleagues. He was, it is true, a peer, but this fact did not at that time constitute so grave a defect as it would today. Other things being equal, no doubt it was better for the Prime Minister to be in the House of Commons, but in this case other things were not equal – indeed they seldom are in real life – and Curzon's nearest rival, Stanley Baldwin, who had only been Chancellor of the Exchequer for a few months, and not a very distinguished one at that, was a mere tyro in politics compared with the great nobleman who had been Viceroy of India and was now Foreign Secretary and Leader of the House of Lords.

No record has survived of Bonar Law's opinion of Curzon. It is indeed highly improbable that he ever committed any such opinion to paper. Those who were intimate with Bonar Law say that he had deep respect for the formidable powers which Curzon possessed both in council and in debate. He never underestimated Curzon's great talents, but on the other hand he found it difficult to take Curzon entirely seriously. He never said anything of Curzon which could be regarded as at all derogatory. Yet when the name of Curzon came up in conversation there would be a twinkle in his eye, just a hint that there was something slightly, very slightly, comical about the whole character of Curzon.[c] The Foreign Secretary was a statesman of the first magnitude, and yet . . . was it really possible to imagine him reconciling all the divergent opinions and conflicting personalities which every Cabinet must contain? Would Curzon's presence at the head of affairs conduce to the unity of the Conservative Party and the smooth running of the governmental machine? Bonar Law had doubts, and some of Curzon's letters, quoted in an earlier chapter, cannot have allayed those doubts. Nevertheless, he continued to regard Curzon as his only possible successor, failing Austen Chamberlain, until at the end of April an episode occurred which brought all his misgivings to the surface. The exact details have never before been published although Sir Winston Churchill, in his account of Curzon in *Great Contemporaries* (p. 284), gives an outline of what happened. The clue to Bonar Law's decision lies in an exchange of letters with Curzon on April 25th.

The letters must be quoted in full.

10 Downing Street,
25th April, 1923.

"My dear Curzon,

"—— called to say that he had been invited to form a syndicate to develop Turkey in various ways including a loan, and wished to know if there was any objection on the part of the Government to his doing this before peace was declared. I see none, but would be glad to have your confirmation before writing him definitely.

"Yours sincerely,

A.B.L."[d]

Foreign Office,
25th April, 1923.

"My dear Bonar,

"If I may say so I think the right thing would be for your private secretary to say that —— should address himself to the F.O. and not to No. 10.

"As a matter of fact I know all about ——. He ran away from his wife – a most charming lady – with another woman: he had to sell his place, and is wholly discredited.

"That anyone should offer a loan to Turkey before peace is concluded would be very doubtful policy. But that that person should be —— renders it quite out of the question. I am sure you did not know all this.

"When these persons go to No. 10 instead of here they are really reproducing one of the least admirable features of the L.G. régime.

                              "Yours sincerely,
                                             Curzon."e

According to those closest in Bonar Law's confidence this letter was the final cause which determined him not to take the responsibility of recommending Curzon as his successor. He was deeply hurt at the tone in which Curzon wrote. He considered that Curzon had no right to address his leader in language of this sort. On the actual merits of the case, and on the rights of the Foreign Office, Curzon was probably correct. He usually was in such matters. But the haughty tone, the lack of proportion shown over so relatively trivial a matter, above all the sting in the last sentence with its innuendo that affairs at No. 10 Downing Street were no better than they had been under the late Prime Minister, all these considerations decided Bonar Law that, whatever else he did, he would not put forward Curzon's name for the succession. Had Bonar Law been well, probably he would not have taken the matter so much to heart. He would have written a sharp rebuke to Curzon and then forgotten about the whole affair. But Bonar Law was far from well, as Curzon knew. That fact was indeed an additional reason why Curzon should never have written such a letter. It was inexcusable to adopt this tone to his tired and ailing leader.

2

Bonar Law felt too ill to make any personal protest to Curzon, nor was he prepared to cancel the arrangement already made for Curzon to act as his deputy. After all it was still possible that no immediate crisis would arise, and in any case past precedent gave the Leader of the House of Lords a claim to preside at Cabinet meetings in the Prime Minister's absence. It did not necessarily mean that he would be the next Prime Minister. Moreover, Bonar Law's reaction to Curzon's letter should not be exaggerated. It was not so much that Bonar Law saw any real alternative to the choice of Curzon, but rather that he was determined to avoid the personal responsibility of recommending Curzon as his successor. No doubt this was an unsatisfactory attitude and no doubt Bonar Law would have taken a more decisive line, had he been less desperately ill.

On May 1st Bonar Law left Southampton in a Dutch liner, the *Princess Juliana*. His orginal plan had been to sail to Canada and Beaverbrook had actually made arrangements for the visit, but Bonar Law decided that there would be too much fuss and publicity. He resolved instead to go on a leisurely Mediterranean cruise touching at Algiers and Genoa. His only companion was his son Dick. Unhappily the sea air brought no relief. On the contrary, the pain in the side of his face became more acute than ever and his voice remained very weak. On May 8th the ship arrived at Genoa, and Bonar Law decided to leave her and go up to Aix les Bains. He was joined at Genoa by his Parliamentary secretary, J. C. Davidson. At Aix he was pleased to find his old friends the Rudyard Kiplings. Kipling, however, was horrified to see how ill he looked. He had not met him for sometime and was therefore more struck by his altered appearance than were those who saw Bonar Law every day. He at once telephoned to Beaverbrook in England urging him to come to Aix without delay.

On arrival Beaverbrook too was shocked at the condition of Bonar Law, and he noticed with alarm that he was taking ten-grain tablets of aspirin sometimes as often as ten times a day in order to ease the pain in his face.[f] Such a heavy dose was producing a most depressing psychological effect. Beaverbrook did not realize the full gravity of the situation, but he saw that something must be done at once and he got in touch with Horder urging the latter to come out to Paris and meet Bonar Law there. On May 16th the party travelled to Paris, Bonar Law and his son staying at the Crillon, Beaverbrook at the Ritz.

On Thursday, May 17th, Horder arrived in Paris. He went at once to the Crillon, saw Bonar Law in the latter's sitting room, and proceeded to examine his throat. At the end of the examination he made some non-committal observations, and then went out to see Beaverbrook who was waiting to hear the verdict. Horder remained silent as the two men walked through the hotel and out into the street. It was brilliant sunshine. The Champs Elysées had all the magic and warmth and gaiety that lends such enchantment to the early summer in Paris. Horder then broke the news: Bonar Law was suffering from an incurable cancer of the throat; there was no possibility of operating; the Prime Minister could not live for more than six months.

To Beaverbrook the news came like the shock of a thunderbolt.

Worried though he was about his friend's health, he had never dreamed that death was imminent. For the last thirteen years, ever since he had lived in England, his whole life had been bound up with that of Bonar Law. They had discussed together every great political problem of the time. To Bonar Law and his family Beaverbrook's house at Leatherhead had been almost a second home. And now it was all over. The man whom he loved and revered was doomed to a lingering painful death, his aims unrealized, his ambitions unfulfilled. But there was no time to reflect upon the full implication of what had happened. It was clear that Bonar Law must resign at once, if only because of the relief which resignation would bring to his weary and depressed spirit. At the same time it was essential to keep the truth about his illness from him. Beaverbrook had hitherto been one of the principal obstacles in the way of the Prime Minister's resignation. Again and again he had urged upon him – and with good reason – the importance of his remaining in office, and had pointed to the dangers which loomed before the Government and the Party if he were to depart. Now this attitude had to be abruptly reversed; yet at the same time all suspicion of the terrible truth must be avoided.

Beaverbrook was intensely distressed by the news that he had just heard. It was vital, however, to put on as cheerful a face as he could. He returned to the Crillon and went up to Bonar Law's sitting room. As soon as he entered, the Prime Minister once again reiterated his anxiety to resign. This time Lord Beaverbrook made no opposition. He said that at last even he had come to the conclusion that Bonar Law would never get well while he remained in office, and that only resignation would relieve the strain from which he was suffering. At once a great load seemed to have been lifted from the tired mind of Prime Minister. Any surprise that he felt at Beaverbrook's apparent *volte face* was submerged in an overwhelming sense of relief at the prospect of laying down a burden which had become all but insupportable. For a short time he was almost cheerful.

But this mood did not last for long. Bonar Law now had once again to face the problem which had been worrying him when he left England and which he had so far left unsolved. Whom was he to recommend as his successor? There was now only a short time in which to make up his mind, and all the doubts which had beset him earlier returned in a more formidable shape than ever. There was no chance of securing the allegiance of any of the ex-Coalitionist Tories. The Party would never tolerate Austen Chamberlain or

Birkenhead until they had formally made their peace with the
official Conservatives. This meant that the choice must lie between
Curzon and Baldwin. A month earlier Bonar Law would have had
no hesitation, but now the memory of Curzon's letter was fresh in his
mind.

How could he recommend as trustee for the interests and unity of
the Conservative Party a man who could display such hectoring bad
temper over so trivial a matter? How could a man of such temperament – however great his talents – preside over the Cabinet and cope
with the hundred and one personal and political problems which
must vex a Prime Minister? On the other hand to ignore his claims
was almost as difficult as to gratify them. The only alternative was
Baldwin and, though Bonar Law liked Baldwin, he had no delusions
about his abilities; if he ever had such delusions they vanished with
the crisis over the American debt. The time might come when
Baldwin would make a suitable Prime Minister, but that time had
not come yet. Bonar Law remained for the rest of the morning in the
Crillon hotel brooding gloomily over this grave problem.

Seeing that he did not wish to be disturbed Beaverbrook left the
hotel and hastened to the Embassy to see Lord Crewe, formerly
leader of the Liberals in the House of Lords, and now Ambassador
in Paris, to which post he had indeed been appointed by Bonar Law
a few months earlier. Beaverbrook hoped to persuade Crewe to
arrange some bridge that afternoon in order to take Bonar Law's
mind off his troubles. Crewe gladly agreed, and in the course of their
conversation Beaverbrook revealed the dilemma which was worrying
Bonar Law. Crewe was able to give encouraging counsel. There was
no need, he declared, for the Prime Minister to worry about the
succession. The choice lay constitutionally with the sovereign, and
the Prime Minister was not obliged to give any advice at all about the
matter. Indeed his advice was not normally asked, and Crewe cited
an example in his own family. He was the son-in-law of Lord Rosebery. When in 1894 Gladstone resigned from the Premiership Queen
Victoria appointed Rosebery without asking for any advice from
Gladstone who would in fact have recommended someone else.
Similarly, Crewe said, King Edward VII had appointed Asquith in
1908 without asking for the advice of the retiring Prime Minister,
Sir Henry Campbell-Bannerman.

Beaverbrook was delighted at this information. He begged Crewe
to guide the conversation round to the question of the succession,
when Bonar Law arrived in the afternoon. He felt sure that Crewe's

advice would relieve the Prime Minister's sick and tired mind. Crewe was only too glad to do what he could to help. Accordingly he told Bonar Law of these two precedents and assured him that there was no need for him to worry: he would not be expected to make a decision; the matter rested with the King, and with the King alone. This information was new to Bonar Law and, as Beaverbrook guessed, it lifted a great weight off his mind. He would now be relieved of the personal responsibility of choosing either Curzon or Baldwin. He did not seriously doubt that the effect of his declining to recommend at all, would be much the same as if he had put forward Curzon's name. The King, he believed, was almost bound to choose Curzon whose claims on grounds of experience and seniority were so strong, but at least he would do so on his own responsibility and not on the advice of Bonar Law.

It is perhaps worth noting that, although Crewe's two precedents were described quite correctly, they were not exactly analogous to the present case, for they did not afford any guidance as to what a Prime Minister ought to do if the sovereign actually pressed him for advice. Queen Victoria refrained from consulting Gladstone, not from any sense of constitutional propriety, but because she detested Gladstone. Edward VII refrained from consulting Campbell-Bannerman partly because he was in Biarritz when Campbell-Bannerman resigned, and partly because Asquith was so obviously the inevitable successor that no problem could arise. It was a different matter if the choice was not obvious and if the sovereign genuinely wanted the advice of the outgoing Prime Minister. However, Bonar Law was far too ill to worry about constitutional niceties of this sort. It was with a real sense of relief that he returned to his hotel that evening. Arrangements for his resignation could now go smoothly ahead, and he would no longer be tormented by the difficult and doubtful problem of the succession.

CHAPTER XXXII

THE END

MAY 19TH – NOVEMBER 3RD, 1923

Bonar Law returns to London – His resignation conveyed to the King on May 20th – Visit from Baldwin – Bonar Law sends for Lord Salisbury – His account of Bonar Law's attitude – "Disinclined to pass over Curzon" – Reasons for Curzon's failure – Memorandum by Lord Davidson – Represented by Colonel Waterhouse as Bonar Law's opinion – Reasons for supposing that it was not – Curious conduct of Colonel Waterhouse – He misleads Lord Stamfordham – Stamfordham consults Balfour who pronounces for Baldwin – The King chooses Baldwin – Bonar Law's surprise – His final retirement from politics – Course of his illness - His fortitude - Bonar Law dies on October 30th, 1923 – Funeral in Westminster Abbey – "The Unknown Prime Minister" – Retrospect

I

BONAR LAW remained one more day in Paris. On Saturday, May 19th, accompanied by his son, Richard, and Beaverbrook, he travelled to London. There was a crowd on the platform at Victoria Station to greet the returning Prime Minister as he stepped off the 5 o'clock boat train. But the cheering died away when it was seen how worn and haggard he looked, and, as he walked past the barrier to his waiting motor car, men removed their hats in a silent and spontaneous gesture of respect – and, perhaps, farewell. Bonar Law could scarcely speak above a whisper to his family and his secretaries who had come to meet him. He was driven immediately to his house in Onslow Gardens.

That evening he completed the arrangements for his resignation. His voice was so weak and he felt so ill that he could not take leave of the King personally. Instead he wrote out a letter of resignation which was to be conveyed the following day to the King at the Royal Pavilion at Aldershot. Bonar Law also arranged for a verbal message to be given to the King if he should ask for advice about the succession. The King was to be told that, owing to ill-health, the Prime Minister would prefer not to be consulted and was unwilling to take the responsibility for any recommendation.[1]

---

[1] Some writers have referred to Bonar Law's "refusal" to give advice. This is incorrect. Bonar Law would not, indeed could not, have "refused" advice, had the King insisted. What he did was to let the King know that he would prefer not to be consulted. The King, properly and naturally, respected the wishes of a very sick man.

Beaverbrook, aware that this negative attitude on Bonar Law's part might be criticized, was anxious to prepare the public, and was, accordingly, busy with the newspapers. A letter from Mary Law (merely dated "Sunday" from the Hotel York, but evidently written on Sunday, May 20th) gives a vivid picture of what was happening.[a]

"My dear Max,

"'Mr. Bonar Law's Health' – 'The Prime Minister by Lord Beaverbrook' and 'Politics Unmasked', are all perfect and to me delightful. In your signed article you have gone over the past ground and brought things up to date so beautifully, and I think it masterly the way the *no need* of the retiring Prime Minister to name a successor to the King is dealt with. The comments appear to me as appearing quite unforced.

"But it was not to say this that I am writing to you. It is from the bottom of my heart to thank you for having gone to Bonar, to have yielded (as I am sure it must have been against your will) to his overwhelming desire to escape, and doing all you have done to help him through. I know you have a real love for Bonar and that love brings you to his rescue when he is in despair. Y'day morning I was filled with a great sorrow that we had arrived at the end of all things political for him but when he arrived home in the afternoon all other feelings gave way to the thankfulness that he could escape. There was a look in his dear eyes that was warning enough for me.

"Thanks once more dear,

"Yours affectionately,
Mary E. Law.

"PS. I hope Bonar's tragedy won't make *you* ill."

There was some discussion at Onslow Gardens as to who should bear Bonar Law's letter of resignation to the King. Colonel Ronald Waterhouse, as Principal Private Secretary, offered to do so. Bonar Law had no objection, but there were members of his family who did not feel entirely happy at the prospect of entrusting this delicate negotiation to Waterhouse alone.[b] They felt that he might possibly have an axe to grind, and, since it was most important that the Prime Minister should not be in any way misrepresented, Bonar Law was persuaded to send another emissary as a companion to Waterhouse – his son-in-law, Sir Frederick Sykes, of whose reliability there could be no question.

It should be emphasized once again that, although Bonar Law was determined not to take the responsibility of recommending, and although he had been convinced by Lord Crewe that there was no need for him to do so, he had little doubt as to what would in fact happen; Curzon would be chosen, but chosen by the King and not by Bonar Law. This attitude is implicit in a letter which he wrote to Curzon the following day:

"I am sorry that I find it necessary to resign. . . . I understand that it is not customary for the King to ask the Prime Minister to recommend his successor in circumstances like the present and I presume that he will not do so; but if, as I hope, he accepts my resignation at once, he will have to take immediate steps about my successor."[c]

The letter recognized the priority of Curzon's claim; for otherwise why write to him at all? But at the same time Bonar Law made it clear that he did not himself expect to take any part in the selection.

On the following morning, Sunday, May 20th, one of Bonar Law's earliest visitors at Onslow Gardens was Stanley Baldwin who had hurriedly returned the night before from Worcestershire. Bonar Law told Baldwin that he did not intend to recommend, but that in his own mind he had no doubt that Curzon would be chosen, that Baldwin's time would come in due course, but that meanwhile he must try to serve loyally under Curzon. Baldwin replied that he would gladly serve under anyone who could hold the Party together. Bonar Law was exceedingly pleased at this answer. He then warned Baldwin that he should, from the outset, come to a clear understanding with Curzon about the division of power between them. In particular Baldwin should keep in his own hands all patronage, appointments, promotions within the House of Commons. Otherwise his position as Leader of the House would be intolerable. Baldwin agreed to all this, and then departed for Chequers.[d]

On Sunday afternoon Colonel Waterhouse and Sir Frederick Sykes went down by motor car to Aldershot. They handed over Bonar Law's letter and in conversation indicated that he did not wish to give advice about his successor. The King then asked whether Bonar Law could recommend anyone else to whom he, the King, could turn for advice. The two messengers returned to Onslow Gardens to consult Bonar Law. His first reaction was to suggest that the King should seek advice from Neville Chamberlain for whom he had come to hold a high opinion. But Neville Chamberlain was a newcomer to the Cabinet, and did not yet have the necessary standing for such a rôle. Instead, therefore, he suggested that the King should consult Lord Salisbury who was Lord President of the Council and a revered, if Die-hard, figure in the Conservative Party.[e] In order to save time Bonar Law took it upon himself to summon Salisbury from the country immediately.

The following morning at 8 o'clock Salisbury came round to Onslow Gardens. Clad in frock coat and top hat he had travelled up to London in the small hours of the morning on a milk train – an

exploit new to him and one upon which he dilated with pride. When
Bonar Law told him what the problem was, he declared that if consulted he would have no choice but to recommend Curzon. He also
had misgivings about Curzon, but, he too did not see how Curzon
could be passed over in favour of Baldwin. Bonar Law agreed and
repeated the gist of this conversation to Beaverbrook who came into
the room immediately after. The story is indirectly corroborated by
Lord Stamfordham's account of his own discussion with Salisbury
later in the day.

"Lord Salisbury then told me that he had seen Bonar Law this morning
and in discussing the question of his successor he gave Salisbury the
impression that in this very grave and complex situation he would on the
whole be disinclined to pass over Curzon: but he added that he would
rather not take the responsibility of any decision. Lord Salisbury particularly begged that this should not be quoted, *as it must be remembered they
were the expressions of a very sick man.*"[f]

As is well known Salisbury's own advice to Stamfordham was in
favour of Curzon.[g]

Thus, then, the stage is set by Monday afternoon. The news of
the Prime Minister's resignation is in every paper. Distressed and
alarmed, ministers, M.P.s and journalists cut short their Whitsun
holiday and come flocking into London. Clubland, normally deserted
on a bank holiday, resounds with the hum of gossip, rumour and
intrigue.

And what of the chief actors? As for Bonar Law his duties are over.
He has done all that he feels entitled to do. His doubts about Curzon
remain unchanged. But there can in the end be no other successor.
Perhaps it will work out satisfactorily. Anyway, the responsibility
now lies with others, with Salisbury, with Stamfordham, with the
King. . . . Bonar Law can rest in peace. As for the rivals, Baldwin has
gone to Chequers. After his talk with Bonar Law he can have little
hope of the succession. Curzon too is out of London. Down in Somerset at Montacute House, one of his numerous country seats, he has
by now received Bonar Law's letter. Only the absence of a telephone
in that venerable mansion prevents him from pursuing his feverish
enquiries personally. He sits all day impatiently awaiting the summons to Buckingham Palace, the summons that will fulfil the
ambition of his life, the summons that must come.

It is a matter of history that Curzon was passed over; that, instead,
Baldwin, "a man of the utmost insignificance", as Curzon was to
prescribe him,[h] received the King's commission to become Prime

Minister of England. What happened to ruin Curzon's chances? The full truth has never been revealed. It is a remarkable tale and, since it indirectly involves Bonar Law, it may appropriately be told in the story of his life.

When Bonar Law's family insisted that General Sykes should accompany Colonel Waterhouse in order to make sure that he did not misrepresent Bonar Law's views, their suspicions were justified. What happened emerges from a significant but hitherto unnoticed document among the Royal Archives. It is unsigned, sand to it is appended the following note by Lord Stamfordham.

"This is the Memorandum handed to the King on Sunday, May 20th, *and which, Colonel Waterhouse stated, practically expressed the views of Mr. Bonar Law.*"[1]

The memorandum must be quoted in full:[i]

"The resignation of the Prime Minister makes it necessary for the Crown to exercise its prerogative in the choice of Mr. Bonar Law's successor. There appears to be only two possible alternatives – Mr. Stanley Baldwin and Lord Curzon.

"The case for each is very strong.

"Lord Curzon has, during a long life, held high office almost continuously and is therefore possessed of wide experience of government. His industry and mental equipment are of the highest order. His grasp of the international situation is great.

"Mr. Stanley Baldwin has had a very rapid promotion and has, by his gathering strength, exceeded the expectation of his most fervent friends. He is very much liked by all shades of political opinion in the House of Commons and has the complete confidence of the City and the commercial world generally. He, in fact, typifies both the spirit of the Government which the people of this country elected last autumn and also the same characteristics which won the people's confidence for Mr. Bonar Law, i.e. honesty, simplicity and balance. There is, however, the disadvantage that compared to many of his colleagues, his official life is short. On the other hand, there can be no doubt that Lord Curzon, temperamentally, does not inspire complete confidence in his colleagues, either as to his judgment or as to his ultimate strength of purpose in a crisis. His methods, too, are inappropriate to harmony. The prospect of his receiving deputations as Prime Minister from the Miners' Federation or the Triple Alliance, for example, is capable of causing alarm for the future relations between the Government and Labour – between moderate and less moderate opinion.

"The choice, in fact, seems to be recognizing in an individual those services which, in Lord Curzon's case, enabled him to act as Deputy Minister but which, as is so often the case when larger issues are involved, might not qualify him in the permanent post. The time, in the opinion of many members of the House of Commons, has passed when the direction

[1] Author's italics.

of domestic policy can be placed outside the House of Commons, and it is submitted that altho' foreign and imperial affairs are of vital importance stability at home must be the basic consideration. There is also the fact that Lord Curzon is regarded in the public eye as representing that section of privileged Conservatism which has its value but which in this democratic age cannot be too assiduously exploited.

"The number of Peers holding the highest offices in the Government, that is, four out of the five Secretaries of State, has already produced comment even among Conservatives. The situation in this respect would be accentuated by placing the direction of Government policy in the Upper House, for any further subordination of the House of Commons would be most strongly resented, not only by the Conservative Party as a whole but by every shade of democratic opinion in the country. It is thought that the truth of this view finds support in the fact that, whereas it would be most unlikely that Lord Curzon could form a Government without the inclusion of the present Chancellor of the Exchequer, on the other hand, it would clearly be possible for Mr. Baldwin to form a Government even tho' Lord Curzon should find himself unable to join it.

"It is believed that Lord Derby would be willing, if necessary, to serve under Mr. Baldwin, but not under Lord Curzon.[1]

"If the King should decide to call upon the Chancellor of the Exchequer he would, no doubt, urge upon Lord Curzon the reasons for his choice and appeal to him to continue his service."

The document is a cogent, vigorous, well argued, plea for Baldwin. On the merits of the case it has much to commend it. Presented by Waterhouse as the expression of the retiring Premier's opinion it could scarcely fail to influence Lord Stamfordham and the King. There was only one thing wrong with it. As the whole of the evidence in the foregoing narrative shows, it was in no sense a true account of Bonar Law's views.

It is not necessary to recapitulate all the reasons for this assertion. There are three pieces of written evidence which prove beyond reasonable doubt that Bonar Law's opinions were not correctly represented in this memorandum. In the first place the letter which Bonar Law wrote to Curzon could never have been written by someone who was ready to damn Curzon behind his back in this devastating fashion. Certainly Bonar Law of all people would never have acted in this way. Secondly there is Stamfordham's account of what Salisbury told him about his discussions with Bonar Law; and here again there is a sharp conflict with the Waterhouse memorandum. Finally there is the evidence of Lord Crewe who wrote to Curzon

---

[1] This was quite true. Derby hated Curzon, and would not have served under him at all readily. Some people believed that a solution to the problem might be for Derby himself to become Prime Minister, but he wisely refused to encourage any such move.

on May 23rd after the crisis was all over. He described his talk with Bonar Law in Paris and ended:[j]

"Of course I had anticipated that you would be asked to succeed him and except for what one sees in the papers I am still quite in the dark about the cause of the actual selection."

But Crewe could scarcely have regarded the selection of Curzon as inevitable or even probable if Bonar Law had shown any sign of sharing the clear pro-Baldwin views which are expressed in the memorandum given by Waterhouse to Stamfordham. If Bonar Law had really felt, as Waterhouse said that he felt, then surely he would have given definite advice in favour of Baldwin Even Mr. Amery, who was personally strongly against Curzon, does not suggest that Bonar Law was prepared to override Curzon's claims. He dined with Bonar Law in Paris on May 18th, the day after the latter's discussion with Crewe, and writes in his memoirs:[k]

"As regards the succession, Bonar on the whole inclined towards Baldwin whose reputation had been greatly enhanced by a very successful 'sound' Budget, but doubted if Curzon's claims on ground of seniority and experience could really be set aside."

It is very difficult to avoid the conclusion that Colonel Waterhouse knew that this document was not an accurate expression of Bonar Law's views. General Sykes who accompanied him to Aldershot remembered nothing about the memorandum. None of the surviving members of Bonar Law's family has any recollection of it, neither has Sir Geoffrey Fry nor Sir Patrick Gower who were Bonar Law's other private secretaries. Lord Beaverbrook was equally ignorant of the document and only saw it for the first time when it was recently copied out from the Windsor Archives. The only explanation would seem to be that Colonel Waterhouse handed the memorandum privately – and behind Sir Frederick Sykes' back – either to Stamfordham or the King.

The document is anonymous, but was in fact composed by Lord Davidson[l] after discussions with Baldwin on Friday night. Of course it does not in the least follow that Lord Davidson authorized Colonel Waterhouse to father his own sincere and perfectly justifiable opinions on to Bonar Law.[1]

---

[1] Although he did not authorize this use of his memorandum, Lord Davidson considers that it did not, in fact, misrepresent Bonar Law. It seems, however, to the author that the memorandum does misrepresent Bonar Law, if only by suggesting decision and clarity where there existed indecision and doubt. The reader must judge which way the balance of evidence inclines.

Indeed it is clear that the document was intended merely as an *aide-mémoire* for Waterhouse[m] in case the King should ask him for his own opinion – a perfectly possible contingency in view of Waterhouse's past connexion with the Court as equerry to the Duke of York – and not as a considered expression of Bonar Law's opinion.

Lord Stamfordham, having read the memorandum on Sunday in the light of Waterhouse's claim that it "practically expressed the views of Mr. Bonar Law", must have been puzzled at receiving on Monday such a very different account of Bonar Law's opinions from Salisbury. He may well have felt that Salisbury had somehow misunderstood the Prime Minister, and, when on Tuesday he received a letter from Salisbury regretting that "the King cannot have the advantage of Bonar's own advice" and offering to enquire whether Bonar Law would see Stamfordham personally, he resolved to send for Waterhouse again. His account of their conversation survives in the Royal Archives:[n]

BUCKINGHAM PALACE

"Memorandum by Lord Stamfordham, Tuesday, May 22nd, 1923.

"Received a letter from Lord Salisbury, on receipt of which I asked Colonel Waterhouse to come and see me. I asked him whether I was at liberty to say that Mr. Bonar Law's family considered that, had he been asked, Bonar Law would have advised the King to appoint Mr. Baldwin, Colonel Waterhouse told me that before leaving London for Aldershot on Sunday, he spoke to Mr. Bonar Law on this point, but he, Bonar Law, said that the King had not asked his advice. Colonel Waterhouse then said, if the King were to ask me, or to sound me, on this point what should I say, and Bonar Law answered – 'On the whole I think I should advise him to send for Baldwin.'

"The memorandum which Colonel Waterhouse brought to Aldershot on Sunday was read by Sir Frederick Sykes,[1] who considers that it embodied the Prime Minister's opinions. Furthermore, Colonel Waterhouse, in order to make sure of what he was coming to tell me, had seen Miss Law, who was in the very closest confidence of her brother, and she endorsed the opinion that Mr. Bonar Law would have favoured the selection of Mr. Baldwin. On this information I wrote my reply to Lord Salisbury. . . ."

Once again Colonel Waterhouse appears to have misled Stamfordham. It is very improbable that Bonar Law used the words attributed to him and it is certain that Sir Frederick Sykes never saw the memorandum. As for Miss Mary Law she was only concerned with her

---

[1] Stamfordham is presumably simply reporting what Waterhouse said. Sir Frederick Sykes told the author that he had never in fact read the memorandum.

brother's health, and was desperately worried. She had no interest in the succession, nor had any other members of Bonar Law's family. Any remark that she made is most unlikely to have gone beyond the undoubted fact that her brother preferred Baldwin personally to Curzon.

Naturally Stamfordham did not question Colonel Waterhouse's bona fides. He presumably decided that Salisbury must have been misinformed, and he wrote as follows to Salisbury after the second interview with Colonel Waterhouse, on May 22nd:[o]

". . . all I have learnt directly or indirectly from Bonar's family is that, eliminating *the personal* factor and having regard to the larger issues involved, he would, if asked to advise the King, have been in favour of the Premiership remaining in the House of Commons.

"With this knowledge, and considering that even *before* the operation the King was asked *not* to seek for Bonar's advice, I do not see that any advantage would be gained by now approaching the family in order to obtain from Bonar an opinion which they consider has [sic] been already expressed and which I have quoted above. . . ."

It has been necessary to quote the original documents in some detail because the whole story would seem scarcely credible but for the written evidence. The papers show beyond reasonable doubt that the King and Stamfordham were misled about the real opinions of Bonar Law. It is impossible to say with certainty what were Waterhouse's motives and how far the deception was deliberate. Waterhouse undoubtedly knew that he was to some extent exceeding his orders. This fact emerges from a little known and obscurely worded book of reminiscences, *Private and Official*, by Lady Waterhouse. According to her, Waterhouse pressed Bonar Law on Sunday morning at breakfast for an answer to the question of the succession, and she reports the conversation:[p]

"Ronald: . . . You *must* tell me what your answer would be if you had to give it.
"B.L.:   But I would not and I will not.
"Ronald: If I give you my word of honour to preserve your confidence?
"B.L.:   In that case . . . I am afraid . . . I should have to say – Baldwin."

Lady Waterhouse describes her husband's reflections on the journey to Aldershot which followed this conversation, and says:

"He found himself being driven fatefully to an immediate choice between unqualified service to the State and the silence imposed by his word of honour given that morning to Bonar. The two were diametrically opposed but the former prevailed. . . ."

Lady Waterhouse presumably bases her account on her husband's papers or on his personal reminiscences, and it is quite clear that, even if we accept her story of Bonar Law's preference for Baldwin – a story for which there is little evidence and against which there is a good deal – Waterhouse had no right to break his word or to claim that Davidson's powerful memorandum expressed Bonar Law's views on the succession. Enough has been said for the reader to judge the ethics of Sir Ronald Waterhouse's conduct. It is perhaps of interest to note that he remained Principal Private Secretary to Baldwin, Ramsay MacDonald, and Baldwin again, until in 1928, as Lady Waterhouse somewhat enigmatically observes:[q]

"it was borne in upon him with abundant clearness that forces beyond his personal control were combining to bring about yet another change in his career."

How much difference did Waterhouse's action make to the final decision? It is impossible to say, but it is hard to believe that such a categorical statement of Bonar Law's views had no effect. The very persistence with which Stamfordham endeavoured to elicit those views suggests that he attached considerable importance to them. Nevertheless the historian who believes that he has discovered new evidence must be very careful not to exaggerate its significance. Waterhouse's use of this memorandum was certainly not the only reason which decided the King to send for Baldwin rather than Curzon. There was, after all, on general grounds – personalities apart – a strong case for keeping the Premiership in the House of Commons when the official Labour Opposition was wholly without representatives in the Lords. There were Curzon's well-known defects of temperament. Above all there was the independent advice given to the King from an altogether separate source – advice which was bound to carry great weight.

Lord Balfour was staying in Norfolk at Sheringham when the crisis broke. He was on a golfing holiday, but had suddenly been struck down by phlebitis. The King decided on Sunday that he must have the advice of so distinguished an elder statesman, an ex-Prime Minister and ex-leader of the Conservative Party, with a long life-time of political experience behind him. From Curzon's viewpoint no more disastrous choice could have been made. For Balfour bore him little love. Behind a front of urbane and unfailing courtesy he regarded the Foreign Secretary with a certain measure of contempt. He considered that Curzon would be an unsuitable Prime Minister.

Although his doctors urged him not to travel, Balfour on receiving

Lord Stamfordham's telegram was determined to go at once to London. On Monday morning he went up from Norfolk to his London house at Carlton Gardens. Lord Stamfordham came to see him during the afternoon. Balfour confined his argument entirely to the question of the House of Lords. He did not discuss the personalities concerned. He merely urged that in a democratic age a peer as Prime Minister would be an anachronism, that it was impossible to have the Prime Minister in the Upper House when the Official Opposition was not represented there at all.[r] These arguments strongly reinforced the King's own views. According to Lord Stamfordham, who discussed the matter with Geoffrey Dawson, the editor of *The Times*, at 8 o'clock on Monday evening, the King was strongly in favour of Baldwin.

"I told him [Dawson] frankly", writes Stamfordham,[s] "that the King was so far convinced that his responsibility to the country made it almost imperative that he should appoint a Prime Minister from the House of Commons. For were he not to do so, and the experiment failed, the country would blame the King for an act which was entirely his own and which proved that the King was ignorant of, and out of touch with the public."

Balfour returned to Sheringham the next day. He was met by some of his party there, which included Lady Desborough and Mr. and Mrs. Edwin Montagu. "And will dear George be chosen?" asked one of them. "No," replied Balfour, "dear George will not."[t]

The rest of the story is well known: how the King, anxious to break the news to Curzon, caused Stamfordham to summon him by telegram on Monday night; how Curzon naturally interpreted this as a summons to the Premiership; how he travelled up from Montacute on Tuesday morning discoursing upon his plans for the Administration; the terrible shock, and the painful scene which followed, when Stamfordham told him at 2.30 that afternoon that within an hour Baldwin would be at Buckingham Palace to receive the King's commission. Nor should we forget the magnanimity, which Curzon displayed after the first shock, in consenting to serve under Baldwin, and even to propose him for the leadership of the Party.

Later that afternoon, May 22nd, Lord Davidson came to see Bonar Law at Onslow Gardens. Lord Beaverbrook was in the room and recalls vividly the surprise with which Bonar Law greeted Davidson's news that the King had sent for Baldwin. Bonar Law had not expected this outcome. He was, indeed, far from displeased, but he had felt all along that Curzon was bound to be his successor, that

Curzon was the man whom the Party and the Cabinet wanted. It had never crossed his mind that any other choice was, in the circumstances, possible. Now that the choice was made he certainly did not condemn it, but he remained astonished nevertheless that Baldwin was to succeed him.

We have seen some of the reasons which led to this surprising result. It will never be possible to state with precision exactly how far the King was swayed by his own personal belief, by Balfour's advice, or by the version of Bonar Law's opinion, which was conveyed to him through Colonel Waterhouse – or by other sources which he may have consulted.

At all events, even if we cannot say exactly what did influence the King, we can say with exactitude what did not. After the event there was no lack of claimants to the glory of having by their advice made all the difference to the decision. Like the fly which pushed the heavy coach to the top of the hill in La Fontaine's famous fable, many people are apt to assume that, because they recommend a certain action, and that action is in fact taken, they are responsible for it. This argument is fallacious. An amusing instance is Mr. L. S. Amery's claim, stated more than once in his writings, that he and Mr. Bridgeman contributed personally to the choice of Baldwin, thanks to a chance meeting with Lord Stamfordham in St. James's Park on the morning of Monday, May 21st. They hastened to talk to Stamfordham and pressed the claim of Baldwin upon him. Their point of view was, says Mr. Amery, "quite new to him, but he was impressed more particularly, I think, when I told him of what Mr. Bonar Law himself thought." Alas, Mr. Amery was deceived by Stamfordham's invariable courtesy. In the Royal Archives there is an account by Stamfordham of this conversation, and the following brief footnote is added in Stamfordham's own hand:

"Earlier in the day Colonel Waterhouse proposed that I should see them: but I said 'No', as I felt sure that they would be in favour of Mr. Baldwin and their advice would not be helpful."

Whatever Mr. Amery and Lord Bridgeman may have accomplished by indirect methods, it seems clear that their only direct approach did not affect the issue.

2

Such was the strange half-accidental manner in which Baldwin became Prime Minister of England. As has been told, Bonar Law played only a negative part in the selection; it was his determination not to recommend Curzon which gave the pro-Baldwin party an opportunity that otherwise might never have come their way. We have seen how skilfully that chance was exploited. Nevertheless, although some of the methods and many of the arguments used against Curzon are open to criticism, there can be little doubt that the right result was achieved. There was no real reason why a peer should not have been Prime Minister in 1923, but there were cogent reasons why a person of Curzon's temperament, whether peer or commoner, should not have been at the head of affairs in the England of the 1920s. Baldwin had many grave defects, but it is clear that Curzon, who was still regarded with intense resentment by the Coalition Conservatives, could never have reunited the Party as Baldwin was later able to do, and it is clear too that Curzon's demeanour would not have made relations with an increasingly radical and egalitarian opposition at all easy.

And now Bonar Law fades from the political scene. His Premiership was one of the shortest in our history. When he resigned on May 20th he had been Prime Minister for only 209 days. The transfer of power to his successor was smooth and easy, helped by the fact that his private secretaries, Davidson, Waterhouse, Fry, all remained in office under Baldwin. From the point of view of his personal convenience no difficulties arose. He had kept his house at Onslow Gardens in readiness for a retirement which he knew could not be long distant, and it was easy to move there from 10 Downing Street.

The public reaction to his sudden resignation was one of unmixed sorrow. It is a favourite platitude to say of any politician who retires that he enjoys the affection of his political opponents as well as of his supporters. In the case of Bonar Law this was genuinely true, and the fact is evidenced by scores of personal and private letters which are far more convincing than the public encomiums invariably pronounced upon these occasions. To many of the writers the true gravity of Bonar Law's condition was not known and their evidently genuine expectations of his speedy recovery make pathetic reading in the light of what lay ahead.

Both at this time and after his death five months later many speakers expressed the view that Bonar Law had sacrificed his health for his country, and that he would never have become so ill if he had not responded to the call of duty at the Carlton Club meeting. Speaking in the House of Commons on November 13th in tribute to Bonar Law, Baldwin said:

Lord Beaverbrook and Bonar Law

The funeral procession of Bonar Law and some of the mourners, November 5th, 1923. *Extreme left:* Mr. Balfour. *On right facing camera:* The Prince of Wales

"There is no doubt that Mr. Bonar Law gave his life for his country just as much as if he had fallen in the Great War."

Such sentiments are comprehensible, and seemed to be confirmed by the fact that Bonar Law took office with such profound doubts about his own health. It is, however, not true to say that his final illness was in any way due to overwork or overstrain. What Bonar Law feared when he became Prime Minister was a recrudescence of the high blood pressure which caused him to resign in 1921 and which can undoubtedly be aggravated by worry and work. But there is no known connexion between cancer and any mental factors of this sort, or between cancer and high blood pressure. It seems probable that Bonar Law would have fallen ill and died at roughly the same time, whatever his decision had been at the Carlton Club meeting of October 1922.

Did Bonar Law himself realize how ill he was when he finally resigned? It is impossible to say for certain. He did not resign his seat in Parliament, although he never attended the House of Commons again. No one told him that he was suffering from cancer. Indeed the word was never mentioned in his presence. Nevertheless those nearest to him during these last months are convinced that in his heart he knew that he had not long to live. Temporarily his health began to improve. He went to Brighton in order to undergo the deep ray treatment which is often prescribed for cancer patients when all other remedies have failed. It alleviated his pain and he seemed better. He remained in Brighton for much of the summer. Lord Beaverbrook vividly recalls how deeply moved he was, despite his usual indifference to public esteem when the diners at a restaurant rose to their feet in a silent gesture of respect as he walked out of the room.[u] He was well enough to pay a short visit to Le Touquet, where he had spent so many happy hours in the past, and he even managed to play a certain amount of golf.

These signs of improvement vanished with the summer. By September his malady was beginning to gain rapidly upon him. During all this time his daughter Isabel looked after him with loving attention, and did everything in her power to help him, despite the fact that her own son, Bonar, to whom his grandfather was devoted, had been born only a few months earlier. Apart from the members of his family Bonar Law's most constant companion during these painful months was Beaverbrook. Ignoring the numerous calls of politics and business upon his time, Beaverbrook devoted all his efforts to alleviating the sufferings of his dying friend. He travelled everywhere

s

with him, endeavoured to amuse him with the latest political gossip, and arranged bridge or chess for him – not always an easy task as the sick man's symptoms became more distressing.

Bonar Law bore his sufferings with a stoic calm. There are no signs that he ever sought consolation in the sombre faith of his ancestors. He remained to the end the sceptic that he had been all his life. He had too much intellectual integrity to turn in sickness to a creed which had long ceased to carry conviction to him. About the middle of October it became clear that the end was near. He was brought back from Brighton, where he had been having further deep-ray treatment, to his house at Onslow Gardens. On Thursday, October 25th, a chill which he had caught developed, as a direct result of the cancer, into septic pneumonia. The illness was mercifully brief. He was still able to talk lucidly and sensibly to Sir Thomas Horder and to his family on the Monday evening, but in the early hours of Tuesday morning, October 30th, 1923, he died peacefully in his sleep.

In his will Bonar Law expressed the wish that he should be buried beside his wife in the cemetery at Helensburgh. His wish was not granted. The Dean and Chapter of Westminster offered to hold the funeral service in the Abbey, and both Mary Law and Beaverbrook favoured acceptance. When it became clear that the Cabinet too was in favour of an Abbey funeral, the family felt bound to agree. It was the first occasion since Gladstone's death in 1898 that a Prime Minister was buried in Westminster Abbey.

On Saturday, November 3rd, the body was cremated at Golders Green and the ashes taken to St. Columba's, Pont Street, the Presbyterian church where Bonar Law's family worshipped, and of which he had himself been an elder. The funeral took place on Monday, November 5th, on a grey windless autumnal morning. The pallbearers were the Prince of Wales, the Speaker, the Prime Minister, Balfour, Asquith, Carson, Austen Chamberlain, Ramsay MacDonald, Beaverbrook, and Lord Edmund Talbot. The coffin was carried into the Abbey by N.C.O.s of the Royal Air Force and of the King's Own Scottish Borderers, the units in which Bonar Law's two sons had served until their deaths in the war. The Archbishops of Canterbury and York took part in the service, and there was present an immense crowd of mourners from the world of politics, including the whole Cabinet and the Dominion Prime Ministers who had assembled for a conference in London. Among the congregation was one of Bonar Law's first admirers, Rudyard Kipling, who heard his own "Reces-

sional" sung at the close of the service. During the afternoon, till long
after dusk, thousands of men and women filed past the burial place
in the second bay below the organ screen on the south side of the
nave. "It is fitting", so Asquith is reputed to have said, "that we
should have buried the Unknown Prime Minister by the side of the
Unknown Soldier."

3

Asquith certainly intended no compliment by this remark, but
Bonar Law would not have resented it. He cared little enough for
fame in his own lifetime, still less for the verdict of posterity. However ambitious he may have been in his earlier days, all who knew
him agree that ambition had died in him long before the end of his
life. He had tried to do his duty as he saw it. He would have been
quite content to go down to history like the unknown soldier – an
anonymous symbol of suffering borne and duty fulfilled.

But Bonar Law's modesty is no reason for accepting Asquith's
verdict. The mere fact that his Premiership was so brief should not
make us dismiss him as a Bute or a Goderich. On the contrary he
exercised a profound influence upon the course of British history.
For twelve critical years he was a key figure in the complicated and
tortuous politics of the times and no account of them would be
adequate without some understanding of his personality, outlook
and ideals.

He himself declared that until the war he had only cared for two
things in politics, Ulster and Tariff Reform: the rest was only a game.
How far did he succeed in attaining those two objectives? Over
Ulster his success was indisputable, and her survival as an autonomous province of the United Kingdom, wholly independent of the
Irish Republic, is in no small measure the achievement of Bonar Law.
His name will ever have one of the most honoured places among
those who fought to preserve Ulster from coming under a Dublin
parliament. Carson may have been a more theatrical figure and a
greater leader of the Ulster Protestant masses. Craig may have
created the solid backbone of indigenous resistance. Yet without the
uncompromising support of Bonar Law, without his much criticized
decision to pledge the whole of the English Conservative Party to the
Ulster cause, it is very unlikely that Ulster would stand where she
does today.

One half of Bonar Law's professed ambitions was thus undoubtedly
achieved, but the other half, Tariff Reform leading to imperial con-

s*

solidation, remained, when he died, as far away as ever. The truth, as we can perhaps now see it, is that the political unity, which Joseph Chamberlain and, after him, Bonar Law sought for the Empire, was contradicted by nearly all the trends of the time, in particular the growth of Dominion nationalism. Moreover the abandonment of Free Trade and the taxation of food, involved in the policy of Tariff Reform, could never be popular in England. No one would deny after the experience of two world wars that imperial unity, anyway among the white races of the Empire, has been a reality. But it has taken a form far more intangible, and less concrete or institutionalized than was envisaged by the Conservative imperialists at the beginning of the twentieth century.

The outbreak of war in 1914 profoundly altered Bonar Law's attitude to politics. The burning issues which had hitherto filled his vision faded away, and he devoted all his efforts to the preservation of his country from the menace of the Central Powers. In the various political upheavals of the war he played a crucial rôle, and his part in overthrowing Asquith has earned him the lasting hostility of that formidable statesman's many partisans – with how little justice has been described in earlier chapters of this book. But even Bonar Law's strongest opponents cannot accuse him of pursuing personal ambition. In 1915 he accepted office far below his deserts because he believed that national interest demanded his self-effacement. In 1916 he readily rejected the chance to become Prime Minister. The contribution which he made as partner and second in command to Lloyd George has never been – and now never can be – fully recorded, but all who knew the two men when they worked together have testified to the value of Bonar Law's cautious sagacity during those troublous years. Not the least eloquent witness has been Lloyd George himself.

In a brilliant sketch[1] – written shortly after Bonar Law's resignation in 1923 – the late Lord Keynes described him as "before everything a party man, deeply concerned for his party, obedient to its instincts, and at each crisis the nominee of its machine". No doubt this is too sweeping a statement. For example, far from being the nominee of the machine Bonar Law aroused much hostility from the Conservative Chief Whip when he intervened in the leadership crisis of 1911. Nevertheless there is a substratum of truth in Keynes's description. Bonar Law *was* deeply concerned for his Party, and while he was leader he undoubtedly regarded himself as being in a sense ...tee for its ultimate interests. He had inherited from Balfour a

Essays in Biography, pp. 42–47.

Party deeply divided, he had united it, and he intended to hand it on intact to his successors. It was this determination which prompted his last decisive action – at the Carlton Club meeting of October 1922. On that occasion he said in his speech:

"I confess frankly that in the immediate crisis in front of us I do personally attach more importance to keeping our Party united than to winning the next election."

Behind these words lay some of his deepest feelings. He was very conscious of the perils of party disunion. For the whole of his political life the Conservative Party, whether divided between Free Traders and Protectionists, or between "hedgers" and "ditchers", or between Coalitionists and Die-hards, had seemed on the verge of dissolution. The successive crises of the war and post-war years increased that danger. Yet in the end the Conservative Party, unlike the Liberals, survived as a united body. More than any one other man Bonar Law can claim the credit for that survival.

Bonar Law never had a brilliant or original mind; he lacked curiosity and was not interested in novel ideas. His great strength as a party politician lay in the fact that he was the ordinary man writ large. It was not from expediency or against his own better judgment that he obeyed his Party's instincts. It was because he genuinely had arrived, if by a different process of reasoning, at the same general conclusions as the vast majority of his supporters. What marked him out from ordinary men were speed of understanding, lucidity of exposition and a phenomenal memory. All these qualities he did indeed possess to an extraordinary degree, but they do not necessarily presuppose an original type of mind. Joseph Chamberlain, Lloyd George, Churchill, Birkenhead, were all capable of vivid flashes of insight wholly denied to Bonar Law. Asquith had a broader mind, Balfour one more speculative and subtle. All these were more liable to disrupt their own Parties by unorthodox words and actions. Bonar Law was a far "safer" man from a party point of view than any of them.

But it does not follow that he was a mere puppet or mediocrity as some of his detractors have suggested. On the contrary, in his latter years he exercised over that most critical body, the House of Commons, a mastery never surpassed and rarely equalled in modern times. It was comparable to that of Walpole or Peel. No man was more adept at giving with an air of sweet reasonableness the soft answer that turns away wrath. No man was more skilful at limiting the debate to precisely those issues upon which his own case was strongest. No man could acknowledge with more engaging candour error where error had occurred. No man could demolish more devastatingly and at shorter notice the arguments of his adversaries. In all that pertained to the speedy absorption of complicated facts, the swift and smooth conduct of business, the clear exposition of thorny and difficult problems, Bonar Law was supreme.

Yet these qualities alone, although they might explain the respect with which Bonar Law was regarded, do not account for the deep affection which he inspired among political opponents as well as friends, and among all classes in society. It was rather his frankness, his modesty, his gentleness, the total absence of pomposity or pride, above all perhaps a certain elusive and wistful melancholy, which made men not merely respect him but love him and seek to do all in their power to help him. The reasons for this affection have perhaps never been better expressed than by Keynes in the short sketch which has been mentioned earlier:

"They [the public] feel him to have been a great public servant whose life of austerity and duty has served them rather than himself. Many politicians are too much enthralled by the crash and glitter of the struggle, their hearts obviously warmed by the swell and pomp of authority, enjoying their positions and their careers, clinging to these sweet delights and primarily pleasing themselves. These are the natural target of envy and detraction and a certain contempt. They have their reward already and need no gratitude. But the public have liked to see a Prime Minister not enjoying his lot unduly. We have preferred to be governed by the sad smile of one who adopts towards the greatest office in the State the attitude that whilst, of course, it is nice to be Prime Minister, it is no great thing to covet, and who feels in office. and not merely afterwards, the vanity of things."

NOTES

1. References

The Bonar Law Papers, which are the principal documentary source for this book, are at present in the possession of Lord Beaverbrook. They will be made available to historians ultimately, and I have therefore given detailed references. The first number refers to the number of the box, the second to the file within the box, and the third, if relevant, to the number of the document within the file. For example, B.L.P. 18.1.13 means document number 13 in file number 1 of box number 18 in the Bonar Law Papers.

The references to the Royal Archives follow a similar principle, the initial letter denoting the series under which the document is catalogued, the figures which follow denoting the file number and document number. All the references in this book are to the reign of King George V.

Of the other collections of documents referred to below, Balfour's papers are in the British Museum, Asquith's are in the Bodleian Library at Oxford, Austen Chamberlain's are in the possession of his son-in-law, Colonel Maxwell, Lloyd George's are in the possession of Lord Beaverbrook.

The other references are self-explanatory. The reader ought, however, to know that the numerous references to Sir Winston Churchill's *World Crisis 1911–18* and to Lloyd George's *War Memoirs* are taken from the two-volume cheap editions of those two works, published by Odhams Press.

The item "private information", which occasionally appears, refers to informants who for various reasons have preferred to remain anonymous. In all such cases I have done my best to satisfy myself of the authenticity of the information.

Chapter I. YOUTH, 1858–1891

The Bonar Law Papers do not date back to this period. The information in this chapter is largely derived from members of Bonar Law's family and from material collected by Lord Coleraine. I have not given detailed references. See also H. A. Taylor, *The Strange Case of Andrew Bonar Law*, Chapters I and II.

Chapter II. FIRST STEPS IN POLITICS, 1900–1909

[a]Churchill, Sir Winston, *Great Contemporaries*, p. 242 – [b]Chamberlain, Austen, *Down the Years*, p. 224 – [c]Amery, L. S., *My Political Life*, Vol. I, p. 387 – [d]B.L.P. 18.1.13, February 6th, 1906 – [e]B.L.P. 18.1.12, January 29th, 1906 – [f]B.L.P. 18.2.16 – [g]B.L.P. 18.8.8, July 29th, 1908 – [h]B.L.P. 18.4.69, July 29th, 1908 – [i]B.L.P. 18.5.84.

Chapter III. THE CONSTITUTIONAL CRISIS, 1909–1911

[a]Beaverbrook, Lord, *Politicians and the War*, Vol. II, p. 57 – [b]Ibid, p. 59 – [c]B.L.P. 21.3.15 – [d]B.L.P. 18.8.13 – [e] Beaverbrook, Lord, *Politicians and the War*, Vol. I, p. 33 – [f]B.L.P. 18.7.151, January 3rd, 1911 – [g]B.L.P. 18.7.181.

Chapter IV. THE LEADERSHIP, 1911

[a]Dugdale, Mrs. Edgar, *Arthur James Balfour*, Vol. II, p. 64 – [b]B.L.P. 18.7.198 – [c]Austen Chamberlain's Papers, a letter to his step-mother – [d]Dugdale, Mrs. Edgar, *Arthur James Balfour*, Vol. II, p. 64 – [e]Chamberlain, Austen, *Politics from the Inside*, p. 387 – [f]B.L.P. 24.1.1 – [g]B.L.P. 33.1.1 – [h]Lord Rankeillour's Papers – [i]Chamberlain, Austen, *Politics from the Inside*, p. 388 – [j]A. J. Balfour's Papers, Sandars to Balfour, November 12th, 1911 – [k]Chamberlain, Austen, *Politics from the Inside*, pp. 390–391 – [l]Ibid., p. 392.

Chapter V. THE PROBLEMS OF THE LEADER, 1911–1912

[a]Sysonby, Lord, *Memories of Three Reigns*, pp. 353–354 – [b]Quoted from the Royal Archives, Nicolson, Sir Harold, *King George V*, p. 165 – [c]Petrie, Sir Charles, *The Life and Letters of Austen Chamberlain*, Vol. I, p. 308 – [d]A. J. Balfour's Papers, Sandars to Balfour, November 10th, 1911 – [e]Ibid., Sandars to Balfour, November 12th, 1911 – [f]B.L.P. 24.3.22, November 13th, 1911 – [g]A. J. Balfour's Papers, Sandars to Balfour, November 12th, 1911 – [h]Oxford and Asquith, Earl of, *Memories and Reflections*, Vol. I, p. 202 – [i]Chamberlain, Austen, *Down the Years*, p. 224 – [j]Lloyd George, David, *War Memoirs*, Vol. I, p. 611 – [k]B.L.P. 41.I.2 – [l]B.L.P. 26.3.39, June 26th, 1912 – [m]B.L.P. 26.4.9, Herbert Praed to Bonar Law, June 5th, 1912 – [n]B.L.P. 26.3.21, May 15th, 1912 – [o]B.L.P. 25.1.34, January 17th, 1912 – [p]B.L.P. 41.I.1(a) – [q]B.L.P. 25.2.49 – [r]B.L.P. 25.2.52.

Chapter VI. FOOD TAXES, 1911–1913

[a]B.L.P. 24.3.11 – [b]B.L.P. 24.3.30 – [c]B.L.P. 33.3.4 – [d]B.L.P. 26.3.2 – [e]B.L.P. 33.4.34 – [f]B.L.P. 33.4.41 – [g]B.L.P. 33.3.32 – [h]B.L.P. 33.4.51 – [i]B.L.P. 27.4.10 – [j]B.L.P. 28.1.52 – [k]B.L.P. 28.1.53 – [l]B.L.P. 33.4.83 – [m]B.L.P. 33.4.86 – [n]B.L.P. 28.1.86 – [o]B.L.P. 33.5.8 – [p]B.L.P. 33.5.6 – [q]Petrie, Sir Charles, *The Life and Letters of Austen Chamberlain*, Vol. I, pp. 334–335 – [r]B.L.P. 33.4.72.

Chapter VII. THE IRISH PROBLEM – THE FIRST ROUND, 1912–1913

[a]Churchill, Sir Winston, *Lord Randolph Churchill* (New Edition, 1951), p. 446 – [b]B.L.P. 33.4.57 – [c]B.L.P. 24.3.25, November 13th, 1911 – [d]Chamberlain, Austen, *Politics from the Inside*, p. 486 – [e]Spender and Asquith, *Life of Lord Oxford and Asquith*, Vol. II, pp. 21–24 – [f]Hyde, H. Montgomery, *Carson*, p. 336 – [g]B.L.P. 32.1.42.

Chapter VIII. THE MARCONI SCANDAL, 1912–1913

[a]Hansard xxxiv, p. 35 – [b]Owen, Frank, *Tempestuous Journey* (the life of Lloyd George), p. 239 – [c]Spender and Asquith, *Life of Lord Oxford and Asquith*, Vol. I, pp. 362–363 – [d]B.L.P. 29.4.21, May 25th, 1913.

Chapter IX. THE IRISH PROBLEM – ATTEMPT AT COMPROMISE, September 1913–February 1914

[a]B.L.P. 39.E.6 – [b]B.L.P. 35.5.20 – [c]B.L.P. 29.2.45 – [d]B.L.P. 39.E.10 – [e]B.L.P. 39.E.7 – [f]B.L.P. 33.5.56 – [g]B.L.P. 33.5.57 – [h]B.L.P. 30.2.15 – [i]B.L.P. 30.2.21 – [j]B.L.P. 30.2.28 – [k]B.L.P. 33.5.61 – [l]B.L.P. 30.2.37 – [m]B.L.P. 33.5.66, October 4th, 1913 – [n]B.L.P. 33.5.67, October 4th, 1913 – [o]B.L.P. 33.5.68 – [p]B.L.P. 30.3.16, October 10th, 1913 – [q]B.L.P. 33.6.80 – [r]Ibid. – [s]B.L.P. 30.3.31 – [t]B.L.P. 33.6.90 – [u]B.L.P. 33.6.93 – [v]Ibid. – [w]B.L.P. 33.6.94 – [x]Spender and Asquith, *Life of Lord Oxford and Asquith*, Vol. II, p. 36 – [y]B.L.P. 33.6.113 – [z]B.L.P. 31.1.23 – [za]Oxford and Asquith, Earl of, *Memories and Reflections*, Vol. I, pp. 205-6 – [zb]B.L.P. 31.2.51 – [zc]B.L.P. 34.1.16 – [zd]B.L.P. 31.3.4 – [ze]B.L.P. 31.2.59 – [zf]B.L.P. 34.1.22 – [zg]Spender and Asquith, *Life of Lord Oxford and Asquith*, Vol. II, p. 39.

Chapter X. THE ARMY ACT, January 26th–March 20th, 1914

[a]B.L.P. 31.1.7 – [b]B.L.P. 31.3.2 – [c]B.L.P. 34.1.25 – [d]B.L.P. 31.3.1 – [e]B.L.P. 34.1.28 – [f]B.L.P. 31.3.7, February 3rd, 1914 – [g]B.L.P. 34.1.31 – [h]B.L.P. 34.1.21 – [i]Callwell, Sir Charles, *Field-Marshal Sir Henry Wilson*, Vol. I, p. 114 – [j]Ibid., p. 138 – [k]B.L.P. 34.2.39, Bonar Law to Sir Henry Craik – [l]B.L.P. 34.2.44 – [m]Spender and Asquith, *Life of Lord Oxford and Asquith*, Vol. II, p. 28 – [n]Callwell, Sir Charles, *Field-Marshal Sir Henry Wilson*, Vol. I, p. 139.

Chapter XI. THE CURRAGH INCIDENT, March 1914

aWhite Paper (Cd. 7329), April 22nd, 1914 – bB.L.P. 39.E.25 – cIbid. – dIbid. –
eB.L.P. 39.E.19 – fGough, Sir Hubert, *Soldiering On*, p. 101 – gIbid, p.100 – hWhite Paper
(Cd. 7329) April 22nd, 1914 – iSpender and Asquith, *Life of Lord Oxford and Asquith*,
Vol. II, p. 47 – jB.L.P. 39.E.19 – kCallwell, Sir Charles, *Field-Marshal Sir Henry Wilson*,
Vol. I, pp. 140–141 – lIbid., p. 141 – mB.L.P. 34.2.45 – nB.L.P. 34.2.47 – oB.L.P.
32.1.51 – pB.L.P. 34.2.49 – qGough, Sir Hubert, *Soldiering On*, p. 107 – rSpender and
Asquith, *Life of Lord Oxford and Asquith*, Vol. II, p. 46 – sB.L.P. 32.1.50 – tSpender and
Asquith, *Life of Lord Oxford and Asquith*, Vol. II, p. 46 – uIbid., p. 46 – vGough, Sir
Hubert, *Soldiering On*, p. 110 – wCd. 7318.

Chapter XII. THE AFTERMATH OF THE CURRAGH INCIDENT, April 1914

aCd. 7329 – bB.L.P. 107.4.18, December 21st, 1921.

Chapter XIII. THE BUCKINGHAM PALACE CONFERENCE, April–August 1914

aB.L.P. 39.E.35 – bB.L.P. 32.3.48 and 32.3.55 – cB.L.P. 32.3.47 – dB.L.P. 32.3.55 –
eB.L.P. 39.E.38 – fB.L.P. 39.E.43 – gIbid. – hB.L.P. 32.4.85 – iB.L.P. 39.E.44 – jIbid. –
kOxford and Asquith, Earl of, *Memories and Reflections*, Vol. II, p. 6 – lSpender and Asquith,
Life of Lord Oxford and Asquith, Vol. II, p. 79.

Chapter XIV. WAR, August and September 1914

aGrey of Fallodon, Viscount, *Twenty Five Years*, Vol. I, p. 337 – bBeaverbrook, Lord,
Politicians and the War, Vol. I, pp. 22–23 – cGrey of Fallodon, Viscount, *Twenty-Five Years*,
Vol. I, p. 337 – dB.L.P. 37.4.1 – eGrey of Fallodon, Viscount, *Twenty-Five Years*, Vol. II,
p. 10 – fB.L.P. 34.3.3. – gBeaverbrook, Lord, *Politicians and the War*, Vol. I, p. 39 –
hB.L.P. 37.4.5 – iB.L.P. 34.3.19 and 20 – jB.L.P. 34.5.34 – kB.L.P. 37.4.18 – lOxford
and Asquith, Earl of, *Memories and Reflections*, Vol. II, p. 33 – mIbid., p. 33 – nB.L.P.
37.4.22.

Chapter XV. PATRIOTIC OPPOSITION, August 1914–May 18th, 1915

aAn unpublished letter from Asquith to Venetia Stanley (Mrs. Edwin Montagu),
November 4th, 1914 – bQuoted by Lord Beaverbrook, *Politicians and the War*, Vol. I,
p. 32 – cIbid., Vol. II, p. 79 – dB.L.P. 37.4.21 – eLloyd George, David, *War Memoirs*,
Vol. I, p. 636 – fAsquith to Venetia Stanley (Mrs. Edwin Montagu), October 5th, 1914 –
gB.L.P. 37.4.21 – hChurchill, Sir Winston, *World Crisis 1911–1918*, Vol. I, p. 54 –
iNicolson, Sir Harold, *King George V*, p. 252 – jB.L.P. 35.4.25 – kB.L.P. 36.2.57 – lB.L.P.
36.2.46 – mB.L.P. 36.2.45, January 27th, 1915 – nB.L.P. 37.5.6 – oB.L.P. 37.5.19 –
pB.L.P. 37.5.15 – qB.L.P. 35.5.17 – rBeaverbrook, Lord, *Politicians and the War*, Vol. I,
pp. 111–112 – sIbid., pp. 112–113 – tB.L.P. 37.2.34 – uOxford and Asquith, Earl of,
Memories and Reflections, Vol. II, pp. 91–92 – vChurchill, Sir Winston, *The World Crisis
1911–1918*, Vol. II, p. 797 – wIbid., p. 805 – xSpender and Asquith, *Life of Lord Oxford
and Asquith*, Vol. II, p. 165 – yIbid. – zLloyd George, David, *War Memoirs*, Vol. I, p. 137

Chapter XVI. THE FORMATION OF THE FIRST COALITION, May–June 1915

aOxford and Asquith, Earl of, *Memories and Reflections*, Vol. II, p. 100 – bPetrie, Sir
Charles, *The Life and Letters of Austen Chamberlain*, Vol. II, pp. 22–23 – cB.L.P. 37.2.37 –
dB.L.P. 50.3.10 – eBeaverbrook, Lord, *Politicians and the War*, Vol. I, p. 140 – fAsquith's
Papers in the Bodleian Library, not calendared – gB.L.P. 53.6.2 – hB.L.P. 50.3.26 –
iB.L.P. 50.3.39 – jB.L.P. 53.6.12 – kB.L.P. 50.3.31 – lOxford and Asquith, Earl of,
Memories and Reflections, Vol. II, pp. 93–94 – mB.L.P. 53.6.21 – nB.L.P. 64.D.3 and 4 –
oB.L.P. 53.6.45.

Chapter XVII. THE DARDANELLES, May–December 1915

aB.L.P.   53.6.38 – bB.L.P.   51.2.11 – cB.L.P.   53.6.39 – dB.L.P.   51.2.12 – eLloyd
George's Papers – fB.L.P. 53.6.33 – gChurchill, Sir Winston, *The World Crisis 1911–1918*,
Vol. II, p. 889 – hB.L.P. 59.5 – iAsquith's Papers – jLloyd George, David, *War Memoirs*,
Vol. I, p. 311 – kQuoted in full by Lord Beaverbrook, *Politicians and the War*, Vol. I,
pp. 164–166 – lB.L.P. 53.6.46 – mBeaverbrook, Lord, *Politicians and the War*, Vol. I,
p. 169 – nAsquith's Papers – oB.L.P. 59.5, Memorandum of November 25th, 1915 –
pB.L.P. 59.5, Memorandum of November 30th, 1915 – qB.L.P. 59.5, Memorandum of
December 4th, 1915 – rBeaverbrook, Lord, *Politicians and the War*, Vol. I, p. 171 –
sIbid., p. 194.

Chapter XVIII. POLITICAL DIFFICULTIES, January–June 1916

aBeaverbrook, Lord, *Politicians and the War*, Vol. II, p. 54 – bYoung, G. M., *Baldwin*,
p. 43 – cRiddell, Lord, *War Diary*, p. 164 – dB.L.P. 52.4.29, March 24th, 1916 – eB.L.P.
53.6.67 – fB.L.P. 53.6.65 – gRiddell, Lord, *War Diary*, p. 178 – hIbid p. 165 – iB.L.P. 53.
6.69 – jB.L.P. 53.6.72 – kBeaverbrook, Lord, *Politicians and the War*, Vol. II, p. 313 –
lRiddell, Lord, *War Diary*, p. 189 – mInformation from Lord Beaverbrook – nIbid. –
oQuoted in Spender and Asquith, *Life of Lord Oxford and Asquith*, Vol. II, p. 230.

Chapter XIX. THE TRIUMVIRATE, July–December 1st, 1916

aB.L.P. 53.6.27 – bIbid. – cSpender and Asquith, *Life of Lord Oxford and Asquith*,
Vol. II, p. 281 – dChurchill, Sir Winston, *The World Crisis 1911–1918*, Vol. II, p. 816 –
eChamberlain, Austen, *Down the Years*, p. 111 – fLloyd George, David, *War Memoirs*,
Vol. I, p. 603 – gBeaverbrook, Lord, *Politicians and the War*, Vol. I, p. 211 – hIbid., Vol. II,
pp. 127–128 – iB.L.P. 53.6.32, July 14th, 1915 – jBeaverbrook, Lord, *Politicians and the
War*, Vol. II, p. 92 – kIbid., p. 106 – lSpender and Asquith, *Life of Lord Oxford and
Asquith*, Vol. II, p. 272, n. 2 – mIbid., p. 248 – nB.L.P. 85.A.1 – oBeaverbrook, Lord,
Politicians and the War, Vol. II, pp. 145–146 – pB.L.P. 85.A.1 – qBeaverbrook, Lord,
Politicians and the War, Vol. II, p. 149 – rIbid., pp. 153–155 – sB.L.P. 85.A.1 –
tBeaverbrook, Lord, *Politicians and the War*, Vol. II, p. 185 – uB.L.P. 85.A.1 – vIbid. –
wLloyd George, David, *War Memoirs*, Vol. I, p. 589 – xBeaverbrook, Lord, *Politicians and
the War*, Vol. II, p. 193.

Chapter XX. THE ATTACK ON ASQUITH, December 1st–3rd, 1916

aChurchill, Sir Winston, *The World Crisis 1911–1918*, Vol. II, pp. 1139–1140 –
bBeaverbrook, Lord, *Politicians and the War*, Vol. II, p. 204 – cIbid., pp. 204–205 –
dIbid., p. 209 – eIbid., p. 211 – fB.L.P. 85.A.1 – gChamberlain, Austen, *Down the Years*,
pp. 117–118 – hBeaverbrook, Lord, *Politicians and the War*, Vol. II, p. 222 – iIbid., p. 223 –
jIbid., pp. 224–225 – kSpender and Asquith, *The Life of Lord Oxford and Asquith*, Vol. II,
pp. 258–260 – lLord Crewe's account appears in full in Asquith's *Memories and Reflections*,
Vol. II, pp. 128–138 – mSpender and Asquith, *Life of Lord Oxford and Asquith*, Vol. II,
pp. 258–259 – nIbid., p. 259 – oB.L.P. 85.A.1 – pSpender and Asquith, *Life of Lord Oxford
and Asquith*, Vol. II, p. 273.

Chapter XXI. THE FALL OF ASQUITH, December 3rd–7th, 1916

aB.L.P. 85.A.1 – bQuoted by Lord Beaverbrook, *Politicians and the War*, Vol. II, p. 233 –
cSpender and Asquith, *Life of Lord Oxford and Asquith*, Vol. II, pp. 262–264 – dHistory of
the Times, Vol. IV, Part I, 1912–1920, p. 297 – eBeaverbrook, Lord, *Politicians and the War*,
Vol. II, pp. 252–253 – fIbid., p. 254 – gB.L.P. 85.A.1 – hIbid. – iIbid. – jChamberlain,
Austen, *Down the Years*, p. 124 – kSpender and Asquith, *Life of Lord Oxford and Asquith*,
Vol. II, pp. 270–271 – lChamberlain, Austen, *Down the Years*, p. 121 – mSpender and
Asquith, *Life of Lord Oxford and Asquith*, Vol. II, p. 271 – nBeaverbrook, Lord, *Politicians
and the War*, Vol. II, p. 270 – oNicolson, Sir Harold, *King George V*, p. 288 – pIbid.,
p. 289 – qRoyal Archives, K. 1048, A.I. – rNicolson, Sir Harold, *King George V*, p. 289 –
sB.L.P. 85.A.1 – tNicolson, Sir Harold, *King George V*, pp. 290–291 – uAsquith's Papers –
vIbid. – wB.L.P. 85.A.1 – xBeaverbrook, Lord, *Politicians and the War*, Vol. II, p. 301 –
yIbid., pp. 313–327.

Chapter XXII. CHANCELLOR OF THE EXCHEQUER, 1916–1918

aB.L.P. 84.6.23, December 27th, 1916 – bLloyd George, David, *War Memoirs*, Vol. I, p. 612 – cRobert Munro (Lord Alness), *Looking Back*, p. 127 – dPrivate information – eAsquith's Papers – fB.L.P. 84.6.22 – gHarrod, R. F., *John Maynard Keynes*, p. 201 – hB.L.P. 65.2.26 – iPrivate information – jB.L.P. 65.3.20 – kIbid. – lInformation from Lord Beaverbrook – mLetter in possession of Lord Coleraine.

Chapter XXIII. THE MISFORTUNES OF WAR, 1916–May 9th, 1918

aBlake, Robert, *Private Papers of Douglas Haig*, pp. 240–241 – bLloyd George, David, *War Memoirs*, Vol. II, p 1293 – cIbid., p. 1293 – dB.L.P. 82.2.12 – eB.L.P. 84.6.113 – fB.L.P. 84.6.99 – gB.L.P. 84.6.127 – hB.L.P. 84.6.133 – iB.L.P. 82.7.3 – jBlake, Robert, *Private Papers of Douglas Haig*, p. 279 – kInformation from Lord Beaverbrook – lLloyd George, David, *War Memoirs*, Chap. LXXVI – mSpender and Asquith, *Life of Lord Oxford and Asquith*, Vol. II, p. 303 – nLloyd George, David, *War Memoirs*, Vol. II, pp. 1786–1787 – oMaurice, Sir Frederick, *Intrigues of the War* – pB.L.P. 68 – qJones, Thomas, *Lloyd George*, p. 149 – rAmery, L. S., *My Political Life*, Vol. II, p. 155 – sJones, Thomas, *Lloyd George*, p. 149 – tBlake, Robert, *The Private Papers of Douglas Haig*, pp. 277–278.

Chapter XXIV. VICTORY AND THE COUPON ELECTION,
May 9th–December 28th, 1918

aPrivate information – bInformation from Sir Horace Hamilton – cB.L.P. 84.7.25, April 28th, 1918 – dB.L.P. 83.4.18 – eB.L.P. 84.7.42 – fB.L.P. 83.4.22 – gB.L.P. 83.6.5, August 2nd, 1918 – hB.L.P. 84.7.37, June 10th, 1918 – iB.L.P. 83.4.21 – jB.L.P. 83.6.43 – kB.L.P. 84.1.10 – lB.L.P. 84.3.1 – mB.L.P. 84.7.97 – nB.L.P. 84.7.98 – oB.L.P. 84.7.103 – pB.L.P. 84.3.1 – qBalfour's Papers – rIbid. – sLloyd George, David, *The Truth about the Peace Treaties*, Vol. I, pp. 173–175 – tSpender and Asquith, *Life of Lord Oxford and Asquith*, Vol. II, p. 313 – uNicolson, Sir Harold, *King George V*, pp. 328–330 – vB.L.P. 95.4 – wIbid.

Chapter XXV. PEACE AND REPARATIONS,
December 28th, 1918–August 5th, 1919

aLloyd George's Papers – bChamberlain, Austen, *Down the Years*, p. 134 – cIbid., p. 139 – dIbid. See whole of Chap. VIII for this episode – eBeaverbrook, Lord, *Politicians and the Press*, pp. 20–21 – fAusten Chamberlain's Papers – gB.L.P. 97.1.16 – hB.L.P. 101.3.39 – iKeynes, J. M., *Essays in Biography*, p. 74 – jB.L.P. 101.3.122 – kB.L.P. 97.5.31 – lB.L.P. 101.3.124.

Chapter XXVI. AFTERMÁTH OF WAR, 1919–March 1921

aPrivate information – bNicolson, Sir Harold, *King George V*, p. 333 – cB.L.P. 101.3.31, March 21st, 1919 – dB.L.P. 97.1.12 – eB.L.P. 95.4 – fIbid. – gIbid. – hB.L.P. 101.3.145 – iInformation from Lady Sykes – jB.L.P. 101.4.40 – kKeynes, J. M., *Essays in Biography*, p. 45.

Chapter XXVII. RETIREMENT, March–December 1921

aB.L.P. 101.5.57 – bLetter in possession of Lady Sykes – cThis and subsequent letters to Miss Watson were in the latter's possession till her death in 1953 – dB.L.P. 107.2 undated – eIbid. – fB.L.P. 107.1.21 – gB.L.P. 107.1.31 – hB.L.P. 107.1.34 – iLetter in the possession of Lord Coleraine – jRiddell, Lord, *Intimate Diary of the Peace Conference and After*, p. 331 – kQuoted by Sir Charles Petrie in *The Life and Letters of Austen Chamberlain*, Vol. II, p. 164.

Chapter XXVIII. RETURN TO POLITICS, January–October 19th, 1922

aSalvidge, Stanley, *Salvidge of Liverpool*, p. 225 – bOwen, Frank, *Tempestuous Journey*, p. 595 – cShown to the author by Miss Watson – dIbid. – eA. J. Balfour's Papers, Memorandum by Balfour, December 22nd, 1922 – fC. P. Scott's Papers, Memorandum by C. P. Scott, December 6th, 1922 – gPrivate information – hB.L.P. 107.2.53 – iChurchill, Sir Winston, *The Aftermath*, p. 343 – jAmery, L. S., *My Political Life*, Vol. II, pp. 233–234 – kNicolson, Sir Harold, *Curzon, The Last Phase*, p. 275 – lAusten Chamberlain's Papers – mIbid. – nIbid. – oIbid. – p*History of The Times*, Vol. IV, Part II, 1921–1948, pp. 755–756 – qIbid., pp. 754–755 – rA. J. Balfour's Papers, Memorandum of December 22nd, 1922 – sRonaldshay, Earl of, *Life of Lord Curzon*, Vol. III, pp. 319–320 – tB.L.P. 107.4.36 – uChamberlain, Austen, *Down the Years*, p. 221 – vRonaldshay, Earl of, *Life of Lord Curzon*, Vol. III, pp. 320–321 – wB.L.P. 108.9.16 – xSalvidge, Stanley, *Salvidge of Liverpool*, p. 239 – yFor the full text of the speeches at the Carlton Club, see *Gleanings and Memoranda* (November 1922), being a monthly record published by the Conservative Central Office.

Chapter XXIX. PRIME MINISTER OF ENGLAND, October 19th–December 1922

aRoyal Archives, K. 1814.1 – bIbid. – cMcKenna, Stephen, *Reginald McKenna*, p. 318 – dPrivate information – eB.L.P. 109.2.11(b) – f*History of The Times*, Vol. IV, Part II, p. 758 – gB.L.P. 108.1.3 – hB.L.P. 108.1.24 – iB.L.P. 108.1.25 – kB.L.P. 108.9.12 – lB.L.P. 108.9.16 – mBeaverbrook, Lord, *Politicians and the Press*, p. 56 – nSalvidge, Stanley, *Salvidge of Liverpool*, pp. 238, 239 and 244 – oIbid., p. 244 – pB.L.P. 108.1.12 – qPrivate information – rB.L.P. 107.2.70 – sIbid. – tB.L.P. 108.6.11, Lord Salisbury to Bonar Law, March 21st, 1923, with attached minute by Lord Davidson – uB.L.P. 107.2.78, undated – vB.L.P. 108.9.16 – wB.L.P. 108.9.21 – xB.L.P. 111.12.42 – yB.L.P. 111.12.43 – zB.L.P. 111.12.44 – zaB.L.P. 111.12.45 – zbBeaverbrook, Lord, *Politicians and the Press*, p. 68 – zcLetter of December 15th, 1922, shown to the author by Sir Patrick Gower.

Chapter XXX. FRANCE AND AMERICA, December 1922–April 1923

aMemorandum by C. P. Scott, December 6th, 1922 – bB.L.P. 111.12.39 – cInformation from Miss Edith Watson – dNicolson, Sir Harold, *Curzon, The Last Phase*, p. 324 – eIbid., pp. 331 and 333 – fB.L.P. 111.12.57 – gB.L.P. 111.12.33, November 9th, 1922 – hIbid. – iB.L.P. 111.12.56 – jB.L.P. 111.12.57 – kB.L.P. 111.12.41 – lB.L.P. 111.12.49 – mB.L.P. 111.12.50 – nB.L.P. 111.12.62 – oYoung, G. M., *Baldwin*, p. 46 – pAmery, L. S., *My Political Life*, Vol. II, pp. 249–250 – qLord Derby's diary, January 30th, 1923 – rIbid., February 1st, 1923 – sB.L.P. 108.4.1 – tB.L.P. 108.9.34 – uB.L.P. 108.4.8 – vAmery, L. S., *My Political Life*, Vol. II, p. 246 – wB.L.P. 115.3.3 – xPetrie, Sir Charles, *Life and Letters of Austen Chamberlain*, Vol. II, p. 212 – yB.L.P. 115.2 – zB.L.P. 111.12.60.

Chapter XXXI. THE SUCCESSION, April 10th–May 18th, 1923

aNicolson, Sir Harold, *King George V*, p. 375 – bLord Derby's diary, describing an interview with Austen Chamberlain – cPrivate information – dB.L.P. 112.15.1 – eB.L.P. 112.15.2 – fThe remainder of this chapter is based on Lord Beaverbrook's personal narrative shown to the author, and on Lord Coleraine's recollections.

Chapter XXXII. THE END

aLord Beaverbrook's Papers – bPrivate information – cB.L.P. 108.9.51 – dInformation from Lord Beaverbrook, who was present – eChurchill, Sir Winston, *Great Contemporaries*, p. 285 – fRoyal Archives, K.1853.8 – gNicolson, Sir Harold, *King George V*, p. 376 – hNicolson, Sir Harold, *Curzon, the Last Phase*, p. 355 – iRoyal Archives, K.1853.5 – jRonaldshay, Earl of, *Life of Lord Curzon*, Vol. III, p. 351 – kAmery, L. S., *My Political Life*, Vol. II, p. 259 – lInformation from Lord Davidson – mWaterhouse, Nora, *Private and Official*, p. 259 – nRoyal Archives, K.1853.17 – oRoyal Archives, K.1853.16 – pWaterhouse, Nora, *Private and Official*, pp. 262–263 – qIbid., p. 359 – rChurchill, Sir Winston, *Great Contemporaries*, pp. 286–287 – sRoyal Archives, K.1853.11 – tChurchill, Sir Winston, *Great Contemporaries*, p. 287 – uBeaverbrook, Lord, *Politicians and the Press*, p. 107.

2. *Chess*

References have been made to Bonar Law's fondness of and skill at chess. Experts may be interested to judge his skill from the following victorious game played while he was Prime Minister. It appears in Irving Chernev's *1,000 Best Short Games of Chess*. Bonar Law had the first move. His opponent was Mr. Brian Harley, chess correspondent of *The Observer:*

(1)	P–K4	P–K4	(8)	Q–Kt4	Kt×Kt
(2)	Kt–KB3	Kt–QB3	(9)	Q×Kt	Kt×B
(3)	B–Kt5	Kt–B3	(10)	Q×KtP	R–B1
(4)	O–O	Kt×P	(11)	B–R6	P–Q4
(5)	P–Q4	P×P	(12)	Q×R ch	K–Q2
(6)	Kt×P	Kt–Q3	(13)	Q×P	K–Q3
(7)	R–K1 ch	B–K2	(14)	R×B	resigns

INDEX